Ethical and Responsible Tourism

Ethical and Responsible Tourism explains the methods and practices used to manage the environmental impact of tourism on local communities and destinations.

The three core themes of the book – destination management, environmental and social aspects of ethical sustainable development and business impacts – are discussed across both topic and case study chapters, alongside explanatory editorial analysis with all chapters clearly signposted and interlinked. The case studies address specific and practical examples from a global range of examples including sites in Australia, Central America, Europe Union countries, Japan, North America and South America.

Used as a core textbook, the linking of theory in the topic chapters, and practice gained through case studies, alongside further reading and editorial commentary, *Ethical and Responsible Tourism* provides a detailed and comprehensive learning experience. Specific case studies can be used as standalone examples as part of a case teaching approach, and the editorial and discussion elements are designed to be suitable for those simply seeking a concise overview, such as tourism professionals or potential investors in sustainable tourism projects.

This book will be essential reading for students, researchers and practitioners of tourism, environmental and sustainability studies.

Marko Koščak held the position of Assistant Professor from 2014 to 2019 and is currently an Associate Professor at the University of Maribor, Faculty of Tourism Brežice, Slovenia. He studied in Ljubljana (Slovenia), Birmingham (UK), Vienna (Austria) and in 1999 completed his PhD on the thesis "Transformation of Rural areas along the Slovene – Croatian border" at the Faculty of Arts, Department of Geography, University of Ljubljana. His academic interests are in the field of Sustainable and Community Tourism, Geography of Tourism and Destination Management. These topics are his research work interest fields in which he also lectures to students. His professional work career started on different activities in the field of Rural Development in Slovenia and abroad since 1986, when he commenced implementation of Integrated Rural Development Projects on local-community level. He was a Project Manager of the Dolenjska and Bela krajina regional sustainable tourism initiative Heritage Trails in South East Slovenia from 1996 to 2009, under the umbrella of the Chamber of Commerce Novo mesto. Since 1986 he was also a Regular Consultant with the Ministry of Agriculture, and employed there from 1999 to 2001 as an Advisor to the Slovenian government in the Sector for Structural policy and Rural development. In the past 30 years, he has worked as an Advisor to UNDP LoSD and sustainable tourism initiative in South East Balkan countries of Croatia, Serbia and Montenegro, Bosnia, Kosovo and Macedonia. He was also involved in the number of sustainable tourism projects and development initiatives and worked on these in Europe and Asia. He is the Founding Member of the Slovenian Rural Development Network, which is part of the European Network "PREPARE". His professional expertise and experiences are primarily in the following fields: Sustainable and Responsible Community Development, Rural and Eco Tourism, Economic Diversification on farms, Product Development, Sustainable Heritage Tourism, Regional and Rural Development and Cross-border Cooperation.

Tony O'Rourke has been actively collaborating with Marko Koščak for a number of years in the area of sustainable and local tourism development. He studied at UK universities in Warwick, Edinburgh and Stirling. His current academic interests are in the fields of Sustainable and Responsible Local Tourism, Financing of Local Tourism / Destination Management organisations and the creation of tourism credit co-operatives. His professional work career began in Higher Education Management connected to training and resources application. From 1990 to 2001 he was working with Scottish Financial Enterprise, the University of Stirling, Heriot-Watt University and the European Commission DG23 on small business financing at a micro level as well as the financing of tourism enterprises in Central and Eastern European transition economies. This included monitoring EU projects in Czech Republic, Hungary, Kazakhstan, Poland and Slovenia. From 1996 to 2001, he was Secretary-General of the Association of European Regional Financial Centres. From 1992 to 2004, he was a part-time Professor in small business financing / small financial market strategy at universities in Ireland, Montenegro and Serbia, and at the same time an Expert Advisor to Dun & Bradstreet Country Risk Services on Bosnia and Herzegovina and Serbia. In 2004, he returned to the University of Stirling as the Director of the programme for continuing professional development in the Scottish finance and investment sector, as well as teaching on the MSc Banking and Finance Programme. Since retiring in 2011, he has taught part-time at MSc and MBA level as a visiting / part-time Professor and also carried out advisory work for Co-operatives UK. He has published widely on tourism issues and expects to continue the latter.

Ethical and Responsible Tourism

Managing Sustainability in Local
Tourism Destinations

Edited by Marko Koščak and Tony O'Rourke

LONDON AND NEW YORK

First published 2020
by Routledge
2 Park Square, Milton Park, Abingdon, Oxon OX14 4RN

and by Routledge
52 Vanderbilt Avenue, New York, NY 10017

Routledge is an imprint of the Taylor & Francis Group, an informa business

British Library Cataloguing-in-Publication Data
A catalogue record for this book is available from the British Library

Library of Congress Cataloging-in-Publication Data
Names: Koščak, Marko, editor. | O'Rourke, Tony, editor.
Title: Ethical and responsible tourism: managing sustainability in local tourism destinations / edited by Marko Koščak and Tony O'Rourke.
Description: Abingdon, Oxon; New York, NY: Routledge, 2020. | Includes bibliographical references and index.
Identifiers: LCCN 2019028175 (print) | LCCN 2019028176 (ebook) |
ISBN 9780367191443 (hardback) | ISBN 9780367191467 (paperback) |
ISBN 9780429200694 (ebook)
Subjects: LCSH: Sustainable tourism. | Tourism—Environmental aspects. |
Tourism—Moral and ethical aspects. | Sustainable tourism—Case studies. |
Tourism—Environmental aspects—Case studies. | Tourism—Moral and ethical aspects—Case studies.
Classification: LCC G156.5.S87 E75 2020 (print) | LCC G156.5.S87 (ebook) |
DDC 910.68/4—dc23
LC record available at https://lccn.loc.gov/2019028175
LC ebook record available at https://lccn.loc.gov/2019028176

ISBN: 978-0-367-19144-3 (hbk)
ISBN: 978-0-367-19146-7 (pbk)
ISBN: 978-0-429-20069-4 (ebk)

Typeset in Sabon
by codeMantra

Contents

Illustrations

Tables

Contributors

Dr Simonetta Acacia, Research Fellow, Department of Architecture and Design, University of Genoa, Genoa, Italy.

Sara Mair Bellshaw, Projects Manager, Postgraduate in Science for Development, Sustainability & Tourism, CU Costa, University of the Highlands & Islands, Fort William, Scotland.

Marcela Costa Bifano de Oliveira, Centro de Estudios para Desarrollo Sustentable, University of Guadalajara, Puerto Vallarta, Mexico.

Daniel Binder, Senior Lecturer, Health and Tourism Management, FH JOANNEUM University of Applied Sciences, Bad Gleichenberg, Austria.

Dr Gary Burke, Director, Production Function, Fremantle/Margaret River, Western Australia.

Dr Carla Pinto Cardoso, Professor & Head of Tourism Heritage Department, Catholic University of Portugal, Braga Campus.

Emir Çekmecelioğlu, Research Assistant, Department of Architecture, Mustafa Kemal University, Hatay/Antakya, Turkey.

Dr Marta Casanova, Student in Postdoctoral Researcher, Conservation of Architectural Heritage, Department of Architecture and Urban Studies, Politecnico di Milano, Milan, Italy.

Fabíola Cristina Costa de Carvalho, Centro de Estudios para Desarrollo Sustentable, CU Costa, University of Guadalajara, Puerto Vallarta, Mexico.

Dr Antonio Alberto Clemente, Professor, Department of Architecture, University G. d'Annunzio, Chieti – Pescara, Italy.

Dr Lesley Crowe-Delaney, Research Fellow, School of Marketing, Faculty of Business & Law, Curtin University, Perth, Western Australia.

Andrew Donaldson, Chief Executive Officer, Comrie Croft, Comrie, Scotland.

Dr Jelena Farkić, Visiting Researcher, Centre for Recreation & Tourism Research, University of the Highlands & Islands, Fort William, Scotland.

Dr Harald A. Friedl, Associate Professor, Institute of Health & Tourism Management Health and Tourism Management, FH JOANNEUM, University of Applied Sciences, Bad Gleichenberg, Austria.

Milan Ilić, Foreign Correspondent, Delo (Slovenia) and MM-Marketing Magazin (Slovenia), Vienna, Austria.

Dr Roy Jones, Emeritus Professor of Geography, School of Design & the Built Environment, Curtin University, Perth, Western Australia.

Maja Klančnik, Independent Researcher, Slovenia.

Dr Mladen Knežević, Professor and Dean, Faculty for International Relations and Diplomacy, Libertas International University, Zagreb, Croatia.

Dr Sérgio Lira, President of the Executive Board, Greenlines Institute for Sustainable Development, Barcelos, Portugal & Professor, Faculty of Arts & Humanities, University of Lisbon, Portugal.

Dr Elena Macchioni, Student in Conservation of Architectural Heritage, Department of Architecture and Urban Studies, Politecnico di Milano, Milan, Italy.

Nika Mernik, Independent Researcher, Slovenia.

Dr James W. Miller, Associate Professor, Institute of Health and Tourism Management, FH JOANNEUM University of Applied Sciences, Bad Gleichenberg, Austria.

Aleksa Panić, HR Manager, Global Logistics Systems, Belgrade, Serbia.

Barbara Pavlakovič, Teaching Assistant, Faculty of Tourism Brežice, University of Maribor, Slovenia.

Dr Thiago Duarte Pimentel, Director CELAT & Professor, Human Sciences Institute, Federal University of Juiz de Fora, Minas Gerais, Brazil.

Dr Federica Pompejano, Postdoctoral Researcher, Department of Architecture and Design, University of Genoa, Genoa, Italy.

Boris Prevolšek, Lecturer, Faculty of Tourism Brežice, University of Maribor, Slovenia.

Dr Camilla Repetti, Student in Conservation of Architectural Heritage, Department of Architecture and Urban Studies, Politecnico di Milano, Milan, Italy.

Dr Maja Rosi, Teaching Assistant, Faculty of Logistics Celje, University of Maribor, Slovenia.

Dr Francesca Segantin, Architect partner with Department of Architecture & Design, University of Genoa, Genoa, Italy.

Dr Tina Šegota, Lecturer in Advertising and Marketing Communications, University of Greenwich, UK.

Dr Laura Stocker, Adjunct Associate Professor, Curtin University Sustainability Policy Institute, Perth, Western Australia.

Dr Aslı Sungur, Associate Professor, Building Design & Theory, Department of Architecture, Yildiz Technical University, Istanbul, Turkey.

Dr Steve Taylor, Head of the Centre for Recreation & Tourism Research, University of the Highlands & Islands, Fort William, Scotland.

Brian Turner, Senior Field Officer, Public Lands Attorney, National Trust for Historic Preservation in the USA.

Bogdan Turnšek, Independent Researcher, Slovenia.

Dr Maja Turnšek, Assistant Professor, Faculty of Tourism Brežice, University of Maribor, Slovenia.

David Valcárcel Ortiz, Scientific Director, Ethnographic Park & Botanical Garden Pirámides de Güímar, Santa Cruz De Tenerife, Spain.

Dr Sandra Luz Zepeda Hernández, Professor, CU Costa, University of Guadalajara, Puerto Vallerta, Mexico.

Maja Žibert, Teaching Assistant, Faculty of Tourism Brežice, University of Maribor, Slovenia.

Preface

This book came to be written as the result of research conducted by the authors over the last five years into various aspects of many elements of responsible and ethical tourism manifested at the local level. This resulted in the presentation of a significant number of conference papers and presentations, peer-reviewed international journal articles and other publications.

We came to the conclusion that there were distinctive gaps between theory and practice, between methodology and actuality, and that a publication of this type could make an effort to bridge those gaps. We had also over the past five years come across a wide range of colleagues – academics and practitioners – whose knowledge and experience called out for wider exposure than necessarily found in conferences and seminars.

Although our contributors came from across the globe, we would immediately make clear that not every continent is covered, nor was it our wish to restrict ourselves by achieving some form of inter-continental balance. Rather we have been impelled by what we feel is interesting and applicable for the widest number of those engaged in any form of ethical and responsible activity. But, on the other side, we believe that the richness of authors from different parts of the world and their views will contribute to understanding of varying views, practices and approaches in the field of local destination development and above all to understanding that there are always different solutions which are required in order to resolve continuing development challenges. It is clear that local problems require local solutions, nonetheless we also understand that local destination issues require an interdisciplinary approach and the contribution of different disciplines and expertise in resolving development challenges.

This underlying impetus and motivation has ensured that we have crossed disciplinary boundaries to include contributors from the fields of architecture, economics, geography, heritage preservation and management, local cultural preservation, the natural environment, rural and urban planning, sociology and tourism.

We hope that this book will be a useful tool for a greater understanding of the many issues connected to "Ethical & Responsible Tourism: Managing sustainability in local tourism destinations". In addition, we also hope that it will be interesting reading material for many differing target groups – whether from a theoretical, practical or indeed a mixed background. At the end we hope that we have contributed a useful and particular view in the challenges facing of local destination development with an ethical and responsible focus.

Marko Koščak and Tony O'Rourke

Acknowledgements

The editors would wish to take this opportunity to thank first of all our families, who have had to endure the effects of the work that we have both been involved in the process of creating this book. It has taken much effort and time, and we appreciate their willingness to give us the space to complete this task.

So therefore very grateful thanks to Branka and children as well as to Elizabeth for their support and resilience.

We also wish to thank our contributors, who have given their time and effort to provide topical chapters and case studies which have been influential and supportive of our goal to create a better understanding of ethical and responsible tourism in local destinations. They are colleagues whom we have relied on for their input, and whom we hope to have continuing contacts with in the future as we progress the ideas and views which are prevalent and paramount in this publication. Hopefully we have started the creation of a community of similar minded individuals who see the value and future of locally oriented responsible tourism activities.

Marko Koščak and Tony O'Rourke

Abbreviations

AUD	Australian dollars
bn	billion
EC	European Commission
EU	European Union
EUR	Eurozone euro (Note in most cases we use the euro as the currency, otherwise we use the USD, unless contributors have specified national currencies and identified these)
km	kilometre
m	million
UNEP	United Nations Environment Programme
UNWTO	United Nations World Travel Organization
USD	USdollar

1 Introduction and background

Marko Koščak and Tony O'Rourke

Objectives of the book

The underlying purpose

The underlying purpose of this publication is to explore a number of varied situations relating to Ethical and Responsible Tourism and based on the concept of how we manage sustainability in local tourism destinations. We are seeking to evaluate in this book, both the methodology and the practice by which we may be able to maintain environmental sustainability in fragile local communities, whilst benefiting from – for example – eco-tourism, cultural and heritage tourism and activity and adventure tourism.

We accept that the material in the book is wide-ranging covering theories, issues and examples across the globe with contributors from Australia, Central America, Europe Union countries, Japan, North America and South America. But in all of the material we have collectively – as contributors and editors – sought to express the underlying concept of how the impact of tourism on the ecological sustainability of local environments may be managed and effected in the most ethical and responsible way at a local destination level.

It should be made clear that the 15 Case Studies, as well as much of the material in the 11 Topic Chapters, are not wholly about planning or developing classic ethical and responsible tourism in terms of locations and facilities. Clearly culture and heritage play a very important role, in that we seek to preserve unique and often fragile tourism environments. But we have also connected to wider issues which relate – for example – to the spatial environment, the management of tourism waste and the concept of the intangible heritage.

Importantly, we are seeking to create a synchronism between theory and practice at the micro and local level. Tourism in its relationship to ecological sustainability and the environmental protection and regeneration of local environments is intensely connected to practice and the practicalities of ethical and sustainable tourism development. Clearly, we may not and should not ignore the significant amount of theoretical material which explains these relationships and synergies. But equally, we should not make a distinction between theory and practice – indeed we should make every effort to connect both together for the benefit of our objective in creating systems of Ethical & Responsible Tourism which are committed to managing sustainability in local tourism destinations.

This then implies an important role in connecting theory and practice – which in a sense is an important and we may suggest a valuable role for this publication. Furthermore, as we explain later, we are also seeking to make the information, ideas and material available important and valuable for a range of individuals, groups and organisations. This does not only include academics as teachers and researchers or practitioners, but other important groups who have a strong interest in the significant longer-term values of Ethical and Responsible Tourism. Beyond that, there are contents in this book which will appeal to those operating in tourism as a wider discipline or practice, as well as those engaged in ethical and responsible issues – also as a wider discipline or practice.

The balancing act

Of course, we have had to face the inevitable and complex issue of the balancing act that local organisations in fragile environments must conduct. On one side they are impelled to improve the sustainability of socio-economic inputs for local inhabitants. We are well aware from European examples, even in the most developed European economies, that rural, coastal, mountainous and other peripheral regions are experiencing population shift and economic decline. Tourism often provides an attractive methodology to improve income flows and maintain viable populations in peripheral regions. Unfortunately, at the same time, whilst such regions seek to strengthen their unique cultural, historical, ethnological and ecological structures that makes them worthy of preservation, the risk of becoming some form of cultural and heritage theme park overrun by tourists is a clear and undeniably certain threat. A number of our case studies amply show that risk made fact.

Thus, tourism in many fragile environments has been a destructive influence on local ecology, culture and heritage. There are areas, which have a high tourism footprint and where we have seen a massive impact on the ability for such areas to remain sustainable and ecologically effective. The economic benefits that tourism is proposed to have brought will tend to be centred on a relatively small group of influential investors – many of whom are not local or indeed even national. Thus striking a balance between important economic inputs to preserve unique environments, cultures and languages, and the risk of wiping out those environments from the detrimental effect of tourism is indeed a very difficult and hard balancing act.

At the same time, we should not discard the potential that local communities may achieve in developing sustainable, ethical local tourism activity, which also provides an equally sustainable and beneficial income flow to local communities. To a certain degree we have tended to view ethical and responsible tourism with a focus on eco-tourism, cultural and heritage tourism and activity and adventure tourism, as having a generally lesser impact on sustainability levels. This is frequently due to the size such activities involve, and their lower environmental footprint. There are contributions which will give readers an impressive view of the value of such levels of ethical and responsible tourism.

However, we hope that this publication will provide a valuable and incisive input into the wider discussion about the management of tourism to ensure that fragile environments are not damaged beyond repair, and that the cultural and historical heritage of such environments will provide significance to future generations.

The local level

Throughout this book, we would suggest that the value of the local level in terms of the development, sustainability and management of ethical and responsible tourism is discussed at a significantly deep level. Without doubt, our view is that one of the most effective developments of eco-tourism, cultural and heritage tourism and activity and adventure tourism has tended to be at a local level. In many cases, such forms of tourism have developed in regions that are geographically peripheral, rural or coastal in nature and have a lower level of socio-economic development than the country in which they are located. Remoteness and what society would perceive as underdevelopment will tend to make such destinations attractive to visitors seeking more natural and authentic experiences. These visitors may also tend to be independent travellers (i.e. groups of 1–5) or small group parties (i.e. groups of 6–15). Groups size may frequently be constrained by the size of local accommodation facilities or the potential difficulties of transport access in terms of cost or carrying capacity.

Nonetheless, despite the many problems faced in seeking the achievement of ethical and responsible tourism development – problems which we trust are clearly identified in this book – we would hope that this collection of ideas and examples from a wide range of individuals will prove both helpful and formative.

An overview of the impact of sustainability processes on local tourism operations

Introduction

A tourist destination may be defined as a geographical area, or a spatial unit, which has its own tourist attractions and is able to offer an experience by providing products and services, associated with the above features that are attractive for tourists. It can be understood as a complex tourism product as a whole, offered by the tourist region, which do not necessarily follow administrative boundaries. This spatial area is a destination to which tourists travel, and that is suitable to meet their needs by providing an appropriate and complex set of tourism-related products and services. Destination governance that both encourages sustainability and promotes competitiveness maximises the benefits of tourism for the destination community. One of the core elements of effective sustainable tourism is the ability to attract and satisfy select markets. Without travellers, the benefits of sustainable tourism cannot be achieved. While it is clear that competitiveness in the marketplace contributes to sustainable tourism, it must be noted that sustainable tourism contributes to competitiveness. Sustainable tourism principles lead to an authentic, quality experience desired by many travellers today.

There is growing concern internationally about how best to direct the sustainable management of local tourism destinations. Sustainable management of local destinations looks beyond the individual performance of a business, company, local authority and other organisations. Sustainable management looks towards a holistic and integrated level where the individual performance contributes to the greater goal of the local destination as a whole. Local tourism destination management has importance in controlling many impacts of tourism, thus insuring its sustainability. Destination management requires the integration of different planning tools, approaches and concepts that help shape the management and daily operation of tourism-related activities. To satisfy the definition of sustainable tourism, destinations must take an interdisciplinary, holistic and integrative approach, which includes four main objectives, namely, to

i   demonstrate sustainable destination management;
ii   maximise social and economic benefits for the host community and minimise negative impacts;
iii   maximise benefits to communities, visitors and cultural heritage and minimise impacts;
iv   maximise benefits to the environment and minimise negative impacts.

Destination planning and development of sustainable local tourism destinations

Tourism destination management can be seen as a continuous, long-term, targeted process, with tourism products and services can be found in the area, taken account into a consistent and complex way, with partners that can be professional and non-governmental organisations, local governments, trustees and independent businesses. Local tourism development and destination planning should be organised as kind of "creative way of tourism" which is a form of tourism that complies with culture and community ways. The community can and should manage their own tourism. In terms of area, it is the tourism in the area that is mainly connected with community ways and nature with natural attractions with the area's identity as well as the culture and history of that particular area. In terms of management, it is the tourism that has no or minimum impact on the environment and has sustainable, preferably local, management by allowing tourists, community and local people as well as affiliated persons to participate in the conservation of culture and environment in the community attractions. In terms of activity and process, it is the tourism that facilitates the learning by educating on culture and community ways as well as environment and ecosystem of tourism to create awareness and consciousness in tourists, community, local people and affiliated persons. In terms of participation, it is the tourism that is aware of the participation from tourists, community, local people and affiliated persons.

Tourism – your everyday life is someone else's adventure

The capacity of tourism for promoting a more sustainable and inclusive development is based, among other factors, on its capacity for taking place in a variety of environments, including rural or underdeveloped areas, on its impact on the economy resulting from the galvanisation of local economies and on the creation of direct and induced employment. The trend is to give tourists the opportunity to live like a local when visiting a destination. Authenticity and more interaction with local population improves contentment on both sides. Tourism is becoming a tripartite activity between providers, tourists, and locals. For a local destination, it is important to live the brand, to run the values of the brand through every act of product creation or communication by all people in the destination. Demand for authentic, experiential and transformative travel experiences is on the rise. Travellers are now more likely to seek out experiences that include cultural immersion and experiential education and have the potential to be eye opening or life changing. This trend is already recognised in many local destinations, up to now unknown and less or not visited.

Adventure travellers desire to explore the backstage of tourism areas, seeking out destinations that will allow them to feel like temporary locals through genuine amicable interactions between locals and visitors. Also demand for health and wellness travel experiences that enrich both mind and body continues to grow. However, travellers are less likely to base their primary motivations for travel in health and wellness, but rather expect a wide availability of physically active and mentally restorative secondary activities during travel. Additionally, companies are responding to demands for wellness elements within travel through innovative programs designed to limit traveller stress and maximise health and wellness outcomes during travel.

Local supply chain and added value

Tourism generates economic opportunities in its environment because it requires the provision of products and services. The impact of tourism on the local economy therefore depends on the strength of its value chain and on the local supplier ecosystem. The more the tourism industry is supplied locally, not only will induced economic growth increase but so will opportunities for new businesses. Therefore, the economic opportunities generated by tourism include the integration of local suppliers and service providers in the destination's value chain and proposition. This is essential for inclusive growth, in which the local communities participate in the benefits of tourism by creating new businesses and taking up new job opportunities. Local and sustainably sourced foods contribute to community economic resilience, reduce environmental impacts and may cultivate an authentic sense of place and culture for visitors. In response to increasing guest demand for local foods, the number of hotels with a local food sourcing policy is on the rise. Cuisine is also claimed to be the only art form that speaks to and involves all five human senses. The sensory stimulants that accompany an experience should support and enhance its theme. The more senses an experience engages, the more effective and memorable it can be. We experience the food itself and the environment in which food is consumed through sight, smell, taste and our tactile senses, and our sense of smell is largely and strongly associated with and appealed to by the dining experience. Food in all its forms is thus a potentially strong element in the branding of a destination.

Last chance and over-tourism

Recognising changes in the natural world caused in part or entirely due to human actions – such as climate change, pollution and habitat loss – tourists are pursuing what is referred to "last chance" tourism. Last chance tourism is travel motivated by the desire to see threatened or diminishing natural attractions, including glaciers, coral reefs and endangered species. Locations featuring these attractions may continue to experience heightened visitation, simultaneously creating opportunities for increased awareness and resource protection as well as increased risk of over-tourism. Over-tourism is acknowledged as a major threat to the industry. Over-tourism describes the tipping point where the costs of tourism outweigh the benefits for local communities due to overcrowding or poor management. If not managed properly, over-tourism is a threat to sustainable tourism development. The growing concern for over-tourism offers opportunities for tourism professionals to implement sustainability best practices and improve site-specific sustainable destination-level management plans. Over-tourism is a complex trend in the travel industry and calls upon destination managers to engage with all sectors and stakeholders involved in tourism towards long-term, fact-based planning to mitigate over-tourism.

Safety, security and social justice

Global threats to political stability, civil liberties and human rights challenge safety and security integral to the travel and tourism industry. Travellers are also increasingly aware of human rights and working conditions, demanding forms of responsible tourism that protect people and give back to communities. Sustainable tourism planners are faced with a unique set of challenges and opportunities in navigating strategies to address to both the needs of travellers and hosts with regard to human rights and social justice.

Inclusive tourism

Inclusive tourism is a growing sector within the industry that emphasises the idea that tourism is for all, and the operators should actively strive to improve accessibility for all persons. An inclusive tourism destination is a destination that offers a tourism experience based on its own, singular attributes; transforms the industry by boosting its competitiveness; creates decent employment; and promotes equal opportunities for all – especially the most vulnerable groups – to participate in and benefit from tourism activity, all in line with the principles of sustainable development. Inclusion can become a factor for competitiveness, both because of the inclusion of groups whose characteristics can help enrich the value proposition and because the inclusion of disadvantaged groups leads, in the medium term, to a healthier society in which tourism enterprises have a greater capacity for growth and success.

Not all tourism models have the same capacity for generating inclusive growth. In destinations with a locally competitive value chain, the economic impact of tourism is high. But in destinations dominated by foreign companies and capital (tour operators, airlines, hotel chains, etc.), the economic impact of tourism could be significantly less if these companies often bring in supplies from outside the destination and send the profits back to their countries of origin. Today, a large proportion of tourism demand, especially the millennial segment, expresses interest in visiting destinations and consuming products that have a clear environmental and cultural value, and in which the presence of the local population is almost essential. Such motivations and the resources that can satisfy them amount to a reality that favours the inclusion of vulnerable groups in tourism development, often enriching the value proposition of destinations.

Economic and social inclusion

At local level, tourism creates new business opportunities within and outside the tourism industry. Such new economic opportunities help diversify local economies, which is strategic for reducing poverty in regions with low levels of development, such as rural areas. In underdeveloped rural areas, tourism is an activity that generates new opportunities, unlike traditional sectors such as farming. It can therefore offer a way out for the most disadvantaged groups. Tourism employment thus helps reduce poverty and economic and social exclusion, and may offer alternatives to migration to cities. Despite the beneficial effects of job creation, it must be borne in mind that tourism employment is very unstable, even in advanced economies, with high levels of seasonality, turnover and part-time work.

Carrying capacity

In order to ensure sustainable tourism development and avoid problems of over-tourism, all voices from different stakeholders groups in the local destination need to be heard and respected. In line with that, sustainable tourism development has to include a carrying capacity study; that is, an estimate of "the maximum number of people who can use a site without an unacceptable alteration in the physical environment and without an unacceptable decline in the quality of the experience to both visitors and residents". The factors that need to be considered are physical impact of tourists, ecological impact of tourists, perceptions of overcrowding and cultural and social impact on local residents. The carrying capacity study is central to meeting the objectives of sustainable tourism development, which is to ensure that the tourists and day visitors attracted to the particular destination will not have a deleterious impact on the cultural or natural sites, that overcrowding will not result in visitor dissatisfaction and that local people will not feel antagonistic towards their "guests". This is essential if tourism is to contribute to the conservation of cultural and natural heritage through the realisation of economic value and raising awareness of, and commitment to, the local patrimony.

Sustainability as a concept within destination management and local tourism

Sustainable development and sustainable tourism

Based on general starting points of sustainable development in 1992, the creation of the set of principles for sustainable tourism was proposed by the World Wildlife Fund (WWF, 1992) and Tourism Concern as following:

- using resources sustainably,
- reducing over-consumption and waste,
- maintaining diversity,
- integrating tourism into planning,
- supporting local economies,
- involving local communities,
- consulting stakeholders and the public,
- training staff,
- marketing tourism responsibly,
- undertaking research.

Sustainable tourism is one of the approaches to the development of the tourism sector, which should assist the decision-maker in tourism to best balance its positive and negative effects on current and future population. Sustainable tourism is defined by the United Nations World Tourism Organization (UNWTO, 1998) as "tourism that takes full account of its current and future economic, social and environmental impacts, addressing the needs of visitors, the industry, the environment and host communities". Sustainable tourism is not a "niche tourism sector"; sustainable tourism principles can apply to all types of tourism including eco-tourism, agri-tourism and even mass tourism. Sustainable tourism principles recognise that tourism must balance economic, social and environmental issues in order to maximise benefits for destination communities. The following four pillars are identifying sustainable tourism development:

- Economic sustainability: The industry is profitable in both the immediate and long terms and maintains growth rates at manageable levels. This includes promoting tourism while keeping an eye on carrying capacities.
- Environmental sustainability: The industry is compatible with the maintenance of biological diversity and environmental resources. A focus must be placed on the capacity of the natural and built environments to handle tourism without damage.
- Social sustainability: The industry helps to increase people's control over their lives and local identity. It also supports communities to absorb increasing tourist arrivals without adversely affecting or damaging indigenous culture.
- Local sustainability: The industry has increasing levels of local involvement in its development, and it benefits local communities. If the tourism stakeholders do not participate in the protection of the attraction or destination, there is a danger of overuse by tourists and the attraction will eventually be destroyed.

Therefore, sustainable tourism should

- make optimal use of environmental resources, maintaining essential ecosystems and helping to conserve biodiversity;
- respect socio-cultural authenticity, conserve built and living cultural heritage and contribute to cross-cultural understanding and tolerance;
- ensure long-term socio-economic benefits, fairly distributed to all community stakeholders, including stable employment and income-earning opportunities, social services and poverty alleviation.

Responsible tourism

The concept of responsible/sustainable tourism brings more hope in this regard by striking a balance between the sustenance of community and sustainability of culture. Responsible tourism aims at the betterment of material well-being, community engagement, cultural identity, cross-cultural interaction, community services, exposure and awareness of the local community along with sustaining the commitment of community towards cultural preservation *(Sustainable Commitment)*. Sustainable Commitment of Community is a sign of cultural sustainability too. Being the custodians of authentic culture, tourism development should take the local community into confidence and strive to make their commitment towards conservation sustainable. Tourism creates both positive and negative impacts. Positive impacts include new employment and business opportunities and enhancement of road networks and the transportation system, as well as more entertainment opportunities. On the other hand, tourism has negative effects on the host community. It may lead to more traffic and demand on public places, and services increase the use and associated problems of drugs and alcohol, and cause damage to the environment. In certain places, tourism activities increase the cost of living.

Sustainable tourism management

Sustainable tourism management requires the core functions of management – planning, organising, leading and controlling – to meet the criteria required to achieve sustainable tourism goals. Sustainable tourism management requires mastery of some important management concepts:

- *Change Management*: Implementing change within systems – whether business practices or personal behaviour change – is difficult and time-consuming.
- *System Management*: Tourism systems are complex and require action by a wide variety of actors – some of which don't even consider themselves in tourism. Tourism systems do not have a hierarchy where one person or organisation is in control – but rely on collaboration and cooperation. Traditional strategic planning models often fail as they assume "command and control" – new models of managing in systems are often required, where participatory planning and partnership approach are base for planning.
- *Strategic Management*: Sustainable tourism management is a strategic activity – it requires long-term commitment. Ensuring all actors in the process to maintain motivation and commitment requires deliberate actions over the long term.
- *Continuous Improvement*: Sustainable tourism management is based on the principle of "continuous improvement". As goals are achieved, new goals are set to further improve performance. As such, sustainable tourism management should be considered a process, not a project.

Sustainable tourism criteria and aims

Sustainable tourism criteria outline a set of activities that should be undertaken by destinations. These actions include the following:

- planning for destination growth and development;
- monitoring sustainability criteria and system performance;
- developing a policy and regulatory framework to support sustainability goals;
- destination marketing;
- infrastructure development and government services to increase competitiveness;
- managing benefits from destination assets – cultural and natural.

More specifically UNWTO and UNEP (UNEP/UNWTO, 2013) identified the following 12 aims for sustainable tourism:

1 ECONOMIC VIABILITY: To ensure the viability and competitiveness of tourism destinations and enterprises, so that they are able to continue to prosper and deliver benefits in the long term.

2 LOCAL PROSPERITY: To maximise the contribution of tourism to the prosperity of the host destination, including the proportion of visitor spending that is retained locally.

3 EMPLOYMENT QUALITY: To strengthen the number and quality of local jobs created and supported by tourism, including the level of pay, conditions of service and availability to all without discrimination by gender, race, disability or in other ways.

4 SOCIAL EQUITY: To seek a widespread distribution of economic and social benefits from tourism throughout the recipient community, including improving opportunities, income and services available to the poor.

5 VISITOR FULFILMENT: To provide a safe, satisfying and fulfilling experience for visitors, available to all without discrimination by gender, race, disability or in other ways.

6 LOCAL CONTROL: To engage and empower local communities in planning and decision-making about the management and future development of tourism in their area, in consultation with other stakeholders.

7 COMMUNITY WELL-BEING: To maintain and strengthen the quality of life in local communities, including social structures and access to resources, amenities and life support systems, avoiding any form of social degradation or exploitation.

8 CULTURAL RICHNESS: To respect and enhance the historic heritage, authentic culture, traditions and distinctiveness of host communities.

9 PHYSICAL INTEGRITY: To maintain and enhance the quality of landscapes, both urban and rural, and avoid the physical and visual degradation of the environment.

10 BIOLOGICAL DIVERSITY: To support the conservation of natural areas, habitats and wildlife, and minimise damage to them.

11 RESOURCE EFFICIENCY: To minimise the use of scarce and non-renewable resources in the development and operation of tourism facilities and services.

12 ENVIRONMENTAL PURITY: To minimise the pollution of air, water and land and the generation of waste by tourism enterprises and visitors.

Participatory approach and partnership

Within tourism literature and practice, a wide range of terms are used to infer inclusivity or participation, including alliances, coalitions, forums and task forces. Over recent years the notion of "partnership" has become particularly prevalent. It is a term that is used particularly by the government and practitioners to describe regular, sometimes cross-sectoral, interactions between groups who aim to achieve a set goal or policy objective. Partnership is seen as a "long-term relationship based on a common cause and mutual respect. Partnerships are believed to have the potential to promote discussion, negotiation and the building of mutually acceptable proposals about how tourism should be developed".

There are a number of reasons why co-operative approaches appear to sit well with the principles of sustainable development:

- Collaboration among a range of stakeholders including non-economic interests might promote more consideration of the varied natural, built and human resources that need to be sustained.

- By involving stakeholders from several fields and with diverse interests, there may be greater potential for integrative/holistic approaches to policy development, which may advance sustainability.
- If multiple stakeholders affected by tourism development were involved in the policy-making process, then this might lead to a more equitable distribution of the resulting benefits and costs. The idea is that participation would raise awareness of tourism impacts on all stakeholders, and this heightened awareness should lead to fairer policies.
- Broad participation in policy-making could help democratise decision-making, empower participants and lead to capacity building and skill acquisition amongst participants.

The ten major groupings of the tools include lists of techniques to assess or measure various aspects of sustainability. These "tools' can also be otherwise referred to as "techniques of sustainability".

Tourism, ethics and responsibility

Introduction

An initial view is that ethical and responsible concepts of tourism development may have the ability to *push* tourism activity into more ethical, responsible and sustainable methodologies. Pushing does, of course, imply that the recipients may be less than happy with the projected direction in which they are moved. Tourism actors may simply see ethical, responsible and sustainable tourism as a new form of marketing which will have an appeal to a wide group of tourists who seek to engage in this form of tourism activity. Clearly that is a rather cynical view, but we have little evidence at the moment as to why tourism consumers may engage with ethical, responsible and sustainable tourism. Probably, it is not cost related and may have a greater connectivity to lifestyle issues and values; it is also a trend which we see across generational groups in tourism – not simply the "back-packer" (18–25 years old) but also the "silver tourist" (60–71 years old).

But should we also look at the *pull* effect? Tourism at the destination and agency level may see ethical, responsible and sustainable tourism as a marketing emblem to attract specific groups who may feel comfortable that they are making some form of ecological contribution (however limited this may be).

So, is it *push* or *pull*? Perhaps it may be a combination of both, although we have no coherent evidence to suggest how these trends may operate. However, we may suggest that to a certain degree this debate about the motivations of tourism engaging at ethical, responsible and sustainable level is overtaken by the serious issues which face many tourism destinations. This is the concept of over-tourism capacity and the destruction of the cultural and heritage environment by a simple overload of tourist activity.

Over-tourism

Whilst the very phrase "over-tourism" has a dramatic capacity, we should be aware of a number of global destinations where tourism is having an increasingly disastrous impact on the local environment, culture and heritage. In many cases this applies to city destinations (we will give as an example the situation in Venice), but equally it will also apply to rural destinations, where excessive tourism is having a dangerous impact on the local society and culture.

There is evidence that certain forms of mass tourism activity – particularly those related to "cruise tourism" involving vessels with thousands of passengers – are having a destructive effect on the level of sustainability of a number of fragile destinations. This is possibly more destructive than the earlier manifestations of day coach visitors on environmental sustainability.

This is more apparent in tourism destinations such as Barcelona and Venice, where what can be described as "day visitors" have no really significant economic input on the local economies, and where the direct spending of such visitors is relatively minimal. At the same time, massive groups of tourists have a detrimental effect on the physical, cultural and ecological infrastructure. In turn, this is promoting angry responses by local inhabitants, who feel threatened and endangered by this substantial tourism influx.

The flawed economic concept

Many tourism operators are driven by the concept of the tourist as a generator of gross domestic product (GDP) growth. As a result they will view this form of mass tourism as highly positive; for example, cruise ships pay large harbour fees and generate income for local coach companies who transfer the visitors from cruise harbours to city centres. But, at the same time, such visitors do not contribute to hotels and other accommodation facilities, and as their visits are relatively brief (e.g. 10:00–15:00) they have a minimal income generational effect on local restaurants and bars.

This therefore returns to the underlying problem in that we continue to measure tourism growth in purely monetary terms – i.e. GDP growth. We value this in terms of personal consumption, business investment, net exports and government expenditure on goods and services. But such an economic model fails to understand the cost of ecological destruction – how do we calculate the real cost of the wearing down of the physical environment of historic cities (e.g. Barcelona, Dubrovnik and Venice) by the constant hordes of low-spending day visitors.

Indeed, in the case of Dubrovnik, it is possible to pose the question that the hordes of cruise ship visitors may continue to have a greater destructive effect in the longer term on the culture and heritage of the city than the dramatic and disastrous military assault by the Yugoslav Army and Navy in 1992–1993. This would lead us to a greater level of concern about considering the balance for future sustainability between short-term economic inputs and long-term ecological, cultural and heritage protection.

The saturation phenomenon

An interesting phenomenon is to examine the so-called saturation of historic tourism centres from three possible negative sources. These included the following:

- low-cost flights;
- Airbnb and similar internet-enabled holiday rental structures;
- cruise tourism.

Low-cost flights

The rapid development of European tourism, particularly flows into the Mediterranean/Southern Europe during the late 1960s onwards, was primarily met by what could be classed as the construction of tourism ghettos – large complexes of hotels and self-catering accommodation with a consequent expansion of associated facilities. Tourists were generally appreciated as being suppliers of income into what were generally "poor economies" by Northern European standards. Many resorts were built on the outskirts of existing settlements (e.g. Benidorm, Tenerife), so did not impact significantly on historic areas. The growth of self-catering apartment tourism, and then the development of rural villas, also tended to be beneficial to host economies, as these tourists would tend to purchase food and meals in local restaurants and bars.

However, de-regulation of the European flight sector by 1997 (European Council Decision 87/602/EEC, 1987) resulted in the rapid growth of low-cost carriers flying not only to existing holiday destinations but also to cities. Initially, this was a boost to hotels and to existing self-catering accommodation (apartments, rooms); whilst local tourism benefited there were some less pleasant by-products. A number of cities with cheap flight connections and relatively cheap living costs (e.g. Tallinn, Prague) began to suffer from the concept of the "hen and stag parties" which generated socially unacceptable levels of alcohol consumption.

Airbnb

However, a more complex problem began to emerge – the concept of the Airbnb apartment. This provided good quality facilities for individuals, couples or family groups in central areas of historic cities; the initial stage was the provision of a room or rooms to travellers sharing with local residents. However, the next stage was the purchase of apartments/houses by entrepreneurs for Airbnb lettings, thereby removing them from the housing stock and also contributing to price inflation in the housing market. This had a direct effect on more price-sensitive groups such as low-income families and students.

Cruise tourism

Cruise tourism has appeared to have expanded phenomenally. If we take the example of the Mediterranean cruise, these were once the prerogative of the wealthy to avoid cold Northern European winters, given that vessels were relatively small (probably less than 900 passengers) and thus did not impact hugely on the destinations they visited. Estimations of current vessel sizes in the Mediterranean are that many will exceed 2,000 passengers (author estimation). Data from Mediterranean cruise port operators (MedCruise, 2017) indicates that the number of passengers has increased from 8.6 million in 2000 to 27.4 million in 2016. This represents an overall increase from 2000 to 2016 of 218.6%.

Without doubt, these cruise vessels provide economic inputs not only to the cruise ship operators, but also to the ports from which they operate, and for the airlines who carry the passengers from their home locations to the embarkation/disembarkation ports. Nonetheless, the fact remains that the direct economic inputs of cruise ship visitors into the local economies visited is minimal. Because they receive all meals and services on the board, the vessels are unlikely to spend other than minimal amounts at onshore destinations. Visits to onshore destinations normally occur between 10:00 and 16:00 hours. The effect of these visitors on historic city centres (e.g. Dubrovnik and Barcelona) is almost catastrophic, as massive groups commandeer the streets and have a harmful footfall effect on the local infrastructure. The same problem applies in rural areas of strong touristic interest (e.g. Cinque Terre in NW Italy – *please see Section 1, Chapter 8, Part B.*

Venice – a city in continuing peril

In the 1960s, Venice was described as a "city in peril", mainly due to the effects of flooding from the high tides in the winter period (the *acqua alta*). The highest level was reached on 4 November 1966 (Commune di Venezia, 2018). Flooding may be seen to have created significant physical problems to the historic infrastructure of buildings although to a degree this has been mitigated by the development of flood control mechanisms protecting the lagoon from the Adriatic Sea. To a strong degree, there were large numbers of day-trippers coming from nearby tourism facilities (e.g. Lido di Jesolo, Padova, Vicenza and Verona). But these numbers were clearly eclipsed by the dramatic rise in the number of cruise ship passengers. As a result there has been the injection of huge numbers of tourists into the central historical area (Centro stórico), which has approximately 20% of the population of the Commune di Venezia.

Between 2003 and 2015, the population of the Commune di Venezia fell by 13.1% (Annuario del Turismo, Commune di Venezia, 2016); at the same time the number of visitors to the city over that same period rose by 63.9% (Annuario del Turismo, Commune di Venezia, 2016). In 2016, it is estimated that 7 million tourists arrived in Venice – but only 3 million of those tourists actually stayed in accommodation in the city (www.veniceinperil.org, 2018). This would indicate that less than half the tourists were resident and engaging in the local economy. Cruise passengers were an important component of the total number of visitors; in 2016, 1.6 million cruise passengers arrived at the port of Venice.

Thus, we have a situation in which the number of tourists, especially those arriving on day visits (i.e. cruise passengers and coach arrivals from other resorts in the Veneto region) is increasing, whilst the number of local inhabitants is declining. It may be suggested (author's estimates) that by 2020 the population of the city may fall to around 180,000. This would be below the population of the city at the height of the Serene Republic's power in the 17th century (albeit excluding what is described as the terra firma – e.g. the mainland of the Veneto region, parts of Friuli-Venezia-Giulia autonomous region as well as the coastal regions of present-day Slovenia, Croatia and Montenegro).

In May 2016, it was suggested that (www.idealista.it) Venice was the most expensive Italian city for housing prices on a square metre (m^2) basis. The average price per m^2 was EUR4,423 compared to Milan (EUR3,460) and Rome (EUR3,386). Such overpricing has the capacity to drive out local residents and at the same time will make it practically impossible for those working in the tourism industry to buy or even rent property in the city. In December 2018, purchase prices per m^2 in the Dorsoduro district (between Santa Lucia railway station and the Rialto) ranged between EUR4,583 and EUR8,214 (www.idealista.it). Local observers claim that there is a direct relationship between the increase in rental and purchase prices for property and the massive increase in the availability of Airbnb accommodation. Before the advent of Airbnb, most holiday lettings were conducted by specialist agencies letting a range of apartments. Airbnb has not only intruded on this market, but at the same time has also edged into the hotel market. The website Inside Airbnb (http://insideairbnb.com) indicated that in 2017 the average price per night for the 6,027 tourist apartments advertised on Airbnb was EUR130. The author's guesstimate is that this has the capacity to generate a rental income of around EUR30,000 per annum and thus place living accommodation well outside the capability of many working in the Centro Stórico.

As well as the examples mentioned above, it is also interesting to look at parallel and comparative evidence from our Turkish contributor about the issues with historic buildings in Istanbul (*please see Section 2, Chapter 21, Part B*). Urban historical monuments, as we have seen in Venice and many other historic cities, are subject to the effects of huge tourism footfall and the resulting degradation of the physical infrastructure. How to ensure sustainable and protective limitations on historic buildings in cities with strong historic implications – in this case Istanbul – is extremely difficult. The authors stress the need for inclusivity as being critical for increasing tourism value but at the same time ensuring a balanced approach to both conservation; the need of an inclusive approach requires a very dynamic approach to the sustainability of heritage sites.

Sustainability or regeneration?

In one of our Topic Chapters (*please see Section 1, Chapter 10, Part C*), the author raises the issue of a focus on regeneration over sustainability. The difference appears to be defined in that regeneration is concerned on a style of management which ensures that the overall environment is in a better condition than before the regenerative process commenced. This would assume that sustainability is concerned with retaining a strong environmental steady state, but not necessarily developing, expanding and improving on that steady state. It would also suggest that sustainable methodologies are concerned to meet immediate needs, whilst regeneration has a longer-term approach. This is certainly an interesting issue to discuss and develop, and it may well be that some aspects of ethical tourism (e.g. active and adventure tourism – *please see Section 1, Chapter 6, Part B*) are more connected to environmental regeneration rather than simply maintaining the status quo.

However, any debate about the role of either sustainability or regeneration must necessarily connect to specific local circumstances. In the book, we are deeply concerned with and connected to the maintenance and growth of local tourism environments both now and in the future; this is in order to protect and enhance local culture, heritage and economic sustainability. Undoubtedly, in ensuring socio-economic development at a local level we must also be concerned with regeneration of the tangible (buildings and environments) as well as the intangible (culture, heritage and language). So perhaps there is no immediate contest between sustainability and regeneration.

At the same time we have to recognise that local communities operate in different ways in approaching the problems of developing ethical, sustainable or regenerative solutions. The Australian case study (*please see Section 2, Chapter 19, Part B*) focuses on a biodiversity "hot spot" famous for premium wine production, gastronomy and eco-tourism. But it also explains that such a community is deeply affected by climate

change; despite having strong demographic growth and an affluent population of retirees, second home owners, 'electronic cottagers' and alternative lifestylers, it cannot
necessarily find mechanisms to successfully cope with the climatic changes which are
envisaged over the next 30–40 years.

This would therefore imply that sustainability and regeneration are not mutually
exclusive; indeed, they may be seen as weapons in a long-term battle with environmental shifts and changes.

Tangible ecological issues

Culture and heritage as social concepts feature strongly in this book, but at the same
time we have evidence of physical rather than social heritage situations. One immediate
example is the use of cycle paths – cycling provides a close relationship to culture, heritage and history – but it is clearly predicated on the need to have a strong and sustainable physical infrastructure. The case study from Montesilvano (*please see Section 2,
Chapter 15, Part A*) demonstrates the role of cycling as an alternative to the car (thus
immediately environmentally supportive) and at the same time indicates the lack of
distinction between the cycling local population and the cycling tourist population.
But importantly, this case also draws attention to problems with the overall environment due to climate changes – urban flooding and extreme weather are mentioned. The
Montesilvano experiment seeks to manage both the impact of climate and the need of
the population to find more ecologically sustainable methods of transportation.

We also have a further example of the physical heritage dealing with tangible ecological issues; the case study on the Sustainable Garden of Pirámides de Güímar (*please
see Section 2, Chapter 20, Part B*) shows how an outdoor museum and botanical garden may also act as a focus for the preservation of critically endangered species as well
as representing something redolent of the rich local culture and heritage. What is important is the degree of collaboration between academic institutions and such physical
environmental activities to demonstrate what tangible environmental results may be
achieved, as this also engages visitors and provides them with a better understanding
of the natural environment. This also indicates that whilst such ventures have the ability to make a contribution to the development and promotion of sustainable tourism,
at the same time they are having a regenerative effect on the local economy.

Economic and political pressures

It is also necessary to examine the effect of economic and political pressures in cultural and heritage centres, where the need to dynamise tourism inflows and incomes
appears to take precedence over the protection of fragile environments. The Mexican
case study (*please see Section 2, Chapter 22, Part B*) examines the effect of overpro-
vision of mass tourism in the north-west of Mexico. Economic pressures from state
and private sector institutions keen to boost revenues resulted in massive tourism
facility expansion as well as attracting significant inflows of workers from outside
the immediate region. Whilst this expansion benefited the developers of mass tourism
accommodation, it had a downscaling effect on local businesses which were more
acclimatised to small-scale tourism activity. It also created a situation in which a large
proportion of the population were dependent on tourist activity and thus sensitive to
any significant shifts in incoming tourism numbers.

Intangible cultural and heritage issues

It is also important to point out that culture and heritage, as part of ethical and sustainable tourism development at a local level, are not wholly based on tangible factors (e.g. buildings and natural physical features). In the case of San Francisco, our contributing author points out (*please see Section 2, Chapter 27, Part C*) that policy tools to protect the cultural heritage have traditionally focused on safeguarding physical assets. This approach tends to overlooks the intangible contributions that define, in this case, American life. The case study therefore examines the protection of one particular class of intangible assets: businesses with demonstrated contributions to their neighbourhood's history and identity – thereby introducing a roadmap that takes into account a broader definition of cultural heritage. This is clearly a valuable and innovative approach that should have resonance for all seeking to preserve the valuable cultural and historical heritage of our surroundings, to the best effect.

Concluding thoughts

Tourism, ethics and responsibility – undoubtedly as we will see in this book, these issues pose a number of contrasting problems. **Tourism** seeks to maximise people flows, but **ethical tourism** seeks to minimise those people flows to ensure that footfall does not damage unique cultural and historical environments. **Responsibility** is about creating and agreeing a balance between socio-economic objectives which benefit local communities in the short to medium term (e.g. boosting wealth) and the effect on those communities over the medium to long term (destroying the ecological environment).

From the comments above we can see that sustainable tourism has a huge problem in major tourism centres such as Venice – similar problems exist in many other urban and rural centres. The advent of the cruise industry, with massive vessels and the capacity to manipulate the local economy, has created a situation in which historic environments are unable to develop ethical, responsible and sustainable tourism. Where such tourism exists, it is economically pushed to the margins of local business activity.

Added to this is the rapid growth of apartment lettings, which although apparently beneficial to tourists, in the longer term appears to be dynamically destructive in terms of the ability of local tourism workers and other residents to access reasonably priced accommodation.

It is therefore interesting to pose the question as to whether ethical, responsible and sustainable tourism may be developed in the large tourism destinations – of which Barcelona, Dubrovnik and Venice are prime examples. Will such tourism in urban areas be pushed to the margins – providing facilities for tourists who have local knowledge? Will such tourism be therefore focused on rural areas, where there is a greater capacity to develop facilities which demonstrate the local culture and heritage and which are also firmly placed in local culture and sustainability? But at the same time, we see evidence of the degradation of local tourism in rural communities as the result of excessive tourism footfall.

Hopefully, the extensive information provided in the Topic Chapters and Case Studies by our wide breadth of contributors from across the globe will enable discussion about these issues.

Explanation of the Topic Chapter and Case Study Themes

The concept

This book has three core themes:

- Part A: Destination Management aspects of ethical sustainable development
- Part B: Environmental & Social aspects of ethical sustainable development
- Part C: The business impacts of ethical sustainable development

These themes are both addressed within the **Topic Chapters** and the **Case Studies**. Therefore, within the Topic Chapters there is a breakdown between the three themes, a similar situation applies to the Case Studies. Furthermore, the editorial analysis also addresses primary issues on the basis of the three thematic approaches, through reviews of the overall impact of both Topic Chapters and Case Studies.

The importance of the themes

Why are the themes important?
    They are important in that we view them as follows:

- Making a specific focus on particular areas in which both theory and practice may be considered in a measured and planned way;
- Providing a conceptual base which connects Topic Chapters and Case Studies potentially through the connectivity between theory and practice.

It is important to stress that the themes do not impose hard boundaries. Ideas can move across each of the themes, and we have reinforced this concept through the **Links** section which can be found in every Topic Chapter. The Links provide a connection from the Topic Chapters to what we have judged to be appropriate and relevant Case Studies over the range of themes. Thus, whilst Links will generally be from Topic Chapters to Case Studies in the same thematic area (i.e. A, B or C), in many cases here will also be links to other important and equally relevant Case Studies in other thematic areas.

    Essentially, all of the themes are inter-related to the overall concept of Ethical & Responsible Tourism which is thereby related to the management of sustainability in local tourism destinations.

    How does this work?
    Our view in seeking to explain the three themes is as follows:

1   Destination Management is about the local operational level and is close to how local tourism operators connect to a local sustainable environment.
2   The Environmental & Social aspects reinforce the sustainable values we expect local operators and local communities to understand and seek to achieve.
3   The business impacts are connected to how we can really make ethical and sustainable tourism work in a practical economic and business sense.

What is the value for the reader?

Having Topic Chapters (which generally address issues) and Case Studies (which generally address specific and practical examples) is a very important understanding and learning tool. As may be seen from Guide to the book this publication is intended to address a range of issues, possibilities and audiences. The role of Topic Chapters and Case Studies, which are all connected to the three themes, is extremely important. It provides a base for understanding and development of the ideas which are mentioned, discussed and, in some cases, actively promoted.

We would not however see the thematic areas as being exclusive; there is hopefully a very essential flow of concepts and ideas between them, which is intended to break down any possible barriers between the three thematic concepts.

We have also been quite demanding in our selection of the material in the book. As well as inviting contributions from well-known experts in the field of Ethical & Responsible Tourism, we have also taken care to include young researchers who have been developing some interesting perspectives. In addition, we have also sought to cross disciplinary boundaries – pulling in contributors from areas outside the immediate tourism field, such as in architecture, planning, marketing, business and economics.

Importantly, the purpose of any publication such as this is to challenge concepts, to promote potentially interesting new ideas and then to see what outcomes may develop and be of value to a wider audience.

A guide to the book

In *Appendix 1*, you will find a simple matrix-based guide to content and applications; in section "Explanation of the Topic Chapter and Case Study Themes" above we explained the differentiation of the book between the Topic Chapters (Section 1) and Case Studies (Section 2) and how these relate to the three core themes.

In addition, we also have the Final Thoughts (Section 3) which looks at some critical thinking in regard to the overall subject of this book.

Additional elements of the book are found in the editorial material:

- Chapter 13 discusses the Topic Chapters, identifies key learning points and poses some further questions.
- Chapter 29 discusses the Case Studies, identifies key learning points and poses some further questions.
- Chapter 31 contains the Conclusions, which seek to answer the open questions about environmental sustainability, the protection of our common heritage and culture, and the role of tourism as a driver or as a participant in the support processes.

The purpose of the matrix is to indicate how the various sections may be applied in varied circumstances according to the requirements of different users. Whilst making general assumptions about the categories of reader, we have tried to be more specific in indicating which parts of the book would be most appropriate to differing groups.

References

Association of Mediterranean Cruise Ports – MedCruise. (2017). *Annual Statistics*. [Online] accessed 23.12.18:
https://www.medcruise.com/node/13

Commune di Venezia. (2018). *Archivo storico – dati di livello a Venezia*. [Online] accessed 21.05.19:
https://www.comune.venezia.it/it/content/dati-e-statistiche-0

Commune di Venezia. (2016).*Annuario del Turismo*. [Online] accessed 21.05.19:
https://live.comune.venezia.it/sites/live.comune.venezia.it/files/articoli/allegati/Annuario%20Turismo%202016_slide%20v6-1.pdf

Council of the European Union. (1987). *European Council Decision 87/602/EEC*. *Official Journal of the European Union*: JOL_1987_374_R_0019_009. Bruxelles: Europa.

Idealista Property Sales Website. (2016). *Listings for Venice*. [Online] accessed 21.05.19:
https://www.idealista.it

Inside Airbnb Website. (2017). *Adding Data to the Debate – Venice*. [Online] accessed 21.05.19:
http://insideairbnb.com/venice/

UN Environment Programme & UN World Tourism Organaisation. (2013). *Making Tourism More Sustainable – A Guide for Policy Makers*. Madrid: UNWTO.

Venice in Peril. (2018). *The Venice in Peril Report*. [Online] accessed 23.12.18: https://www.veniceinperil.org/projects/the-venice-report-project

World Wildlife Fund (WWF). (1992). *Tourism Concern: Beyond the Green Horizon: Principles for sustainable Tourism*. Godalming: WWF UK.

World Tourism Organization (WTO). (1998). *Guide for Local Planner Authorities in Developing Sustainable Tourism*. Madrid: UNWTO.

Section 1

Topics

Part A

Destination Management aspects of ethical sustainable development

2 Cultural and heritage tourism – a potential for local sustainable tourism development?

Marko Koščak and Tony O'Rourke

Summary

In this chapter we discuss the interrelationship between heritage and cultural tourism, within a local rural environment. This is based on two examples:

1 Heritage Trails in Slovenian Istria
2 The Green Box network in NW Ireland

Both projects developed as a programme of action for rural regeneration through sustainable tourism – promoted at national and international levels – which at the same time retained local focus and personality. In the Slovenian example we view the experiences gathered over some 15 years of activity enabling taking an historic and developmental viewpoint. In the Irish example, we show how a cross-border tourism initiative, with international support, created the possibility to overcome centuries of ethno-religious and cultural conflict. A beneficial methodology for growing and developing a level of sustainable tourism that enhances the totality of local and regional environments is the multi-stakeholder approach. A key feature is the need for small-scale tourism entrepreneurs to develop a promotional mechanism to market their product or service at a wider national and international level. The Slovenian experience (Koščak and O'Rourke, 2018) displays the critical success factor of co-ordinated action between local and regional stakeholders from public, private and NGO sector for common benefit.

There is a shared opinion between tourism experts that cultural tourism involves four elements:

• overall tourism experience;
• application of cultural heritage assets;
• consumption of experiences and products;
• role of the individual tourist.

It is obvious that cultural tourism offers an activity in which a destination's cultural and heritage assets are presented for the consumption of tourists – domestic or foreign. We present development of the heritage/cultural tourism product in SE Slovenia and SW Ireland whilst critically evaluating results and impacts – positive and negative – achieved and reflected in the local/regional economic, social and environmental livelihoods over the past 20 years.

Links

The following Case Study links may be of interest to readers of this Topic Chapter:

- Case Studies Part A (Destination Management aspects of ethical sustainable development) – Chapter 14/Chapter 16/Chapter 17/Chapter 18;
- Case Studies Part B (Environmental & Social aspects of ethical sustainable development) – Chapter 19/Chapter 20/Chapter 21/Chapter 23;
- Case Studies Part C (The business impacts of ethical sustainable development) – Chapter 27.

Please see the Contents on pages v–viii, and the Guide to the text-book in Appendix 1 for further information.

Alternative tourism concepts

The classic "sun and sand" tourism destinations in Europe are finding it increasingly difficult to hold onto their share of the market as new areas develop elsewhere in the world and become more affordable.

"Alternative" forms of tourism, on the other hand, are booming. According to figures by the end of millennium they are growing almost three times (8%) as fast as the classic tourism market. Recent market surveys reveal that more and more people are interested not only in trying out new places but also in discovering different forms of tourism. They are also placing greater emphasis on quality products, on more environmentally conscious forms of tourism and on shorter but more frequent trips.

One way to meet these new challenges and to capitalise on changing market preferences in Europe is to consider developing sustainable tourism based on rich natural and cultural heritage. For example, with so many different landscapes, climates, cultural particularities and traditions, dialects and natural environments, Slovenia offers an ideal platform for these more specialised and increasingly popular forms of tourism. This also includes region of Southern Primorska, the most visited tourist region in Slovenia, when considering tourism volumes in the most recent decades.

Ireland presents a different perspective – a single geographic zone as an island in the Eastern Atlantic, but containing the territory of two states, the Republic of Ireland and the UK. Antagonism between the Irish and British heritage remains a compelling and dangerous issue. Furthermore, the UK withdrawal from the European Union (EU) creates new problems and potentially new antagonisms.

Facts and figures in Europe – the challenge for tourism destination with heritage and cultural tourism products?

The UN World Tourism Organisation (UNWTO) has predicted that much of the increase in European tourism receipts over the coming decade will come from alternative forms of travel not involving the classic "sun and sand" tourism. This type of tourism is expected to account for over 20% of all travel in the period between 2018 and 2028 and is set to grow faster than any other market segment. Some of the growth will come from a greater volume of tourists, but a significant portion will result from a shift in tourist numbers between the different segments (Source: Eurobarometer, Flash EB No 258, 2009).

There may be several reasons for these shifting trends:

- People are becoming more experienced in their travel choices and more discerning in their selection of destination. This leads them to search for new places and new tourism products.
- They are more mobile – cross-border travel is easier than ever thanks to the liberalisation of the airlines, construction of new roads and European integration.
- They are taking shorter but more frequent holidays throughout the year.
- They are more active whilst on holiday, seeking out different activities.
- The European population is getting older but staying active longer.
- Finally, we may discern from research that tourists are more increasingly concerned about the environment.

From the Figures 2.1 and 2.2, we may conclude that the sea remains a popular choice (20%), but a significant number of European citizens mentioned rest and recreation (36%) as a preferred destination. As to the criteria for choosing one area over another, not surprisingly the climate figures are prominent (45%) but so are other factors such as scenery, historical interest and the environment. These are on a par with the cost of accommodation and travel. These interesting findings indicate that the main expectations from non-traditional, emerging destinations focus on local culture, lifestyles and traditions as the primary magnets of non-conventional destinations of tourism in Europe (see Figure 2.3).

When deciding on holiday destinations, most Europeans named the location's environment (e.g. its overall attractiveness) as the key consideration (31%). Cultural heritage (24%) and the options for entertainment (15%) were the second and third most widespread responses in regard to factors that influenced a choice of destination (see Figure 2.4).

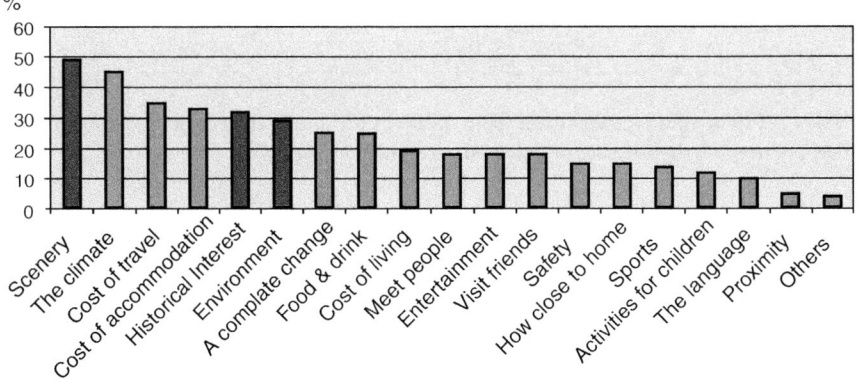

Figure 2.1 Criteria for choosing a tourism destination.
Source: Eurobarometer Survey, Europeans on holiday, 1999.

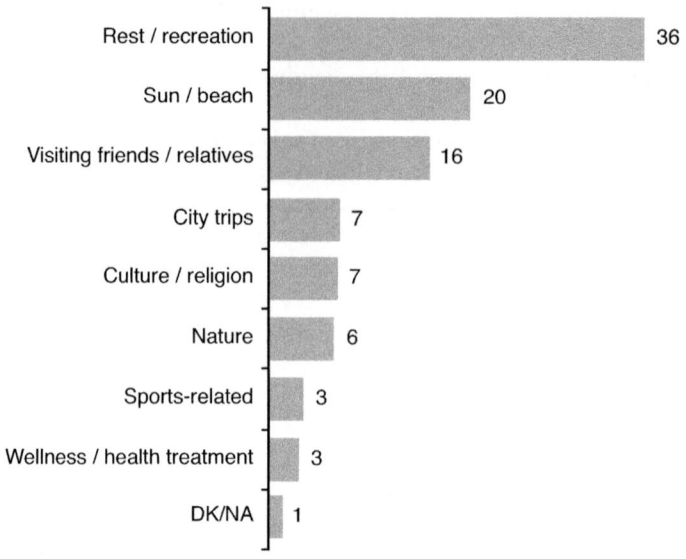

Figure 2.2 The major motivation for EU citizens' main holiday trip.
Source: Survey on the attitudes of Europeans towards tourism, 2008.

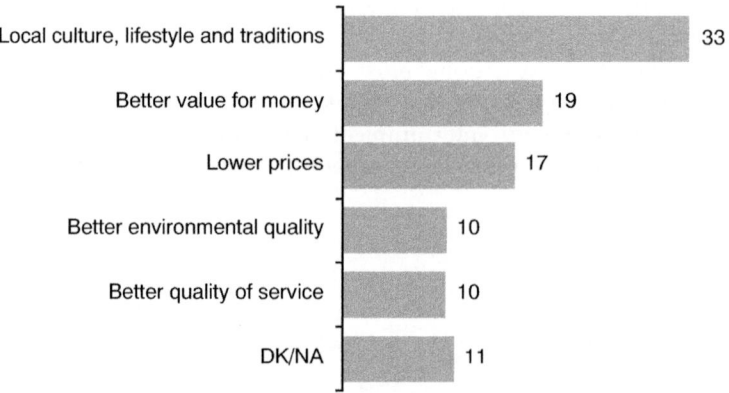

Figure 2.3 The main expectation from a non-traditional, emerging destination.
Source: Survey on the attitudes of Europeans towards tourism, 2008.

Heritage and cultural tourism – tourism profiles and issues

Heritage is defined as the elements of our inherited past that we value. Heritage tourism is defined as tourism markets and industry which have evolved around heritage. Heritage tourism is the form of tourism whose objective is, among other aims, the discovery of monuments and sites. It has become a more popular tourist activity in making visits to historical cultural heritage sites, in this electronic era. Culture, heritage, environment and tourism are interconnected and taking significant attention globally (Perera, 2013).

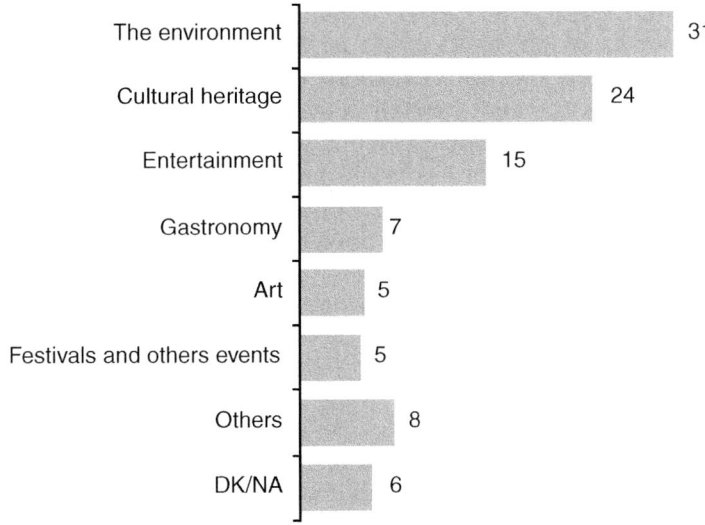

Figure 2.4 Attractions influencing the choice of destination.
Source: Survey on the attitudes of Europeans towards tourism, 2008.

Heritage tourism, in line with the global trend in cultural tourism, has emerged as one of the most popular tourism categories (Chen and Chen, 2010). The economic contribution of heritage resources is a major means to achieve sustainable tourism development (Apostolakis and Jaffry, 2005). Therefore, a better understanding of heritage tourist behaviour in terms of heritage service attributes, specifically tourist preferences, may provide insightful information leading to the ability of heritage managers to create effective sustainable development strategies (Chen and Chen, 2012). Chen and Chen have clearly described the importance of heritage tourism for sustainable economy.

Creating a visitor profile for the kind of tourists interested in natural and cultural heritage tourism is very difficult due to their diversity of interests and the general lack of targeted market research. Thus, only general comments may be given here, based on the results of practical experience in different tourism destinations. Tourists in search of natural and cultural heritage appear to look for a wide range of different attractions and activities that are designed to satisfy different needs, be they for learning, relaxation, recreation or adventure. The following are examples of activities that may be developed using natural and cultural heritage and are related to cultural tourism:

- festivals and events, banquets;
- music, theatre, shows;
- village life and rural life (e.g. farms, Sunday markets,);
- gastronomy, visiting/tasting local products;
- general sightseeing, village buildings and "atmosphere";
- visiting historic and religious monuments or vernacular buildings, ruins;
- sites connected to famous people in the region.

It is also worth mentioning that nature- and culture-orientated tourists are also strongly influenced by the quality and type of accommodation and food on offer. It seems that tourists in search of nature or culture are rarely attracted to large luxury hotels. They will be much more interested in smaller establishments of good quality which provide a personal service and a certain level of comfort and quality – the demand for two- and three-star accommodation is generally very strong. There is also a small but growing proportion of tourists looking for character and "charm" in their accommodation. Rural accommodation, family hotels and pensions that use local quality crafts or are located in vernacular buildings are becoming increasingly popular.

There are, however, a number of additional factors that should be borne in mind when dealing with natural and cultural heritage (Source: Tourism in Europe – at a crossroads?, 1999):

- Cultural and environmental heritage cannot be easily re-produced: They exist because of history and geography and cannot be created easily in the short term. This means that destinations need to work with what they have. If their intrinsic appeal is low or only moderate it will be very difficult for the area to gain a competitive edge over other destinations.
- Cultural and natural attractions are mostly a public resource: Tourists rarely have to pay to see nature and most of the culture – e.g. visiting nature reserves, landscapes and village architecture. It is therefore primarily the private businesses which develop a derived product around this public resource and thus reap the economic rewards. But there is no automatic mechanism for ensuring that some of this income is remitted back into maintaining and enhancing the cultural and natural heritage itself.
- Damage to natural and cultural resources is extremely difficult to measure: Tourism inevitably impacts on the natural and cultural resources of a particular destination but its interrelationship is extremely complex and very difficult to quantify. There is no universal formula for determining carrying capacities for sites (i.e. the number of people that can visit the site without causing significant damage to it) as so much depends on the particular circumstances of the area.
- Finally, the pricing structure of heritage-based tourism is not as clear as in other services or other forms of tourism. There is little guidance available in this area due to the lack of established benchmarks. Comparable attractions in other regions might exist but in a different economic climate which makes comparisons difficult. Consequently, businesses might be pricing themselves out of the market, or more likely undercharging.

The example of the Heritage Trails of Slovenian Istria and Dolina (Italy)

In 2001 the municipalities of Piran, Izola and Koper, and many public and private organisations in Slovenian Istria expressed enthusiasm for the concept of a Heritage Trail. They were fortunate in being able to observe what has been achieved in the pioneer Heritage Trail in Dolenjska and Bela krajina in SE of Slovenia. It should be recognised, however, that there is no standard model of Heritage Trail. The initiative in each area should be suited to the character of that area.

Seen from a European perspective, Slovenian Istria is a compact rural area of very distinctive character. It is green and fertile, with a Mediterranean climate and vegetation. It has a remarkable structure of deep valleys and flat-topped hills, with a plateaux which offers very fine views west to the sea, north into mountainous Slovenia and south into Croatian Istria. The profile of these hills is accentuated by the location of many villages on the rim of the plateau, with church spires marking the end of each ridge. The villages, hamlets and isolated buildings are mainly of strong traditional character, built of local limestone or blue-stone, with tiled roofs and many graceful features. The plateaux and the valley floors contain cultivated fields and pastures. The slopes are graced by rich and varied woodland, and by terraces with vines, olive trees, maize fields and orchards.

The overall effect is of a fine and distinctive landscape. The area is rich in wildlife, and in features of cultural heritage, including fine churches (some with remarkable frescoes and other features), vernacular buildings, water-powered mills and other monuments. It has traditional local products of high quality; a notable variety of good wines; a distinctive regional cuisine; and a local dialect and tradition of customs, dress, music and decorative arts which are remembered and valued by the older local people.

Heritage Trails consultancy

The main implementation institution for the project beside three already mentioned municipalities of Koper, Izola and Piran was the Regional Development Centre of Koper, which was supported by regional institutions on the field of natural and cultural heritage. Partners and stakeholders in the project were institutions from the public, private and NGO sector in this part of Slovenia.

Methods

Initially, the shared opinion among experts who were responsible for the development of the concept was that the Heritage Trail in Slovenian Istria should take account of this distinctive character of the territory, which included also the area's location, immediately behind and above the zone of coastal tourism, and adjoining the Croatian part of Istria, to which it is linked by history, character and a pattern of inland roads and tracks. It is possible to build on this existing pattern of tourist enterprises and of flows of visitors. These elements were taken into account when developing a model for the Heritage Trails in 2001 in Slovenian Istria, namely:

- First, there was and remains a rising demand, throughout Europe, for rural tourism. Such tourism includes both day visits into rural areas from cities and coastal resorts, and overnight stays by holiday-makers and others. Visitors may be drawn to the rural areas by attractions such as heritage sites; by activities such as walking, horse-riding, cycling and scenic driving; or by opportunities to eat and drink in agreeable surroundings. The accommodation that they use may vary from simple campsites through bed-and-breakfast establishments and farm guesthouses to hotels, spas, etc. Slovenian Istria is already quite rich in such attractions, and has human, natural and cultural resources through which these attractions can be further enriched. The existing pattern of visitors shows that there are lucrative categories of tourists who can be further attracted to use those resources.

- Second, the existing tourism trade on the Slovenian coast can benefit from the development of inland attractions. Tourists today are able to choose amongst a rapidly growing number of coastal tourism resorts in the Mediterranean, the Caribbean, South Asia and elsewhere. There is, and will be, intense competition among these coastal resorts. If it is to survive and thrive in this competitive climate, the Slovenian coast must maintain high standards and it must apply its distinctive assets. One major, and currently under-used, asset is the rural hinterland. This hinterland can offer activities – such as scenic driving, horse-riding, cultural tourism and dining out in a quiet and spectacular setting – which are complementary to the beach-based activities, water sports, casino and entertainments on the coast.

- Third, the rural part of Slovenian Istria needs the development of rural tourism, in order to boost its rural economy and to sustain its heritage and its settlements. This is by tradition an agricultural area. But it suffered a decline in farming activity and in the farm-based population after Second World War. During the last two decades, there has been some revival of farming, with a focus on wine, olives, maize, vegetables, fruit and livestock. But the farm economy is not robust yet; and it was adversely affected, when Slovenia joined the EU in 2004, by competition from farmers in the present Union and by the demands of EU regulations. For this and some other reasons (i.e. small-scale and scattered farm units for agricultural production), local farmers would benefit greatly from opportunities to sell more of their products directly to tourists or to hotels, guesthouses and restaurants in the area. Farm families, and other families resident in this rural area, will benefit also from the employment and added value which growth of rural tourism will bring. Existing and new attractions, based on the natural and cultural heritage, will benefit from spending by visitors. Tourism may permit new uses to be made of the under-used and often derelict houses and other structures which are common in the villages in this rural area.

- Fourth, an initiative in sustainable tourism in this area should build on the past and future interest of the government and the EU in rural development. Since its independence in 1991, Slovenia has pursued the CRPOV[1] programme of integrated rural development. Much has been learned from the many small projects assisted by CRPOV, and notably from the more ambitious area-based projects such as Wine Routes and Heritage Trails: one of the Wine Routes passes through Slovenian Istria. The rural areas of Slovenia have also benefited from PHARE, SAPARD and other pre-accession programmes of the EU in case of Slovenian Istria and also from CBC (Cross Border Co-Operation) with Italy.

Finally, a model was drawn in order to illustrate all these elements and justify why the concept of the Trail was structured in the method proposed (Figure 2.5).

This model presents historical movements from inland rural parts (fingers) of the territory which supplied main towns on the coast (palm). In the context of sustainable tourism development product, as Heritage Trails should be structured, the model anticipated a range of integrated tourism products. This included an interaction in terms of the tourism offer comprised as an ideal product mix between the coastal and the rural elements, which may be seen as sustainable in the longer-term perspective. Furthermore, such a plan will have the intrinsic capacity in helping to revitalise the rural part of Slovene Istria, which to a degree has suffered from a level of peripherality

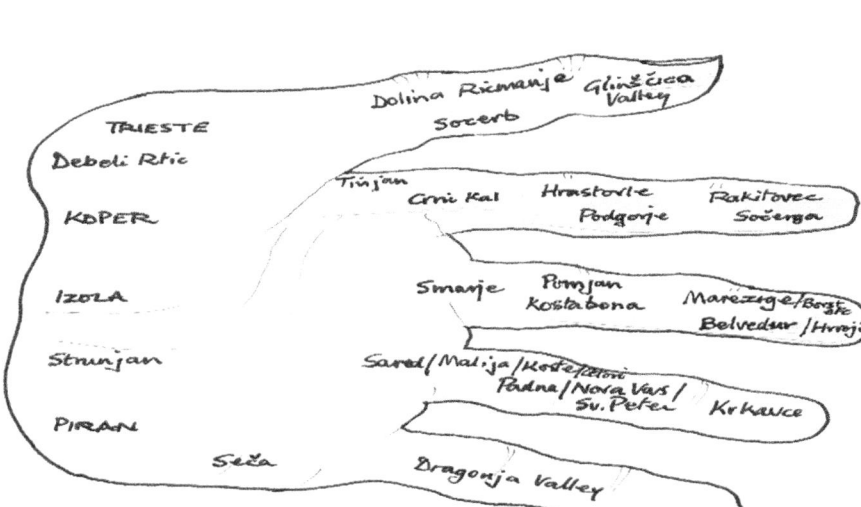

Figure 2.5 The "hand" model.
Source: Dower and Koscak (2001).

from the more intensive touristic development of the coastal region. The main aim of the project was therefore to stimulate tourism development in the hinterland of the Slovene coast. This aim should be pursued by offering support to rural business initiatives, by improving the infrastructure and by intensive marketing activity with focus on rural hinterland of Slovene Istria.

Stages of commercial product adaptation and implementation

For a change from Heritage Trails in Dolenjska and Bela krajina, Heritage Trails in Slovenia Istria was sadly never officially launched, neither on the domestic nor on the international market. The reason for this failure lay in the fact that tourist stakeholders in this coastal region, which was traditionally and remains now the most visited tourism region in Slovenia, were fixated in the past achievements of tourism activity. As a result, in the current contemporary environment, which holds greater challenges and demands, they have been unable and to a degree unwilling to make that critical step forward to co-operate, to engage and to agree an efficient and long-term public-private partnership and co-operation, which would perform as a Destination Management Organisation (DMO). Such a DMO would and should act on behalf of all tourist stakeholders in the region and by the synergies thus created dynamise the entire tourism offer for this region. Regrettably, such an organisation does not exist in this region of Slovenia, and unfortunately, it is the only Slovenian tourism region which is without such an important capacity. This remains a kind of paradox, but, on the other side, a painful reality which already reflects in some tourism figures and statistics (Figure 2.6).

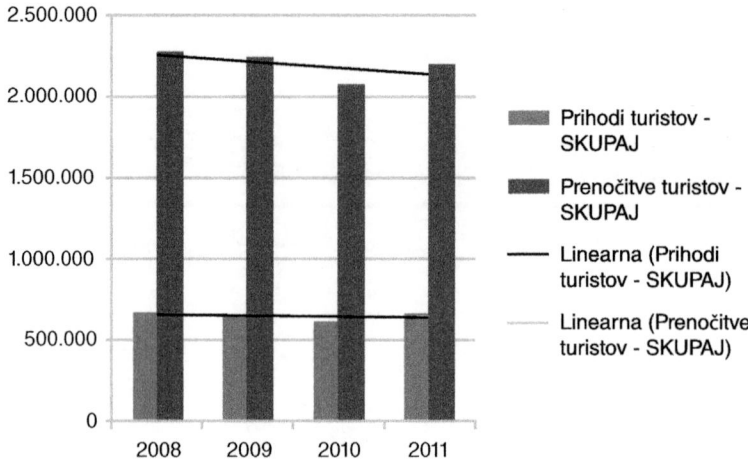

Figure 2.6 Tourist arrivals (blue) and overnights (red) with trends.
Source: RRC Koper, 2015.

This figure shows, and we can interpret it as such, that the traditional sun, sea and sand (3S) product is not in trend anymore and that its life cycle is declining. Unfortunately, it was a lost opportunity to launch a Heritage Trail and to focus more on the rural offer some years ago when the opportunity was ripe for such actions. It is not our intention to speculate and insist that this will change the figures presented above, but we believe that a Heritage Trail-type structure would open immense opportunities for rural entrepreneurs and offer them new challenges for new jobs in their home-yards in rural Istria.

Learning points and conclusions

- It is evident from the example quoted that the heritage-resource tourism in this part of Slovenia has huge opportunities to be developed far more than it is at the moment. Many excellent products and offers of cultural tourism exist and remain but these are insufficiently developed and inefficiently presented on major tourism markets at both a national and an international levels. Currently, it appears that the overall tourism offer is dominated by the interests of some large hotel chains, which are not local and who are neither interested nor motivated to put forward local interests and engage local resources. Beside this it is unlikely that they really understand the concept of a DMO, despite the fact that just a few kilometres distant exists an extremely successful DMO – namely, Croatian Istria with an excellent experience and results.
- It is also obvious and clear that sustainability of the product, in our case cultural tourism, must be secured. Without detailed carrying capacity research of sites which potentially would become resource-zones in the Heritage Trails and without involvement of rural community from the very early stage of initiative, the entire process will fail to operate as ideally as they should. Namely, the rural

community, which is involved and committed to tourism, must and should be responsible, in co-operation with professional institutions for cultural and natural heritage, for site management and should also gain added value from their involvement in the rural tourism.

- Slovenian Istria is a known tourist destination, not only on the domestic market but as well on some immediate international markets – particularly Italian, but also Austrian, German and lately (despite decline in 2014) Russian market. But its identity is still greatly dependent on the 3S product. Unfortunately, very little has been done in recent years to open up the rural hinterland by offering new, innovative and exciting tourism products in rural area that has high potentials for tourism development of superb class. For a successful destination offer it would be imperative to create a unique mix of characteristics, which are determined by its geographical location, culture and history. This should be a focus of those who are responsible for the destination management and wish to influence the experiences of both visitors and residents.

- The failure, which has extended over the last ten and more years, in the creation of an efficient DMO is one of the most painful elements and reasons why Slovenian Istria did not perform as coherent, modern tourist destination and lacks in application of its best tourism potentials being offered on both domestic and international markets. Lack of co-operation and trust between key stakeholders, which are driving their own interests rather than working together in promotion of the destination, development of integrated tourism products and performing through well-organised destination management frameworks, seems to be a long and lonely path towards an evidenced decline of the most successful tourism destination in the country.

- In the light of above, continuity of personnel in DMO is extremely important. In the region there exists a number of experienced managers possessing professional expertise and skills, which are important to be invited and applied in the process of establishment of an efficient DMO. Beside these characteristics it would be also important that DMO management should gain trust and support from key tourism stakeholders, namely hotel chain owners, who are at the moment failing to respond to initiatives for the creation of a regional DMO. Therefore, both the economic and political environments must seek to find consensus for an acceptable and efficient DMO.

- In this region, as well as other tourism stakeholders, there is the Faculty of Tourism Studies – Turistica, together with other Faculties and departments, which are active in the field of tourism research, have sufficient expertise, are experienced in development and management of cultural tourism products and above all are willing to assist the process of establishment of sustainable, transparent and efficient DMO in the region. Such expertise and energy should be used in the process of creation of DMO.

The tourist sector is one of the fastest growing economic sectors in the world, but also the one where there is the greatest competition. In present times of globalisation, liberalisation and deregulation, tourist subjects are facing fearsome competition. That is the reason why the success of a destination depends on the overall level of services quality, which represents the function of a whole series of variables which are united under the same denominator of the destination management (DMO). Slovenian Istria is not an exemption. Key players in tourism will need to urgently agree how to organise regions tourism management unless they want to face further tourism decline and as consequence also other negative economic trends in tourism.

The case of the Green Box network – culture and heritage on a troubled border

The background

This example looks initially at the issues that exist in a geographic and cultural region which shares a common natural heritage but which is divided by ethno-religious tensions and some eight centuries of conflict. Add to this a state frontier that passes through the region and the complexities of seeking to establish a common purpose in pursuit of protecting the same environment and boosting shared socio-economic uncertainties.

Post-1945 border regions

Most of the difficult border areas in post-1945 Europe derive from the difficulties in applying the settlements agreed by the major powers in the aftermath of the Second World War. This, for example, created issues for Slovenia in regard to the frontier with Croatia post-independence in 1991 (see section "Heritage Trails consultancy" above) as well as leaving unresolved issues regarding ethnic/linguistic frontiers in areas such as Trentino-Alto Adige/Sud Tirol. Yet many of these problems were resolved through the application of EU cross-border and inter-regional programmes, which focused on cultural and heritage commonalities irrespective of state frontiers. Importantly, the issue of fixed state frontiers was also to a degree resolved by the Schengen agreement, which removed fixed frontiers and allowed freedom of movement across the frontiers of the EU Schengen participants. EU programmes also often engaged in shared common cultures and heritage across existing state frontiers.

A pre-existing frontier

Yet one frontier pre-dated the solutions of the 1945 settlement – the frontier between the Republic of Ireland and the UK. Until 1921, Ireland existed – in international law – as a kingdom within the UK, sharing the same head of state and participating in the political connection of the UK parliament. Yet in 1918, a 75% majority of Irish UK parliamentary constituencies had elected members of Sinn Féin – the Irish republican political party – to represent them; those representatives then refused to participate in the UK parliament, and given their overwhelming national mandate established an Irish parliament – Dáil Éireann. Following the War of Independence, a treaty was signed with the UK, which established an Irish Free State in 26 of the 32 Irish counties. The remaining six counties remained as part of the UK, but with their own parliament. Partition created huge resentment across the island of Ireland, as the boundary agreed in 1921 – effectively a political demarcation line – left some 40% of Irish Catholics supporting independence within Northern Ireland and under British rule, whilst at the same time stranding some 7% of Irish Protestants (wishing to remain in Britain) within the Free State. In 1937, the Free State declared itself a self-governing republic outside the British Empire, and in 1939, declared itself a neutral territory in terms of the conflict between the UK and Germany.

The "Emerald Curtain"

The border divided communities and socio-economic structures; towns which were the major economic centres for large rural communities suddenly found themselves on the wrong side of an international frontier. The border became an economic frontier, due to differing levels of taxation between the republic and the North. Smuggling became almost an economic necessity as cattle, butter, vehicle fuel and other commodities were moved back and forth across the frontier. Furthermore, when Ireland joined the eurozone, there was a disconnection between the existing Irish pound and the UK pound, which created further problems in cross-border trade.

As a result, the border region – the republic's counties of Louth, Cavan, Monaghan, Leitrim, Sligo and Donegal and the Northern Ireland counties of Armagh, Fermanagh, Tyrone and Derry – suffered huge economic disadvantage. This disadvantage was increased as a result of the Second World War, when the republic suffered economic problems in terms of trade. Conditions were made worse as a result of the IRA Border campaign, involving attacks on British forces in the North. Conditions worsened from 1969, when sectarian attacks on Catholics in the North by Protestant paramilitaries and state forces created the civil rights movement, and resulted in the UK's decision to station UK army troops in the North. From that point, the frontier became the most militarised frontier in Europe after the former Iron Curtain between Western and Eastern Europe.

Economic conditions across the whole border region – in the republic and in the North – worsened. In 2001, the EU Economic and Social Committee reported that the 15% of the total population of the island of Ireland living in the border area suffered the most serious socio-economic problems, the lowest incomes, the worst unemployment, the highest levels of emigration and the most appalling levels of rural poverty. Added to this were a high numbers of displaced persons who had left their homes as a result of ethno-religious threats – in 1972–1994 this amounted to 11,000 persons. In addition, even after the Good Friday peace agreement, which ended the conflict and resulted in de-militarisation of the frontier, in the six border counties of the republic some 10% of the population were ex-political prisoners.

Solutions from culture and heritage

One of the most constructive issues was the implementation of two EU programme activities – The EU Peace I and II programmes and the inter-related LEADER and INTERREG programmes which were operated from 1998 onwards. These programmes were distinctively connected to cross-border activities and importantly sought to find common and cultural heritage issues which would unite both the Catholic and Protestant communities.

A key feature was the establishment at a macro-level of all Ireland tourism marketing facilities that connected both the republic and the north's tourism agencies mirrored by cross-border and inter-regional activity at a local level. Whilst some of these activities built on existing tourism mechanisms, others also developed to connect together disjointed and mutually suspicious communities. This, for example, brought together ex-political prisoners from both paramilitary groups – (the IRA and the Ulster loyalists) as well as the wives and families of the political prisoners. At the same time, efforts were made – despite the differing currency systems – to connect tourism activities in areas where the natural touristic heritage saw the border as an unnecessary barrier to tourism development. This saw projects developing in such areas as re-building old canals and waterways, and as developing old railway lines as walking/cycling paths. Both waterways and railways had been terminated purely because the border imposed a massive strain on them – in some cases post-1921 railway services were passing through more than six border crossings and customs posts.

The challenge of the new border post-December 2020

Many of the solutions achieved are highly constructive and highly efficient, but they are now facing a much more difficult challenge, the UK's exit from the EU/EEA after the transition period, and the fact that the only land border between the UK and the EU will be in Ireland. This presents immense challenges, and in particular it has the potential to de-rail and destroy the strong co-operation between the two cultural and heritage communities across, within and without the existing state frontier. The shared culture and heritage is already fragile, and the economic effects of the re-creation of a hard frontier between the 6 counties of Norther Ireland and the 26 counties forming the Republic of Ireland are difficult to imagine.

The Green Box experiment

Green Box constitutes a Peace Process initiative seeking to bridge frontiers and conflicting attitudes by boosting those common factors which people on either sides of the frontier share together.

Eco-tourism in Ireland

We define eco-tourism as "responsible travel to natural areas that conserves the environment, sustains the well-being of the local people, and involves interpretation and education" (The International Ecotourism Society, 2015). Eco-tourism in Ireland developed in a number of local areas, mainly those which were outside the traditional large-scale tourism activity involving groups of 30–60 individuals, which in general occurred on the urban region around Dublin as well as other urban areas such as Cork, Limerick and Galway. Eco-tourism relied on individuals who realised the value of ecologically sustainable tourism in local areas, managed locally and developed locally. This resulted in visitors reacting to a situation in which they saw an essentially valuable area of landscape being preserved for future generations, as well as the potential to assist in the socio-economic development of fragile, remote and peripheral communities.

Primarily, we need to understand that Ireland, as the whole island irrespective of political jurisdiction, consists of a bio-diverse landscape, and that such a landscape cannot be wholly constrained by tourism which is focused on large groups visiting urban areas and being immersed in what can only be described as "ersatz Irish culture". Importantly, Fáilte Ireland (Fáilte Ireland, Carbon Strategy, 2008) began from 2008 to put in place a number of ecologically supportive initiatives to measure the carbon footprint of the 18,000 tourism businesses in Ireland. The initiative would appear to be based on the fact that Fáilte Ireland research (Fáilte Ireland Carbon Strategy, 2008) demonstrated that emissions from tourism accommodation alone would increase by 170% between 2005 and 2035.

However, it would appear that by 2020, the majority of visitors to Ireland will be 55 years old or more (Fáilte Ireland, Tourism Product Development Strategy, 2007). We may discern that visitors in this age profile (Koščak and O'Rourke, 2018) will have a stronger desire to connect into the environment which they visit, will prefer to understand and engage with local culture and heritage, and will also have a greater compulsion to see the unique environment which they visit preserved over future generations. We would also suggest that there are two further age groups which have similar objectives – the "back-packer tourist" (age 18–25) and the "family tourist" (age 25–40) – both are connected to the 55+ "silver tourist" in seeking unique and natural experiences and the willingness to absorb and be immersed in a wide cultural heritage (Koščak and O'Rourke, 2018).

Green Box explained

The Green Box was developed as a cross-border project to link together the communities in the Irish border community. These communities shared a common ecological land space and the same history and to a great extent a common desire to attract tourism. But at an organisational level, their attitudes were shaped by religion and politics (i.e. Catholic Nationalist or Republican against Protestant Unionist or Loyalist). The matrix of beliefs and political affiliations was complex and extremely difficult for those outside the border counties to understand or comprehend, unless it was compared with ethnic-religious complexities in Kosovo or in Bosnia and Herzegovina. Attitudes were hardened and complicated by events that occurred over 8 centuries ago, and defined into an "us" and "them" situation.

Green Box took a radical alternative concept in creating a pilot project across religious and political divides by promoting the injection of tourism activities which would support sustainable development and environmental protection, and help the development of ecologically supportive tourism growth. In that sense it was the first eco-tourism DMO on the whole island of Ireland. We should note that when looking at the provision of bed/nights across the island of Ireland, the region covered by the project in 2005 only provided 4% of the total, compared to Dublin with 47%

(O'Rourke, 2015). We should also understand that in general most of the tourism providers had between 1 and 25 employees and thus fell within the EU definition of micro/small enterprises.

The Green Box project delivered

At the start of the project in 2005, the management team provided training to 30 eco-tourism providers, by 2015 this had expanded to 80 providers, with 30 providers providing mentoring to a far wider group of individual tourism operators. In addition further education institutions in the border region were involved in delivering eco-tourism programmes to entrepreneurs. From 2005, the project was supported by the EU Peace Initiatives, through the "Peace through tourism" workshops. Mentoring was a powerful tool, where successful entrepreneurs under the initial parts of the programme were then able to apply the lessons learned to new entrants.

This also contributed to great cross-border tourism activity, particularly in areas where tourists had no concept that a rural walk of 3 km may involve crossing an international frontier on two or three occasions. Tourists expected integrated services, and cross-border actions were powerful in creating such a potential. The engagement of Green Box under the EU programmes INTERREG and LEADER had a strong influence in boosting engagement with 100 members and a strong connectivity into the ongoing "Peace & Reconciliation" programme.

Conclusions

The task of bringing together disparate and in many cases emotionally wounded communities has been assisted by such projects as Green Box. It demonstrates that in areas where individual communities have differing views of their past history, and are affected by latent fear of those who hold differing religious or cultural beliefs, the willingness to create a pleasant and agreeable environment for visiting tourists has a remarkably healing effect. It joins individuals, families and communities together to realise that although there are potent issues which divide them, they also have much in common – preserving a distinct historical and cultural environment and probing care of the ecological environment.

Reflections

Both of the examples described have a strong connectivity to rural regimes which have significant underlying socio-economic problems. To an extent the source of those problems (whether lack of resources from central government or a tense political-military situation) is to a degree irrelevant. The argument is that fundamentally local solutions may only be determined by local communities acting coherently together, whether in Istria or in the NW of Ireland. Despite the geographic and cultural differences, the problems remain the same – local problems require local solutions, and local solutions require a level of community involvement which may be difficult to manage, but which is fundamentally necessary.

Questions

1　Which are the critical success factors in promoting, developing and sustaining locally based cultural and heritage tourism?
2　What kind of marketing and promotion tools and delivery channels and mechanisms should be applied for the most optimal operational implementation in case of local cultural and heritage tourism?
3　Which is the most efficient way to organise local stakeholders in the process of joint action and effective partnership? Are there different options depending on the situation in the local destination, i.e. economic, cultural, political, etc.?
4　How important is the process of carrying capacity before and during the implementation of development, promotion in order to achieve optimal sustainability and responsible management of cultural and heritage tourism in the destination?
5　What are the measures based on carrying capacity assessments which should sustain the action and development on economic, social and environmental aspects of cultural and heritage tourism in the destination?

Note

1　CPROV is the Slovenian name for the "Integrated Rural Development & Village renovation Programme".

Further reading

Beaumont, N., & Dredge, D. (2010). *Local tourism governance: A comparison of three network approaches. Journal of Sustainable Tourism*, 18(1), 7–28.
Koščak, M., & O'Rourke, T. (2018). *Practical and Conceptual Strategies for the Re-evaluation of Local Tourism Destinations – a Scientific Monograph*. Harlow: Pearson.
Mariani, M. M., Buhalis, D., Longhi, C., & Vitouladiti, O. (2014). *Managing change in tourism destinations: Key issues and current trends. Journal of Destination Marketing & Management*, 2(4), 269–272.
UNWTO (2007). *A Practical Guide to Tourism Destination Management*. Madrid: World Tourism Organization.
UNWTO & European Commission. (2013). *Sustainable Tourism for Development Guidebook*. Madrid: World Tourism Organisation.

References

Sources & literature

Apostolakis, A., & Jaffry, S. (2005). Stated preferences for two creative heritage attractions. *Annals of Tourism Research*, 32(4), 985–1005.
Chen, C.F., & Chen, P.C. (2012). Research note: Exploring tourists' stated preferences for heritage tourism services – the case of Tainan City, Taiwan. *Tourism Economics*, 18(2), 457–464.
Chen, C.F., & Chen, F.S. (2010). Experience quality, perceived value, satisfaction and behavioral intentions for heritage tourists. *Tourism Management*, 31, 29–35.
Dower, M., & Koscak, M. (2001). *Heritage trails through Slovenian Istria and Dolina, Sustainable Tourism strategy for rural Istria*, RRC Koper.

Eurobarometer. (2009). Analytical report. Flash EB No 258 – *Survey on the Attitudes of Europeans Towards Tourism*, page 4. Introduction. This *Flash Eurobarometer* survey (*Flash Eurobarometer 258* on the "Survey on the attitudes of Europeans towards tourism".

The International Ecotourism Society. (2015). "What is ecotourism". Retrieved December 16, 2017, from www.ecotourism.org/what-is-ecotourism

Koščak,M., & O'Rourke, T. (2018). *Practical and Conceptual Strategies for the Re-evaluation of Local Tourism Destinations – a Scientific Monograph*. Harlow: Pearson.

O'Rourke, T. (2015). "Tourism & conflict", unpublished paper presented at University of Stirling (May, 2015).

Perera, K. (2013). *The Role of Museums in Cultural and Heritage Tourism for Sustainable Economy in Developing Countries*. International Conference on Asian Art, Culture and Heritage, Sri Lanka.

3 Active and adventure tourism in the planning of local destination management

Marko Koščak and Tony O'Rourke

Summary

In this chapter we will suggest that in line with global tourism trends, destination managers are more and more likely to design their destination products in a direction where elements of active tourism – such as recreation and education, respect and contemplation, action, exercise and active involvement in company of an expert local friend or an academically competent tour guide – are an important part of their destination offer.

We consider evidence suggesting that the role of active tourism is understood and defined as the "way of visiting", including the attitude of the tourist and the activities that are carried out during the tourist visit. Importantly, we regard these as essential elements within the sustainable framework, a framework that benefits tourists; local inhabitants; and the existing culture, heritage and physical environment.

Links

The following Case Study links may be of interest to readers of this Topic Chapter:

- Case Studies Part A (Destination Management aspects of ethical sustainable development) – Chapters 15, 16 and 17;
- Case Studies Part B (Environmental & Social aspects of ethical sustainable development) – Chapters 19, 20 and 24.

Please see the Contents on pages v–viii, and the Guide to the text-book in Appendix 1 for further information.

Introduction

If as one of the potential definitions, Active Tourism is seen as responsible travel to foreign areas requiring both physical and mental participation from the tourist and following the maxims of sustainability, protection of biodiversity and conservation of culture, then the product preparation and management requires a highly professional and sensitive touch by destination stakeholders and managers. It is therefore a responsibility of both visitors and hosts to take an active role in this process of responsible travel.

Active Tourism is no longer to be viewed as a new travelling philosophy that combines adventure, eco-tourism and cultural aspects of a discovery tour. Active Tourism should be low-impact, ecological, socially compatible and of high quality. Active Tourism should aim to combine recreation and education, and deliver benefits to both the tourist as well as to the visited destination. Active Tourism has many values in common with eco-tourism and nature tourism, and it also integrates some activities of action and adventure tourism. Additionally, it also includes aspects of cultural tours, academic and scientific expeditions. An important application of the concept "active tourism" is by linking it to activities. Tourists' visiting destinations and attractions are offered a range of activities to learn more about the destination, to cater to different needs and requirements of tourists and to present experience offered in specific regions (www.active-tourism.org, 2002).

An important element of active tourism is also support to local economies. Direct income from tourism is the amount of tourist expenditure that remains locally after taxes, profits and wages are paid outside the area and after imports are purchased; these subtracted amounts are referred to as "leakage". The United Nations Environment Programme (UNEP) cites that in most all-inclusive mass tourism package tours, about 80% of travellers' expenditures go to the airlines, hotels and other international companies (who often have their headquarters in the travellers' home countries), not to local businesses or workers. Of each USD 100 spent on a vacation tour by a tourist from a developed country, only around USD 5 actually stays in a developing destination's economy (UNWTO, 2014).

Active tourism, as a concept, is frequently applied in connection with sports, adventure and physical activities – but there are also definitions of active tourism that views it as a variation of responsible tourism, a development of eco-tourism or a version of local tourism. In the more common uses of the concept "Active tourism", we regularly find "action", the etymological cousin of active, and linked to action we often find "adventure" mentioned. There is significant research that combines sports, active leisure and active tourism – and is naturally one method of understanding the concept (Edelheim, 2017).

Adventure tourism as an underlying part of the active tourism concept has grown exponentially worldwide over the past years with tourists visiting destinations previously undiscovered. This allows for new destinations to market themselves as truly unique, appealing to those travellers looking for rare, incomparable experiences. Adventure tourism is often divided into soft and hard dimensions. Soft adventure vacations include biking, bird-or-animal watching, hiking, horseback riding, rafting, scuba diving and snorkelling. Caving, climbing and trekking are ranked among the hard adventure activities. Studies indicate that there has been a shift in classification. At the beginning of the 21st century, rafting and scuba diving were classified as hard adventure activities at that time. It seems currently that these activities have lost some of their thrill content and more adventurous travellers are seeking more risky, more unusual and more novel experiences. Soft adventure activities are pursued by those tourists apparently interested in a perceived risk and adventure with little actual risk. As the example of bird-or-animal watching shows, soft adventure activities blend physical adventures (in this case, visiting the natural area) with enriching activities (learning from the birds' observation). On the contrary, hard adventure activities are known by both the participant and the service provider to have a high level of risk and involve more physically demanding activities as well as training and preparation.

Generally, the following core characteristics or qualities are regarded to be the basis of adventure activities (Wolter, 2014):

- Involvement with a natural environment;
- Uncertain outcomes;
- Danger and risks;
- Challenge;
- Anticipated rewards;
- Novelty;
- Stimulation and excitement;
- Escapism and separation.

Similarly, in a World Tourism Organization (UNWTO, 2014) report on types of adventure tourism, the authors stressed that there are two main categories of adventure activities – hard adventure or soft adventure. Vigorous debate often surrounds which activities belong to which category. The easiest way to identify an adventure trip as hard or soft adventure is by its primary activity.

Regardless of how tourism professionals organise or categorise adventure travel, adventure will always be a subjective term for travellers themselves, because it is related to one's individual experience. Adventure to one traveller may seem mundane to another. Adventure tourists push their own cultural, physical and geographic comfort limits, and those limits differ for each person (ATTA, Global Sustainable Tourism, 2014).

Active tourism can also be defined by what it is not – mass tourism. Mass tourism includes large-ship leisure cruises, "sun and sand" package vacations, bus tours around city centres that stop only at iconic attractions, theme parks, etc. Both public and private sector stakeholders understand that adventure tourism is inextricably linked with human and nature capital. Protection and promotion of these resources is important, and the continued development of this sector must seek to protect these valuable assets.

Because of the documented benefits to the environment, local people and local economies, governments are increasingly identifying adventure tourism as a tool for sustainable and responsible economic growth that delivers benefits to every level of society. In many destinations, adventure tourism has been developed without extensive new infrastructure. It may also deliver benefits, from creating local jobs rapidly to relying on traditional knowledge of local people for guiding and interpretation (UNWTO, 2014).

Components of Active Tourism and its market

Active Tourism is a special way to spend your vacations. It is a new travelling philosophy that combines adventure, eco-tourism and cultural aspects of a discovery tour. Active tourism is low impact, ecological, socially compatible and of high quality. Active tourism has three major aims (www.active-tourism.org, 2002):

1 *Recreation*: Distraction from daily working during vacations. Active tourism is fun and can provide you all the pleasure you can desire. Relax your mind and recharge your body energy by practising exercise and actively participating in your entertainment.

2   *Education*: An active tourist is eager to learn and wants to know closely another culture and way of living. Your vacations should broaden your horizons. Willingness to learn the language, eat the typical food, value local traditions and respect foreign cultures and beliefs.
3   *Benefit*: Tourism not only brings advantages to visitors but also helps the local economy and promotes development of the visited land. Active tourism is low impact, ecologically and socially sustainable. Active tourism uses and values nature, protects biodiversity and offers work to people.

Some of the most interesting activities of a region are only available to the local population. However, the international tourist can have access to them through a "local friend". Active Tourism offers this type of activities, such as dancing, cooking lessons and language learning. It also offers visits to local cultural events as football matches, concerts, theatres and art expositions.

Active tourism and tourism activities are important for destinations because they promote the objectives of making destinations distinctive, they allow a wider range of stakeholders to present their offerings to tourists and they may act as a reason for visitors to stay longer in a region. All of these elements are important to limit the negative effects of travel which is exaggerated by short holidays (Edelheim, 2017). Active Tourism is the contrary to passive tourism. This travelling concept is also opposed to Mass Tourism in the sense that is small scale, low impact, run and administrated locally. Active Tourism is socially and ecologically sustainable.

Destinations that have prioritised active and adventure tourism frequently create regional associations that regulate the quality and safety of this category of tourism offered in their area. Many of these associations provide certification for members who comply with sustainability or safety criteria. The reasons people engage in active tourism are diverse, but the most frequently cited motivations are relaxation, exploring new places, spending time with family and learning about different cultures. When compared with non-active travellers, active and adventure travellers are more likely to use professional services, such as guides, tour operators and boutique service providers. In examining only active and adventure travellers, however, it is found that 56% of travellers still handle everything on their own (UNWTO, 2014).

Active and adventure travellers rank areas of natural beauty as the most important factor in choosing their most recent destination, followed by the activities available and the climate. Such travellers are early adopters by nature, meaning they are generally more willing to try new destinations, activities and travel products. Popular activities change rapidly, and it seems there is a new twist on an existing sport every year. Non-active travellers ranked having friends and family at the destination as the most important factor, followed by areas of natural beauty and climate (UNWTO, 2014).

In the active tourism sector as a whole, the trend has been towards disintermediation, meaning the removal of the middle man—a tour operator or travel agent—who has traditionally connected the consumer in the source market to the provider or ground handler in the destination market. As the traveller can access information and trusted consumer reviews online, he is more likely to go straight to the provider.

Travellers are increasingly more connected, and active travellers also rarely leave without a phone or tablet to capture their holiday moment or stay in touch with loved ones. This trend is breaking down geographic boundaries and allowing travellers to venture further afield than ever before. The internet helps bring market access to active and adventure tourism businesses located in the most remote corners of the world. From small guiding outfits to big hotels, tourism businesses need a reliable internet connection, a website and other online platforms to successfully market and effectively communicate with clients (UNWTO, 2014).

The demand and supply side

To understand the structure of the active and adventure sector, it is important to understand how demand is created by the consumer. Demand refers to the amount of desire within the market to purchase active and adventure tourism holidays. People must be motivated to travel, and they must have access to information and resources that allow them to plan their trips and ultimately book them.

Factors influencing the demand for adventure tourism include (UNWTO, 2014) the following:

- The cost of an adventure tour;
- The cost of related products (e.g. airline tickets);
- The capacity or income of target markets;
- Marketing, which appeals to the preferences or motivations of travellers.

Businesses and destinations involved in adventure tourism need to understand and consider these factors if they are to successfully create demand for their offerings.

On the other hand, the adventure tourism supply chain is more complex. Niche products often require specialised knowledge and operations. Adventure tourism's supply chain linkages go very deep, and this is one of the key reasons that adventure tourism delivers greater benefits at the local level. Supply chains vary from destination to destination. The makeup of the most involved adventure tourism supply chain does not always follow the traditional tourism pattern (ATTA, 2013). Parts of the chain might be minimised or overlooked, and the connection to those actually providing the product or service might be much more direct, depending on the scope or type of offering. The chain may be shortened depending on the product, the size of the local supplier companies and the distance between the customer and the destination (UNWTO, 2014).

Issues: the role and concept of other types of tourism interacting with Active Tourism

The differences between adventure tourism and mass tourism are clear, but the differences between adventure tourism and other types of tourism may be more nuanced. Below are definitions of other popular types of tourism, which share characteristics with adventure tourism, such as minimising negative impacts and increasing local benefits (UNWTO, 2014):

Sustainable Tourism is tourism that takes full account of its current and future economic, social and environmental impacts, addressing the needs of visitors, the industry, the environment and host communities (UNEP & WTO, 2015).

Conservation Tourism, as defined by tourism researcher Prof. Ralf Buckley (Millich, 2011), is "commercial tourism which makes a net positive contribution to the continuing survival of threatened plant or animal species". Buckley notes that while there are a variety of ways for tourism to add positive contributions to conservation, the key issue is to calculate net outcomes after subtracting the negative impacts. A broader definition of conservation tourism is tourism that delivers experiences that support the protection of natural and cultural resources through the following:

- Impact: creating financial incentives for conservation;
- Influence: engaging travellers, communities and other stakeholders on the value of protecting the integrity of nature and culture;
- Investment: driving financial support from the travel sector and the travellers for conservation.

Responsible Tourism is tourism "that creates better places for people to live in, and better places to visit". Responsible tourism can take place in any environment, and many cities have adopted responsible tourism policies (Cape Town Declaration, 2002).

Pro-Poor Tourism is tourism that provides net benefits to poor people as defined by the Pro-Poor Tourism Partnership.

Community-Based Tourism (CBT) is defined by The Mountain Institute and Regional Community Forestry Training Center as a visitor-host interaction that has meaningful participation by both, and generates economic and conservation benefits for local communities and environments (The Mountain Institute, 2000).

Volunteer Tourism is "the practice of individuals going on a working holiday, volunteering their labour for worthy causes". Volunteer tourism includes work that is not remunerated and is sometimes also called "Voluntourism" (Tomazos, 2009).

SAVE Tourism encompasses Scientific, Academic, Volunteer and Educational Tourism, as defined by the SAVE Travel Alliance. SAVE tourism may include remunerated work (SAVE Travel Alliance, 2008).

Geo-Tourism is defined as tourism that sustains or enhances the geographical character of a place – its environment, culture, aesthetics, heritage and the well-being of its residents (What is Geo-tourism?, 2010).

Eco-Tourism is defined by The International Ecotourism Society as

> purposeful travel to natural areas to understand the culture and natural history of the environment, taking care not to alter the integrity of the ecosystem, while producing economic opportunities that make the conservation of natural resources beneficial to local people.
>
> (The International Ecotourism Society, 2012)

It is important to note that none of these types of tourism, including adventure tourism, are mutually exclusive and definitions can be overlapping. These "brands" of tourism have a specific or even niche market value, because they resonate with a particular segment of consumers.

The "Active Tourism" and "Eco-Tourism" crossover

If we see Active Tourism as responsible travel requiring both physical and mental participation from the tourist and following the maxims of sustainability, protection of biodiversity and conservation of culture, then Eco-tourism may be seen as aligning with those stated maxims. Indeed, the International Ecotourism Society defines eco-tourism as "responsible travel that conserves the environment and improves the well-being of local people" (http://www.ecotourism.org/ties-overview). From our perspective we see some important "cross-over factors"; in our view the first is between eco-tourism and active tourism as these forms of tourism are not mutually exclusive; indeed, in some cases they appear to thrive off and be supportive of each other. For instance, it may be that mountain biking, hiking, trail biking and hill running combine with an environment in which man-made structures seek to conform to the sustainable environment (wind and solar power, ecological waste treatment and natural heating methods).

But there are further cross-over factors; those engaged in what we may describe as "eco-tourism with an active component" will come from three main markets, segregated on a lifestyle/age basis:

- The "silver tourist" (aged 60+) – this tourist segment may be interested in walking/cycling in the natural environment, visiting historic locations, fishing, etc. whilst at the same time staying in a eco-lodge, up-market hostel facility or bringing their own caravan.
- The "family tourist" (aged 35–45) – this tourist segment may be interested in family activities, cycling, nature trails, outdoor sports as well as child-specific activities; they would tend to stay in the hostel, a family tent, or bring their own caravan and camping accommodation.
- The "backpacker tourist" (aged 16–25) – this tourist segment may be interested in high activity sports, running, mountain biking or joining community volunteer activities to restore old buildings or pathways; they would tend to stay in the hostel with basic facilities or low-cost camping facilities.

Whilst their inputs into to active tourism and eco-tourism will generally be located at different ends of the physical and risk activity scales, they tend to share a common interest in the total tourism environment (nature, people, culture and heritage) as well as the common need to engage in a meaningful experience. Such tourists are also discerning about the qualities and scale of sustainability impact. In the above-mentioned case study, we demonstrate the age-lifestyle cross-over in a situation where all three market segments mentioned above will also share access to ecological catering (e.g. the eco-cafe) and food sources (e.g. the ecological market garden), whilst enjoying together an evening of Scottish traditional music.

Another important area is that "active tourism and eco-tourism cross-over" displays tendencies of developing in tourist locations that have previously been poorly developed or are distant from mass tourism locations. In many ways, underdeveloped capacity and the existence of poor transport connections may be considered as positive advantages in shaping tourism markets that are environmentally sustainable and sensitive to capacity controls. This would then substantiate our view that Active Tourism aims also to help the sustained development of such peripheral regions. The tourists should be invited to help actively and to contribute morally and economically to local social organisations and ecological initiatives (non-profit, non-governmental or mutual organisations). The tourists should not come to watch passively but to interact actively, to learn, to help and to enjoy the richness of cultural diversity. They should come to observe biodiversity to respect and value the miracle of millions of years of natural evolution (www.active-tourism.org, 2002).

Challenges for active tourism

We would suggest that there are three critical challenges for Active Tourism when operated at a local level within concurrent support at a regional and national/EU level. These challenges are as follows:

- **Low financial capacity** – local Active Tourism providers will tend to be micro/ small enterprises which do not have immediate and medium/long-term access to funding for both ongoing cash-flow and business development.
- **Low promotional capacity** – again given the size of these enterprises, unless they are able to combine at either a local or sectoral level, they lack the capacity to promote themselves at the necessary marketing level to attract new business.
- **Low management capacity** – Active Tourism enterprises inevitably require "active engagement" by the owners, whether leading walking/cycling tours, white water rafting, etc. Such engagement mitigates very strongly against their ability to provide strong management capacity at a strategic, financial accounting and human resources level.

Necessarily our fundamental question should be "How may such challenges be addressed?" In this chapter, we are suggesting that the value of strongly organised, professionally competent and dynamic local Destination Management Organisations (DMOs) should not be overstated or undervalued. There is ample evidence not only from tourism, but from other sectors of small business activity that entrepreneurs combining for mutual and collective benefit may achieve a greater synergistically driven result than the sum of all individual entrepreneurs.

Discussion – outcomes and concepts

In an effort to spread the benefits of tourism to a wide range of regions and communities, destinations are often seeking to diversify their traditional offerings by promoting adventure tourism to bring visitors out of urban centres and into more rural places. As with any sector, adventure tourism does not operate in a vacuum. It both affects and is affected by a myriad of social, cultural, economic, ecological and geographic factors, as well as political regulations and social norms; some of these support its development and others hinder it (UNWTO, 2014).

In adventure tourism, it is often difficult to reach places and often affects vulnerable people. Ideally, prior to any tourism development, the network of potentially affected stakeholders or communities should give input, e.g. "participatory planning input". This is referred to as "social licence". Social licence is an intangible priority, but it is critical to the success of the development of any project.

Social licence must be earned and maintained. Social licence has three critical components (UNWTO, 2014):

Legitimacy: This must be established by demonstrating that the development project adheres to cultural and social rules. It typically involves an initial consultation process, which includes preparation of accurate and accessible communication to community members and other stakeholders about planned projects. Mechanisms to receive community views, suggestions and concerns need to be established, and community input should be taken into account the project design. It can be useful to establish forums, such as local community advisory committees, to ensure on-going community engagement through the life of a project or program.

Credibility: This must be created by providing accurate and consistent access to information about the project, which may involve a signed agreement.

Trust: This will be gained between the parties when both sides feel that they are benefiting from the project and that the other is maintaining their best interests as much as possible. Destinations both large and small should strive to obtain social licence before adventure tourism development occurs. Social licence should also lead to another intangible characteristic, which is referred to by the World Travel and Tourism Council 1 as an "affinity for tourism". This is demonstrated by characteristics such as the society accepting foreigners' presence, which is especially critical for adventure tourism.

We may suggest that Active Tourism occurs and combines both natural areas and rural and urban areas – such as rural market towns, villages and smaller cities. The product is designed in the way of "slow travel"; it offers interesting cultural experiences and close human interaction between guests and hosts, despite the fact that visitors may speak another language. This is an essential part of what the tourist seeks to achieve, in terms of the nature of experiences offered by these two regions. The almost intact nature, the local architecture, archaeological ruins, both rural and urban features and civilisation products may all be objects of visiting in Active Tourism markets – be it domestic or international. Furthermore, to discover the diverse results of human creativity as living culture elements – local traditions, language, music, dancing or cooking – may be the most interesting ingredients of the Active Tourism experience in these two contrasting regions of both Slovenia and Scotland. The idea of the products offered is that visitors not only go to visit a natural and beautiful site, but they practise exercise, activate their body energy and enrich their mind. This means that body and mind are in harmony with nature and at the same time connected to human civilisation. As visitors wander through the untouched forest, they should listen to the local guides who will inform them of the most interesting facts about animal and plant species, about the ecosystem, about conservation issues and explain local history and legends.

Best practices often evolve into standards over time (UNWTO, 2014). Standards are typically endorsed and/or recognised by an institution of the sector, but are also frequently developed from within the market and adhered to voluntarily. Adherence to standards are not always enforced, but over time it may become obvious to business owners that the following standards are in their best interest.

Active tourism market-driven standards are as follows:

- Owned by sector stakeholders, such as tour operators and guides, because they are developed over time by the stakeholders themselves;
- Cost effective, in that they are developed organically from within the sector;
- Capable of widespread adoption as it becomes obvious the standards are in the best interest of stakeholders;
- Slower to develop, but have long-term applicability, because they are often observed consistently and without significant oversight;
- Not enforceable or officially regulated.

While the future of the active tourism sector has many challenges, including carrying capacities, environmental fragility and limitations, and others, the sector is equally ripe with opportunities for growth.

Tourism capacity and planning has always been crucial for sustainable tourism markets. Officials and stakeholders must strategically address the impacts of adventure tourism – additional consumption, traffic and waste caused by non-residents, potential deterioration of natural and historical sites, cultural impacts and pressures for host destinations to develop infrastructure for the benefit of tourists rather than local needs – to prevent degradation and negative effects (UNWTO, 2014).

Active Tourism commonly occurs in or near natural environments, social environments with distinct culture and/or sites inhabiting historical artefacts. As such, adventure tourism destinations are often fragile and in need of protection from overcrowding. While significant numbers of visitors can offer a financial incentive to conserve attractions, they also increase threats to destination integrity through overuse, uneven resource distribution and pressures to develop in non-sustainable ways in order to capture and maximise profits.

Concluding thoughts

Our approach in this chapter has been to suggest that in line with global tourism trends, destination managers are more and more likely to design their destination products in a direction where elements of active tourism – such as recreation and education, respect and contemplation, action, exercise and active involvement in company of an expert local friend or an academically competent tour guide – are an important part of their destination offer. We would suggest that there are tree important issues:

1   **The three critical capacity challenges for Active Tourism at a local level:** i.e. solving low financial capacity, low promotional capacity and low management capacity. Resolution of these challenges is a critical success factor.
2   **The important role of ensuring that the development of active tourism does not develop in a vacuum at a local level** (UNWTO, 2014): This can be ensured through the concept of the "social licence" (UNWTO, 2014), but it requires three essential components – legitimacy, credibility and trust.
3   **Managing capacity through locally inspired, community-driven and multi-agency approaches:** Over-capacity is rapidly becoming a dangerous issue in mass tourism destinations, but the problem is now spreading to small tourism destinations.

In addition, when considering the potential impact of active tourism on local destinations, consideration should be given to the following (UNWTO, 2014):

*   **Care for environment:** Interestingly, because the majority of adventure travel businesses are small-to-medium business enterprises and entrepreneurial, innovative ideas and products often emerge from this segment; this is where many trends start. There is not much status quo to protect, so businesses in this space quickly jump to incorporating initiatives such as composting, recycling, alternative energy sources and reclaiming land.
*   **Transformation of consumers into active advocates:** A week on the trail, a day in the mountains or an afternoon at an archaeological site – interacting closely

with nature and culture has an impact on a traveller that is impossible to replicate any other way. And it will take transformation and disruption to change unconsciously destructive and consumptive traveller behaviours, which are so deeply ingrained and increase carbon footprints worldwide. Adventure travel bridges the gap between the problem and the consumer. The more that people see, feel and interact, the more they will understand what is happening to the world around them. They must, and will, take this important learning back to their lives and businesses. Consumer demand for responsible tourism will help give destinations and businesses a reason to pursue change in their own operations.

- **Protection of the nature:** A key element of adventure travel is that it takes place in nature and often in rural locations. The adventure travel industry is among the most vocal and self-interested in protecting these assets. If travellers cease coming into a region and delivering important income, people will extract every last bit of value from the land – either directly or by selling to non-local parties who care primarily about profit instead of the negative environmental impact.
- **Adventure travel requires less development than traditional industry:** Paved roads, large airports and expensive infrastructure are not always required by the adventure customer or product. This is especially ideal for emerging economies who can maximise what they already have.
- **Adventure travel keeps revenue in the destination:** It gives alternatives to extractive one-use industries and pushes revenue to the rural outreaches – 66% of revenue spent stays in the local destination.
- **Adventure travel gives people a reason to stay rural and be proud of their cultures:** Migration to overcrowded megacities is a problem in many emerging economies, and adventure tourism can be used as a tool to give young people and entrepreneurs a way to create products that attract high-value, low-impact customers.

Active tourism, linked to an ecological base and driven, inspired and sustained by the local communities, can offer a rich experience to a number of growing tourism segments and tourism lifestyles. Developed compassionately and carefully it will add social, environmental and economic benefits; developed under conditions where economic growth is the paramount factor, it may become a social and environmental disaster.

Reflections

1   Active Tourism has a significant impact on local environments, as it is driven by the structure of local ecology, culture and heritage. In a sense this is the Unique Selling Point of Active Tourism – it is closely engaged and interactive with the natural environment in which it is located.
2   By ensuring that Active Tourism is under the control of a local DMO, does this confer a degree of protection of the local cultural, heritage and ecological environment from the depredation and destruction that mass tourism can bring.
3   Nonetheless, it is important that local DMOs adhere to best practice in the management of tourism within the local area, and are not deflected by the short-term potentials of mass tourism. Mass tourism brings short-term economic advantage, but fails to provide longer-term sustainable development.

4   We would suggest that the three critical capacity challenges are important issues – solving low financial capacity, addressing low marketing and promotional capacity and facing up to potential low management capacity. Dealing with these capacity issues requires a community-led consensus to provide the necessary level of resourcing to improve the three capacity deficits.

Questions

1   How do we isolate and address the Unique Selling Point for Active Tourism in local destinations?
2   How can we assess interaction between the social, economic and physical environment in such a way as to preserve the fragile balance of maintaining local culture, heritage and ecology, whilst benefiting from economic growth?
3   What is the critical role of a local DMO?
4   In what way may fragile environments (addressing fragility in culture, heritage and ecology) be protected from excessive tourism activity?
5   How do we solve the problems of local tourism management activities which derive from a lack of financial, marketing and management capacity? May it be solved by training or is something more comprehensive required?

Further reading

Adventure Travel Trade Association (2013). *Industry Snapshot 2013*, Seattle.
Edelheim, J.R. (2017). *Active Tourism – Definitions, Uses, Challenges and Opportunities for Researchers and Operators. Tourism and development 2017: Active & Sports Tourism: Feel the Freedom of the Water*. Brežice: Faculty of Tourism Brežice, University of Maribor Press.
Millich, L. (2011). *Conservation Tourism: Interview with Ralf Buckley, International Centre for Ecotourism Research, yourtravelchoice.org, The International Ecotourism Society*. Retrieved 24.09.14 from: www.yourtravelchoice.org/2011/06/conservation-tourism-interview-with-ralf-buckley-international-centre-for-ecotourism-research/.
Tomazos, K. (2009). *Volunteer Tourism, an Ambiguous Phenomenon: An Analysis of the Demand and Supply for the Volunteer Tourism Market*. Glasgow: University of Strathclyde.
World Tourism Organization (2014). *AM Reports, Volume Nine – Global Report on Adventure Tourism*. Madrid: UNWTO.
Wolter, L. (2014). *The Benefits of Tourism for Natural Areas*. Wiesbaden: Springer Gabler, ISBN 978-3-658–04536-4.

References

Active Tourism Website (2002). Retrieved 25.08.17 from: www.active-tourism.org.
Adventure Travel Trade Association (2013). *Industry Snapshot 2013*, Seattle.
Breadalbane Tourism DMO Promotional Website (2016). Retrieved 14.12.17 from: www.breadalbane.org/rings-of-breadalbane.
City of Cape Town (n.d.). *Responsible Tourism in Cape Town*. Retrieved 16.12.17 from: www.capetown.gov.za/en/tourism/Documents/Responsible%20Tourism/Responsible_tourism_bro_web.pdf.
Comrie Croft Ltd. Promotional Website (2017). Retrieved 14.12.17 from: www.comriecroft.com.

Edelheim, J.R. (2017). *Active Tourism – Definitions, Uses, Challenges and Opportunities for Researchers and Operators, Tourism and Development 2017: Active & Sports Tourism: Feel the Freedom of the Water*. Brežice: Faculty of Tourism Brežice, University of Maribor Press.

Global Sustainable Tourism (2014). Retrieved 16.12.2017 from: www.gstcouncil.org/about/learn-about-gstc.html.

International Conference on Responsible Tourism in destinations (2002), *The Cape Town Declaration*, Cape Town, SA

KOMPAS Novo mesto. (2012). *Unpublished Statistical Data*. Novo mesto.

Koščak, M. (2002). Heritage Trails: Rural Regeneration Through Sustainable Tourism in Dolenjska and Bela krajina. *Rast, XIII*, 2(80), 204–211, MO Novo mesto.

Koščak, M. (2012). *Po poteh dediščine – od teorije k praksi, Priročnik za načrtovanje trajnostnega razvoja in turizma z vključevanjem naravne in kulturne dediščine s praktičnimi primeri*. STUDIO MKA d.o.o.

Millich, L. (2011). 'Conservation Tourism: Interview with Ralf Buckley, International Centre for Ecotourism Research', yourtravelchoice.org, The International Ecotourism Society. Retrieved 24–09–14 from: www.yourtravelchoice.org/2011/06/conservation-tourism-interview-with-ralf-buckley-international-centre-for-ecotourism-research/.

Propoortourism. Retrieved 16.12.17 from: www.propoortourism.info.

Responsible Tourism Development Fund (n.d.). 'What Is Responsible Tourism'. Retrieved 16.12.17 from: www.responsibletourism.mn/why-responsible-tourism/what-is-responsible-tourism.html.

SAVE Travel Alliance (2008). Retrieved 16.12.17 from: www.save-travel.org.

The International Ecotourism Society (2012). 'What Is Ecotourism'. Retrieved 16.12.17 from: www.ecotourism.org/what-is-ecotourism.

The International Ecotourism Society (TIES) (2017). *Society Overview and Objectives*. Retrieved 25.08.17 from: www.ecotourism.org/ties-overview.

The Mountain Institute (2000). *Community-Based Tourism for Conservation and Development: A Resource Kit, The Mountain Institute*. Retrieved 16.12.17 from: http://mountain.org/sites/default/files/attachments/community_based_tourism_for_conservation_and_development.pdf.

Tomazos, K. (2009). *Volunteer Tourism, an Ambiguous Phenomenon: An Analysis of the Demand and Supply for the Volunteer Tourism Market*. Glasgow: University of Strathclyde Glasgow.

United Nations Environment Programme and World Tourism Organization (2015). 'Making Tourism More Sustainable', a Guide for Policy Makers, UNEP and WTO. Retrieved 16.12.17 from: www.unep.fr/ shared/publications/pdf/DTIx0592xPA-TourismPolicyEN.pdf.

'What Is Geotourism?' (2010), National Geographic, Center for Sustainable Destinations. Retrieved 16.12.17 from: http://travel.nationalgeographic.com/travel/sustainable/about_geotourism.html.

Wolter, L. (2014). *The benefits of Tourism for Natural Areas*. Springer Gabler, ISBN 978-3-658-04536-4.

World Tourism Organization (2014). *AM Reports, Volume Nine – Global Report on Adventure Tourism*. Madrid: UNWTO.

World Travel & Tourism Council. Retrieved 16.12.17 from: www.wttc.org.

4 The challenges of integrating sustainable wine-growing into wine tourism

Examples from Slovenia and abroad

Marko Koščak

Overview

In an increasingly competitive tourist market, wine and enogastronomy are becoming key elements in the development of tourist products in regions that cultivate grapevines, in Slovenia and internationally. It has been claimed that no kind of tourism can develop in regions without wine; however, from today's perspective, this claim seems an exaggeration. Nevertheless, enogastronomy is an integral part of many contemporary tourist products. As such, it combines tradition, history and heritage and also improves the recognisability of a given destination on which modern wine tourism products rest. On a global scale, wine tourism is growing, and the forecast for the future is likewise promising.

The essence of a wine tourism product is to connect food and wine, i.e. enogastronomic or culinary experiences, and to follow new trends. The trend is to consolidate this segment of tourism services, in particular through leisure activities and relaxation at the destination of choice. Food and wine thus become part of the cultural experience of the visited destination and equal the experience of visiting a museum or a concert or may be an equal component of such a package.

Links

The following Case Study links may be of interest to readers of this chapter:

- Case Studies Part A (Destination Management aspects of ethical sustainable development) – Chapter 14/Chapter 16/Chapter 18;
- Case Studies Part B (Environmental & Social aspects of ethical sustainable development) – Chapter 19.

Please see the Contents on pages v–viii, and the Guide to the text-book in Appendix 1 for further information.

Introduction

On a global scale, wine tourism is a fast-developing tourist product that grew out of the expectations and activities of the wine industry in the New World (USA, Australia and New Zealand). One reason for encouraging this type of tourism was that global consumption of wine had decreased, and an effort was made to increase its consumption through tourism. In Europe, around 600,000 trips take place annually that are primarily tied to wine tourism as a tourist product; indirectly, this tourist segment accounts for around 20 million tours. Tourist experts are optimistic about the future of wine tourism and predict that the demand will grow between 7% and 12% per annum (UNWTO, 2012).

As part of the tourist package, wine and food may be used to outline the image of a particular destination and represent part of its additional and diversified offering. This can be a powerful element in addressing new tourist markets as well as an opportunity for innovative and high-quality experiences within the existing products. Wine and food can also mitigate the problem of seasonality; they have the potential to extend the season of a tourist destination, encourage engagement by the local community in the processes of creating such tourist products and enable visitors to discover destinations from new perspectives and with new features that were previously unknown.

The product of wine tourism should thus be visible and understood as a business opportunity with considerable development potential for a tourist destination. Some regions can use it to overcome economic crises; by marketing regional products, it is possible to include small producers and family businesses, which thereby generate new jobs and foster prosperity by giving added value to local products. This is a good reason for family hotels, restaurants, tourist farms, vineyard cottages, etc., to include in their portfolio local and home-made products as these are both diverse and of high quality.

The wine tourism product range includes not only conventional wine-growing products but increasingly the products of sustainable wine-growing and related eno-gastronomic services. This trend is particularly evident in countries such as Italy, France and Spain, where sustainable wine-growing is well developed. In Slovenia, sustainable wine-growing is developing with individual wine-growers in the Styria (Štajerska) and Primorska regions. Wine-growers in the Goriška Brda region have made the most progress in this segment of tourist products, and it thus comes as no surprise that Goriška Brda became the European Destination of Excellence in 2015. The region has become recognisable precisely through wine tourism.

What is wine tourism as a product?

This field has been the subject of many studies since the turn of the century, when this product commenced appearing more frequently in the plans and operations of individual destinations. The majority of some ten cited authors have defined wine tourism as "visitation to vineyards, wineries, wine festivals and wine shows for which wine tasting and/or experiencing the attributes of a grapevine region are the prime motivating factors for visitors" (Hall et al., 2000, p. 3). Getz and Brown (2006) define the key success factors of a given wine-tourist region (Figure 4.1), considering wine tourism simultaneously as one form of consumer behaviour, the strategy that tourist destinations use to create local development and market local wines, but also as a marketing opportunity for wineries that can sell their products directly to the buyer.

The development of wine tourism may be connected with the planning and development of "wine trails". The first wine trails appeared in 1934 in Burgundy, France; later, other European countries followed the same model. The key objective was to help the wine-makers market their products. When wine trails appeared in California and South Africa, they were originally planned as integral itineraries, which, in addition to the experiences and flavours, i.e. wine and gastronomy, offered the experience of a cultural landscape, its natural and cultural heritage, the life of the local population, etc., i.e. as a product of wine tourism. Wine tourism as a concept represented a link between wine-making, first and foremost the wineries, and other tourist offerings of the

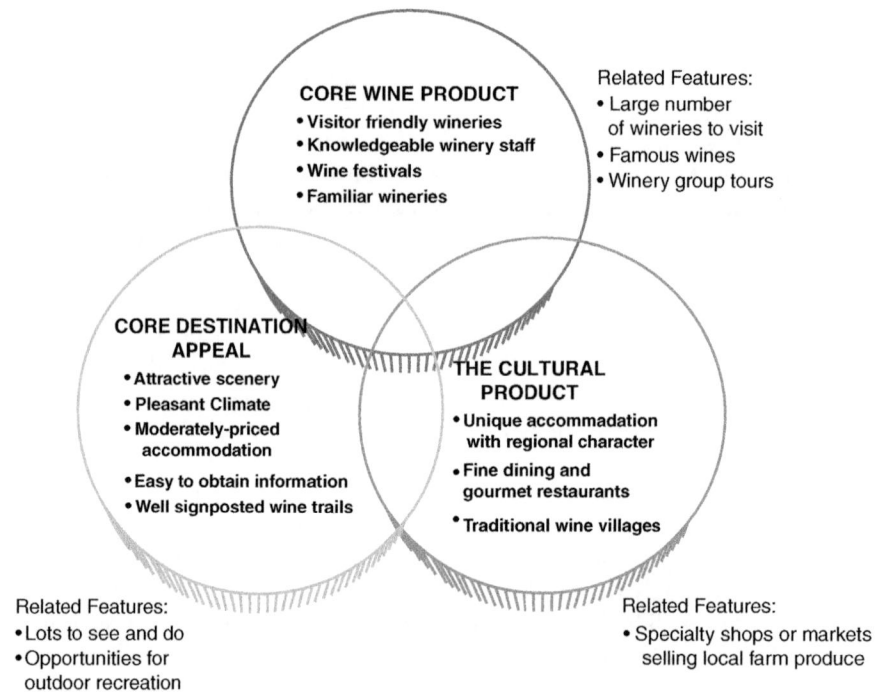

Figure 4.1 Critical factors of success according to Getz and Brown.
Source: Based on Getz and Brown (2006).

destination, i.e. the tourist industry of the destination (Manila, 2010). In Europe, this concept developed slowly and expanded over the last few decades of the 20th century.

However, this concept is not new in Slovenia. After independence in 1991, the project of Tourist Wine Trails (Vinske turistične ceste – VTC) was initiated by the Ministry of Agriculture, Forestry and Food of the Republic of Slovenia; however, not all VTC locations in Slovenia reached their full potential. The concept was based on a special kind of agricultural product marketing, according to which farms offer their products and services under the label of "wine trails". Of course, in developing the package, the concept presupposed partnership between stakeholders from the public, private and non-governmental sectors, which turned out to be the most difficult step in organising VTCs in Slovenia. Cooperation between wine-makers, i.e. wineries, tourist experts and tourist stakeholders, remains vital for the development of wine tourism as a quality tourist product.

In some environments, wine tourism is offered in combination with eco-, cultural, adrenaline and other types of sustainable tourism, so that visitors typically do not distinguish between individual types of tourism (Charters & Ali-Knight, 2002) (Figure 4.2).

It is necessary to introduce new business activities that are local and compliant with the environment, utilising the local natural and demographic potential. Using this approach, the responsibility and thus motivation for success is transferred to the actual owner (farmer), who is able to generate a higher income with additional engagement. Opportunities no doubt exist, including the segment of sustainable, integrated or

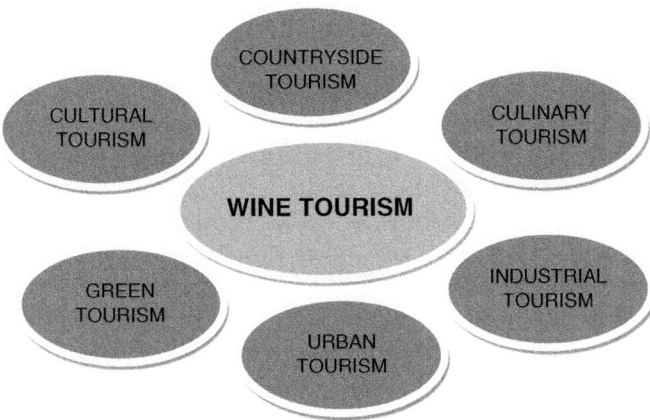

Figure 4.2 Wine tourism – at the crossroads of other types of sustainable tourism.
Source: Charters & Ali-Knight, 2002.

organic crop production, depending on the situation in the market and above all, on awareness of these opportunities among the stakeholders at a particular destination (Koščak, 2014).

Wine tourism thus comprises products that may be ranked into several categories. The development of these products presupposes close cooperation between protagonists of two key sectors – tourism and wine culture – both of which are part of a national strategy and operate in the context of local partnership. It should be assumed that wine tourism is based on three key dimensions: the regional, the local heritage and the wines offered. The following table includes the typology of wine products (Table 4.1):

Table 4.1 The typology and elements of the wine tourism product (Mănilă, 2010)

Wine tourism products	*What these products constitute*
Wine trail	Marked itineraries in wine-growing regions for the discovery of the vineyards, wine, cellars, etc.
Vineyard hiking	Marked itineraries enabling discovery of the vineyards in a ride.
Organised tours and stays in the vineyards	Packages including accommodation, catering and transport, with a variable duration, in which they are proposed activities involving the discovery of the vineyards in one or more components (oenological, gastronomical, cultural, technical, formal dining).
Wine cellar visits	Visiting the cellars; wine producers are known for their wine cellars.
Museums of wine	Places of culture with the goal of presenting the world of wine and transmitting a "savoir-faire" and ancestral traditions.
Holidays and festivals	Events aimed at keeping local traditions, encouraging the promotion of wine and animating the territory; e.g. the local wine festival "Cviček Week".
Professional salons, local fairs, wine sales promotion	Strictly commercial activities to promote wine sales.

Wine tourism in Europe…and in Slovenia

On the other hand, the European Charter on Oenotourism (2006, p.2) defines wine tourism as "the development of all tourist and 'spare time' activities, dedicated to the discovery and to the cultural and wine knowledge pleasure of the vine, the wine and its soil". Wine tourism is a very complex concept covering several research fields, stakeholders' interests, territorial strategies and business perspectives. Firms and the territories where they are located are interlaced realities. The evolution of territories is influenced by the strategies adopted by firms, as well as regional characteristics and dynamics. The interconnection between firms and territories is thus a key issue for territorial sustainable development. This issue is particularly important for the tourism industry as regional attractiveness depends not only on a territory's endogenous resources and on the landscape but also on the interaction of spatial enterprises.

Wine tourism products are increasing in Europe, in particular with the development of wine trails/roads. It is interesting that, although 70% of global wine production takes place in Europe, wine tourism products are best developed in California, South Africa, Argentina, Australia and New Zealand. In these countries, such products are part of the tourist presentation of entire wine-making regions, including the necessary tourist logistics and infrastructure. In Italy, wine tourism has been an integral part of the national tourist programme since 1987 ("citta del vino"), in Spain since 1994 (ACEVIN) and in France since 1997 (RAVIVIN), after national and international exchange networks were established between cities and local producers with the aim of integrating and competing with countries where this product was more developed (Lingon-Darmaillac, 2011). It should be noted that the proportion of sustainable wine-growing is not always indicated by these statistics. Some data from Austria suggests that the proportion of organic vineyards in Austria has exceeded 6% (Krautgartner, 2014).

An analysis of the autonomous community of Aragon in Spain (based on a sample of 43 wine-makers in the community) demonstrates that approximately 33% of all producers are family businesses with fewer than ten employees. Exports generate 50% of their income. However, almost 73% of all wine-makers offer one type of wine tourism product, whereby they averaged 5,573 visitors per year, most of them over the summer. The majority are open throughout the year and have longer working hours in the summer. They mostly do not charge an entry fee; if they do, the fee is around EUR 6. Profit is generated by direct sales, which on average represents 15–20% of the total market share. Regarding the particular example, wine tourism has made the area more recognisable and has improved the image of the wine-makers, the tourist image of the area, the tourist destination trademark, etc. (Iglesias&Navarro, 2014).

The general global trend in the consumption segment (agriculture, cuisine and the energy sector as well as tourism) is to look for products that comply with the principles of respect for the environment, sustainability and environmental protection. This also applies to the narrow sector of wine-growing or wine-making. The experience of pioneering countries in the field shows that sustainability and integrated production are becoming increasingly important factors for the industry. Their experience also shows that the proportion of sustainable products in the portfolio of tourist products will have to expand in the future. However, a few conscientious individuals are not enough; instead, a well-planned and organised approach is required that will allow the story of sustainability or sustainable production to become an integral part of the comprehensive story of a given wine and tourist destination. Sustainability is an opportunity for wine tourism; however, its economic feasibility must also be considered. If these trends turn out to be economically viable, wine-growers will no longer be able to ignore it.

Vineyards and wine are components of a cultural heritage, which is connected to history and has been an essential element for the economic, social and cultural development of different wine regions. Wine culture has grown as part of the life, culture and diet of these regions since time immemorial. As a cultural symbol the importance of wine has changed over time, moving from an imperative source of nutrition to a cultural complement to food and conviviality and compatible with a healthy lifestyle. Promoting wine culture adds authenticity to its origins, and creates a product strongly linked to gastronomy, the pleasures of taste as well as the underlying heritage. According to the Deloitte European Enotourism Handbook Vintur Project (2005, p.4)

> Without the wine culture, wine tourism does not exist. The wine culture is the thematic axis of this product and the tourist must be able to perceive that during all the steps of their wine tourism trip and in any component of the Wine tourism value chain. One should be able to "breathe" the winemaking culture. The enological-cultural value determines the weight of the wine element as an axis or a vertebra of the tourist experience.

In Portugal, the cultural appreciation of wine reflects the diversity of the 14 wine regions, the savoir-vivre and culinary habits. The art of viticulture and winemaking has also developed in improving the association of wine with gastronomy, history, tradition, origin, local quality products and dignified social settings. One important issue is the geographical characterisation – the role of the land, the physical climatic environment as well as the social nature of the various wine-growing regions. This therefore plays a distinctive role in the historical, natural and winemaking heritage as well as focusing on their singular identities. The wine tourism holistic landscape is important, as it is an authentic cultural element of great value which extends to all of the territory and has a sufficient potential to shelter a significant quantity of tourist services, activities and singular experiences (Salvado, 2016).

The Vulkanland tourist destination in the south of Austrian Styria is a telling example. After the whole area identified with the Vulkanland trademark, the initiative attracted individual wineries, which formed a consortium or started developing new types of wines on their own, using names such as Eruption, Caldera, etc., which merged with the overall image and orientation of the destination. Today, Vulkanland is a recognisable tourist destination in Austria, and local wines and cuisine represent two of its most important developmental goals (more details are available here: http://www.kloecherweine.at/cms/weinbaumuseum/). Vulkanland is interesting for a further reason, its key orientation in enogastronomy is to emphasise local specialities and specific features. The local winery thus saw an opportunity in the old self-rooted grapevine variety "jurka" and created a prestigious sparkling wine that became extremely successful with visitors and wine tasters due to its organic production methods.

This necessarily raises the question of the potential of our self-rooted grapevine, the "šmarnica" from Slovenia and the Dolenjska region, which has been seen as a poisonous and harmful wine because of its methanol content, which apparently causes madness, blindness, irrational behaviour and aggressiveness (Malnič, 1990). Its real name is *Noah* and originates from Hebrew; the grape was named "šmarnica" because it grows ripe around the Christian feast day of the Nativity of Mary ("Mali šmaren"). The grapevine belongs to the species of self-rooted grapevines that are a cross between two or more varieties of vine. They are typically more resistant than cultivated grapevines, do not require propagation and are less labour intensive. In the past, "šmarnica" typically grew in condensed vineyards with vines trained to individual stakes or wire and not trained over a trellis, as was typical of other self-rooted grape wines (Malnič, 1990).

The harmful "šmarnica" stereotype developed gradually to become widespread in Slovene society. It was only later, after sample analysis showed that wine made from the "šmarnica" grape contained only small quantities of methanol, but that "šmarnica", in fact, was dangerous for other reasons. Its main problem was not the methanol but the competition that this wine is represented for quality varieties of wine that experienced a major crisis in the market after the First World War (Slabe, 2007).

Our purpose is not to advocate the quality of wine from this grapevine from Dolenjska but to emphasise that this and other self-rooted grapevines are an opportunity to create tourist products that are based on a "story". The story is the guiding principle in successful tourist products in Slovenia and abroad. The Austrians created a successful story out of the Uhudler wine blend that comprises several self-growing varieties of grape. It is interesting that the European Parliament has granted Austria the exclusive right to make and sell wine from self-growing grapevine varieties until 2030.

Similar to the self-growing grapevines, a few endemic grapevines from Dolenjska likewise have specific development potential. The endemic "lipno" grapevine is a particularly important variety; however, it has almost disappeared from the Dolenjska vineyards. The largest vineyard that features this variety is owned by the well-known wine-maker Marjan Jelenič in Jablance nad Kostanjevico na Krki (Štepec, 2013, pp. 86–87). A good example of the revival of endemic varieties of grapevine that can serve as a role model comes from the region of Vipavska dolina. This region has managed to create a good wine story from the reintroduction of endemic varieties such as "zelen", "pinela", "klarnica", "vitovska grganja" and "pikolit".

Regarding the integration of sustainable wine-growing in the tourist sector, another successful story is that of The Matjaž Farm in Paha and The Story of Cviček (more information is available at http://www.matjazeva-domacija.si/klasicen-program.html), which is an upgrade of what "cviček" means in Dolenjska as the odd man out among the wines. In a nutshell, the story is not just about wine and its associated cultural landscape, but about so much more. The Story of Cviček first and foremost presents the local architecture of a typical Dolenjska poor peasant farmer (today it is part of the prestigious international Houses of Tradition tourist network), and it takes the visitor into the past by offering a visit to the old house and its cellar, culminating in the barn where the visitor is introduced to the processes taking place in the vineyard throughout the year. With the help of multimedia, the visitor learns what "cviček" means as a wine and how it is made. Of course, an integral part of the story is the pleasant enogastronomic experience of tasting local and home-made food and various sorts of "cviček"; the highlight of the visit is the tasting of the winning "King of Cviček", the top award-winning wine from the annual "Cviček Week" festival, which rounds off this tourist product from the region of Otočec.

Conclusion

It is unrealistic to expect Dolenjska to compete in wine tourism with other regions and countries as a wine-growing area given its quality, production volume, natural and cultural potential, reputation in the tourist market and the current marketing input in the field of tourism. However, it is necessary to point out the "Tourism in Vineyard Cottages" tourist package, which was a major step forward and proved that systematic work and cooperation could help Dolenjska become more recognisable in this segment of its tourist industry.

Nevertheless, additional research into tourist markets, more coordinated activities and approaches are required for the successful future development of wine tourism in Dolenjska. It would be important to integrate and unite all stakeholders in the tourist industry, private, public as well as the enthusiasts in order for them to work together in a coordinated manner. This includes cooperation of wineries, hotels, tour operators, restaurants, wine cellars, farmers, food producers and wine merchants. All should be guided by an analysis and assessment of whether wine tourism can be integrated across the various fields and place the idea of a sustainable product, including wine and food; the main objective should be how to turn this into a convincing and marketable tourist product. In my opinion, successful examples from other countries show that more emphasis should be given to sustainability as a new orientation.

Of course, this requires a long-term commitment, whereby both providers of services and visitors must understand that the satisfaction of both is key to ensuring the sustainability of the product. Nevertheless, the rich natural and cultural heritage that includes wine tourism products in Dolenjska represents an opportunity and a challenge for better cooperation among all stakeholders. The challenge for the future lies in following the principle "Act cooperatively, promote the collective and deliver the individual".

Reflections

Wine and enogastronomy are becoming very important elements in the development of tourist products in regions that cultivate grapevines, both in Slovenia and internationally. The essence of a wine tourism product is to connect food and wine, i.e. enogastronomic or culinary experiences, and to follow new trends, which is to consolidate this segment of tourism services, in particular through leisure activities and relaxation at the destination of choice. As part of the tourist package, wine and food may be used to outline the image of a particular destination and represent part of its additional and diversified offering. This can be a powerful element in addressing new tourist markets as well as an opportunity for innovative and high-quality experiences within the existing products.

The product of wine tourism should be visible and understood as a business opportunity with considerable development potential for a tourist destination, particularly by inclusion of small producers and family businesses, which thereby generate new jobs and foster prosperity by giving added value to the local products. This is a good reason for family hotels, restaurants, tourist farms, vineyard cottages, etc., to include in their portfolio local and home-made products as these are both diverse and of high quality. The role of the land, the physical climatic environment as well as the social nature of the various wine-growing regions play a distinctive role in the historical, natural and winemaking heritage as well as focusing on their singular identities. The wine tourism holistic landscape is important, as it is an authentic cultural element of great value which extends to all of the territory and has a sufficient potential to shelter a significant quantity of tourist services, activities and singular experiences.

Questions

1   How may destinations efficiently integrate and unite all stakeholders in the tourist industry, private, public as well as the enthusiasts in order for them to work together in a coordinated manner?
2   How may we assess whether wine tourism should be integrated across the various fields and place the idea of a sustainable product, including wine and food; the main objective should be how to turn this into a convincing and marketable tourist product?
3   How may we create a well-planned and organised approach in the wine destination that will allow the concept of sustainability and sustainable production to become an integral part of the comprehensive story of a given wine and tourist destination?
4   How should we ensure that sustainability, being an opportunity for wine tourism that includes or challenges economic feasibility, may be considered simultaneously? What are the consequences if these sustainable trends turn out to be economically viable, then will wine-growers no longer be able to ignore them?
5   How should we manage and sustain a successful wine destination – where vineyards and wine are components of the cultural heritage, are connected to history and have been an essential element for the economic, social and cultural development of that destination?

Further reading

Alant, K., & Bruwer, J. (2004). Wine tourism behaviour in the context of a motivational framework for wine regions and cellar doors. *Journal of Wine Research, 15*(1), 27–37.

Alonso, A.D., Bressan, A., O'Shea, M., & Krajsic, V. (2014). Educating winery visitors and consumers: An international perspective. *Current Issues in Tourism, 17*(6), 539–556.

Alonso, A.D., Bressan, A., O'Shea, M., & Krajsic, V. (2015). Perceived benefits and challenges to wine tourism involvement: An international perspective. *International Journal of Tourism Research, 17*(1), 66–81.

Bruwer, J., Pratt, M.A., Saliba, A., & Hirche, M. (2017). Regional destination image perception oftourists within a winescape context. *Current Issues in Tourism, 20*(2), 157–177.

Charters, S., & Ali-Knight, J. (2002). Who is the wine tourist? *Tourism Management, 23*(3), 311–319.

Grimstad, S., & Burgess, J. (2014). Environmental sustainability and competitive advantage in a wine tourism micro-cluster. *Management Research Review, 37*(6), 553–573.

Kerma, S., & Gačnik, A. (2015). Wine tourism as an opportunity for tourism development: Examples of good practice in Slovenia. *Journal of International Food and Agribusiness Marketing, 27*(4), 311–323.

References

Charters, S., & Ali-Knight, J. (2002). Who is the wine tourist? *Tourism Management, 23*, 311–319.

European Enotourism Handbook – Vintur Project. (2005). *Deloitte*, www.recevin.net/userfiles/file/VINTUR/VADEMECUM_ENOTURISMO_EUROPEO1_engl%20sept05.pdf

Getz, D., & Brown, G. (2006). Critical success factors for wine tourism regions: A demand analysis. *Tourism Management, 27*, 146–158.

Hall, C.M., Sharples, L., Cambourne, B., & Macionis, N. (2000).*Wine Tourism around the World*. Oxford: Elsevier Butterworth-Heinemann.

Internet source 1: Matjaževa domačija na Pahi. 17 April 2016, www.matjazeva-domacija.si/klasicen-program.html

Internet Source 2: *European Charter on Oenotourism*. (2006). 17 April 2016, www.recevin.net/userfiles/file/VINTUR/Charte_EN.pdf

Koščak, M. (2014).*Cviček, vzrok in posledica za razvoj vinskih poti. Zbornik Cviček v dolenjski deželi turizma/42. Teden Cvička*. Kostanjevica na Krki: Društvo vinogradnikov Dolenjske and Fakulteta za turizem, pp. 161–164.

Krautgartner, R. (2014). *Austrian Wine 2014*. GAIN Report Number: AU 1405, Vienna, https://gain.fas.usda.gov/Recent%20GAIN%20Publications/Austrian%20Wine%202014_Vienna_Austria_2-3-2014.pdf, accessed 17 April 2016.

Lignon-Darmaillac, S. (2011).*Vin, vignoble et tourisme: des relations à construire*, Vin, vignoble et tourisme – Les Cahiers Espace, nr.111, pp. 8–15.

Malnič, A. (1990). *Slovenci, vino in država: Štajerci in šmarnica* [graduation thesis]. Univerza v Ljubljani, Oddelek za etnologijo.

Mănilă, M. (2010). Wine tourism – a great offer face to new challenges. *Journal of Tourism*, (13), 54–60.

Pedraja Iglesias, M., & Marzo Navarro, M. (2014). *Wine Tourism Development from the Perspective of Family Winery, Cuadernos de Turismo*, Vol. 34. Spain: Universidad de Murcia, pp. 233–249, 415–418.

Salvado, J. (2016). A pathway for the new generation of tourism research. In *Proceedings of the EATSA conference 2016*, ISBN: 9789892072173.

Slabe, J. (2007). *Proč s šmarnico. Zgodovina za vse, leto XIV, št.2*. Celje: Zgodovinsko društvo Celje, pp. 89–105.

Štepec, D. (2013). *10 let Društva vinogradnikov Lisec Dobrnič (2003–2013) in oris vinogradniške tradicije na Liscu*. Dobrnič: Društvo vinogradnikov Lisec Dobrnič.

UNWTO. (2012).*Global Report on Food Tourism*, Madrid, Spain.

5 The role of planned events on the promotion of the destination Maribor-Pohorje

Maja Rosi, Nika Mernik, Tony O'Rourke and Marko Koščak

Introduction

Event tourism has become an increasingly important industry, with significant economic effects, whilst at the same time attracting visitors to visit the destination and its various associated events. Tourists are a good source for spreading positive or negative feelings and opinions about the destination all over the world. Destinations that seek to become successful require to plan strategically their destination marketing, including all planned national and international events. Planned events are part of the tourist attractions offered by a particular destination and have a significant role in destination marketing, the promotion, positioning and branding of the destination itself. For that reason, a number of destinations are building their image on the visibility and recognition of events as an important part of their offer. The aim of this research was to explore the impact of planned events on promotion of destination Maribor-Pohorje and destination's promotional strategy regarding chosen events. This chapter examines the results of a strengths, weaknesses, opportunities and threats (SWOT) analysis of impact of planned events on chosen destination, which was structured upon a personal interview survey and relevant secondary data review. Based on the findings, several recommendations regarding SWOT analysis are proposed to improve the current situation regarding the impact of events on chosen destination promotion and creating a greater attraction for visitors.

Links

The following Case Study links may be of interest to readers of this chapter:

- Case Studies Part A (Destination Management aspects of ethical sustainable development) – Chapter 14/Chapter 16/Chapter 17/Chapter 18;
- Case Studies Part B (Environmental & Social aspects of ethical sustainable development) – Chapter 19/Chapter 21;
- Case Studies Part C (The business impacts of ethical sustainable development) – Chapter 26/Chapter 27.

Please see the Contents on pages v–viii, and the Guide to the text-book in Appendix 1 for further information.

Concepts of destinations and events

Marketing is used as a mechanism to achieve strategic objectives of destination regions and is becoming extremely competitive worldwide. Consumers associate destinations with the entire range of local producers and suppliers that why it is important for tourism marketers to appreciate travel motivations in order to develop appropriate offer and brand destinations for the right target markets (Buhalis, 2000). The motivation and motives of people in tourism are very important. When tourists decide which tourist destination to choose for their holiday destination, their motives are a very important element and thus taking into consideration the process of destination marketing. If destination marketing understands tourists' needs and motives, it will also understand their way of thinking and acting; this will also help tourist destinations to predict future tourism trends. Tourist motives are changing accordingly to their habits, lifestyle and current tourism trends. Therefore, tourist destinations are also changing and adapting their marketing policies as well as aligning their marketing activities and tourist promotion to their targeted visitor segments. Doyle (2002) defines the concept of tourist promotion as the transmission of messages in order to create products and business services that attract target groups. Good examples of this are events that destinations are offering in order to attract as many visitors as possible. Thus, events have become an increasingly significant component of destination branding (Jago et al., 2003) and planned events are of increasing importance for destination competitiveness (Getz, 2008). Throughout they can directly communicate with their target groups, e.g. sport , gastronomic and cultural events. All of these events have a common purpose, and this is to gain people's attention (Kotler et al., 2014) and to build up positive image of destination. According to Chi and Qu (2008), the image that tourists hold of a destination affects tourists' satisfaction with the travel experiences, and organising cultural events that appeal to tourists is one of crucial elements that contributes to the shaping of the image of a destination. Getz (1997) defined the event or event tourism as the planning, development and marketing of events that are a guide for further development of the destination, helping to strengthen its reputation. When promoting a tourist destination, it is necessary to focus on the content of events, since they reflect the image of the destination and impact of its visibility.

This chapter is designed to determine the impact of the most important planned events on the promotion of the destination Maribor-Pohorje, and to explore the promotion strategy of chosen events and the flow of foreign visitors to these events. By using the term "planned event", the paper refers to Getz (2008) typology of the main categories of planned events, where some are for public celebration (cultural celebration – festivals, carnivals), whilst others are planned for the purpose of competition, fun, entertainment, business or socialising. The paper commences with a theoretical background by outlining existing challenges of collaboration between stakeholders that form the tourist destination. It continues with the importance of the proper promotion for attracting as many visitors as possible and exposes the impact of planned events on the destination marketing. For the research purposes, the destination Maribor-Pohorje was chosen for the following reasons: (a) favourable position at the crossroads of major European routes; (b) many cultural, historical and natural attractions; (c) many sporting, cultural and other domestic and international events; (d) according to various media, one of the top ten tourist destinations in the world.

Sustainable management of tourism destinations

There is growing concern internationally about how best to direct the sustainable management of tourism destinations. Sustainable management of destinations looks beyond the individual performance of a business, company, local authority and other organisations. Sustainable management looks towards a holistic and integrated level where the individual performance contributes to the greater goal of the destination as a whole.

One of the first terms related to the sustainable management of tourism was sustainable tourism destinations. The tourist destination was defined as "the main place of consumption of tourist services and, therefore, the location and place of activity of tourist businesses". This term emerged from the need to develop tourism destinations in a sustainable manner (Lee, 2001). The impact of a well-managed tourism destination can provide important benefits. Poor management can have a serious impact on ecosystems and contribute to the loss of cultural integrity and identity of the destination (Charters & Saxon, 2007; Rio & Nunes, 2012). Destinations are complex and dynamic systems consisting of subsystems that have a direct or indirect impact on tourism development. Development of tourism in the destination is typically spontaneous, unless specifically influenced by destination management organisations. It can be analysed quantitatively and qualitatively using statistical data, indicators and models that contribute to the detection of patterns as well as a prediction of future development of tourism.

A tourism destination is an important unit of analysis, albeit difficult to define (Haywood, 1986), but may be considered as a cluster of interrelated stakeholders embedded in a social network (Scott et al., 2008). Such a network of stakeholders interacts, jointly meeting visitor needs and producing the experience that travellers consume. These destination stakeholders include accommodation businesses, attractions, events, tour companies and others providing commercial services; government agencies; and tourism offices as well as representatives of the local community. The interaction of these stakeholders is complex, dynamic and subject to external shocks. The basic premise of tourism destination management is that through cooperative planning and organisational activities, the effectiveness of these joint interactions can be improved to the benefit of individual stakeholders. Governance is a concept that refers to relationships between multiple stakeholders and how they interact with one another. It involves how stakeholders determine, implement and evaluate the rules for their interaction (Beritelli et al., 2007). Thus, differences in the governance arrangements of tourism destinations may be presumed to lead to differences in the effectiveness of joint stakeholder interactions and hence to improvements in destination competitiveness (Beaumont and Dredge, 2010).

Much research on the topic of tourism destination highlights how single players within a destination are not self-sufficient, implying a high level of interdependencies among the plurality of local actors. Thus, in order to survive, destinations at local, regional and national level must be comprehensively governed and coordinated through new form of collaborations. One of these is re-inventing the structure in terms of collaboration and leadership, which may add value to a destination in terms of growth, innovation and competitiveness. Destinations are difficult bodies to manage due to the dynamic of benefits and interests sought by stakeholders. Although they have numerous linkages and interdependencies, they do not collaborate, and they often have different development visions but none of them can control the destination (Buhalis, 2000; Sainaghi, 2006).

The tourist destination is constructed from different tourism providers and interest groups from public, private and civil sector (Vodeb, 2014). Their mutual connection and cooperation is odecrucial for the development, planning, existence and competitiveness of tourist destinations as well as the proper organisation of tourism at the destination. According to Mariani et al. (2014) for improving the attractiveness of the destination, it is crucial to have the collaboration of tourism companies for destination marketing purposes. Difficulties may arise because of conflicts of interest of different tourism providers at the destination. For this reason, coordination and cooperation between tourism providers and the public sector is crucial. The result of this kind of cooperation reduces the negative impacts and increases the positive impacts of tourism. On the other hand, Alič and Cvikl (2011) add that it is necessary to maintain primary natural and cultural sights and heritage, to minimise adverse impacts and interventions in nature and climate and to increase the level of development and profitability. All this has to be done in respect of the principles of sustainable tourism development. Uran and Juvan (2009, p. 175) state that "Long-term success of tourism is conditional on proper involvement of every tourism provider".

Key elements of a particular destination are shown in Figure 5.1, where Koščak (2015, adopted from UNWTO (2007)) differentiates between (a) attractions, (b) infrastructure and (c) services – products.

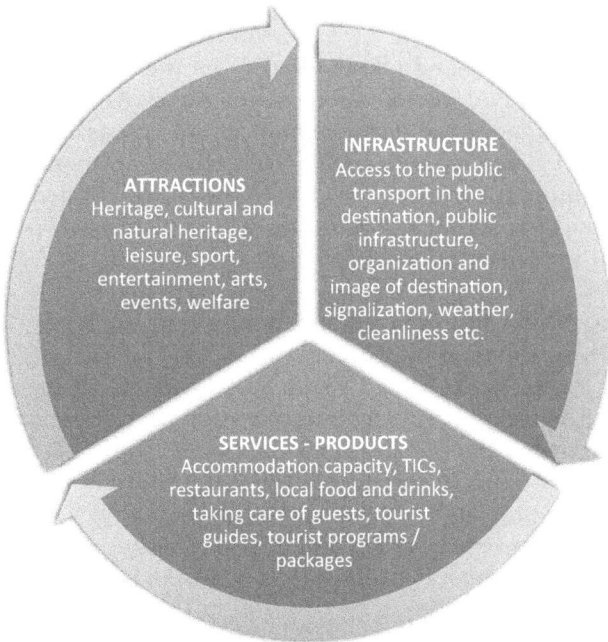

Figure 5.1 Key elements of particular destination.
Source: Koščak (2015, adopted from UNWTO (2007)).

The success of individual actions at a tourist destination is the subject of common features, and it depends on actions of every single stakeholder in the destination, which collectively create the tourism product in that destination. In order to attract visitors, a complete offer of interesting and attractive services at the destination should be developed and designed, because such an offer is the main driver at the destination offering a holistic tourist experience (Nemec Rudež & Zabukovec Baruca, 2011). An important element is effective and successful tourist promotion, which Doyle (2002) defines as the transmission of a communication process with the aim of showing the attractiveness of a product or service to its target segments. Marketing communication or tourist promotion integrates and coordinates all promotion tools and channels for the transmission of consistent and compelling messages about the organisation or product (Middleton et al., 2009).

An important part of tourist promotion is the effective destination positioning strategy that enables the creation of a place attractive in the minds of the target groups (Echtner and Ritchie, 1991). Positioning has a decisive impact on shaping of perception about a particular destination; how the visitor perceives it in his consciousness and consequently directly affects the growth of the attractiveness of the destination. Vodeb (2014) states that effective positioning of destination is based on the search for uniqueness, which is part of a destination's identity. If identity is simple, clear and easy to explain, also the uniqueness is more acceptable and more understandable. The destination's identity actually represents the key features that distinguish it from others. Especially in tourism, is it important to be unique and so more attractive for tourists.

Middleton et al. (2009) claim that tourist destinations constantly communicate; they are always (im)personally and (un)intentionally in interaction with their consumers or even the whole public. Therefore, every form of tourist promotion is primarily designed to manipulate demand and the impact on the shopping behaviour of consumers. The authors (Ibid.) define promotion strategy as a design and implementation of promotional and integrated communicational programs, as well as communication with target potential segments of visitors. For promotion strategy and its components planning is essential; the clear goals must be stated, target segments have to be identified and effective messages have to be developed and monitored through careful implementation of promotional strategies and evaluation (Doyle, 2002).

Events, as part of the promotion strategy of destination, are strong factors to attract tourists and to gain their attention for visiting a particular destination – they are destination attractions themselves. Getz (2008) defines events as an important motivator of tourism, which figure prominently in the development and marketing plans of most destinations. Further on, Richards and Wilson (2004) describe events as a particular valuable form in terms of their image effects. A primary purpose of event tourism is to enrich the leisure time of visitors and inhabitants as well. Avraham (2014) outlines the importance of events impact on destination image, since they are considered a good opportunity to attract outsiders to a destination they might never consider visiting.

Between tourist events Sikošek (2010) considers all events that enrich and expand the destination tourist offer. Tourist destination and events are totally separated and different fields of tourism, but they have to collaborate with each other for their own success, because they serve the same purpose. Without successful destination, there are no successful events and vice versa (Koščak, 2015). Marzano and Scott (2006) are claiming that events are an important part of attractions at a destination, which has, beside the financial benefits, a significant impact on the positioning and branding of the destination itself. For these reasons, all events should be considered and included in promotional strategy of any destination.

In planning promotional strategy, Brezovec and Nemec Rudež (2009) point out important questions to be answered:

- To whom we communicate (tourism providers, local community, investors, etc.)?
- Why we communicate (persuasion of buyers, sales promotion, creating an image about the product or service…)?
- What and how we communicate (content, structure, format…)?
- How often we communicate (depends on how often we want the target segment to be informed about the product)?
- Where we communicate (choice of communication channels and communication tools)?

Every community or destination should have promotional strategy and also appropriate tourist events plan, because there is a correlation between events and community, as well as development of tourist destinations is therefore enhanced. Getz (2008) argues that event tourism is not usually recognised as a separate professional field. Instead, it is important part of destination marketing/management organisations and national tourism offices. Interrelation between event tourism, tourism management and event management is presented in Figure 5.2, showing that tourism and event studies consist of both the marketing of events to tourists and the development and marketing of events for tourism and economic development purposes.

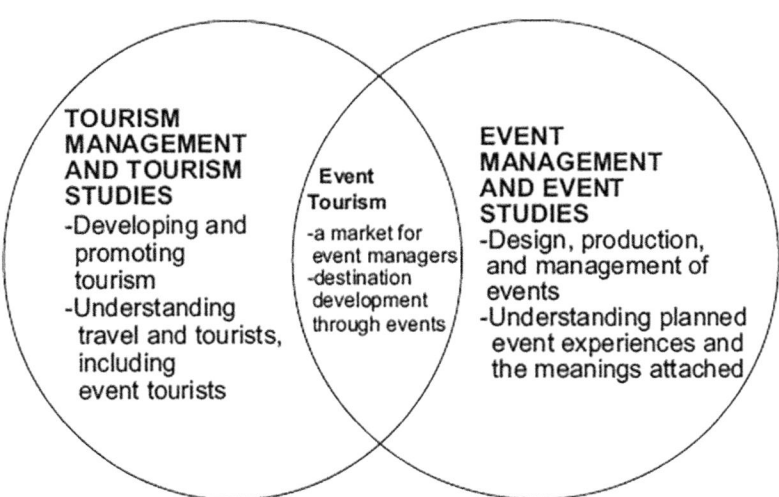

Figure 5.2 Event tourism at the nexus of tourism and event studies.
Source: Getz (2008).

UNWTO (2007) considers events as bearers of important tourist features:

- *Events as brand builders.* Major events could play a vital role in building and re-enforcing the destination brand. The fact that the destination is capable of bidding for and hosting major events is an indicator of destination's capability and provides global exposure via print and TV media. By investing in an appropriate portfolio of events that complement the brand image, the destination can re-enforce the brand in the marketplace.
- *Events as indirect stimulators of business growth.* Carefully selected and supported portfolio of appropriate events in accordance with the economic growth strategy of the destination, events could act as stimulants for sectoral business growth. An example of this is the opportunity for boat building that could arise from stopovers of major ocean races. Similarly, major film or fashion events could stimulate the development and expansion of these market sectors.
- *Events as tactical levers, e.g. to offset seasonality.* Events that are appropriately positioned could act as catalysts to offset fluctuations in demand due to seasonality and other factors. In addition, they could serve as magnets for tactical marketing drives – e.g. a Whale Festival as lever for a whale-watching package, flower festival, as levers for botanical travel packages, etc.
- *Events as direct generators of tourism business.* A portfolio of major events could draw substantial numbers of new visitors to the destination. Each visitor that attends an event spends a considerable amount in the destination, and such expenditure permeates through the local economy resulting in indirect and induced economic benefits.
- *Events as vehicles for local pride and community building.* Local events can provide opportunities for rallying community pride and ensure enjoyment and involvement of local citizens.

Events may be primary attractions of some destination and a main consideration in creating a topic and image of destination, tourist packages, etc. Tourist destinations should consider, think about and determine the extent to which existing events will continue to develop and be promoted as a tourist attraction and what will be the extent of support for the development or creation of new events. The role of events is also lengthening tourist seasons; the geographical spread of tourism; creation and improvement of the image of destination; and the promotion of arts, culture, sport, recreation, conservation of natural and cultural heritage and community development. Because of so many different roles, there is a need for organisational development on the level of stakeholders, local communities, destinations and country in order to support the event tourism (Getz, 1997).

Methodology

This is an explorative study about impact of events on destination promotion in the chosen case of the destination Maribor-Pohorje in Slovenia. Maribor – the second largest city in Slovenia, and the capital of the Štajerska region lies in the embrace of the green Pohorje Mountains and the wine-growing Slovenske gorice hills. The river Drava makes its way between the Pohorje Mountains and the Kozjak hills, and flows through Maribor continuing across the Dravsko polje plain. Destination

Maribor-Pohorje, the central Štajerska region, comprises 22 municipalities. The heart of the region is the city Maribor. Its tourist attraction is complemented by the attractions of the surrounding municipalities (Zavod za turizem Maribor-Pohorje, 2014). The most important tourist offers are the wine and food; recreation and sport; culture, urban and rural; natural environment (eco-tourism, wellness); congress and business tourism; gambling; and shopping (Zavod za turizem Maribor-Pohorje, 2016). At this destination a variety of planned events are taking place, but the problem is that they overlap each other and are not specially categorised for target groups of visitors.

To address the purpose of the research, a qualitative research method was used. Information was gathered through a semi-structured interview. In order to increase the credibility of the research, the results were compared with previous research findings from the Annual Report of the Institute of Tourism Maribor-Pohorje. Interviews were conducted with six research participants – the main promoters from the organisation board of the most recognisable destination events: Lent Festival, Old Vine Festival, Maribor Theatre Festival, St. Martin's Day and Magic December in Maribor.

The individual interviews were conducted in 2016. The interview questions are presented in Table 5.1.

Triangulation implies looking at the same research purpose from differing angles and may be used to corroborate, elaborate or illuminate a research problem (Decrop, 1999). With this method, interview findings were complemented with a literature review and important findings from the Annual Report of the Institute of Tourism Maribor-Pohorje.

Porter's five forces were used to consider the chosen destination and its events potential market dynamics (competitors, buyers, suppliers, etc.). Porter's five forces model analyses entrepreneurial attractiveness and likely profitability within a strategic management concept. Porter saw that whilst closely observing the actions of rival enterprises was important, organisations should be encouraged to look beyond the actions of competitors and examine what other factors could affect the business environment. Porter's five forces are as follows: *threat of new entrants, intensity of rivalry, threat of substitutes, bargaining power of buyers* and *bargaining power of suppliers* (Porter, 1985).

Table 5.1 Questionnaire for personal interview survey

Questions
Since when your event is taking place?
How visible is your event between domestic guests and how between foreign guests?
Have there been some evident changes regarding organising this event (in quality, content, visitor structure)?
Do you include the local community when organising the event? Did you establish any local partnership?
What are your target groups for addressing the event?
What is the budget of organising the event?
When do you usually first activities for organising the event begin?
Where and on which markets in your event promotion taking place?
Is event program suitable for foreign speaking guest? To what extent?
Do you think that your event has a positive influence of the promotion of the Maribor-Pohorje destination? How?

To synthesise the main findings, a SWOT analysis was conducted, with application of Porter's five forces model resulting:

supplier power strengths,
buyer power opportunities,
rivalry weaknesses and strengths,
threats of new entrants and threat of substitutions threats.

SWOT analysis was used to identify the strengths and weaknesses of an organisation (internal environment) and the opportunities and threats from the external environment (Dyson, 2004) and has been used as strategic planning tool from the 1960s onwards (Hill & Westbrook, 1997; Mintzberg, 2000). According to Lordkipanidze et al. (2005) the SWOT analysis has a qualitative nature and in aspect of this paper, it helps to discover information about impacts of different events on chosen destination. It contains a discussion on SWOT regarding the impact that chosen events have on destination Maribor-Pohorje. Combining Porter's five forces model, SWOT analysis and the findings of personal interview surveys, a study of the literature and the Annual Report of the Institute of Tourism Maribor-Pohorje, so that the final results reflect the common situation of chosen organisations and their events. This enabled the present and future view of analysed events at chosen destination.

Interpretation of results and synthesis of findings

The impact of planned events on the destination marketing of Maribor-Pohorje was examined through interviews with representatives of the organisational board of the events such as Lent Festival, Old Vine Festival, Maribor Theatre Festival, St. Martin's Day and Magic December in Maribor. For the purpose of this chapter, only the main findings were reported. Based on a transcription of interviews, the results are reported as a synthesis of the main interviewees' conclusions.

The events that were subject of this research have been periodically organised for three decades and are therefore traditional events, deeply rooted in the consciousness of the local population. Most events are in Slovenia connected with the following superlatives: the largest, the oldest, highest quality, most reputable, etc. All events have over these three decades developed their identity and improve the content of events and other accompanying tourist products, lengthen the duration of the programs and constantly make efforts to raise the quality of the events. As a result, organisers are observing the trend of increasingly demanding visitors who know what they want and expect what they require. Events that have been a subject of this research are international, multicultural and mostly oriented towards the whole public. They are also almost entirely suitable for foreign visitors, which is a possible reason for the growth of foreign visitors (mainly from Austria). Organisers of the event are very pleased with the good relations with local media and foreign media, which report on these events and compare them with other European events, thus promoting them free to a broader market. Events are organised throughout the whole year with no time overlap, and thus, there is no "stealing" of the visitors (although observation of a higher frequency of events occurs in the second half of the year). It is also good for destinations to avoid excessive seasonality. Organisation of events is taking place throughout the whole year; the first activities commence after the conclusion of the previous event. Promotion activities are usually carried out approximately six to three months before the start date of the event.

Unfortunately, due to the current economic situation, all events are affected by decreased budgets; in particular, the share of sponsorship funds has decreased, whereby sponsorship is mainly connected with free material, less money and more compensation arrangements. Nevertheless, the share of the budget devoted to event promotion ranges between 12.6% and 25.0% of the total budget of the event.

All of these event organisers believe that events definitely have a positive impact on the promotion of the destination Maribor-Pohorje. There are many reasons for this:

- Organising an event interconnects individual stakeholders at the destination, and encourages their participation and contribution to the development of cultural tourism.
- Foreign tourists and visitors are exploring the city of Maribor, because of the dispersal of event venues, and thus are getting to know many cultural, historical and natural attractions.
- At the events, visitors get different kinds of promotional materials related to the destination Maribor-Pohorje and other information about the destination.

According to their opinion, satisfied visitors are certainly the most important part of the promotion, because they are able to spread and communicate their positive impressions and feelings about the events and the event destination itself, everywhere and to everyone.

Porter's five forces model

Intensity of rivalry

The degree of competition differs from industry to industry. Claiming for a better competitive position, companies/organisers use a variety of tools, such as price competition, aggressive communication strategy, aggressive introduction of new products and after-sales service (Porter, 1985). Destination Maribor-Pohorje is positioned in a very competitive environment, geographically very close to well-known players, e.g. Ljubljana (December in Ljubljana, Open Kitchen); Graz (the design festival assembly), Austria; and Zagreb, Croatia (Advent in Zagreb). All of them have plenty of international known and quality events that have great promotion all over the Europe and also well visited from domestic and international guests. Since the rivals are strong and regarding the identified weaknesses of chosen events at destination Maribor-Pohorje (e.g. budgeting, sponsorships, additional service offer, promotion), a lot of attention must be paid to sustain the number of visitors and especially to attract new one. For destination Maribor-Pohorje it is essential to build a differentiation and increase promotion in order to attract more visitors. The collaboration with competitors must also be the priority in order to increase the market size.

Threat of new entrants

When new companies enter the industry, they increase the overall capacities and resources. Because of greater competitiveness, the prices of products and services can be reduced and thus the profitability of the industry. This is certainly not in interest of existing competitors (Porter, 1985). Tourism has over the past two decades exhibited a huge shift in destinations; the advent of cheap flights has opened up low-cost destinations previously not available. New entrants are strengthening the competition by offering new products and services, which are attractive to customers/visitors. Chosen events at destination Maribor-Pohorje have (too) wide target segment of the visitors, and also regarding the interviewees, there is too much effort given on rising events' attractiveness among young people. Regarding these threats and also identified weakness, there may be a potential (threat) that new entrants with new products (events) can attract our target visitors.

Bargaining power of suppliers

In the case of tourism, suppliers are both tangible (those providing tangible products to tourism – food, accommodation, transport, connected service providers) and intangible (national and local taxes, availability of labour, availability of intellectual skills and speed of communications/IT networks). For organisers of chosen events at destination Maribor-Pohorje are of great importance especially accommodation suppliers for visitors, who decide to stay at destination. If the prices of accommodation are not suitable for visitors, that can influence also their decision of visiting the event.

Bargaining power of buyers

Chosen events have a variety of customers (event attendees/tourists) coming from different countries. They want as more as possible for money they pay. Since chosen events have much competition among events of other near destinations, the bargaining power of buyers is present. According to Porter (1985), only a few customers do have more power, but power of organisation increases if there are many customers. In order to sustain the power of buyers and according to interviewees there are opportunities in development of additional target markets and development of tourism products, e.g. parallel tourist products related to the events, cooperation and networking with important stakeholders.

Threat of substitutes

This is probably a minimal threat, but the threats of substitution do always exist – namely when near destination offers a similar event that meets the similar visitors' need, there is a potential to lose a number of visitors. According to Porter (1985), the presence of substitutes can lower attractiveness and profitability because they limit price levels.

SWOT analysis and discussion of common key research findings

Based on Porter's five forcers model and the results from interview, literature review and findings of Institute of Tourism Maribor-Pohorje Annual Report, the SWOT analysis of the impact of events on the destination promotion Maribor was conducted and is presented in Table 5.2.

Table 5.2 SWOT analysis of common key research finding

Tradition of events	Advanced visitors – the higher price segment
Good relations with the media	Development of additional target markets
Raising quality of events	Cooperation and networking with important stakeholders
Event programs appropriate for foreign visitors	Development of cultural tourism
Growth number of foreign visitors	Greater visibility of the destination at the domestic and foreign markets as a result of quality events offer
Distribution of the events throughout the year	Development of parallel tourist products related to the events
Strengths	**Opportunities**
Weaknesses	**Threats**
Budget reductions for the events	(Too) wide target segment of the visitors
Sponsorship assets in the material and less in cash	Reduction of public resources for cultural activities
Events don't offer full package program for visitors (accommodation, transport, etc.)	Impact of safety factor on organising public events and the resulting increase of the cost for events security
Events don't influence on rise of tourists overnights	No activities to introduce young target groups with those kind of events
Destination doesn't have any promotional strategy in the form of a written document	

The promotion of the destination significantly impacts on the visibility of the destination and the subjective perception of destination visitors (Blain et al., 2005; Doyle, 2002; Sirgy & Su, 2000). Each visitor creates in their consciousness their own experiences, their impressions about a particular destination and their assessment and evaluation of it. For this reason, the examined events have an impact on the promotion of the destination, because they are all periodical and the destination Maribor-Pohorje can therefore then gradually build up and develop. Events help to create the identity of the destination, so it is necessary to select very carefully those type of events that will satisfy increasingly demanding visitors and transmit the message throughout the destination wishing to represent and promote itself. This means also attracting appropriate target market segments, what can according to Buhalis (2000) assist the reduction of seasonality and strategically planned events can enable destinations to increase their demand during the low season.

The findings reveal that at the destination Maribor-Pohorje there are sufficient number of quality events, particularly in the second half of the year, and they do not overlap. All events are suitable for foreign visitors, but still do not meet the desired or expected growth of overnight stays at the destination. Chosen events at destination Maribor-Pohorje certainly have a positive impact on the promotion of it, since the organisation of events interconnects individual stakeholders in the destination, encourages their participation and contributes to the development of event tourism at destination. Foreign tourists and visitors can through the diversification of the planned events' venues experience the city of Maribor with the many cultural, historical and natural sights. Satisfied visitors are certainly the most important part of the promotion, as they are able to spread and communicate their positive impressions and feelings everywhere and to everybody.

Overall, planned events may inter alia also serve as one of the attractions of the destination and are the great opportunity for tourists to come not only to visit the destination, but also to stay for few days or more. Therefore, is it essential to connect the tourism products and to form them into integral tourist products (which have the benefit of the offer) and promote them on time in all target markets, as well as to define target markets and the segmentation of visitors.

The Maribor-Pohorje destination is already following the principles of promotional strategies, but a unified promotional strategy must be developed in the future for solving the gaps, as mentioned on Weakness and Threats side of the SWOT analysis undertaken. A unified and properly coordinated promotional strategy that would include key events at the Maribor-Pohorje destination should enable a more targeted and focused promotion. This would also have a greater effect in convicting potential visitors; at the same time, promotional and marketing costs may also be streamlined. In fact, planning is essential for communication and consequently for the promotion of destination; it is only in that way that target markets and segments may be explored, and a good and effective message developed. Every institution organising a major event should have a promotional and marketing strategy consistent with the promotion and marketing strategy of the whole destination. Such communication does not only inform audiences, but also convinces, inspires, invites and reminds (potential) visitors at destination events. When designing a promotional strategy, the stakeholders in a destination are very important. They require to be involved at the inception of the process of designing the strategy, so they may therefore share their own opinions and suggestions. The promotional strategy of key events and destinations itself would be a good example to all the stakeholders in the destination Maribor-Pohorje, whereby they could more systematically and strategically connect, participate and promote themselves.

Conclusion

The results of the literature review, survey findings and all information summarised in the SWOT analysis demonstrate how planned events may affect the attractiveness of the destination Maribor-Pohorje – for visitors, for promotion of the destination and for the overall situation regarding visibility of these events. There have been identified a number of positive relationships in chosen events that are influencing directly or indirectly on the destination promotion and presented on the strengths side of SWOT analysis. Nevertheless, there remain significant opportunities for making these events more visible and thus attracting more visitors to the destination, such as increased numbers of visitors from the higher price segments. This includes the development of additional target markets, cooperation and networking with important stakeholders, as well as development of cultural tourism products. The analyses also reveal some strategic weaknesses and potential threats – issues that event organisers require to take into consideration in their planning and organising of future events. Examples include the fact that events may not offer a full package programme for visitors (accommodation, transport, etc.); events may not impact on increasing tourist-overnights and the lack of activities that introduce younger target groups into this kind of events. Planned events, as part of the tourist offer, are and will continue to be one of the key marketing tools for attracting visitors. It is very important that both tourism sector and tourism collaborate and together build the destination image through promotion of various events at the destination – as explored on the destination Maribor-Pohorje. This could be obtained through a unified promotion strategy of destination, which is still missing at the destination Maribor-Pohorje. Due to the obvious limitation on some planned events at the chosen destination, the future research has to broaden the research population, whereby a larger number of events and their organisers require to be covered. In addition, the survey among the local population has to be spread to gather their opinion regarding this re-search topic. In the future research, a more holistically approach has to be taken for proposing a guideline for a unified promotional strategy of this chosen desti-nation. It would be of a great importance to look closer to other destinations, e.g. Zagreb, Ljubljana, Graz, and compare their events (statistical data, appearance, strategy, promotion, etc.) with chosen events at destination Maribor-Pohorje.

Reflections

Event tourism at a destination level is the development and marketing of planned events as tourist attractions, catalysts, animators, image-makers and place marketers. This process includes bidding on, facilitating and creating events, and the manage-ment of portfolios of events as destination assets. For individual events, event tourism means taking a marketing orientation to attract tourists, sometimes as an additional segment and sometimes as the core business. In this chapter, we demonstrate how planned events may affect the attractiveness of the destination Maribor-Pohorje – for visitors, for promotion of the destination and for the overall situation regarding visi-bility of these events. Planned events, as part of the tourist offer, are and will continue to be one of the key marketing tools for attracting visitors. It is very important that both tourism sector and tourism collaborate and together build the destination image through promotion of various events at the destination – as explored on the destina-tion Maribor-Pohorje.

Questions

1 Where does the event planning process begin?
2 To what extent does the event compliment the unique attractions of the destina-tion and is in accordance with the product and attractions portfolio?
3 What is the optimal planned event strategy, i.e. where the event falls within low-season periods or alternatively the event supports and compliments a year-round calendar of events?
4 What are the community benefits associated with the event and potential spread of economic benefits to the destination and its disadvantaged areas and the hinterland?
5 How would you choose the location/venue for an event? What are your priorities after choosing a location/venue?

6 How do you choose partners (e.g. caterers) when organising an event? What are your criteria to assess their eligibility/quality?
7 Have you ever had to plan more than one event simultaneously? How did you do it? What was the result?
8 How do you use social media for your event planning or for attracting customers?
9 Describe a time when you went over budget. What went wrong and what did you do to fix it?
10 How would you manage stress as the date of an event draws near?
11 How would you react to technical problems during an event? What are the most common/serious problems you have encountered during an event and what did you do about them?
12 Describe a time when you provided a creative solution to a problem. What was the result?
13 Describe your most successful event planning experience. What did you do that made it so successful?
14 Describe an event management experience that didn't have the results you aimed for. What happened and what did you learn?

Further reading

Avraham, E. (2014). Hosting events as a tool for restoring destination image. *International Journal of Event Management Research*, 8(1), 61–76.

Getz, D. (2008). Event tourism: Definition, evolution, and research. *Tourism management*, 29(3), 403–428.

Marzano, G. & Scot, N. (2006). *Consistency in Destination Branding: The Impact of Events*. Brisbane: The University of Queensland Press

Richards, G. & Wilson, J. (2004). The impact of cultural events on city image: Rotterdam, cultural capital of Europe 2001. *Urban Studies*, 41(10), 1931–1951.

UNWTO (2007). *A Practical Guide to Tourism Destination Management*. Madrid: World Tourism Organization.

References

Alič, A. & Cvikl, H. (2011). *Uvod v turizem in destinacijski menedžment*. Maribor: Višja strokovna šola za gostinstvo in turizem Maribor.

Avraham, E. (2014). Hosting events as a tool for restoring destination image. *International Journal of Event Management Research*, 8(1), 61–76.

Beaumont, N. & Dredge, D. (2010). Local tourism governance: A comparison of three network approaches. *Journal of Sustainable Tourism*, 18(1), 7–28.

Beritelli, P., Bieger, T., & Laesser, C. (2007). Destination governance: Using corporate governance theories as a foundation for effective destination management. *Journal of Travel Research*, 46(1), 96–107.

Blain, C., Levy, S. E., & Ritchie, J. B. (2005). Destination branding: Insights and practices from destination management organizations. *Journal of Travel Research*, 43(4), 328–338.

Brezovec, A. & Nemec Rudež, H. (2009). *Marketing v turizmu: izhodišča za ustvarjalno razmišljanje in upravljanje*. Portorož: Univerza na Primorskem, Fakulteta za turistične študije – Turistica.

Buhalis, D. (2000). Marketing the competitive destination of the future. *Tourism management*, 21(1), 97–116.

Charters, T., & Saxon, E. (2007). *Tourism and mountains. A practical guide to managing the environmental and social impacts of mountain tours.* United Nations Environment Programme, Conservation International, Tour Operators' Initiative.

Chi, C. G. Q., & Qu, H. (2008). Examining the structural relationships of destination image, tourist satisfaction and destination loyalty: An integrated approach. *Tourism management, 29*(4), 624–636.

Decrop, A. (1999). Triangulation in qualitative tourism research. *Tourism management, 20*(1), 157–161.

Doyle, P. (2002). *Marketing Management and Strategy.* Fourth edition. Harlow: Prentice Hall.

Dyson, R. G. (2004). Strategic development and SWOT analysis at the University of Warwick. *European Journal of Operational Research, 152*(3), 631–640.

Echtner, C. M. & Ritchie, J. B. (1991). The meaning and measurement of destination image. *Journal of Tourism Studies, 2*(2), 2–12.

Getz, D. (1997). *Event Management & Event Tourism.* New York: Cognizant Communication Offices.

Getz, D. (2008). Event tourism: Definition, evolution, and research. *Tourism management, 29*(3), 403–428.

Haywood, K. M. (1986). Can the tourist-area life cycle be made operational? *Tourism Management, 7*(3), 154–167.

Hill, T. & Westbrook, R. (1997). SWOT analysis: It's time for a product recall. *Long Range Planning, 30*(1), 46–52.

Jago, L., Chalip, L., Brown, G., Mules, T., & Ali, S. (2003). Building events into destination branding: Insights from experts. *Event management, 8*(1), 3–14.

Koščak, M. (2015). Eventi & dogodki kot ključni spodbujevalci razvoja turizma v destinaciji. *Globoke korenine cvička – 43. teden cvička* (pp. 97–101). Brežice: Fakulteta za turizem Univerze v Mariboru.

Kotler, P., Bowen, J. T., & Makens, J. C. (2014). *Marketing for Hospitality and Tourism.* Sixth edition. Essex: Pearson Education Limited.

Lee, K. F. (2001). Sustainable tourism destinations: The importance of cleaner production. *Journal of Cleaner Production, 9*(4), 313–323.

Lordkipanidze, M., Brezet, H., & Backman, M. (2005). The entrepreneurship factor in sustainable tourism development. *Journal of Cleaner Production, 13*(8), 787–798.

Mariani, M. M., Buhalis, D., Longhi, C., & Vitouladiti, O. (2014). Managing change in tourism destinations: Key issues and current trends. *Journal of Destination Marketing & Management, 2*(4), 269–272.

Marzano, G. & Scot, N. (2006). *Consistency in Destination Branding: The Impact of Events.* Brisbane: The University of Queensland Press.

Middleton, V. T. C., Fyall, A., & Morgan, M. (2009). *Marketing in Travel and Tourism.* Fourth edition. Oxford: Butterworth-Heinemann.

Mintzberg, H. (2000). *The Rise and Fall of Strategic Planning.* London: Pearson Education.

Nemec Rudež, H. & Zabukovec Baruca, P. (2011). *Trženje turističnih destinacij.* Koper: Univerzitetna založba Annales.

Porter, M. E. (1985). *Competitive Advantage.* New York: Free Press.

Richards, G. & Wilson, J. (2004). The impact of cultural events on city image: Rotterdam, cultural capital of Europe 2001. *Urban studies, 41*(10), 1931–1951.

Rio, D. & Nunes, L. M. (2012). Monitoring and evaluation tool for tourism destinations. *Tourism Management Perspectives, 4*, 64–66.

Sainaghi, R. (2006). From contents to processes: Versus a dynamic destination management model (DDMM). *Tourism Management, 27*(5), 1053–1063.

Scott, N., Cooper, C., & Baggio, R. (2008). Destination networks: Four Australian cases. *Annals of Tourism Research, 35*(1), 169–188.

Sikošek, M. (2010). *Management prireditev: Organizacija študentskih prireditev.* Koper: Univerza na Primorskem, Fakulteta za management Koper.

Sirgy, M. J. & Su, C. (2000). Destination image, self-congruity, and travel behavior: Toward an integrative model. *Journal of Travel Research, 38*(4), 340–352.UNWTO (2007). *A Practical Guide to Tourism Destination Management.* Madrid: World Tourism Organization.

Uran, M. & Juvan, E. (2009). *Strateški management v turizmu: Oblikovanje strategije turizma in vloga deležnikov.* Koper: Društvo za akademske in aplikativne raziskave Koper.

Vodeb, K. (2014). *Turistična destinacija: sodobna obravnava koncepta.* Koper: Univerza na Primorskem.

Zavod za turizem Maribor-Pohorje (2014). *Presenečenj polna destinacija.* Available at: https://maribor-pohorje.si/files/presenecenj-polna-destinacija-2014.pdf, 2.8.2016.

Zavod za turizem Maribor-Pohorje (2016). *Poslovno poročilo 2015.* Available at: http://maribor-pohorje.si/files/letno-porocilo-2015.pdf, 2.8.2016.

Part B

Environmental and social aspects of ethical sustainable development

6 Slow adventure in remote and rural areas
Creating and narrating the tourism product

*Jelena Farkić, Steve Taylor and
Sara Mair Bellshaw*

Summary

In postmodernity, characterised by fast-paced life, social alienation, workaholism and prevalent electronic entertainment, people have become somewhat detached from the natural environment and other people. For this reason, to overcome a feeling of disconnectedness, and get life back to its slower, immersive pace, a number of global initiatives for slowing down have arisen – slow food, slow cities or slow tourism, to name but a few. In a way, slow activities attempt to strengthen or restore a local, place-specific pattern of living, as well as allow opportunities for the generation of rich, immersive and more meaningful experiences for the consumer.

More recently, the concept of "slow adventure" has been introduced by Varley and Semple (2015). Grounding it in the Nordic philosophy of *friluftsliv,* as the basic and simple activity of just being, or dwelling, in nature, they suggested four critical elements: time, nature, passage and comfort, all of which suggest deeper appreciation of and bodily engagement with the environment. Commercially, the concept of slow adventure is being increasingly used. By way of example, the tourism industry in northern Europe has been successful in taking the concept of slow adventure further through a transnational project Slow Adventure in Northern Territories (SAINT, 2015). The project sought to raise awareness of the concept and introduce contemporary consumers to an alternative dimension of "adventure." As an outcome of the project, travel providers are now increasingly offering slow adventure activities in order to bring the marginal or remote areas closer to visitors through activities as simple as star gazing, open water swimming, creel fishing, wild camping or cooking foraged foods. In so doing, an emphasis is placed on authenticity and sustainability of the local community, natural environment and cultural heritage, all being vital principles of the slow adventure philosophy and its ethos.

Links

The following Case Study links may be of interest to readers of this chapter:

- Case Studies Part A (Destination management aspects of ethical sustainable development) – Chapters 16 and 17
- Case Studies Part B (Environmental & social aspects of ethical sustainable development) – Chapters 20, 23 and 24

Please see the Contents on pages v–viii, and the Guide to the textbook in Appendix 1 for further information.

Introduction

Inspiring connections with the outdoors. Creating memories through meaningful experiences as you invest time in a place, in its traditions and community. Surrendering to the natural forces of the environment as you reflect, reconnect and become closer to nature.

Discussions around the development of tourism in European peripheral areas are far from new (Müller and Jansson, 2006; Saarinen, 2007; Kauppila, Saarinen and Leinonen, 2009). Their descriptions as "remote," "peripheral" or "liminal" are mostly applied to rural or wild areas that are spatially distant from frequently visited centres, are sparsely populated and not particularly accessible. For this reason, the viability of tourism and its benefits for local communities have been questioned (Hohl and Tisdell, 1995). Furthermore, the major limitation of tourism in the northern peripheries in particular may be its seasonality, whereby existing package tours may be limited to several months a year. For this reason, despite their attractiveness and strong "territorial capital" (Pezzi and Urso, 2016) embodied in rich cultural and natural heritage, it has been a challenge for local tourism planners to reinvent a destination and build a recognisable tourism product.

More recently, however, this sense of remoteness is what many tourists increasingly seek in their adventurous leisure pursuits. Individuals wish to explore both the physical and emotional geography of wild places. The peripheral regions have thus received an increased recognition among tourism scholarship and industry experts alike (Carson and Harwood, 2007; Hall et al., 2013; Heimtun, 2016; Heimtun and Lovelock, 2017). In recognition of this trend, local tourism managers and activity providers have made efforts to commodify the sense of remoteness and uniqueness of the cultural landscapes, offering a wide range of activities, for example, crossing a glacier, chasing the northern lights, ice fishing or coastal foraging, to name just a few. Tourism in peripheral areas has experienced steady growth in the past decades, from which they have benefited to an above average extent. However, this growth brings many opportunities for these regions – as well as risks. Therefore, different approaches to responsible consumption of natural resources have been proposed, mostly through tourism (Zurick, 1992; Hall and Boyd, 2005). It is all the more important to actively support the development of tourism and create adequate conditions that can contribute to creating sustainable destinations in peripheral areas. This, however, is not done only through regimented management activities but also through education of the local population and raising awareness about the fragility of resources through various initiatives and campaigns.

Current thinking about sustainability recognises the importance of identifying and understanding the needs and interests of all stakeholders and the value that is created in the interaction with them. One such initiative that aids tourism development in peripheral regions has been a transnational project, Slow Adventure in Northern Territories (SAINT hereafter). To address the issues of remoteness, underdevelopment of tourism or its seasonality, the project proposed a product that is less seasonally dependent, creates potential for year-round employment and income, while at the same time not exerting pressure on natural or cultural assets. Furthermore, it fosters collaboration at the local level among small and medium-size enterprises (SMEs) while at the same time introducing contemporary, affluent consumers to an alternative dimension of "adventure." Building on Varley and Semple's (2015) conceptual work on slow adventure, it engaged seven northern European countries (Scotland, Northern Ireland, Ireland, Sweden, Finland, Iceland and Norway) in their development of analogous tourism products and transnational marketing.

In this chapter, we highlight crucial aspects and benefits of developing slow adventure products in peripheral areas through the case of the SAINT project. We first introduce the concept of slow adventure as an alternative adventure tourism form and discuss it in relation to the broader adventure tourism context. This is followed by an overview of the SAINT project and the process of slow adventure tourism product development, illuminating its two crucial stages: (1) clustering of local SMEs and their involvement in developing collaborative slow adventure tourism products and (2) their collective promotion through a transnational digital marketing campaign. We conclude by restating the benefits of the slow adventure product and its potential to act as a vehicle for sustainable and responsible development of tourism in other "remote," or underdeveloped, regions.

An "alternative" dimension of adventure

Restoring life back to a slower, more immersive pace, a number of global initiatives for slowing down have arisen in the past few decades, slow food or slow cities, for example. In a way, they attempt to strengthen or restore a local, place-specific pattern of living, whilst at the same time offering deeper, richer and more meaningful experiences for the consumer. They offer apparently "authentic" experiences through sensual engagement with a place through "the mix of feelings and emotions by seeing, holding, hearing, testing, smelling and moving through the extraordinary array of goods and services, places and environments, that characterise contemporary consumerism organised around a particular culture" (MacNaghten and Urry, 1995, p. 213).

Likewise, marketeers and tourism workers have also "packaged" adventure. It has become commodified, commercialised and a commodity for sale (Holyfield, 1999; Beedie and Hudson, 2003; Cater and Smith, 2003; Cater, 2005; Hudson and Beedie, 2006; Varley, 2006). Whilst excitement and thrilling activities are no doubt desirable selling points for most commercial operators, they are not the only source of competitive advantage in the adventure tourism industry. The new adventure consumers, as illustrated in the UNWTO (2014) report on global adventure tourism, seek deep, meaningful, "slow(er)" experiences, authentic in their engagement with local culture, arts and crafts or foods. The wider adventure tourism market has thus been recognised, and "softer," less risky and less dangerous forms of adventure and experiences beyond sport and physical recreation have been increasingly offered. Travel providers are now offering activities as simple as star gazing, open water swimming, creel fishing, wild camping or cooking foraged foods. Such activities trigger the immediate mental and bodily sensations of the taste of food; of being connected to nature and of being comfortable with place, with one's self and the others.

To that end, the academic attention has focused on sensual, emotive, spiritual and deeply immersive dimensions of the outdoor experience (Valkonen, 2009; Rantala et al., 2011; Røkenes et al., 2015). In particular, Varley and Semple (2015) introduced the concept of "slow adventure" with its focus on the extension of time, comfort and convenience while pursuing journeys in the outdoors. The concept is grounded in the Nordic philosophy of friluftsliv, as the basic and simple activity of just "being" in nature for extended periods of time. Varley and Semple (2015) suggested four critical elements of slow adventure: time, nature, passage and comfort. Time embodies itself in awareness of its passing during the outdoor journeys; nature refers to the natural setting and access to it; passage, both physical and spiritual, is the navigation through time, space and the self; comfort implies being at ease with the unusual challenges throughout the journey, or reconnection with the place, and the self. Discovering wild and nature-rich landscapes at a slower pace through softer, more immersive activities epitomises the essence of slow adventure.

Semple (2013) explained that "the deepening familiarity and acuity which arises from extended immersion within a relatively wild environment suggests a kind of *sinking-into* an *other-worldliness*" (p. 65). "Slowness," as a luxurious commodity in the contemporary world, must therefore follow two important principles: firstly, taking time to dwell in nature and secondly, performing a lived attachment to a particular place, often augmented via the presence of skilled guides, as a crucial element of a package adventure holiday. This has been further interrogated into studies on the importance of the provision of ontological security for tourists and creating comfortable dwellings in the outdoors (Farkic, 2018; Varley et al., 2018). These conceptual ideas were the impetus for a transnational project that would aid tourism development in peripheral areas of northern Europe and offer contemporary consumers slower, richer and more immersive experiences in remote natural environments.

SAINT's ideas and approaches

With advances in consumer society at the turn of the 21st century, a major paradigm shift occurred in services marketing and management strategies. A new thinking that recognises intangible resources and the co-creation of experiences and value has taken primacy in the market (Vargo and Lusch, 2004). In particular, experiential marketing was claimed to be a key proposition to provide consumers with unique and memorable experiences, create added value and gain competitive advantage (Pine et al., 1999; Grönroos, 2006; Binkhorst and Den Dekker, 2009). This gave rise to the strategic selling of experiences as a prime objective in marketing, a main endeavour for companies and a driver for business success (Prahalad and Ramaswamy, 2004). With consumers striving for and readily purchasing high-value experiences, tourism service providers have therefore entered a new paradigm of crafting and selling, with the aim of fostering growth and innovation, thus generating new sources of competitive advantage.

Such approaches to value creation for consumers have also been pronounced in the tourism context; however in remote, less visited places, this seems to have been more difficult to realise. In particular, peripheral northern European regions are facing a number of challenges in their tourism development, such as fragile local economies, lack of customer base, sparse population and youth out-migration. However, these places offer a number of opportunities for economic growth through the development of innovative, region-specific tourism products. In recognising that sparsely populated wild spaces offer experientially rich opportunities for entrepreneurs in tourism, as well as the value of joint participation and co-creation of tourism products, attempts have been made to address the challenges through proposing operationalisation of the new marketing concepts. Commodification of and packaging distinct cultural landscapes in novel ways have the potential to generate vibrant, competitive and sustainable communities, by harnessing innovation, expanding the capacity for entrepreneurship and seizing the unique growth initiatives and opportunities of the Northern and Arctic regions in a resource efficient way (NPA, 2019).

In particular, the slow adventure concept, developed by Varley and Semple (2015), has been taken forward as an applied marketing concept through the SAINT transnational project (SAINT, 2015). It was co-funded by the EU Northern Periphery and Arctic Cooperation Programme 2014–2020 (NPA), a cooperation between nine programme partner countries, seven of which (Scotland, Norway, Finland, Sweden, Iceland, Ireland and Northern Ireland) took part in the project. Its overall aim was raising awareness of the slow adventure concept and introducing affluent consumer groups from international markets to alternative dimensions of "adventure." The idea is attracting those who would buy, and buy into, new, softer and slower experiential products, for example, canoe trails in Northern Ireland or yoga and sailing in Scotland, thereby contributing to the sustainable and responsible development of tourism in peripheral areas through the valorisation of distinct regional resources.

The process of co-creation assumes a management initiative that brings together diverse agents in order to jointly produce a mutually valued outcome (Prahalad and Ramaswamy, 2004). Thus, a triple helix approach to project implementation was recognised as vital (Etzkowitz and Leysdorf, 1997). The main pillars were the universities, the state and the businesses, all of which made their contributions equally important in the project delivery. In doing so, the priority was to make SMEs in partner countries more aware of how to capitalise on business opportunities through, for example, (1) identifying new, lucrative markets to which to promote slow adventure activities; (2) effectively targeting these markets through the use of new, technology-oriented marketing models and clustering approaches, locally, regionally and transnationally and (3) developing engaging, insightful and meaningful slow adventure consumer experiences through collective workshops or individual sessions.

Furthermore, this approach allowed for the continual sharing of experiences and learning from previous projects and initiatives of all stakeholders in the partner regions. Co-created value was developed in the form of personalised, unique experiences for the customer on the one hand, and new knowledges, higher revenues/profitability and/or superior brand value/loyalty on the other. Subsequently, each partner area developed a case study to test how its specific region might advance and/or implement slow adventure as a business development opportunity, based on these tourism clustering and marketing concepts. In what now follows, we illustrate the process of building the slow adventure product through highlighting its two crucial stages: (1) clustering of the local SMEs and their involvement in joint slow adventure tourism products and (2) their clustering on a transnational level and promotion through a digital marketing campaign.

Clustering, collaboration and developing the product

One way of achieving responsible and sustainable tourism development in peripheral areas is through clustering and collaborative participation in the creation of tourism products. A couple of decades ago, Porter (1998, p. 78) broadly defined clusters as "geographic concentrations of interconnected companies and institutions in a particular field," aimed at increasing the competitiveness of a regional industry (Rocha, 2004; Delgado et al., 2010). The objective of a tourism cluster is to bring together companies that generally work alone, to build a successful tourism product in a region (Novelli et al., 2006). In the tourism context, clusters represent spatially concentrated groups of service providers (e.g. accommodation, food and beverage, transportation or recreational activity providers) and supporting institutions (e.g. public agencies, destination marketing organisations, non-governmental organisations and local communities) that are focused on the delivery of tourism products. However, in developing a brand for their destination, small, or micro, clusters are claimed to have a vital role (Michael, 2003, 2007b). They tend to be associated with constellations of complementary firms that collectively deliver specialised products in the region.

Michael's (2007a) conceptualisation of micro-clusters suggests the potential to gain competitive advantage through economies of scope. In other words, market share and profitability may be achieved through co-creating products or diversifying the range of products to attract new consumer groups (Grimstad and Burgess, 2014). Micro-clustering can be especially beneficial for small communities in remote or peripheral areas, as in northern European territories. The appeal of the place is a primary attraction for tourists; however, their satisfaction also depends on the quality and efficiency of related business (Porter, 2008). Therefore, the key to success of this project lies is the participation of SMEs collaborating in clusters, along with the involvement of other related players such as membership bodies and academic partners. A cluster is recognised as a vertical value chain and includes, for example, providers involved in activities, accommodation, tour guides, transport, etc. Extending the slow adventure value chain to other regional stakeholders outside of the business cluster gave significant results in the SAINT project.

Cluster initiation requires a significant investment of time, engagement and cultivation, and the project demonstrates how marketing and clustering are mutually interdependent. The SAINT case studies, and an attendant business survey, provided insight into the ways that SMEs form clusters in order to market and deliver a full range of slow adventure experiences and ultimately build the slow adventure experience and associated brand. In all of the SAINT case studies, marketing activities required the initiation of local/regional slow adventure clusters, and at the same time, the process of cluster development also catalysed and shaped marketing activities.

By reaching out to micro-businesses and SMEs working within the sector and testing various cluster models, each region adopted new "ambassadors" for slow adventure. With close cooperation between each partner and partner regions, this group of ambassadors has naturally formed a transnational cluster. The SAINT case study identified the core pillars of the brand which constitute the essence of "slow adventure" as a product concept and include the following key elements (Figure 6.1):

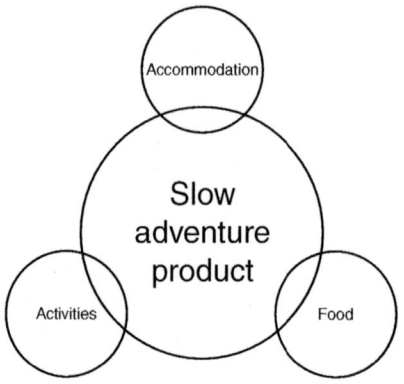

Figure 6.1 Slow adventure product.

- human-powered slow journeys – nature-based activities that are typical for the northern periphery region include expeditions into nature by hiking, kayaking, canoeing and cycling
- foraging, cooking and eating local, wild or slow food – collecting, catching or hunting for food combined with slow or wild cooking exemplifies how people have connected with nature to survive in a place
- a place to spend time in nature – overnight stays combined with a nature experience to enhance the connection with place.

All three core pillars are connected through a common thread and, combined with activities such as wildlife watching, nature interpretation, cultural or heritage activities, storytelling and honing outdoor skills, create a seamless experience and a deeper connection with landscape, nature, people and culture. The range of activities is country-specific and demonstrates how multifaceted a slow adventure experience can be. For example, a Finnish slow adventure offers activities with a focus on the winter season, which includes snowshoeing, cross-country skiing, sauna, dog-sledding, reindeer farm programs and swimming. Activities that distinguish Iceland include unique experiences such as ice cave tours, glacier hiking and ice hiking. Biking on roads is the core country-specific slow adventure activity in Ireland, complemented by jogging, meditation and yoga in nature, picnicking and food tours.

Therefore, in their process of building the slow adventure product by combining various "slow" and "authentic" experiences specific to the region, service providers recognised the strength and benefits of micro-clustering and offering their services as part of a collective, hybrid product. As a result, a number of slow adventure products were developed in each country. For clarity, they are presented on a country-by-country basis in alphabetical order in Table 6.1, alongside the number of SMEs involved in each case study.

The idea that the overall slow adventure experience should be the result of a collaboration between local SMEs has been additionally strengthened by the physical and emotional connections with the place, illustrated by the project's tagline, presented as this paper's epigraph. The strength of micro-clusters is thus determined by the level of cooperation, trust and synergies between the members, and consequently one of its fundamental aspects is sharing the same values and their implementation in a common territory (Hall et al., 2007). The SAINT project has highlighted that sharing the same values is a vital principle not only of the slow adventure philosophy and its ethos, but also of the sustainable development of tourism in peripheral areas.

Table 6.1 The effects of clustering on a local level

Partner countries	Number of products developed	Number of SMEs involved
Finland	3	12
Iceland	10	11
Ireland	15	9
Northern Ireland	15	13
Norway	21	23
Scotland	7	37
Sweden	2	17

Building a transnational digital marketing campaign

The awareness of competitive international opportunities, and threats, has put regional interests, and hence the interests of SMEs, back on the agenda. To achieve success in this techno-economic innovation paradigm requires new ways of thinking and the synergy of cooperative behaviour which facilitates actions in a dynamic marketplace (Konstadakopulos, 2005). What has been particularly insisted on in the contemporary business environment is a dynamic interaction among SMEs, whereby emphasis on their trust and collaboration is placed at the heart of innovation (Dodgson, 2018). Furthermore, it has been recognised that "Internet portals and new e-commerce technologies are necessary to transform business capabilities from a parochial to a global level" (Braun, 2002, p. 15). The application and dissemination of new tourism technologies to SMEs in this sector also displays elements of innovation, in that it facilitates and encourages businesses to consider and adopt new digital marketing approaches.

The nature of interaction between tourists and service suppliers, host communities and the physical environment in which tourism is taking place provides the core of the tourist experience (Prebensen et al., 2014), from which stems the construction of personal narratives (Binkhorst and Dekker, 2009). Thus, creating unique and memorable experiences for consumers has become of primary importance for both tourism practice and research. Subjects often discussed in literature are online information finding and sharing, seen as a new paradigm in destination marketing, and the interaction between service providers and tourists (Mathisen, 2013; Mossberg et al., 2014). Information and communication technologies have represented a catalyst of change that has opened unprecedented possibilities for tourist experience creation and enhancement. They have the power to transform the ways in which tourism businesses and organisations produce, deliver and sell their products (Buhalis and Law, 2008) and also the ways in which tourists buy and experience tourism (Buhalis, 1998; Buhalis and Licata, 2002; Kim and Fesenmaier, 2008).

The success of the project's core work package, which was aimed at transnational clustering, was therefore contingent upon SMEs acting as case studies for developing new online marketing models. With the rise of portals and Internet-based marketing, and the online customer journey being a vital part of the overall tourist experience, slow adventure was in an excellent position to extend into a web-based cooperative marketing campaign. Thus, to market the product transnationally in supporting the development of greater market reach, a digital marketing campaign, Slow Adventuring, was initiated.

A review of "state of the art" in tourism technology was conducted, concentrating in particular on the pre-booking aspects of slow adventure experiences: how to effectively communicate with targeted consumer typologies, how to portray the essence of slow adventure to the customer, and how to connect with customers using mobile technologies in particular. As it is difficult to adequately "explain" slow adventure, visual solutions were explored that could be used at trade fairs or available through tourist offices for example. Recognising the power of digital storytelling (Burgess, 2006; Lambert, 2013) as a means of making SMEs more visible in the marketplace, this approach was also pilot tested in the initial stages of the project.

Each region has developed its own regional campaign page to promote its slow adventures, and the transnational landing page links to each regional landing page via a map. Consequently, a transnational platform, Slow Adventure International (2019), was created, which has coalesced the slow adventure products developed in each partner country, providing corresponding online representation. The campaign website (or landing pages for each country) has been used as a place to link posts on social media and to divert enquiries to slow adventure SMEs.

Social media have gained significant value in marketing a destination and thus represent an inevitable part of destination marketing strategies as a powerful tool for reaching global audiences (Hays et al., 2013). To that end, social media platforms, such as Facebook, Twitter, Instagram, Pinterest and Flickr, have been also created as part of the Slow Adventuring digital marketing campaign. They have been regularly used to reach and inspire the consumer by creating, curating and promoting various slow adventure content (i.e. photos, descriptions, emotions, videos, podcasts, etc.) and sharing globally through social media and other relevant digital marketing tools. Most posts have been supported by the hashtag #slowadventuring to catalogue content related to the SAINT project and slow adventure. All content using this hashtag is streamed onto the landing page and is a strong visual representation of the transnational cluster.

Furthermore, the contributions of Let's Go Slow (2019) bloggers have been invaluable in creating and promoting content. They visited each partner region to experience slow adventures developed through the SAINT project and created content (which visually unifies each region) to share on both the Let's Go Slow blog site and the Slow Adventuring pages. Additionally, Instagram takeovers were scheduled over weekends in order to showcase one region at a time. By collaborating closely with independent influencers who already blogged about slow adventure, it allowed both businesses and partner organisations to treat the bloggers as "test consumers" and extended the reach of both content and brand to a wider industry and consumer audience.

Concluding remarks

The slow adventure sector of the tourism industry in the Northern Periphery and Arctic (NPA) region holds great potential for the sustainable development of peripheral and fragile communities. These environmentally and socially responsible experiences can form a new framework for tourism and destination development. The SAINT project has largely supported the SMEs in the region in exploiting opportunities to develop tourism products specific to each area, capitalising on their key assets – their landscapes, food, culture and people.

In peripheral regions, formal collaboration is still relatively rare. The SAINT project, however, achieved effective, formalised collaboration within the tourism industry and across other sectors and helped to demonstrate the benefits of clustering to the wider industry. It also enabled the businesses to broaden their knowledge of the sector with regards to, for example, customers to target, the potential for future collaborations and the role of and support available from the academic sector. SAINT has provided the evidence to show that the slow adventure initiative could bring positive economic and societal impacts for the tourism industry of the partner countries. The change brought about by the initiative is embodied in a number of ways.

Firstly, there has been an increase in the number of businesses in the region collaborating on tourism development. SMEs across the seven countries perceive the brand as a tool for enhancing collaboration between local SMEs and other stakeholders, as well as a mechanism to promote international cooperation. Businesses have therefore embraced the common brand as a way to increase the exposure of peripherally located micro-enterprises, especially to new international markets, and to associate remote areas with a high-quality experience.

Secondly, tourism marketing activity and exposure for the region has significantly increased. SMEs extolled the benefits of a common brand, including participation in joint online marketing and social media campaigns and access to new (e.g. online) booking channels, targeting customers willing to stay longer and try other, more immersive ways of being in nature.

Thirdly, the project tackled the issue of seasonality through increasing shoulder-season activities in order to help to obviate this structural weakness of the sector. SMEs operating across the transnational area offer slow adventure activities all year round, and the low season period in countries in the far north, such as Finland, coincides with the high season in others. Therefore, the countries complement each other to a degree and offer year-round opportunities for the consumption of slow adventure experiences.

Fourthly, the project has been committed to increasing employment in rural areas, particularly of young people, attracted to the lifestyle opportunities. SMEs highlighted that slow adventure as a concept offers a ready-to-use profile for companies that already offer or are able to offer slow adventure activities but lack experience or capacity to develop their product or reach the market. This is particularly useful for the creation of jobs for a young workforce which identifies its lifestyle as an "adventure," helping to combat youth out-migration.

Likewise, the project has significant implications for both influencing consequent projects that extend slow adventure to new areas and contributing to academic knowledge. There has been demonstrable enthusiasm and support for developing these experiences in other regions of the partner countries, as well as in countries new to slow adventure. While the cooperation was regionally focussed at inception, the possibility of extending it geographically means that the benefits, and change in the industry, could be extended to other areas as a means of community development. Showcasing the value of clustering and collaboration both within the tourism industry, and through cross-cutting with other sectors, such as creative industries and food and drink, may help in strengthening the brand and its expansion. Developing the slow adventure "movement," and cross-marketing it internationally, may secure significant transnational economic and societal benefits, facilitate transformational change in consumer perspective and engender a more forward-thinking attitude towards the sustainable development of tourism in peripheral areas.

Reflections

1   This chapter introduces the concept of slow adventure tourism, as a vehicle for developing destinations in peripheral areas in sustainable and responsible way.
2   In doing so, it argues for the importance of collaboration and joint participation of SMEs, at local, regional, national *and* transnational levels, in value co-creation and developing the product.
3   Another crucial aspect is transnational collaboration in product promotion under the umbrella of slow adventure, achieved through building a joint marketing campaign and harnessing social media to market the products developed in each partner country.

4   The project helped to illustrate to the partner SMEs the benefits of clustering, from increasing the exposure of peripheral, isolated micro-enterprises, to new, distant international markets in particular, to participation in collaborative social media campaigns to access affluent customer groups and to foster a sense of a slow adventure "community."

Questions

1   How can slow adventure play a role in reducing well-documented tourism pressures in popular but fragile areas?
2   How can a quality visitor experience balance the conflicting needs and attitudes of tourists and local communities?
3   How can the antagonistic demands of using smartphone technology in wild areas be reconciled without compromising the digitally savvy slow adventurer's experience?
4   What role should the Destination Management Organisation and/or policymakers play in the development of sustainable destinations?

Further reading

www.slowadventure.org
www.keep.eu/sites/default/files/project_files/Saint_Business%20strategy.pdf
www.rmf.is/static/research/files/05-2016-slowadventurer_lokpdf

References

Beedie, P., & Hudson, S. (2003). Emergence of mountain-based adventure tourism. *Annals of Tourism Research*, 30(3), 625–643.

Binkhorst, E., & Den Dekker, T. (2009). Agenda for co-creation tourism experience research. *Journal of Hospitality Marketing & Management*, 18(2–3), 311–327.

Braun, P. (2002). Networking tourism SMEs: E-commerce and e-marketing issues in regional Australia. *Information Technology & Tourism*, 5(1), 13–23.

Buhalis, D. (1998). Strategic use of information technologies in the tourism industry. *Tourism Management*, 19(5), 409–421.

Buhalis, D., & Law, R. (2008). Progress in information technology and tourism management: 20 Years on and 10 years after the Internet—The state of eTourism research. *Tourism Management*, 29(4), 609–623.

Buhalis, D., & Licata, M. C. (2002). The future eTourism intermediaries. *Tourism Management*, 23(3), 207–220.

Burgess, J. (2006). Hearing ordinary voices: Cultural studies, vernacular creativity and digital storytelling. *Continuum*, 20(2), 201–214.

Carson, D., & Harwood, S. (2007). Tourism development in rural and remote areas: Build it and they may not come! *Queensland Planner*, 47, 18–22.

Cater, C. I. (2005). Looking the part: The relationship between adventure tourism and the outdoor fashion industry. In R. Buckley (Ed.) *Taking tourism to the limits* (pp. 155–164). London: Taylor & Francis.

Cater, C., & Smith, L. (2003). *New country visions: Adventurous bodies in rural tourism*, Country Visions.

Delgado, M., Porter, M. E., & Stern, S. (2010). Clusters and entrepreneurship. *Journal of Economic Geography*, 10(4), 495–518.

Dodgson, M. (2018). *Technological Collaboration in Industry: Strategy, Policy and Internationalization in Innovation*. London: Routledge.

Etzkowitz, H., & Leydesdorf, L. (1997). *Universities and the Global Knowledge Economy. A Triple-Helix of University-Industry-Government Relations*. London: Pinter.

Farkic, J. (2018). Outdoor guiding as hospitality work. *Annals of Tourism Research*, 73(C), 197–199.

Grimstad, S., & Burgess, J. (2014). Environmental sustainability and competitive advantage in a wine tourism micro-cluster. *Management Research Review*, 37(6), 553–573.

Grönroos, C. (2006). On defining marketing: finding a new roadmap for marketing. *Marketing Theory*, 6(4), 395–417.

Hall, C. M. (2007). North-south perspectives on tourism, regional development and peripheral areas. In D. Muller and B. Jansson (Eds.) *Tourism in peripheries: Perspectives from the Far North and South* (pp. 19–37). Reading: CAB International.

Hall, C. M., & Boyd, S. W. (Eds.). (2005). *Nature-based tourism in peripheral areas: Development or disaster?* (Vol. 21). Bristol: Channel View Publications.

Hall, C. M., Harrison, D., Weaver, D., & Wall, G. (2013). Vanishing peripheries: Does tourism consume places? *Tourism Recreation Research*, 38(1), 71–92.

Hays, S., Page, S. J., & Buhalis, D. (2013). Social media as a destination marketing tool: Its use by national tourism organisations. *Current Issues in Tourism*, 16(3), 211–239.

Heimtun, B. (2016). Emotions and affects at work on Northern Lights tours. *Hospitality & Society*, 6(3), 223–241.

Heimtun, B., & Lovelock, B. (2017). Communicating paradox: Uncertainty and the northern lights. *Tourism Management*, 61, 63–69.

Hohl, A. E., & Tisdell, C. A. (1995). Peripheral tourism: Development and management. *Annals of Tourism Research*, 22(3), 517–534.

Holyfield, L. (1999). Manufacturing adventure: The buying and selling of emotions. *Journal of Contemporary Ethnography*, 28(1), 3–32.

Hudson, S., & Beedie, P. (2006). From Inuits in skin boats to bobos on the high seas: The commodification of sea kayaking through tourism. *Tourism in Marine Environments*, 2(2), 65–77.

Kauppila, P., Saarinen, J., & Leinonen, R. (2009). Sustainable tourism planning and regional development in peripheries: A Nordic view. *Scandinavian Journal of Hospitality and Tourism*, 9(4), 424–435.

Kim, H., & Fesenmaier, D. R. (2008). Persuasive design of destination websites: An analysis of first impression. *Journal of Travel Research*, 47(1), 3–13.

Konstadakopulos, D. (2005). From public loudspeakers to the Internet: The adoption of information and communication technologies (ICTs) by small enterprise clusters in Vietnam. *Information Technologies & International Development*, 2(4), 21.

Lambert, J. (2013). *Digital storytelling: Capturing lives, creating community*. Abingdon: Routledge.

Macnaghten, P., & Urry, J. (1995). Towards a sociology of nature. *Sociology*, 29(2), 203–220.

Mathisen, L. (2013). Staging natural environments: A performance perspective. *Advances in Hospitality and Leisure*, 9, 163–183.

Michael, E. J. (2003). Tourism micro-clusters. *Tourism Economics*, 9(2), 133–145.

Michael, E. J. (2007a). Development and cluster theory. In E. J. Michael (Ed.), *Micro-clusters and networks: The growth of tourism* (pp. 21–31). Oxford: Elsevier.

Michael, E. J. (2007b). Microclusters in tourism. In E. J. Michael, L. Gibson, C. M. Hall, P. Lynch, R. Mitchell, A. Morrison, & C. Schreiber (Eds.), *Micro-clusters and networks. The growth of tourism*. Oxford: Elsevier.

Mossberg, L., Hanefors, M., & Hansen, A. H. (2014). Guide performance: Co-created experiences for tourist immersion. *Creating Experience Value in Tourism*, 234–247.

Müller, D. K., & Jansson, B. (Eds.). (2006). *Tourism in peripheries: Perspectives from the far north and south*. Wallingford: CABI.

NPA (2016). *Northern Periphery and Arctic Cooperation Programme 2014–2020*.

Novelli, M., Schmitz, B., & Spencer, T. (2006). Networks, clusters and innovation in tourism: A UK experience. *Tourism Management, 27*(6), 1141–1152.

Pezzi, M. G., & Urso, G. (2016). Peripheral areas: conceptualizations and policies. Introduction and editorial note. *Italian Journal of Planning Practice, 6*(1), 1–19.

Pine, B. J., Pine, J., & Gilmore, J. H. (1999). *The experience economy: Work is theatre & every business a stage*. Brighton: Harvard Business Press.

Porter, M. E. (1998). *Clusters and the new economics of competition* (Vol. 76, No. 6, pp. 77–90). Boston, MA: Harvard Business School Press.

Porter, M. E. (2008). *Competitive strategy: Techniques for analyzing industries and competitors*. New York: Simon and Schuster.

Prahalad, C. K., & Ramaswamy, V. (2004). Co-creation experiences: The next practice in value creation. *Journal of Interactive Marketing, 18*(3), 5–14.

Prebensen, N. K., Chen, J. S., & Uysal, M. (2014). Co-creation of tourist experience: Scope, definition and structure. In *Creating Experience Value in Tourism* (2nd edition, pp. 1–10). Wallingford: CAB International.

Rantala, O., Valtonen, A., & Markuksela, V. (2011). Materializing tourist weather: Ethnography on weather-wise wilderness guiding practices, *Journal of Material Culture, 16*(3), 285–300.

Rocha, H. O. (2004). Entrepreneurship and development: The role of clusters. *Small Business Economics, 23*(5), 363–400.

Røkenes, A., Schumann, S., & Rose, J. (2015). The art of guiding in nature-based adventure tourism – how guides can create client value and positive experiences on mountain bike and backcountry ski tours. *Scandinavian Journal of Hospitality and Tourism, 15*, 62–82.

Saarinen, J. (2007). Tourism in peripheries: The role of tourism in regional development in Northern Finland. *Tourism in peripheries: Perspectives from the far north and south*, 41–52.

Semple, T. (2013). The semiotics of slow adventure: Narrative and identity. In S. Taylor, P. Varley, & T. Johnston (Eds.), *Adventure tourism: Meanings, experience and learning* (pp. 77–90). Abingdon: Routledge.

UNWTO (2014). *Global report on adventure tourism*. AM Reports. Madrid: UNWTO.

Valkonen, J. (2009). Acting in nature: Service events and agency in wilderness guiding, *Tourist Studies, 9*(2), pp. 164–180.

Vargo, S. L., & Lusch, R. F. (2004). Evolving to a new dominant logic for marketing. *Journal of Marketing, 68*(1), 1–17.

Varley, P. (2006). Confecting adventure and playing with meaning: The adventure commodification continuum. *Journal of Sport & Tourism, 11*(2), 173–194.

Varley, P., Farkic, J., & Carnicelli, S. (2018). Hospitality in wild places. *Hospitality & Society, 8*(2), 137–157.

Varley, P., & Semple, T. (2015). Nordic slow adventure: Explorations in time and nature. *Scandinavian Journal of Hospitality and Tourism, 15*(1–2), 73–90.

Zurick, D. N. (1992). Adventure travel and sustainable tourism in the peripheral economy of Nepal. *Annals of the Association of American Geographers, 82*(4), 608–628.

7 Strategies for sustainable tourism in Porto

The host community perspective

Carla Pinto Cardoso

Introduction

Over the last decade, demand for sustainable tourism practices has risen considerably in Porto, as the city experiences one of the most noteworthy tourism growths in Europe. Most stakeholders recognise that sustainability is the way to meet the needs of present visitors and host communities, without compromising the ability of future generations to meet their own needs.

As a result, a wide variety of different strategies for dealing with tourism growth have been suggested and debated among tourism stakeholders. However, the perspective of the local community is not still clear in the literature. Hence, this chapter explores the strategies for the development of sustainable tourism adopted in Porto and examines whether or not the host community support these strategies and the extent to which they support.

For this purpose, the study combines a comprehensive desk research based on secondary data from key industry and academic sources and a quantitative survey conducted among a sample of 140 residents from the city of Porto.

The results can be used to support the continued competitive and sustainable future of Porto, while at the same time offering guidelines for practitioners in other cities which are experiencing a growth in tourism or are seeking to develop this sector, since many of the points raised from Porto's experience have a more general application.

The remainder of the chapter proceeds as follows: section "Sustainable tourism concept and principles" presents the theoretical background to the context of the study, by briefly reviewing the meaning and key elements of sustainable tourism. Then, the third section offers the case study drawn from the experience of the city of Porto. The concluding section summarises the main findings obtained based on Porto's experiences and makes suggestions for addressing successful development of future tourism.

Links

The following Case Study links may be of interest to readers of this chapter:

- Case Studies Part B (Environmental & social aspects of ethical sustainable development) – Chapters 21 and 22
- Case Studies Part C (The business impacts of ethical sustainable development) – Chapters 26 and 27

Please see the Contents on pages v–viii, and the Guide to the textbook in Appendix 1 for further information.

Sustainable tourism concept and principles

In 1993, the World Tourism Organization, using the definition of sustainable development from the Brundtland Report (WCED, 1987) as its basis, defined sustainable tourism as follows:

> Sustainable Tourism development meets the needs of present tourists and host regions while protecting and enhancing opportunities for the future. It is envisaged as leading to management of all resources in such a way that economic, social and aesthetic needs can be fulfilled while maintaining cultural integrity, essential ecological processes, biological diversity and life support system.
>
> (UNWTO, 1993. p. 19)

Since then, the debates on defining issues and insights of sustainable tourism have taken on greater importance (Bramwell and Lane, 2011). It has become one of the subfields of the sustainable development literature, where the list of existing studies is extensive and significant. According to Buckley (2012), it has been estimated that there are in excess of 5,000 published works on sustainable tourism.

Within these studies, topics such as tourism impacts, eco-tourism, visitor attitudes and behaviour and planning are consistently popular. The use of empirical studies is also very common in sustainable tourism research (e.g. Blowers, 1993; Buckley, 2012; Butler, 1999; Canna and Theuma, 2013; Ciegis et al., 2009, Coccossis, 1996; Duran et al., 2015; Faulkner and Tideswell, 1997; Fyall and Garrod, 1998).

At the same time, various international conventions and declarations have elaborated principles for sustainable tourism (e.g. International Guidelines for Biological Diversity and Tourism Development, 2004; Marrakesh Task Force Sustainable Tourism, 2006, among many others).

In a general sense, much of this literature suggests that any tourism development should respect the basic principles of sustainable development under a holistic approach (see Table 7.1).

In this line of thought, in its publication *Sustainable Tourism for Development*, UNWTO (UNWTO, 2013) adds that tourism should embrace the 2030 Agenda, adopted by United Nations for ending poverty and promoting economic, social and environmental development. More specifically, it is argued that tourism has a fundamental role to play in the achievement of the 2030 Agenda, since it has a

Table 7.1 Principles of sustainable development

---

1. **Environmental sustainability**: development must be compatible with the maintenance of resources, ecological processes and biodiversity.
2. **Sociocultural sustainability**: sustainable development must be compatible with the values of the people and strengthen the identity of the community.
3. **Economic sustainability**: development must be economically efficient, it has to benefit all people and the resources must be managed so as to preserve them for future generations.

UNWTO, "World Summit on Sustainable Development" (2002).

profound and wide-ranging impact on societies, the environment and the economy (UNWTO, 2019).

It is also evident from the literature that sustainable tourism is commonly perceived as an effective vehicle of development (e.g. Fyall and Garrod, 1998). The main arguments presented, as well summarised at the *International Forum on Sustainable Development of Tourism and Innovation* (2014), were that tourism, developed in a sustainable manner,

- improves prosperity and well-being for all stakeholders (**social equity**) (see Haralambopoulos and Pizam, 1996)
- maintains the quality of the environment for both the local population and visitors (**environmental protection**) (see Kuvan and Akan, 2005)
- promotes the cultural exchange and preserves the cultural identity of the host population (**cultural issues**) (see Haralambopoulos and Pizam, 1996)
- increases the economic profitability of tourism, as source of income, employment, tax revenues and foreign exchange (**economic growth**) (see Andereck et al., 2005; Brida et al., 2010; Brida et al., 2011).

In other words, it is widely recognised that tourism, preferably planned and managed in such a way as to minimise potential economic, sociocultural and environmental negative impacts (such as changes in values and customs, congestion, inflation, overcrowding, air and noise pollution) as far as possible and, at the same time, to provide a variety of returns that generates mutual benefits to hosts and visitors.

It is not surprising, therefore, that the concept of sustainable tourism has also become popular in the discourses of policymakers and planners and has been regularly used by the business sector as a marketing argument. In fact, tourism is commonly perceived as an important driver of broader economic, environment and social development policy that, as underlined by Sharpley and Telfer (2002), justifies the relevance of the tourism by itself.

Nonetheless, it is important to note that tourism authorities responsible for developing destinations need to be able to simultaneously satisfy the expectations of visitors and investors and the residents' needs. In this context, as refereed by Farsari et al. (2007), sustainable tourism can be considered a malleable concept, fitting different perceptions.

The next section presents the case of Porto, the second city of Portugal, with a view to understanding how the host community perceive sustainable strategies for tourism.

The case of the city of Porto

Strategic approach for sustainable tourism

Tourism is crucial to the economy of Portugal and its regions. Indeed, it is the main export sector, representing almost 17% of the exports of goods and services (Turismo de Portugal, 2017). In 2017, tourism accounted, directly and indirectly, for 17.7% of the Gross Domestic Product and employed 20.4% of workers (UNWTO, 2018). In addition, according to UNWTO, Portugal should enter the world's top ten tourist destinations in the year 2020, as 40 million annual visitors come to the country with a population of less than 10 million people (UNWTO, 2011).

In line with the national scenario, over the last ten years, Porto has experienced unprecedented tourism growth, with two-figure growth almost every year (Cardoso and Silva, 2018). In 2018, for the first time ever, Porto's Francisco Sá Carneiro Airport exceeded 11 million passengers in a single year (11% more than in the previous year), and the amount of revenue generated by tourist tax has exceeded the city's expectations by 50%. Last year, the city saw its best performance ever in terms of number of international tourists and tourist spending. It reached nearly 5.2 million tourist overnights and a revenue with figures above the goals set for 2020. Moreover, it is estimated that this trend will remain globally positive in the following years (CMP, 2019).

As a result, the importance of tourism in Porto as an engine of economic development, welfare and competitiveness is repeatedly referred to by practitioners and politicians alike. On the other hand, the paradigm to promote sustainable tourism has been one of the central concerns for private sector businesses and government bodies. Therefore, they have recently made a stronger commitment to developing sustainable practices to enhance future sustainability opportunities and reduce the adverse impacts of tourism. Amongst the most important measures are the following.

National Tourism Strategy for 2027 (ET27)

Resulting from an unprecedented open and participatory process with the stakeholders set up in Portugal by the Tourism National Board – Turismo de Portugal – the ET27 provides a strategic framework for the development of tourism in Portugal for 2017–2027. This plan is aimed at a desired scenario in which tourism becomes a hub for economic, social and environmental development, reinforcing **Portugal's position as one of the most competitive and sustainable leader destinations on the international tourism market**. Sustainability is perceived as a key element for maintaining natural resources and landscapes and attracting investment for their protection.

For this purpose, five overarching principles were identified, and the overall sustainable targets were defined. They are illustrated in Figure 7.1. It should be noted that ET27 underlines that an important part of the overarching principles of sustainability

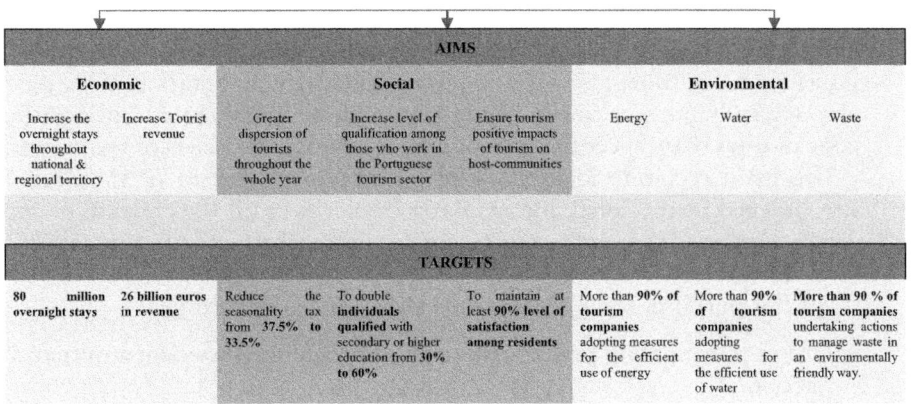

Figure 7.1 ET27: Aims and targets for sustainability.

Table 7.2 Strategic principles of Portuguese national ten-year strategy (2017–2027)

Estratégia Turismo 2027
• **Add value to the offer** (e.g. preserve and improve coastlines and emphasize the sea in the tourism economy; enhance the cultural and natural heritage; encourage sustainable tourism in unprotected areas; …) • **Boost the economy** (e.g. guarantee the economy solidity of the industry; attract and support investment; promote equal opportunities; …) • **Enhance knowledge** (e.g. enhance tourism professionals; support professional training and entrepreneurship; develop R&D; …) • **Improve networks and connectivity** (e.g. improve roads, railways and sea connections; encourage stakeholder networking; endorse Portugal as a smart destination; …) • **Create awareness** (e.g. reinforce Portugal's internationalisation as a tourism destination; encourage authentic and innovative tourism offers; …)

(Source: Estratégia 2027, TP)

is the involvement of local communities and socio-economic systems and enhancement of the role of tourism businesses and the regional and municipal authorities. Meanwhile, in line with Portugal's Strategy for Tourism 2017, two Sustainable Tourism Observatories were already created in Portugal with the aim to study and monitor tourism performance in the areas of economic, social and environmental sustainability. They are located in Alentejo and Algarve regions.

Regional and municipal strategic aims and actions

A review of the *Tourism Plan for Porto And North of Portugal* (TPNP, 2015), advisory reports and published newspaper articles evidence that, at a regional and municipal level, the aims of sustainable tourism are shaped around four key areas, strongly related to the national priorities for sustainable tourism. (A summary of these key areas is illustrated in Table 7.2.)

a   Tourism policy and regulatory framework

The importance of effective policy and governance has been confirmed by *Tourism Plan for Porto and North of Portugal* (TPNP, 2015), which provides direction for the development and management of sustainable tourism, supported by necessary legislation (e.g. rights, responsibilities and obligations of different stakeholders in tourism) and a multi-stakeholder collaboration. This seems to play a very important role in shaping tourism development and prioritising actions in ways that reflect the specific characteristics and needs of the destination.

The main recommendations of this plan are related to (i) the need for a strengthened institutional and regularly framework; (ii) the creation of consolidated, diversified tourism products and targets markets and (iii) the stakeholders' involvement.

For this purpose, some actions have already been undertaken:

improved coordination between national and local level tourism governance and action

provided capacity building for tourism stakeholder bodies at a local level

improved local awareness and knowledge of sustainability issues in tourism through communication and training

adoption of new legislation for accommodation, restaurants and transport.
b   Sustainable economic growth, investment and competitiveness
    Amongst the priorities identified by public authorities was the need to ensure that the economic development of Porto is fully integrated into and synchronised with national sustainable strategies. These included:

a **measure of the robustness and knowledge of the extent of tourism activities** (e.g. regular collection of data on visitors' arrivals, profiles and activities)

a **marketing plan** which identifies target markets and provides a framework for promotion (e.g. *Tourism Marketing Strategic Plan of Porto and North of Portugal, 2015–2020*, TPNP, 2015)

the **presence of policies and strategies for investment** that meet the needs of the sector (e.g. licensing requirements, security safety, economic incentives, training and other support to investors).

c   Natural and cultural environment
    To make sure that tourism activities do not damage the natural and cultural environment, but rather help to sustain them, through the awareness and income that they generate, a range of initiatives and interventions has been implemented in Porto by national and local authorities. These include:

establishing codes of conduct for tourism operations and activities. For example, in April 2017, Porto adopted the first tourism transport regulation in Portugal. Park-and-ride systems in accordance with new routes were also created

involving tourism stakeholders and other local communities (e.g. holding workshops)

using tourism income to support conservation and local livelihoods. In March 2018, a tourist tax (2 euros per tourist overnight) was implemented. The aim is to reduce the "tourist footprint" in the city, as explained by the mayor of Porto. It is expected that the total amount earned through the scheme will be reinvested in housing, mobility and improved services for locals. For example, as the mayor explained, the City Hall is buying and rebuilding houses in downtown area with a view to putting them on the market with more affordable prices for those locals who want to live there as permanent residents.
    Porto also launched a programme called "Porto de Tradição" or "Porto of Tradition" as a way to preserve and conserve establishments with cultural heritage or significance (CMP, 2019).

introducing incentives for sustainable tourism development (e.g. ecolabels, sustainability certification, financial support, promoting responsible use of natural resources such as renewable energy)

preparing and disseminating guidelines and practical tools for environmental best practices (e.g. including actions and measures in fields such as the environment, housing and mobility)

creating alternative modes of travel (e.g. itineraries, paths and roads) as tools to reinforce knowledge of the extensive and complex history and heritage present throughout the city.

d   Inclusive and sustainable growth for human development
    The local authorities intend to affirm tourism as a relevant instrument to promote inclusive economic growth that creates jobs, attracts investment and encourages local culture and products. The aim is to make tourism more sustainable and innovative, with a focus on equitable benefits for all players.

To achieve these goals, several actions were already introduced, among which are the following:

facilitating business partnerships
encouraging knowledge and technology transfer
promoting the development of policies
supporting training and educational programmes.

Summing up, it is evident from the above that sustainable tourism strategies are discussed and practised in Porto on diverse scales, ranging from the local to the national level.

The aim is to understand how sustainable strategies are perceived by the host community. Nonetheless, before exploring the research findings, some methodological notes should be presented.

Methodological notes

The data used in this chapter to analyse the host community perceptions towards strategies for the development of sustainable tourism in Porto are based on the outcomes of a quantitative survey carried out among 140 residents of the city of Porto.

The survey was conducted in 2018, using face-to-face questionnaires in each civil parish of Porto (seven in total), whether more or less touristic. The target sample was Porto residents (more than one-year residency) who were aged 18 and older. They were randomly selected until 20 responses were obtained per civil parish.

Using a questionnaire survey instrument was helpful to request uniform data from respondents, as it facilitates comparative statistical analysis. At the same time, face-to face survey allowed the integration of views from residents who might be difficult to reach otherwise. Also, this was found useful to provide contextual insights (e.g. it captures verbal and non-verbal behaviours and emotions). Nonetheless, there was a need to limit sample size, since the gathering of data from residents could take longer.

Thus, the results obtained are presented in the context of the selected sample and should not be generalised to the population of the city.

The questionnaire contained questions related to personal characteristics, tourism impacts, support for strategies to deal with tourism development and attitudes towards tourism development. In designing questions, theoretical and empirical literature was consulted and considered. This included studies on sustainable strategies in the tourism context and studies dealing with residents' perceptions and attitudes towards tourism development (e.g. Ap, 1992; Brida et al., 2011; Jurowski et al., 1997; Liu and Var, 1986; Koens and Postma, 2017; Postma and Schmuecker, 2017).

Finally, it should be noted that the data were analysed using descriptive methods, which helps describe and summarise data in a meaningful way. Indeed, the frequencies used for categorical variables provide a clear description of the number and percentages of observations in any given category. In this case, each variable was examined separately – univariate technique – with the aim of illustrating patterns and tendencies in the data, both for the ease of presentation of the respondents' profile and the viewpoints studied. The mean was used as measure of central tendency.

Inferential statistical procedures were not used because there is no need to infer from the sample to the population from which the sample was selected and which only accounts for a small part (Balnaves and Caputi, 2001). The samples were effectively too few. It is expected that in the future, a second stage of this study will be carried out involving a large sample.

The results are presented in following.

Strategies for tourism development as perceived by the host community

Generally speaking, the literature review on residents' perceptions towards tourism evidences that this is a complex analysis since a number of distinct elements and frameworks can be involved. For instance, some authors argue that host perceptions depend on those elements that tourists bring to the destination, such as numbers of visitors (see Vargas-Sanchez et al., 2009), links to community residents or social differences (Johnson et al., 1994) or seasonality (see Belisle and Hoy, 1980), while many other authors state that factors influencing residents' perceptions embrace the elements that are part of the destination itself, such as personal values (see Choi and Murray, 2010), community attachment (see Andereck et al., 2005), pace of tourism development (Brougham and Butler, 1981), demographic variables (see Fredline and Faulkner, 2000) or personal reliance on tourism (see King et al., 1993).

As explained before, the intention here is to identify patterns and trends in the host-community views towards sustainable strategies. Therefore, the particularly popular conceptual frameworks and theories in research into resident's perceptions towards tourism (e.g. Social Exchange Theory (Ap, 1992) and Social Representation Theory (Pearce et al., 1996) were not explored in this analysis. Furthermore, the correlation between the various determinants influencing residents' perceptions towards tourism proposed by several authors (such as Andereck et al., 2005; Andriotis, 2005; Belisle and Hoy, 1980; Pearce, 1989; Sharma and Dyer, 2009, among many others) was also not studied. Thus, the results presented here are descriptive and structured in a way that can also support further investigation.

Main findings and discussion

Profile of the respondents

The overwhelming majority (75%) of respondents were females between 31 and 44 years old. Most of the respondents had a good educational background, with almost 53% of them having completed a graduate degree and approximately 38% having completed an undergraduate diploma. A considerable percentage of respondents (50%) indicated that they were employed in public or private services, while 25% indicated that they were business people and 20% that they were students. The large majority of respondents (82%) were not engaged in the tourism sector.

Level of host-community support towards strategies for sustainable tourism

To gain the overall view of the host community towards strategies for the development of sustainable tourism, respondents from Porto were invited to consider a range of 18 tourism strategies and different actions suggested by theoretical and empirical literature and to rate their support for these strategies on a scale of 1–5, where 1 is "strongly disagree" and 5 is "strongly agree." Then they were asked to explain their answers.

The strategies were presented in random order. But, for the purpose of this analysis, these strategies/actions are grouped into the three key dimensions of sustainability: social, economic and environmental.

The findings, summarised in Table 7.3, are explained below.

Overall, the above results indicate that respondents hold strong views (agree or strongly agree) on many strategies. In addition, it is also evident that strategies with social impacts were the most popular among the host community. In fact, if we rank them by mean (see Table 7.4), the top three listed strategies are directed at the social field, and among the most eight supported strategies, six include actions developed in the social dimension.

Table 7.3 Residents' strategies

	1 Strongly disagreed	2 Disagree	3 Neutral	4 Agree	5 Strongly agree
Social dimension					
Create city experiences that benefit both visitors and local residents	–	4.5	22.7	**43.2**	29.5
Create conduct codes for visitors	11.4	2.3	20.5	25	**40.9**
Incentives to maintain residents in the historical centre	–	–	20.5	34.1	**45.5**
Reinforce regulatory framework	2.3	13.6	27.3	15.9	**40.9**
Encourage networking with the various agents in the sector	–	2.3	15.9	**47.7**	34.1
Improve city infrastructure and facilities	–	4.5	22.7	22.7	**50.0**
Economic dimension					
Time-based rerouting (e.g. price differentiation along the year)	9.1	6.8	22.7	**43.2**	18.2
Support professional training and educational programmes	9.1	6.8	4.5	36.6	**43.2**
Business incentives (entrepreneurship)	6.8	15.9	25	**36.4**	15.9
Visitor segmentation	20.5	**36.4**	18.2	18.2	6.8
Promotion	–	13.6	34.1	**31.8**	20.5
Control number of visitors	13,6	20.5	**27.3**	15.9	22.7
Environment dimension					
Spreading visitors around the city (e.g. alternative itineraries)	4.5	9.1	25	**38.6**	22.7
Spreading visitors to city surroundings	2.3	6.8	18.2	**47.7**	25
Offer new apps to achieve time-based rerouting	6.8	13.6	22.7	25	**31.8**
Encourage authentic products	18.2	11.4	29.5	**31.8**	9.1
Preserve and improve cultural and natural heritage	18.2	11.4	27.3	**31.8**	11.4
Improve the bicycle path	22.7	4.5	20.5	**31.8**	20.5

Table 7.4 Residents' support for strategies/action (by rank)

Strategy/action	Mean	Dimension
Reinforce regulatory framework	4.4	Social
Incentives to maintain residents in the historical centre	4.2	Social
Improve city infrastructure and facilities	4.1	Social
Support professional training and educational programmes	4	Economic
Spreading visitors to city surroundings	3.9	Environment
Create city experiences that benefit both visitors and local residents	3.9	Social
Encourage networking with the various agents in the sector	3.9	Social
Create conduct codes for visitors	3.8	Social
Time-based rerouting (e.g. price differentiation along the year)	3.8	Economic
Business incentives (entrepreneurship)	3.8	Economic
Spreading visitors around the city (e.g. alternative itineraries)	3.7	Environment
Promotion	3.6	Economic
Offer new apps to achieve time-based rerouting	3.3	Environment
Improve the bicycle path	3.2	Environment
Control number of visitors	3.1	Economic
Encourage authentic products	3.0	Environment
Preserve and improve cultural and natural heritage	3.0	Environment
Visitor segmentation	2.5	Economic

As can be observed, **reinforcing** a **regulatory framework** is the most supported strategy among the respondents. This, in turn, reflects the respondents' major concerns related to the large number of houses that are rented out as tourist apartments. As the majority of the respondents explained, they hold concerns related to:

rises in the prices of land and housing
loss of local residents living into the historic city
the decrease in houses for residents as a result of the growing number of tourist accommodations/apartments.

As result, a large group of respondents (82%) suggests that the growing demand for holiday flats (such as *Airbnb*) needs to be more restricted in the historical centre. There were also views (12% of the respondents) that holiday apartments should be limited to peripheral areas and/or that tourists should not be accommodated in residential buildings (14% of respondents). This seems to also justify why the growth of incentives to maintain residents in the historical centre was strongly supported by the majority of the respondents.

The importance of **improvement of city infrastructures and facilities** was also well supported by most of the respondents. In fact, Porto residents (38%) appear to be concerned about traffic congestion brought about by the increasing number of tourists in the historical centre. Few respondents (10%) mentioned that nowadays they avoid going downtown.

Nonetheless, findings also showed that even though they have some concerns about traffic congestion, almost half of the **respondents did not consider it necessary to**

improve the bicycle path. In a general way, they said that the bicycle flows are not significant in the city.

From the results, it was also evident that respondents from Porto emphasised strong support for the **development of experiences that benefit residents and visitors** alike. When they were asked to explain their answers, the majority of them recognised that new investments brought about by tourism growth (such as new business) were relevant to create a pleasant living environment for residents and stimulate cultural exchange between residents and visitors. As they argued, this could not exist without tourism. They exemplified this with the new restaurants, festivals and other events.

With regard to the importance of **encouraging networking with local agents**, the data from the survey revealed that more than 80% of the respondents agree or strongly agree with this measure. Moreover, it was evident that they believe that involving residents, business managers and public authorities in the decision-making process would help to achieve more success.

On the other hand, it is important to note that, in general, strategies directly related to environment dimension were less supported by the participants. For example, a high number of respondents said that they strongly disagree with measures such as *encouraging authentic products* and *preserving and improving cultural and natural heritage*. This may be related to the fact that the large majority of the respondents did not recognise significant negative tourism implications at this level. Issues such as the increase in noise and air pollution, frequently cited in the literature as negative impacts of tourism, were not perceived by the majority of the respondents in this study.

Concerning measures adopted in the economic field, initiatives to promote **educational and training programmes** were deemed important for a large majority of respondents (almost 80%). As it was explained, they recognised that tourism brought about more business and jobs, which requires a demand for qualified people.

Also, the possibility of **time-based rerouting** was well supported by the majority of the respondents (more than 50%). As they explained, they believed that rerouting visitors would help to make the city lively during more quieter periods and would help to deal more effectively with future extra disturbance caused by the rise of visitors. This also justified why a large number of respondents argued that **visitors should spread to city surroundings or around the city**.

However, the **use of new apps to achieve time-based rerouting** was less supported by the respondents. The reason for this may be because, in general, the respondents did not perceive visitor pressure, which also may explain why approximately 35% of the respondents strongly disagree, disagree or have neutral views according the **establishment of conduct codes for visitors**. Also, there was no significant support for **implementing visitor controls**, with around 62% of respondents saying that they strongly disagree, disagree or have neutral views on any control.

Findings also demonstrated that the majority of the respondents believed that certain **business incentives** (e.g. legislation, tax reductions, training) should be created. As the majority explained, some Portuguese businesses need to be supported in order to become more competitive in the international market.

Finally, this study also found that comparatively less attention was given to factors such as **visitor segmentation** and **promotion**, both considered a fundamental requirement by most stakeholders. According to the majority of the respondents, there is no need to target visitors to Porto, because, as they explained, the city offers a huge variety of products and services that can attract people from everywhere. Additionally, they believed that Porto is already well known in international markets. This suggests that actions on marketing still need to be explained.

Concluding remarks and suggestions for addressing future success in tourism development

Within a context of a continuous growth in tourism experienced by the second city of Portugal – Porto – over the last decade, this chapter uses the case of Porto to explore the strategies for sustainable tourism and examine the host-community views towards those strategies.

The results demonstrate that Porto is already undergoing considerable work on sustainability for tourism development, with tourism authorities adapting their practices and activities to steer local tourism development along the sustainable development path. As result, a systematical approach with an economic-social-environmental three-way system has been implemented and managed over recent years. This process includes, among others, the following aims:

to work in a partnership model (e.g. open discussion to involve the full range of stakeholders)

to promote host community well-being (e.g. accommodation and services)

to ensure ongoing satisfaction with visitors' experience and locals' quality of life (e.g. cultural programmes)

to add value to the offer (e.g. protect cultural and natural heritage, encourage sustainable tourism schemes)

to boost the economy (e.g. attract and support investment, entrepreneur and professional training and education).

From the experience of Porto, it was also noted that the strategic options and actions for locals' tourism development were in line with the national policy strategy.

On the other hand, regarding host-community perceptions, the study found that, overall, respondents had positive views towards sustainable strategies. In general, respondents from Porto recognised that the implementation of different strategies to develop tourism can mitigate negative impacts brought about by tourism and, simultaneously, provide additional benefits not only for visitors or businesses, but also for residents.

Moreover, it also became clear that strategies which focus on social matters were the most supported from the residents. Indeed, the claims of residents were more extensively focused on the adequate quality of life of the host community (e.g. calls for greater efforts towards effective regulation to control local accommodation/real estate and calls for greater incentives for maintaining locals in downtown). This confirms previous outcomes found in the literature (see Postma, 2003).

Findings also revealed that strategies related to environmental factors were less supported by respondents from Porto. As mentioned earlier, the large majority of respondents did not perceive any negative environmental factor, which seemed to justify these views.

From a practical perspective, the contribution of this study gathered from the results found is threefold:

to enhance stakeholders' awareness of the **need to implement and manage sustainable strategies,** not only because strategies help to mitigate potential negative tourism impacts, but also because they will determine the way that tourism activities will be configured into a long-term period

to emphasise the need of the prerequisite to take into consideration the interest of all the stakeholders involved to ensure sustainable tourism. Indeed, while visitors look essentially for tourism experiences and managers for business opportunities, host communities demand quality of life

to underline that the involvement of the host community should go deeper than consultation, including appropriate engagement and discussion in decision taking. A co-operative approach is recommended.

Questions

1   Describe what is meant by sustainable tourism and why it is important.
2   Explain the most typical types of objectives that are sought through sustainable tourism strategies.
3   On what scale is tourism likely to contribute most to development – at the national, regional or local level?
4   Which of the principles best describes Porto's approach to strategies for sustainable tourism?
5   Explain how collaboration between tourism stakeholders can contribute to the acquisition of competitive advantage?
6   What do you see as the likely major developments in strategic management in the future?

Further reading

European Commission, European Tourism Forum. (2002). *Agenda 21 – Sustainability in the European Tourism Sector.*
International Guidelines for Biological Diversity and Tourism Development, available at: www.cbd.int/doc/publications/tou-gdl-en.pdf
Sustainable Travel International, available at: www.sustainabletravelinternational.org
The Marrakesh Task Force Sustainable Tourism, available at: www.veilleinfotourisme.fr/taskforce
The Responsible Tourism Partnership, available at: www.responsibletourismpartnership.org

References

Andereck, K.L., Valentine, K.M., Knopf, R.C. and Vogt, C.A. (2005). Residents' perceptions of community tourism impacts, *Annals of Tourism Research*, 32, 1056–1076.
Andriotis, K. (2005). Community groups' perceptions and preferences to tourism development. Evidence from Crete, *Journal of Hospitality and Tourism Research*, 29(1), 67–90.
Ap, J. (1992). Residents' perceptions on tourism impacts, *Annals of Tourism Research*, 19 (4), 665–690.
Balnaves, M. and Caputi, P. (2001). *Introduction to Quantitative Research Methods: An Investigative Approach*. London: Sage.

Belisle, F.J. and Hoy, D.R. (1980). The perceived impact of tourism by residents, *Annals of Tourism Research*, 7, 83–101.

Blowers, A. (1993). *Planning for a Sustainable Environment.* London: Earthscan.

Bramwell, B. and Lane, B. (2011). Critical research on the governance of tourism and sustainability, *Journal of Sustainable Tourism*, 19(4–5), 411–421.

Brida, J.G., Osti, L. and Barquet, A. (2010). Segmenting resident perceptions towards tourism – a cluster Analysis with a Multinomial Logit Model of a Mountain Community, *International Journal of Tourism Research*, Wiley InterScience. doi:10.1002/jtr.778.

Brida, J.G., Osti, L. and Faccioli, M. (2011). Residents' perception and attitudes towards tourism impacts: a case study of the small rural community of Folgaria (Trentino–Italy), *Benchmarking: An International Journal*, 18(3), 359–385.

Brougham, J.E. and Butler R.W. (1981). A segmentation analysis of resident attitudes to the social, impact of tourism, *Annals of Tourism Research*, 7(4), 569–590.

Buckley, R. (2012). Sustainable tourism: research and reality, *Annals of Tourism Research*, 39, 528–546.

Butler, R. (1999). Sustainable tourism: a state-of-the-art review, *Tourism Geographies*, 1(1), 7–25.

Canna, R. and Theuma, N. (2013). *Strategies and Tools for Sustainable Tourism Destination Management: Applying the European Tourism Indicator System in Malta*, available at: www.researchgate.net/publication/299985794_strategies_and_tools_for_sustainable tourism_destination_management_applying_the_European_Tourism_Indicator_System_in Malta.

Cardoso, C. and Silva, M. (2018). Residents' perceptions and attitudes towards future tourism development: a challenge for tourism planners, *Worldwide Hospitality and Tourism Themes*, 10(6), 688–697.

Choi, H.C. and Murray, I. (2010). Resident attitudes toward sustainable community tourism. *Journal Sustainable Tourism*, 18, 575–594.

Ciegis, R., Ramanauskiene, J. and Martinkus, B. (2009). The concept of sustainable development and its use for sustainability scenarios. *Inzinerine Ekonomika – Engineering Economics*, 2, 28–37.

CMP (2019). *Primeiro ano de taxa turística gera receita de 10,4 milhões de euros*, available at: www.porto.pt/noticias/primeiro-ano-de-taxa-turistica-gera-receita-de-104-milhoes-de-euros (28-02-2019).

Coccossis, H. (1996). Tourism and sustainability: perspectives and implications, in Priestley, G. et al. (eds.), *Sustainable Tourism? European Experiences.* Wallingford, UK: Cab International.

Duran et al. (2015). *The Objectives of Sustainable Development – Ways to Achieve Welfare.* available at: www.researchgate.net/publication/283237277_The_Objectives_of_Sustainable_Development_-_Ways_to_Achieve_Welfare (04-02-2019).

Farsari, Y., Prastacos, P. and Butler, R.W. (2007). Policy and implementation issues of sustainable tourism in the Mediterranean, *International Journal of Tourism Policy*, 1(1), 58–78.

Faulkner, B. and Tideswell, C. (1997). A framework for monitoring community impacts of tourism, *Journal of Sustainable Tourism*, 5(1), 3–28.

Fredline, E. and Faulkner, B. (2000). Host community reactions: a cluster analysis, *Annals of Tourism Research*, 27(3), 763–784.

Fyall, A. and Garrod, B. (1998). Heritage tourism: at what price, *Managing Leisure*, 3(4), 213–228

Haralambopoulos, N. and Pizam, A. (1996). Perceived impacts of tourism: the case of Samos, *Annals of Tourism Research*, 23, 503–526.

Johnson, J.D., Snepenger, D.J. and Akis, S. (1994). Residents' perception of tourism development, *Annals of Tourism Research*, 12(3), 629–642.

Jurowski, C., Uysal, M. and Williams, R.D. (1997). A theoretical analysis of host community resident reactions to tourism, *Journal of Travel Research*, 36(2), 3–11.

King, B., Pizam, A. and Milman, A. (1993). Social impacts of tourism: host perceptions, *Annals of Tourism Research*, 20, 650–665.

Koens, K. and Postma, A. (2017). Understanding and measuring visitor pressure in Urban Tourism. A study into the nature and methods used to manage visitor pressure in six major European cities, *Centre of Expertise in Leisure, Tourism and Hospitality* (CELTH), Breda and Leeuwarden and Vlissingen.

Kuvan, Y. and Akan, P. (2005). Residents' attitudes toward general and forest-related impacts of tourism: the case of Belek, Antalya, *Tourism Management*, 26, 691–706.

Liu, J. and Var, T. (1986). Resident attitudes towards tourism impacts in Hawaii, *Annals of Tourism Research*, 13(2), 193–214.

Pearce, P. (1989). *Social Impacts of Tourism, in the Social, Cultural and Environmental Impacts of Tourism*. Sydney, Australia: New South Wales Tourism Commission.

Pearce, P., Moscardo, G. and Ross, G. (1996). *Tourism Community Relationships*. Oxford: Elsevier.

Postma, A. (2003). "Quality of life, competing value perspectives in leisure and tourism", Keynote presentation, *ATLAS 10th International Conference*, "Quality of Life, competing value perspectives in leisure and tourism", Leeuwarden, June.

Postma, A. and Schmuecker, D. (2017). Understanding and overcoming negative impacts of tourism in city destinations: conceptual model and strategic framework. *Journal of Tourism Futures*, 3(2), 144–156.

Sharma, B. and Dyer, P. (2009). An investigation of differences in residents' perceptions on the Sunshine Coast: tourism impacts and demographic variables, *Tourism Geographies*, 11(2), 187–213.

Sharpley, R. and Telfer, D.J. (2002). *Tourism and Development: Concepts and Issues*. Clevedon: Channel View Publications.

TP (2017). *Estratégia 2027*. available at: http://estrategia.turismodeportugal.pt/sites/default/files/Estrategia_Turismo_2027_TdP.pdf) (04-02-2019).

Turismo de Portuga (2017). *Statistical Data*, available at: http://travelbi.turismodeportugal.pt/pt-pt/Paginas/HomePage.aspx

TPNP, Turismo do Porto e Norte de Portugal, ER (2015). *Estratégia de Marketing Turístico do Porto e Norte de Portugal: Horizonte 2020*. Lisboa: TP.

UNWTO (2018). *Travel & Tourism Economic Impact 2017 – Portugal*. Madrid: UNWTO.

UNWTO (2011). *Tourism Towards 2030*. Madrid: UNWTO

UNWTO (2013). *Sustainable Tourism for Development*. Madrid: UNWTO.

Vargas-Sánchez, A., de los Ángeles Plaza-Mejía, M. and Porras-Bueno, N. (2009). Understanding residents' attitudes toward the development of industrial tourism in a former mining, *Journal of Travel Research*, 47 (3), 373–387.

WCED (1987). *Our Common Future. World Commission on Environment and Development*. Oxford: Oxford University Press.

World Tourism Organization (1993). *Sustainable Tourism Development: Guide for Local Planners*. Madrid: World Tourism Organization.

World Tourism Organization (2019). *Tourism and Sustainable Development Goals – Journey to 2030 Destinations: A Guidebook*. Madrid, Spain: World Tourism Organization.

8 Terraced landscape preservation and tourism sustainability in Cinque Terre, Liguria

Simonetta Acacia, Marta Casanova, Elena Macchioni, Federica Pompejano, Camilla Repetti and Francesca Segantin

Summary

Cinque Terre's terraced landscape represents an example of a peculiar relation between nature and humankind, thanks to its characteristic shaped territory. This area, vulnerable to natural disaster and anthropic degradation, has been involved in several actions aimed at its preservation since the 80s. The site was inscribed in the World Heritage List, and various laws and agencies were created to support local agriculture and landscape preservation. Through the analysis of the regulations, context and related requirements, this chapter aims to explore the relationship between mass tourism effects and landscape vulnerability and the conflict between conservation needs and the site's real economy.

Links

The following Case Study links may be of interest to readers of this chapter:

- Case Studies Part A (Destination management aspects of ethical sustainable development) – Chapter 15
- Case Studies Part B (Environmental & social aspects of ethical sustainable development) – Chapters 19, 20, 22 and 23

Please see the Contents on pages v–viii, and the Guide to the textbook in Appendix 1 for further information.

Introduction

The word Cinque Terre, used for the first time in 1448, identifies a territory located in the eastern part of Liguria, around the villages of Monterosso al Mare, Vernazza, Corniglia, Manarola and Riomaggiore, distinguished by rugged and steep slopes. The closeness of the ridge to the coast entails a very mild climate, also due to the favourable exposure, but at the same time some isolation from the neighbouring region (Verbas, 1978). These factors determined the marked homogeneity of this area and the community bond, strengthened by the increasing relationships between villages after the annexation to the Republic of Genoa in the 13th century (Marengo, 1924).

Vine growing is Cinque Terre distinctive feature: it defines its landscape, by means of farmed terraces built in a large part of this territory, and economy, with all the

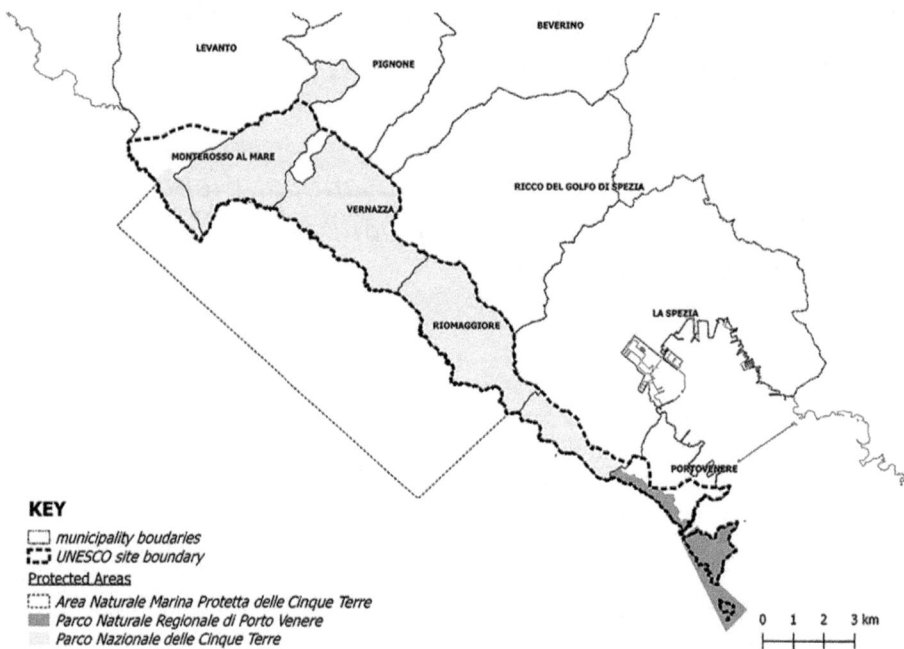

Figure 8.1 UNESCO site and Cinque Terre National Park.

works related to wine production and distribution (Verbas, 1978). During the 19th century, economic and societal changes occurred, railway construction In 1874, five stations were opened on the Sestri Levante-La Spezia section of the Genova-Pisa line. The spread of grapevines' devastating diseases (Gasparini, 2014) caused the decline of wine-producing industry in the area.

In the 20th century, the great value of Cinque Terre landscape and culture was acknowledged and protected. In 1959, the territory was listed according to the Italian law, and a regional (later national) park was issued (see paragraph "Cinque Terre National Park between planning through and action"). In 1997, the site was inscribed in the UNESCO World Heritage List (WHL) as cultural landscape (Figure 8.1). Moreover in 1973, Cinque Terre and Cinque Terre Sciacchetrà DOC labels were established to protect the local wine production (Verbas, 1978).

The Park Authority, UNESCO, Region of Liguria (Regione Liguria) and other local authorities, beyond preparing their own government and management tools, undertook many actions (such as scientific studies and resolutions) aiming to support agriculture and regulate tourism, as well as to restore and preserve the environment and terraced system.

Hydrogeological risk and terracing in the Cinque Terre area

From a geomorphological point of view, this area is prevalently mountainous and hilly, and the seaside is characterised by the presence of a high coast, mainly rocky and impervious. The rare small beaches, composed of deposits of pebbles and gravel, are made of landslide material or by shingle transported by watercourses. Further-more, the coast is exposed to storms and permanent wave action, causing its erosion, especially where streams emerge into the sea (Cevasco, 2007). Even if mountains are not particularly high (with a maximum height of ca. 800 m), the whole territory is extremely steep and sprinkled by waterways with a torrential regime. Many slopes are affected by detachments of blocks, landslides and debris flow (Figure 8.2).

Over the centuries, human intervention interacted with the structural vulnerability of the soil, modifying the slope shape and the water flow, by means of a vast terraced system allowing farming (Besio, 2004): terraces are supported by dry-stone walls that need constant maintenance. Nowadays cultivation abandonment (and subsequent lack of maintenance) mainly occurs in those areas that are high, far from the seaside, or hillside villages. Another factor causing abandonment is the extreme split of land property. The local custom wants each parcel to be equally divided among heirs, so that one person can eventually own little patches of cultivations very far from each other (Verbas, 1978) (Figure 8.3).

Regardless of the quality of constructive technique and employed materials, the lack of maintenance causes degradation of dry-stone walls, including collapse of up-per course of stones, with the consequent confluence of surface water, and wall defor-mation (Martini et al., 2004).

Due to its conformation and man-made alterations, most part of the area is naturally subjected to a high hydrogeological risk. According to the 2016 update of Cinque Terre Piano di Bacino, a great part of the territory is classified with high and very high hydrogeological risk, further increased by the so-called land

Figure 8.2 Cinque Terre coastal view.

Figure 8.3   Cinque Terre terraced landscape.

consumption phenomenon (DiAP et al., 2009). Piano di Bacino is a Regional planning tool that controls the actions and rules about conservation, defence and valorisation of the soil and correct use of waters (L. 183/1989). High risk (R3 class) corresponds to a high probability of phenomena such as landslides, soil erosion and river flooding. They can cause dangers for person safety, functional damage to buildings and infrastructures, interruption of functionality of socio-economic activities and damage to the environmental heritage. Very high hydrogeological risk (R4 class) corresponds to a higher damage degree that could involve injuries and loss of human lives.

Land consumption is caused not only by buildings and infrastructure construction, but also by mass tourism, significantly grown after the inclusion of the site in the UNESCO WHL. The presence of tourists affects the territory with demand of facilities and intense use of the trails (Martini et al., 2004) that follow ancient itineraries beside the ridge, coast or hillside and the diagonal paths joining them (De Marco, 2006). Land consumption can be generally defined as an anthropogenic process that involves progressive transformation of natural or agricultural surfaces through the construction of buildings and infrastructures (Figure 8.4).

In the area, there are more than 88 active landslides (Data available at http://www.banchedati.ambienteinliguria.it (February 2019), and, in the last decades, the territory was devastated by two floods (in 2000 and 2011) and two landslides. The first landslide caused the closure of the so-called Via dell'Amore path in 2012, while the second one determined the closure of Sentiero Azzurro path, between the villages of Manarola and Corniglia, in 2014. Following further landslides, the entire coastal

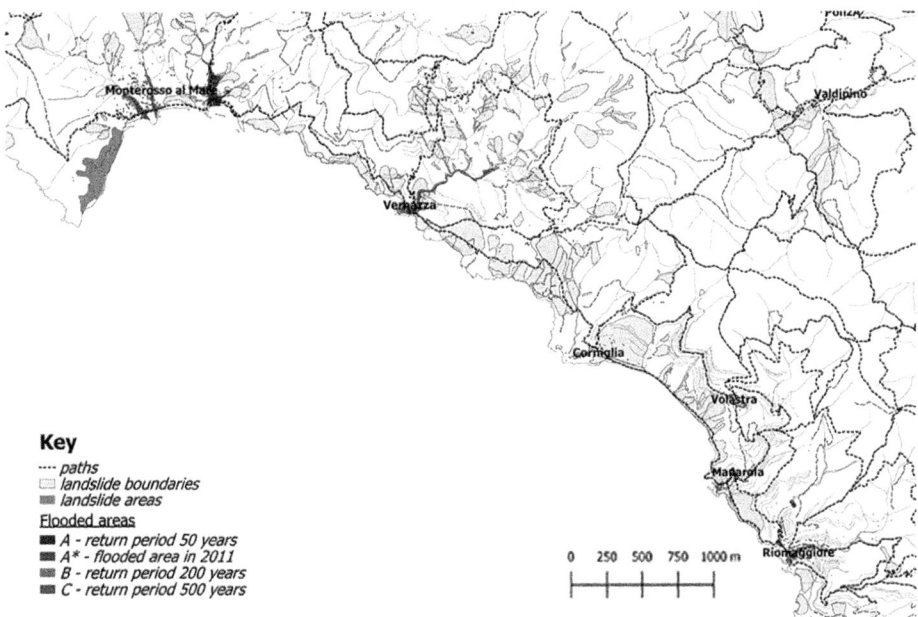

Figure 8.4 Map of paths and landslide areas.

itinerary is now not accessible. Its reopening, scheduled for 2021, is linked to the implementation of the safety measures in the territory. Via dell'Amore is a pedestrian path overlooking the sea, about 1 km long, connecting the villages of Riomaggiore and Manarola. It is a segment of Sentiero Azzurro that crosses the whole Cinque Terre area. It was built in the 1930s (D.M. 2015); therefore, it does not match with any historical path.

Most landslides correspond to abandoned terraces, whereas flows are related to neglect, lack of maintenance of forests and terraces, and cementing of the territory (in addition to heavy rains and huge debris falls).

The return to a natural state of the slope is the inevitable future for abandoned and faraway terraces: in fact the restoration of the whole Cinque Terre terraced system is not sustainable from the economic point of view. However, the recovery of the natural slope can be an additional risk, if it is not properly managed until the achievement of a new balance (Besio, 2004).

Tourist growth: promotion and sustainability

A distinctive aspect of Cinque Terre is its economy nowadays mainly based on tourism. While generating positive outcomes for the economy of the area, tourism has also a strong impact on its landscape and population. Cinque Terre tourist tradition dates back to the period after World War I, when a lodging, a small hotel and two bath facilities were opened in Monterosso (Verbas, 1978). During the 1930s, there were around 800 visitors per year, including about 50 foreigners, with an average stay of 20 days each (Consiglio Provinciale Economia Corporativa, 1934). After 1955, tourism expanded, with more than 50% of foreign visitors. Apart from Monterosso, tourism is a quite recent phenomenon for the Cinque Terre hamlets: given the features of their territory, they could not develop large hotel facilities but rather developed small non-hotel properties. As for other touristic destinations marked by a fragile environment, the tourism infrastructure growth had a strong impact on the territory, causing the increase of urban settlements and the continuing touristification of territorial resources (Tizzoni, 2014). At least, however, it did not degenerate into the massive urban growth characterising other Ligurian coastal areas.

The analysis of data regarding the number of visitors and length of stay between 1998 and 2018 (Figure 8.5) reveals an evident increase of arrivals, both for the municipalities included in the UNESCO site and for neighbouring municipalities displaying similar characteristics (Bonassola, Framura, and Levanto). Riomaggiore has the most significant increase (from 12,333 to 96,285 visitors). On the contrary, Bonassola and Framura display the smallest increase. The distribution of tourists within the borders of the UNESCO site also reflects the accommodation capacity. The number of beds in hotels remained almost unchanged for all the analysed municipalities between 2002 and 2016, while the beds in non-hotel properties had a significant increase, except for Bonassola and Framura. The length of stay decreases or is almost unchanged for the analysed timeframe: 2–3 days for the municipalities of the UNESCO site, with a peak of 3.5 days for Monterosso al Mare in 2009. The length of stay for the municipalities of the UNESCO site is slightly lower than the national and regional average.

Foreign tourists represent 76% of total arrivals and 77% of total stays between 2010 and 2015; this emphasises the international vocation of Cinque Terre. These values are above the Italian, regional and also provincial average (MiBACT et al., 2016). According to ENIT (Agenzia Nazionale del Turismo) 2016 report, analysing the main foreign tour operators selling Italian destinations, Cinque Terre is among the favourite destinations for Spanish, US, Canadian, Indian and Australian tourists. Data regarding touristic flows come from the survey of customers' movements in accommodation facilities. Data regarding accommodation capacity from Indagine sulla Capacità degli esercizi ricettivi by ISTAT – Istituto Nazionale di Statistica –is available at http://dati.istat.it/ (February 2019). (Data regarding municipalities, courtesy of Osservatorio Turistico – Regione Liguria.)

In addition to visitors staying overnight in the UNESCO site, the ones visiting on a day trip must be considered for their strong impact on landscape and population. Most of these visitors come from cruise ships docked at La Spezia harbour, the most important in the area. In 2017, 163 cruise ships reached this harbour, with 426.024 passengers in total, 80% arriving from May to October (data available at www.crocierelaspezia.com (February 2018)). For example, 8,000 cruisers arrived in a single day in August, because of a lack of planning. In 2015, the excursions in Cinque Terre offered by cruise ships were mainly by boat, and included a visit to Portovenere and Monterosso and lunch in a traditional restaurant.

Although tourism is usually an important factor for the revitalisation of an area, its increase can dangerously affect the natural and cultural features of the territory (Musso, 2014). Thus, a concrete and conscious tourism strategy, addressed to the development of sustainable tourism activities, can play a key role in the preservation of the outstanding values of Cinque Terre site.

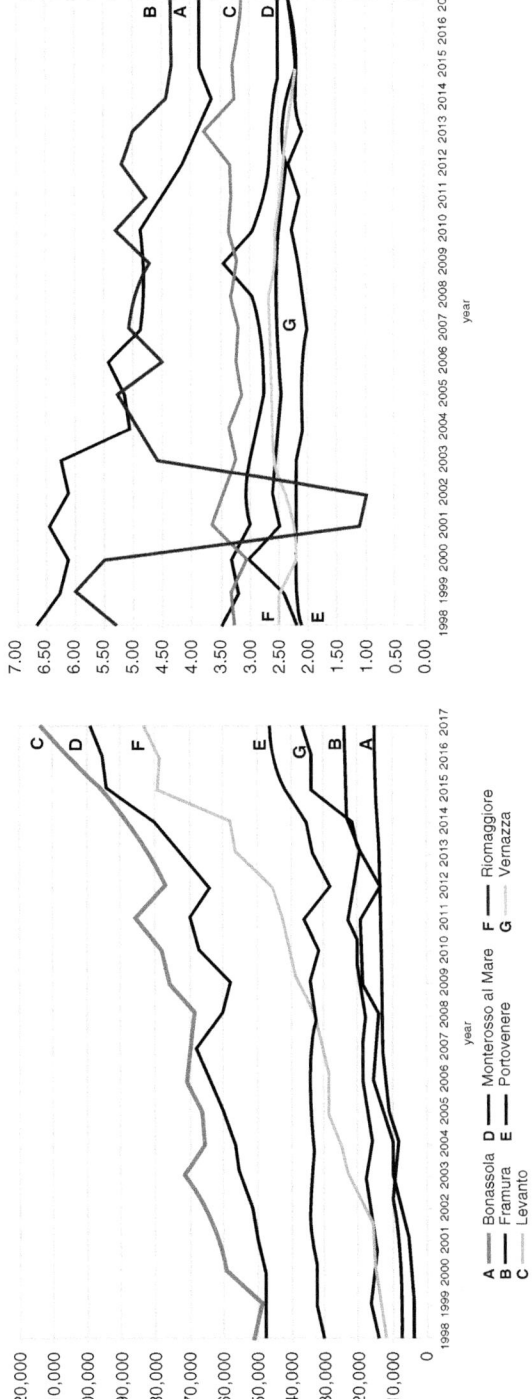

Figure 8.5 Visitors' arrivals and average stay for the analysed municipalities 1998–2018.

Sustainable tourism takes into account current and future impacts on economy, society and environment, considering demands from visitors, industry and local communities (UNEP & UNWTO, 2005). In 2014, the Cinque Terre Park Authority complied to the European Charter for Sustainable Tourism in Protected Areas (CETS). The Strategy and Action Plan 2014 objectives are not limited to the preservation of Cinque Terre peculiarities but include calibrated actions addressing a continuous life quality improvement and sustainable development. The declared goal is to restore a harmonious balance between the human element and environment, starting from current conditions (PNCT, 2014).

The document identifies several weaknesses, and among them, the disorganised tourist offer suffering from the lack of overall coordinated management. In fact local institutions do not cooperate with each other in the efficient promotion of the UNESCO site: none of their official institutional websites directly refers to the UNESCO website.

Excluding the phenomenon of mass tourism, especially aroused by cruise traffic, the main type of visitors is certainly the one interested in outdoor, cultural, wine and gastronomic activities, aimed to experience the local culture and traditions (PNCT, 2014).

Local institutions' main websites are analysed focusing on the promotion of seaside/mountain trekking itineraries. To obtain an effective web publicity of a tourism product, as the Cinque Terre trails and related cultural activities, a strong horizontal cooperation is necessary in order to develop a common strategy between the various local institutions. In fact, only a conscious promotion considering both the fragilities (among them, the high hydrogeological risk) and strengths of the territory could live up to the European Charter for Sustainable Tourism in Protected Areas (CETS) commitments. This strategy should improve the influence on the market of the offered tourist products, trying to widen their degree of coverage (ratio between current and potential visitors).

The organization and management of an effective tourist promotion turns to be important to attract a specific kind of visitors, directly involved in the sustainable development process stated and promoted in the Strategy and Action Plan 2014.

Also the analysis of the Cinque Terre trails network tourist promotion highlights a low degree of horizontal cooperation between local institutions. Their websites promote the Park's trails network incompletely, often offering ambiguous and complex web references, especially for foreign tourists (that are the most part, according to the Strategy and Action Plan 2014). On the other hand, the website of the Park Authority is very exhaustive, with a well-assorted web page of the entire hiking network and many references, for example, to local food and wine producers.

Finally, it has been observed that direct reference to the UNESCO Cinque Terre main page is lacking on the institutional websites, and the UNESCO logo is scarcely present (MiBACT et al., 2016). Thus, the need of a conscious and common promotional strategy should start through the creation of a unique or integrated web tourist promotion management (e.g. on the trails network and related activities), linking the efforts from the involved local institutions, while sharing a common sustainable long-term vision.

Cinque Terre National Park between planning and action

[*In this section, references to laws and decrees are made using the following abbreviations: L. (law), L.R. (regional law), D.P.R. (decree by the President of the Italian Republic), D.G.R. (regional decree), D.M. (ministerial decree), D.lgs. (legislative decree).*]

First activities carried out for the conservation of Cinque Terre terraced landscape date back to the second half of the 20th century, with the national law for use of cultivated land (L. 440/1978) and the regional one on the protection of agricultural activity in the Cinque Terre area (L.R. 41/1985). In 1995, three protected areas, instituted in 1985 (L.R. 12/1985), were reunited in the Cinque Terre Natural Regional Park (L.R. 12/1995). In the wake of these actions and of the UNESCO nomination, the Municipalities of Monterosso, Vernazza and Riomaggiore sought the institution of the Cinque Terre National Park, which was granted in 1999 (D.P.R. 6 October 1999). After the institution, while the Park Plan was approved, the area was subjected to Disciplina di Tutela, a document focused on protection of traditional agricultural, pastoral and craft activities (D.P.R. 6 October 1999). In 2002, the Park Authority approved the new Park Plan: it was based on the principle that, to preserve this landscape, it was necessary to allow the permanence of dwellers and their agricultural activity, providing their oversight on the territory. The Plan focused on the creation of a market system that could support the Cinque Terre agro-food production, aided by new forms of sustainable tourism. However, after judicial scandal of the Park Authority (2010), the Park Plan was revoked (D.G.R. 1482/2010) and required to be updated. In August 2018, a call for tenders was published in order to entrust a multi-disciplinary working group with the writing of Cinque Terre Park planning tools (PNCT, 2018a), and currently it has been won provisionally. The required Park planning tools are Park Plan, Park Rules and Regulations, Long-term Economic and Social Plan, and strategic environmental assessment documents (PNCT, 2018a). The special contract specifications attached to the call for tenders require the planning which indicates, on the one hand, the fundamental directions for territory long-term transformation based on structural provisions and, on the other hand, short-term actions based on programmatic provisions. Moreover, the document identifies targets and strategies to be pursued through the planning tools. The Park Authority recognises as its mission, beyond the preservation of the natural environment, the recovery and preservation of Cinque Terre landscape whose survival is put in danger by complex economic and social reasons. So it identifies as strategies the vineyard and agriculture maintenance as well as quality tourism. The Park Authority acknowledges that tourism activities are the most important sources of revenue in the Park area, while the agricultural ones are the fundamental means to ensure landscape preservation: only the search for a new balance between these factors (and other ones) can lead to the territory's sustainable development.

Until the entry into force of the new Park Plan, the safeguard measures contained in the 1999 Disciplina di Tutela would be considered valid again. Since that moment until today, the Park Authority has no longer adopted a management plan, despite the numerous environmental emergencies and the evidence of a precarious situation that requires long-term planning, as soon as possible.

If, on the one hand, there is a deficiency by the Park Authority due to the absence of a plan, on the other hand, the Park Authority itself promoted numerous initiatives for the protection of the territory that, in some way, suggest the idea of a long-term vision for the Cinque Terre area. The aim of the National Park is to encourage the development of a new balance between economic competitiveness and landscape protection, traditional know-how and development of responsible tourism, involving public and private subjects (D.M. 22/2012). In December 2015,

Europarc (Europarc is a federation for the protection of natural and cultural heritage in European protected areas with particular attention on sustainable tourism, economics and health issues) included the Cinque Terre National Park in the network of Parks that obtained the CETS, activity that the Park has implemented with two paths it has already undertaken: the Environmental Certification ISO 14001 and Environmental Quality Label (MQA), with the aim of promoting sustainability policies that involve public and private subjects (PNCT, 2014). Starting from the analysis of dwellers' quality of life, pressure of tourism on natural resources and tourism offer quality, the Action Plan identifies targets, intervention strategies, funding and required professional skills. On the analysis and comparison phase carried out, three work areas and relative activities were identified, reflecting the main underlined problems: original and innovative tourism offer, enhancement of local culture and know-how and territory and tourist flow management (PNCT, 2014). Among these activities, the Action Plan provides for the reinforcement of the tools adopted by the Park Authority in order to maintain a specific environmental quality standard (ISO 14001 and MQA), both in management and protection activities. Specifically, the MQA is based on voluntary participation by private subjects (restaurants, hotels, producers) who pledge to keep a certain service sustainability (For example, for raw materials supply, restaurants and accommodation facilities must choose from a list of local producers to obtain the MQA (PNCT, 2014).) in exchange for enrolment in a virtuous circle of private activities, ensuring them some visibility. In the same year, the Park Authority published the Sustainability Report (PN5T, 2015) to clearly disseminate its activities and the economic resources spent to increase the Park sustainability.

However, despite the numerous actions carried out for landscape protection and sustainability, in almost 20 years since the establishment of the National Park, there has been a lack of long-term management vision for this fragile heritage that can be compromised under the interests of various subjects and tourist pressure. The increase of institutions (This territory is under the provisions not only of the Park Authority, but also of UNESCO, Ministry of Cultural Heritage and Tourism, Regione Liguria, local administrations, associations and foundations.) who must (or voluntarily) produce a management or protection plan for the Cinque Terre landscape creates a complex situation and documents overlapping. (Among others, the Cinque Terre landscape and built heritage protection and management is defined by D.lgs. 42/2004, L. 394/1991 and D.lgs. 151/2006.) Some of the protection and management tools active in the area are landscape coordination plan according to L.R. 431/1985 (1990); town plans of Vernazza (1995), Monterosso (1977) and Riomaggiore (1997); Disciplina di Tutela (1999); Piano di Bacino (2016) and UNESCO Management Plan (2016). In this framework, the UNESCO Site Management Plan (MP) could be one of the tools for their coordination.

World Heritage List inscription and Management Plan development

Starting from 2003, MP is required for UNESCO sites and was included in the Italian legislative framework in 2006 (L. 77/2006). Its scope is to define strategies to maintain Outstanding Universal Value (OUV) and increase positive outcomes for environment, society and economy. Despite the introduction of MP as essential for UNESCO sites management, and several calls for its development from the UNESCO World Heritage Centre (WHC), it was only in 2016, almost 20 years after its inscription on the WHL, that the site was provided with one.

In 1997, the site of Portovenere, Cinque Terre and the Islands (Palmaria, Tino and Tinetto) was inscribed in the WHL as a continuing cultural landscape based on criteria (ii), (iv) and (v). Created by the work of humankind and nature, its significance relies in the active relationship between the two factors (UNESCO WHC, 1997).

From the WHL inscription onwards, the WHC documents recognise that the traditional lifestyle has been preserved, despite pressures from social and economic developments. In 1997, economic and social crises were identified as the biggest threats to the site, since the trend of speculative investments for mass tourism seemed adverted by then (UNESCO WHC, 1997). Nevertheless, even in 1997, ICOMOS (International Council on Monuments & Sites) recommendations highlighted the potential risks connected with the increase of tourism, possibly connected to the inscription on the WHL (UNESCO WHC, 1997). In fact, the inscription usually implies an average +30% increase in the number of visitors (Puglisi, 2012). Therefore, ICOMOS requested the State Party further information on tourist management and community involvement activities.

Problems connected to the lack of maintenance of terraced fields were already evident in 1999 and 2000, when the site was inscribed in the World Monuments Watch of the World Monuments Fund, and received funding for the implementation of scientific studies concerning the terraced landscape (e.g. project PROSIT). Concern related to an uncontrolled tourism development and lack of an overall planning grew over the years. The 2006 periodic report warned on the effect of tourism on the integrity and authenticity of the site (UNESCO WHC, 2006). Major threats were identified with the increase of visitors (mostly day trippers), soil erosion, and the low coordination between the subject involved in protection and management.

At the time of 1997 inscription, MP was not mandatory, the protection of the site being ensured by the existing regulatory framework. At the same time, a buffer zone was not defined, in consideration of the features of the terrain, having a natural border on the landward side. The buffer zone usually includes areas displaying similar values to that of the inscribed property but with a minor degree of authenticity and integrity; the definition of a buffer zone can increase the level of protection to the site. Among other planning instruments, the approval of 2002 Cinque Terre National Park Plan further regulated interventions in one area of the UNESCO site. However, the need for an MP was urged in the report by the advisory mission invited to the site after the 2011 flood and landslides (UNESCO WHC, 2012a) and started again in 2013, alongside the development of tourism and risk management strategies (UNESCO WHC, 2013). After the 2011 flood and landslides, the State Party invited an advisory mission to assess the overall state of conservation of the property and provide technical advice on remedial measures and risk preparedness (UNESCO WHC, 2012a, 2012b). According to the 2012 report, the degradation of the cultural landscape was due to social and economic pressure, rather than to natural disasters (UNESCO WHC, 2012b).

In 2014, an agreement between MiBACT Segretariato Regionale of Liguria and FILSE S.p.a. was signed for the elaboration of the MP for the site. The workgroup involved MiBACT Segretariato Regionale of Liguria, Regione Liguria, Cinque Terre

National Park, Porto Venere Municipality and consultants. Finally, the buffer zone proposal and MP (MiBACT et al., 2016) were delivered to the World Heritage Centre in 2015 and 2016.

Preliminary studies were developed in three macro areas: analysis of the context including the cultural landscape, territory and safety and tourism. The research involved study regarding landscape transformations and residents' sense of identity.

The MP provides the site with an overall strategy, assuming the existence of a complex regulatory framework in place. Identifying the social capital of the territory as a priority, it envisions a site where all dwellings are inhabited and all terraced fields are cultivated. The MP goals include increase of cohesion, identity and integration between the stakeholders and improvement of management and administration. The MP envisions recovery of terraced fields still used and maintenance of dry-stone walls, the modernization of agricultural sector and integration between farming and promotion of local products.

For the MP section about tourism management, the workgroup followed the methodology of UNESCO World Heritage and Sustainable Tourism Program, with the goal of making tourism contribute to the conservation of the site and the territory belong primarily to the inhabitants. The impact of mass tourism is worsened by landscape morphology and lack of overall management strategies and coordination between tourism and agriculture.

Regarding tourism, the MP for the UNESCO site includes initiatives aimed at increasing awareness of the value and vulnerability of the site among residents and tourists. It encompasses several objectives and related actions. First, create an overall assessment of the flows of tourists making it possible to control the carrying capacity of the site as a whole (with a specific focus on the impact of day trippers). This includes the implementation of a unique system of reservation (bus, hotel, activities) and access to the site, allowing the harmonisation of touristic services and the diversification of the offer (for high and low season). Second, link the seaside and the landward side: this means decreasing the number of tourists staying only in the coastal towns also through wine-tourism, fostering the transmission of knowledge between rural and touristic sector, involving tourists in agricultural activities and maintenance of the rural landscape (as an educational tool for visitors), connecting agriculture production and restaurants (widening the product marked of origin) and thus increasing local entrepreneurship. Third, improve the social capital through educational activities aimed at different public and to address specific needs.

Finally, the MP also suggests creating a single municipality, to better integrate and coordinate the governance for the site, and identifying a mediator between the various stakeholders and institutions. Besides, in 2017, Regione Liguria accepted the proposal by the Mayors of the three municipalities to compile an Inter-municipal Town Plan (Piano Urbanistico Intercomunale) that includes the entire Cinque Terre territory.

A management office was created in April 2018, involving Regione Liguria, Cinque Terre National Park and the municipalities involved, to define strategies for the area, encompassing three main sections: logistics and transportation, agriculture and tourism (more information available at https://www.regione.liguria.it/giunta/item/18590-5-terre-cabina-regia.html – January 2019).

The agreement for the protection, management and sustainable development of the site was signed in August 2018 between Regione Liguria, Cinque Terre National Park, Porto Venere Regional Park, the municipalities included in the UNESCO site and buffer zone and the Ministry of Cultural Heritage and Tourism. Among other actions, the agreement involved the creation of the "Cinque Terre, Porto Venere and the Islands UNESCO Site Office," as a technical and administrative body formed by the National and Regional Parks. The main duties of the appointed Site Manager, working within the office, are coordinating the relationships between UNESCO and local authorities and organisations, and supporting the implementation of the MP initiatives. More specifically, the site manager oversees the MP actions as defined by the working groups and the coordination committee, is responsible for the efficiency of the management system and the MP effectiveness, transmits the periodic report to UNESCO compiled by the permanent workgroup and coordinates the involved stakeholders. Moreover, the Cinque Terre, Porto Venere and the Islands UNESCO Site Office works to improve the services to the users of the site, according to the territory emerging needs.

Further actions for the Cinque Terre landscape protection and promotion

In order to decrease the hydrogeological and territorial risk, the Region allocated funds to monitor landslides, implement anti-landslide mechanisms (such as laying of barriers, armed nets, rock fall), restore dry-stone walls and damaged trails and carry out some interventions on watercourses (as hydraulic checks and for safety of overflowing areas). Funds were allocated for repair works on Via dell'Amore and the hillside path called Strada dei Santuari, reopened in 2017 after a six-year closure.

In addition, the Regional Authority and European Union assigned funds for the conservation of Cinque Terre terraced landscape, by means of Piano di Sviluppo Rurale (Rural Development Program), co-financed by the State, that provides grants to restore dry-stone walls, specifically in regional or national parks and areas with a high hydrological risk. However, to carry out an effective slope reinforcement, this provision requires allocation of grants to be coordinated and aimed to recover entire areas that are still cultivated.

The Park Authority finances a centre for hydrological risk studies, coordinating actions regarding research and distribution of stones to be employed in maintenance of the dry-stone walls and promoting educational programs on territory maintenance addressed to disadvantaged people. Furthermore, the Park organises and promotes initiatives related to agricultural activity support. Among them are the recovery of abandoned farmland and planting of new vineyards following traditional techniques, such as the actions of TRA Monti project; the restoration of Case Lovara on behalf of the FAI (Italian Environment Fund) and the New Farmers initiative. Performance Planning is a tool introduced by D.lgs. 150/2009 to manage Public Administrations performance; it allows to know year by year the directions and targets the Park Authority sets itself and how it wants to achieve them (PNCT, 2019).

Other educational activities related to agricultural tradition include the agreement with the Building School of Spezia and Manarola Cinque Terre Foundation (2015) to teach dry-stone wall construction technique in schools and the ones carried out by the National Park Environmental Education Centre.

All these initiatives involve young generations and aim to increase awareness about landscape problems and sense of belonging.

In order to decrease mass tourism impact on the environment, MSC and Royal Caribbean cruise companies changed their excursion itineraries excluding the villages of Manarola, Riomaggiore and Vernazza, starting from 2015. In 2014, an agreement between the La Spezia Port Authority and National Park established an Info Point for cruisers to warn visitors on the fragility and features of Cinque Terre Landscape; an adequate planning and distribution of cruise arrivals are necessary to contain and reduce the impact of day trippers.

Another existing tool is the Cinque Terre Card for tourist access to the National Park area and its paths. Introduced in 2001, it encourages public transportation, reducing the number of private vehicles, and aims to generate resources for territory and local services maintenance.

Moreover, numerous activities are organized to develop a new form of conscious and innovative tourism, such as the Sciacchetrail, a race through the vineyards to learn about traditional wines and Sciacchetrà liquor, or the training activities regarding Cinque Terre terraced landscape organized by Tu quoque organization. Finally, the Committee for the Safeguarding of the Intangible Cultural Heritage inscribed the "Art of dry stone walling, knowledge and techniques" on the Representative List of the Intangible Cultural Heritage of Humanity at the end of 2018 (UNESCO ICH, 2018). The dry-stone walling know-how transmission plays a crucial role in the creation and maintenance of the living societal environment. In fact, several cultural and educational activities at regional and local levels are aimed to booster existing synergies between communities and associated organisations and practitioners. In addition, the fundamental role of the dry-stone terraces in preventing landslides and floods of the land in Cinque Terre terraced landscape has been already recognised by the Piano di sviluppo rurale (Rural Development Program 2014–2020).

Conclusions

Despite ICOMOS first warnings, it has been difficult to find effective tools to manage the increasing flow of visitors. In the last years, international media have focused their attention on the issue of Cinque Terre tourism and on its effects on its fragile landscape. Cinque Terre and Venice were included by CNN in a list of 12 destinations to be avoided in 2018 because of tourist overcrowding. These recent events can be interpreted as the sign of a new consciousness about the negative effects of mass tourism on landscape preservation and tourism itself. Moreover, the increase of visitors does not ease the phenomenon of agricultural activities abandonment, but rather it has led workforce to move to the profitable tourist industry.

The critical situation of Cinque Terre landscape requests feasible strategies to avoid delisting from UNESCO WHL and above all the loss of its identity. This landscape must find a new balance between mankind sustainable presence and natural environment preservation. Achieved and ongoing actions for a sustainable tourism offer should be supported by an effective rationalisation of visitors, in the villages and on widely known paths, and by a strict scheduling of cruisers' landing. Tourist flow should be controlled so that it is adequate to Cinque Terre vulnerability and suitable for the enjoyment of the place identity.

Giving a unique body the responsibility of balancing tourist promotion and landscape preservation can foster the effectiveness of these strategies, through a subject who can mediate between the parks, UNESCO, State, Region, local institutions, associations and private citizens.

This study demonstrates how the coordination between the various planning and management tools involving Cinque Terre territory can run into obstacles when put into action considering the regulatory framework. Therefore, the MP offers an opportunity for a real change in the site management, given the fact local institutions incorporate its recommendations in their planning tools (An evaluation on MP results and its reception by local bodies is hard due to its recent publication.) and recognise the inhabitants' role for landscape maintenance and implementation of actions aimed to preserve residents on site (Besio, 2004).

Reflections

1 Today, the Cinque Terre economy is mainly based on tourism, having strong impacts on natural and cultural features of the territory. The highest pressure comes from day trippers, mostly from cruises.
2 The significance of the site relies in the active relationship between humankind and nature. Landscape preservation can only be ensured by allowing the permanence of dwellers and their agricultural activity.
3 The return to a natural state of the slope is the inevitable future for abandoned and faraway terrace, but the recovery of the natural slope can be an additional risk, if it is not properly managed.
4 The definition of general tools to ensure coordination between the various subjects involved in the management and protection of the site to promote a long-term management vision is critical. In 2018, the "Cinque Terre, Porto Venere and the Islands UNESCO Site Office" was created as a technical and administrative body formed by the National and Regional Parks, working on the main sections of agriculture, tourism and transportation.
5 The conservation of the site requires the implementation of a conscious tourism strategy, encompassing the promotion of sustainable tourism activities, life quality improvement for residents and sustainable development.

Questions

1 Is restricting the number of tourists accessing the site an effective strategy to ensure landscape preservation and livability?
2 How is it possible to limit the negative pressures on natural and cultural features of the site coming from mass tourism on the most accessed paths?
3 By which means is it possible to address the problems related to waste produced by day trippers?

4   How to effectively promote active and slow tourism, contributing to the preservation of natural and cultural features of the site?
5   How to retain (or increase) the number of dwellers and rural workers, recognizing their role in the maintenance of the site?

Further reading

Agnoletti, M., et al. 2019. "Terraced Landscapes and Hydrogeological Risk. Effects of Land Abandonment in Cinque Terre (Italy) during Severe Rainfall Events." *Sustainability* 11: 1–12. MDPI.

Bartolini, F., Penerai, S., Panico, C., and Pappalepore, I. 2004. "Sviluppo turistico ed economia della cultura: verso un turismo sostenibile. Il caso delle Cinque Terre." *Risposte Turismo.* 1 vols. Venezia: Nicola Longobardi Editore.

Boato, A., Martini, S., and Pesce, G. 2003. "Ricerche sui terrazzamenti delle Cinque Terre." *Notiziario di Archeologia Medievale* 75: 7–8.

Boato, A., Martini, S., and Pesce, G. 2005. "La costruzione dei terrazzamenti a secco nel parco nazionale delle Cinque Terre (SP): codificazione di un sapere empirico." In *International Seminar "Theory and Practice of Construction: Knowledge, Means, Models,* 963–973. Ravenna: Moderna.

Brancucci, G., Tarolli, P., and Rizzo, D. 2019. "Terraced Landscapes: Land Abandonment, Soil Degradation, and Suitable Management." In Varotto M., Bonardi L., and Tarolli P. eds. *World Terraced Landscapes: History, Environment, Quality of Life. Environmental History,* 9 vols. Cham: Springer.

Franco, G. 2015. "Sito UNESCO Cinque Terre, Porto Venere e Isole. Eco-efficienza degli edifici tradizionali e applicabilita di sistemi alimentati da fonti rinnovabili." *Il Progetto Sostenibile* 36–37: 263. Monfalcone: Edicom.

Franco, G. 2018. "Solar Powered Energy and Eco-efficiency in a UNESCO Site. Criteria and Recommendations for the National Park of Cinque Terre, Italy." *Energy and Buildings* 174: 168–178. Amsterdam: Elsevier.

Franco, G., De Marco, L., and Magrini, A. 2014. "Solar powered energy and eco-efficiency in a UNESCO site. Criteria and recommendations for the National Park of Cinque Terre, Italy." In Toniolo, L., Boriani, M., and Guidi, G., eds. *Built Heritage: Monitoring Conservation and Management,* 21–32. Berlin: Springer.

Franco, G., and Musso, S.F. 2003. "Una guida per il recupero nel Parco delle Cinque Terre." In A.A. V.V., *Atti del Convegno Internazionale. Napoli, Aprile 2003,* 323–332.

ICOMOS. 2015. *Evaluation of Nomination of Cultural and Mixed Properties to the World Heritage List.* ICOMOS Report for the World Heritage Committee. 39th ordinary session. WHC-15/39.COM/INF.8B1. Add.

Musso, S.F., and Franco, G. 2006. *Guida agli interventi di recupero dell'edilizia diffusa nel Parco Nazionale delle Cinque Terre.* Venezia: Marsilio Editore.

Musso, S.F., and De Marco, L. 2008. "La gestion de la transformacion de un paisaje aterrazado. Rehabilitacion del parque nacional "Cinque Terre", Liguria (Italia)." In Casanovas, X., eds. *Experiencias de rehabilitacion mediterraneas.* Barcelona: Rehabimed.

Raso, E., et al. 2019. "Landslide Inventory of the Cinque Terre National Park, Italy." In Shakoor A., and Cato K., eds. *IAEG/AEG Annual Meeting Proceedings, San Francisco, California, 2018.* 1 vols. Cham: Springer.

UNESCO WHC. 2014. *State of Conservation of World Heritage Properties. Portovenere, Cinque Terre, and the Islands (Palmaria, Tino and Tinetto) (Italy). Periodic report.*

UNESCO WHC. 2017. *Adoption of Retrospective Statements of Outstanding Universal Value. Decision: 41 COM 8E.*

References

Besio, M. 2004. "Le Cinque Terre: una presentazione." In Parco Nazionale delle Cinque Terre, ed. *Life 00 ENV/IT/000191 P.R.O.S.I.T.; Conference Proceedings, Riomaggiore, 26 July 2004*, 5–10. La Spezia: Tipografia Ambrosiana.

Cevasco, A. 2007. "I fenomeni d'instabilità nell'evoluzione della costa alta delle Cinque Terre (Liguria Orientale)." *Studi costieri* 13: 95–111.

Consiglio Provinciale Economia Corporativa. 1934. *Relazione statistica per gli anni 1931–32*, La Spezia.

De Marco, L. 2006. "Il paesaggio delle Cinque Terre." In Musso, S.F. and Franco, G., eds. *Guida agli interventi di recupero dell'edilizia diffusa nel Parco Nazionale delle Cinque Terre*, 37–43. Venezia: Marsilio.

DiAP, Politecnico di Milano, Legambiente, I.N.U., and Osservatorio Nazionale sul Consumo di Suolo. 2009. *Primo rapporto nazionale sui consumi di suolo*. Santarcangelo di Romagna: Maggioli Editore.

Gasparini, G.P. 2014. "Il vino delle Cinque Terre e le trasformazioni ottocentesche." In Carassale, A., and Lo Basso, L., eds. *Terra vineata. La vite e il vino in Liguria e nelle Alpi Marittime dal Medioevo ai nostri giorni*, 88–108. Ventimiglia: Philobiblon.

Marengo, E. 1924. "Le Cinque Terre e la genesi di questo nome." *Atti della Società Ligure di Storia Patria* LII: 289–302.

MiBACT – Ministero dei beni e delle attività culturali e del turismo, FILSE s.p.a. – Finanziaria Ligure per lo Sviluppo Economico, Parco Nazionale delle Cinque Terre, Comune di Porto Venere, Parco Naturale Regionale di Porto Venere, and Regione Liguria. 2016. *Piano di Gestione per il sito UNESCO. Porto Venere, Cinque Terre e Isole (Palmaria, Tino e Tinetto)*.

Musso, S.F. 2014. "The destiny of the built landscapes, between nature and culture. The Cinque Terre in Liguria." In Russo, V., eds. *Landscape as Architecture. Identity and Conservation of Crapolla Cultural Site*. Firenze: Nardini Editore.

Martini, S., Pesce, G., and De Franchi, R., eds. 2004. *Manuale per la costruzione dei muri a secco. Linee guida per la manutenzione dei terrazzamenti delle Cinque Terre*. La Spezia: Tipografia Ambrosiana.

Parco Nazionale delle Cinque Terre (PNCT). 2014. *Adesione alla Carta Europea per il Turismo Sostenibile nelle Aree Protette. Strategia e Piano di Azione. Ministero dell'Ambiente e della tutela del territorio e del mare*. Federparchi – Federazione Italiana Parchi e Riserve Naturali.

Parco Nazionale delle Cinque Terre (PNCT). 2018a. *Gara a procedura aperta per la redazione degli strumenti di pianificazione del Parco Nazionale delle Cinque Terre. Bando di Gara*.

Parco Nazionale delle Cinque Terre (PNCT). 2018b. *Gara a procedura aperta per la redazione degli strumenti di pianificazione del Parco Nazionale delle Cinque Terre. Capitolato Speciale d'Appalto*.

Parco Nazionale delle Cinque Terre (PNCT). 2019. *Piano della Performance*.

Puglisi, G. 2012. "Il valore del brand UNESCO." *Siti patrimonio italiano UNESCO* 8: 8–12.

Tizzoni, E. 2014. "Paesaggio e sviluppo turistico nelle Cinque Terre: il ruolo della viticoltura." *Territoires du vin* 6.

UNEP & UNWTO. 2005. *Making Tourism More Sustainable – A Guide for Policy Makers*.

UNESCO ICH. 2018. *Art of Dry Stone Walling, Knowledge and Techniques. Croatia, Cyprus, France, Greece, Italy, Slovenia, Spain and Switzerland. Decision: 13.COM 10.b.10*.

UNESCO WHC. 1997. *Inscription on the World Heritage List. Portovenere, Cinque Terre, and the Islands (Palmaria, Tino and Tinetto) (Italy). Decision code: CONF 208 VIII.C.*

UNESCO WHC. 2006. *State of Conservation of World Heritage Properties. Portovenere, Cinque Terre, and the Islands (Palmaria, Tino and Tinetto) (Italy). Periodic report: PR-C1-S2–826.*

UNESCO WHC. 2012a. *State of Conservation of World Heritage Properties. Portovenere, Cinque Terre, and the Islands (Palmaria, Tino and Tinetto) (Italy) (C826). Decision: 36 COM 7B.77.*

UNESCO WHC. 2012b. *Report on the Joint WHC–ICOMOS Advisory Mission to Portovenere, Cinque Terre, and the Islands (Palmaria, Tino and Tinetto) (Italy). 8–12 October 2012.*

UNESCO WHC. 2013. *State of Conservation of World Heritage Properties. Portovenere, Cinque Terre, and the Islands (Palmaria, Tino and Tinetto) (Italy). Decision: 37 COM 7B.78.*

Verbas, C. 1978. "Le Cinque Terre." *Studi e ricerche di geografia* 1: 17–114.

9 Inter-generational concepts of sustainability and the role of children in local tourism destinations

Mladen Knežević, Tony O'Rourke,
Tina Šegota and Marko Koščak

Summary

The concept of sustainable tourism is more than a piecemeal policy solution which Agyeman and Evans (2004) described as "just sustainability"; it indicates above all the concept of holistic development and finding such solutions that solve the integrity of the human problems. Therefore, the current generation that is undertaking the governance of tourism and sustainability (Bramwell and Lane, 2011) should be aware that, at this moment, there is a generation of young people that seeks to feel and see the impact of sustainability in their lives. Young people's views on tourism are very often neglected, making the sustainability concept incomplete. However, at the end of the day, these young people will be part of the community that will live and work in the tourism sector in the future. Hence, in this chapter, we focused on young people to explore their role in a tourism community and how they engage in a participatory way in the planning of their tourism environment. In our study, we have demonstrated that young people are not only 'residents' in tourist areas, towns and villages, but participants in events in these areas and careful observers of the environment around them.

Links

The following Case Study links may be of interest to readers of this chapter:

- Case Studies Part A (Destination management aspects of ethical sustainable development) – Chapters 16 and 17
- Case Studies Part C (The business impacts of ethical sustainable development) – Chapter 27

Please see the Contents on pages v–viii, and the Guide to the textbook in Appendix 1 for further information.

Review of existing ideas and concepts

By analysing the various approaches to the concept of sustainable tourism, Bill Bramwell and Bernard Lane stressed that, based on the famous Brundtland Report (World Commission on Environment and Development, 1987), which is considered as a source of ideas on sustainable tourism, it can be defined "as tourism that meets the needs of present generations without compromising the ability of future generations to meet their own needs" (Bramwell and Lane, 2011: 413). This certainly does not refer only to the future generations that will live in our areas for 500 years or more; future generations are our children who live here now and in the future and therefore will have to endure the consequences of our environmental management. This was the initial thought in the thinking of researchers who participated in this study. If the fundamental rationale of the concept of sustainability is "without compromising the ability of future generations to meet their own needs," then it is logical to conclude that for these future generations someone has to ask about the development of tourism in the places in which they live and where they will probably continue to live.

The first of the four basic principles for the concept of sustainability for many authors is a principle of holistic planning and strategy-making (Lu and Nepal, 2009: 5). The concept of holistic planning includes the principle of participatory planning; participatory planning is one of the most important elements and a key approach of tourism development if one wishes to satisfy the requirements of the modern paradigm of sustainability and responsibility in tourism. Furthermore, a community-based approach to tourism development with the involvement of a broad number of stakeholders is a prerequisite to sustainability. Inclusion of the widest possible range of stakeholders in tourism development, based on the concept of sustainability, requires the local community to adopt fundamental principles that are derived from the theory of social learning (Wray, 2011). That certainly includes young people who live in a particular destination; specifically, this young generation is in the process of social learning in order to understand elements of sustainability for the future of their local community. Inclusion of this generation in the planning process at the local level implies a departure from the traditional "top-down" approaches and requires the inclusion of needs of a broader community (Wray, 2011). This of course emphasises the sustainable future of tourism in certain destinations. Maximising benefits to local residents typically results in tourism being better accepted by them and their active support in the conservation of local resources (Inskeep, 1994). This collective planning for the tourism industry, at the same time, is a significant step in the advancement of education of young people and their sensitising to community life (Iorioa and Corsale, 2014).

Participation may only be guaranteed if decision-making processes are fully transparent. Logistic, technical and financial support and the means of communication should be made available to ensure the participation of all those possibly affected. This applies especially to disadvantaged population groups. In order to ensure a comprehensive, prior-informed and active equal participation of all stakeholders in tourism, the flow of information, education and communication must be improved. The relevant authorities and the tourism industry in particular are requested to support this process at international and local levels (FernWeh, 2002).

Planning for sustainable tourism development is an effort to shape the future. The younger generation, who clearly have the largest stake in the future, should therefore have the right to participate in planning sustainable tourism development. Adult attitudes towards place reflect immediate (largely short term) concerns and motivations; children's perceptions of place are free from adult concerns. In this regard, children are much more objective in their assessment of what matters. Furthermore, adults' perceptions and evaluations of place are dependent on their instrumental evaluation of place; place is frequently a commodity, a resource to be exploited. For children, place represents an inherent value in itself. Thus, favourite places are often those that are remembered from childhood, and this explains why children ought to have a voice in the planning of tourism destination, in pursuit of a sustainable and responsible long-term life (Sancar, 2005).

Youth in tourism

Unfortunately, there is little or no theoretical and empirical literature that considers the voices of the younger generation in the planning and development of tourism. Little has changed since Graburn's (1983) observation, almost 35 years ago, of the absence of children in the tourism literature. Research which discusses children as tourists has primarily focused on children's influence on parental decision making (Filiatrault and Ritchie, 1980; Fodness, 1992; Seaton and Tagg, 1994; Wang et al., 2004) and children's influence on adult tourists' experiences (Johns and Gyimothy, 2002; Salma, 2001; Thompson et al., 1996). With few exceptions, the studies of children have been from an adult perspective, though some writers have recognised the importance of children as a market segment (Cullingford, 1995; Ryan, 1992; Swarbrooke and Horner, 1999). For instance, Connell (2005) refers to the phenomenon of "toddler tourism," which emerged in the United Kingdom stimulated by the British TV program, *Balamory*, set on the Isle of Mull in Scotland.

It is only in the last two decades that researchers have begun to examine how children experience holidays. Cullingford (1995), in a study of attitudes towards overseas holidays of British children, aged 7–11 years, found that children had clear ideas of which countries were attractive as holiday destinations. It was the developed world which was most desirable; in other words, that which was culturally familiar. The author found, for most of the children in the study, that travel meant beaches, good weather and eating out rather than cultural sightseeing. He explained that "for the most part, children are confined to their clearly demarcated 'holiday' and while they enjoy the entertainment of a beach holiday with friends, they are also aware of the differences in being abroad" (p. 125).

The dramatic influx of visitors to destinations and the reconstruction of destinations to appeal to children highlight the role of the child in today's holidaying family. However, the value of researching children goes beyond the commercial incentive. Graburn (1983) and Cullingford (1995) have called for research that enquires more broadly about perceptions children have of other countries and peoples and the impact childhood experiences have on their later adult holidays.

Almost 30 years ago, Graburn (1983) pointed out the importance of studying the impact of tourism on the life cycle of the individual, the formation of "identity and aspirations" and the development of "attitudes toward other peoples and places in the world" (1983, p. 2). He also called upon tourism researchers to begin to study the impact of tourism on children. Substantially lacking are studies of the effects of tourism on the historical, natural and geographical awareness of growing children.

The importance of including the traditionally excluded voices of children and youth in the planning of public spaces is also an issue articulated in the literature. For example, Parnell and Patsarika's (2011) work focuses on children's contributions to the planning of school-related spaces, while Laughlin and Johnson's (2011) work deals with the role of youth in informing decisions related to housing developments (Laughlin and Johnson, 2011). Very few researchers have studied how children in destination areas perceive tourists.

According to Gamradt (1995), tourism affects the lives of children particularly if one or more of their relatives and/or acquaintances are employed in the industry: "[S]uch children will have acquired knowledge of, and may even have formed strong opinions about tourists and the tourism industry" (p. 735). The aforementioned extant studies offer a strong foundation on which to understand the life worlds of children within host communities located in tourism destinations. However, except for a few studies, such as that of Buzinde and Manuel-Navarrete's (2013) exploring Mayan children's perceptions of boundaries caused by tourism enclaves, and that of Gamradt's (1995) with Jamaican children, analyses of children's perceptions of their surrounding landscapes, particularly those zoned in favour of tourism at the expense of locals, have been under-examined.

There are several possible factors that might help explain the deficiency of research on children and tourism. First, research with children demands special expertise (Measelle et al., 1998). As far as implementing the research is concerned, interviews and surveys with children must be conducted by researchers who are familiar with specific techniques (e.g., doll-play, storytelling and pictorial questions) and procedures (e.g., the Berkeley Puppet Interview) used for investigating children at various developmental stages.

Furthermore, in many countries, scholars who wish to involve children in their studies need permission not only from parents but also from government agencies and ethics committees inside and outside the university. An additional factor that hinders scholars from studying children is the state of the current body of tourism knowledge and unfamiliarity with theories needed to conceptualise children's behaviour. Most lines of thinking in tourism studies are based on the assumption that tourists are free agents who can choose from a wide range of travel options, many of which form an escape from daily routines and social obligations (Obrador, 2012).

The development of the child and her/his understanding of the world around them takes place in constant interaction with the environment. One of the most important interactions is certainly their interaction with their parents. So parental views on the environment are passed on to their children, either through explicit or through implicit attitudes. Both of these attitudes are recognised and adopted in their own way by children in the socialisation process (Holden and Hawk 2003). Implicit attitudes are those that are activated automatically, and parents are rarely aware that they express them. Implicit attitudes are mainly forms of traditional parenting rooted in family traditions. Parents have difficulty recognising such in their relations with children (Holden and Hawk, 2003). Explicit attitudes are also apparent through parental reflection and analysis in the process of interaction with their child (Holden and Hawk, 2003). The attitudes expressed by parents towards tourists are often implicit. Parents are often unaware of the content of these attitudes. These attitudes are often coloured by prejudices and stereotypes, and this gives them a special significance in the process of interaction with children. In the process of growing up, children are very attentive listeners, and they recognise the views of their parents. Although the adoption of parental attitudes is not automatic and also draws on children's own experiences, parents' attitudes have a strong influence on the development of children's views.

Thus, the parallel study, which the authors have been engaged in, explored the perceptions of the 11-to-12-year-old children of tourists, hosts and their parents' opinion of tourists, taking into account the stages and development of the tourist destinations and whether the children's parents or relatives were employed in the tourism industry. Children are very careful observers of the attitudes of their parents, though even from an early age, it is not always certain whether they will agree with those attitudes. Ozturk et al. (2013) examined how children view their parents' attitude towards smoking and found that they can clearly distinguish between positive and negative attitudes. Exploring how children see the racial attitudes of their parents, Castelli et al. (2007) observed that parents of white children prefer their children to play with whites. This research shows that children very closely monitor the attitudes of their parents. This has led us, in our study, to examine how children view their parent's attitudes towards tourists.

A traditional theme often explored in terms of the attitudes of the host population to tourists is prejudice. As is well known, prejudices are a phenomenon which occurs relatively early in human development (Raabe and Beelmann, 2011, p. 1715). Prejudices are not just a simple ratio of intolerance towards others who are different; they are very complex categories which depend on a complex interaction between sociocontextual and sociocognitive variables (Raabe and Beelmann, 2011, p. 1717). Therefore, it is necessary that the various dimensions of tourism appearance, shape and development are explored.

Over-tourism and the importance of participatory planning

When discussing the problems of over-tourism in many tourism destinations across Europe and globally, this is concerned with not only what may be perceived as a realistic number of tourists on some destinations, but also the perception of the local population regarding that level of tourism input. In effect, over-tourism occurs when there are too many visitors to a particular destination. "Too many" is of course a subjective term, but it may be defined in each destination by local residents (amongst whom are children and youth), hosts, business owners and tourists. One is too much if he/she is too much. And if this perception is then passed on to children, then a very uncertain fate will impact on the dimensions of tourism activity. When rent prices push out local tenants to make way for holiday rentals, that is over-tourism. When narrow roads become jammed with tourist vehicles, that is over-tourism. When wildlife is scared away, when tourists cannot view landmarks because of the crowds, when fragile environments become degraded – these are all signs of over-tourism.

Over-tourism is, therefore, not a new problem (Francis, n.d.). However, while the term itself was coined in 2012, it did not hit the headlines until the summer of 2017. This was not because of the increase in tourist numbers, which had not been particularly dramatic. What made the news in 2017 was the sudden backlash from local residents, a phenomenon which had not occurred previously before on any significant scale. There had been a slow drip feed of tourism into cities, such as Barcelona, Venice and Dubrovnik, into places one thought of as remote such as Iceland and Skye, and finally, as the balance tipped and this new concept was given a name, the protests spread. There were marches in the streets, graffiti saying "Tourist go home" (Coldwell, 2017), and in some cases local authorities responded by increasing fees, refusing to issue permits for more tourist-focused businesses in city centres, and even closing entire islands to visitors (McKinsey and Company and WTTC, 2017). It was these responses which made the news.

Problems of over-tourism occur when there is no application of a correct process of participatory planning. Primarily, an important element to avoid the problem of over-tourism is to study the impacts of tourism upon host communities, as well as upon host cultures. "Culture" (Tylor, 1871) was defined as "culture or civilisation, taken in its wide ethnographic sense, is that complex whole which includes knowledge beliefs, arts, morals, law, customs, and any other capabilities and habits acquired by man as a member of society." Malinowski (1931) gave a more universal and less anthropocentric definition, namely, "a culture is functioning, active, efficient, well-organised unity, which must be analysed into component institutions in relation to one another, and in relation to the environment, man-made as well as natural." In a report on Wales, Jones and Travis (1983) defined culture as "the system of values, beliefs, behaviours, morals, and other social phenomena shared by a group of people, based on their common experience of life, language and history." This testifies to tourism not simply being an economic branch, but it is also, amongst others, a culture in the wider contextual sense. It is a culture that is transmitted inter-generationally, as indeed the wider concept of culture is transmitted. Efforts to address the complex linkages between culture and development require, on the one hand, promoting the inclusion of minorities and disadvantaged groups in social, political and cultural life and, on the other hand, harnessing the potential of the creative sector for job creation, economic growth and poverty reduction efforts more broadly. The inclusion of minorities and disadvantaged groups in social, political and cultural life remains an ongoing development priority. Tourism can play a great role in achieving all of this, due to its character as a horizontal sector with a value chain that goes across almost every existing economic, human or cultural activity in each place. Compared with other economic activities, the special relationship of tourism with the environment and society makes it an ideal tool for sustainable development. This is due to its unique dependency on quality environments, cultural distinctiveness and social interaction, security and wellbeing. On the one hand, if poorly planned or developed to excess, tourism may destroy those special qualities which have such a central relationship to sustainable development. On the other, it may be a driving force for their conservation and promotion – directly through the raising of awareness and income to support them and indirectly by providing an economic justification for the provision of such support by others.

In order to ensure sustainable tourism development and avoid problems of over-tourism, *all voices* need to be heard (Byrd, 2007; Šegota et al., 2017). In line with that, sustainable tourism development has to include a carrying capacity study, that is, an estimate of "the maximum number of people who can use a site without an unacceptable alteration in the physical environment and without an unacceptable decline in the quality of the experience" (Mathieson and Wall, 1982) to both visitors and residents. The factors that need to be considered are (1) physical impact of tourists, (2) ecological impact of tourists, (3) perceptions of overcrowding, and (4) cultural and social impact on local residents. The carrying capacity study is central to meeting the objectives of sustainable tourism development (Koščak, 2002), which is to ensure that the tourists and day visitors attracted to the particular destination will not have a deleterious impact on the cultural or natural sites, that overcrowding will not result in visitor dissatisfaction and that local people will not feel antagonistic towards their "guests." This is essential if tourism is to contribute to the conservation of cultural and natural heritage though the realisation of economic value and raising awareness of, and commitment to, the local patrimony.

Parallel research

We have already referred to the parallel and as yet unpublished research which the authors and some colleagues have been engaged in involving young people aged 11–13, who were attending school and lived in tourist-intensive cities. This research initially focused on four Slovenian tourism destinations (Brežice, Lucija, Piran, Trebnje), although subsequent research is currently expanding quite significantly to include a large number of other European destinations, but is still in progress.

However, the initial research has some important resonance in looking at the concept of sustainability and the importance of children in tourism destinations in Slovenia. This initial research (Knežević et al., 2016) found that children from the least-developed tourist area – the town of Trebnje – had a more positive assessment of tourists. Slightly less positive, albeit with positive ratings, were the assessments given by children from Brežice, the city in which tourism is not developed but which has a large spa complex outside the town. Children from the most developed Slovenian tourist destinations of Lucija and Piran, with large hotel complexes, assessed tourists least positively. The differences were statistically significant when compared by location.

What was very interesting to the researchers were the differences when analysing individual locations. Children in tourism centres without a significant tourist industry (Brežice and Trebnje) had a higher assessment of the role of tourists, whilst children in those tourist areas with the most intense touristic activity (Lucija and Pirana) evaluated tourists in a more negative perspective.

This view of tourists should be interpreted in the context of the nature of individual destinations. Lucija and Piran are coastal destinations for summer vacations on the beaches – sun, sea, sand – with a large proportion of tourists coming from Germany and Austria and, to a degree, Switzerland and Hungary. Children will perceive tourists as persons who lay on the beach and do not move around very much. This perception appears to be enhanced, in those destinations, by what the children hear from their parents, who evaluate the nature of tourist activity somewhat more negatively than children do. On the other hand, children in centres such as Brežice and Trebnje, where tourism is focused on health, wellness, activity and a strong engagement with local culture, have an entirely different perspective. Clearly this research is work in progress and is being developed to cover a greater number of international tourism destinations.

Results

However, this research indicates that young people have very clearly defined attitudes towards tourists coming to the destinations in which they live. Hence, young people's views are of extreme importance for tourism destination planners and managers since tourists are constantly entering into young people's living space. The simplified answer, that tourism is an economic activity that allows young people an orderly life, is clearly not a sufficient answer in terms of neglecting the views of young people and their attitudes towards tourism. Since young people are obviously part of what is called a tourist destination, it is imperative for them to be consulted on tourism development in the community. Otherwise, as seen in this study, young people carry negative biases onto the next generation, because prejudice, as it is well known, is transferred inter-generationally.

At this stage, we may introduce the concept that tourism activity may be regarded as either tangible or intangible. To a degree, we are impelled to recognise this when measuring the response of children to the tourism environment. Mass tourism – as located in seaside resorts of which Piran and Lucija are prime examples – is very tangible in the physical aspect of buildings (hotels, guest houses and related tourism facilities) as well as in the overwhelming level of impact tourism has on the socio-economic environment. It is also tangible in the organisation and deployment of tourists; they will tend to arrive in groups, they will make visits in groups and they will conduct social activities in groups. They are thus a tangible and demonstrable feature. Sustainable tourism – whether cultural, heritage or environmental – will tend to have a far lower profile. Groups will be of a far lower size, and many sustainable tourists will come as individuals or as couples. Carrying capacity of sustainable and heritage tourism sites also tends to downsize the number of visitor groups. In this sense, sustainable tourism is far less tangible and far less evident. However, we do not as yet have physical evidence (e.g. tourism spend per capita) as to the extent to which Large Scale tourism activity spends less or more than sustainable tourists or of the socio-economic variances between these two contrasting forms of tourism activity. This should undoubtedly provide a further topic of investigation and research.

Limitations

There are two significant limitations to this chapter and the research behind it. The first is cultural; the study was conducted in the Slovenian cultural environment. In this case, while it is only relatively applicable to other European cultures, we can still talk about the possibilities of its application in non-European conditions. Gamradt (1995), in his research with children in Jamaica, showed a very positive attitude towards "visitors" to Jamaica. To be able to generalise the results, the study should be repeated in other cultures.

A second limitation is that children in areas where tourism has a low profile (albeit not a necessarily low economic input) may tend to have little relationship with tourists unless their family is directly engaged in some tourism activity (e.g. agro-tourism). Children in areas where tourism has a high level of intensity will have a strong relationship to tourism – albeit positive or negative. This tends to highlight one of the dilemmas of sustainable tourism; it seeks to exploit the fact that sustainable destinations are "off the beaten track" but at the same time tries to promote sustainable destinations to increase inflows and revenues. The tipping point between profitability and sustainability is very difficult to judge and to reach a balance. Whilst sustainable tourism has a low profile, its environmental impact is low, but its socio-economic impact from evidential tourism economic inputs is low. If the profile is made greater, the socio-economic impact will increase, but the potential environmental damage may also increase. We may envisage that this an issue affecting children in sustainable tourism areas – may they see tourists as an advantage (income, economic development) or a threat (destruction of the environmental, cultural and heritage environment)?

A third limitation is related to the locations where the research was conducted. These are all small towns due to the nature of tourist activities in Slovenia, which mainly relate to small towns. It is quite possible that in a larger city, results would be different; this compels future research to be extended to different cultural environments, as well as to larger cities.

This survey explored children's attitudes towards tourists at one point in time. Our subjects were children who were 11–12 years of age. In further investigations, it would be competent to see how these concepts change over time as they grow up, such as, for example, in later adolescence and early adulthood. We would then obtain better answers about relations between the local populations and their visitors.

Conclusions

Primarily we are of the view that what is most important in this chapter is demonstrating the view that children are not only "residents" in tourist areas, towns and villages, but also participants in events in these areas and careful observers of the events around them.

However, in spite of all the research conducted on tourism, no one – it appears – has ever asked children and young adults their views about tourism and the impact tourism may have on their lives and their future.

There is almost no evidence that young people are invited and asked about their views on destination development plans in the participatory planning process. This study showed that the mere presence of tourists is an important socialisation factor in the development of young people. They observe and listen to what their parents say and how they behave towards tourists. They see how their parents treat tourists. Perceptions that they see in their parents and their own experiences with tourists define their "social competence." Many analyses of the workforce employed in hospitality and tourism have shown that young people are reluctant to enter professions in tourism and hospitality. Many authors emphasise that there is a very high turnover of staff in the tourism industry. One result of this research shows that young people in tourism-intensive areas are internalising the relatively negative perception of tourists that their parents have. Therein lays one of the important problem factors with labour that is found in the tourism and hospitality industry. Some tourist destinations are facing serious problems in lack of professional and educated staff, such as chefs or waiters. They face a serious problem since less and less young people wish to work in the tourism industry. Therefore, it is mistaken to neglect young people's views and attitudes towards tourists, because these are the basis for the future development of tourism activities.

We would also suggest that there is significant value in adding a subjective view, to overlay the research conducted to date. This is to introduce the concept that tourism activity may be regarded as either tangible or intangible, and to a degree, we must recognise this when measuring the response of children to the tourism environment. Mass tourism, such as that located in seaside resorts of which Piran and Lucija are prime examples, is very tangible. It is tangible in the physical aspect of buildings – hotels, guest houses and related tourism facilities – as well as in the overwhelming level of impact tourism has on the socio-economic environment. It is also tangible in the organisation and deployment of tourists; they will tend to arrive in groups, they will make visits in groups and they will conduct social activities in groups. They are thus a tangible and demonstrable feature.

Sustainable tourism – whether cultural, heritage or environmental – will tend to have a far lower profile. Groups will be of a far lower size, and many sustainable tourists will come as individuals or as couples. Effective carrying capacity policies for sustainable and heritage tourism sites will tend to depress or cap the size and volume of visitor groups. In this sense, sustainable tourism is far less tangible and far less evident, simply because it is not predicated by the volume of numbers who visit but by the intangible socio-economic inputs on the host communities. However, we do not as yet have physical evidence (tourism spend per capita) as to the extent to which larger-scale tourists spend less or more than sustainable tourists. This is an area which requires to be developed and investigated.

We may also suggest that a critical theme is to move away from the concept of viewing tourism destinations purely in economic and financial capacity terms. This includes valuing outputs in relation to what are frequently intangible financial markets or inputs categorised solely in relation to consumer choices. Sustainable tourism, by its ethical basis, attracts those who to a degree reject consumerism and the commoditisation of tourism products. Thus, to engage and incorporate that tourism base, we require to employ parallel concepts which have a strong and vibrant relationship to ethical/sustainable tourism issues. These are developments which are based on the cultural heritage and that seek to protect and preserve often fragile environments (physical, historical and cultural) within the sensitive rural/urban location. This concerns tracking and determining carrying capacity as well as analysing the point at which levels of tourism activity may commit serious damage to that fragile environment. This has a profound impact on children, as it is their future (and the future of their own children) which we are often failing to assess and comprehend.

Reflections

Young people's views on tourism are very often neglected, making the sustainability concept incomplete. However, at the end of the day, these young people will be part of the community that will live and work in tourism sector in the future. Young people are not only "residents" in tourist areas, towns and villages, but also participants in events in these areas and careful observers of the environment around them. They should have a voice in the planning of tourism development in their destinations which should be heard.

Among the complexities of co-researching with children and young people, entering the field and engaging young people in the participatory process was probably one of the most challenging aspects. Young people were intentionally not approached through schools given complexities around adult–child power relations.

We urgently need to access the views of children and young people living in host communities and involved in the tourism industry through, for example, child labour, sexual exploitation and orphanage tourism. These are all neglected areas in tourism research which may, in turn, challenge and expand current theorising within the sociology of childhood.

Some tourist destinations are facing serious problems in lack of professional and educated staff, such as chefs or waiters. They face a serious problem since less and less young people wish to work in the tourism industry. Therefore, it is mistaken to neglect young people's views and attitudes towards tourists, because these are the basis for the future development of tourism activities.

Questions

1   Stakeholders in tourist destinations should be aware that, at this moment, there is a generation of young people that seeks to feel and see the impact of sustainability in their lives. Therefore how should we ensure that the voice of young generations is heard and respected in the participatory planning process?

2   If the United Nations Convention on the Rights of the Child (UNCRC – United Nations, 1989) has drawn international attention to children's rights in relation to not only their protection from harm, provision of care and resources, but also their participation in matters that affect them, such as research about their lives, what are the reasons are that this is not respected as it should be the case?

3   How should we overcome probably the "biggest barrier to children's participation, which is the need in every case for an adult to consent to their participation" in research or an interview?

4   What are the other reasons why children and young people have been an "under-researched" and "under-valued" field of enquiry in Tourism Studies. Almost 20 years after this initial situation, recent studies continue to acknowledge the absence of children in the tourism literature?

5   May we say that problems of over-tourism occur when there is no application of a correct process of participatory planning including neglected voices of the younger generation?

Further reading

Canosa, A., Moyle, B., & Wray, M. (2016). Can anybody hear me? A critical analysis of young residents' voices in tourism studies. *Tourism Analysis: An Interdisciplinary Journal, 21*(2), 325–337.

Canosa, A., Wilson, E., & Graham, A. (2016). Empowering young people through participatory film: A postmethodological approach. *Current Issues in Tourism*, 1–14. doi:10.1080/1 3683500.2016.1179270.

Coldwell, W. (2017). First Venice and Barcelona: Now anti-tourism marches spread across Europe, *The Guardian*. Available at: www.theguardian.com/travel/2017/aug/10/anti-tourism-marches-spread-across-europe-venice-barcelona (Accessed: 10 March 2018).

Francis, J. (n.d.). *Overtourism – What is it, and how can we avoid it?* Available at: www.responsibletravel.com/copy/what-is-overtourism (Accessed: 15 May 2018).

Kellett, M. (2010). Small shoes, big steps! Empowering children as active researchers. *American Journal of Community Psychology, 46*(1 and 2), 195–203.

Khoo-Lattimore, C. (2015). Kids on board: Methodological challenges, concerns and clarifications when including young children's voices in tourism research. *Current Issues in Tourism, 18*(9), 845–858.

References

Agyeman, J., & Evans, B. (2004). 'Just sustainability': The emerging discourse of environmental justice in Britain? *The Geographical Journal, 170*(2), 155–164.

Byrd, E.T. (2007). Stakeholders in sustainable tourism development and their roles: Applying stakeholder theory to sustainable tourism development. *Tourism Review, 62*(2), 6–13.

Buzinde, C.N., & Manuel-Navarrete, D. (2013). The social production of space in tourism enclaves: Mayan children's perceptions of tourism boundaries. *Annals of Tourism Research, 43*, 482–505.

Bramwell, B., & Lane, B. (2011). Editorial: Critical research on the governance of tourism and sustainability. *Journal of Sustainable Tourism, 19*(4–5): 411–421.

Castelli, L., Carraro, L., Tomelleri, S., & Amari, A. (2007). White children's alignment to the perceived racial attitudes of the parents: Closer to the mother than the father. *British Journal of Developmental Psychology, 25*(3), 353–357.

Coldwell, W. (2017). First Venice and Barcelona: now anti-tourism marches spread across Europe, *The Guardian*. Available at: www.theguardian.com/travel/2017/aug/10/anti-tourism-marches-spread-across-europe-venice-barcelona (Accessed: 10 March 2018).

Connell, J. (2005). Toddlers, tourism and Tobermoray: Destination marketing issues and television-induced tourism. *Tourism Management, 26*(5), 763–776.

Cullingford, C. (1995). Children's attitudes to holidays overseas. *Tourism Management, 16*(2), 121–127.

FernWeh, (2002). *Tourism Review – Working Group on Tourism & Development, Rio: Ten years on – Red card for tourism?*

Filiatrault, P., & Ritchie, J.R.B. (1980). Joint purchasing decisions: A comparison of influence structure in family and couple decision-making units. *Journal of Consumer Research, 7*(2), 131–140.

Fodness, D. (1992). The impact of family life cycle on the vacation decision-making process. *Journal of Travel Research, 31*(2), 8–13.

Francis, J. (n.d.). *Overtourism – What is it, and how can we avoid it?* Available at: www.responsibletravel.com/copy/what-is-overtourism (Accessed: 15 May 2018).

Gamradt, J. (1995). Jamaican children's representations of tourism. *Annals of Tourism Research, 22*(4), 735–762.

Graburn, N. (1983). Editor's page. *Annals of Tourism Research, 10*(1), 3–5.

Holden, G.W., & Hawk, C.K. (2003). Meta-parenting in the journey of child rearing: A cognitive mechanisms for change. In L. Kuczynski (Ed.), *Handbook of dynamics in parent-child relations*. Thousand Oaks: Sage Publications INC.

Inskeep, E. (1994). *National and regional tourism planning*. London: Routledge, 8.

Iorioa, M., & Corsale, A. (2014). Community-based tourism and networking: Viscri, Romania. *Journal of Sustainable Tourism, 22*(2), 234–255.

Johns, N., & Gyimothy, S. (2002). Mythologies of a theme park: An icon of modern family life. *Journal of Vacation Marketing, 8*(4), 320–331.

Jones, A., & Travis, A. (1983). *Cultural Tourism: Toward a European Charter: Report to WTB*. Birmingham, UK: EW Tourism Consultancy.

Koščak, M. (2002). Heritage Trails: Rural regeneration through sustainable tourism in Dolenjska and Bela Krajina. *Rast, XIII*, 2(80), 204–211.

Knežević, M., Koščak, M., & O'Rourke, T. (2016). *No one asks the children, right?* [unpublished paper].

Laughlin, D. L., & Johnson, L. C. (2011). Defining and exploring public space: Perspective of young people from Regent's Park. *Children's Geographies, 9*(3/4), 439–456.

Lu, J., & Nepal, S.K. (2009). Sustainable tourism research: an analysis of papers published in the Journal of Sustainable Tourism. *Journal of Sustainable Tourism, 17*(1), 5–16.

Malinowski, B. (1931). Culture. In E.R. Andreson Seligman & A. Saunders Johnson (Eds.), *Encyclopedia of the Social Sciences* (pp. 621–645). New York: Macmillan.

Measelle, J. R., Ablow, J. C., Cowan, P. A., & Cowan, C. P. (1998). Assessing young children's views of their academic, social and emotional lives: An evaluation of the self-perception scales on the Berkeley puppet interview. *Child Development, 69*(6), 1556–1576.

Mathieson, A., & Wall. G. (1982). *Tourism: Economic, Physical and Social Impacts*. Essex, UK: Longman.

McKinsey & Company & WTTC. (2017). *Coping with success: Managing overcrowding in tourism destinations*. WTTC. Available at: www.wttc.org/priorities/sustainable-growth/destination-stewardship/.

Obrador, P. (2012). The place of the family in tourism research: Domesticity and thick sociality by the pool. *Annals of Tourism Research, 39*(1), 401–420.

Ozturk, C., Kahraman, S., & Bektas, M. (2013). Effects of perceived parental attitudes on children's views of smoking. *Asian Pacific Journal of Cancer Prevention, 14*(4), 2615–2624.

Parnell, R., & Patsarika, M. (2011). Young people's participation in school design: Exploring diversity and power in a UK governmental policy case-study. *Children's Geographies, 9*(3/4), 457–475.

Raabe, T., & Beelmann, A. (2011). Development of ethnic, racial, and national prejudice in childhood and adolescence: A multinational meta-analysis of age differences. *Child Development, 82*(6), 1715–1737.

Ryan, C. (1992). The child as visitor. *World Travel and Tourism Review, 2*, 135–139.

Salma, U. (2001). Kids call the shots: How Aussie children affect travel. *BTR Tourism Research Report, 3*, 43–49.

Sancar, F. (2005). *Participatory Learning and Action: Children Voices in Municipal Planning*. Boulder: Department of Planning and Design College of Architecture and Planning, University of Colorado, 27–36.

Seaton, A.V., & Tagg, S. (1994). How different are Scottish family holidays from English? In A. Seaton (Ed.), *Tourism: The state of the art* (pp. 540–548). Chichester: John Wiley & Sons.

Swarbrooke, J., & Horner, S. (1999). *Consumer behaviour in tourism*. Oxford: Butterworth-Heinemann.

Šegota, T., Mihalič, T., & Kuščer, K. (2017). The impact of residents' informedness and involvement on perceptions of tourism impacts: The case of the destination Bled. *Journal of Destination Marketing and Management, 6*(3), 196–206.

Thompson, W.N., Pinney, J. K., & Schibrowsky, J. A. (1996). The family that gambles together: Business and social concerns. *Journal of Travel Research, 34*(3), 70–74.

Tylor, E. B. (1871). *Primitive Culture: Researches into the Development Mythology*. New York: Harper Collins.

Wang, K., Hsieh, A., Yeh, Y., & Tsai, C. (2004). Who is the decision-maker: The parents or the child in package group tours? *Tourism Management, 25*(2), 183–194.

World Commission on Environment and Development (1987). *Our Common Future*. New York: United Nations.

Wray, M. (2011). Adopting and implementing a transactive approach to sustainable tourism planning: Translating theory into practice. *Journal of Sustainable Tourism, 19*(4–5), 605–627.

Part C

The business impacts of ethical sustainable development

10 Micro-financing a sustainable, ethical, local project

Andrew Donaldson

Introduction

Comrie Croft is an award-winning 93 ha ecofarm in the southern edge of the Scottish Highlands. Formerly a traditional agricultural holding, by the early 1990s, changes in farming meant it was no longer economically viable. Now a wide range of synergistic activities and micro-enterprises are established onsite including a barn wedding venue; visitor accommodation; camping and glamping; mountain bike trails and bike shop; a fruit, vegetable and flower market garden; a café; a farm shop; a tea leaf growing and processing facility and an event hire business. Ultimately, the vision for Comrie Croft is to pioneer a form of holistic, regenerative enterprise where visitors, employees, owners, local people and the natural environment all benefit through collaborative enterprise including ecotourism.

The desire of Comrie Croft is to see life and the abundance and beauty of nature flourish in rural areas. That includes human repopulation, together with increased biodiversity and quality of life. This chapter is written from the very unique perspective of the author, who has a strong and immense capacity to weave together concepts, theories and real applicable practice in the creation of this project.

Links

The following Case Study links may be of interest to readers of this chapter:

- Case Studies Part B (Environmental & social aspects of ethical sustainable development) – Chapters 20–22
- Case Studies Part C (The business impacts of ethical sustainable development) – Chapters 25–28

Please see the Contents on pages v–viii, and the Guide to the textbook in Appendix 1 for further information.

Background to the development

The way Comrie Croft came about is part of the author's story, and this is wholly relevant and extremely important in creating a strong and direct link between theory and practice in this chapter. As a student of Countryside and Environmental Management in Scotland in the 1990s, the author was excited by the ecoenterprise potential of rural areas. But the reality of what was happening on the ground was often a different story; he recalls walking where the hills and glens were devoid of wildlife due to overgrazing; where the local school, hotel and shop had closed; where farm buildings lay abandoned and where the remaining local economy and community only survived due to a combination of agricultural subsidies, increasingly industrialised agricultural and forestry systems and the investment of financially endowed landowners in their large private hunting estates.

Global issues such as climate change were also becoming increasingly obvious on the ground. Perhaps part of the solution involved tackling local rural problems that would also be part of the solution to these bigger global problems.

In 1996, the author's summer job included an opportunity to assist in the operation of a new tourist hostel, Braincroft Bunkhouse. The hostel was a first for Strathearn – an area often bypassed by visitors heading for more famous places in the Highlands such as Loch Ness or Skye. Here was a beautiful 200-year-old building that had been rescued from dilapidation (or from being turned into commuter housing) and was now pulling in visitors to stay, spend money and experience the wonderful scenery and outdoor attractions of the area. This led to an academic dissertation examining how the company could use genuine ecotourism to increase business success and achieve positive environmental and social impacts. Then fast-forward 10 years and an intervening career in community-based wildlife conservation in East Africa, after which the author was back to where he had originally been inspired, first as an employee, then forming a new company that leased the premises. Eventually in 2008, together with his wife and brother, the author led a buyout of the entire farm and hostel, by this time renamed "Comrie Croft."

Other pioneer community-led enterprises springing up over the Scottish Highlands, such as the community of Laggan, provided inspiration. The people of Laggan bought their closure threatened village shop in the 1980s and are still the owner-operators today. Perhaps, the thinking at Comrie Croft went, a hybrid family-employee-community-owned structure could be developed. This would recognise the existing private investment in the company, while also opening the opportunity of ownership to the company's employees, local people, family and friends.

The financing model for Comrie Croft

So this is what they did: The author, together with the staff team, jointly developed a comprehensive business plan setting out the vision and action plan for the business. The plan was given to the staff team, friends and family and local people who were known to have some empathy with the vision for the Croft. In many ways, this was a very early example of crowd-funding, but instead of a global online audience, at Comrie Croft, they chose to focus on a selected local audience in order to reduce the risk of knowledge of the impending (off-market) property sale encouraging other (higher) bids. In this respect, the goodwill of the seller must be acknowledged, for he may have been able to secure a higher price on the open market.

The sale of shares in the company (equity) formed approximately one-quarter of the money required to buy the farm. The business plan was also used to raise finance in the form of deferred payment to the landowner of a portion of the property (one-eighth of the total), another gesture of goodwill; a loan from a friend who believed in the project (also one-eighth of the total) and a bank loan (50% of the total property cost) from an ethical bank. Triodos only lends to businesses that benefit people and the environment. The business plan gained credibility because the financial projections were based on the actual trading history of the company to that point. Expectations were set for it to be a relatively safe investment backed by the value of the property, and with a modest financial return in the form of dividends and capital growth, alongside social and environmental achievements.

The only condition on the bank loan was that the company would achieve and maintain the gold standard in the ecotourism certification programme, the Green Tourism Business Scheme. This was achieved shortly after the loan was secured and has been maintained ever since.

Organisational structure

The business and land-holding is held by approximately 50 people in the form of shares in a limited liability company (a private company rather than a publicly listed one). Ownership between overlapping categories is as follows: the founders, their family and friends 82%; employees 51% and the local community 68%. The company has a Board of Directors with a breadth and depth of different knowledge, skills and experience gained in particular from non-executives from other ecotourism businesses. Leadership and operational management is provided by two executive directors. Despite having many of the characteristics of a community body – such as a broad-based local ownership – Comrie Croft is more of a hybrid community-private enterprise: It shares as many governance characteristics with private enterprises as it does with community organisations. Decision-making is consultative and at most times consensual, but ultimately it is not governed by committee; it has an organisation structure with a lead social entrepreneur who has the vision and is mandated with final responsibility and to take decisions decisively and quickly when required.

Several strategic decisions have guided the development of Comrie Croft. Perhaps foremost amongst these is a focus on regeneration over sustainability, the difference being that regeneration is about focusing on stewardship which leaves things in a better state than they started out in. Others define regenerative design as

> processes that restore, renew or revitalize their own sources of energy and materials. Regenerative design uses whole systems thinking to create resilient and equitable systems that integrate the needs of society with the integrity of nature... Whereas the highest aim of sustainable development is to satisfy fundamental human needs today without compromising the possibility of future generations to satisfy theirs, the goal of regenerative design is to develop restorative systems that are dynamic and emergent, and are beneficial for humans and other species.
> (https://en.wikipedia.org/wiki/Regenerative_design)

Goals of a regenerative enterprise in a rural community

One of Comrie Croft's primary goals is to get people outside and connecting with nature and the great outdoors. Within this objective, the business also aims to educate and enthuse people about the challenges and solutions associated with its regenerative mission. This can take many forms from informing people onsite about how Comrie Croft operates – such as the businesses' "smart" energy system with renewable generation and battery power storage – to social media posts encouraging engagement with important environmental and societal issues.

The second important strategic direction taken by Comrie Croft is to be unashamedly for-profit even though the group has a clear and strong environmental and social mission. It was decided from the beginning that the best way to achieve the holistic goals of the organisation (social, community, environmental and commercial) was to make reasonable profits which could be reinvested, rather than being dependent on grants from external funding bodies. The company believes that this enables greater focus on achieving goals than would be achievable under grant funding criteria.

The third strategic decision taken by the Comrie Croft team is to focus on localisation: using the decisions and spending power of the Croft and its visitors to build up and increase the resilience of the local community and environment. One of the most obvious ways that this works in practice is in how the weddings offer has been designed. Couples are encouraged to use trusted local suppliers to provide their catering, photography, flowers, etc., etc. This policy alone pumps an estimated £750,000 annually into the local economy, encouraging existing businesses to invest and new businesses to form.

An example of the emphasis placed on building up local environmental resilience is the investment put into tree planting designed to link woodlands so that the whole length of Strathearn valley has wildlife corridors with woodland cover where before there was a missing link at Comrie Croft.

The final pillar of Comrie Croft's strategic direction is collaboration: identifying and building on synergies between different objectives, activities, and enterprises so that the whole is greater than the sum of the parts. For example, the Croft has established a farm shop serving locally produced food. It is commercially viable because it combines the demand from local people with the demand from visitors. Another example is a waste product from one enterprise – large numbers of cardboard boxes from the bike shop – which are reused within the market garden – as a zero-cost ground cover/mulch to suppress weed growth around fruit trees and bushes. These kinds of collaboration take mutual respect, a positive attitude and plentiful, open communication to make them happen.

The framework of the financing model

The financing model used by Comrie Croft is an interesting form of multi-financing, which blends private equity investment with term loans and a deferred-loan facility (effectively a private bond). A major problem with access to mainstream finance for micro/small enterprises is that in the past the main reliance has been on fixed-term loan or overdraft facilities. Private equity or private bond investment has been a more problematic area as the levels of financing required are often below the cost-effective level (EUR 1m) or the types of enterprises concerned do not have the methodologies which enable them to approach such forms of investment inputs. Blending different financing models, including variations on the crowd-funding equity approach, can make propositions more attractive.

The solution proposed by Comrie Croft as a methodology for financing and sustaining the regenerative development provides a very effective model for other micro/small financing projects in rural, coastal and peripheral locations. Such a model may have a specific application to ethical, responsible and sustainable tourism with an innovative blending of equity funding, crowdfunding, deferred loan and ordinary term-loan financing.

An important issue is that the financing model for Comrie Croft took place within a cohesive community which already had experience of community-driven ethical and sustainable projects. Clearly there was

- a local culture of community development
- an ability among the energetic and highly-focused primary movers of the project to look towards self-reliance and self-sufficiency
- a strong concern towards engagement in ecotourism and regeneration of the local rural community

[*Readers with a particular interest in this area are encouraged to read Chapter 11, "SMART Sustainable Finance," in Section 1, Part C, which includes a proposed model for funding micro/small rural and coastal enterprises which have ethical, environmental and sustainable/regenerative capacities.*]

Achievements and issues

What has been achieved and what has not worked well in the 11 years since the buy-out of Comrie Croft?

- From a financially non-viable farm that had one employee, Comrie Croft now has more than 25 Full-Time Equivalent people working onsite either in the core business or in associated owner-operated businesses. Of these, Comrie Croft Ltd employs a team of 17 Full Time Equivalent staff mostly in year-round, permanent positions. Comrie Croft Ltd is an accredited payer of the voluntary Living Wage which is significantly higher than the UK minimum wage. The ratio between the lowest and the highest pay is just over 1:2.
- The Croft has established a unique selling point that is part friendly informality, part social and environmental credentials and part simply doing things differently. Guest and visitor feedback is overwhelmingly positive with people praising the atmosphere, trust, welcome and other aspects not always associated with commercial enterprises.
- Staff report that jobs at Comrie Croft entail a high degree of autonomy and a feeling of a community working together. The community aspect also comes into play with local and international volunteers supporting the work that goes on in a wide variety of ways from volunteer mountain bike trail-building to horticulture.
- Four other synergistic businesses have been established by entrepreneurs who have been invited in, namely, Tomnah'a Market Garden, The Tea Garden at Comrie Croft Café, The Scottish Tea Factory and the Wee Event Hire Company. The management team see land as a unique and special resource, and as stewards of this resource, they see it as one of their roles to use Comrie Croft as an incubator of complimentary land-uses and enterprises. All the people working at Comrie Croft are either from the local area or have integrated into the local community.
- Financially, Comrie Croft Ltd has grown steadily year-on-year from revenues of £63,000 in 2005 to over £1,000,000 in 2018. While always profitable, profits have varied from only 1% of total revenue (2012) to a high point of over 20% (2014).

- The Croft is fortunate to be part of the thriving community of Comrie, a village of approximately 2,000 people perhaps most famous as the place where the world's first earth tremor observation centre was built, hence the village's nickname, the "shakey toun." The ecofarm has worked hard and with intentionality to build connections, positive relationships and mutual benefit with the community. For instance, a great deal of staff time has gone into development work to improve the local paths network. One output of this effort is a 4 km way-marked walking and mountain-biking route connecting the village and Comrie Croft. This enables local people to safely access the facilities at Comrie Croft, as well as forming an enjoyable route for visitors to gain access, take part in the life of the village and add something to its economic prosperity.
- The collaborative business strategy also results in various mutual benefits within the community. One good example is that of the custom-built ("Do It Yourself") weddings hosted by the Croft. Couples choose their own independent suppliers, with positive encouragement given by the Croft team to use the wide range of fantastic local suppliers be it for catering, flowers, audio equipment or anything else.
- Within the 93 ha of the farm, approximately 20 km of dedicated mountain bike trails have been created and continue to be maintained for free public use. The backbone of the bike trails network was created with public funding from the Scottish Rural Development Programme, the Commonwealth Games Legacy Fund and Perth and Kinross Countryside Trust and built by a specialist trail designer-builder, Rik Allsop. Volunteers and Comrie Croft's own staff have built additional trails and do all the maintenance.

Environmental & ecological issues

Most of the land at Comrie Croft is either former pasture or former forestry plantation, much of which was clear-felled just before the author became involved in the farm. In both the pasture and woodland area, the main land stewardship policy can be summarised as "rewilding." A very low level of management intervention is allowing nature to take its course. For this to be achieved, the property had to be fenced from deer on the mountain to the north, and sheep were removed from all but one of the fields. Relieving this grazing pressure has allowed extensive natural regeneration of native woodland, particularly birch. This has been supplemented by the planting of native tree species to increase diversity and the woodland area. Native woodland is now the predominant land use on more than 50% of the land. In these rewilded areas, no building is permitted, and human intervention is limited to small-scale tree thinning and recreational use for walking and mountain biking.

The Croft is working towards being energy self-sufficient from onsite renewable sources. Currently electricity is generated by 65 kW of photo-voltaic panels. In sunshine, these generate more power than the Croft consumes, so there is also a 15 kWh capacity battery bank where the power is automatically stored and then drawn from when the amount generated falls below what is being used. On average over a year, the Croft is generating more than 75% of the power used onsite.

For heat, the Croft has installed a mini-district heating system with a 200 kw wood chip boiler that is fuelled from locally grown and processed FSC (Forests For All Forever) certified sustainable wood.

Zero % of Comrie Croft's waste goes to landfill/incineration, thanks to a partnership with one of Scotland's most innovative recycling companies, Binn Group. The key objective now is further reducing resource consumption in the first place and reusing what can be reused in novel ways onsite in order to reduce the tonnage of recyclates transported offsite and the associated carbon and financial costs.

Extending the strategic principle of collaboration discussed earlier, one of the hallmarks of Comrie Croft is cooperation beyond its own boundaries, both formally through active membership of cooperative groups, such as the regional Breadalbane Tourism Cooperative and the global Long Run Initiative, as well as informally through business and friendship networks.

Challenges

Of course, not everything at the Croft have gone as planned, and a number of challenges remain. Notably, an attempt to establish a wildlife visitor attraction primarily based on viewing raptors at close hand (Ospreys and Red Kites) was attempted between 2011 and 2014. A large hide was built, interpretive materials developed and attempts made to habituate the Red Kites to humans, using methods similar to those successfully employed elsewhere in the UK (e.g. Argaty Red Kites, Bellymack Hill Farm). Sadly, the Osprey nest was destroyed in winter storms two years running after which they did not return to the same site, and the Red Kites never became sufficiently habituated to allow reliable viewing to take place. So despite a large investment, the decision was eventually made not to pursue this enterprise any further.

Two significant issues in rural Scotland are keenly felt at Comrie Croft, namely a shortage of accessible affordable housing and the availability of staff to help take the business forward. At Comrie Croft, a lack of local affordable housing has prevented the hiring of staff who required housing. At the same time, the business has been unable to find suitably qualified people already living locally. Combined, these have acted as a constraint on the development of the ecotourism business. At the time of writing, planning permission to create a pioneering eight-home regenerative and affordable co-housing scheme is being sought from the local authority.

Reflections

What lessons can be learned from Comrie Croft, and how replicable is the Comrie Croft model in other places and countries?

1   In Scotland, it is very difficult to acquire land due to policies that support the status quo and severely limit the land use possibilities for ecotourism and social enterprise entrepreneurs. It would help to see policies that make acquiring the use or ownership of land easier, particularly policies that lower the purchase price of land.
2   Comrie Croft also shows that it is not always best to approach developments with a large investment and a plan that in itself takes a lot of time and money (and often external consultants) to prepare. The more organic approach – try something on as small a scale as possible to test the market and then grow it in response to customer demand – has been very successful.
3   The Tea Garden café at Comrie Croft is a good example of this approach. It started life as a small garden shed with a coffee vending machine and, at the time

of writing, has recently been ranked the number one café/restaurant from 33 in the Strathearn area. This "organic" investment approach lowers the need for large capital sums while also lowering the risk to those investments. It does require a flexible approach and greater in-house capacity to undertake development work, such as Comrie Croft's in-house construction and maintenance team.

4   Finally, based on his experience at Comrie Croft, the author would advocate a well-balanced approach to the question of commerce versus values. The experience at Comrie Croft demonstrates that the two can be mutually beneficial to the achievement of the other if that purpose is held in clear focus at all times.

Questions

1   Describe the challenges faced by ecotourism start-ups in rural locations.
2   The goal of regenerative design is to develop restorative systems that are dynamic and emergent and are beneficial for humans and other species – is this appropriate for ecotourism developments?
3   The Comrie Croft financing model is a rather unique blend of family, crowd funding and bank funding structures – clearly it works, but how applicable is it to other rural tourism activities?
4   An essential component of the Comrie Croft tourism offer is active & adventure tourism – should we see this as a rapidly growing feature of the ecological and sustainable tourism offer?

Further reading

Please see the following websites.
www.comriecroft.com
www.comriecroftbikes.co.uk
www.scottishteafactory.co.uk
www.tomnaha.com

Reference

This chapter is based on the personal experiences of the author and is intended as a practical approach to issues in managing ecologically sustainable and socially regenerative projects. In that sense, it is a groundbreaking approach for which there is no clearly apparent literature. This is important in the context of this textbook which is seeking to blend practice and theory closely together.

11 SMART Sustainable finance

Tony O'Rourke

Introduction

Ethical finance is a relatively new entrant into the general area of financial activity, particularly in regard to the creation of ethical solutions for micro and small-scale tourism enterprises. Investment into sustainable goals has primarily been evidenced in the Nordic countries – with data published by RobecoSAM (RobecoSAM, 2018) of the Top five countries indicating that Sweden has the highest score, Denmark the second highest, Switzerland the third highest, Finland the fourth highest and Norway the fifth highest.

At a wider level sustainable investment implies careful scanning of not only the policies of investment targets, but also their corporate policies towards environmental objectives, social responsibility and ethical governance. The concept of sustainability does not solely apply to large corporate entities, but to all business activities– including those in the micro and small business sector. This policy has been given impetus and weight by the European Parliament, which in April 2014 approved legislation ensuring access by the public to the environmental and sustainability policies of listed companies. However, a crucial issue is that often sustainable ethical and sustainable investment can be seen as something trendy, a key issue for this year, but lacking real commitment for those indulging– superficially – in it. What is less evident, and more difficult to track and evaluate, is the development of sustainable financial solutions for micro and small enterprises in the tourism sector, especially those operating at a local level.

In this chapter, we will explore how there is a potential for greater levels of SMART investment activity into micro and small enterprises in the tourism sector. SMART means finance that is technologically assisted and enabled, has a high degree of transparency and is easily accessible.

Links

The following Case Study links may be of interest to readers of this Topic Chapter:

- Case Studies Theme B (Environmental & Social aspects of ethical sustainable development)– Chapters 21 and 22;
- Case Studies Theme C (The business impacts of ethical sustainable development)– Chapters 25, 26, 27 and 28.

Please see the Contents on pages v–viii, and the Guide to the text-book in Appendix 1 for further information.

The need for SMART financial development into sustainable and ethical tourism

For certain, we have seen a strong growth in the availability of access into investment in small businesses which have an ethical and environmental background. There has also been a strong growth in crowd-funding platforms which promote ethical and sustainable investment (through bonds or equity structures) into micro and small business enterprises, including those which are mutually or co-operatively owned.

For small-scale tourism enterprises in rural, coastal and other peripheral areas, there is a strongly motivating requirement for SMART finance. This is finance which is adaptable and blends elements of loan, deferred payment/bonds and equity engagement to provide flexible and coherent financing for small-scale tourism enterprises over the medium to longer term. At the same time, we should also relate such forms of financing to grant aid, loan guarantee projects and public financing initiatives which complement other lending methodologies.

Thus given these trends and general movements, we require in this chapter to examine more carefully as to how we can realistically structure and develop financing for small-scale tourism enterprises in rural and coastal communities which suffer from not only geographic peripherality but also from disconnectivity to SMART financial solutions.

General concepts connected to small business financing

We should note that from the 1990s there was a strong drive, backed by the European Commission, to provide new systems of access to finance for the small and medium enterprise (SME) sector, with an emphasis on micro-enterprises (one to nine employees). This resulted in a number of new initiatives– e.g. small-scale equity markets and state-backed equity funds, but at the same time there were also structural and on-lending credit funds focused on SMEs (such as COSME).

Problematically the equity route tended to gravitate towards the upper level of the SME sector, normally above EUR 1 million. For example, EASDAQ and AIM were supposed to be "small equity markets" but clearly failed to provide financing for those enterprises which were seeking funding below EUR 1 million. Undoubtedly, EASDAQ, AIM and other "junior" markets did fulfil a market financing gap, but they did not provide the access to credit which was strongly required during that era. At the same time a number of "off-exchange" equity markets appeared, which grew out of the rapidly expanding business angel/archangel structures, and were in effect an exit strategy for business angels and archangels. Yet again, these tended to operate at the EUR 1 million plus level. Attempts to provide small internet-based equity markets in a number of EU countries were defeated first by the concerns of the regulators prior to 2007–2008, and then after 2008–2010, by the lack of coherent liquidity for small enterprise financing in the wake of the financial crisis.

During the financial crisis from 2008, and through the immediate post-crisis period, the major European commercial banks (i.e. those with shareholder ownership as well as those failed banks taken into public ownership) proved incompetent at managing the needs of the small business sector. Given that the primary need for financing of small enterprises tends to fall below EUR 250,000, existing institutions have been unable or unwilling to engage in lending into this sector. Access to finance has continued to remain a critical and partly unsolvable issue for micro and small enterprises in the ethical and sustainable tourism sector. In part, this is due to the fact that many of these enterprises are located in rural, coastal, mountainous and other peripheral regions where financing has traditionally been on a term-loan model. At the same time, as banks have become more centralised and have deserted peripheral regions, accessibility to banking services and contact with the providers of loan finance has begun to shrink.

The provision of finance for tourism at a local level

It may be suggested that in general the provision of finance in local areas for tourism and tourism-related industries (including cultural and heritage tourism, agri-tourism, aqua-tourism, adventure/active tourism and more specialist capacities such as gastronomic and vinicultural tourism) has generally been related to a top-down structure, where national governments trickle down resources through regional structures to a local level. Inevitably, the seepage of resources when passing through these structural levels may result in a strong diminution of resourcing for local communities. Bottom-up systems in terms of local and community action are preferable– they will view needs and requirements from the local perspective and understand local conditions and requirements. They may also engage a multi-agency approach involving public, private, social and local community agencies into a harmonious structure (Koščak & O'Rourke, 2018).

At the same time we should take cognisance of the fact that the provision of external funding may tend to create a grant-junkie culture, in which local communities become increasingly dependent on external aid (international, state or regional). It may therefore be problematic when this type of funding ends or is reduced, and communities have no ability to quickly generate new financial inflows. Tourism is not simply about visitor flows – this involves counting numbers and not comprehending the inputs that tourism may have. We require to examine the wider picture that pulls in agriculture, arts and crafts, catering, fisheries, food production and a whole range of other local and ethnic industries. It may also engage with such issues as local energy initiatives – wind or hydro farms producing local energy for local communities. Financing these activities is about matching the needs of local communities – this may involve establishing mutually owned, community-owned or other forms of social enterprise as an alternative to continuing reliance on traditional lending systems which failed to support small local enterprises in the fall-out from the 2008 financial crisis. It may be suggested that there is a potentially positive benefit – an indication that community-driven financial initiatives may have a strong potential for successful engagement in local tourism activity (Koščak & O'Rourke, 2018).

The local concept

Localisation of tourism activity will generally tend to engage with local sustainable activities, and thus create an impetus for programmes enhanced and driven by tourism activity. It is therefore important to examine a range of sustainable financial solutions for local tourism activity and for connected sectors (e.g. agri-tourism and aqua-tourism). This connects to potential solutions which may help us to understand the role of sustainability in the creation of financial solutions for micro and small tourism enterprises. We should therefore consider the role of a number of innovative models in providing the necessary flexible financing for start-ups and development in the micro and small tourism sector. In the past, innovative solutions have focused on the provision of venture capital initiatives, which tend to have a top-down orientation and focus on larger enterprise structures.

However, more recently, we are seeing the growth of small-scale financing in local areas. It should be taken into account that many sustainable tourism enterprises, because of their focus and underlying concept (e.g. eco-tourism, activity tourism and cultural tourism), will inherently coincide with the lower end of the small business sector, either as owner-managed or with under ten employees.

It has been suggested above that tourism, for example, should not wholly be predicated on visitor flows – success being judged by the number of visitors who pass through the doors of tourism attractions. We should also look at quality flows – i.e. the real expenditure of visitors passing through tourism attractions. The experience of major tourism destinations affected by mass tourism flows (Venice, Dubrovnik, Barcelona) indicates that cruise tourists spend very little in destinations. For example, data collected by the Institute of Tourism in Dubrovnik indicated that traditional, hotel-based tourists spend EUR 170 a day while guests in private accommodation spend EUR 114 per day. These figures include accommodation and spending on food and drink. Passengers from cruise ships will spend EUR 59 per day, as their visit will be relatively brief (between 10:00 and 16:00 hrs for one day only) and their food and drink consumption is mainly on the cruise vessel (TOMAS Research Report, 2018). The author's own (unpublished) research into agri-tourism destinations has indicated that visitors to such destinations– which generally have relatively smaller numbers of visitors – will still have spending per capita of around EUR 125 per day. This will include accommodation, food, payments for visits to monuments and museums, drinks and purchases. The impact of that level of spending, which in economic terms will generally remain within the local tourism area, has a great dynamic than mass tourism inputs.

Financing the local concept

The problem is that mass tourism (i.e. cruise ships, large-scale tourism groups) tends to be financed by the huge income flows deriving from financial market activity. The companies offering such tourist activities are generally listed on one or more international financial market or are owned by large private financial agglomerates. On the other hand, small-scale and local tourism is heavily dependent on credits provided by the banking structure or by the personal financing of individual entrepreneurs, their family or friends. Since 2008, the banking system in many European countries has taken a seriously adverse position towards small-scale tourism financing. Flight from what banks assume are high credit exposure scenarios has ensured that they are not prepared to take on the risk of many small-scale businesses, unless they can obtain a commensurate level of credit amelioration (i.e. securitisation of property or credible assets). The banks have tended to blame this on the regulators, but clearly it is a knee-jerk response to their earlier actions in entering into high-risk lending situations in the corporate sector prior to the financial crisis.

On that basis, innovation solutions and relevant financial support for small-scale business are therefore seriously hampered. For businesses operating in both the agricultural and aquamarine sectors, the conditions are significantly worse. Nonetheless, we can see very clear and ultimately sustainable examples of financing small-scale tourism activities in a number of European peripheral regions, which operate through mutual guarantee societies, public banks or mutual/public organisations.

As explained above, the financing of micro and small enterprises has been a problematical issue for Europe since the early 1990s. At that stage, there was a view that risk capital (i.e. equity investment through small markets or through business angel mechanisms) would provide an immediate solution. For sure, this did provide a channel of financing development for the high-tech and biotech sectors, but it failed to provide any real support for those micro/small-scale businesses seeking capital inputs below the EUR 0.5 million level. Thus, for those enterprises, traditional credit financing remained the preferred plan; we should also take account of the fact that micro & small Enterprises in rural, coastal and other peripheral regions suffer from the following:

- Seasonality of demand;
- Peripherality – e.g. poor access to transport, distance from national commercial and financial centres, a lower level of social infrastructure;
- Poor levels of financial structure and availability of flexible financing;
- Lack of understanding by mainstream banking entities which tend to be focused in larger population centres;
- Similar lack of understanding by small-scale entrepreneurs of the operation of financial system infrastructures;
- Frequent reliance on public subsidies and grant aid, which can often stimulate and extend the public financing junkie culture.

What have we come up with so far in innovative responses?

As always, innovation and new technologies appear to provide apparently SMART and impressive answers. The main problem is that such solutions provided by technological innovation often upscale and rapidly detach any connectivity to micro and small business financing as they focus into companies in the SME sector (rather than the micro/small sector) which have the potential to move rapidly into equity markets or attract high-end wealth investment. Thus, rural, coastal and other peripheral tourism sectors – which display the more impressive abilities to embrace ethical and ecologically sustainable practices – fail to be able to gain access to innovative and technology-embedded financial systems.

So, do we therefore look at crowd-funding platforms in terms of Peer-to-Peer (P2P) or Business-to-Business (B2B); such platforms have easy access, they have wide coverage in terms of likely investors and the lending costs reflect the risk of the investment. But an immediate issue is that the crowd-funder platform is generally an intermediary/introducer not a lender; furthermore, as they become more successful they will upscale to larger size deals, and this then ensures that they will be required to meet continually tighter regulatory conditions over capital adequacy and risk levels. Thus, the original concept of flexible, connected and accessible financial structures is undermined by the need to become more greatly aligned to mainstream financial activity, which thereby implies accepting a consequently greater level of regulatory control.

However, it should be accepted that at the same time we have seen the emergence of community financing and mutual/co-operative credit solutions and that such ventures have generally been successful. The weakness is that these programmes are only successful in small communities where there is knowledge of borrowers, they are reliant on traditional bank loan systems and they require an infrastructure where there are co-operative or mutual local bank partners with a strong social and community enterprise ethos. It is clear that in Italy– with the *confidi* organisation and its links to the *banca populare*– peer assessment of loan guarantee financing is based on either a local basis or a sectoral basis (e.g. fishing, farming, tourism or artisan activity). Similarly, in France there is close alignment between local rural co-operative banks and regional mutual guarantee societies. In the Italian and French cases, the bottom-up structures are augmented by national federations backed by both national and EU-wide funding mechanisms (e.g. COSME) to provide financial stability. Similarly, there are other examples of local/regional micro-credit solutions in Germany and Austria; these provide local control, decision-making and development but they do require a reliable local financial partner/intermediary and a degree of "soft" regulatory control from the national banking/financial regulator.

Other forms of financing local enterprise

Importantly all of those structures mentioned above relate to the provision of loans over a fixed period of time; this requires repayments from the outset, so therefore such financing models do not have the flexibility of equity financing or bond financing where effective repayment of the debt is deferred. For example, small-scale agri-tourism, aqua-tourism, adventure tourism, cultural and heritage tourism find significant problems of reliance on credit financing (e.g. fixed term loans). Loan finance is undoubtedly inflexible in terms of adapting to trends and shifts in seasonal and market patterns due to repayment structures. Overdraft finance is more flexible, but if a bank has capital adequacy problems it may call in overdrafts as a means of reducing the size of its loan books to meet regulatory requirements.

Alternative financing models

We must recognise that equity finance is far more flexible but that it requires the following:

- The entrepreneur to pass a share of the business to the "risk taker" investor; many entrepreneurs are very unhappy at the thought of an external investors having significant control of the business and a share of the profits (O'Rourke, 1999).
- The investor to have a method to exit the investment – many investors (e.g. business angels) will have a five- to seven-year investment horizon. If the business becomes profitable, they may expect the entrepreneur to either buy back their equity stake, find another investor to buy that stake (e.g. private sale) or in some cases list the equity of the enterprise on a public market or private off-exchange market. That potential issue – the exit from the investment – may cause potential investors to hesitate.
- The investor to accept that although their liability is limited to the amount of their shareholding, they have no security over their investment if the enterprise fails; it is clearly risk capital.

Also, in rural, coastal and peripheral regions– particular for tourism – locating potential equity investors will usually require state intervention through publicly supported business angel networks or through public investment funds.

Deferred borrowing is also a possibility; this involves a loan instrument for a fixed period of time on which only interest is paid (annually or every six months) and at the end of the time period the loan falls due for payment. The investor in this situation will be a preferred creditor if the enterprise fails. In recent years there has been a steady growth in platforms which connect potential lenders to ethical and sustainable investments offering bonds across Europe (e.g. www.ethex.org.uk). However, both equity investment and deferred loan instruments imply and incur legal and accountancy costs, costs which may be disproportionately high for many small-scale entrepreneurs.

Blending?

A solution for small-scale tourism financing with specific application to ethical, responsible and sustainable tourism in local destinations may be an innovative blending of equity funding, crowd funding, deferred loan and ordinary term loan financing. This would take place within the "wrapper" of a community investment vehicle (e.g. a co-operative, social enterprise or not-for-profit community benefit society). Using a community wrapper would then reduce legal, accounting and administrative costs, as these would be shared. Furthermore, financial institutions and external investors would be attracted by an investment vehicle which spreads risk (they would be investing in a range of enterprises, not a single enterprise). The wrapper would raise funding from the following:

- Equity crowd funding through ethical, sustainable platforms (e.g. 40% of total capital);
- Bond funding – deferred bond repayable after five years with annual interest payments to the bond-holders (e.g. 20% of total capital);
- Bank/Credit Union funding on a fixed term loan basis (e.g. 40% of total capital – underwritten by appropriate national/international/European investment funds).

For the individual entrepreneurs they would seek financing from the "wrapper" in one, all or any of the following three formats:

- A fixed term loan (which in the case of the purchase of property, land or equipment would be secured on that asset);
- A deferred term loan on an interest-only basis, with the capital repaid at the end of a defined period – but with interest paid half-yearly or annually through the term of the deferred loan;
- An equity investment in the enterprise of a maximum of 49% of total share capital.

Entrepreneurs would be required to be members of the "wrapper" organisation and subscribe a share/equity contribution to be members (e.g. EUR 100). They would also have the capacity to subscribe capital as a loan to the "wrapper" and receive a relevant rate of interest on that loan. In other words, the "wrapper" would operate as a form of a business credit co-operative with both borrowing and lending members.

Clearly such a community-based local financing system requires the following:

- A local culture of self-reliance and self-sufficiency;
- Energetic and highly-focused local actors;
- Appropriate local infrastructure– e.g. a community-based support group or co-operative;
- Ability to have soft regulatory control at the outset;
- Ability to connect/access guarantee/underwriting from national/international/ European programmes.

Risk

It should be noted that where the concept of mutually owned credit organisations is not well understood, regulators and policy makers may tend to exhibit potentially irrational fears about the level of risk inherent in such financial co-operatives or mutual/community organisations. In part this is based on a perspective that financial co-operatives and community organisations are pyramidical structures in which ownership is focused at the bottom and management at the top in which the gap between ownership and decision-making creates a form of perilous risk.

At the same time, whilst such groups may employ professional managers, decision-making is frequently in the hands or members of local communities. Yet the past decade has demonstrated to us that classic corporate financial models are unable to protect society from perilous risk and have frequently demonstrated a significant gap in shared knowledge and understanding between the ownership level (shareholders) and the decision-making level (boards of directors). Equally, evidence from community-based financial models has tended to indicate that loan default rates are frequently at 50% of the level encountered by the commercial banking sector (European Commission Paper No 3 – *Guarantees and mutual guarantees*. No 3, 2006. 65 pp. (EN) Cat. No NB-AL-05-001-EN-C).

Community ownership and direction is an important concept within the development of local tourism initiatives; it ensures that those engaged in local tourism have a controlling role, but at the same time that those controlling local tourism do not lose touch with the need to ensure community engagement and involvement.

Reflections

- The current situation – this provides significant challenges to the ongoing development of ethical and sustainable tourism development in local destinations. Financing development is a major challenge, in that the traditional banking sector will tend to gravitate towards large projects with a potentially fast repayment profile and where they hold significant securitisation of assets. Financial institutions, apart from those which have a specific environmental profile and commitment, will tend to take a short-term concept of financial commitment, which tends to ignore the longer-term pay-backs that sustainable and ethical investment may bring.
- Solutions – we continue to be faced by the "one size fits all" concept in regard to tourism. Clearly, the issues encountered in places such as Barcelona and

Dubrovnik due to the ravaging effect of massive inflows of tourism exhibiting minimal spending profiles, has failed to register with many decision-makers. They continue to be obsessed with the exponential need to grow tourism numbers, rather than observing and understanding the importance of value and quality from tourism visits. Thus, solutions are difficult to grasp, and we do require a wider and more engaging debate about the role of ethical and sustainable tourism as part of the viable and valuable infrastructure for our fragile rural and coastal communities.

- Objectives – we need to carefully examine how we can use innovative and SMART financial capabilities to solve the issues about the financing of tourism in our fragile rural and coastal communities. If we can find local, community-driven solutions that rely on local knowledge, understanding and expertise, then we have made a very important leap forward.
- Where next? – this requires greater engagement with and understanding of the needs and demands of local communities in terms of viable ethical, sustainable and environmentally sound tourism development. This involves having a full and detailed understanding of local heritage and culture – this benefits local communities in protecting and prolonging the value of that culture and at the same time allows careful and sensitive tourist travellers to such destinations to experience, enjoy and participate in those cultural and heritage potentials.

Questions

1   Is the loan financing model for local eco-friendly and ethical small-scale tourism enterprises less relevant and less appropriate than it has been in the past due to its inflexibility?
2   Is it not true that equity and bond models do not operate efficiently for local eco-friendly and ethical small-scale tourism enterprises, due to inherent imbedded costs?
3   Is there a general lack of understanding of the most efficient methodologies for investment in ethical, sustainable and regenerative tourism?
4   Is the "blended model" suggested a potential answer?
5   How do we ensure, however SMART the financing packages are, that they are firmly rooted in the community, operate on a locally managed basis and have the protection of fragile culture and heritage as a primary objective?

Further reading

This is a developing area, and to be both consistent and contemporary, there are no valid Further Reading references to propose.

References

Bank for International Settlements Working Paper 290. (2017). Basel. ISBN 978–92–9259–022-2 [online]. Retrieved 02.05.19:www.bis.org/publ/work290.pdf
Most of the material is taken from the author's unpublished work over the last 25 years, albeit the material was used at seminars and in discussions on an international level. The references given therefore reflect any external material used:

Dubrovnik Tourist Board Assembly at the Hilton Imperial Hotel [Press Release]."*TOMAS Dubrovnik 2018*". Retrieved 02.05.19:www.thedubrovniktimes.com/news/dubrovnik/item/ 6451-tourists-spend-almost-three-times-more-than-cruise-ship-passengers-in-dubrovnik

Ethex website. [online]. Retrieved 02.05.19:www.ethex.org.uk/savings-and-investments_16. html

Koščak, M.& O'Rourke, T. (2018). *Practical and conceptual strategies for the re-evaluation of local tourism destinations*. Pearson: Harlow.

RobecoSAM (2018). *Country Sustainability Ranking*. [online] Retrieved 02.05.19:https:// www.robecosam.com/en/key-strengths/country-sustainability-ranking.html

O'Rourke, T. (1999). *Equity pooling and profit sharing innovations in the Vipava Valley, Republic of Slovenia*. Bruxelles: Association of European Regional Financial Centres.

12 Japanese tourism in the late 20th and early 21st centuries

An aim for economic recovery

Lesley Crowe-Delaney

Summary

Japanese domestic tourism has a long history based on pilgrimage and travel, possibly from the year 794. Tourism development thus within Japan is based on two premises, tourism destinations already in place heritage and culture, and those that are added to improve local economies. While this has been argued as a context of core-periphery geography (Crowe-Delaney, 2015) or core favoured (historic) sites for tourism policy development over the peripherally less developed (Funck and Cooper, 2013), there is also a chronological approach, synonymous to an add-on to each new strategic plan of five or ten years (Soshiroda, 2005). However, major influences contribute to Japan's tourism industry sustainability. While the phenomenal increase in tourism globally has increased travel flows, this has not been the case for Japan, suffering an inbound deficit in tourism figures in the 1980s. Since the early 1990s, tourism policy has been scattered throughout many ministerial portfolios aimed at where government policy stakeholders aiming for tourism to improve the domestic economic, including the construction industry, rural and regional revitalisation. The rush for resort developments, including those overseas investments, came to a halt as the Great Hanshin Earthquake 1995 took charge of Japan's focus and financial resources to rebuild. This disaster for Japan arguably had dire consequences for its tourism industry development as projects for rural revitalisation were put aside. The aim of this book is to investigate the consequences of tourism impact on fragile environments. The Japanese chapter indicates that tourism policy and long range policy strategies should not use tourism as a prop up of other industries. Tourism, while having negative consequences on fragile environments of heritage, religious and natural significances are at risks unknown as in Japan, prone to major disruption due to disasters and long-term economic disruptors such as ageing populations, urbanised culture and infrastructure that depends on the latest and short-term tourism scheme.

Links

The following Case Study links may be of interest to readers of this chapter:

- Case Studies Part B (Environmental & Social aspects of ethical sustainable development) – Chapter 21/Chapter 22;
- Case Studies Part C (The business impacts of ethical sustainable development) – Chapter 25/Chapter 26/Chapter 27.

Please see the Contents on pages v–viii, and the Guide to the text-book in Appendix 1 for further information.

Introduction

For Japan, in-country travel was a precursor to its modern tourism practice. Two travel forms widely acknowledged are pilgrimage to religious sites (periodically since 794) and the compulsory alternative residence system of the Edo or Tokugawa period of 1603–1867. Mercantilism followed as business travellers were allowed to travel for entrepreneurial purposes. Accommodation, hospitality and sightseeing of natural and built attractions all grew from these travel systems. A diverse touristic activity in Japan was set in place, though arguably, an idiosyncratic one which has challenged successful tourism policy formation particularly for inbound tourism to 2019 (Funck and Cooper, 2013).

While this domestic tourism has a long history it has not a sophisticated one in international tourism policy suited to its domestic provision, despite its mature industry application in hospitality, accommodation and gourmet food. As such early tourism as pilgrimage and sightseeing was additional to these travel requirements. The idea of 'reja' or leisure was introduced from the 1970s, when controversially, non-Japanese observers believed that the hard-working Japanese had introduced this pastime because there was no Japanese cultural equivalent. This was one of the many stereotype concepts supposedly unique, a Japanese-ness (nihonjinron) that anthropologists, social scientists and sociologists have argued about until the early 21st century. The Japanese used travel, tour routes via hot springs (onsen) as well as spiritual pilgrimage to enjoy rest (Graburn, 1983; Funck and Cooper, 2013).

This chapter does not have the space to detail the history of travel and tourism in Japan, and there is already a broad literature base for further reading is attached at the end of this chapter. The aim here then is to give a synopsis of the foundation of Japanese travel and pre-tourism activity and then move into the late 20th century and the current period to 2019. The reasons for this timeframe are as follows:

- International tourism has had its greatest impact so far in the 21st century on the global economy and cultures;
- Japan has lagged behind the rest of the post-industrialised nations impacting inbound and domestic tourism strategies;
- Geography of historic locations, travel and heritage sites determine tourism routes and attractions;
- The impact of disaster on Japanese tourism policy from 1995;
- The influence of the Koizumi era;
- The catchup of the Abe era.

International and domestic tourism policies have been intertwined and often been a policy that supports other economic portfolios, particularly construction in the 1990s onwards and recently rural revitalisation, including the national promotion of returning to a country lifestyle – counter urbanisation. Therefore, this chapter takes up the domestic tourism discussion from the late 20th century into the Koizumi government where in that short time, much change led to a different approach to tourism marketing to the international markets. Nonetheless, the discussion commensurate with the aims of this book is to evaluate how Japanese tourism requires to be managed at the rural and regional levels. It highlights a period in Japan where tourism policy was regarded as a critical element for economic revitalisation, but due to uncontrollable factors has gone down a path of trial, error and questionable efficacy to develop a sustainable industry. This chapter will end in the era of 'Abe-nomics', the economic catch cry describing the current Prime Minister and his government to manage and rapidly ageing and economically challenged national tourism strategy.

Geography and economy

The term 'regional' for Japan often means those nations that sit in the outer Indo-Pacific. This author uses it in a core-periphery geography context of the outlying areas of major city centres within a country. Having said that, as with many anomalies in Japan (population 126.71 million in 2017), policymakers also use 'regional' for the peri-urban areas, such as the outskirts or the hinterland beyond central Tokyo (population 9.23 million 2015 and its outer metropolis of 13.25 million 2015), where tourism funding to support the outer regions finds its way to this most populous city of Japan (36.4% of population), rather than to the rural towns of 13,000 or less. For additional statistics of population density in 2015, the last published census, there were 6,168.7 persons per km^2 compared to the rest of Japan of 340.8 per km^2. With 12 cities with a population over 1 million, they had a total of 29 million people or 23.2% of the national population, followed by the cities of Yokohama (3.72 m), Osaka (2.69 m) and Nagoya (2.3 m). In 2015, 52% of the population were concentrated in the Kanto, Chukyo and Kinki metropolitan areas.

The population has decreased rapidly from the 1980s. The period from the 2010–2015 censuses indicated a decrease of 962,607 people. Between 2016 and 2017 the decrease was 227,000. Its ageing population (of 35.15 m in 2015) means that 21.71 million households were 65 years of age and over, accounting for 40.7% of all private households and where there are twice the number of women as men. This demographic decline also means that births are down since the 1970s (19 per 1,000) to 2017 (7.6 per 1,000). Life expectancy is the highest globally, with 2016 births expected to live to 87.1 for women and 81 for men. The death rate in 1987 was 6.3 per 1,000 and in 2017 was 10.8 per 1,000.

As part of its economic and political management since the 1800s, Japan has amalgamated municipalities. While some have earned city status, that is population criteria of over 500K, this has occurred due to local municipality amalgamation (*gappe*) from 1999 of 3,232 to 2018 of 1,718.

In 2017, tourists numbered 25.44 million of foreign visitors to Japan or 88.7%. The highest was from the Republic of Korea, with 6.59 million tourists then China, with 6.45 million.

Recent economic trends since the 1980s saw the collapse of a bubble economy driven by low unemployment and stable prices. Since then Japan's economy while still one of the largest in the world has experienced a variety of fluctuations and a downward trend in the 21st century. Its economy has suffered impact from natural and human induced disasters, industry privatisation, plummeting stock and land prices. Global impacts include the U.S. economic financial crises, declining exports and a rise in unemployment. In 2010, it began a rise in economic positive trends only to be beset with a weakening economy following the

Figure 12.1 Map of Japan.

2011 tsunami and the subsequent Daiichi nuclear power plant collapse. In 2013 this economic stagflation has been given a three-pronged approach for change, of aggressive monetary and flexible fiscal policies and growth strategies for promoting private investment (Statistics Bureau of Japan, 2019) (Figure 12.1).

A synopsis of the history of Japanese tourism

From the early 1700s, for industrialised countries, such as the Britain or the Netherlands, the activity of tourism had been the reaction to such industrialisation. Densely urbanised and polluted central or peripherally located cities and townships also brought along ill-health and the perception of earlier, better times. The countryside became a rural idyll despite its agrarian hardships (Bunce, 1994) as workers were encouraged to day trip and the wealthy to travel by horse and carriage entourage to the clean and rejuvenating countryside.

In contrast, Japanese tourism travel did not begin like this European model because a different internal economic market system had developed due to pilgrimage routes, the isolationist, restricted foreign trade system with the outside world and later the enforced alternative residence system (*Sankin kōtai*). While the industrialists followed this capitalistic venture and a colonialist theory of economics, Japan closed itself from the rest of the world except through the port of Nagasaki.

Originally as a form of purposeful travel away from one's home for more than a day due to the demands of pilgrimage, travel then became compulsory in the Tokugawa period for the elite warlords to offer homage to the central government of Edo. As this form of governance settled Japan and matured strategic policies, so too did the growth and maturing of mercantilism. This meant that several members of business families could travel for work purposes throughout Japan. Women family members could conduct business travel without men though they would have staff accompany them if their financial means and distances allowed.

After the Meiji Restoration of 1868 tourism policy strategies for the international market commenced alongside the rest of world as cruise ship lanes opened up for elite travel and railways expanded to allow these early tourists inland. This short period to WWI allowed Japan to develop its international tourism and again before WWII. The purpose of early tourism was to direct the visitor to the magnificence of Japan's artistic history of Kyoto and the Emperors castle in Tokyo, with the Mt Fuji looming in the distance. Wealth, pomp and circumstance of the upper echelon of heritage tourism was well promoted in simple guidebooks bound in traditional folded rice paper with sewn bindings, while the Japan Tourism Bureau established around 1912 its precursor the Japanese Tourism Agency, produced similar books to the Bradshaw rail guides of 1861.

Rapid ascension of the railways opened up Japan from the 1860s nearby the historic routes of the Tōkaidō and Nakasendo, formerly established for the enforced travel system to the central city Edo of the Shogun of the Tokugawa period. Initially only Japanese inns at registered posts, specially designated local villages and townships provided accommodation and food, later as the numbers of travellers going and returning increased, other accommodation and hospitality developed including important village leaders and their associates. In the 17th and 18th centuries, artists such as Hokusai (1760–1849) and Hiroshige (1797–1858) and 17th-century poets such as Bashō (Bashō and Keene, 1996) travelled along these routes recording delightful scenes of villages and natural landscapes and innkeepers (Figure 12.2).

Early forms of advertising and marketing developed with hanging lanterns and flags fluttering near signposts. Innkeepers of famous standing would encourage poets to write about them and artists to include their portraits and businesses within larger

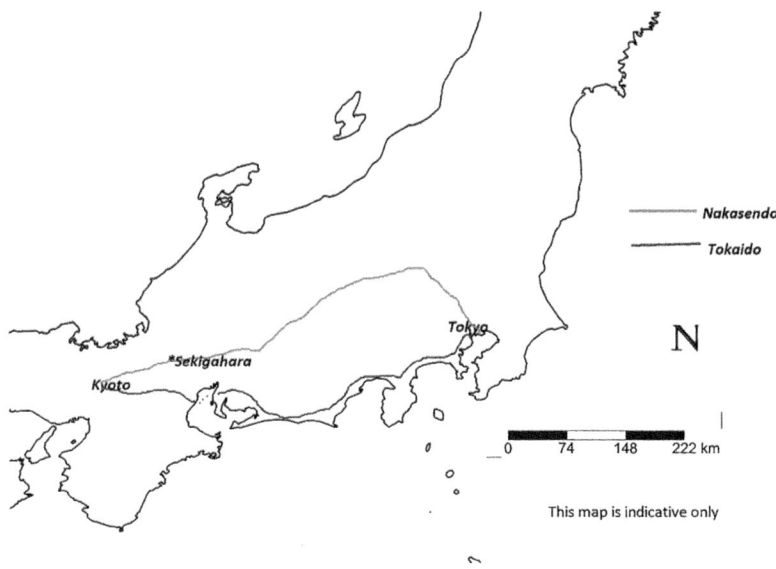

Figure 12.2 Travel routes of the Tokugawa period. Approximate and used for walking travel tours.

village landscapes. These artisans were encouraged to depict essential standards of accommodations and hospitality as well as local sightseeing and religious artefacts and shrines (for wealth, health and other wishes). The natural beauty of coasts and onsen (hot springs) was also depicted in drawings of maps. Small histories of patrons would sometimes accompany the illustrations and maps so that those who could read or afford such works would also know where to visit. Standards as the wealth of the travelling Daimyo and samurai varied due to the decline of the system. It was losing its efficacy and popularity due to upcoming Meiji political activists who challenged the archaic system, but also as the samurai clans lost power and money. Roadside food stalls and private houses were then established by local villagers along the way providing local produce. The boarding houses for the elite samurai and daimyo remained. At the end of this period, the class of mercantilist was able to move about for business purposes. This included women and accompanying staff.

As Japan moved into its first 20th-century expansion into Manchuria in 1931, cruise lines had established travel for leisure into the region since the 1920s. The guidebooks in both western and Japanese styles described Japan's rapid global presence. The Japanese militarist government promoted itself as a unique and exceptional nation, the beginnings of its own stereotyping called *nihonjinron*.

The party leadership, lead mostly by a military regime for the next 45 years in between wars, promoted Japan as a place to visit in order to educate the world about Japanese culture, its modernisation and adaptation of 'westernisation'. This showcasing of Japan meant that the poorer undeveloped districts were not publicised or were put under tour guide headings of agriculture, sericulture, forestry and fisheries. The rail system not only allowed for transportation of goods to regional areas of Japan, but also carried foreigners. They later carried local urbanites who were encouraged to help expand Japan industrially to the regions of Kobe and Himeji.

Again after the WWII and the rewriting of the constitution under the authority and supervision of SCAP (Supreme Commander for Allied Powers), Japan advertised itself to the rest of the world marketing its historic features that had been the enforced route attractions for over 200 years, and by the 1960s including the Tokyo Olympics of 1964 had also included the growing industrial areas that featured production to be traded with the rest of the world, cars and electrical goods. International visitors were encouraged to partake of the delights of geisha houses in the artisanal areas of Kyoto or the upmarket bars of the Roppongi and later the Shinjuku, the Kabukichō of host and hostess clubs all in Tokyo.

Three categories of Japanese tourism

For the study of Japanese tourism and its multiple purpose use for the economy, its foundation can be categorised into two broad characteristics. Type one includes historical and significant sites that include pilgrimage, historic and heritage sites, religious sites of the built and natural environment and castle towns. This category includes attractions such as major cities of Tokyo, Kyoto, Osaka and Himeji for their emperor and castle town history; then other large city visitor hotspots such as Kobe and then the more delightful restored cities such as Okayama or Kawagoe for their historical value. Included in this category are towns and small cities that have more recent historical and spiritual significance. These are the dark tourism sites of Hiroshima and Nagasaki for the nuclear bombing and Ibaraki and Chiran, Kagoshima on the island of Kyushu, where kamikaze pilots, some as young as 14 years old, were sent out to fly planes never to return. On a lighter note, included in this category are the historic walks, the Shinto shrines, Buddhist temples buildings and natural sites of World Heritage Listing. Most of these destinations are also places of international inbound tourism interest. They are established in the tourism industry, both as in-country and internationally marketed tourist destinations.

Type two includes more recent tourism destinations and attractions developed for the purpose of regional and rural location revitalisation and various economic sectors, mainly the construction industry for development opportunities such as resorts, roads works, coastal protection, fisheries protection and other development ideas. The aims were to grow rural and regional areas that were suffering as a result of depopulation and outmigration. Tourism development was a strategy for rural revitalisation. However, the problems sat in the national policy to determine what is regional and rural and who deserves the funding.

This dual categorisation is therefore a socio-cultural-economic geographic polarisation. By the late 20th century, various national ministries included domestic tourism within their sphere of activities. It had become an annexure in many planning strategies, in both national and prefectural cross-departmental projects, and as local municipals were expected to take greater input into tourism, they too had a difficult burden as the governments' projects took precedence in the municipal areas. Prime Minister Koizumi's Welcome Japan 2005 policy, given his government's aim for greater transparency in government policy and practice, is useful one to examine.

It is important to note here that Funck and Cooper (2013, 37–39) contend tourism categorisation in Japan in a different context where her purposeful positioning of Japanese tourism development is in a well-organised and comprehensive publication. This core-periphery approach has also been extensively discussed in case study context (Crowe-Delaney, 2019) as is marginalising 'the other' in a broader context (Shields, 1991). Chronological investigation of Japanese tourism has also been well discussed (Soshiroda, 2005). The two categorisations outlined in this section encompass not only the core-periphery and illustrated in tourism maps and guides websites that focus on the historic and heritage places *and* their peripheries, but contrast with 'the other', those of the 'new' touristic focus, attached to economic revival.

There is a third categorisation, however and that is the digital age of tourism, Japan's Cool Tourism policy. This began arguably with the Koizumi government tourism to incorporate not only a younger generation of domestic tourists to rediscover Japan, but to harness the power of innovation, technology and Web3.0 to attract younger international tourists, Japan enthusiasts, and to utilise Research and Development and Artificial Intelligence to manage the next generation of tourists. This third category also includes the management of tourism in a country with an ageing demographic, but to also facilitate a broader aged tourist cohort both domestic and inbound.

Nationalism and policy change for regional development

Japan, cultural extension, trade imbalances and having fun with tourism

With the beginning of the Yasuhiro Nakasone government (1982–1987), internationalisation (*kokusiaka*) was a key aim. This included the principles of economic trade such as capital, goods technology and the movement of people within companies to their new international regional grounds. The next stage was to introduce Japanese culture as a diplomatic effort (McCormack, 1994, 167).

Although Japan had changed its constitution after 1945, it still maintained a cultural self-scrutiny, an introspection that was termed *nihonjinron* (a theory of uniqueness). This ideology grew from *Nihon fukeiron*, the Japanese landscape by geographer and philosopher Shiga Shigetaka (1863–1927) in 1894 . Later, literature from international academic research or from the curious travellers fostered this unique nationalistic observation and became a nation under reconnaissance due to its increasingly aggressive militarist government (Yokoyama, 1987, Hendry, 1998). Nakasone was a proponent of *nihonjinron* following the philosopher's teachings of Tetsuro Watsuji. Travel books followed this uniqueness and propagated this ideology. '*We Japanese*' published by the Japanese tourist bureau is an example (Yamaguchi, 1950).

Major descriptions of this nationalistic theory are as follows:

- Japanese attributes are all shared through class, gender, occupation and all social variables.
- There is no variation of characteristic or attribute.
- No other society has a characteristic of uniqueness (Sugimoto, 1997).

While this 'theory' has been disproved from medical to social to geographical research, there is a tendency for remnants of it to persist, particularly when tourism policy (Crowe-Delaney, 2015) and nationalism are examined (Morris-Suzuki, 1998). Human and physical geographers address some variables of the Japanese archipelago, where there are

- forty-seven prefectures;
- four major islands and several inhabited smaller ones;
- three major climatic zones: subtropical in the southern area, temperate in the central region and sub-arctic in the north;
- geomorphological features ranging from high mountains to land areas below sea level;
- households that vary widely from one person, employed part-time or full-time or unemployed living in a tent for over ten years in a major city, to a family of four generations living under one large house in rural mountainous or coastal villages;
- culturally significant societies of the indigenous Ainu and the Ruuchuu minzuku of Okinawa;
- distinct regional dialects;
- rural communities whose economies are based on one, or all, of primary production in agriculture, fisheries and forestry, as well as tourism.

Japanese tourism policy has inherited past strategies and styles of national policy-making and includes significant natural sites as iconic such as the *nihon sankei* or 3 Japanese landscapes along with 12 other meaning sites since 1932 (Funck and Cooper, 2013, 38). They have geographically anchored tourism policy to include well-known heritage sites. Modern tourism policy design has used the similar mechanisms (Soshiroda, 2005).

Other specialists in Japanese culture and policy argue similarly of cultural devices with strong traditional elements embedded such as in the fisheries (Seidenstecker, 1951), a symbol of Japan's nationalistic food source, and more recently urban policy (Sorensen, 2002), growth based on historic and Topophilia elements (Tuan, 1974). As such, from the 1970s to 2016, clumsy additions to tourism policy and development have been a reactive approach to economic repair. Along with the support of the construction industry, there was also the development of what may be described as "unique" markets in specific local tourism destinations support as part of rural and regional revitalisation. This would include such features as "one village-one product", the "best of" or "the most famous". While Tourism White Papers were developed from the 1990s, other portfolio white papers evidenced tourism to enhance their projects. It has not been until rewriting policy for the 2019 rugby games that inbound tourism issues are being addressed indicating that there is a change in the direction of government comprehension of the industry and one that needs to function for its own sake.

Until the Koizumi era, tourism in Japan incorporated heritage sightseeing into inbound and domestic tourism strategies under various banners of 'Welcome' policies each always focussing on internationalism (Soshiroda, 2005). These were not successful due to distance, cost of travel and slow and crowded roads in peak times, along with a general disinterest in Japanese nationals own culture beyond the cities. Policy and advertising created a city focus, but the urbanite has become far removed from his agricultural and fisheries backgrounds.

Nonetheless, as tourism policy updates occur between major development initiatives, local municipalities of rural towns and regional cities bear the burden of fulfilling remnants of previous policy strategies. They are then one step behind their city counterparts. Along with ageing populations and disinterest in agriculture, forestry and fisheries, the food and primary production sectors, the efficacy of these peripheral tourism attractions is questionable for local economic growth and tourism in the 21st century. Further regional development also remains questionable. Prime Minister Shinzo Abe's variety of funding for economic policy and associated construction policies are based on growing population demographic statistics in this country suffering rapid depopulation (Janowski and Kaneko, 2013, Sieg and Miyazaki, 2018).

Disaster interrupting tourism

Tourism policies also incorporate challenges. Interruptions of local disasters on a grand scale as in the Great Hanshin Earthquake of 1995 closed Kobe port and gave future growth promise to the smaller sister port in Himeji. The later Fukushima disaster following the 2011 Tsunami is one which has only just surfaced to indicate the devastation to the economy and tourism in that region. For the Hanshin area, its tourism industry had begun to be promoted into the university sector where the prefectural government recognised the value of students' own tourist behaviour and their welcoming of family and friends. This was additional to international business visitors' tourism behaviour and the few international wealthy tourists who visited the area and the university academic sector. This came to be an abrupt halt when the earthquake occurred.

The Table 12.1 is an example of the impact of disaster on policy redevelopment following the 1995 earthquake indicates the challenges of interpretation and management of tourism policy strategies. In the period of 2002, for example, municipal level role-players were led by senior officials who still maintained that Japan's economy

Table 12.1 An example of four tourism policies for the period 2000–2010 for Hyogo Prefecture

Hyōgo 2001 Plan Main Themes	Hyōgo Vision 2010 (MAFF prefectural Division) Main Themes	White Paper MLITT 2002 Main Themes	A New Vision (2000–2001), Real Japan & Visit Japan (2001–2002). Main Themes
Incorporating elements the Welcome Plan 21 for tourism. Focussed on rebuilding after the Great Hanshin earthquake of 1995 including the incorporating of the Phoenix Plans and the earlier 1990s projects. Connecting urban to rural	Rural revitalisation through tourism via MAFF not MLIT Revitalisation of the farming, mountain and fishing villages. Volunteers to support the rural. Tourism specifics include Tajima – product branding, local foods, attracting people to the local nature and coastal culture. Tourism for the purpose of agri-business	Focussed on the low increase in domestic travel of 0.02% from 1999–2000. Nature based themes Domestic tourists encouraged by way of 'low cost pastimes' such as nature sightseeing, festivals and inexpensive activities. Visit traditional Japan: Okinawa, Aomori, Hakodate and Nagano. Increase foreign and domestic tourism through movies (NHK supported), special travel tickets and better internet service	Incorporated regional tourism development to increase international inbound tourism 'Vision' a precursor to 'Real' and 'Visit' Koizumi's domestic policy, nationalism and rural revitalisation
Phoenix Plans for Tourism Main Themes		*White Paper MAFF 2002*	*Yokoso Japan (International 2001)*
Hyogo tourism revitalisation inspired by Kobe and the marketing of 'resurrection'		Green Tourism, interconnections between urban and rural peoples, improve fisheries	Tourism Action Plan, international tourism income, Regional revitalisation

and tourism would turn around with some local 'deals'. This uninformed localised approach was the way a top-down approach system for Japan from the prefectural (state or province) and national level could be managed at the municipal level for tourism and local infrastructure projects.

Nature and tourism

The movement of travellers throughout Japan led to an acknowledgment of nature, already supported in the religion of Shinto. The beginnings of a new integration of nationalism and economic management by the government incorporated the philosophical works of writers and social scientists. Philosophy publications used nature to influence culture and to understand nature in order to improve Japanese daily lifestyles (Morris-Suzuki, 1998, 45–46). In the Tokugawa era of the regional financial crises that followed as fiscal wealth found its way into the metropolises of Edo and Osaka, everyday Japanese were encouraged to use nature as a resource for improvement.

Alongside this was mercantilism justified as significant and connecting Shintō with nationalism for a reflective wisdom of the nature and the environment. This ideology appealed to both urban and rural dwellers and a sense of superiority Shintō mythology. These ideas were then combined with the Chinese classics and with the Dutch to create an ideal society where aggressive development and enrichment of the nation were core themes (Morris-Suzuki, 1998, 49). As the Meiji period changed, Japanese lyrics were combined with western music to further develop a sense of nature to Japanese culture. Tradition making and philosophical thought led to the 'reinventing of Japan, through time, space and nationhood' (Morris-Suzuki, 1998, 49) to create a 'national heritage' (Robertson, 1995, 92).

This is problematic in 21st-century rural Japan, where the national governments perceive the rural environment (e.g. farming forestry and fisheries) as being the connection to and the guardian of nature. This implies protection of Japan's food-producing regions and coastal environment as well as the supervision and control of tourism growth.

The Koizumi era, while trying to promote nationalism through promoting regional tourism, overlooked that the urban Japanese were not interested in returning to their roots *furusato* for *muraokshi undo* village regeneration movement. Moreover, rural food producers have questioned the efficacy of counter-urbanites through tourism promotion as the tourism-induced settlers do not know how to manage their hobby farmland, and, in the coastal areas, their boats and jetties.

Koizumi plan, do, see

The new welcome campaign, 'Yokoso Japan' campaign, aimed to improve Japan's international tourism trade deficit. At the same time, it encouraged Japanese to visit regional areas of Japan (Koizumi, 2005). The Koizumi approach was to develop tourism to a level commensurate with Japan's position in the world economy, and this tourism comparison goal looked to France's tourism strategies. In 2005, the inbound-outbound tourism budget deficit meant 6 million inbound visitors compared to 17 million outbound Japanese.

According to the president of the Japan National Tourism Organisation and the United Nations World Tourism Organisation by 2020, an estimated 40 million visitors would have passed through East Asia and the Pacific region. Japan would be seeking an increased share of this market focussing on tourists from Korea, Taiwan, the United States, China, Hong Kong, the United Kingdom, Germany and France. Koizumi publicly claimed that not only for the Japanese economy, but local municipalities would receive support to develop their own tourism plans. The Japanese tourism industry needed to tap into these cash resources and aim for tourism levels comparable with those of France (Koizumi, 2005).

Koizumi also recognised the need for strategies to redress the younger generations of Japanese who were estranged from the Japanese culture and a knowledge of its geography. The tourism objectives would be combined to re-establish local arts and crafts and to offer these 'new' domestic tourists the experience of their home country's various cultures of the furusato, something that rural locals argued had not been successful in previous village regeneration movements.

Regional development and sustainable tourism initiatives in Japan should include the following:

- Academic research into a diverse range of tourism-related problems, including language barriers;
- Tourism summits;
- The promotion of youth tourism;
- Bus and rail passes for locals;
- More flexible transport passes for foreign tourists;
- Call centres staffed with translators for foreign tourists with specially designed hired mobile telephones or access to telephone booths;
- A single focus tourism market approach for China and South Korea through re-establishing the traditional Asian gateway of Fukuoka, Kyushu.

Thus, the government (Koizumi, 2005) publicly identified tourism as offering an opportunity to bring about regional economic diversity and sustainability through:

- Enhancing the population's awareness of Japanese culture;
- Encouraging the continuation of folk arts and crafts and traditional farming and food processing by locals;
- Maintaining existing populations while encouraging re-population from densely populated cities;
- Targeted initiatives for tourism change and renovation included;
- Advertising regional Japanese destinations instead of the popular hotspots such as Tokyo and Kyoto;
- Reducing national tourist agency domination whereby little of the tourist dollar filters down to the local communities;
- Moving away from mass or group tourism in favour of smaller numbers. In recognition that not only should cultural and environmental heritage be preserved, but that some tourism impacts should be reduced. (Although it was not acknowledged smaller groups would use a larger number of smaller vehicles, such as family cars.)

Tourism statistics

Whilst tourism statistics have become more accurate since the Abe government, tourism itself is divided amongst various ministries in terms of the provision of data and statistics. This results in situations where the Ministry for Land, Infrastructure, Transport and Tourism (2017) has a two year time lag behind information supplied by the Ministry for Economy, Trade and Investment (Ministry of Economy Trade and Investment, 2018a). Generally, prefectures have different methods of statistics gathering and differing criteria. Within those groups who do collect data, there are a host of volunteers in rural locations in tourism associations and chambers of commerce. All this adds to interesting data findings (Funck and Cooper, 2013). This indicates that

Japan has yet to seriously realise the potential of tourism strategies and is in peril of repeating the same mistakes in terms of how tourism policy is developed. Ministry of Economy Trade and Investment (METI) is aiming to model Japanese tourism development on the French wine regions model, one that is popular in various parts of the world already and in terms of provincial licensing (Ministry of Economy Trade and Investment, 2018a, 445–448). Some of the most reliable statistics therefore are between 1995 and 2015, the latest provided by METI in English. Consecutively, the number of arrivals in 1995 was 5 million–20 million arrivals in 2015 and 1995 departures 15 million–16 million in 2015.

Japan's analysis of its tourism income statistics, value-added aims and other initiatives and challenges indicates that strategies are concern-making tourism improved by comparing other countries' successful strategies, most importantly that of France, as forecast by Prime Minister Koizumi in 2005. The approach of talking domestic and international tourism, expecting that the domestic providers will help support the international strategies, is worrying. While Japanese tourism is currently focussing on a Cool Japan as one of its latest strategies to attract a younger tourist cohort and one focussed on anime and manga, METI argues that there appears to be low interest in Japanese culture (Ministry of Economy Trade and Investment, 2018a, 458). So basically tourists are interested in spending on accommodation (Y4000), and food and tourist-related products, but least on cultural services and tours (Y200) (approximate exchange rate Y141.92 = 1 Euro in 2017).

Domestic tourism figures were not available to be included in this thesis, to indicate the success of the Yokoso Japan campaign. The main features in Yokoso Japan feature heavily throughout the tourism white paper of 2001. Additionally, the Japanese economy was still in recession, yet anecdotal evidence indicated that following the 9/11 terrorist attack in New York, some students from Himeji University were planning to capitalise on the cheap flights and travel to Hawaii due to the early stages of Japan and US tourism support as a result of the attack.

Tourism themes

Heritage tourism is well embedded into Japanese tourism policy. To revitalise economies in rural, regional and peri-urban areas throughout Japan by attracting tourists to these locations, other tourism themes have been initiated. There is difficulty with analysing the success of such themed tourism attractions due to some initiatives being incorporated under other revitalisation schemes, being attached to functioning local industry such as the fisheries or vinegar making, or as in some very small villages due to tax-avoidance tactics. Here are a few main themes of the second category to revitalise regional economies.

Theme park tourism

Large theme parks have had varying success and connected as original parks such as Universal Studios and Tokyo Disneyland. Smaller amusement parks have developed since the decline of the economy and focus on feudal Japan, with samurai villages based on the Edo era of 1603–1868, some of the most violent times before a more peaceful era from about 1615 of Japan. Nonetheless, this is an example, like the *furusato* of Japan, where the difficulties of an agrarian lifestyle are swept away to promote a connectedness with nature. The violence and upheaval and the social stratification and enforced alternative residence system that held families to ransom are now tourist attractions.

Local municipalities and communities are encouraged to develop tourism attractions for domestic and international tourism. Problematic, as the non-Japanese speaker will note, on various websites is the lack of smaller towns and villages to have multi-lingual links. While larger theme parks have detracted from smaller themed community attractions, the latter do maintain their community connectedness. Efforts to maintain and sustain local tourism themes often depend on the primary production or artisanry and culture of the township or village. Therefore, a sense of pride and community obligation means that for some small towns and villages, despite the cost of maintaining themes, volunteerism contributes to tourism industry. In contrast, some spectacularly efficient are those linked to Hyogo Prefecture one of the earliest to maintain and foster internationalism and which overcame the issues of the 1995 earthquake, while seeking local industry, and prefectural and national funding support. Large theme parks on the whole, however, remain only as strong as their popularity.

Industrial tourism

Japanese domestic tourism has a long history due to its religious pilgrimage, enforced system of political travel to the Shogun capital and the locals along these transportation links, mostly along the Tōkaidō who opportunistically and often enforced by Samurai, to provide food and accommodation. Tourism across Japan has focussed on the local produce, people and scenery; with the introduction of international tourism in the mid-Meiji period of the 1880s, tourism policy segregated the important modernisation of Japan highlighting this globally, while managing to direct its domestic tourism to the regional and rural areas and to encourage a new urban growth corridor to favourite internal travel destinations such as Kobe and other outer regions onto the Kyushu, such as at Fukuoka to that island's north. Artisanal production was fostered, at various stages, but also challenged to remain sustainable as the thrust for industrial growth was pursued after the 200 years of exclusionist policy from the Tokugawa period.

Some of these artisanal productions could be transformed to large-scale industrial production such as rope making, iron and steel smelting, and that would eventually be targets for destruction in the WWII. Many of these industries post-WWII then were rebuilt, transforming into modern commercial shipbuilding, car manufacture and the many steel and iron 'accessories' to these industries, such as anchor making. With the relaxation of the defence policies in the late 1990s and with the Koizumi policy to send in a defence force to Iran, defence shipbuilding and submarine making gained traction into these heavy industries while more polluting industries included Artificial Intelligence and reduced space led to a closure or decline in these industries. Many of the building sites remained empty in the economic downturn of the 1990s, but with the increase in sustainable production, environmental sustainability and a direction toward environmental and ecologically sustainable industry, some buildings and sites were transformed to recycling plants, or were locations for decentralising industry that was no longer suitable for large city-fringe industrial development.

As was the case in the previous year, Japan had many opportunities to share the country's attractiveness with the world in 2015. In June, the 2016 G7 Summit in

Ise-Shima on May 26 and 27 was announced. In July, "Sites of Japan's Meiji Industrial Revolution: Iron and Steel, Shipbuilding and Coal Mining in Japan" were inscribed on the UNESCO World Heritage List. The Sites of Japan's Meiji Industrial Revolution consist of 23 assets in 8 prefectures (Iwate, Shizuoka, Yamaguchi, Fukuoka, Saga, Nagasaki, Kumamoto and Kagoshima). These are the first World Heritage industrial sites in Japan that have facilities which are still partly in operation, such as the Yahata Steelworks.

Farm and craft experience tourism

Like farm tourism in many parts of the world, Japanese farmers offer a touristic experience for short stays on working farms, but mostly for day or a few hours experience picking fresh produce to take home such as soy beans or digging for potatoes among other more familiar vegetable and fruit picking.

As expected in regional areas, some of the local artisanry remains and Japan is well known for its living cultural heritage recognition. While the older artisans may only perform their artworks for short showings, younger experienced artists can teach groups, such as basket weaving or pottery.

Sister-city relationships, educational exchanges and international tourism

Since 2005, the attraction for university tourism took on a new prospect as again the Koizumi strategies aimed for tourism markets from China, Taiwan, Korea and Southeast Asia. When sister-city relationships first developed, some Japanese prefectures were keen to establish relationships particularly for business, cultural and educational exchanges as well as through the public service sector. Sister-city relationships, like the current Japanese Partnership for Quality Infrastructure, had a 'harmony and peace' theme that included strong economic relationship building. For tourism in Japan on the international stage, this was an opportunity to promote Japan in a multiple cost-effective manner. However, sister-city relationships rely heavily on enthusiastic volunteers or strong relationship builders for trade and economic exchange such as Western Australia for the mining sector. Educational exchange while fostering goodwill has limited value for tourism balance for Japan.

Universities that attract international students have had tourism-rebound benefits in Japan, particularly those focussed on English language learning and tourism and hospitality courses, mostly for the Asian market and managed by private companies. While there is a possibility that 32 universities have tourism studies in their courses, little research informs the efficacy of Tourism and Hospitality education (Friedman, 2018). From a domestic service providers context, while anecdotal discourse laments the lack of English usage in the most rural areas of Japan, which advertise in English on their websites, a more formal report supports this (Fitch Solutions Group Limited, 2019, 5).

International tourism

Mentioned earlier in this chapter, tourism guidebooks for international travellers had already developed for the late 1800s 'foreign' tourist market, mostly English, but with some produced in German as well. They included steering the foreign traveller from

regional and rural areas to encourage foreigners to the established sightseeing destinations and away from the rural and regional areas.

International tourism policies now aim for large numbers to travel not only to the
historic sites, but to all that rural and regional providers offer. In 2019, Kyoto has
already felt the consequences of increased tourism numbers and is considering regu-
lating its numbers. Additionally, in a 'be careful what you wish for may come true'
scenario, Japan has a single market focus on China and as the chapter on Queensland
indicates, such dependency may warrant a renegotiation of strategies on such over-
reliance (Fitch Solutions Group Limited, 2019, 9).

Furthermore as inbound tourism figures are expected to rise, outbound tourism
expected to wane due to the slow economic outlook for Japan, there is an expectation
that domestic travel will increase (Fitch Solutions Group Limited, 2019, 12). However, like many tourists, crowded spaces are not an enjoyable touristic experience
and Japanese expect the reason that they travel to rural areas are for a peaceful and
harmonious experience (Ito and Miyano, 2019).

Reflections

As already noted, various versions of Tourism White Papers in Japan have reported
that tourism provided an opportunity to regenerate regional economies despite both
the central and prefectural governments experiencing varying success rates in fulfilling their development and construction goals (Ministry of Land Infrastucture and
Transport, 2001, 2002, 2003; Miyano 2004, 2006). The Nakasone period of tourism
through to the Koizumi period used a philosophy in the inbound tourism context that
if Japan advertises a welcome, they will come. The consequences of this approach are
that for 53 years, Japan's travel balance was in deficit until 2015 (Ministry of Economy Trade and Investment, 2018a, 443).

The economic stagnation of the 1990s can be blamed on a government system
based on construction interests and complex forms of systemic corruption. For
example, political support by the central government for theme park developers
amidst the financial investment pressures of the stagnating 1990s (Williams, 1998,
192), and the unyielding control by the triangle of central government, and the
tourism and construction industries often justified tourism developments in terms
of their apparent commercial and actual construction opportunities (Cooper and
Flehr, 2006, 71).

Several projects that had been initiated by Koizumi's predecessor, Yōshiro Mori,
and commenced in the 1990s were re-evaluated in lieu of their political viability by
2002. The Koizumi government's philosophy declared that planned, approved and
publicly announced development projects must reach completion, and tourism projects were included in this directive. This was a management strategy to contain the
construction industry and make it accountable. Instead, for small rural municipalities the consequence was cessation or lengthy pauses in planned development. While
decentralisation policies were being introduced for tourism management at the local
level, national infrastructure policies overrode and at times eroded local initiatives
(Crowe-Delaney, 2019).

Furthermore in terms of risk and rewards ratings, Japan appears to be high in both
evaluations of these sectors. While it has been questionable regarding the likelihood
of tensions between China and North Korea, these tensions have existed over two

centuries and figures do not indicate that such tensions impact on Japanese tourism. In fact in the months following the 9–11 terrorist attacks on New York, Japanese students from Hyogo prefecture were keen to exploit the availability of cheap airfares to Hawaii. However, this author does acknowledge that there are risks to focus on single markets being China and South Korea, both countries that can change tourism plans due to political tensions.

In terms of safety and fear factors for travel, the difficulties in language, business corruption, geographic safety and complex financial and banking systems still need to be addressed. Japan is just now adopting a cashless system (Ministry of Economy Trade and Investment, 2019, 2018b). This means that not only is its reputation at stake in terms of administration, but that its ability to manage large numbers of international tourists (Brasor, 2018). With the Olympic Games in 2020 and the 2019 Rugby games, international visitors have been used to, and competent with, advanced technology in finance systems and ticketing systems accommodation, and hospitality is in contrast to what is perceived to be managed on the domestic front. Japan set up its first working group in 2016 and updated in 2017 (Commerce and Distribution Policy Group, 2016). It is fortunate that the cashless providers are only too please to support Japan's enthusiastic, though late, approach.

These modern-day ideological approaches have a far deeper history that has only been changed with progressive understanding of global tourism strategies. The other understanding for Japan is that tourism can inject foreign capital into the country and creates increases in spending locally. While the latter has been an economic process for centuries, like other countries, the accumulation of foreign exchange is relatively new to Japan compared to the rest of the industrialised and port industrialised world.

Questions

1   What can we learn from Japanese tourism in its home country?
2   How does this help us understand Japanese tourists?
3   What is meant by the term 'regional'? How does this play a role in Japanese tourism policy?
4   What is the Partnership for Quality Infrastructure? Discuss its predecessors such as the retirement and golf resorts planned for Australia in the 1980s (Cooper and Flehr, 2006)
5   After reading this chapter, do you consider that Corporate Social Responsibility principles extend to government in respect of close involvement with aggressive developers?
6   How does this relate to underperforming rural and regional economies of local municipalities in Japan or elsewhere?

Further reading

Geography

Murayama, Y. 1994. The Impact of Railways on Accessibility in the Japanese Urban System. *Journal of Transport Geography*, 2, 87–100, www.journals.elsevier.com/journal-of-transport-geography/ [accessed 9 December 2009].

Witherick, M. E. and Carr, M. 1993. *The Changing Face of Japan*. Kent, England: Hodder and Stoughton.

Tourism

Edgington, D. W. 2010. *Reconstructing Kobe: The Geography of Crisis and Opportunity.* Vancouver: UBC Press.

Funck, C. and Cooper, M. 2013. *Japanese tourism: Spaces, Places and Structures.* New York: Berghahn Books.

Hendry, J. 1995. *Understanding Japanese Society.* New York: Routledge.

Hendry, J. (ed.).1998. *Interpreting Japanese Society: Anthropological Approaches.* London: Routledge.

Hendry, J. 2000. Foreign Country Theme Parks: A New Theme or an Old Japanese Pattern. *Social Science Japan Journal*, 3, 207–220.

Soshiroda, A. 2005. Inbound Tourism Policies in Japan from 1859 to 2003. *Annals of Tourism Research*, 32(4), 1100–1120, www.sciencedirect.com.dbgw.lis.curtin.edu.au/science [accessed 20 July 2007].

History

Totman, C. 2000. *A History of Japan.* Malden MA: Blackwell Publishers Inc.

Wigen, K. 1995. *The Making of a Japanese Periphery, 1750–1920.* Berkeley: University of California Press.

Stereotypes and nihonjinron

Mouer, R. and Sugimoto, Y. 1986. *Images of Japanese Society: A Study in the Social Construction of Reality.* London: KPI Limited.

Mouer, R. and Sugimoto, Y. 1995. *Nihonjinron at the End of the Twentieth Century: A Multicultural Perspective.* La Trobe University Asian Studies Papers-Research Series No. 4, La Trobe University.

Nature

Asquith, P. J. and Kalland, A. 1997. Japanese Perceptions of Nature: Ideals and Illusions. In: Asquith, P. J. and Kalland, A. (eds.) *Japanese Images of Nature: Cultural Perspectives.* London: Curzon Press, 1–35.

References

Bashō, M. & Keene, D. T. 1996. *The Narrow Road to Oku*, Tokyo, Kodansha International.

Brasor, P. 2018. Japan is struggling to deal with the foreign tourism boom. *The Japan Times.*

Bunce, M. 1994. *The Countryside Ideal: Anglo-American Images of Landscape.* London, Routledge.

Commerce and Distribution Policy Group. 2016. The Working Group for the Standardization of Credit Card Data- to realise a cahsless society and full utilisation of data-report. In: Ministry of Economy, T. A. I. (ed.). Tokyo: METI.

Cooper, M. & Flehr, M. 2006. Government intervention in tourism development: Case studies from Japan and South Australia. *Current Issues in Tourism*, 9, 69–85.

Crowe-Delaney, L. 2015. *Back to nature or forward planning?: Regional policy, cultural perceptions and coastal tourism development in Hyōgo prefecture, Japan.* PhD Research, Curtin University.

Crowe-Delaney, L. 2019. *Tourism and Coastal Development in Japan.* Palgrave, UK: Palgrave Macmillan.

Fitch Solutions Group Limited. 2019. *Japan tourism report – Q2 2019.* London.

Friedman, G. L. 2018. Cross-cultural promotional competence: A comparison of student and DMO marketing text. *Journal of Teaching in Travel & Tourism*, 19(3), 171–190.

Funck, C. & Cooper, M. 2013. *Japanese Tourism: Spaces, Places and Structures*. New York: Berghahn Books.

Graburn, N. 1983. *To Pray, Pay and Play: The Cultural Structure of Japanese Tourism*. Wisconsin: University of Wisconsin.

Hendry, J. 1998. Introduction. In: Hendry, J. (ed.) *Interpreting Japanese Society: Anthropological Approaches*. London: Routledge.

Ito, M. & Miyano, T. 2019. Bad behavior forces facilities to reject foreign group tourists. *Asahi Shinbun*.

Janowski, T. & Kaneko, K. 2013. Analysis: Japan's mission impossible: To spend $100 billion in 15 months. *The Japan Times*, February 22, 2013 / 5:07 AM.

Koizumi, J. 2005. Conference Speech. *World Tourism Student Summit, 2005 Ritsumeikan University*. Beppu Oita Prefecture, Japan.

McCormack, G. 1994. Kokusaika, Nichibunken, and the question of Japan-bashing. *Asian Studies Review*, 17, 166–172.

Ministry of Economy Trade and Investment (ed.). 2018a. *Current Status of Tourism and Future Challenges for Enhancing Value Added 2016*. Tokyo: MEIT.

Ministry of Economy Trade and Investment (ed.). 2018b. *METI Releases Cashless Vision and API Guidelines for Utilization of Credit Card Data*. Tokyo: MEIT.

Ministry of Economy Trade and Investment. 2019. METI starts accepting Provisional Registration of Cashless Settlement Businesses under the Point Reward Project for Consumers using Cashless Payment. *METI Journal*.

Ministry of Land Infrastructure and Transport (ed.). 2006. *White Paper on Land, Infrastructure and Transport, 2005*. Tokyo: MLIT.

Ministry of Land Infrastucture and Transport (ed.). 2001. *Ministry of Land, Infrastructure, Transport and Tourism, Whitepaper on Tourism (sightseeing). Kankō hakushyo, heisei 13 nenban*. Tokyo: MLIT.

Ministry of Land Infrastucture and Transport. 2002. *White Paper on Land Infrastructure and Transport in Japan 2001: Challenge for Reform-Toward New Administration of Ministry of Land Infrastructure and Transport for the 21st Century*. Tokyo: MLIT.

Ministry of Land Infrastucture and Transport. 2003. *White Paper on Land, Infrastructure and Transport in Japan, 2002*. Tokyo: MLIT.

Ministry of Land Infrastucture and Transport (ed.). 2004. *Welcome 21 Plan*. Tokyo: MLIT.

Ministry of Land Infrastructure, Transport and Tourism. 2017. *White Paper on Land, Infrastructure, Transport and Tourism in Japan, 2017*. Tokyo: MLIT.

Morris-Suzuki, T. 1998. *Re-Inventing Japan: Time, Space and Nation*. New York: M.E. Sharpe.

Robertson, J. 1995. Hegemonic Nostalgia, Tourism and Nation-Making in Japan. *Senri Ethnological Studies*, 38.

Seidenstecker, E. G. 1951. Japanese Fisheries Reform. *Far Eastern Survey* [Online], 20, http://links.jstor.org/sici?sici=0362-8949%2819511024%2920%3A18%3C185%3AJ-FRACS%3E2.0.CO%3B2-9 [accessed 27 February 2007].

Shields, R. 1991. *Places on the Margin: Alternative Geographies of Modernity*. New York: Routledge.

Sieg, L. & Miyazaki, A. 2018. Aging Japan: Military recruiters struggle as applicant pool dries up. *The Japan Times*, September 19, 2018.

Sorensen, A. 2002. *The Making of Urban Japan: Cities and Planning from Edo to the 21st Century*. London: Routledge.

Soshiroda, A. 2005. Inbound Tourism Policies in Japan from 1859 to 2003. *Annals of Tourism Research*, 32, 1100–1120.

Statistics Bureau of Japan. 2019. *Statistical Handbook of Japan 2018* [Online]. Tokyo: Statistics Bureau Ministry of Internal Affairs and Communications, https://www.stat.go.jp/english/data/handbook/c0117.html.

Sugimoto, Y. 1997. *An Introduction to Japanese Society.* Cambridge, UK: Cambridge University Press.

Tuan, Y. 1974. *Topophilia: A Study of Environmental Perception, Attitudes and Values.* Upper Saddle River: Prentice-Hall.

Yamaguchi, H. S. K. (ed.) 1950. *We Japanese.* Yokohama: Yamagata Press.

Yokoyama, T. 1987. *Japan in the Victorian Mind: A Study of Stereotyped Images of a Nation.* London: Macmillan.

13 An assessment of the Topics

Marko Koščak and Tony O'Rourke

Discussion

The purpose of the Discussion section is to seek to review the main contents of each of the Topics (Chapters 2–12) by theme.

Theme A: Destination Management aspects of ethical sustainable development

In *Chapter 2* entitled *"Cultural and heritage tourism – a potential for local sustainable tourism development?"* authors M. Koščak and T. O'Rourke discuss the interrelationship between heritage and cultural tourism, within a local rural environment. This is based on two examples:

1 Heritage Trails in Slovenian Istria
2 The Green Box network in NW Ireland

Both projects developed as a programme of action for rural regeneration through sustainable tourism – promoted at national and international levels – which at the same time retained local focus and personality. In the Slovenian example the experiences gathered over some 15 years of activity enabling taking an historic and developmental viewpoint are presented. The Irish example showed how a cross-border tourism initiative, with international support, created the possibility to overcome centuries of ethno-religious and cultural conflict. In both cases authors presented a beneficial methodology for growing and developing a level of sustainable tourism that enhances the totality of local and regional environments, namely the multi-stakeholder approach.

In *Chapter 3*, with the title *"Active & Adventure Tourism in the planning of local destination management"* the same authors suggest that in line with global tourism trends and their own experience working in practice, destination managers are more and more likely to design their destination products in a direction where elements of active tourism – such as recreation and education, respect and contemplation, action, participation and hands-on exercise and experience as well as an active involvement in the company of an expert local friend or an academically competent tour guide – are an important part of their destination offer.

Authors consider evidence suggesting that the role of active tourism is understood and defined as the "way of visiting", including the attitude of the tourist and the activities that are carried out during the tourist visit. Importantly, they regard these elements as kind of experience and as such essential elements within the sustainable framework, a framework that benefits tourists; local inhabitants; and the existing culture, heritage and physical environment.

In *Chapter 4* entitled *"The Challenges of Integrating Sustainable Wine-growing into Wine Tourism – Examples from Slovenia and Abroad"* M. Koščak discusses the creation of an experience through the aspect of senses. This has been identified among destination tourism experts as an important aspect of destination management and marketing. The five human senses are in a direct connection to customers' emotions. Implementing sound, smell, sight, taste and touch is crucial for managing a positive emotional experience, when presenting destination products.

One of the most frequently used senses is, beside sight, taste. In an increasingly competitive tourist market, wine and enogastronomy are becoming key elements in the development of tourist products in regions that cultivate grapevines, in Slovenia and internationally. It has been claimed that no kind of tourism can develop in regions without wine; however, from today's perspective, this claim seems an exaggeration. Nevertheless, enogastronomy is an integral part of many contemporary tourist products. As such, it combines tradition, history and heritage, and also improves the recognisability of a given destination on which modern wine tourism products rest. On a global scale, wine tourism is growing, and the forecast for the future is likewise promising.

The essence of a wine tourism product is to connect food and wine, i.e. enogastronomic or culinary experiences, and to follow new trends. The trend is to consolidate this segment of tourism services, in particular through leisure activities and relaxation at the destination of choice. Food and wine thus become part of the cultural experience of the visited destination and equal the experience of visiting a museum or a concert or may be an equal component of such a package.

In *Chapter 5*, with the title *"The role of planned events on the promotion of the destination Maribor-Pohorje"* authors Maja Rosi, Nika Mernik, Tony O'Rourke and Marko Koščak discuss event tourism as an important element of destination marketing. An event has been defined as a planned occasion or activity such as a social gathering or an activity that is planned for a special purpose and usually involves a lot of people, a meeting, party, trade show or conference. A growing number of tourism organisations have planned and held events such as local product festivals, community fairs or sporting events to attract residents and travellers, and bring economic and social benefits to communities.

Event tourism has therefore become an increasingly important industry, with significant economic effects, whilst at the same time attracting visitors to visit the destination and its various associated events. Tourists are a good source for spreading positive or negative feelings and opinions about the destination all over the world. Destinations that seek to become successful require to plan strategically their destination marketing, including all planned national and international events. Planned events are part of the tourist attractions offered by a particular destination and have a significant role in destination marketing, the promotion, positioning and branding of the destination itself. For that reason, a number of destinations are building their image on the visibility and recognition of events as an important part of their offer. The aim of this chapter was to explore the impact of planned events on promotion of destination Maribor-Pohorje in NE Slovenia and destination's promotional strategy regarding chosen events. This chapter examines the results of a SWOT analysis of impact of planned events on chosen destination, which was structured upon a personal interview survey and relevant secondary data review. Based on the findings, several recommendations regarding SWOT analysis are proposed to improve the current situation regarding the impact of events on chosen destination promotion and creating a greater attraction for visitors.

Theme B: Environmental & Social aspects of ethical sustainable development

In *Chapter 6* entitled *"Slow adventure in remote and rural areas – Creating and narrating the tourism product"* authors Jelena Farkić, Steve Taylor and Sara Mair Bellshaw suggest that in postmodernity, characterised by fast-paced life, social alienation, workaholism and prevalent electronic entertainment, people have become somewhat detached from the natural environment and other people. For this reason, to overcome a feeling of disconnectedness, and get life back to its slower, immersive pace, a number of global initiatives for slowing down have arisen – slow food, slow cities or slow tourism, to name but a few. In a way, slow activities attempt to strengthen or restore a local, place-specific pattern of living, as well as allow opportunities for the generation of rich, immersive and more meaningful experiences for the consumer.

Grounding it in the Nordic philosophy of *friluftsliv,* as the basic and simple activity of just being, or dwelling, in nature, they suggested four critical elements: time, nature, passage and comfort, all of which suggest deeper appreciation of and bodily engagement with the environment. Commercially, the concept of slow adventure is being increasingly used. By way of example, the tourism industry in northern Europe has been successful in taking the concept of slow adventure further through a transnational project Slow Adventure in Northern Territories (SAINT, 2015). The project sought to raise awareness of the concept and introduce contemporary consumers to an alternative dimension of "adventure". As an outcome of the project, travel providers are now increasingly offering slow adventure activities in order to bring the marginal or remote areas closer to visitors through activities as simple as star gazing, open water swimming, creel fishing, wild camping or cooking foraged foods. In so doing, an emphasis is placed on authenticity and sustainability of the local community, natural environment and cultural heritage, all being vital principles of the slow adventure philosophy and its ethos.

In *Chapter 7,* with the title *"Strategies for sustainable tourism in Porto: the host community perspective"* author Carla Pinto Cardoso offers a suggestion that over the last decade, demand for sustainable tourism practices has risen considerably in Porto, as the city experiences one of the most noteworthy tourism growths in Europe. Most stakeholders recognise that sustainability is the way to meet the needs of present visitors and host communities, without compromising the ability of future generations to meet their own needs.

As result, a wide variety of different strategies for dealing with tourism growth have been suggested and debated among tourism stakeholders. Hence, this chapter explores the strategies for the development of sustainable tourism adopted in Porto and examines the extent to which the host community supports these strategies or not. For this purpose, the study in this chapter combines a comprehensive desk-research based on secondary data from key industry and academic sources and a quantitative survey conducted among a sample of 140 residents from the city of Porto. The results can be used to support the continued competitive and sustainable future of Porto, while at the same time offering guidelines for practitioners in other cities which are experiencing a growth in tourism or are seeking to develop this sector, since many of the points raised from Porto's experience have a more general application.

In *Chapter 8*, with the title *"Terraced landscape preservation and tourism sustainability in Cinque Terre, Liguria, Italy"* authors Simonetta Acacia, Marta Casanova, Elena Macchioni, Federica Pompejano, Camilla Repetti and Francesca Segantin discuss the development challenges of the Cinque Terre, a string of five fishing villages perched high on the Italian Riviera which until recently were linked only by mule tracks and accessible only by rail or water. The Cinque Terre is noted for its beauty. Over centuries, people have carefully built terraces to cultivate grapes and olives on the rugged, steep landscape right up to the cliffs that overlook the Mediterranean Sea. The breath-taking views of harbours far below the wild but hospitable coastline along with the medieval fortresses and plentiful vines and vibrant colours make this a memorable holiday.

Cinque Terre's terraced landscape represents an example of a peculiar relation between nature and humankind, thanks to its characteristic shaped territory. This area, vulnerable to natural disaster and anthropic degradation, has been involved in several actions aimed at its preservation since the 1980s. The site was inscribed in the World Heritage List, and various laws and agencies were created to support local agriculture and landscape preservation. Through the analysis of the regulations context and related requirements, this chapter aims to explore the relationship between mass tourism effects and landscape vulnerability, and the conflict between conservation needs and the site's real economy.

In *Chapter 9* entitled *"Inter-generational concepts of sustainability and the role of children in local tourism destinations"* authors Mladen Knežević, Tony O'Rourke, Tina Šegota and Marko Koščak suggest that modern tourism planning and development of a destination should include input from all levels of society, including different age groups and varying interest groups within a local community. However, it is very rare that, in the process of participatory planning, youths and school groups are invited to express their views on development plans or have the opportunity to take an active part in decision-making.

The concept of sustainable tourism is more than a piecemeal policy solution, described as "just sustainability"; it indicates above all the concept of holistic development and finding such solutions that solve the integrity of the human problems. Therefore, the current generation that is undertaking the governance of tourism and sustainability should be aware that at this moment there is a generation of young people that seeks to feel and see the impact of sustainability in their lives. Young people's views on tourism are very often neglected, making the sustainability concept incomplete. However, at the end of the day, these young people will be part of the community that will live and work in the tourism sector in the future. Hence, in this chapter, authors focused on young people to explore their role in a tourism community and how do they engage in a participatory way in the planning of their tourism environment. In the study presented in this chapter, authors have demonstrated that young people are not only "residents" in tourist areas, towns and villages, but participants in events in these areas and careful observers of the environment around them.

Theme C: The business impacts of ethical sustainable development

In *Chapter 10*, with the title "*Financing a sustainable, ethical, local project*", Andrew Donaldson provides an extremely interesting narrative of the development of an eco-farm in the southern edge of the Scottish Highlands. The chapter relates to the challenges faced in converting what was a traditional farm which was no longer economically viable into an enterprise which has a wide range of synergistic activities and micro-enterprises established onsite. The author also provides readers with a vision which seeks to pioneer a holistic, regenerative enterprise where visitors, employees, owners, local people and the natural environment all benefit through collaborative activity including eco-tourism. Clearly the desire of the founders of this enterprise is to see nature flourish in rural areas. This desire includes the necessity for human re-population, increased biodiversity and improved quality of rural life.

An important element of this chapter is the interesting financing structure which the author, his friends and family embarked on to create Comrie Croft. The model they employed – a blending of equity financing from friends, family and local supporters together with deferred loan finance (a private bond), and finally a bank loan is an interesting structure which may be applicable to a number of peripheral rural, mountainous and coastal regions. The chapter also connects very well to the concept of adventure and activity tourism – getting people to connect with nature and informing people onsite about such issues as "smart" energy systems with renewable generation and battery power storage and waste treatment. Added to this is the focus on localisation – i.e. engagement with the local community – and equally importantly the identifying and building on synergies between different objectives, activities and enterprises so that the whole is greater than the sum of the parts.

In *Chapter 11*, with the title "*SMART sustainable finance*" Tony O'Rourke explores how the potential for greater levels of SMART financial activity into micro and small enterprises in the sustainable tourism sector. He defines SMART finance and investment as finance that is technologically assisted and enabled, has a high degree of transparency and is easily accessible. The chapter looks at the needs for SMART financial activity in terms of investment in small businesses which have an ethical and environmental background. A strong motivation, the author suggests, is for the problems faced by small-scale tourism enterprises in rural, coastal and other peripheral areas in terms of accessing finance. After exploring the background to various European and global initiatives to finance the micro-small and small-medium enterprise sectors as well as the impact of the failures of the banking system in 2007–2010, the author goes on to examine the problems of financing in local areas for tourism and tourism-related industries (including cultural and heritage tourism, agro-tourism, aqua-tourism, adventure/active tourism and more specialist capacities such as gastronomic and vinicultural tourism).

The author then discusses issues relating to resourcing at a local level for the ethical and sustainable tourism sector – top-down or bottom-up, reliance on external funding, those roles of the multi-agency approach bringing public, private and social agencies together. He then relates the problems of the ethical and sustainable tourism sector in accessing finance – including the problems of small enterprises in meeting critical issues such as seasonality of demand, the problems of peripheral locations and the withdrawal of financial capacity in peripheral areas. A potentially interesting element of the chapter is the author's promotion of a new financing model for ethical and sustainable tourism which analyses loan, equity and bond financing and then proposes a "blending" model operating through a community investment wrapper and providing a mix of equity, deferred loan and fixed term loan financing facilities. The chapter concludes by stressing the value of community ownership and direction within the development of local ethical and sustainable tourism initiatives.

In *Chapter 12*, with the title *"Japanese Tourism in the late 20th/early21st century: an aim for economic recovery"*, Lesley Crowe-Delaney discusses the Japanese domestic tourism industry, which has a life span of some 1200 years based on pilgrimage and travel. Thus, it has a strong basis in cultural and heritage tourism, but the author argues that those added to this have been activities to improve local economies. This therefore provides an interesting example to add to the European, American and other material in this book. An interesting issue which the author raises is that whilst there has been a phenomenal increase in global tourism, Japan suffered an inbound deficit in tourism figures in the 1980s. Physical and economic disasters had a profound effect, but added to this appears to be a short-termist approach in national tourism thinking. What is of course interesting is the deeply cultural heritage aspect of Japanese domestic tourism, which has its base in over a millennium of domestic tourism activity. The problem appears to be difficulties in promoting Japan's cultural heritage to external tourist markets without destroying what is clearly a unique and very fragile resource in both physical and cultural terms.

The author identifies the fact that Japanese tourism travel parallels the European model based on industrial development and the outward-facing interests of the ruling classes. Its isolationist political and trade system hindered such developments. Whilst external tourists were welcomed in the period from 1868 to 1939, it was not until the 1960s that Japan's cultural heritage was re-opened to global visitors. The author reminds us of three categorisations of the tourism offer – the first are historical heritage and religious sites of the built and natural environment and castle towns. The second are more recent tourism destinations such as resort tourism. The third is the digitalised "Cool Tourism" policy to attract both domestic and international younger tourists.

This chapter contains a wide variety of fascinating information about the development, problems and current issues of Japanese tourism, but importantly it highlights many tensions between the tensions of a traditionalistic society to preserve culture and heritage with the demands of an internationalised economy to maximise income from the international tourism market.

Learning points

The Learning Points are an addition to the Reflections in this chapter. In a sense they seek to summarise some of the key factors and may be used to demonstrate a number of critical issues which affect Responsible and Sustainable Tourism at a local level.

Theme A: Destination Management aspects of ethical sustainable development

- The key **Learning Point** in relation to "Cultural and Heritage Tourism" (Chapter 2) is concerned with the fact that cultural tourism is insufficiently developed and presented on major tourism markets at both national and international levels, and this provides a lack of security for sustainability of this product. There is also a necessity not only for detailed carrying capacity research of Cultural and Heritage sites but a failure to connect local and rural communities into the planning process at a very early stage. The geographical, cultural and historical elements are an important focus for those who are responsible for the destination management. Unfortunately, lack of co-operation and trust between key stakeholders, who are driving their own interests rather than working together in promotion of the destination, creates a long and lonely path towards an evidenced decline in many local tourism destinations.

- The key **Learning Point** in relation to "Active and Adventure Tourism" (Chapter 3) connects to how to solve low financial capacity, low promotional capacity and low management capacity and thus ensure that the development of active tourism does not develop in a vacuum at a local level. This can be ensured through the concept of the "social licence", but it requires three essential components – legitimacy, credibility and trust. It also requires the management of capacity through locally inspired, community-driven and multi-agency approaches. Over-capacity is rapidly becoming a dangerous issue in mass tourism destinations, but the problem is now spreading to small tourism destinations.

- The key **Learning Point** in relation to "Integrating Sustainable Wine-growing into Wine Tourism" (Chapter 4) relates to the fact that both wine and enogastronomy are becoming very important elements in the development of tourist products in wine-producing regions. New trends indicate a consolidation of this segment of tourism through leisure activities and relaxation at the destination of choice offering multi-sensory experiences. As part of the tourist package, wine and food may be used to outline a diversified image of a particular destination. Wine tourism represents a holistic landscape; it is also a considerable development potential by including small producers and family businesses – generating new jobs and local economic growth.

- The key **Learning Point** in relation to "the destination Maribor-Pohorje" (Chapter 5) is concerned with the potential for event tourism at a destination level to promote the development and marketing of planned events as tourist attractions, catalysts, animators, image-makers and place marketers. This process includes bidding on, facilitating and creating events, and the management of portfolios of events as destination assets. For individual events, event tourism means taking a marketing orientation to attract tourists, sometimes as an additional segment and sometimes as the core business. Planned events, as part of the tourist offer, are and will continue to be one of the key marketing tools for attracting visitors. It is very important that both tourism sector and tourism collaborate and together build the destination image through promotion of various events at the destination.

Theme B: Environmental & Social aspects of ethical sustainable development

- The key **Learning Point** in relation to "Slow adventure in remote and rural areas" (Chapter 6) emphasises the importance of collaboration and joint participation of small business, at local, regional, national and transnational levels, in value co-creation and developing the product. Another crucial aspect is transnational collaboration in product promotion under the umbrella of slow adventure, achieved through building a joint marketing campaign and harnessing social media to market the products developed in each partner country. It is clear that the project helped to illustrate to the partner small enterprises the benefits of clustering, from increasing the exposure of peripheral, isolated micro-enterprises, to new, distant international markets in particular, to participation in collaborative social media campaigns to access affluent customer groups and to foster a sense of a slow adventure "community".

- The key **Learning Point** in relation to "Strategies for sustainable tourism in Porto" (Chapter 7) connects to the important issue of enhancing stakeholders' awareness of the need to implement and manage sustainable strategies. This is not only because such strategies assist in mitigating potential negative tourism impacts, but also because they have the potential to determine the methodology by which tourism activities may be configured into a long-term period. This emphasises the need to take into consideration the interest of all the stakeholders involved to ensure sustainable tourism. Indeed, while visitors look essentially for tourism experiences and managers for business opportunities, host communities demand quality of life. This underlines the fact that the involvement of the host community must develop more deeply than consultation and should include appropriate engagement and discussion in decision-taking. A co-operative and participatory approach and involvement is recommended.

- The key **Learning Point** in relation to "Terraced landscape preservation and tourism sustainability in Cinque Terre" (Chapter 8) highlights the important fact that at present, the Cinque Terre economy is mainly based on tourism, which has strong impacts on the natural and cultural features of the territory. The greatest pressure derives from day trippers, who are primarily from cruise ship passengers. It is important to understand that significance of the Cinque Terre relies on an active relationship between humans and nature. Landscape preservation can only be ensured by allowing the permanence of dwellers and their agricultural activity. The conservation of the site requires the implementation of a conscious tourism strategy, encompassing the promotion of sustainable tourism activities, life quality improvement for residents and overall sustainable development.

- The key **Learning Point** in relation to "Inter-generational concepts of sustainability and the role of children in local tourism destinations" (Chapter 9) is that the views of young people about tourism are very often neglected. This has the tendency to make the sustainability concept incomplete as these young people will be part of the community that may live and work in the tourism sector in the future. Young people are not only "residents" in tourist areas, towns and villages, but participants in events in these areas and careful observers of the environment around them. It would therefore be appropriate that they should have a voice in the planning of tourism development in their destinations. There is an urgent need to access the views of children and young people living in tourism communities; unfortunately, this represents a neglected area in tourism research. Connected to this is the fact that some tourist destinations face serious problems in lack of professional and educated staff as fewer young people wish to work in the tourism industry.

Theme C: The business impacts of ethical sustainable development

- The key **Learning Point** in relation to "the Comrie Croft model of an ethical, re-generative and sustainable rural eco-tourism activity" (Chapter 10) is concerned with a primary focus on an organic approach – testing the market and then growing it in response to customer demand. All of the business activities at Comrie Croft were predicated on a model of "test and try". This "organic investment approach" has the capacity to reduce the need for large capital inputs and simultaneously lowers the investment risk for those participating. It does require a flexible approach and greater in-house capacity to undertake development work, such as Comrie Croft's in-house construction and maintenance team.
- The key **Learning Point** in relation to "SMART finance" (Chapter 11) connects to a current situation which provides significant challenges to the ongoing development of ethical and sustainable tourism development in local destinations. Financing development is a major issue given that the traditional banking sector will tend to gravitate towards large projects with a potentially fast repayment profile and where they hold significant securitisation of assets and will tend to take a short-term concept of financial commitment. Growing tourism numbers is not an answer, the solution may appear to be in developing quality sustainable and ethical tourism products and services. This requires greater engagement with local communities and having a full and detailed understanding of local heritage and culture.
- The key **Learning Point** in in relation to "Japanese tourism" (Chapter 12) connects to the failure of various national administrative systems to develop tourism in a meaningful, ethical and sustainable way. Japan's past concept of tourism was very much located into culture and heritage – but this was primarily for the domestic market. The official approach for foreign tourism appears to reflect a desire to create a mass market of large-scale groups which is very much similar to cruise tourism. It is very clear that Japan has a strong vibrant cultural heritage, as well as a fragile environment which is constantly under threat from urbanisation. It is therefore a situation which is very resonant to all of those who live in developed economies.

Further questions

The Further Questions are connected to the issues raised from the Topics discussed in Chapters 2–12. They may be used for teaching or training purposes, or as a method for stimulating concepts and ideas about the fundamental topics in this book.

Theme A: Destination Management aspects of ethical sustainable development

- How important is the process of carrying capacity before and during the implementation of development and promotional actions in order to achieve optimal sustainability and responsible management of cultural and heritage tourism in the destination?
- Does the interaction between the social, economic and physical environment have the ability to preserve the fragile balance between maintaining local culture,

heritage and ecology, whilst ensuring local communities benefit from sustainable economic growth?
- What is the critical role of a local Destination Management Organisation in the process of developing ethical and sustainable tourism?

Theme B: Environmental & Social aspects of ethical sustainable development

- In what way is it possible to reconcile providing a quality and meaningful visitor experience with the needs of local communities and the more negative environmental impacts of tourism on those communities?
- Is there a requirement to consider a move towards tourism activity which involves restricting visitor numbers and ensuring less environmental impact in terms of developing sustainable tourism strategies?
- By excluding young people from the tourism planning process and engagement in how future sustainable tourism can be developed? Are we inevitably excluding those who future lives will be negatively affected by such issues as over-tourism?

Theme C: The business impacts of ethical sustainable development

- Should we take greater notice of regenerative capacity which is about the development of restorative systems which are dynamic and emergent, and are beneficial for humans and other species?
- SMART financing is about connecting access to finance to the needs of local communities which operate on a locally managed basis and have the protection of fragile culture and heritage as a primary objective. Does this then require us to design financial structures which operate on a local community basis?
- Japanese tourism development indicates a classic conflict between domestic tourism seeking to protect a unique cultural and heritage environment and globalised tourism which is highly invasive. Is it possible to resolve the differences?

Section 2
The case studies

Part A

Destination Management aspects of ethical sustainable development

14 The ethics of sufficiency

The Edelsbach Tulip Festival as a best practice example of sustainable event culture

Daniel Binder, Harald A. Friedl and James W. Miller

Summary

This chapter examines how events, when managed in a truly sustainable way, can contribute to the identity of a rural community, while at the same way helping to preserve its economic and social foundations. It begins with a discussion of the ethical aspects of sustainable development and how they are connected to questions of community identity. A specific case, the Edelsbach Tulip Festival, illustrates how concentrating on core values such as sustainability and sufficiency when designing and managing an event can help fend off rural decline.

Introduction

Research on sustainability in connection with events has focussed especially on issues such as waste management and transportation (Yuan, 2013; Hottle, Bilec, Brown, & Landis, 2015; Chirieleison & Scrucca, 2017; Zelenika, Moreau, & Zhao, 2018). Sustainable events in the context of ethical issues related to the well-being of rural communities have received less scholarly attention. This chapter aims to explain this connection by first laying a groundwork for the discussion be examining the literature on ethics and sustainability with regard to events and tourism and then explaining the connection in detail by examining a specific case – a festival held in a rural community in Austria.

Sustainability, ethics and well-being: a theoretical background

Ethics reflect the individual search for and re-establishment of the "good life" (Aristotle, 1999, p. 12), or to use a more current buzzword, "well-being" (Morand & Lajaunie, 2018, p. 119) in the context of changing situations. Ethical reflections should result in concrete guidance for individuals on how to take personal responsibility for reaching the "good life" personally (Sacks, 2005; Croitor, 2014; Mantatov & Mantatova, 2015). Because an individual can exist only in an interdependent relationship with his or her social and natural environments, in the final analysis ethics ends up consisting of questions about how to best cope with these environments in order to survive in the long run (Friedl, 2007). To put it simply, ethics are about individual sustainability.

In contrast to ethics, the focus of sustainability is usually on the long-term balance of complex natural or social systems, such as communities within their specific and changing environment. Reflections about sustainability should provide communities with concrete answers about what to do in order to take their collective responsibility for approaching the collective "good life". As complex systems produce complex and dynamic interactions, both within the system itself and with its environment (Fath, 2014), research about sustainability focusses on how to cope with both the system itself (the community) and its environment in order to ensure survival in the long run. From this perspective, it can be concluded that sustainability represents a kind of collective, systemic ethics (Oliveira de Paula & Cavalcantib, 2000).

Sustainability, ethics and identity

The crucial, never-ending question for both ethics and sustainability concerns the "right" way to reach the good life. The simplest and only right answer would be as follows: It depends on who is asking! Just as the best shoes are the ones that fit the specific feet in question, the best answers to both ethical and sustainability questions depend on the specific identity of the "target" in question. In the case of an individual, identity is the expression of that person's individual history: how the individual has coped with his life (successful practices, ideas and values), and where the person wants to go in the future (visions) (Pappas, Pappas & Sweeney, 2015). As already stated, an individual exists in permanent interaction with his or her environment, and personal identity will always reflect this relationship in some way. No ethical answer is possible outside the context of personal identity. Knowing who I am is the precondition for answering what I should do. That was what was meant by the Temple of Delphi's dictum, "Know thyself" (Jopling, 2000, p. 1).

For a community, basically the same approach applies, although in a much more complex way. Collective identity, from this perspective, is the expression of a permanent coordination process engaged in by all individual community members in the context of their specific environment or "culture" (Serpe & Stryker, 2011; Friedl, 2015a). It is not possible to know how to maintain or to reach sustainability without defining the collective identity of the group striving for sustainability. Knowing who "we" are, based on knowing who our members "are", is the precondition for answering what "we" should do. These structural determinants are the reason why the first step in destination strategy processes must be the participative development of a common mission statement (Rey & Bastons, 2018).

The role of events in promoting sufficiency as a way toward community sustainability

Modern society is characterised by permanent change and growth. One result is that "de-growth" is normally associated with "underdevelopment" or even economic decline. Rural regions experiencing outmigration to highly dynamic urban areas are classic examples of such "de-growth" (Schneider, Kallis & Martinez-Alier, 2010). "Sustainable growth", on the other hand, is frequently presented as a desirable end in tourism discourses, a prime example being the UN sustainability development goals (UNWTO, 2015). The "Limits of Growth" (Meadows, Meadows, Randers & Behrens, 1972), on the other hand, are increasingly gaining the attention of tourism scholars. In this context, de-growth is seen as healthy downsizing of over-dimensioned systems plagued by over-tourism in order to reach "sufficiency" (Hall, 2009; Higgins-Desbiolles, 2010; Friedl, 2015b).

Usually, however, community-based tourist projects, such as events, are implemented in order to foster economic growth. New economic dynamism should be achieved by attracting more visitors, earning additional money and maintaining or creating additional jobs (Pablo-Romera & Molina, 2013; Antonakakis, Dragouni & Filis, 2015). According to common sustainability discourses, these kinds of events can be judged to be more or less "sustainable" if significant parts of the earnings stay in the community (economic sustainability); natural resources such as water and energy are used in reasonable ways, and waste production is minimised (environmental sustainability); the majority of the community's population tolerates the event (socio-cultural sustainability). Practically, "sustainable events" use local products and manpower as much as possible, rather than outsourcing them (Boggia, Massei, Paolotti, Rocchi & Schiavi, 2018).

Unfortunately, this growth-based approach leads to several paradoxes in contradiction to sustainability in the sense of a systemic long-term balance (Higgins-Desbioles, 2018). We have yet to sever the connection between economic growth and growing consumption of natural, non-renewable resources. Until we do, growth per se will continue to result in critical waste emissions and diminished resources. Furthermore, the permanent growth of such events can also cause social tensions within a community. The desire on the part of some stakeholders for even more economic growth is then met by resistance on the part of others within the community who do not like the side effects (Curcija, Breakey & Driml, 2019). This leads to fundamental conflicts over the event's future, which clearly runs counter to the idea of a "sustainable event".

The constitutive role of community participation in the sustainability of events

According to Saarinen, the conviction that sustainability in tourism should serve first and foremost the destination's population instead of the tourism industry was rather slow in coming. This new stakeholder orientation was not the result of a sudden ethical realisation that those who must live with the consequences of decisions should also be the ones to make them. Quite the contrary, it was the result of a painful learning process associated with the resistance of the residents of protected areas to top-down decisions (Saarinen, 2006).

What does this imply for a sustainable community event? "Community sustainability" in connection with an event can be achieved if there is

- a high degree of community participation in the process of formulating a vision for the event,
- a high degree of critical reflection about the community's identity (a common understanding of the community's history, present values and practices, as well as a common vision for the future).

This common concept can then work both as the reflection of the community's identity AND as the benchmark for the design and the control of the event. This means that local products won't be used only to maximise economic growth, but especially because the community members are proud of these products, which nourishes socio-cultural sustainability. They won't just use local manpower in order to maximise local jobs, but especially because all community members identify with the event and are proud to be an indispensable part of it. Thus, such a community event ends up being much more than a strategy to fight economic decline. Instead, it becomes an integral part of the community's culture, and at the same time an expression of their way of life and an instrument to maintain and develop it.

In consequence, the question of growth suddenly loses its paradigmatic meaning. The immediate connection with the socio-cultural needs of the community members means that they can maintain their authority over the degree of growth. If further growth fits their enthusiasm and needs, then it can be accommodated. If de-growth becomes necessary in order to sustain rather than undermine the identity and well-being of the community, then this becomes clearly the way to go. No growth may well be the best option, as part of an overarching "sufficiency mind-set and a steady-state strategy" (Higgins-Desboilles, 2018, p. 158).

The Case: the Edelsbach Tulip Festival

An excellent example of this approach to sustainability in connection with events is an annual two-day community festival held in Edelsbach bei Feldbach in the Federal State of Styria in southeastern Austria. The Edelsbach Tulip Festival has been attracting on average about 6,000 visitors annually to this village of 1,400 souls since 2008. Since then, the village has branded itself as the Tulip Village, since it is the only place in Austria to host such a festival. The way the event was originally conceived and then organically developed has resulted in the strengthening of local identity. In the process, the residents have also committed themselves to sustainable event management practices and no-growth (Tourismusverband Edelsbach, 2019).

Edelsbach bei Feldbach is located 40 km from Graz, Austria's second largest city. Day tourists are attracted by Austria's only bridge museum, a bee-keeping attraction; stations of the cross conceived by contemporary artists; and the "World Machine", a quirky room-sized Rube Goldberg apparatus that was the life's work of a local cottager—a cross between a work of art and a metaphor for the world (Moick, 2007). Finding a theme to tie such disparate attractions together was nigh impossible, so the Edelsbach Tourism Association decided to create a festival that would draw guests and introduce them to what the village has to offer in addition to the short-blooming tulips. The goal was to raise awareness of the village in order to increase visitorship to its attractions throughout the year. Tulips were chosen as a festival theme, because no other Austrian village had identified itself with the flower, and because the early blooming time would position the festival at the very beginning of the tourism season. It should be mentioned that tulips had not been grown in large numbers in the village before 2008. A total of 100,000 bulbs were planted that first year. In recent years greater efficiency in how the bulbs are placed has made it possible to reduce the annual planting to about 60,000 (Tulpenfest in Edelsbach, 2019).

Minimising leakage

The Tourism Association took pains from the beginning to ensure that the proceeds from the festival would remain to a very large extent within the village (Zarnhofer, 2012, p. 10). Catering is done by local restaurants, direct farm marketers and village organisations, such as the local band, volunteer fire brigade, seniors' club and tennis club. The beer served comes from a microbrewery in the next village and a larger commercial brewery in Graz, which provides the tables and benches for free as part of the contract. Wine is supplied by two village wineries and the mineral water comes from springs located 30 km away. No soft drinks are served—instead the guests can choose from a wide range of fruit juices from local farmers. The meat served comes from the local butcher, who actually still slaughters and processes animals from local farmers. The pastries sold are produced by local people, the village bakery and a local sheltered workshop. This strong commitment to local sourcing means that leakage is minimal. But it also has a second benefit. This commitment is also communicated to the guests, and so reinforces the message that the festival is a celebration of local identity and may also serve to mollify the odd guest who is unhappy about not being able to order a Coke.

Local cultural identity

Local financial participation in the event is not the end of the story, however. The programming is also a product of local identity. Local choirs, the local marching band, dance groups and the local theatre group provide the entertainment at the event. Some international colour is provided by dance groups and choirs from a partner village in Hungary. This partnership, however, is intensely "lived", with multiple visits back and forth between the two villages each year. This "foreign" element in the programme is therefore not really foreign at all, because the partnership is also part of the two villages' identity. Evidence of the close interaction between the cultural programme and identity is extensive. The elementary school choir, for example, named itself the "Tulpinis"—an idea that came from the children, not the teachers. And a member of the men's choir composed a "Tulip Festival Song", which is now sung at the festival opening each year. The tulip beds themselves provide a further opportunity for identification, because various groups, such as the kindergarten, the pottery club and even the radio-controlled model car club "adopt" beds and then compete with one another to come up with the most creative and colourful design. The visitors to the event then vote on the best bed.

Other examples of the high degree of identification between villagers and "their" festival include a number of products that have been developed in connection with the festival. The baker sells gingerbread with a Tulip Festival logo. One of the village's vintners has created a tulip wine. A cocktail stand at the festival sells tulip-themed cocktails. And the Tourism Association worked with a regional chocolatier to create a chocolate bar with honey, jelly made from the tulip wine and dried tulip blossoms as decoration.

Waste avoidance

Resident identification is only part of the reason for the event's ongoing success. Another has been the firm commitment from the beginning to making the event as ecologically sustainable as possible. It has to be said that the groundwork for this mindset has been laid in the last 20 years by an initiative of the Styrian state government called "G'scheit feiern" (Celebrate Intelligently). It provides small subsidies to events that are managed in such a way as to minimise waste (Land Steiermark, 2016). As a consequence of the initiative, infrastructure has been created that permits neighbouring communities to cooperate in this effort. All the food and beverages at the Tulip Festival are served using reusable glasses, plates and silverware, which are immediately collected and washed onsite in portable washing stations as soon as the patrons are finished eating. Such washing stations are shared among several villages, as they are almost never needed simultaneously. A factor which makes this solution workable is the fact that the festival is supported by the work of asylum-seekers who live just over the municipality's border in the next village. Over the last several years, several groups of asylum-seekers have helped bus tables, and the villagers are glad to see "their" refugees included in the festival.

The local sourcing also reduces wastes. All of the beverages are supplied in return-able bottles which go back directly to the farmers for reuse at the end of the festival, and all of the containers in which the pastries are supplied also go back to the sup-pliers. The net result of such practices is that only 240 litres of residual waste were generated by the festival in 2018 (Tourismusverband Edelsbach, 2019). The commit-ment to keeping waste to a minimum is reflected in numerous decisions taken over the years by the organisers. For example, when the idea of reducing the need for labour by using bamboo plates instead of ceramic was raised, it was immediately rejected by the group. Even though the plates would be recyclable, they still represent waste and furthermore are transported half-way around the world before they get to Edelsbach.

Attitudes toward growth and quality of life

The commitment to sustainability also influences the residents' attitude toward growth. There is a general consensus among the organisers that the festival should not grow. Although the marketing of the event is not especially professional (with only a very rudimentary homepage and very limited social media presence, for example), the organisers have made a conscious decision not to expand it in any significant way. The annual visitor numbers of about 6,000 is viewed as the village's carrying capacity. If more people come, there would not be enough parking, the present catering system would not work anymore and additional suppliers would have to be brought in from outside. There is the fear that if that were to take place, one could not be certain that the new catering firms would keep to the same standards regarding food sourcing and waste. At present the festival is seen by residents as contributing to the quality of life of the village. The concern on the part of the organisers is that growth might turn opinion in the opposite direction (Tourismusverband Edelsbach, 2019).

Social considerations have played a central role in the organisers' thinking from the beginning. After the festival had been running for five years, in-depth interviews were conducted with 21 individuals who were involved in the organisation. One of the main reasons they said they remained involved, despite the large amount of work involved, was related to the role of the festival in promoting social cohesion and pride in the village (Zarnhofer, 2012, p. 5).That was, by extension, associated with main-taining the high quality of life in the village. This appears at least as important as motivator for the villagers as the financial gains made through sales to the festival's visitors (Zarnhofer, 2012, p. 5).

Sufficiency as a sustainable goal

At the outset of this discussion, the recent assertion that sufficiency is a more ap-propriate guiding principle for sustainable tourism than "sustainable" growth was explored. For rural communities, sufficiency may be understood in such basic things as the local shop staying open, young people having sufficient perspectives to stay

Census and Registry* Figures						Population Predictions			
1971	1981	1991	2001	2011	2019*	2015	2020	2025	2030
1295	1295	1309	1371	1398	1402*	1363	1329	1314	1299

Figure 14.1 Population of Edelsbach bei Feldbach.
Sources: Land Steiermark, 2019a; Land Steiermark, 2019b.

put rather than moving away and the local school having enough children to make it pay to keep its doors open. When a village community also functions socially, then the prospects for avoiding depopulation are good. In proper dosages tourism can well contribute to such a healthy development. While it would certainly be a stretch to maintain that the Tulip Festival alone is responsible for minimising depopulation in Edelsbach, it may play a small role as one of many measures to maintain the local quality of life.

Bottom-up initiatives resulting in desirable rural lifestyles have been shown elsewhere to contribute to reversing rural decline (Li, Westlund, Zheng & Liu, 2016). Edelsbach appears to have figured that out. While the county in which Edelsbach is located has suffered a 2.4% population decline since 2001, Edelsbach has actually grown slightly in the last 20 years and appears to be bucking population predictions made by the state government regarding its demographic development (Figure 14.1):

Furthermore, despite being located only 7 km from the county seat, the economic drawing power of which has led to the closing of many shops and other infrastructure in surrounding villages, Edelsbach has managed to hang on to its kindergarten, elementary school, two small grocery stores, a bakery, a butcher, automotive mechanic, assisted living facility, general practitioner and veterinarian. If sustainably organised events such as the Tulip Festival do indeed contribute to social cohesion and local pride, as well as to the economic viability of local businesses, then they may also very well contribute to a socio-economic steady-state and the "good life" that is, we have argued, ultimately the goal of sustainability.

Reflections

1   Self-understanding and reflection are prerequisites for ethical and sustainable behaviour. This applies to both individuals and groups. In times in which change is the only constant, it is especially important for a community to know its residents and what they want to achieve. Only then can common goals be identified and reached.

2   Sustainable economic activity at the local level means minimising waste and conserving resources, while ensuring that the income generated by such economic activity remains to as large a degree as possible within the community. For this to work, the local population has to be led in their actions by these guiding principles of sustainability, which will lead them to make use of local products and labour. The better the inclusion of local residents works, the lower the potential for conflict that might interfere with the success of such economic activity in the long term.

3   If community residents begin to define themselves through common goals that lead to a steady-state in which all of them can survive economically, then unlimited growth may lose its meaning as the be-all and end-all of economic development. The local population then can decide which activities are conducive to the steady-state and which are not. Taking control is an important prerequisite for sustainable development of societies.

4   The Edelsbach Tulip Festival could probably grow significantly if it were more professionally and aggressively marketed. The organisers have made a conscious decision against additional growth, because profit maximisation is not their primary goal. Instead, sufficiency, social coherence and community pride are the main driving motivators for the festival. By always keeping the interests of the local residents in mind, the organisers have established a basis for ethical and sustainable event management.

Questions

1   Can the demands of economic growth and sustainable development be reconciled? If so, how?

2   How can regional sustainable development contribute in the long run to protecting local jobs that might otherwise be threatened by global and digital competition?

3   What lessons can be learned from the Edelsbach Tulip Festival that might be applied to other communities and touristic endeavours?

4   The Edelsbach Tulip Festival was originally intended to enhance the visibility of the village and its attractions and bring in more guests throughout the year, rather than to create a "green event". In the meantime, the positive effects are more varied than originally imagined. Based on what you have read, do you think the Festival has proven to be a learning experience for the local residents? In what ways?

5   How can a well-developed local cultural identity influence tendencies toward out-migration in rural regions?

Further reading

Agyeiwaah, E., McKercher B. & Suntikul, W. (2017). Identifying core indicators of sustainable tourism: A path forward? *Tourism Management Perspectives*, 24, 26–33.

The Austrian Ecolabel for Green Meetings and Green Events. www.umweltzeichen.at/en/green-meetings-and-events/home.

BMLFUW. (n.d.) *Green meetings and green events.* Retrieved on May 17, 2018, from www.umweltzeichen.at/cms/upload/20%20docs/2016/web_green_meetingsbroschre_2016.pdf.

Buathong, K. & Lai, P.-C. (2019). Event sustainable development in Thailand: A qualitative investigation. *Journal of Hospitality, Leisure, Sport and Tourism Education*, 24, 110–119.

George, W., Maier, H. & Reid, D. (2009). *Rural tourism development. Localism and cultural change.* Bristol: Channel View Publications.

Hallak, R., Brown, G. & Lindsay, N. (2012). The Place Identity – Performance relationship among tourism entrepreneurs: A structural equation modelling analysis. *Tourism Management* 33, 143–154. doi:10.1016/j.tourman.2011.02.013. Retrieved on April 9, 2017, from www.sciencedirect.com/science/article/pii/S0261517711000574.

Hanna, P., Font, X., Scarles, C., Weeden, C. & Harrison, C. (2018). Tourist destination marketing: From sustainability myopia to memorable experiences. *Journal of Destination Marketing & Management*, 9, 36–43.

Hjalager, A. & Kwiatkowski, G. (2017). Entrepreneurial implications, prospects and dilemmas in rural festivals. *Journal of Rural Studies*. Retrieved on April 9, 2017, from http://doi.org/10.1016/j.jrurstud.2017.02.019.

Laing, J. & Frost, W. (2010). How green was my festival: Exploring challenges and opportunities associated with staging green events. *International Journal of Hospitality Management*, 29(2), 261–267.

McCabe, S. (2006). The making of community identity through historic festive practice: The case of Ashbourne Royal Shrovetide Football. In D. Picard& M. Robinson (eds.). *Festivals, Tourism and Social Change*. (pp. 99–118). Cleveland: Channel View Publications.

Nierling, L. (2012). "This is a bit of the good life": Recognition of unpaid work from the perspective of degrowth. *Ecological Economics*, 84, 240–246.

Picard, D. & Robinson, M. (2006). *Festivals, Tourism and Social Change*. Clevedon: Channel View Publications.

Tölkes, C. (2018). Sustainability communication in tourism – A literature review. *Tourism Management Perspectives*, 27, 10–21.

References

Antonakakis, N., Dabouni, M. & Filis, G. (2015). How strong is the linkage between tourism and economic growth in Europe? *Economic Modelling*, 44, 142–155.

Aristotle. (1999). *Nicomachean Ethics*. Kitchener: Batoche Books.

Boggia, A., Massei, G., Paolotti, L., Rocchi, L. & Schiavi, F. (2018). A model for measuring the environmental sustainability of events. *Journal of Environmental Management*, 206, 836–845.

Chirieleison, C. & Scrucca, L. (2017). Event sustainability and transportation policy: A model-based cluster analysis for a cross-comparison of hallmark events. *Tourism Management Perspectives*, 24, 72–85.

Croitor, E. (2014). Ethics of Responsibility? Some postmodern views. *Procedia—Social and Behavioural Sciences*, 149, 253–260.

Curcija, M. Breakey, N. & Driml, S. (2019). Development of a conflict management model as a tool for improved project outcomes in community based tourism, 70, 341–354.

Fath, B. (2014). Sustainable systems promote wholeness- extending transformations: The contributions of systems thinking. *Ecological Modelling*, 293, 42–48.

Friedl, H. (2007). Kybernetische Tourismusethik: Zukunftsweisendes Instrument des nachhaltigen Tourismusmanagements? In R. Egger & T. Herdin (eds.), *Tourismus. Herausforderung. Zukunft* (pp. 561–586). Salzburg: Lit-Verlag.

Friedl, H. (2015a). Communication. In C. Cater, B. Garrod & T. Low (eds.), *The Encyclopedia of Sustainable Tourism* (pp. 112–113). Wallingford: CABI.

Friedl, H. (2015b). Degrowth. In C. Cater, B. Garrod & T. Low (eds.), *The Encyclopedia of Sustainable Tourism* (p. 161). Wallingford: CABI.

Hall, C.M. (2009). Degrowing tourism: Decroissance, sustainable consumption and steady-state tourism. *Anatolia: An International Journal of Tourism and Hospitality Research*, 20(1), 46–61.

Hjalager, A. & Kwiatkowski, G. (2017). Entrepreneurial implications, prospects and dilemmas in rural festivals. *Journal of Rural Studies*. Retrieved on April 9, 2017, from http://doi.org/10.1016/j.jrurstud.2017.02.019.

Higgins-Desboilles, F. (2010). The elusiveness of sustainability in tourism: The culture-ideology of consumerism and its implications. *Tourism and Hospitality Research*, 10(2), 116–129.

Higgins-Desboilles, F. (2018). Sustainable tourism: Sustaining tourism or something more? *Tourism Management Perspectives*, 25, 157–160.

Hottle, T., Bilec, M., Brown, N. & Landis, A. (2015). Toward zero waste: Composting and recycling for sustainable venue based events. *Waste Management*, 38, 86–94.Retrieved on May 17, 2018, from www.sciencedirect.com/science/article/pii/S0956053X15000562?via%3Dihub#s0050.

Jopling, D. (2000). *Self-Knowledge and the Self*. New York: Routledge.

Land Steiermark. (2016). *G'SCHEIT FEIERN: No waste! Serve healthy food! Travel by bus, taxi or car-pooling*. Retrieved on May 17, 2018, from www.gscheitfeiern.steiermark.at/cms/dokumente/10209129_27662367/7339f462/Infofolder_GF_EN_V1.1.pdf.

Land Steiermark. (2019a).*Datenkatalog: Metadaten-Details—Bevölkerungsentwicklung in den Gemeinden der Steiermark, 1869–2011.* Retrieved on February 17, 2019, from http:// data.steiermark.at/cms/beitrag/11822084/97108894/?AppInt_OGD_ID=50.

Land Steiermark. (2019b).*Datenkatalog: Metadaten-Details-Bevölkerungsprognose Steiermark, 2015–2030.* Retrieved on February 17, 2019, from http://data.steiermark.at/cms/beit rag/11822084/97108894/?AppInt_OGD_ID=42.Li, Y., Westlund, H., Zheng, X. & Liu, Y. (2016). Bottom-up initiatives and revival in the face of rural decline: Case studies from China and Sweden. *Journal of Rural Studies, 47,* 506–513.

Mantatov, V.& Mantatova, L. (2015). Philosophical underpinnings of environmental ethics: Theory of responsibility by Hans Jonas. *Procedia – Social and Behavioral Sciences, 214,* 1055–1061.

McCabe, S. (2006). The making of community identity through historic festive practice: The case of Ashbourne Royal Shrovetide Football. In D. Picard& M. Robinson (eds.). *Festivals, Tourism and Social Change.* (pp. 99–118). Cleveland: Channel View Publications.

Meadows, D. H., Meadows, D. L., Randers, J.& Behrens, W. (1972). *The Limits to Growth.* New York: New American Library.

Moick, D. (2007). *Gsellmanns Weltmaschine: Volkskunst der anderen Art im bäuerlichen Milieu der Oststeiermark* (Unpublished doctoral dissertation). Karl-Franzens Universität Graz.

Morand, S. & Lajaunie, C. (2018). *Biodiversity and Health. Linking Life, Ecosystems, Societies.* London: ISTE Press.

Oliveria de Paula, G. & Cavalcanti, R. (2000). Ethics: Essence for sustainability. *Journal of Cleaner Production, 8*(2), 109–117.

Pablo-Romero, M. & Molina, J. (2013). Tourism and economic growth: A review of empirical literature. *Tourism Management Perspectives, 8,* 28–41.

Pappas, E., Pappas, J., & Sweeney, D. (2015). Walking the walk: Conceptual foundations of the sustainable personality. *Journal of Cleaner Production, 86,* 323–334.

Picard, D. & Robinson, M. (2006). *Festivals, Tourism and Social Change.* Clevedon: Channel View Publications.

Rey, C. & Bastons, M. (2018). Three dimensions of effective mission implementation. *Long Range Planning, 51*(4), 580–585.

Saarinen, J. (2006). Traditions of sustainability in tourism studies. *Annals of Tourism Research, 33*(4), 1121–1140.

Sacks, J. (2005). *To Heal a Fractured World: The Ethics of Responsibility.* London: Continuum.

Schneider, F., Kallis, G. & Martinez-Alier, J. (2010). Crisis or opportunity? Economic degrowth for social equity and ecological sustainability. Introduction to this special issue. *Journal of Cleaner Production, 18*(6), 511–518.

Serpe, R. & Stryker, S. (2011). The symbolic interactionist perspective and identity theory. In S. Schwartz,K. Luyckx & V. L. Vignoles (eds.) *Handbook of Identity Theory and Research*(pp. 225–248). New York: Springer.

Tourismusverband Edelsbach. (2019). Minutes of the Annual Meeting held on 14 February, 2019.

Tulpenfest in Edelsbach. (2019).Retrieved on February 15, 2019, from www.steiermark.com/ de/reiseplanung/veranstaltungen/tulpenfest-in-edelsbach_e963934.

UNWTO. (2015). *Tourism and the Sustainable Development Goals.* Madrid: UNWTO.

Yuan, Y. (2013). Adding environmental sustainability of the management of event tourism. *International Journal of Culture, Tourism and Hospitality Research, 7*(2), 175–183.

Zarnhofer, C. (2012). *5 Jahre Tulpenfest in Edelsbach: Endbericht zur Befragung unter Helfern und Beteiligten der letzten Jahre.* Unpublished Report.

Zelenika, I., Moreau, T. & Zhao, J. (2018). Toward zero waste events: Reducing contamination in waste streams with volunteer assistance. *Waste Management, 76,* 39–45.

15 Bicycle networks as a new ground project

The Montesilvano case study

Antonio Alberto Clemente

Introduction

The Adriatic city is a linear conurbation that runs along the coastline of six regions: Veneto, Emilia, Marche, Abruzzo, Molise and part of Apulia. Its construction began in the early 1900s and was resumed, with great intensity, after the Second World War, mainly for tourist purposes. Such construction continued, in the following decades, with a single common factor: the coastline. However, for many years, cities and towns along the coast continued to assert their identity, rather than their belonging to a same territorial denominator. In the 1980s, it became clear that alongside specificities, a common feature existed which was distinctive from a geographical viewpoint: a filiform heart that belonged to "a seaside metropolis that has no equal in Europe" (Tondelli, 1986). One that goes well beyond municipal boundaries, beyond both the provincial and the regional scales until it includes

> the entire Adriatic coast: an amusement park defined in relation not so much to real landscapes, but rather to the landscapes of our imagination. And that these beaches, these hotels, have much to do with our imagination, with our myths and with the history of our most recent decades is an indisputable fact.
>
> (Tondelli, 1990)

Construction continued, incessantly, in the following years as well, to the point that the Adriatic city now appears as a compact whole in which the rarefaction of the fabric is an exception with respect to a rule that never changes: its alignment with the coast. The saturation of space, however, is not only an indicator of a specific building paradigm, but also a testimony to the fact that the Adriatic city has never lost its appeal and, even today, continues to remain one of Italy's major tourist attractions (www.bancaditalia.it). This is also the case in Abruzzo. The region's view of the sea seen

> from above meets the eye as an undifferentiated segment of the larger agglomeration which borders the entire western Adriatic area. A segment consisting of now thicker, now more rarefied portions, furrowed by infrastructural lines, almost a reproduction of the coastline, rhythmically variegated by portions which move inland towards the Apennines.
>
> (Bianchetti, 2003)

A construction process that now appears to have reached its final stages. Almost crystallised in an image where everything seems to be coming to an end. Where the future perspective is the restructuring of what already exists, rather than the addition of anything new. If, however, one looks carefully at the specific territorial features of Abruzzo, the characteristics of its landscapes and its environmental values, then what emerges clearly is that there is still a lot of work to be done in favour of a more sustainable type of tourism.

Cycling network and urban flooding

Specific features of the Adriatic city of Abruzzo are its urban and area cycling infrastructures. Elsewhere too, along the coast, there are examples of virtuous municipalities in this respect, but what happens in Abruzzo is particular. From Ortona to Martinsicuro there is an almost seamless route through Francavilla, Pescara, Montesilvano, Silvi, Pineto, Roseto, Giulianova, Tortoreto, Alba Adriatica: about 100 km of coastline where the bicycle is a concrete alternative to the motor car, so we are informed by a survey (www.comuniciclabili.it/2019), carried out to identify the Italian cities which best cater to the needs of cyclists. Since the assessment concerns both daily mobility and holiday experience, an exclusively quantitative approach was set aside, as this would have given primacy to those urban conglomerates with the most extensive cycling paths in terms of kilometres, without saying anything about their quality, the extension of the network, its safety and the services made available to the public, including tourists. This is precisely the reason why the indicators taken into consideration belong to four large families. The first is amateur cycling, which interprets the ability of a city to connect with cycling paths on a territorial scale and whether adequate accommodation facilities are available to meet the needs of those who choose a cycling holiday.

The second family refers to the need to integrate the moderation of car traffic with the extension of pedestrian areas and cycling paths, above all in specific areas. The third concerns governance

> because the process of transforming mobility and therefore the city, requires strategic objectives, planning (Sustainable Urban Mobility Plans, Biciplan), dedicated bodies (mobility manager, bicycle department) and measures which are not only infrastructural, such as the organisation and management of pedibus and bicibus services.
>
> (www.comuniciclabili.it/2018)

Lastly, the effectiveness of communication policies was assessed, since changes in urban mobility mainly concern a radical transformation of the idea of cities (Bernardi, 2013) in which "the use of bicycles offers a concrete dimension to the dream of a utopian world in which the joy of living is finally a priority for everyone and ensures respect for all" (Augé, 2009).

Urban and area cycling infrastructures are accompanied by another fact: in July 2018, the National Agency for new technologies, energy and sustainable economic development (ENEA) included Pescara and Martinsicuro among the coastal areas at greatest risk of flooding due to the rise of the Mediterranean Sea (www.enea.it/2018). Alongside this phenomenon is another which makes the situation even more serious:

in recent years, along the entire Abruzzo coastline, the frequency of urban flooding resulting from extreme weather conditions is increasing. This is largely due to the reduction of vegetation, excessive soil sealing and an obsolete and insufficient drainage network.

Symbol of this difficult condition is Montesilvano which, despite being one of the municipalities which best caters to the needs of cyclists, is the emblem, in positive and negative, of the Adriatic city. One of its main characteristic is its extraordinary demographic growth. According to data from the Italian Institute of Statistics (www.istat.it/2013), the population has increased from just over 7,000 (1951) to almost 30,000 (1981) and, in 2011, exceeded 50,000. And it continues to grow, considering that, according to the municipal registry office, there are now over 54,000 residents (www.comune.montesilvano.pe.it). To such demographic data must be added the productive, commercial and service areas (www.istat.it/2014), the phenomenon of holiday homes and that of accommodation facilities built to satisfy the demand of the seaside tourist industry. What is more, to better understand the phenomenon of soil sealing, it should be noted that the municipal area of Montesilvano extends over just 23.57 sq km (2,300 inhabitants/sq km), compressed between the coastline, the major area infrastructures (Adriatic railway, State Road 16, Motorway A14), the dual carriageway and the river Saline. In this context, urban flooding is a priority issue from the environmental point of view – the pollution of the sea and the river resulting from the flow of surface water into which runs not only rain but also the return flow of the sewage system – and from an economic and social point of view – the damage which infrastructures, the cultural heritage, the residential fabric and production areas are liable to suffer, and the risks affecting the population.

Cycling infrastructures and urban flooding are two issues which the Adriatic city of Abruzzo has always addressed separately. The first is seen as a contribution to slow mobility, often too sectoral because it is linked to the creation of the largest number of kilometres of cycling paths. The second continues to be treated as a periodic emergency to be faced from time to time so as to get the situation back to normal in the shortest possible time.

An effort is probably needed to overcome such separateness. And to imagine a sustainable cycling network in terms of its environmental, social and economic benefits, which can also contribute to the resilience of the urban system through measures to combat urban flooding. Of course, this intention is, in reality, a working hypothesis which requires a verification of sources in order to understand whether the possibility actually exists of dealing with the two aspects as closely linked phenomena.

Regulations, guidelines and good practices

The study began by looking at urban planning regulations. In 1995, the principal concern expressed in the *Direttive per la redazione, adozione ed attuazione dei Piani Urbani del Traffico* (Directives for the Preparation, Adoption and Implementation of Urban Traffic Plans) in relation to pedestrians and cyclists was to "provide all interventions useful and necessary for guaranteeing safety". Successively, in 1998, the *Norme per il finanziamento della mobilità ciclistica* (Regulations for Financing Bicycle Mobility) anticipated, on the one hand, an intermodal relationship between bicycles and public transport and, on the other hand, identified priority areas for the realisation of cycling lanes along abandoned or unused rail lines and riverbanks.

The following year, the Ministry of Public Works, together with the Ministry of Transport, issued the *Regolamento recante norme per la definizione delle caratteristiche tecniche delle piste ciclabili* (Regulation Containing Rules for Defining the Technical Characteristics of Cycling Lanes). The aims of this regulation included

> favouring and promoting an elevated level of bicycle and pedestrian movement, as an alternative to the use of combustion engine vehicles in urban areas [...]; focusing on the attractiveness, continuity and recognisability of cycling routes [...]; evaluating the profitability of investments in relation to real and potential users and in relation to the objective of reducing the risk of accidents and levels of atmospheric and acoustic pollution; verifying the concrete feasibility and real utilisation of cycling lanes by users.

In 2013, the strategic objectives for urban bicycle mobility in the region of Abruzzo were as follows: increasing the existing network of cycling lanes (privileging the creation of a network), improving safety and including the introduction of specific signage and the connection with the system of public mobility (Fleury, 2012). The regulations for the preparation of the *Biciplans* (Bike Plans) contained in Law 2/2018 can be ascribed to a vast register:

> towns not part of metropolitan cities and metropolitan cities are to prepare and adopt, in relation to their budget [...] and its eventual modifications, plans for urban bicycle mobility, known as "biciplans". These *Piani Urbani della Mobilità Sostenibile* (PUMS), or plans for sustainable urban mobility, are to focus on defining objectives, strategies and actions necessary to promote and intensify the use of the bicycle as a means of transport for daily movements and activities related to tourism and recreation and to improve safety for cyclists and pedestrians.

Another analytical approach is tied to the comparison between the extraordinary production of guidelines. There are substantially five main areas of investigation: the identification of the network, signage, safety, materials and dimensional characteristics of cycling lanes. The objectives of the guidelines include the promotion of using the bicycle as a means of transport for movements between the home-work/school; clarifying the environmental, social and economic benefits linked to the use of the bicycle with respect to traditional forms of motorised mobility; guaranteeing an elevated standard of safety by minimising the risk of accidents or any other risk to cyclists; defining the most effective signage; identifying the geometric standards for the various typologies of paths, also considering that

> without cohesion there is no network, only a bunch of single routes. This is a matter of degree: the more routes interconnect and allow cyclists to freely choose their itinerary, the stronger the network is. For cyclists, cohesion is a very real quality: it is the extent to which they can reach their destination via the route of their choice.
>
> (European Commission, 2010)

As regards good practices, the reference is L'ABiCi – 2° Rapporto Legambici on the economy of the bicycle in Italy of 2018 edited by Legambiente (www.legambiente.it).

The assessments of the guide move in four main directions: the modal share of the communal area, i.e., the type of vehicle used to move from home to the town centre; the splitting up of cycling paths by type (separate or promiscuous, in carriageway or on pavement); the thematic surveys produced by the Istituto Superiore di Formazione e Ricerca per i Trasporti (ISFORT), Confartigianato, including those on the current lack of safety of cycling paths and on the fact that, in Italy, over the last ten years, there has been an increase of such paths in terms of kilometres, while the same cannot be said of cyclists. Fourth and last direction of investigation is the economic value of the bicycle for which the main reference was The EU Cycling Economy (www.ecf. com). From these premises, despite the fact that they are only very briefly described here, it emerges that, more than any others, Bolzano, Pesaro, Ferrara and Treviso are Italy's most bike-friendly cities.

These brief considerations reveal how regulations, guidelines and good practices are functional to the achievement of five objectives: inter-modality, technical functionality, safety, design and comfort, and closure of the network (Giuliani and Maternini, 2018). The background on which they work is that of a cycling path intended, exclusively, as an infrastructure for slow mobility. A sort of small highway in which controlled speed, mono-functionality aimed at ensuring movement from one place to another and specialisation due to transit dedicated to bicycles only, appear as phenomena which rule out any relationship with the surrounding context. This is why it is possible to assert that the greatest challenge still remains open: to escape from a sectorial logic entirely internal to cycling. However, our intention is not to discuss the usefulness of legislation, guidelines or the interest of good practices, but to point out that these are not enough to build an environmental infrastructure able to take on responsibility, albeit only to a certain extent, for the problems and opportunities of a project and the areas involved in it. And it is precisely on the basis of these observations that we should ask ourselves: can the bicycle network be just this? Or can it play other roles as well? Some cities have gone further. Philadelphia, Melbourne, Boston, San Rafael and Copenhagen have asked themselves which are the most appropriate responses to transform water from a potential risk element into a strategic resource for the resilience of the urban system seen as

> the ability of a system, community or society exposed to hazards to resist, absorb, accommodate, adapt to, transform and recover from the effects of a hazard in a timely and efficient manner, including through the preservation and restoration of its essential basic structures and functions through risk management.
>
> (www.unisdr.org)

These cities have worked on the basis of the idea that the soil of the cycle network is not only a support for cycling traffic but also a layer or, rather, a series of superimposed layers, which can contribute to the construction of an environmental infrastructure, including with a view to improving water collection and management, both under normal and extreme conditions, as in the case of urban flooding.

Philadelphia

In Philadelphia, the *Green City-Clean Water plan* (www.phillywatersheds.org/doc), whose general aim is to avoid overloading the sewer network, is based on a number of cardinal criteria such as recharging water tables and maintaining and expanding water infrastructures. It is precisely in this direction that a network of cycling lanes, as part of an infrastructural system, enters the realm of planning. In particular, in the *City of Philadelphia Green Streets Design Manual* (www.phillywatersheds.org/img) identifies six green stormwater infrastructures for the collection and management of stormwater in densely urbanised areas:

permeable pavement. Its porous surface and subterranean stone reservoir provide temporary storage, before the water filters into the ground. Naturally, there are many types of porous surfaces, including permeable asphalt and permeable pavers. These latter function differently than permeable asphalt and concrete. Instead of allowing water to penetrate through the paved surfaces, the pavers typically allow water to pass through the joint spacing between the pavers.

stormwater planters or rain gardens. Similar to flower beds, they tend to be longer than they are wider. Flanking sidewalks they are used to manage runoff from the street and sidewalk. The level of the planting media in the planter is lower than the sidewalk and paralleled by a drain at the street edge. Rain gardens are used to manage rainwater by allowing for its storage, infiltration and evapotranspiration. Excess runoff is channelled into an overflow pipe connected to the existing sewer network.

stormwater bump-outs (midblock and corner). These planted extensions of the sidewalk project out into the street, midblock or at intersections to create what is to all intents and purposes a new curb located close to the existing one. A bump-out consists of a layer of stone covered with soil and plants. The slope of the sidewalk deviates the flow of rainwater so that it can be stored, filtered and collected by plants (evapotranspiration). Excess runoff can be channelled into the existing sewer network.

stormwater trees. This term refers to a tree planted in a bed set into the sidewalk. The upper surface of the planting media is set below street level, and runoff is managed by drains. Water from the sidewalk runs directly into the bed. It is possible to imagine a series of tree beds that are able to manage the highest volume of rainwater, which can successively be filtered or channelled into the sewer system.

stormwater tree trenches. This is a system of trees connected to an underground infiltration system. On the surface, it resembles a normal sequence of planted trees. However, in reality it is a system composed of trenches dug beneath the sidewalk, finished with a permeable geotextile fabric and filled with stones or gravel, covered by the amount of terrain required to support the trees' root balls. Rainwater flows from the sloping sidewalk and from the street into a horizontal drain connected to the underground infiltration system. Water can be stored in void spaces between stones and used to irrigate the trees and slowly filter through the base layer, green gutter. This narrow, elongated and shallow landscaped strip along the street curb (or that of a bicycle lane) that manages stormwater runoff. The upper layer of the planting media is set lower than the street level to aid runoff from the street and sidewalk. The system attenuates stormwater flows, provides for storage and, in some cases, filtration and evapotranspiration. In flow-through green gutters, overflow runoff can be conveyed to the existing storm drain system, either through an underdrain tied to the existing storm drain system, or as shallow concentrated flow that is conveyed downstream to an existing inlet.

Melbourne

The La Trobe Street green bicycle lane is a new cycling lane with its own dedicated space (http://urbanwater.melbourne.vic.gov.au). The design involves the narrowing of the roadbed and the modification of parking stalls. The lane is separated from the street by a traffic divider that also serves as a planting bed for trees. This bed is used to channel stormwater from the street and water that penetrates through the porous asphalt finish of the bike lane. The structure of the planting bed is designed to favour the passive irrigation of the tree roots. On the one hand, this limits the risk of flooding and, on the other hand, helps reduce stormwater pollution. Thermal imagery has shown La Trobe Street to be one of the hottest areas in the city. The planting of trees that cover the bicycle lane serves not only to collect and manage stormwater, but also to create shade and cool the air. However, the trees can also have a negative impact on safety for cyclists. A study identified three actions for reducing this risk: the use of bike-friendly drain covers, pruning of the trees up to a height of 2.4 metres above street level to maintain the efficiency of sunlight and the selection of trees with slender trunks.

The La Trobe Street green bicycle lane belongs to a vaster understanding of the contribution to the implementation of the Total Watermark (http://melbourne.vic.gov.au/getinvolved): City as a Catchment Strategy for the integrated water cycle management; the Urban Forest Strategy program to create a more resilient, healthier and diversified city by increasing urban plantings; the Bicycle Plan whose primary aim is to increase the safety and attractiveness of cycling lanes and the Climate Change Adaptation Strategy, which includes a line of specific actions designed to contrast urban flooding caused by extreme climatic events (www.melbourne.vic.gov.au/doc).

In light of these brief considerations, The La Trobe Street green bicycle lane is more than a bicycle lane. It is also an environmental infrastructure that integrates soil permeability with stormwater catchment, passive irrigation and the objective of contrasting heat islands (Figure 15.1).

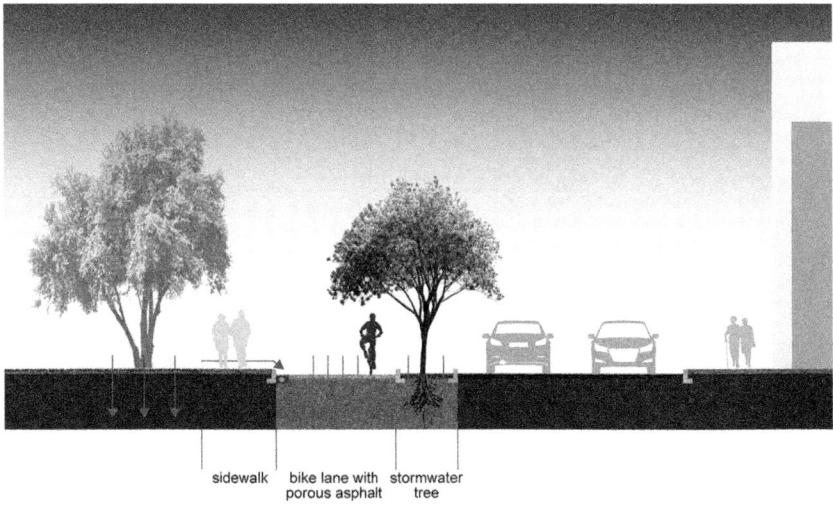

Figure 15.1 Melbourne, section of La Trobe Street green bicycle lane.

Greater Boston

"Scientists have predicted an overall increase in sea level of 4 to 6 feet by the end of this century, which will place a large portion of existing infrastructure networks in Greater Boston under water" (www.boston.uli.org). "Developing resilience: Living with water strategies for Greater Boston" represents the policy of the metropolitan area of Boston to counter flood risks. The starting point was to realise that the lack of a public debate on the social and economic implications of floods has led to a general underestimation of the risks to be faced. That is why raising the awareness of the population and stakeholders as regards the fact that the effects of climate change are the most important challenge for the future of cities was such a fundamental step. Developing resilience is a systematic set of measures on a supra-municipal scale the overall aim of which is to improve the sustainability and resilience of the urban system. From a programmatic point of view, a series of projects are planned in the residential sector in order to improve the environmental performance of buildings; in the infrastructural sector in order to reduce the vulnerability of the electricity, natural gas, drinking water and sewage networks; in the transport sector in order to make public and private mobility more sustainable. And this is precisely the sector into which the redevelopment of Western Avenue falls. A road that plays a major role in linking Central Square and the Charles River in Cambridge. The project has two main objectives: to moderate car traffic flows and to improve rainwater treatment. The first of these objectives was pursued by reducing the carriageway and expanding the cycle/pedestrian section. The second resulted in the construction of a cycling path out of permeable material while the part immediately adjacent to it consists of green stormwater infrastructures. Both these solutions allow the water to flow towards a pipeline completely separate from waste waters. From the hydraulic point of view, this pipeline dedicated to filtered water, both from the permeable floor and from the vegetation, has a double positive effect: it increases rainwater drainage capacity and reduces the pressure on the sewage system. Western Avenue is both a sustainable and resilient project because the soil becomes not only a support for cycling but also an environmental infrastructure which fits perfectly into the urban context (Figure 15.2).

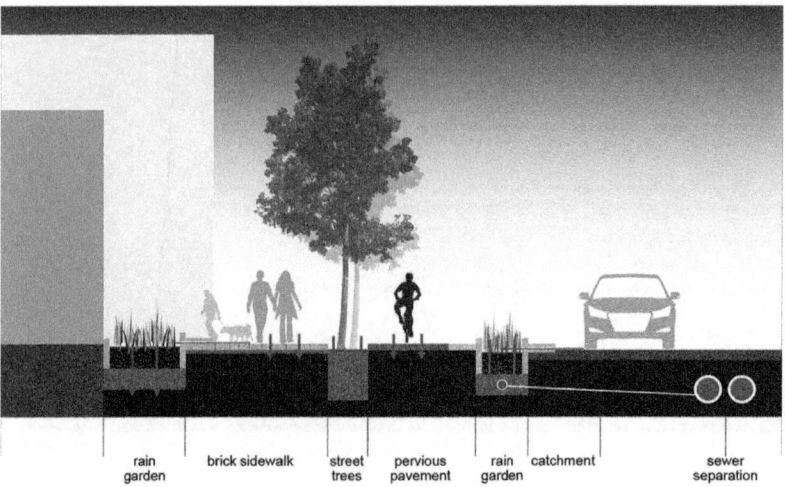

Figure 15.2 Greater Boston (Cambridge), section of Western Avenue.

San Rafael

San Rafael is the city most exposed to flood risk in the whole of San Francisco Bay. In the face of this problem, more traditional solutions no longer seem sufficient, not only to counter the dangers of urban flooding but also to return the city, in a short time, to the condition it was in prior to the stress situation caused by heavy rains, rising sea levels or both. The current situation requires a radical change: we can no longer contemplate simply raising banks to counter the disastrous effects of urban flooding; we must counter the trends underway, with which everyone is well acquainted, in order to plan the most appropriate measures in advance. In other words, we must move from the logic of emergency to that of priority. It is on the basis of these considerations that the "Elevate San Rafael" project was born. A project characterised by a multidisciplinary approach to the theme of urban flooding in which

> Elevate San Rafael is a new paradigm to respond to the complexity of environmental change. We propose that the city evolve by employing time-tested approaches to coastal adaptation in combination with a moral, financial, and infrastructural agenda for large scale preparedness. In this process of strategic change and redefining the relationship to the bay, we see the singular opportunity to elevate all aspects of life. To physically elevate habitation, and the bonds of community and dignity. To elevate ones social and financial position in life, and policy for urban change. To lift infrastructure to new elevations and purposes, and allow for ecology to persist and expand.
>
> (www.resilientbayarea.org/elevate-san-rafael)

The strategy is based on an immediate response which includes a series of measures called pilot and catalyst projects with the aim of protecting San Rafael now, to better prepare for the future, and a longer-term response consisting in the re-elaboration of the entire urban structure, its mobility, its infrastructure and its residential and productive areas.

As part of the pilot and catalyst projects, a new elevated cycling path is planned along Canal Street and Francisco Boulevard, which, on the one hand, would complete the Bay Trail route and, on the other hand, would protect the city closest to the sea from flooding. Such solution envisages the Bay Trail being raised by 30 cm to about 130 cm in all its parts to ensure the community is protected until the middle of the century and reduce the need for additional short-term protection measures along the coast. This is a special case for a cycling path: it is not only a bike path but also a project that, through soil modelling, relates to the needs of the urban context because it links the coast with the downtown areas and becomes a tool for sustainable local development. The prerogatives of this bike path do not however stop there. The track is, in fact, a new environmental infrastructure for the drainage of water that works in two directions: it provides for the replacement of existing metal pipes, now corroded, with new materials and increases the dispersion of water in the landfill used for the elevation. A real stormwater infrastructure that contributes to the greater resilience of the urban system (Bionic Team, 2018) (Figure 15.3).

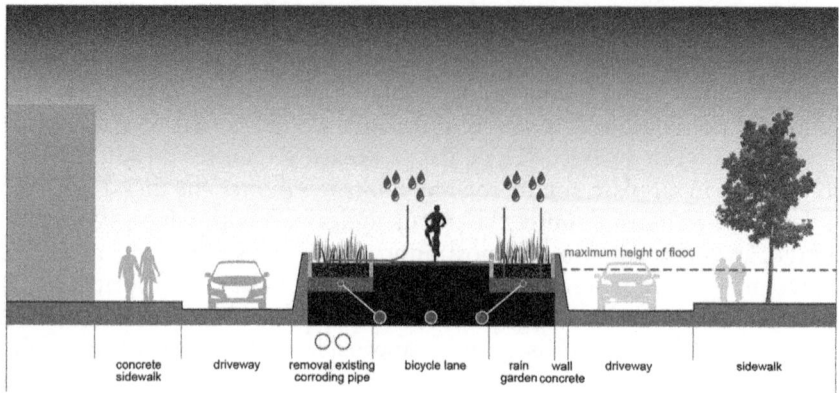

concrete sidewalk   driveway   removal existing corroding pipe   bicycle lane   rain garden   wall concrete   driveway   sidewalk

Figure 15.3 San Rafael, section of Canal Street.

Copenhagen

Climate change challenges are clearly defined in Copenhagen and in Denmark. 1000 km of dikes protect many parts of the country from the sea, but the new threat is the water from within and from above. Our fate has become being inundated with torrential rain that floods entire neighbourhoods. The existing sewer system is completely inadequate to tackle the volume of water from cloudbursts.

(www.copenhagenize.com)

Among the remedies tested, within the Climate Adaptation Plan (http://international. kk.dk), are cloudburst streets, i.e., a series of design solutions, relating to the various types of urban space, in which the roads and the space associated with them, also play the role of rainwater storage and drainage infrastructure (http://en.klimatilpasning.dk/). However, these infrastructures require a certain section of road, which is not always available. This is precisely why The Copenhagenize Current – Stormwater Management and Cycle Tracks was created: with this project solution, even the narrowest streets can contribute to contrasting urban flooding. The strong idea is to provide the space beneath the city's vast network of bicycle lanes with a secondary system of stormwater channels and to improve the city's cycling infrastructure. The system consists of prefabricated concrete channels covered by prefabricated concrete slabs that create the surface of the bicycle lanes. They offer the necessary support for the weight of the city's thousands of cyclists, as well as automotive traffic at lane crossings. In addition, the slabs are fitted with LED lights that improve visibility and heating coils that melt ice during the winter (Figure 15.4).

The system also includes drainage channels at the edge of lanes and street curbs that drain runoff from both sides and capture any detritus. The entire system is easy to install and maintain and, among other things, also provides the possibility to reserve space for the eventual passage of underground urban services. The Copenhagenize Current integrates the existing sewer network to accelerate stormwater drainage by channelling water toward the river, the sea and Sankt Jørgens Lake.

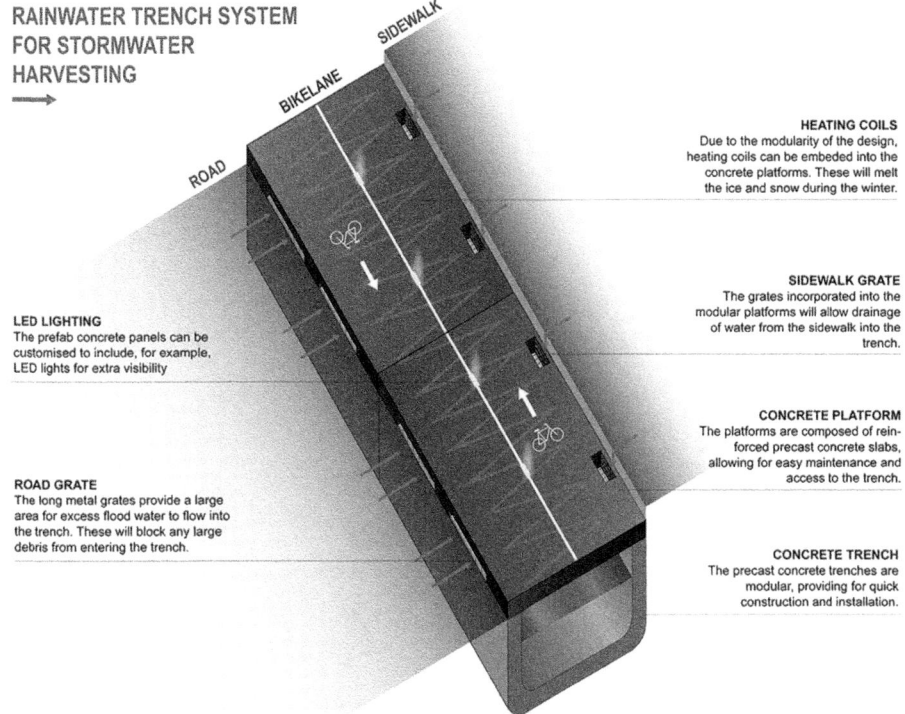

RAINWATER TRENCH SYSTEM
FOR STORMWATER
HARVESTING

SIDEWALK

BIKELANE

ROAD

HEATING COILS
Due to the modularity of the design,
heating coils can be embeded into the
concrete platforms. These will melt
the ice and snow during the winter.

LED LIGHTING
The prefab concrete panels can be
customised to include, for example,
LED lights for extra visibility

SIDEWALK GRATE
The grates incorporated into the
modular platforms will allow drainage
of water from the sidewalk into the
trench.

CONCRETE PLATFORM
The platforms are composed of reinforced precast concrete slabs,
allowing for easy maintenance and
access to the trench.

ROAD GRATE
The long metal grates provide a large
area for excess flood water to flow into
the trench. These will block any large
debris from entering the trench.

CONCRETE TRENCH
The precast concrete trenches are
modular, providing for quick
construction and installation.

Figure 15.4 The prefabricated concrete canals assumed in Copenhagen.

Despite Copenhagen having one of the largest (369 km) and busiest networks in Europe, two bicycle-only bridges, a high level of safety and security, the city continues to invest in innovation (www.klimakvarter.dk/).

Both in the sense of sustainability: the public administration is giving priority to the bicycle over any other means of transport, is implementing a series of policies to discourage the use of private cars and, what is more, is creating the conditions for ever faster cycle crossings.

And on the resilience side, as is demonstrated by The Copenhagenize Current – Stormwater Management and Cycle Tracks, a project in which the soil acquires a different (and deeper) thickness than that strictly necessary for the transit of bicycles. Thanks to prefabricated channels, the network, in addition to its role as a support for mobility, has another function: it helps to improve rainwater collection and management. And it is not the only experiment in this direction. The University of Copenhagen has set up the chair of Urban Landscapes Adapted to Climate Change which has been assigned to Marine Bergen Jensen, who has developed an urban resilience project. This involves the construction of a green wall which acts both as an acoustic barrier, because it separates car traffic from cycle/pedestrian traffic, and as an element for the capillary rise of rainwater which accumulates in the channel below the bike path (Climate Resilient Cities, 2015).

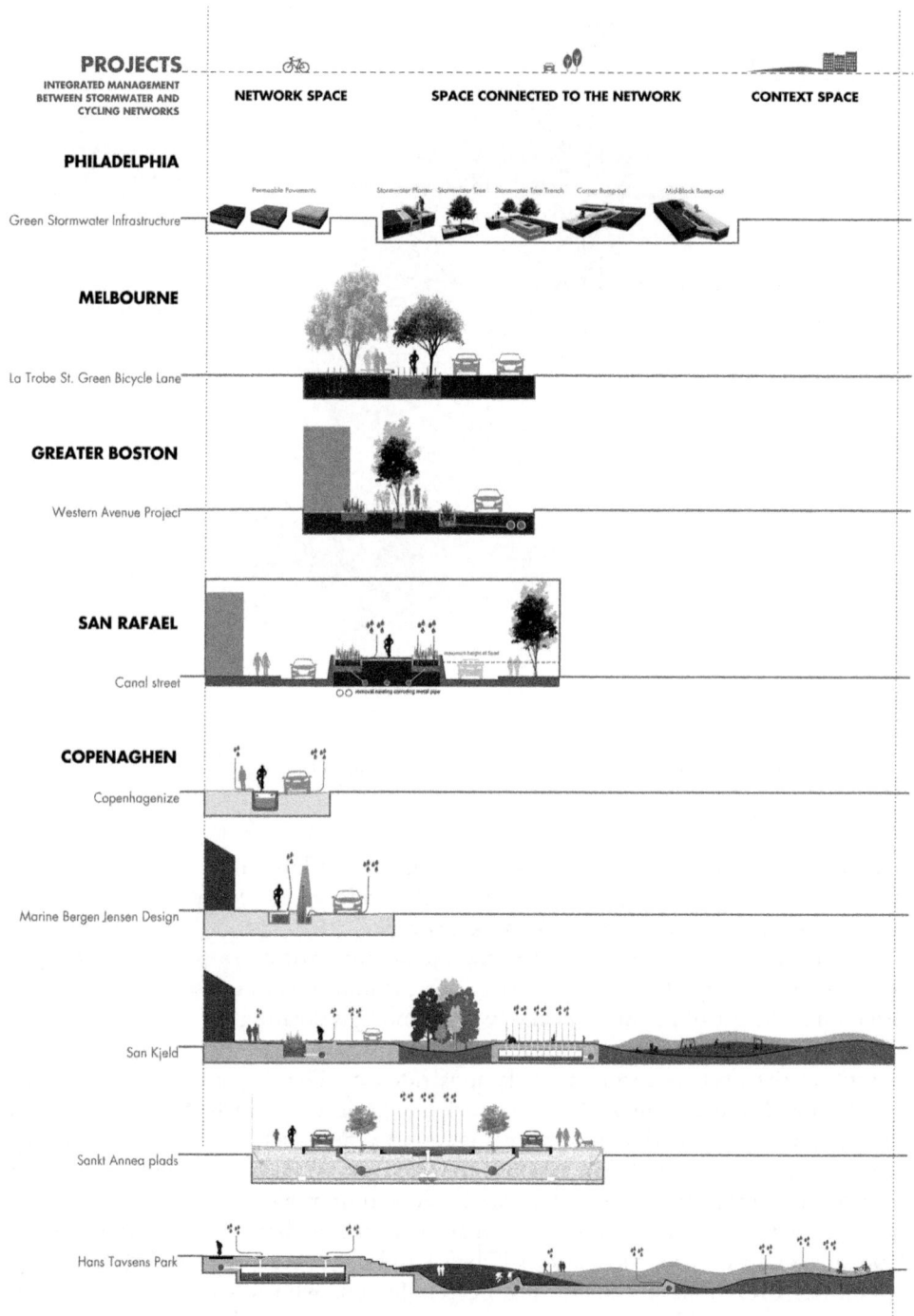

Figure 15.5 Comparison of project actions related to network space, space connected to the network, context space.

And resilience is again a central issue in the redevelopment of a number of public spaces such as Saint Kjelds called "The first climate district" (www.tredjenatur.dk), Sankt Annae plads (www.realdania.dk) and Hans Tavsens Park (www.sla.dk). Although with different architectural solutions in these public spaces, during extreme weather events, urban greenery has the purpose of draining the large flow of water and, when it is no longer able to cope, to convey it to underground tanks. This is a landscape in which the cycling path helps achieve these objectives by means of gradients whereby the water flows towards the stormwater infrastructures positioned so as to separate the traffic (Figure 15.5). Maybe that's the reason why

> the Little Mermaid is a brilliant fairy tale, but the statue, in my opinion, is a lame monument for a city like Copenhagen. I firmly believe that the greatest monument we have ever erected is our bicycle infrastructure network. It is an intricate and complex work, ever changing and in constant motion and constantly modified and improved by hundreds of thousands of citizens and visitors alike who use each day. An organic structure of such overwhelming beauty. There is no ownership of this moment. It is completely open-source and it's not reserved for Copenhagen alone.
>
> (Colville-Andersen, 2018)

Provisional findings

This review of experiences has clearly shown that the cycle path can be an environmental infrastructure capable of responding to both the needs of slow mobility and to contribute to a better collection and management of water in urban areas. This is the main teaching of Philadelphia, Melbourne, Greater Boston, San Rafael and Copenhagen. A teaching that also has another positive characteristic: easy replicability.

Applying it to Montesilvano, in Abruzzo, means integrating a multiplicity of lines of action. Three main ones are explained as follows. The first one concerns the need to change point of view. The cycle path is not a ring road which, by always staying on the side of something, fails to activate any link with it. On the contrary, it is a work that relates to the places it passes through, that establishes privileged relationships with the public space and that opens to the interdependence between infrastructure and environment. Working on this hypothesis forces us to think differently about traffic engineering which in Italy, since the second post-war period, has imposed the idea that to solve mobility and accessibility problems (Borlini and Memo, 2009), one had to invest only in big infrastructure networks. Montesilvano was no exception: the construction of the city was strongly influenced by the Adriatic Railway, of the Strada Statale 16, the Autostrada A 14 and the interchanges connecting to the urban viability. The time has come to change direction. It is essential to start again from the smaller networks and, in particular, from the cycling ones (Castrignanò et al., 2012). And this is precisely the premise from which the second line of action must start. The municipality of Montesilvano, whichbuilt all its part of the Ciclovia Adriatica, and a significant number of kilometres of other cycle paths, is now called upon to take the next step: building the network.

Reflections

This is why it is necessary to start a reflection as much on the role of the two north-south roads (Parkway and via Aldo Moro), which as parallel lines never meet, as on the perpendicular ones of potential east-west connection (via Lago di Bracciano, via Torrente Piomba, via Marinelli). Only in this way will it be possible to build an efficient cycling system that works in an integrated manner both as a transport infrastructure, to guarantee accessibility throughout the territory, and as a permeable body, to counter the negative effects of urban flooding. To do this, the third line of action is essential: giving importance to the relationship with the context. Understanding where to invest in the network space that concerns the soil of the cycle path and the technological devices, placed under the track, to allow the collection and management of water; where on that associated with the network which is the ideal place to place stormwater infrastructures; where to activate the links with the urban areas that the network crosses. These choices concern geomorphological conditions, the width of the road section, the possibility of integrating or not, the system of underground utilities and, more generally, the possibility of creating an alternative network to the sewage system for the collection and management of waters. Probably this is the analytical itinerary to arrive at a soil project that does not remain pure description of the phenomenon but is able to imagine architectural devices capable of becoming, in the first place, a vision of the future of the city; subsequently, hypothesis of intervention; and then concrete realisation. A project in which the soil is shaped, in depth or in elevation, to respond to a double objective: to support the transit of bicycles and to combat urban flooding. This is the responsibility that ultimately must be assumed by those planning a cycle network: it must be the infrastructural part of a broader soil project capable of triggering sustainable development and urban resilience processes (Figures 15.6 and 15.7).

Figure 15.6 First feasibility evaluations: the two parallel roads north-south.

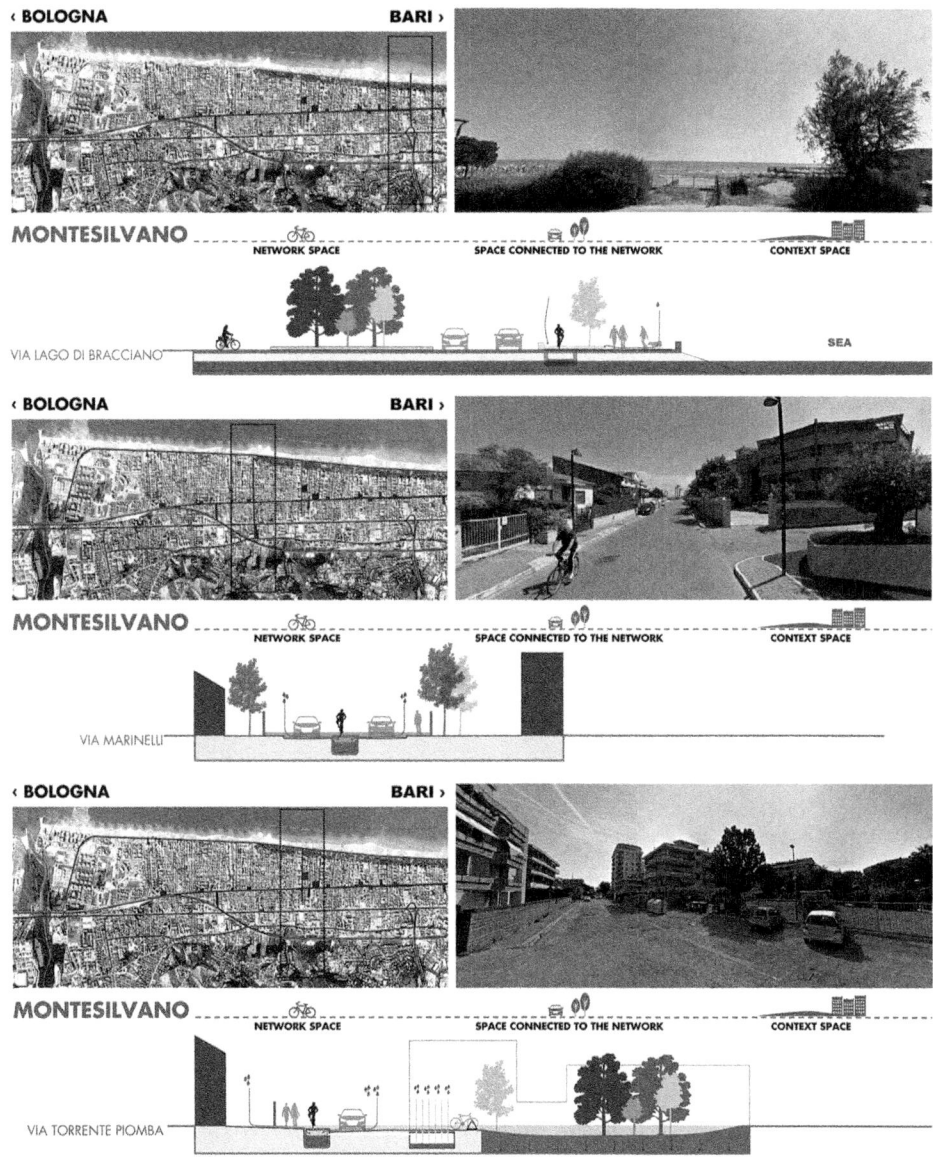

Figure 15.7 First feasibility evaluations: the three perpendicular roads of potential east-west intersection.

Questions
1 Is the cycling network only a slow mobility infrastructure or does it also have to be a soil project?
2 Can the cycling network contribute to a better water collection and management?
3 Is there the possibility to think about a relationship between the cycling network and urban resilience?

Further reading

There is no relevant Further Reading due to the innovative nature of this case study which is currently in a leading edge situation.

References

Augé, M. (2009). *Il bello della bicicletta*. Torino: Bollati Boringhieri.

Australian Government Department of Climate Change. (2009). City of Melbourne climate change adaptation strategy. Available at www.melbourne.vic.gov.au/.

Banca d'Italia. (2018). *Turismo in Italia. Numeri e potenziale di sviluppo*. Available at www.bancaditalia.it/pubblicazioni/collana-seminari-convegni/2018-0023/rapporto_turismo_finale_convegno.pdf.

Bernardi, W. (2013). *La filosofia va in bicicletta*. Milano: Ediciclo.

Bianchetti, C. (2003). *Abitare la città contemporanea*. Skira, Milano.

Bionic Team. (2018). *San Rafael Elevate. Resilient by design: Bay area challenge*. Available at www.resilientbayarea.org/elevate-san-rafael.

Borlini, B., Memo, F. (2009). *Ripensare l'accessibilità urbana*. Roma: Cittalia-Fondazione ANCI ricerche.

Castrignanò, M., Colleoni, M., Pronello, C. (eds.). (2012). *Muoversi in città. Accessibilità e mobilità nella metropoli contemporanea*. Milano: Franco Angeli.

City of Copenhagen. (2011). *Copenhagen climate adaptation plan*. Available at http://international.kk.dk/artikel/climate-adaptation.

City of Copenhagen. (2012). *Cloudburst management plan 2012*. Available at http://en.klimatilpasning.dk/.

City of Copenhagen. (2016). *Copenhagen climate resilient neighbourhood*. Available at www.klimakvarter.dk/.

City of Melbourne. (2013). *La Trobe Street green bicycle lane*. Available at http://urbanwater.melbourne.vic.gov.au/.

City of Melbourne. (2014). *Total watermark-City as a catchment*. Available at http://melbourne.vic.gov.au/getinvolved.

Colville-Andersen, M. (2018). *Copenaghenize. The Definitve Guide to Global Bicycle Urbanisme*. Washington: Island press.

Comune di Montesilvano. (2019). *Dati demografici 2018*. Available at www.comune.montesilvano.pe.it/index.php/news/4896-dati-demografici-2018-montesilvano-stabile-sopra-quota-54-mila.

ENEA. (2018). *Sette nuove aree costiere a rischio inondazione in Italia*. Available at www.enea.it/it/Stampa/comunicati/clima-enea-sette-nuove-aree-costiere-a-rischio-inondazione-in-italia.

European Commission (2010). *Promoting Cycling for Everyone as a Daily Transport Mode*. Available at www.rupprecht-consult.eu/

European Cyclist' Federation. (2016). *The EU Cycling Economy. Argument for an integrated EU cycling policy*. Available at https://ecf.com/sites/ecf.com/files/FINAL%20THE%20EU%20CYCLING%20ECONOMY_low%20res.pdf.

Federazione Italiana Ambiente e Bicicletta. (2018). *Guida ai comuni ciclabili d'Italia*. Available at www.comuniciclabili.it/wp-content/uploads/2018/03/GUIDA-ComuniCiclabili-Italia-2018.pdf.

Federazione Italiana Ambiente e Bicicletta. (2019). *Guida ai comuni ciclabili d'Italia*. Available at www.comuniciclabili.it/2-edizione-2019/.

Fleury, D. (2012). *Sicurezza e urbanistica. L'integrazione della sicurezza stradale nel governo urbano*. Roma: Gangemi.

Giuliani, F., Maternini, G. (2018). *Mobilità ciclistica e sicurezza*. Forlì: Egaf.

Greater Boston. (2015). *Developing resilience: Living with water strategies for greater Boston.* Available at https://boston.uli.org/uli-in-action/sustainability/.

ISTAT. (2013). *15° Censimento generale della popolazione.* Available at www.istat.it/it/files//2013/01/Comunicato-Abruzzo.pdf.

ISTAT. (2014). *9° Censimento dell'industria e dei servizi e Censimento delle istituzioni non profit.* Available at www.istat.it/it/files//2014/04/CIS_Abruzzo.pdf.

Legambiente. (2018). *2° Rapporto Legambici sull'economia della bici in Italia.* Available at www.legambiente.it/sites/default/files/docs/a_bi_ci_2018.pdf

Marine Bergen Jensen. (2015). *Climate resilient cities.* Available at www.youtube.com/watch?v=OOd4vOKPzEg.

Philadelphia Water Department. (2011). *Green city clean waters.* Available at www.phillywatersheds.org/doc/.

Philadelphia Water Department. (2014). *City of Philadelphia green streets design manual.* Available at www.phillywatersheds.org/img/

Realdania. (2016). *The Sankt Annæ project.* Available at https://realdania.dk/samlet-projektliste/sankt-ann%C3%A6-projektet.

SLA. (2016). *Hans Tavsens Park.* Available at www.sla.dk/en/projects/hanstavsenspark/.

The Blog by Copenhagenize Design Co. (2015). *The Copenhagenize Current – stormwater management and cycle tracks.* Available at www.copenhagenize.com/.

Tondelli, P.V. (1986). *Rimini.* Milano: Bompiani.

Tondelli, P.V. (1990). *Un weekend Postmoderno. Cronache dagli anni ottanta.* Milano: Bompiani.

Tredje Natur. (2016). *The first climate district.* Available at www.tredjenatur.dk/en/portfolio/the-first-climate-district/.

United Nations Office for Disaster Risk Reduction. (2016). *Report of the open-ended inter-governmental expert working group on indicators and terminology relating to disaster risk reduction.* Available at www.unisdr.org/we/inform/terminology#letter-r.

16 The Importance of stakeholder involvement in the strategic development of destination management

Maja Žibert, Boris Prevolšek and Marko Koščak

Summary

The aim of this case study is to develop the importance of stakeholder involvement in the strategic process of destination management, which has the purpose of achieving a deeper understanding of how different stakeholders perceive to the critical features of destination management. The key concepts of strategy and of destination management are explained in the theoretical part of the paper. Based on this, we have developed the following critical research question: What are the desires of different stakeholders in the development of the destination in the light of strategic management? The explanations and viewpoints of other authors were summarised, and attempts were made to derive new viewpoints based on this research questions. Our results confirmed the findings that the life of the local population should be included and engaged actively when developing the destination and identifying the potential of that destinations. Each group of stakeholders plays a specific role in the development of the destination, and thereby, this case study offers an overview of the analytical challenges and trends in the development of a small tourist destination. The most effective and appropriate structure for small destinations is to operate on a 'bottom-up' basis and to consider a common brand, which will provide recognition of the place and its key tourism products.

Introduction

When a destination seeks to be classified as a tourism objective, it should provide a range of activities that tourists are able to identify as a 'tourist' experience (Bornhorst, Ritchie, & Sheehan, 2010). In regard to this development, destinations should define challenges and identify trends according to what they may assume as a transparent image. These trends form a group of good examples and practices that tourist destinations experience throughout their development. Ovsenik (2003) points out that it is important for the environment to identify itself with the industry in the shortest possible time if they adopted a decision about destination management according to the principles of destination management.

Morgan, Pritchard and Piggott (2003) have, through their research, confirmed that, while the provision of direction for development is implicit in visioning, what is important is the emphasis on formulating the destination vision through a publicly driven process based on stakeholder values and consensus, rather than through a more private expert-driven process based solely on market forces. The same authors further stress that stakeholders must agree that the final vision statement provides both a meaningful and an operational dream for the future of their destination – one that reflects the values of destination stakeholders while not ignoring the realities and constraints of the marketplace.

When conducting research about stakeholder involvement into the strategic development of a destination, Aas, Ladkin and Fletcher (2005) identified that in-depth interviews were the best way to understand the importance of this involvement, since they gave them what they called 'a wealth of information on the stakeholder project and the development of tourism.' In Australia, research has been conducted to find out to what extent strategic planning supports real planning in tourism. Ruhanen (2010) conducted 31 structured interviews with the representatives of five tourist destinations. She came to the conclusion that planning in tourism is focussed on short-term and immediate effect, while real strategies are lacking. She also emphasised that the policy of sustainable development has the appearance of some kind of movement; nevertheless, concerns about the financial effect are still predominant.

New destinations in formation may therefore follow those examples and conspicuous trends in their development. The Mirna Valley is a geographic entity within the broader Dolenjska tourism destination. It is located on the territory that used to be part of the Municipality of Trebnje; today, it consists of the Municipalities of Mokronog-Trebelno, Mirna and Šentrupert, and forms part of central Slovenia – particularly the south-eastern part of central Slovenia, bordered by the nearby Municipalities of Ivančna Gorica, Šmartno pri Litiji, Litija, Sevnica, Škocjan, Šmarješke Toplice, Novo mesto, Mirna Peč and Žužemberk.

In entering this research, our presumption was that the development of the region and tourism proceeds as anticipated and in line with the development strategy conceived by the documented Strategic Action Plan for establishment of the tourist destination Mirna Valley. This action plan does not discuss the meaning of the strategic management. Through this case study, we will discuss the importance of strategic management and the inclusion of various stakeholders from the public, civil and private sectors. It would, thus, be more than welcome if they associated and cooperated in the development. During the research, we wanted to verify how the individual sectors perceive and experience the development of tourism and environment in the Mirna Valley area.

Theoretical background

Cooperation of stakeholders in strategic management

In their work, Haugland, Ness, Gronseth and Aarstad (2011) state clearly that research on destination development is very fragmented, since some studies focus primarily on one or a few selected areas of destination development, thus paying limited attention to multilevel issues and theoretical integration, while, on the other hand, there are studies that take a more holistic, phenomena-driven view, making theoretical delimitation difficult. With the importance of continuous development, it is also very hard to determine when destination development ends and destination management begins. Based on the views of many other authors, it was Haugland et al. (2011) who claim that tourism destinations can be considered as complex networks that involve a large number of co-producing actors delivering a variety of products and services. This complexity mentioned by the authors can be seen as something that clearly differentiates destination development and destination management from organisational development and organisational management.

As is pointed out by Dimovski, Penger and Žnidaršič (2003), the strategic management is often considered to equal executive management. Brownman (1994) claims that the key feature of the strategic management is taking decisions continuously, influencing the effect of organisation and implementation in practice. Belak (2002) says that the basic duty of the strategic management is searching for, creating and controlling the strategic potentials of the organisation. On the other hand, Uran (2006) views the role of the strategic management as dealing with the understanding of the nature of competitive advantage and the manner of how to create and retain that advantage over the others. In the opinion of Tavčar (2008), long-term and comprehensive control of the organisation, focussed on the important matters, is in question. Tavčar (2002) said: 'The assumption that the conditions from the past will continue in the future, has become less and less probable.' In that way, she defines one of the key reasons for the appearance of long-term and, later on, strategic planning.

In their paper, Mackey and Zundel (2016) show that worldwide, many classifications of the Strategic Business Management Schools are known; for example, McKiernan, Mintzberg and Whittington (Whittington, 2001) divide the Strategic Business Management Schools as follows: conventional, process, evolutionary and system schools. The conventional school advocates the attitude that the strategy can be developed on the basis of rational system process, while the model of strategy forming should be simple and as little formalised as possible. The process school starts from the assumption that differences occur between the planned and realised strategy, while, during the implementation process, the in-process strategy still appears. The evolutionary school denies that the business managers are qualified enough to form strategy. That implies that the profit maximisation is governed by the market and not strategy. The system and the conventional schools advocate the capacity of organisations to plan and act effectively inside their environment (Pučko, Čater, & Rejc Buhovac, 2009).

Strategic management in tourism

Understanding historical and modern trends and movements in the business environment is the basic prerequisite for strategic planning in tourism. New initiatives for such planning will require for successful planners to have the capacity to predict new key movements and developments. This will lead to creating innovative and effective strategies. In the area of tourism, the relation between bidders and the market/business environment is unique, since the latter embraces the entire world. The tool PEST is one of the most convenient tools for the analysis of the business/market environment. That analysis governs the survey of political, economic, social and technical factors. Because of the unique and specific business environment, and characteristic of tourism, Mountinho, Ballantyne and Rate (2011) propose another model of analysis of the business environment. That is the tool *SCEPTICAL* – S – social factors, C – cultural factors, E – economic factors, P – physical factors, T – technical factors, I – international factors, C – communications and infrastructure factors, A – administrative and institutional factors, and L – legal and political factors (Mountinho et al., 2011).

In Jordan, strategic planning is exploited by the use of various techniques. In his research, Aldehayyat (2011) investigates the importance of strategic thinking in tourism in Jordan. One of the principal findings was that this was done only by the people, stakeholders and creators of the destinations, and that outside consultants were not hired. Nevertheless, Guiver and Stanford (2014) have found that a Destination Manager seldom applies the concept of strategic judgement of influences. In their research into countryside destinations in Great Britain, these authors have concluded that successful introduction of integrated planning is prevented by the structure of the tourist industry, public financing and difficulties in coordination of several agencies having equal goals.

Okumus and Wong (2005) have found that strategic management incorporated different views and models, implying great variety in concepts from the point of view of teaching. The two authors recapitulate that modern curricula should focus on the implementation of strategies, *RBV* (resource-based view) management of know-how, establishing new companies, learning organisation, managing a non-profit organisation and multi-national company. Strategic management should aim at maintaining the tourist destination and the long-term stable position competitively, while strategic marketing should promote combining the tasks of the tourist destination management and its perception in the eyes of the tourists.

Destination management

The basic definition of management and/or planning refers to organising, managing and control. The same competences are also attributed to the destination management concerning the tourist offer, but it is also necessary to add the marketing and communication component as a key to achieve transparency and, consequently, economic and development success of the destination (Magaš, 2003). Laesser and Beritelli (2013) see destination management (*DMO*) as the management process that aims to attract visitors and allocate time and money in a specific geographic space. As they said, destination management should comprise different domains of activity, such as planning, lobbying (on behalf of all stakeholders), marketing in a comprehensive way, and coordinating a seamless customer experience. As Munar (2012) pointed out, *DMOs* have several main functions as follows.

First, the coordination of marketing strategies, including the destination brand, and the management of information and knowledge about the tourism destination; second, the establishment of networks and initiatives to improve the destination offer; and third, the coordination of tourism planning and development. The *DMO* should lead and coordinate this different aspect of destination, as is shown below.

In Figure 16.1, we can see the proposed scheme of the *DMO's* activities and organisation as seen by United Nations World Tourism Organization (2007). On the top part, we see the possibilities that the destination provides, and on the bottom part, we see the issues around which DMOs have to work in order to take full advantage of what a destination has to offer to potential visitors. Tourism is nowadays a sector in a state of transition. Therefore, the traditional role of *DMO* is changing. As Presenza, Sheehan and Ritchie (2005) pointed out: 'DMO's are becoming more prominent as "destination developers" by acting as catalysts and facilitators for the realisation of tourism developments.'

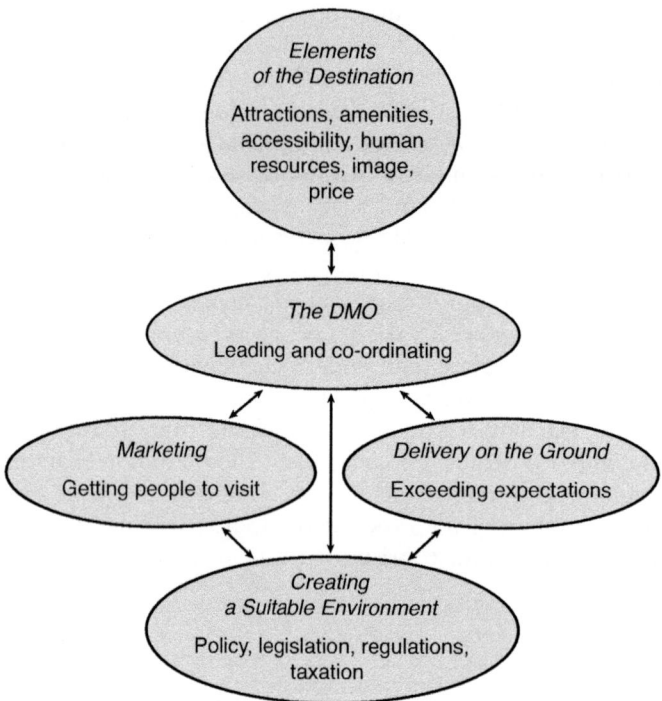

Figure 16.1 Destination Management (DMO).
Source: Adapted from United Nations World Tourism Organization, 2007.

Stakeholders at the destination

The connection point inside all three groups of stakeholders (private, civil and public sectors) at a destination is destination management. It acts to coordinate all interests and encourages a consistent and sustainable development, as well as the overall marketing impetus. Within the destination, each of the stakeholders has their interests, wishes, expectations and favours. Ackermann and Eden (2011) indicated that one stakeholder's actions may generate a dynamic of responses across a range of others. Relations between stakeholders at a destination are both formal and informal. Tourism organisation operates on several levels, and among them are related tasks. It is necessary to define clearly the tasks and scope of the work of each stakeholder. Uran (2014) prepared a structure, which shows us the relationship between the private and public sectors and civil society on the one hand, and the relationship between them at national, regional and local levels (see Figure 16.2 below). This level of organisation of tourism can also be found within the destination of the Mirna Valley. In this way, we can see that the stakeholders from the private sector are oriented to the features of the destination in the short and long term. They are interested primarily in the promotion and growth of the destination on the common tourist market. The public sector is concerned about the social and economic interests in the long term and puts much emphasis on the destination development. The civil society expects primarily

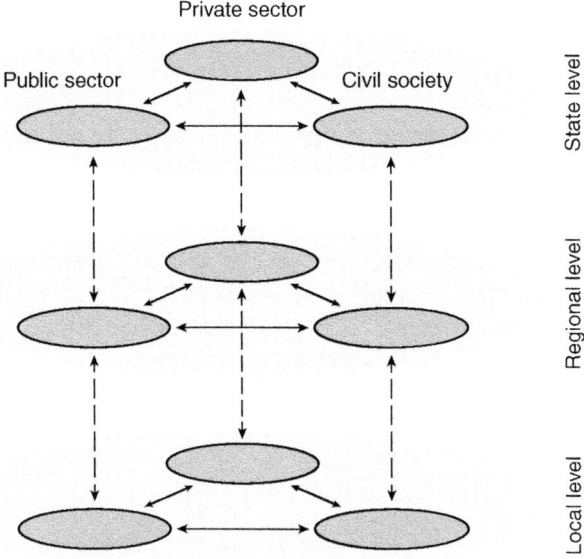

Figure 16.2 Stakeholders.
Source: Adapted from Uran, 2014.

the improvement of life quality within the destination with personal engagement. Adequate development of the destination and successful functioning of the system within the destination requires cooperation of the key three sectors of stakeholders, and well-qualified strategic managers and managers active at the destination itself. Sautter and Leisen (1999) said that for tourism planners, it is important to consider the interests or perspectives of the different stakeholder groups.

According to Wall and Mathieson (2006), 'Stakeholder perceptions are accepted as crucial for evaluating participatory processes and devising effective strategies for implementing sustainable tourism,' but there is no clear understanding of how best to increase the involvement of stakeholders in sustainable tourism. The importance of stakeholder involvement in strategic development of destination management was classified in a research paper about a multi-stakeholder involvement management framework. Waligo, Clarke and Hawkins (2013) explained that the inclusion of stakeholders affects development and establishment of sustainable tourism. The argument was based on three assumptions. First, stakeholders represent a core component of the implementation of sustainable tourism (stakeholder identification); second, stakeholder perceptions are sought to facilitate the development of effective stakeholder involvement strategies (stakeholder engagement); and third, 'stakeholder involvement' can facilitate the achievement of sustainable tourism objectives (multi-stakeholder involvement).

Based on a theoretical overview, we can confirm the fact that the life of the local population should be included and engaged actively in the development when developing the destination and identifying the potentials. A tourist destination changes in the course of time in accordance with changes in all the environments forming it. Through the view of Magaš (1997), who talked about the destination cycles, we could conclude that Mirna Valley is in the early development phase. That time, the destination management becomes a necessity, as the complete offer must be integrated into the environment.

At present, it is still too early to speak about the consolidation phase, but an important question is what is desired after that phase, either an autonomous way or development of the tourist offer within a wider destination? It is well known that problems, ranging from social, ecological to economic, start to appear at the destination. Such difficulties are faced even sooner, if the destination is too little for singular development and organisation in terms of human capacities and environmental offer. Therefore, it is an appropriate moment now to ask the question how to go on. The answer is by organising efficient destination management; however, the first thing is to define clearly the tasks and scope of work of each stakeholder, and then start to coordinate all aspects by stakeholders. However, the positive effects of destination development are caused by (1) exchange of information, (2) use of synergies and (3) coordination of action (Volgger and Pechlaner, 2014).

Methodology

Preparation of the research contents was based on the document Strategic Action Plan for establishment of the Mirna Valley destination (Koščak, 2013) and on the study of implementation concerning individual priorities between the stakeholders at the destination. The Strategic Action Plan for establishment of Mirna Valley destination is a document that was presented to the stakeholders in tourism in the Mirna Valley area, and presents ideas about how to establish Mirna Valley as a tourism destination.

Based on the theoretical overview and the knowledge of the Strategic Action Plan for establishment of the Mirna Valley destination, we have created the following research questions:

1　What are the current challenges in the destination management of Mirna Valley?
2　How can we ensure the key stakeholders (i.e. civil society, private sector, public sector) are involved more actively in the destination management of Mirna Valley?
3　What are the expected future trends in destination management of the Mirna Valley?

On the basis of the examination of the Strategic Action Plan for establishment of the Mirna Valley location as a tourist destination, and after identifying individual priorities stated therein, a questionnaire has been prepared. Consequently, the implementation of priorities and the destination development were verified. The questionnaire was prepared in conjunction with the purpose of the research work to find answers to the research questions.

Representation of the research sample

In total, we have conducted 14 interviews with representatives in all sectors and in each Municipality separately, receiving a wide insight into the situation in the field. The tourist destination of the Mirna Valley consists of three Municipalities. We interviewed all three representatives of local self-government – Mayors in this part the sample are equal to the entire population. Among the private and civil sectors, we interviewed key players in each. In the civil sector, those were institutions covering most of the organised public events. With the interviews, we covered only the part of the private sector, which is linked to tourism services, and they recorded the highest number of visitors. It is also important to note that the Land of hay-racks was interviewed – a representative of the largest tourist service provider in the Mirna Valley. In this part, the population represents 20 individuals, and in this sample, we included 11 of them. The aforementioned 14 in-depth interviews were made in the field in June 2015 and July 2015.

In the Mirna Municipality, those included the Mayor and a member of the Municipal Administration, the President and some members of the Sports Society Partizan, and the 'Aladin' adventure ranch head. In the Šentrupert Municipality, the Mayor, the President and some members of the Ethnic Society Draga and the guesthouse workers from the Winehouse Frelih and the Land of hay-racks were interviewed, while in the area of the Mokronog-Trebelno Municipality, we interviewed the Mayor, a member of the Municipal Administration, the President and some members of the Tourist Society and employees of the Guesthouse Deu.

The result of the research shows that 14 participants in the selected sample comply with the preparation target of the work contents. In the field, we contacted the key persons in the Mirna Valley destination organisation. We were interested in the key targets of priorities formed by their creators. We selected the persons at an executive level in the individual area of the development and promotion of tourism at the Mirna Valley destination. In our opinion, they were able to present in detail the actual state of the destination management development and organisation, preparation of various touristic and cultural events. Based on the recording of statistics of tourist arrivals, we divided them into two groups: first 'the small group' and another 'the biggest group.' From each of the groups, we took five interviewees; the 11th was the Land of hay-racks – a representative of the largest tourist service provider in the Mirna Valley.

We were also keen to know what concrete activities had already been carried out by them as members of the individual sector to make the priority live, and what, in their opinion, the indicators controlling the implementation and functioning of priorities at the destination were. Below, the basic questions asked in the interviews and the principal research findings are presented. We contacted the interviewees personally and recorded their answers on the spot according to the key items. By means of a computer, the transcripts were analysed and the principal findings written in sets as follows: public sector, private sector and civil sector. Afterwards, interviews were interpreted sector by sector, first individually and then by making a SWOT analysis of findings. The interviewees took part in interviews voluntarily. Interviews were, therefore, agreed upon in advance.

Research methods

The interview consisted of two parts. The first part comprised four sets, each set having three questions. The sets covered priorities given by the authors of the document Strategic Action Plan for the establishment of the Mirna Valley destination regarding development orientations and the overall vision for managing the future development of sustainable tourism in the Mirna Valley. Priorities, on which the questions posed to the interviewees were based, had been devised on the basis and principles of participative planning, the representatives of public, private and civil sectors having the possibility to give operational proposals at the time of preparation of the Strategic Action Plan for forming the vision and for future action.

In the main part, the interviewees were invited to propose, what, in their opinion, were the key targets which they were prioritising; what concrete activities had already been performed by them in their individual sector to bring that priority to life; and what were, in their opinion, the indicators controlling the execution and functioning of priorities at the destination. In addition to this substantive part, a number of basic demographic questions were raised (e.g. age, education and profession). With the help of field research, we were able to verify the implementation of the development strategy in the Mirna Valley region, in order that we should be in a position to ascertain that the area develops in the planned way and at the rate directed by the development strategy.

Data interpretation and analysis

Public sector

After the interviews, we set out to analyse the answers we received from the interviewees within the public sector. The most important issue for the public sector is to activate internal potentials and to include the local community. It is important that the destination should be managed and formed on the principle 'bottom-up'; that is, the local actors should see the potential behind it, while the public sector seeks to provide responsible leadership management. One of the interviewees stated very clearly: 'Sometimes it is felt that some people lack the sense of community and would like to fly solo.' They have a common opinion, capable management linking together the entire destination is needed; especially now, the destination has been established, and an important step will be its managing.

They are convinced an important area is also the cultural heritage, but they said the state, nevertheless, follows the traced path. 'It is important to recognise the development-vision steps; the vision is carried on and, in that way, the desired management, i.e., the management "bottom-up" is reached,' said one of the interviewees. They said it is hard to speak about the operational phase of the project, as the project has been stopped due to financing constraints when their objective – one of the joint goals – was to have a common brand name. In the project of establishing the Mirna Valley as a specific destination, it is necessary to have all actors appearing to have a common and homogeneous purpose. The document – Strategy of establishment of Mirna Valley tourist destination – should be viewed from a wider strategic standpoint and seen also in the light of economy.

They said it is well known that the prospects of the *EU*, today, are centred in tourism. Therefore, they are confident that they are turning in the right direction; regrettably, wider cooperation between them is missing. 'We must be aware that the destination is attractive to tourists, therefore, statistical research is needed to be able to design tourist packages which, so far, have been missing,' said one of the interviewees. At present, only the Land of hay-racks has such packages as a tourist product of the Mirna Valley destination. They also mentioned that sustainable development should not be neglected. 'That is the preferred topic of tourism development in the entire EU. Experiences in nature and the rich heritage must be our priorities.'

Civil sector

Their activities link together the people and inhabitants beyond the borders of the Municipality. They are also active in tourism, particularly in organisation of events. They feel that the Municipalities, so far, have not yet managed to agree on joint management of the destination, as would be desirable. In that way, they would know when various projects and events take place within all societies; 'maybe the system financing would be organised better' said one of the interviewees. Their activities include publishing of folding booklets; they are active in cultural activities, in organising various events, including events for tourists. In addition, they also receive funds from membership fees, donations and sponsorship. They admit that in the sphere of protection and preservation of cultural and natural heritage, a lot more could be done. 'Tourism is sold by good stories. Will we win them by preserving natural and cultural heritage? Something more is needed,' was convinced one of an interviewees. 'Our management must know precisely what it wants and conduct a common policy. The management must proceed step by step, not in a hurry,' said someone else. In their opinion, management could be better, and they are concerned how a function, linking together the Mirna Valley area, could operate. They are asking if they have to act together and conduct a common policy, or would they then branch away and be an autonomous destination within the broader Dolenjska region. They are sure that the idea of a common brand name is an excellent idea. They are sure that the destination also needs indicators of control, telling them whether they are going in the right direction.

Private sector

By system and transparent destination management in the private sector, its members are eager to see the result, i.e., an increased number of tourists at the destination. From their point of view, the result of all priorities would be an increase in profit. They belong to a group that offers special tourist services at particular destination microlocations, and without them, the destination could not be imagined such as it is. 'An important component here is the private sector of stakeholders in the destination,' they are convinced. They said the private sector drew attention to the choice in the Land of hay-racks emphasising that they must work hard on their promotion and deliberate according to their best appearance on the promotion market, since the image in the right market groups of consumers is important. 'Protection and sustainable development of cultural and natural heritage are today, of course, of great importance, as the sustainability priority,' they pointed out again and again. A lot has been done on that priority, in comparison with the past. In their opinion, they must continue working on that priority at an accelerated rate and more concretely. As they pointed out, for them, it is the market activity that counts the most. What seems for the most important at the destination is the coordination of individual representatives within the public sector, since, from there onwards, the destination is managed. 'The connecting link is missing,' they also said.

SWOT analysis of the Mirna Valley

By the comparative research method, we compared the interviews from individual sectors and tried to find mutual links, common points and/or differences; at the end of the research, by use of the synthesis method, we tried to link theoretic knowledge and explanations with practical facts, gained thanks to interviews. The SWOT analysis of the Mirna Valley area is presented below. Thus, some strengths, as well as weaknesses, opportunities and threats, apply not only to the Mirna Valley but also to wider Dolenjska. Table 16.1 presents strengths according to the SWOT analysis.

The Strategic Action Plan for establishment of the Mirna Valley destination (Koščak, 2013) proposed several steps in establishing the Mirna Valley destination,

Table 16.1 SWOT analysis

Strengths	Weaknesses
• Favourable geographic position (airports Ljubljana, Zagreb, Xth motorway corridor, proximity of frontier, proximity of principal EU markets) • Attractive landscape (natural, cultural heritage) for residence and tourism • Natural resources (forests, waters, etc. • The Mirna Valley area is an example of active tourism • Rich cultural heritage of countryside • Local organisation: established and active structures • Hospitality and friendliness of locals • Opportunities for free and safe walking • Experience in acquiring EU funds	• Increase in the percentage of jobless young people • Lack of green fields • Weak cooperation culture and skills • Poor offer for high-rank guests wanting to spend more money (Russians) • Lack of tourist programs and new interesting and innovative products in spite of potentials offered by the region • Deficient statistics' research; lack of public sanitary conveniences, parking lots, scarce and inappropriate multi-purpose facilities for tourism, illicit dumping sites • Low transfer for know-how, tradition and skills to younger generations and familiarisation of the young with the importance of tradition
Opportunities	*Threats*
• Accessibility and good quality of environment (factor attracting creative people and investments) • Associating of sectors (technological development – tourism – farming – education) • Growth of individual tourism in the area • Relaxation and anti-stress programs as a type of offer of integral tourist products • Chances for development of green tourism • The area features intact and preserved nature offering potential for tourism and quality of life itself • Protected and naturally preserved areas may be visited by tourists and visitors	• (Too) slow responding (indecision) and low readiness to take risks • Lack of developing – managing know-how and regional Project Managers • Deepening of social inequality • Lack of development cooperation within various development strategies and proposals for joint area management • Unfavourable circumstances for investments, particularly, because of excessively expensive loans • Changes in the labour market – the increasing number of jobless people in the farming sector • Keeping of statistics – decrease in overnight accommodations, good and ready integral tourist products

and one of the very important tasks was to determine priorities on the basis of SWOT analysis and to determine actions, how to realise them. In the following part, we are presenting the priorities and certain ideas about what actions to take.

Priority 1: promoting business growth for jobs and economic growth for a better developed area

In comparison with Slovenia, the Mirna Valley area is marked by low added value below average, low *GDP* and lower salaries. The Mirna Valley area also features bad transfer of know-how, tradition and skills to young generations; bad familiarisation of the young with the importance of tradition; deficient keeping of statistics; lack of public sanitary conveniences and parking lots; rare and inadequate multi-purpose facilities; and some illicit dumping sites that can be found.

Measures

1 Continuous learning, innovation and the adoption of the necessary knowledge.
2 Prepare an attractive environment for the development of the company.
3 Pay attention to the surrounding tradition and handicrafts.

Priority 2: farming friendly to the environment and the development of additional activities on the farm

Tourism at the destination of the Mirna Valley must be connected to agriculture. The area of the Mirna Valley is predominantly rural. We have to maintain farming and forestry. For these activities, for their further development, we should promote the use of new technologies. We need to create conditions for further conservation of the countryside. Also, we should increase and exploit better the potential of tourism in the spa, wellness, business, recreation, winter, event areas, etc.

Measures

1 On farms to introduce additional activities (sleep in the hayloft).
2 The increase in production and quality of products on the farm (certification).
3 Execution of practical learning through educational programs.
4 The increase in sales of agricultural products and foodstuffs.
5 Local farmers supply the local population with their food.

Priority 3: Tourism and infrastructure

Dolenjska region has the longest number of nights of domestic guests. For overnight stays by foreign guests, they were overtaken by a number of other Slovenian regions. It would be necessary to establish a linkage between heritage and tourism. It is necessary to accept the changes and trends of globalisation. It is necessary to be on the visibility of the area, to draw a good competitive bid to restore the natural and cultural heritage, and to develop sustainable tourism. A crucial key to success in tourism is the individual approach to guests. We can offer relaxation in thermal water, learning about the natural and cultural heritage, and traditional cuisine and wines.

Measures

1   Better infrastructure for access and indications to the facilities, attractions and heritage.
2   Larger and more varied tourist offer and services.
3   Improve the organisation of cooperation between all providers in the Dolenjska region.
4   Young people present interest in tourism.

Main findings

A tourist destination changes in the course of time in accordance with changes in all the environments forming it. At the beginning, a destination is, usually, still displaying some attributes of intact nature and not as yet infested with tourism. Here, the destination still has many chances of being integrated into the life of the local population in the course of development. Engagement implies that much effort is applied to the development of the destination. At this stage, authors Jamal and Getz (1995) said that tourism development takes on the characteristics of a public and social good. The result is the increase in the number of tourists, enhancement of the offer, building of tourist infrastructure, etc. The so-called tourist seasons are formed, and also many 'tourist' benefits could be shared by numerous stakeholders at the destination.

Later on, the destination management becomes a necessity, as the complete offer must be integrated into the environment. It may happen that the tourist destination stagnates. This is the time when the destination is no more attractive than before. Thus, a change of offer is necessary to retain the guests or to attract them anew. Slowly, the destination starts to face social, ecological, economic and other problems. During the decline, the destination usually loses its value. In the tourist destination, the management is changed, and the accommodating capacities become lost. In this phase, the programs must necessarily be redefined, products renewed and modified, and in short, the system must be established anew if the destination is to revive again. This is the step of some kind of destination revival. In each stage of development, stakeholders perform a special task.

All sectors of stakeholders mentioned the importance of a common brand; therefore, developers should take into consideration the need to design a common brand. It was also stated by Blain, Levy and Ritchie (2005) that: 'destination logos can facilitate many DMO marketing activities to establish brand image and identity, particularly relevant before the actual visitor experience.' Involvement of stakeholders in strategic management of a destination is important in each stage of development. The case study shows the importance of cooperation of the key stakeholders (i.e. civil society, private sector, public sector) at different levels. Moreover, the case study demonstrates the importance of the 'bottom-up' development in a destination, which we can frequently interpret as a pressure on public institutions and the public sector, for example, the additional building of infrastructure. Reid (1996) mentions two approaches to the process of achieving the goals of destination development. In the model of 'bottom-up' approach, there is the decentralisation of authorities at a lower level. Local authorities have an important role in the local ecosystem management and development activities – also in terms of tourism organisations and other activities (for example, arranging local transport infrastructure). The 'top-down' approach is the opposite, in implementing the principles of tourism development; the state plays a major and distant role.

In the area of the Mirna Valley, a joint managing policy must be found, representatives of individual destination sectors should be more incorporated into its management, and, at the same time, the financing arrangements intended for the development must be examined concretely and thoroughly. To solve the problem of non-constructive destination, better running of the management would have to be established. A Destination Manager is needed and considered to act as the principal driving wheel in the region. For the time being, in this relatively small area of Slovenia within the Dolenjska destination, a common development policy and appearance on the market have not yet been introduced.

Through interviews, we may conclude that the Mirna Valley destination management is led to a large extent by the development centre Novo mesto. An independent management centre in the Mirna Valley area within the Dolenjska tourist destination has not as yet been established, although the vision and strategy anticipated its establishment within one year after publishing the document. With a common interest in the development and destination marketing of the Mirna Valley, including all three Municipalities, the Mirna Valley can be developed as an important tourist destination. The number of visitors is increasing every year at the destination of the Mirna Valley. This is evidenced by the statistical recording by a representative of the largest tourist service provider in the Mirna Valley – the Land of hay-racks. Only with destination management, with new lodgings capacity and some other parts of the tourist infrastructure, will it become a strong and distinctive sightseeing attraction.

Limitations and suggestions for future research

Every research has some limitations. In this case, we can consider the limitations concerning the size of the research population; to minimise its effect, we conducted interviews with all Mayors within the destination and selected carefully a sample of 20 of the most important tourist providers at the destination; we managed to capture the opinions of 11 of them. For future research, it would be proper to use another research method – for example, a survey which would cover a larger number of respondents. It would be appropriate to think about a common brand name in the wider destination, but, today, we do not have any concrete concepts of such a brand. In the Mirna Valley area, also the cultural and natural landscape changes. With the change of generations, many vineyards are abandoned in the valleys, especially in comparison with the past, and there are more quarries in some way spoiling landscape. When thinking about the future, we must ask ourselves what impact will a new road link between north and south (known as the third development axis) have on us when it is constructed, not only in the sphere of tourism but also in the spheres of economy and transit. The Tourist Information Center should not be a building or organisation only. There must be informers, who will be capable of providing useful information to tourists on the premises, in the flower shop or in the street. Let us not forget that we are living in the age of advanced technology, when smartphones play an important role. Applications by smartphone (about the offer of Mirna Valley and its contents too) should become one of the priorities to be established. Our work is an appropriate starting point for further researches in the Mirna Valley destination, particularly from the point of view of sustainable tourism, since, according to modern trends, the sustainability and development of the destination must go hand in hand.

Conclusions

The starting point of any strategic tourism policy is a tourist destination (city, region, country) as a group of interconnected stakeholders. The activity of each individual affects the activity of the others. Certain common objectives must be defined and achieved in a coordinated way. The public sector should be responsible for the future development of the destination (the development plans). The tasks of the public sector are interest rate subsidies, employment assistance, infrastructure in the Municipality, taking care of monuments, organisation of events and market research.

The private sector of the Mirna Valley is well represented. The leading group at the destination is the Land of hay-racks. For the private sector, it is important to ensure and monitor the quality. They have to implement additional tourist offers to keep the tourist longer at the destination. The private sector must consider these challenges. Civil society is very important for the development of tourism, as they supply additional activities, such as organising events or information. These events are lacking in the Mirna Valley. Here are included tourist associations, cultural associations, the Association of Rural Women, choirs, wine clubs and sports associations. They are responsible for landscaping. Civil society is financed from the municipal budget.

During the formation of the Regional Development Strategy, experts proposed some solutions that were put into the time schedule. To a large extent, those solutions have not been implemented. According to the findings, the area still has many opportunities for further development and research.

Reflections

The critical issues that we can derive from this case study would appear to be as follows:

- The role of the local tourism destination actors in implementing and developing local destination management strategies and longer-term developmental concepts.
- Questions about the ability of the various agencies concerned in the promotion of the Mirna Valley (private, public, social, regional, national) to develop appropriate and efficient skills in terms of effective and efficient collaboration.
- Concerns about the interface between local tourism entrepreneurs and the other actors which appear to have resulted in the lack of a coherent development strategy for the Mirna Valley. In other words, where is the local development strategy and who is implementing it?

Questions

1   How is it possible to enable and motivate cross-sectoral development of local destination management strategy when there is a mix of sectoral partners from public, private, social and voluntary sectors?
2   How can we explain the gap in local destination management strategic planning in the Mirna Valley?
3   To what extent may the use of smart technology (local destination apps, mapping and smart tourism guides) overcome the lack of physical facilities on the ground?

Further reading

Bornhorst, T., Ritchie, J. B., & Sheehan, L. (2010). Determinants of tourism success for DMO's & destinations: An empirical examination of stakeholders' perspectives. *Tourism Management, 31* (5), 572–589.

Ruhanen, L. (2010).Where's the strategy in tourism strategic planning? Implications for sustainable tourism destination planning. *Journal of Travel and Tourism Research, 10* (1/2), 58–76.

Volgger, M., & Pechlaner, H. (2014). Requirements for destination management organizations in destination governance: Understanding DMO success. *Tourism Management, 41,* 64–75.

Waligo, V. M., Clarke, J., & Hawkins, R. (2013). Implementing sustainable tourism: A multi-stakeholder involvement management framework. *Tourism Management, 36,* 342–353.

References

Aas, C., Ladkin, A., & Fletcher, J. (2005). Stakeholder collaboration and heritage management. *Annals of Tourism Research, 32* (1), 28–48.

Ackermann, F., & Eden, C. (2011). Strategic management of stakeholders: Theory and practice. *Long Range Planning, 44* (3), 179–196.

Aldehayyat, J. (2011). Organizational characteristics and the practice of strategic planning in Jordanian hotels. *International Journal of Hospitality Management, 30* (1), 192–199.

Belak, J. (2002). *Politika podjetja in strateški management: management in razvoj.* Gubno: MER Eurocenter.

Blain, C., Levy, S. E., & Ritchie, J. B. (2005). Destination branding: Insights and practices from destination management organizations. *Journal of Travel Research, 43* (4), 328–338.

Bornhorst, T., Ritchie, J. B., & Sheehan, L. (2010). Determinants of tourism success for DMO's & destinations: An empirical examination of stakeholders' perspectives. *Tourism Management, 31* (5), 572–589.

Brownman, C. (1994). *Bistvo strateškega managementa.* Ljubljana, Slovenia: Gospodarski vestnik.

Dimovski, V., Penger, S. & Žnidaršič, J. (2003). *Sodobni management.* Ljubljana, Slovenia: Ekonomska fakulteta.

Guiver, J., & Stanford, D. (2014). Why destination visitor travel planning falls between the cracks. *Journal of Destinational Marketing and Management, 3* (3), 140–151.

Haugland, S. A., Ness, H., Gronseth, B. O., & Aarstad, J. (2011). Development of tourism destinations: An integrated multilevel perspective. *Annals of Tourism Research, 38* (1), 268–290.

Jamal, T. B., & Getz, D. (1995). Collaboration theory and community tourism planning. *Annals of Tourism Research, 22* (1), 186–204.

Koščak, M. (2013). *Strateško akcijski načrt za vzpostavitev turistične destinacije Mirnska dolina* (Unpublished document). Studio MKA, Mokronog, Slovenia.

Laesser, C., & Beritelli, P. (2013). St. Gallen consensus on destination management. *Journal of Destination Marketing and Management, 2* (1), 46–49.

Mackey, D., & Zundel, M. (2016). Recovering the divide: A review of strategic and tactics in business and management. *International Journal of Management Reviews, 19* (2), 175–194.

Magaš, D. (1997). *Turistična destinacija.* Opatija, Croatia: Hotelijerski fakultet.

Magaš, D. (2003). *Management turističke organizacije i destinacije.* Opatija, Croatia: Fakultet za turistićki i hotelski menadžment.

Morgan, N. J., Pritchard, A., & Piggott, R. (2003). Destination branding and the role of the stakeholders: The case of New Zealand. *Journal of Vacation Marketing, 9* (3), 285–299.

Mountinho, L., Ballantyne, R., & Rate, S. (2011). The new business environment and trends in tourism. In Moutinho, L. (Ed.), *Strategic management in tourism* (2nd ed., pp. 1–19). Cambridge, UK: Cambridge University Press.

Munar, A. M. (2012). Social media strategies and destination management. *Scandinavian Journal of Hospitality and Tourism, 12* (2), 101–120.

Okumus, F. & Wong, K. F. (2005). In pursuit of contemporary content for courses on strategic management in tourism and hospitality schools. *Hospitality Management, 24* (2), 259–279.

Ovsenik, R. (2003). *Perspektive in protislovja razvoja turističnega področja: model turističnega managementa na območju slovenskih Alp* (Unpublished doctoral dissertation). Fakulteta za organizacijske vede, Kranj, Slovenia.

Presenza, A., Sheehan, L., & Ritchie, J. B. (2005). Towards a model of the roles and activities of destination management organizations. *Journal of Hospitality, Tourism and Leisure Science, 3* (1), 1–16.

Pučko, D., Čater, T., & Rejc Buhovac, A. (2009). *Strateški management 2.* Ljubljana, Slovenia: Ekonomska fakulteta.

Reid, D. (1996). *Sustainable development: An introductory guide.* London, England: Routledge EarthScan.

Ruhanen, L. (2010).Where's the strategy in tourism strategic planning? Implications for sustainable tourism destination planning. *Journal of Travel and Tourism Research, 10* (1/2), 58–76.

Sautter, E. T., & Leisen, B. (1999). Managing stakeholders a tourism planning model. *Annals of Tourism Research, 26* (2), 312–328.

Tavčar, M. (2002). *Strateški management.* Koper, Slovenia: Visoka šola za management.

Tavčar, M. (2008). *Management in organizacija: celostno snovanje politike organizacije.* Koper, Slovenia: Fakulteta za management.

United Nations World Tourism Organization. (2007). *Practical guide to tourism destination management.* Madrid, Spain.

Uran, M. (2006). *Strategija v turizmu.* Portorož, Slovenia: Turistica.

Uran, M. (2014). Organiziranost slovenskega turizma. Retrieved from www.slovenia.info/pictures%5ccategory%5catchments_1%5c2014%5corganiziranost_turizma_v_sloveniji_-_dr._maja_uran_18945.pptx.

Volgger, M., & Pechlaner, H. (2014). Requirements for destination management organizations in destination governance: Understanding DMO success. *Tourism Management, 41,* 64–75.

Waligo, V.M., Clarke, J., & Hawkins, R. (2013). Implementing sustainable tourism: A multi-stakeholder involvement management framework. *Tourism Management, 36,* 342–353.

Wall, G., & Mathieson, A. (2006). *Tourism: Changes, impacts and opportunities.* Harlow, England: Pearson Prentice Hall.

Whittington, R. (2001). *What is strategy – and does it matter?* London, England: Thomson Learning.

17 Evolution of a gentle mobility in an Alpine rural municipality

The case of Werfenweng

Milan Ilić

Introduction

A village with 1,000 inhabitants and a summer and winter tourist resort with 2,000 beds and 290,000 overnight stays per year, Werfenweng developed a concept of "gentle mobility" (*Sanfte Mobilität* – SAMO) in the late 1990s. Supported by the federal and provincial government and launched in the winter season 1999/2000, the SAMO gradually became more successful as a role model for a holiday without the privately owned car. The example of Werfenweng shows that success for the concept is based on the deliberate and gradual introduction of new, attractive, high-quality and reasonably priced mobility services, as well as the voluntary participation of both tourist enterprises and guests. The smart concept of alternative mobility during holidays addressed social trends relevant to marketing in target markets, such as the increased environmental awareness of tourists. The municipality continues to register a constant tourism growth, particularly of guests who arrive by train. However, daily visitors and their avalanche of private cars on many weekends in the area continue to be a significant challenge.

Background

Tourism has a visible share in the Austrian economy, with total tourism revenue in absolute terms, much higher than in many other countries in the world. In 2017, direct added value from tourism amounted to EUR26bn; the share of tourism in Austrian GDP has been constant in recent years at about 7.0%, with 335,000 persons directly employed in tourism activity (www.statistik.at).

In 2018, Austria had a record year with 149.8 million overnight stays in its tourist facilities (a 3.6% year-on-year increase), of which 110.4 million were foreign tourists (4.2% year-on-year increase). The most numerous tourist group are from Germany, with 56.3 million overnight stays in 2018 (up to 5.0% year-on-year); German tourists make up more than one-third of the total and more than half of foreign overnight stays. They are followed by domestic tourists, with 39.4 million overnight stays (up to 2.2% year-on-year). In the third place, as usual in recent decades, are Dutch tourists, with 10.0 million overnight stays in 2018 (up to 2.7% year-on-year). The average length of stay is 3.34 nights (www.austriatourism.com). (Note: day excursions – whether domestic or from neighbouring countries – are not included in these statistics.)

The Alps cover 62% of landlocked Austria, of which only 28% of the landscape is moderately hilly or flat. Whilst the cities of Vienna and Salzburg are global tourism attractions, a larger part of Austrian tourism income is earned in the mountain regions with tourists visiting Alpine area in winter as well as in summer. Austria has a long history of skiing in winter and hiking during summer; the Austro-Hungarian emperor Franz Josef I, one of the longest reigning monarchs in European history, nurtured a habit of "summer freshness" for 60 years. He spent every summer in Bad Ischl (a brine spa town in the province of Salzburg) until 1914– and thus encouraged the development of summer Alpine tourism.

A similar location for "summer freshness" as well as winter snow-sports is Werfenweng, located – as the imperial Bad Ischl – in the province of Salzburg. Werfenweng is in the Pongau region, 50 km south of the city of Salzburg and 12 km from the regional centre of Bischofshofen, in an alpine side valley of the Salzach River Valley. Surrounded by the mountains of Tennengebirge, at more than 900 million above the sea level, Werfenweng is a village with only 1,017 permanent inhabitants in 2018 (www.gemeinde-werfenweng.at). It has a few hamlets, scattered within a perimeter of a few kilometres. Without industry and with a traditional dominance of agriculture, Werfenweng is today a highly intensive tourism resort, with 2,000 tourist beds – i.e. almost two per inhabitant. In 2017, there were 290,008 overnight stays (up to 6.6% year-on-year) which were almost equally distributed between 49% during May–October 2017 and 51% during November 2017–April 2018 (www.salzburg. gv.at). The Werfenweng area is known for cross-country skiing (26 km of trails), alpine skiing and snowboarding (25 km of slopes), daily and nightly sledging and also as an internationally known paragliding centre. During summer, hiking, mountain biking and local gastronomy are popular.

Werfenweng launched the concept of SAMO (gentle mobility) in 1999. Tourists and importantly the local population were motivated to take a holiday away from their private cars. Because of SAMO, Werfenweng became famous, and the success of the SAMO concept was an ignition spark for the foundation of the international tourism marketing association, Alpine Pearls, with Werfenweng having a pivotal role. The Alpine Pearls association describes itself as "a necklace of pearls ... strung across the entire Alpine area of Germany, Austria, Italy, Slovenia, and Switzerland". The 23 members have in common a concern for the environment and a methodology to protect it in a quest for gentle mobility and climate-friendly holidays (www.alpine-pearls. com).

Public sector cooperation

Mobility as a factor in the transportation of tourists is believed to account for over 50% of the total environmental adverse effects caused by tourism. Individual tourist arrivals with a personal car and its subsequent usage in the holiday region create numerous problems that can be counterproductive for local tourism.

Aware of these problems from the early 1990s, Austrian experts began to intensively consider how to link economy and ecology, tourism development and environmental friendliness. The goal on the local level was to make synergies between high ecological quality, sought by both domestic population and tourists, and high mobility of guests, according to their individual wishes and needs. The essence of the tourist freedom is to go wherever and whenever they wish, and this degree of mobility is, in fact, one of the main pillars of tourist satisfaction. However, the optimisation of a tourist's individual satisfaction, the minimisation of the negative impact of tourism on the natural and social environment, and the maximisation of the income from tourism is a lengthy and complex process. Nonetheless, the case of Werfenweng indicates that it is possible to progress in this direction.

The Austrian Federal and Provincial ministries of economy, transport, agriculture, sustainability and tourism are increasingly promoting and supporting projects of mobility with an environmentally less damaging effect. The former Federal Minister for Sustainability and Tourism, Elisabeth Köstinger, has indicated that 11,600 projects of the Austrian climate programme are in realisation and subsidised with a total of EUR108m; they generated total investments of around EUR645m by 2018 ("Mission 2030", Bundesministerium für Nachhaltigkeit und Tourismus, 2018). Werfenweng was one of the least populated but the first and most innovative places participating in the environmentally friendly concept of gentle mobility supported by the relevant Austrian federal ministries and the Province of Salzburg.

In the early 1990s, independently from considerations on the federal level, local politicians and entrepreneurs began to think about the longer-term tourism strategy of Werfenweng. This was a period of difficulty for Austrian tourism, after decades of constant growth. The year 1992 was a record one for the Austrian tourism, with a total of 130.4 million overnight stays, but over the following five years, there was a constant decrease in tourist numbers. This decline lasted until 1997, a year with 109.1 million overnight stays, in effect almost one-sixth less than in 1992. (www.wko.at).

The tourism community of Werfenweng responded very promptly. Mr. Romain Molitor, an expert on traffic development and general manager of *komobile w7*, a Vienna-based engineering bureau for traffic planning commented that

> at that time, Werfenweng had fewer than 700 residents and almost 2,000 tourist beds. Managers were aware that they had to create a settlement that has to function smoothly for up to 3,000 people, not just for 700 or 1,000 permanent inhabitants.

Mr. Molitor added that Austrian tourist destinations generally have a relatively good ratio between the number of inhabitants and tourist beds, especially in alpine regions. "In some places in Italy, France, and Switzerland this ratio is 1:7". In 1994, Werfenweng created a new tourism marketing strategy. They announced a new market positioning and presented ideas on how to stop the "avalanche of cars", aware that uncontrolled growth in passenger car traffic could potentially endanger tourism in the area. Another important motivation factor for the implementation of the SAMO model was the desire of Werfenweng to be specifically positioned in tourism marketing and thus different from the increasingly fierce competition. Close to Werfenweng are several famous winter sports resorts: Sportworld Amadé, Gasteinertal, Flachau, Obertauern, and the towns of Schladming, Zell am See and several others. The main challenge for Werfenweng was how to continue to develop tourism, increase its accommodation capacities (especially for holidays on a farm), enlarge its network of hiking and cross-country ski trails, and ensure other necessary infrastructure. Simultaneous goals for Mr. Brandauer and his aides were the preservation of natural and cultural landscapes, mountain pastures, meadows, traditional crafts, and regional food specialties.

Great dream, gradual evolution

The main points of the "Werfenweng 2000" development strategy, created in 1994, are even today a bright vision because of its focus on the environmental issues in tourism and comprehensive development of the municipality. The original dream of Mr. Brandauer and his supporters was to make Werfenweng a car-free place (like Zermatt in Switzerland) and to transform the village into an air spa. At the same time, this little place was very suitable for testing the models of gentle mobility that were deliberated at the time by experts at Austrian federal ministries and their think-tanks who were looking for partners at the local level.

"Gentle Mobility – Car-Free Tourism" in Werfenweng listed the following main objectives:

- better environmental quality and the quality of life for the local population and guests
- environmentally friendly mobility and change of the mobility behaviour of residents and guests
- sustainable tourism, which should also serve as a model at home and abroad
- broad application of environmentally sound technologies (www.alpine-space.eu)

Decision-makers in Werfenweng understood that soon it would not be possible to create an Austrian version of Zermatt. Lifestyles of the local population and the habits of guests did not allow any radical solutions, and thus, a ban on private cars was not a viable solution. The inhabitants of Werfenweng decided to follow a strategy of "thousand small steps" in which they focussed on finding new ideas and practical, gradual solutions. At the same time, they planned to make both local people and tourists sensitive for alternatives to individual mobility based on overwhelming usage of private fossil-fuel-powered cars. Although conceived primarily as a tourist concept, one of the main premises of the SAMO was the inclusion of the local population, from the beginning of its implementation. The intention of Mr. Brandauer and his associates was not the construction of a Potemkin village, with some media attractive, superficial actions. They wanted to make substantial changes in mobility habits in the area.

The decisive part of the SAMO programme was to interface Werfenweng as a holiday destination with tourist mobility. During vacations, the latter is complex given that a tourist has to arrive at the destination. If this journey is completed by public transport (plane, train, bus), they must be then transferred to the accommodation facility. In a provincial destination, such as Werfenweng, a tourist normally seeks to visit surrounding attractions (e.g. Amusement Park Wengsee, *Eisriesenwelt* – "Giant Ice World", the world's largest ice caves, Hohenwerfen Castle, the Salt Mines in Hallein, Salzburg, Bischofshofen, etc.). If the tourist reaches all of these destinations in their personal transport, it is an environmental burden for the holiday destination, for permanent inhabitants and other tourists. This is particularly evident in the alpine environment; mountain topography is a natural limitation factor for car parking, among others.

A car remains indispensable for the majority of tourists in Werfenweng. "The vast majority of German guests, who are the most numerous in our house, would prefer to have a garage for their car – or at least a parking place in the yard they can see from the room", indicated Ms. Christine Huber in an interview. She operates the

Höchhäusl, a family-run guesthouse in Werfenweng. As with most accommodation facilities in the municipality, the Huber family participates in the SAMO model. Ms. Huber is a part of the absolute majority of Werfenweng residents who are convinced proponents of the SAMO.

SAMO is not a compulsory programme for all facilities and guests in Werfenweng. It is a cooperative model based on voluntary membership of participating companies and guests. By 2019, a large majority of hotels and other tourist accommodation facilities were members of SAMO. Around 75% of all accommodation capacities are part of the programme. "We do not force anybody to abandon his car during his stay here. We simply invite people to participate. At the same time, we point out that if one arrives by train or bus, he will have many advantages", emphasised Mayor Brandauer in an interview. He added, however, that the overall environmental adverse effect greatly differs if someone travels from Hamburg to Werfenweng by train or if he drives his car 1,000 km in each direction. Therefore, Werfenweng would like to greet a greater number of tourists who arrive by train.

The E-car experience

SAMO implies the implementation of new technologies, new products and services, and the change of established tourist habits. Mr. Brandauer also reminds us that in the mid-1990s, it was not easy at all to find proper electric cars. "Technologically, it was a different era. We analysed what is offered on the electric car market – and found almost only prototypes!" The market launch of SAMO was in the winter season 1999/2000. For the first time, the guests of Werfenweng were offered a SAMO card. The first precondition was and remains that an overnight guest must be located in a SAMO participating hotel/guesthouse. Facilities which are members of SAMO pay EUR1.68 for each guest's night, regardless of whether or not they acquire the SAMO-card during his stay. A tourist who seeks to buy a SAMO-card obtains this at the Tourist-information centre in Werfenweng after showing their arrival train ticket or depositing their car keys. The SAMO card costs EUR10 per person (the family of four has to pay EUR40, for example), regardless of the duration of the stay in Werfenweng. These two financial sources fund the entire SAMO model, except the Werfenweng-Shuttle (see below) which is funded differently.

Tourism companies, as members of SAMO, decide cooperatively on what form of services is included in the programme. SAMO members meet at least twice a year, to discuss the management of the SAMO structure; the tourism organisation of Werfenweng is responsible for programme implementation and management, through one of its companies specifically established for that activity. The SAMO card includes services and various discounts that would otherwise cost over EUR350. For example, a winter evening trip with the horse-sleigh costs EUR12 per person. In principle, the SAMO card is designed as a "guarantee of mobility". The first concept was to assure the mobility the tourists seek during their holiday, whether in summer or in winter. The second concept was that quality of SAMO services should be lower than the costs of a tourist driving their own car.

The function of SAMO function is fairly straightforward. The tourist arrives in Bischofshofen or Werfen, either by train or by bus (buses are frequent in recent years, fully occupied and environmentally not much more adverse than trains). The Werfenweng-Shuttle is waiting for the tourist at the station. The guest is transported with this shuttle to the hotel/guest house in Werfenweng. This service, transfer to/from the station on arrival/departure, is free of charge if the tourist's accommodation facility is a SAMO member.

Inside the municipality of Werfenweng, there is another shuttle-bus, called E-LOIS; SAMO-card owners have the possibility to use it every day. Their "personal driver" will take them with E-LOIS wherever they want inside Werfenweng. The service, free of charge for SAMO-card owners, is available every day from 08:00 AM until 10:00 PM; on Friday/Saturday, Saturday/Sunday, and nights before public holidays, E-LOIS runs until 04:00 AM.

Electric vehicles for personal use are another mode of mobility in Werfenweng. The SAMO card is the "ignition key" for the fleet of current 11 modern electric cars (mostly BMW i3 for up to four passengers, and some Smart cars for two passengers). The only problem with electric cars in Werfenweng is their limited number. It is, therefore, necessary for a tourist to plan their excursions and organise when they need a car. Before the first journey, they are required to obtain brief directions for driving the vehicle, as electric cars are not identical to fossil-fuel-powered cars; electric cars are taken and subsequently returned to the parking lot in the centre of Werfenweng. The parking lot is also an electric car charging station. The operating range of the BMWi3 is over 200 km, so they are usable for longer excursions, e.g., to the city of Salzburg and similar.

The SAMO-card includes many other complimentary services, such as the renting of electric bikes and Segway transporters in summer. The total number of all such available vehicles reached 106 in 2018. A free trip to Salzburg is also included in the SAMO-card, as well as a ticket for the Lake Amusement Park Wengsee (in summer), the hiring of equipment for cross-country skiing, snowshoeing, and other related services in winter. The SAMO-card covers one horse-sleigh ride as well during the winter, but during the summer, the SAMO-card holders may access trekking tour with lamas.

SAMO was an immediate success. In the period 2000–2004, when the number of tourist beds in Werfenweng was constant, overnight stays jumped from 152,000 to 212,000 per year. This was an extremely important argument for the acceptance of SAMO among the local population. In the beginning, the people of Werfenweng were rather sceptical. They did not believe that tourists, mostly Germans (who make 75% of tourists in Werfenweng), wanted to have a holiday apart from their car. In the early days of the programme, 13 different tourism enterprises in Werfenweng were members of SAMO; by 2019, the number increased to 45.

No less important, the new concept of tourism mobility in Werfenweng has attracted many new tourists. Environmentally friendly tourism has become increasingly relevant to marketing and market communication. It was not easy to convince people of Werfenweng to re-orient to environmentally aware tourists as they were afraid to specialise in specifically defined environmental market segments. Clearly, the number of environmentally aware guests tourists is constantly increasing; before 1994 and the introduction of SAMO, only 6% of all tourists came by train. In 2017, they represented 25%, and the emission of CO_2 has decreased by 2,000 tons annually as a result.

Community transport in Werfenweng

The fleet of electric cars has been increasing as there is a growing demand for this form of transportation; each electric car is driven, on average, for more than 30,000 km yearly. Local residents may also use electric cars from the SAMO programme, under somewhat different conditions from tourists, but certainly these conditions are very advantageous. To an extent, it is possible to predict a trend for the community electric cars to replace ownership of second cars given the low costs of usage.

Prior to the launching of SAMO, buses between Werfenweng and Bischofshofen operated only three times daily – in the morning, around noon and in the evening. Now, a shuttle bus is available every hour based on the fact that a passenger must call for the bus at least one hour before the needed ride. The bus comes directly to the passenger's address, but if a bus is full, the company provides an additional back-up service. In rush hours in the high tourist season, there are sometimes six buses simultaneously on the road. Whilst SAMO-card owners have free transport in these buses, domestic residents have the ability to access the local use service as a reasonable price. This is due to a development in Werfenweng's traffic policy for the introduction of the SAMO-card for domestic residents. There are several target groups among the domestic inhabitants – if they choose not to use a private car and wish to be driven by the Werfenweng-Shuttle, they may obtain an annual ticket for this bus, a number of tickets for E-LOIS, the right to use e-bikes and other benefits. Households with children who go to school alone (are not driven by parents) receive a seasonal swimming pool ticket and some family excursions free of charge. The households who choose not to drive their car on a particular day of the week have the right to use electric vehicles on that day. By the beginning of 2019, about 50 such contracts were signed.

The electrical energy required to fill SAMO cars is obtained from a solar power plant in the southern part of the village. The annual output of almost 300,000 kWh far exceeds the power consumption of the SAMO fleet of electric cars and other vehicles. Since September 2013, a further power plant based on renewable energy sources (biomass – wood chips) began operating, with a 2.5 MW of installed power. There are also many hydropower plants on mountain creeks and rivers in and around Werfenweng, so all the electricity consumed in the village is provided by renewable sources.

Yet apart from the environmentally friendly policies reflected in the mobility of tourists and energy from renewable sources, the tourism policy of Werfenweng is also promoting a local supply of food and other products needed in tourism, with short transport routes whenever possible.

Day excursions

A segment in which Werfenweng has failed to make a big turnaround with its SAMO policy relates to day excursion visitors. These will be visitors who during the winter weekends are seeking to access winter-sports facilities, which results in a mass of cars blocking the centre of the resort and ski lift ground stations. Clearly, one of the main goals of the SAMO policy has been to attract even more guests to arrive by public transport.

The plan for the near future is to introduce SAMO-cards for daily visitors as well. The main prerequisite for that is innovative solutions and an incentive system that would intelligently reward those who arrive by public transport. Werfenweng would also like to position itself as a great place for one-day visitors who want a superb experience without a car. This involves the construction of a new mobility centre which would provide parking facilities for those switching from traditional to environmentally friendly transport. Clearly, moving to electrical mobility in Werfenweng may not appeal to all citizens, but the justification of this policy is the huge success in attracting many new tourists and the excellent image that the municipality provides in Austria and abroad.

Concluding comments

Werfenweng was placed on the Global 100 Sustainable Destinations list in 2017 and received a number of other relevant awards. SAMO has been copied in a number of tourism destinations – not wholly those which are members of the Alpine Pearls association. Establishment of Alpine Pearls was a significant milestone in the development of gentle mobility in this part of Europe. The existence and activities of Alpine Pearls also provides greater political weight to Werfenweng and all the other members, making it easier to negotiate with other relevant travel and tourism organisations.

We should also not ignore the fact that Werfenweng has become an increasingly popular place to live, with an expanding population. The Province of Salzburg statistics reveal that Werfenweng was the third municipality in terms of population growth – 9.3% growth over 2014–2019 – with only higher growth registered in Hollersbach in Pinzgau – 10.4% growth over 2014–2019 (Salzburger Landesstastik, 2019). The overall provincial population grew by 3% in 2014–2019, but numerous villages and small towns are constantly losing their populations. Werfenweng is, on the contrary, attractive for younger families, because it has good traffic connections and is surrounded by beautiful nature. Qualities which attract tourists are obviously appealing for many other people from the province of Salzburg and have led to an increase in the number of families settling in the village.

Annually, a number of global tourism experts gather to understand and review the experience of Werfenweng. This involves learning more about the local practice of gentle mobility and environmentally friendly tourism. This would indicate that Werfenweng is an interesting example and role model for gentle mobility in many tourist resorts around the world.

Reflections

The Austrian alpine village municipality Werfenweng confirms the concept that tourists, as well as the domestic population, do not necessarily require private cars but need efficient transport. Werfenweng has positioned itself as a practical model of "gentle mobility" development, initiated by the Austrian ministry of environment and based on expert knowledge. It has addressed the need of Werfenweng to reposition its tourism and the transport habits of the local population very specifically and not only in augmenting its image as a tourist destination. Political will at the local level and the provision of expert advice were prerequisites for the success of the "Gentle mobility – Car Free Tourism".

"SAMO" in Werfenweng is not a compulsory system for all hosts and other tourism enterprises, all guests, and all inhabitants of Werfenweng. Everybody is simply invited to participate in this voluntary programme with its many advantages. Mobility continues to have a significant environmental impact; there are no miracle solutions. The strategy of a thousand small steps is convincing tourists to come to Werfenweng by public transportation – and the local population to drive their cars less frequently – and to use the SAMO. "Gentle mobility" was also one of the common denominators for the establishment of the Alpine Pearls, an international tourism marketing association.

Questions

1 What may be done at the EU, national and regional levels to promote environmentally friendlier transportation in tourism?
2 What is the role of regional, national and international transport companies in gentle mobility development at the local level?
3 If you were a mayor of one of the Alpine Pearls member municipalities, what would you wish to achieve? Are the growth of overnight stays and income the only indicator of tourism success?
4 What should be the target tourism segment for Werfenweng? Young individuals? People who do not own a car? Families with children who would like to try electric cars, Segways and other e-vehicles? Highly educated, environmentally aware bourgeoise bohemians? Older people? All overseas guests who arrive in Austria by plane?
5 How may SAMO be advertised in different target markets?
6 What should be the main motivational factors for tourists to change their transportation habits?
7 In a discussion about Werfenweng, what are the positive and negative arguments regarding SAMO versus private cars?

Further reading

Kalteis, F. and Bergmann, B. 2007. *Werfenweng. Sanft Mobil auf neuen Wegen (Werfenweng – Soft Mobile on New Paths*, in German, with shorter text versions translated in English, French and Italian). Tourismusverband Werfenweng

References

The material collected for this case study was primarily from personal interviews by the author, Milan Ilić, with Austrian government officials as well as with provincial and local tourism representatives.
In addition the following web-sites were accessed:
www.statistik.at/web_de/statistiken/wirtschaft/tourismus/index.html
www.austriatourism.com/tourismusforschung/studien-und-berichte/statistik-kalenderjahr-2018/
www.gemeinde-werfenweng.at/Unser_Werfenweng/Zahlen_und_Fakten
www.salzburg.gv.at/statistik_/Documents/statistik-Tourismus-Kalenderjahr2017.pdf
www.alpine-pearls.com/en/about-us/alpine-pearls/
Mission2030: Klimaaktiv Mobil unterstützt Österreichs Unternehmen, Städte, Gemeinden und Regionen bei sauberer Mobilität, Wien, September 2018, Bundesministerium für Nachhaltigkeit und Tourismus
http://wko.at/statistik/jahrbuch/tourismus-naechtigungen.pdf
www.alpine-space.eu/projects/astus/mtc/06_brandauer.pdf. Salzburger Nachrichten, Feb. 16, 2019, based on data from the Salzburg Landesstatistik

18 Experience design in interpreting cultural heritage

A case study on the Land of Hayracks, Slovenia

Bogdan Turnšek and Maja Turnšek

Introduction

The aim of this chapter is to introduce the concepts of experience design within the so-called "Experience Economy" (Pine and Gilmore, 1998) and apply the model of the 4Es in experience design to heritage interpretation: the 4Es being education, entertainment, aesthetics and escape. We apply the model to a case study from Slovenia: The Land of Hayracks and discuss the implications the model has for the management of the product and its value in interpreting local cultural heritage to tourists.

Today's long-established tourism industry emerged from a purely economic approach. This was before transforming into a distinctly multidisciplinary area that now has the potential to integrate key social and environmental pillars into the restoration of values that are being slowly forgotten in the developed world. Managers working in modern tourist services do not treat tourists simply as customers, but also as guests who are looking to fulfil their dreams through unforgettable experiences which satisfy the highest human needs for self-realisation. The global economy has also adapted to this change. In 1998, Pine and Gilmore coined a new term for a modern economic range of services – the "experience economy" or the "adventure economy". This concept represents the most recent stage in the industry's economic evolution and represents an enhancement of an economy based on just goods, products and services.

Since the way that natural and cultural heritage is interpreted not only enhances meaning but also stimulates the desire to protect and preserve, it is crucial to take this into account when planning a tourist experience.

In essence, "Dežela kozolcev" (The Land of Hayracks – see Figure 18.1) doubles up as an outdoor ethnological museum and a tourist product that displays and interprets a diverse typography of Slovenian cultural heritage – all in one location. Its success with incorporating modern tourist trends was appraised by a qualitative content analysis and a quantitative survey research conducted on a random sample of Slovenian museum visitors. The study revealed that the managers of the "Dežela kozolcev" tourist product are not very familiar with the most recently developed cutting-edge concepts that ensure high-quality experiences.

Figure 18.1 Hayrack.

The educational role of heritage interpretation

Interpretation of natural and, in our case, cultural heritage is, above all, a profession which plays a pivotal role in the design and creation of high-quality tourist products, and has its basis in the preserved nature, history and culture in developed tourist destinations. This is evident from several destination development plans which refer to the interpretation of heritage and its importance in creating authentic experiences as one of the key priorities (Schumacher Farm Park, 2005; Fort Nisqually Living History Museum, 2010; Fort St. James, 2013; Patapsco Heritage Greenway, 2015).

A useful interpretation is one in which there is a communication process that helps guests enhance their understanding of history and heritage, establishing a meaningful relationship with both. Rather than simply providing information and cold facts, it is primarily an educational activity devoted to finding meaning in heritage through direct personal experiences when coming into contact with its authentic elements (Tilden, 1977). By becoming personally involved in experiencing natural and cultural heritage, the interpretation process leads to understanding the final goal. This is to gain respect and, as a result, better understand the design and active preservation of the natural or cultural heritage being interpreted (as referred to by Tilden, 1977; Herbert, Prentice and Thomas, 1989; Moscardo, Woods and Saltzer, 2004; and Mohamed, Noor and Mohamed, 2014).

This method also stimulates a desire among visitors to actively preserve the heritage site in question (Jacobs and Harms, 2014), which in turn ensures its economic success. Moreover, as seen by Ham and Weiler (2002), this also results in the ability to satisfy modern tourist demands on the one hand and to create local jobs on the other. Interpretation consistently fulfils the three core principles of sustainability and plays a pivotal role in the establishment of sustainable tourism. In addition to raising the standard of visitors' experiences, it also contributes to a better local environment and quality of life for the local population (Moscardo, 2003).

The way something is interpreted is often dependent on the power ratio between all the interest groups and stakeholders involved with the destination. Decisions are often made by non-local "experts" who are trained in completely different areas and are in place to implement the will and policies of higher authorities (Graham and Howard, 2008). Bramwell and Lane (2011) also warn of the pitfalls that may arise when planning the interpretation process at a destination and that these are a result of economic imperatives. They argue that there is significant risk of so-called "pre-interpretations", i.e. unwarranted interference in the experience, excessive transformation of space, simplification and the impoverishment of content, elitism, etc. This relates to a fear of commodifying the inheritance and the loss of its identity, which is ultimately a consequence of differing views on authenticity. This is currently one of the most hotly debated concepts in tourism studies (for an example of such a debate, see Wang, 1999).

Therefore, the primary double-edged sword in this debate on the sustainable management of natural and cultural heritage, especially when seen through the prism of developing the tourism experience, appears to hinge on striking a balance between the profitability of the product and its educational role. Approaching the economic aspect, Pine and Gilmore (1998) offer the so-called 4Es model of experience design, which in turn goes beyond the dichotomy between education and profitability, and define the educational dimension as a cornerstone of profitable product design.

Sustaining added value through experiences

Pine and Gilmore (1998, 1999) claim that we are transitioning into a new phase of economic development as we find new ways to increase added value for the customer and financial gain for the organisation. They claim that the economy has undergone four stages thus far. The first concerns the era when agrarian companies predominated. Goods and raw materials were obtained from the natural environment; when refined, they were sent to monopolised wholesale markets where the price was set depending on supply and demand. The goods were expandable and substitutable, and the differentiation level negligible since the only relevant criterion for purchase was their market price. When companies became industrialised, moving away from the agrarian model, the automation of labour brought increased productivity. This in turn led to the emergence of the second stage of the economic supply, which was dominated by production. The production of tangible goods and products intended for individual buyers made from raw materials began, and the price was determined by production costs. The first brands were established and competition between them started, which opened the way to differentiation. This in addition to production costs had a decisive influence on the identification and determination of final prices. Over time, the technological progress has also gradually diminished the need for workers; compounding the issue, the vast assets belonging to the manufacturing sector and the accumulated inventories of manufactured goods have triggered the need for a new economic supply based on services and service workers. Services are intangible activities that are adapted to the specific demands clients in order to perform an activity, or a task in order to satisfy some specific needs or perform tasks that the clients would otherwise have to do by themselves. Products constitute the basis for the provision of services, but services in this third stage of economic supply are more valued. They represent a new form of added value and an even higher level of differentiation between providers. Although, for example, restaurants serve food, which is tangible, economists classify them in the service sector. This is because their range of services is not standardised, nor is it a part of a stock, but is ready and served according to the customer's specific order. In its present state, the service economy could reach a turning point where only products and services in themselves are no longer sufficient. The time has come for a new level of economic supply, with experience at its foundation.

According to the authors (Pine and Gilmore, 1999), adventure or experience occurs when the company deliberately uses its services as a staged event and its products as props when engaging with an individual on a personal level. If the raw materials are expendable, the products tangible and the service intangible, the experiences will be unforgettable. When consumers pay for the experience, they essentially pay for the time they spend with the provider, but the memories stay forever. Experience providers are no longer just sellers, but participants; and customers are no longer simply customers, but guests who appreciate the experience gained far more than just the product or service itself. They are willing to pay more for something if it might stay in their heart and memory. And because experiences take place on the individual level, the degree of differentiation between individual products is also the highest.

Good product design and marketing are crucial for goods and services as well as experiential economics, while inventiveness and innovation are essential for income growth. In any case, experiences have completely different qualities and characteristics to goods and services, and their design is a unique challenge. In this study, experiences are defined through two dimensions. The first refers to the level of inclusion or guest participation. On the one hand, guests are passive, which means they do not have an effect on the event at which they are participants. Examples of such guests include audience members at classical music concerts who experience the event merely as observers and listeners. On the other hand, there are active guests who play a key role in co-creating an event – an experience. Examples of such participants would be skiers in competition. It is also worth noting that even spectators at skiing competitions are not completely passive participants because they also contribute to either the beautiful scenery or the sound effect created with others by their presence at an event. The second dimension of an experience concerns the connection or nature of the relationship that brings guests together with an event or performance. At one polar extreme of the connection is the absorption, which results in enthusiasm, and on the other end, we have immersion, which results in being enticed. For example, most students accept content more enthusiastically in lectures than they would by simply reading the material – the absorption rate is therefore higher when listening to lectures than reading. Another example of different levels of absorption is the viewing of a film in the cinema. The environment, the large screen and good level of audio all contribute significantly to the feeling of being drawn in and connecting with the film, as opposed to the experience of watching a film at home. Pine and Gilmore classify experiences according to the different stages of the two dimensions, but into four categories. They claim that the word "adventure" evokes a feeling of having a good time among the majority of people. Watching television or visiting a concert is a passive form of participation, and their connection with the event is closer to absorption than immersion or active inclusion. Educational events such as lectures or ski courses require the active participation of participants, but these participants do not get involved in the creation of the event, instead accepting it merely for what it is and how it is presented. The so-called escapist experience, which typically features an escape from everyday life or as a getaway to somewhere else, to another place or time, offers us education and fun at the same time; however, unlike in the aforementioned categories, the guest in this case is much more connected with the experience. Performing in a theatre production, playing in an orchestra or walking through the Grand Canyon includes both the guest's activity and the consequent delight. As the visitor's level of activity reduces, the escapist experience becomes aesthetic. In this case, the visitors are part of the experience. They are merged with it, but have either very little or no influence on it. An example of such a visitor would be a tourist observing the Grand Canyon, but from afar, or someone visiting a gallery. It is clear that the richest experiences are those which include all four areas of experience, forming a sweet spot with the best from all areas coming together at once.

In an attempt to provide further insight into how tourism providers and destinations create successful experiences, Oh, Fiore and Jeoung (2007) developed a research instrument. This took the form of a questionnaire based on the four areas of experience identified by Pine and Gilmore (1998). They developed and tested the model using a quantitative survey on the B&B (Bed and Breakfast) sector in the United States of America. The questionnaire was designed to be appropriate for all tourism sectors, requiring only slight adjustments, and can clearly show deviations in favour of one or more areas of experience. Even prior to this, certain authors (Zeithaml, 1988; Kotler, 2004) had developed a model for measuring the experience and consequent customer satisfaction based on so-called perceived value, which is in fact an individual's own assessment of the value of the product, depending on how much that individual wants or needs product in question. Other authors (Williams and Soutar, 2009; Song et al., 2015) studied two aspects of the experience that form guest satisfaction. Taking into account their studies, there are two types of values involved: (i) functional, resulting from educational experience; and (ii) emotional, resulting from aesthetic experiences. They found that emotional values are always perceived differently and in unique manner by each individual. Oh, Fiore and Jeoung (2007) found that the dominant dimension in experiences in the American B&B industry was the area of aesthetics. For a musical festival in Norway, the two dominant areas were escapism and aesthetics, and in a museum in Norway, the areas were education and aesthetics (Mehmetoglu and Engen, 2011). Quadri-Felitti and Fiore (2012) also used the Four Areas of Experience model to analyse experiential theory in the management and planning of viniculture and rural tourism the world over. Sidali, Kastenholz and Bianchi (2015) did the same with the management and planning of rural tourism based on local food, and Gabova (2016) applied the model on the Santa Park case in Rovaniemi, Finland. When assessing Santa Park, Gabova's results showed the highest experiential level of Russian guests in the aesthetic and escapist fields and lower levels in the areas of entertainment and education.

Pine and Gilmore's (1998, 1999) approach therefore appears to find a compromise between the educational function and the economic imperative of heritage interpretation in tourism products. This is achieved by providing a model of experience design where education is one of the experience functions and the perception of how much one has learned is an important added value for the guest. At the same time, it is important to mention the critical perspective that deals with the experience economy as a tool for achieving globalisation processes and, consequently, cultural homogenisation and commercialisation. Thematically, we are yet again faced with the concept of pre-interpreting heritage and MacCanell's staged (fake) authenticity, which only proves the connection between the topics discussed. As Richards (1996) already concludes, both globalisation and the attempt to cater for the tourist demand for experiences and adventure caused the culture to commoditise and transform into a new, non-authentic form – solely for the purpose of making easy sales. Many global corporations are intentionally building their marketing and sales strategies on being able to provide experience; however, their aim is not cultural diversity but the imposition of western values (MacLeod, 2004; Reisinger and Dimanche, 2010). The authors also refer to several terms that summarise these processes, such as corporate Westernisation, Americanisation, McDonaldization and Cocacolonization. Bryman (1999) concludes by noting that Disneyization is in fact a notion that complements the most widespread process – the McDonaldization of society. This is because the stated principles of Disney's thematic parks increasingly dominate more sectors in both American society and companies around the world. We conducted a survey to ascertain whether this was also the case with the Land of Hayracks.

Land of Hayracks – description

In its development strategy in 2005, Slovenia clearly set out its position in support of sustainable development. One of the key priorities for achieving the set goals was the development of Slovenia's national identity and culture (Slovenia's Development Strategy, 2005, p. 9). Twelve years later, in its development strategy until 2030, cultural heritage is still defined as a reflection of values, beliefs, knowledge and traditions, and as an important developmental aspect of society (Slovenia's Development Strategy 2030, 2017, p. 30). Museums in particular can contribute significantly to preserving and building a cultural identity. In essence, the Land of Hayracks is an outdoor ethnological museum that displays and interprets a varied typography of Slovenian rural cultural heritage in the form of guided tours, events and various workshops – all in one place. It is located in a small village called Šentrupert in the valley of the Mirna river in Dolenjska, which is in the south-east of Slovenia, not far from the Ljubljana-Novo Mesto motorway link. The museum was founded by the Municipality of Šentrupert and opened its doors to visitors in 2013 to the proud claim of being the first hayrack museum in the world. Every year, it attracts around 25,000 visitors. The outdoor museum was partly financed by the European Regional Development Fund, and the museum's access point and the Cultural Heritage Protection Centre were partly funded by the Leader programme funds.

The definition provided on their website (Land of Hayracks, 2019) states that a hayrack is a roof-covered independent building; sometimes, it leans against another building or takes the form of a drying device made primarily of wood. A hayrack is part of the homestead but can also be a self-standing structure in a meadow or field. They are used to dry and store hay, various cereals, maize, flax, hemp, legumes, tuberous plants, ferns and other products. The hayracks became a place where a wide range of activities were carried out. They became venues for various celebrations, social events and farm work, while the local people sold home-made food and drinks under their shade, and children played in safe hay shelters. They also offered a place of refuge for various travellers, and young men would often use hayracks as makeshift beds all summer. Since hayracks have evolved into several types and typical forms which cannot be found elsewhere in the world, they are considered a Slovenian speciality. It is for this reason that the hayrack became an identifying characteristic of the country.

There are currently a total of 19 different dryers on display in the Land of Hayracks. The facilities were transferred to the outdoor museum in a professional manner and in adherence to all relevant principles of restoration. Almost all of the objects originate from the surrounding area – the Mirna Valley. The purpose of the installation was to demonstrate the development of hayracks from temporal, spatial and social points of view. This was represented in the form of simple dryers through to single hay racks and all the way to the more developed forms of double hayfields – toplars. These represent the pinnace of a centuries-old tradition concerning agricultural and livestock activities in the environs of peasant, monastic and castle estates. The museum stretches over 2.5 hectares of landscaped real estate, through which winds a kilometre-long network of walking paths. The oldest toplar is the Lukatov toplar, which was constructed in 1795, making it one of the oldest preserved double hayracks in Slovenia and, indeed, the whole world.

On their website, the Land of Hayracks refers to itself as an innovative project run by the Šentrupert municipality which connects the all-round value of rural building heritage with modern forms of tourism and commerce. The project's stakeholders include the municipality, educational and scientific institutions, local societies and businesses, as well as several individuals. Through its various activities, the museum strives to acknowledge and preserve the existence of its heritage and to help develop positive approaches and attitudes towards heritage generally. Each hayrack belongs to a homestead and is a manifestation of the story of the people who used it and the craftsmen who built it. In their opinion, these stories did not conclude when the hayracks were moved into an outdoor museum. They maintain their development through continued interpretative content. The current practice involves the creation of new heritage content and stories, taking care not to over-exploit the commercial potential available. We examined how this works from an experiential economy perspective.

Four areas of experience in the Land of Hayracks

For the remainder of the study, an evaluation was conducted on how the museum incorporates the four areas of designing experience put forward by Pine and Gilmore (1998, 1999). In terms of the experiential economy, otherwise known as the experience economy, we were interested in ascertaining which area of experience – entertainment, education, the aesthetic experience or the escapist experience – dominated among visitors to the Land of Hayracks. In search of the answer, a quantitative method of research was adopted, taking the form a survey with a questionnaire that was developed and used by Oh, Fiore and Jeoung (2007) and based on Pine and Gilmore's theories of experiential economics or the economies of experience. In addition to general questions, the survey module also includes questions covering the content in all four areas of experience. At the end of the survey, the goal was to understand the level of excitement about the product, how memorable it was, the overall quality of the product and customer satisfaction. The survey was conducted on a sample of Slovenian visitors to the museum which were taken from individual guests and guided group participants. The survey was carried out through the online 1k survey. The visitors were asked to fill out the questionnaire at the end of their visit. The questionnaire was also available to be completed in physical form at the museum's entrance-exit point and inside the museum as well for all wishing to fill it out directly after the tour had concluded.

The survey ran during the period 21 April 2018 to 15 November 2018 in electronic form on the "1ka" internet portal and in physical form at the museum's entrance-exit point. With the agreement of the museum, a covering letter was prepared for a request to complete the survey. It contained a preface, a link to a survey on the web portal and a QR code to connect to the web portal via mobile phones, and was available to all visitors. A total of 183 visitors started filling out the survey, of whom 46 only read the preface, while 20 respondents did not complete it fully. We took only fully completed surveys into account, which ultimately resulted in 117 useful surveys, of which 65 were in written and 52 in electronic form.

The sample comprised 59 women (50.4%) and 58 men (49.6%). A total of 31 (26.5%) participants were up to 30 years of age, 47 (40.2%) were aged between 31 and 50, and 39 (33.3%) over 51 years of age. A total of 10 (8.5%) participants were with elementary school education, 35 (29.9%) with high school education, 57 (48.7%) with bachelor's degree and 15 (12.8%) with a master's degree or doctorate.

Aesthetic area

As can be seen from Table 18.1, the surveyed visitors to the Land of Hayracks mostly agreed with the assertion that it was very pleasant to be there (average 4.11), followed by the notion that the setting looked very attractive (average 3.99). The next most popular assertion was that a real sense of harmony could be felt at the setting (average 3.88), then that the museum paid a lot of attention to small but important design details (average 3.58), and that the setting appealed to all their senses (an average of 3.55). It appears that the lowest average was the claim that the scene was quite bland (an average of 2.44, median 2), but note should be made that this claim was semantically incongruent, which was taken into account in all statistical calculations. Thus, the overall average in the aesthetic area was 3.78. In addition to the median, a standard deviation is displayed for each statement.

Table 18.1 Aesthetic area

	Number	Median	Average	Standard deviation
Just being here was very pleasant.	117	4.00	4.11	0.888
The setting was very attractive.	117	4.00	3.99	0.895
I felt a real sense of harmony.	117	4.00	3.88	0.873
The setting really showed attention to design detail.	117	4.00	3.58	1.108
The setting appealed to my senses.	117	4.00	3.55	0.978
The setting was quite bland. (reverse coded)	117	2.00	2.44	1.094

Source: Turnšek (2019).

Table 18.2 Educational area

	Number	Median	Average	Standard deviation
The experience has made me more knowledgeable.	117	4.00	4.06	0.893
I learned a lot.	117	4.00	3.86	0.928
It stimulated my curiosity to learn new things.	117	4.00	3.77	0.950
It was a real learning experience.	117	4.00	3.74	0.968
The experience was highly educational for me.	117	4.00	3.56	0.951
The experience really enhanced my skills.	117	3.00	3.01	1.055

Source: Turnšek (2019).

Educational area

As can be seen from Table 18.2, the Land of Hayracks visitors who fully completed the survey agreed with the assertion that the experience in the museum had expanded their knowledge (an average of 4.06). Slightly fewer participants agreed with the claim that they had learned a lot (average 3.86), that the experience had stimulated their interest in learning new things (an average of 3.77) and that this was a real educational experience (an average of 3.74). Slightly fewer again agreed with the claim that education provided had been a high-level experience for them (an average of 3.56), and the visitors agreed least with the assertion that the experience had helped them to improve certain skills (average 3.01, median 3). The overall average in the educational area was 3.67.

Escapist area

As can be seen from Table 18.3, the Land of Hayracks visitors who fully completed the survey agreed with the assertion that they completely forgot about their daily work during their museum visit (average 3.63, median 4). However, they agreed somewhat less with the claim that they felt like they had found themselves living in a different time and place (an average of 3.38). Slightly fewer visitors agreed with the claim that they were able completely escape from their realities (averaging 3.22) and slightly fewer again claimed that the experience allowed them to imagine they were somebody else (an average of 3.09). The smallest agreement was expressed with the assertion that they felt like they were playing a different role in their lives (an average of 2.97). The total average in the escapist area was 3.26.

Table 18.3 Escapist area

	Number	Median	Average	Standard deviation
I totally forgot about my daily routine.	117	4.00	3.63	1.063
I felt like I was living in a different time or place.	117	3.00	3.38	1.187
I completely escaped from reality.	117	3.00	3.22	1.123
The experience here let me imagine being someone else.	117	3.00	3.09	1.103
I felt I played a different character here.	117	3.00	2.97	1.137

Source: Turnšek (2019).

Entertainment area

As can be seen from Table 18.4, visitors who completed all of the survey agreed with the assertion that they had lot of fun at the Land of Hayracks (an average of 3.63). However, somewhat fewer agreed with the assertion that it was amusing to observe the activities of others (an average of 3.59). The next most popular assertion was that they really enjoyed seeing what other people were doing (average 3.11, median 3), and the semantically opposite claim that they were bored by what others did (an average of 2.50, median 2). This altered claim was taken into account in all statistical calculations. The visitors agreed least with the statement that the activities of others were amusing to observe (an average of 2.44). The total average for the entertainment area was 3.26.

As can be seen from Table 18.5, the average estimate of the level of experience level in all four areas was greater than 3 out of 5, and the average in all four areas together was 3.49. This is also confirmed by the results of the *t*-tests, which were statistically significant for all four areas ($p < 0.05$). It is therefore evident that the level of experience for the visitors to the Land of Hayracks was high in all four areas.

Checks were conducted on which area of experience recorded the statistically highest rating among visitors to the Land of Hayracks. Since this is a product that emphasises education as its basis, we expected the experiential level to be the highest in this area. Since the Shapiro–Wilk test revealed that the distribution of the variables deviated from the norm to a statistically significant degree, the Wilcoxon signed-rank test was used to verify the hypothesis.

As can be seen from Table 18.5, the level of experience is not the highest in the educational area but in the aesthetic area. All the differences between the areas are also statistically significant, with the exception of the entertainment and escapist areas (Table 18.6). It can therefore be concluded that the level of experience is the highest in

Table 18.4 Entertainment area

	Number	Median	Average	Standard deviation
It was an entertaining experience.	117	4.00	3.63	1.039
The activities of others were amusing to watch.	117	4.00	3.59	1.108
I really enjoyed watching what others were doing.	117	3.00	3.11	1.216
What others did was boring to watch. (semantically opposite)	117	2.00	2.50	1.215
Activities of others were fun to watch.	117	2.00	2.44	1.110

Source: Turnšek (2019).

Table 18.5 Comparison of the average level of experience in four areas

	Number	Average	Standard deviation	t	p
Aesthetic area	117	3.78	0.72	11.704	<0.001*
Educational area	117	3.67	0.74	9.775	<0.001*
Escapist area	117	3.26	0.88	3.136	0.001*
Entertainment area	117	3.26	0.67	4.133	<0.001*

Source: Turnšek (2019).
*The difference is statistically significant ($p < 0.05$).

Table 18.6 Comparing the level of experience between the four areas

	Number	Wilcoxon Z	p
Aesthetic vs. Educational	117	1.747	0.041*
Aesthetic vs. Entertainment	117	7.098	<0.001*
Aesthetic vs. Escapist	117	7.133	<0.001*
Educational vs. Entertainment	117	5.806	<0.001*
Educational vs. Escapist	117	6.282	<0.001*
Entertainment vs. Escapist	117	0.168	0.433

Source: Turnšek (2019).
*The difference is statistically significant ($p < 0.05$).

the aesthetic area and in the educational area, and third place is shared by the escapist and entertainment areas.

Discussion – outcomes and concepts

As far as the aesthetic field is concerned, the conclusion can be reached that attending the museum was a pleasant experience for the majority of visitors. The venue was considered attractive, although the museum should devote more attention to small but important design details and to triggering as many senses as possible. In the field of education, the visit to the museum allows visitors to expand their theoretical knowledge, but not their practical expertise, as the results demonstrate. If the museum were to allow its visitors to take a more active role in daily activities (for example, the live history shows), the experience would also be taken to a higher level. In this way, it would also be possible to encroach upon the areas of escapism and entertainment since it would make it easier for visitors to escape from the "real world" and to imagine they are someone else. At the same time, it would also make watching other people's activities more enjoyable. As proposed by Sidali, Kastenholz and Bianchi (2015), experienced planners working with tourism providers would simply need to incorporate these findings into the strategy for their experiential range of services and to strive to continue making the right decisions through monitoring and further research.

From an experience economy perspective, the assumption was made that the educational area would reach the highest experiential level in the Land of Hayracks, but the results of the research showed a slight positive deviation towards aesthetics. This represents an important finding that can greatly benefit the museum in enhancing their existing range of services. As mentioned in the theoretical part of the task, aesthetics is an important element in the construction of the spirit and the character of the destination. In English, there is a very apt expression for this – *a sense of place*, which is wonderfully explained by many authors (Walsh, Jamrozy and Burr, 2001; Moscardo, 2008; Davis, 2011; Campelo, Aitken, Thyne and Gnoth, 2014). The Land of Hayracks has a high aesthetic value, with a good starting point for further thematic development and brand recognition. Now, with the systematic enhancement of its aesthetic and other elements, it can emerge from being simply an outdoor museum to become a museum of living history. This will merge the direct experiences of locals and visitors with the values of another time in the most authentic environment possible, which represents one of the most complete forms of heritage interpretation (Tilmans, Van Vree and Winter, 2010). The Museum of Living History is a welcome vision for the future development of the Land of Hayracks. Its base is an outdoor museum in the form it exists today. Although scores of around 4 out of 5 have been achieved thus far in aesthetics and education, unfortunately escapism and entertainment are considerably weaker with a score of 3 out of 5. This could encourage the museum to take measures to attract visitors experiences to that sweet spot where all areas merge as seamlessly as possible (Pine and Gilmore, 1999).

This is a serious note of caution to the museum that its management should be approached in a planned and professional manner. Every guided tour does not represent an interpretation, and a cultural heritage, which is merely an end in itself, does not necessarily convey the same deep message in the eyes of the visitors as it might with the aid of a well-planned interpretation. Or maybe it does in terms of the aesthetics of the Land of Hayracks? The question here is whether the articles in the museum and the space itself could simply speak for themselves? This could be more the case for natural heritage, where a superfluous (or incorrectly assigned) interpretation often defaces the aesthetic worth of unspoiled natural values (Xu, Cui, Ballantyne and Packer, 2013), while Hall and Piggin (2003) similarly identify these problems in both natural and cultural UNESCO heritage sites. Is it possible that the Land of Hayracks could be dealing with pre-interpretation, as described by Bramwell and Lane (2011)? At this point, it would be eminently sensible to appeal to the museum for further research and analysis to be conducted, along with a comparison of the interpretation of heritage in all the experiential areas. There should be an emphasis on the aesthetic dimension, since without such analysis, it is impossible to provide an answer to this sensitive topic. It is for precisely this reason that such further studies are required as part of the regular monitoring of the museum. In the potential absence of any planned development, these would be able to provide the regular updates required on the current situation.

Reflections

1   Cultural heritage interpretation is an educational activity that has an important role for the tourists to understand the local history and culture and is often considered as the hallmark of creating a positive and knowledgeable impression of a visited destination.
2   Pine and Gilmore propose that the current search for the added value in economy is shifting towards the so-called "experience economy" whereby the guests are more and more willing to pay for the overall experience and included memories, and not only services, or tangible products.
3   The experience economy model proposes that in order for an experience to be satisfying, it needs to find a balance between the four "E's of experiences": education, aesthetics, entertainment and escape.
4   The case study Land of Hayracks shows that is it not easy to find a balance between all four dimensions of experience design and that the product would benefit from paying more attention to the experience of the interpretation.

Questions

1   What role does heritage interpretation play in local destination management?
2   Can we really talk about the experience economy replacing the service economy? Can you think of any of examples of experience economy business models in your destination?

3   What are the four dimensions of experience design within the "4Es" model of experiences? Do you agree that for a quality experience all four should be included?
4   What could be the critiques of the "4Es" model of experiences?

Further reading

Davis, P. (2011). *Ecomuseums: A sense of place*. London: A&C Black.
Hodges, Sue. (2006). *Hands-on history: The essential guide to researching, recording and creating historical products*. South Melbourne, Vic: Sue Hodges Productions.
Pine, B. J., & Gilmore, J. H. (1999). *The experience economy: Work is theatre & every business a stage*. Brighton: Harvard Business Press.
Tilden, F. (1977). *Interpreting our heritage*. Chapel Hill: University of North Carolina Press.
Tilmans, K., van Vree, F., & Winter, J. M. (Eds.). (2010). *Performing the past: memory, history, and identity in modern Europe*. Amsterdam: Amsterdam University Press.

References

Bramwell, B., & Lane, B. (2011). Interpretation and sustainable tourism: The potential and pitfalls. *Revista Interamericana de Ambiente y Turismo-RIAT*, 1(1), 20–27.
Bryman, A. (1999). The Disneyization of society. *The Sociological Review*, 47(1), 25–47.
Campelo, A., Aitken, R., Thyne, M., & Gnoth, J. (2014). Sense of place: The importance for destination branding. *Journal of Travel Research*, 53(2), 154–166.
Davis, P. (2011). *Ecomuseums: A sense of place*. London: A&C Black.
Fort Nisqually Living History Museum. (2010). *Business plan*. Tacoma: Metro parks Tacoma.
Fort St. James National Historic Site of Canada. (2013). *Management plan*. Gatineau: Parks Canada.
Gabova, M. (2016). *Managing the customer satisfaction of tourists in an experience economy*. (Master's Thesis). Finland: University of Oulu.
Graham, B., & Howard, P. (2008). Heritage and identity. *The Ashgate research companion to heritage and identity*, 1–15.
Hall, C. M., & Piggin, R. (2003). World Heritage sites: Managing the brand. In A. Leask, B. Garrod, & A. Fyall (Eds.), *Managing Visitor Attractions: New Directions*, 203–219. Amsterdam: Elsevier.
Ham, S. H., & Weiler, B. (2002). Interpretation as the centerpiece of sustainable wildlife tourism. In R. Harris, P. Williams, & T. Griffin (Eds.), *Sustainable Tourism*, 35–44. Oxford: Butterworth-Heinemann.
Herbert, D. T., Prentice, R. C., & Thomas, C. J. (1989). *Heritage sites: Strategies for marketing and development*. Aldershot: Avebury.
Jacobs, M. H., & Harms, M. (2014). Influence of interpretation on conservation intentions of whale tourists. *Tourism Management*, 42, 123–131.
Kotler, P. (2004). A three-part plan for upgrading your marketing department for new challenges. *Strategy & Leadership*, 32(5), 4–9.
Land of Hayracks. (2019). Available at: www.dezelakozolcev.si/en/museum-of-hayracks/, 29 March 2019.
Macleod, D. V. (2004). *Tourism, globalisation, and cultural change: An island community perspective* (Vol. 2). Bristol: Channel View Publications.
Mehmetoglu, M., & Engen, M. (2011). Pine and Gilmore's concept of experience economy and its dimensions: An empirical examination in tourism. *Journal of Quality Assurance in Hospitality & Tourism*, 12(4), 237–255.
Mohamed, M. N. E. Z. H., Noor, S. M., & Mohamed, R. (2014). Creating mindful tourists at heritage sites through tour guide's interpretation: A case of Georgetown World Heritage sites. *GSTF Journal on Media & Communications (JMC)*, 1(2).

Moscardo, G. (2003). Interpretation and sustainable tourism: Functions, examples and principles. *Journal of Tourism Studies*, 14(1), 112–123.

Moscardo, G. (Ed.). (2008). *Building community capacity for tourism development*. Wallingford: CABI.

Moscardo, G., Woods, B., & Saltzer, R. (2004). *The role of interpretation in wildlife tourism*. Altona: Common Ground Publishing.

Oh, H., Fiore, A. M., & Jeoung, M. (2007). Measuring experience economy concepts: Tourism applications. *Journal of Travel Research*, 46(2), 119–132.

Patapsco Heritage Greenway. (2015). *Patapsco Heritage Area Management Plan*. Patapsco, MD: Salient Group.

Pine, B. J., & Gilmore, J. H. (1998). Welcome to the experience economy. *Harvard Business Review, 76*, 97–105.

Pine, B. J., & Gilmore, J. H. (1999). *The experience economy: Work is theatre & every business a stage*. Brighton: Harvard Business Press.

Quadri-Felitti, D., & Fiore, A. M. (2012). Experience economy constructs as a framework for understanding wine tourism. *Journal of Vacation Marketing, 18*(1), 3–15.

Reisinger, Y., & Dimanche, F. (2010). *International tourism*. Abingdon: Routledge.

Richards, G. (1996). *Cultural tourism in Europe*. Wallingford: CABI.

Schumacher Farm Park. (2005). *Master plan report*. Waunakee: Dane Country Parks Department.

Sidali, K. L., Kastenholz, E., & Bianchi, R. (2015). Food tourism, niche markets and products in rural tourism: Combining the intimacy model and the experience economy as a rural development strategy. *Journal of Sustainable Tourism, 23*(8–9), 1179–1197.

Slovenia's Development Strategy. (2005). Ljubljana: Urad Republike Slovenije za makroekonomske analize in razvoj.

Slovenia's Development Strategy 2030. (2017). Ljubljana: Služba Vlade Republike Slovenije za razvoj in evropsko kohezijsko politiko.

Song, H. J., Lee, C. K., Park, J. A., Hwang, Y. H., & Reisinger, Y. (2015). The influence of tourist experience on perceived value and satisfaction with temple stays: The experience economy theory. *Journal of Travel & Tourism Marketing, 32*(4), 401–415.

Tilden, F. (1977). *Interpreting our heritage*. Chapel Hill: University of North Carolina Press.

Tilmans, K., van Vree, F., & Winter, J. M. (Eds.). (2010). *Performing the past: Memory, history, and identity in modern Europe*. Amsterdam: Amsterdam University Press.

Turnšek, B. (2019). *Izkustvena ekonomija na primeru dediščinskega turističnega produkta Dežela kozolcev na Dolenjskem: magistrsko delo*. Brežice: Faculty of Tourism, University of Maribor.

Walsh, J. A., Jamrozy, U., & Burr, S. W. (2001). Sense of place as a component of sustainable tourism marketing. In S.F. McCool & R. N. Moisey (Eds.) *Tourism, recreation and sustainability*, 195–216. Wallingford: CABI Publishing.

Wang, N. (1999). Rethinking authenticity in tourism experience. *Annals of tourism research, 26*(2), 349–370.

Williams, P., & Soutar, G. N. (2009). Value, satisfaction and behavioral intentions in an adventure tourism context. *Annals of Tourism Research, 36*(3), 413–438.

Xu, H., Cui, Q., Ballantyne, R., & Packer, J. (2013). Effective environmental interpretation at Chinese natural attractions: The need for an aesthetic approach. *Journal of Sustainable Tourism, 21*(1), 117–133.

Zeithaml, V. A. (1988). Consumer perceptions of price, quality, and value: A means-end model and synthesis of evidence. *The Journal of Marketing, 52*, 2–22.

Part B

Environmental and Social aspects of ethical sustainable development

19 Climate change, tourism and rural sustainability in the Margaret River wine region of W Australia[1]

Roy Jones, Gary Burke and Laura Stocker

Summary

The Margaret River region is within a biodiversity 'hot spot' and is an agricultural region famous for its premium wine production and wine, gastronomic and ecotourism. These activities are vulnerable to climate change, especially to reductions in rainfall and runoff. The region has experienced demographic growth as the wine and tourism industries have expanded, and as an educated and affluent population of retirees, second home owners, 'electronic cottagers' and alternative life-stylers has moved into the area. Two projects, a local study as part of a national evaluation of the adaptation of tourist areas to climate change and a more focused identification of vulnerable locations and activities were supported by local government, business and community organisations and several adaptive strategies were identified. The success of these projects can in part be attributed to the relatively high levels of both education and environmental awareness possessed by the local population as a matter of happenstance. Nevertheless, the original contention of this chapter is that these initiatives also allow communities like Margaret River to take on the role of front-runners, providing demonstrations and learning opportunities on how to manage the transition to sustainability and guidance on how such methods might be adapted in other tourism areas facing the challenges of climate change.

Introduction

Since World War Two, the Margaret River region, in the far South West of Western Australia, has experienced rapid demographic and economic growth. It is an amenity rich area (Argent et al., 2014) with a Mediterranean climate, scenic coastline, rolling topography, large limestone cave systems and impressive and unique forest flora and fauna. Furthermore, it is within three hours driving time of Perth, Western Australia's state capital, a growing city with a population of over 2 million (Western Australian Planning Commission, 2018). The region can be said to have passed through all the stages the tourism area life cycle (Butler, 1980, 2006) from its discovery by 'pioneer' groups of tourists in the early and mid-20th century to its current status as an internationally renowned wine, surfing and ecotourism destination.

However, in common with many rural regions of Australia with a high degree of dependence on tourism, the prospect of climate change presents a significant threat to Margaret River's environmental and economic, and therefore its social, sustainability (Turton et al., 2009). In this chapter, we will, firstly, provide some historical and geographical information on the Margaret River region, where an early 20th century agricultural initiative failed but, in doing so, provided some of the bases for the region's subsequent tourism and more general success (Jones et al., 2015). We then summarise the recent and prospective changes in Margaret River's climate, and especially its rainfall regimes, which threaten the sustainability of the local tourism industry and thereby of the local community more broadly. This will be followed by a consideration of two local community consultation exercises which demonstrated a high degree of community confidence in the ability of the region to adapt to the climatic challenges and resulted in a series of constructive initiatives to sustain the local environment and economy. In conclusion, we contend that Margaret River's ability to adapt to climate change is, at least in part, related to its success in attracting an educated, environmentally aware and relatively well-off population in recent decades. In view of this, we suggest that Margaret River may have the potential to become an exemplar to and offer guidance for other rural regions facing sustainability challenges as a result of climate change.

Economic and tourism development in Margaret River

Aboriginal populations have lived in Margaret River region for around 50 millennia (Turney et al., 2001) and the Devil's Lair limestone cave is a nationally and internationally significant archaeological site which has yielded some to the earliest examples of the production of symbolic objects (jewellery) by humans anywhere in the world (Bednarik, 1997). Nevertheless, European attempts to settle and develop the area met with little initial success (Sanders, 2006). Although a few farms were established in the early 19th century, most early development centred on the extractive and hardly sustainable timber industry.

In the early 20th century, however, the British government sought to alleviate a major unemployment problem following World War One by encouraging emigration and pioneer settlement (Considine, 1980). At the same time, the Western Australian government was encouraging agricultural development to diversify the economy at the end of the state's gold rush. The two governments entered into an agreement, the Group Settlement Scheme (Gabbedy, 1988), to finance the passages of British migrants and to provide them with advice and initial assistance to clear the forest and develop dairy and fruit farms in the South West of the state. In the 1920s, 6,000 British settlers moved into the South West with the largest concentration being settled in the Margaret River region. The scheme was spectacularly unsuccessful. The soils were often poorly drained, the forest was difficult to clear, the migrants were unfamiliar with both farming and the local environment and the advice and support offered to them were inadequate. The blocks allocated to the settlers were hardly large enough to provide a family with an adequate living and the fall in agricultural prices during the 1930s Depression was often the final straw. Brunger and Selwood (1997) found that almost half of the settlers abandoned their blocks within five years and, after 25 years, only 12% of the original owners remained on their properties. While this initiative was clearly unsustainable, it did leave behind a patchwork of relatively small, and often only partially cleared, rural blocks of land, and a skeletal set of tracks linking them to small local service centres. At the same time, the first beginnings of a tourist industry could be discerned. Early in the 20th century, a hotel was constructed between a popular beach and the first of the limestone caverns to be opened up to the public. By 1930s this had become a popular honeymoon destination.

After the Second World War, several of the abandoned farm blocks were reallocated to returned Australian soldiers who were more familiar with the local environment and who benefitted from the rising commodity prices of the post war boom. The exceptional surfing potential of the area was also discovered by newly affluent and mobile members of the postwar 'youth culture' (McDonald-Lee, 2016). Initially, these young people would simply drive from Perth and camp on the beaches or sleep in their cars and vans. In the 1960s and 1970s, however, both surfers and members of the countercultural (hippy) movement sought more permanent places to live in pleasant rural surroundings near the surf beaches. The run-down and often abandoned Group Settlement properties were cheap to purchase and attracted not only surfers but also those who wished to develop more self-sufficient life-styles including growing organic produce and producing arts and craft items.

Simultaneously, agricultural research was being conducted on the soils of the limestone ridge extending north and south of the Margaret River town site (Gladstones, 1965). This area was found to share soil and climate characteristics with the Bordeaux region and to have the potential for the production of high-quality wines. Western Australia experienced a mining boom, and therefore a period of prosperity, in the 1960s and many Perth professionals invested in the development of vineyards and wineries in Margaret River, again often buying up former Group Settlement blocks for this purpose. The first vines were planted locally in 1967. Four decades later about 140 wineries were producing 20% of Australia's premium wine from around 5,500 hectares of vines.

Following on from these developments, Margaret River has developed a broad-based tourism industry focusing on wine, gastronomy and a wide range of coastal, forest and subterranean environmental attractions. The town of Margaret River now has a population approaching 5,000 and is the centre of a Shire containing ca. 15,000 people. This has prompted a considerable expansion in the town's commercial and community services, and the shire has therefore also become an attractive destination for both retirees seeking a sea or tree change (Burnley and Murphy, 2004) and 'electronic cottagers' (Gold, 1991) who can carry out their businesses remotely while residing in a pleasant rural environment (Curry et al., 2001).

The threat of climate change

Margaret River's success story of the previous half century is largely the result of its environmental assets. Its economy is therefore highly vulnerable to any adverse impacts on these assets that might result from climatic shifts. These shifts are currently occurring and are predicted to intensify. Hennessey et al. (2008), a study commissioned by the Sustainable Tourism Cooperative Research Centre from Australia's Commonwealth Science and Industrial Research Organisation, provides a comprehensive account of the anticipated climatic change impacts as follows. Compared to the 1970–2000 mean, a 1.4 degree centigrade increase in temperature is predicted by 2050 if a high carbon emissions scenario remains in place. Changes in rainfall are more significant. Between the mid-1970s and 2008, an 11% decrease in rainfall has taken place. Most of this decrease has been occurred in the winter peak rainfall period, and this has produced a 50% decrease in runoff. By 2050 a further

20% decrease in rainfall is predicted with a larger drop off in runoff and a significant reduction in groundwater levels. A slight increase in extreme weather events (e.g. an increase of one in the number of days over 35 degrees centigrade per year and of ca. 2% in heavy rainfall intensity) by 2050 and a rise in sea level of 1.1 metres by 2100 are also predicted.

The potential impact of these changes on the Margaret River tourism industry and its economy more widely varies. Premium wine grapes are highly sensitive to temperature change and even a small shift may have a disproportional impact on the reputation and profits of local brands. Furthermore, to ensure the maintenance of a premium product, the viticulture industry requires specific levels of natural rainfall. While these can be, in part, substituted by irrigation, this will draw on already decreasing supplies of groundwater and there is likely to be increased competition for groundwater between viticulturalists and (often organic) horticulturalists. Furthermore, water levels have recently been falling in the underground limestone caverns reducing the visual impact of the reflections of the stalagmites and stalactites in the underground pools.

The giant eucalypt (karri) forest ecosystem is also vulnerable. An increase in temperatures, combined with a decrease in rainfall and ongoing population growth, significantly increases the risk of bushfires in an already fire-prone area. More seriously, this unique ecosystem only exists in a strip, a few tens of kilometres wide adjacent to Australia's south westernmost coast. If significant climatic shifts occur, this forest system has limited potential to shift polewards in response to increasing temperatures or westwards in response to decreasing rainfall. It could therefore become even smaller or even disappear. Since the geomorphological nature of the coastal zone is the most important contributor to the quality of the wave breaks, surfing would seem to be the form of tourism least likely to be adversely affected by climate change. But the prospect of sea level rise and increased frequency of extreme weather events have the potential to disrupt this industry also.

Nevertheless, there is a counterargument to these concerns. Margaret River will remain as one of the cooler and wetter parts of Western Australia. It is already an attractive destination for residents and tourists seeking to avoid the summer heat in the inland and northern parts of the state. This comparative advantage may remain or even increase under the prospective impacts of climate change.

Community consultation and adaptation strategies

As a follow-up to a national investigation of the impact of climate change on tourism regions (Turton et al., 2009), Australia's Cooperative Research Centre for Sustainable Tourism commissioned a further case study of the Margaret River wine region (Jones et al., 2010). In addition to literature and archival sources, this study reported on the findings of 377 questionnaires, 12 in-depth interviews and a 1 day workshop with stakeholders. Jones et al. 2010 (Chapters 5–7) provides detailed information on the methodologies used. The questionnaires were administered to visitors at (local government operated) tourist information centres across the region. The interviews were conducted with three government, three tourist industry, three environmentalist and three community representatives. Ca. 50 local, regional and state community and government stakeholders attended the workshops. Interview schedules and further information is contained in Jones et al. (2010). While many respondents expressed some concern over the potentially adverse effects of climate change on their community, a more notable and general finding was that the vast majority felt that these challenges could be overcome. They acknowledged that higher levels of government (state, national and international) would need to regulate in order to slow the increase in the rate of production of greenhouse gases, to raise popular awareness of the problem and to inform and facilitate local response efforts. But they were generally confident that the local community had the skills and resources to steer the tourism industry and the region more generally through the likely climatic challenges ahead.

There was a consensus that the region's 'premium' reputation in viticultural terms could be built on and adopted more widely. The rapid success achieved by the area's current wines such as cabernet sauvignon could be built on through ongoing research into grape types suited to slightly warmer temperatures, such as Tempranillo, which could replace the currently favoured Cabernet Sauvignon. Many of these modern vineyards were already using best practice forms of water conservation. This information could be shared among all the area's viticulturalists and agriculturalists, and similar high standards could also be adopted and even mandated for building design and other local forms of water use. Such initiatives would be likely to gain the support of the progressive local council and could be showcased to tourists in their holiday accommodation and vineyard visits.

Furthermore, and again with the support of the sympathetic council, the area's environmental and planning controls needed to be at least maintained and, in some areas, increased. Suggested measures included larger coastal development setbacks, greater watercourse, wetland and bushland protection and restrictions on pesticide use. If was felt that the adoption of these initiatives would enable Margaret River to apply for and attain prestigious national and international environmental awards. Most of the stakeholder interviewees also felt that the successful pursuit of these initiatives would enable the area to market itself as a 'green', and therefore a premium, tourism and residential destination. Even if some adverse effects of climate change eventuated, the diverse nature of the area's attractions and the adaptable nature of the area's population would enable shifts in tourism emphasis, for example to 'more beach and less bush', to be made with no more difficulty than a gradual change from one grape type to another.

These positive sentiments would appear to have been borne out by subsequent developments. In 2012, a local community organisation Sustain Margaret River affiliated with the global Transition Network to become Transition Margaret River and the first Transition Town in Australia. The first Transition Town group was established in Totnes, Devon by Rob Hopkins in 2006, and this has become the basis for a global network (Hopkins, 2008). Transition Margaret River's facebook page (https://www.facebook.com/TransitionMargaret River/ accessed 17/8/17) defines 'Transition' as "a community-led local approach to creating a more resilient society in the face of challenges we face in today's world, especially climate change and economic uncertainty".

Since its establishment, Transition Margaret River has collaborated with academic and state and local governments to identify strategies related to this aim. In 2016, it participated in a workshop co-sponsored by the Shire of Augusta Margaret River, the Curtin University Sustainability Policy Institute and the Cape to Cape Catchment Group (a locally based state government environmental and land use management instrumentality). The workshop used participatory mapping techniques to identify specific social, cultural, environmental and economic sustainability hotspots and, from these, to devise adaptation pathways. These entailed the further identification of responsible stakeholders, objectives, actions and trials and evaluation processes of any initiatives to be undertaken.

One example of this process relates to the goal of effectively managing overall water supply, which is linked to two Sustainable Development Goals, namely, 13 Climate Action and 6 Water. Relevant Stakeholders were identified as the Augusta Margaret River Shire, local wineries, the Wadandi (the local Aboriginal population), the Water Corporation, Forest Products (the local timber industry body) and the state's Department of Fire and Emergency Services. Suggested actions included:

> holistically review water cycle for Shire to understand use and recharge; pursue partnerships, e.g., with viticulture; investigate reinjection of aquifers; investigate desalination using renewable energy; understand Indigenous and biodiversity values around key water assets; manage and monitor 10 Mile Brook Dam for multiple use; (encourage) citizen science at Ellensbrook (a creekside historic homestead, now publicly managed as a heritage tourist site) to evaluate changes to waterways and dams; develop Shire Water Management plan against multiple criteria including for emergency needs.

While this is an aspirational goal at present, it is an interesting reflection of the level of environmental and political awareness and, potentially therefore, of the level of resilience of the local community, its organisations and its council. As with the other initiatives cited in this section, we present this information in order to offer examples of appropriate community consultation, strategisation and implementation techniques, rather than as potentially transferable examples of environmental remediation techniques, since these will invariably require adaptation to local circumstances.

Conclusion: demography, sustainability and the wider applicability of the Margaret River experience

The unsustainability of the Group Settlement Scheme between the Wars stands in stark contrast to the successful development of a diverse and prosperous community in Margaret River over the postwar period. While both the Group Settlers and the postwar immigrants to the region arrived with high hopes and a determination to meet the challenges that faced them, it is the contrasts between the two populations that are perhaps the most notable and the most relevant. The Group Settlers came from the other side of the planet. They were poor, largely urban and generally possessed low levels of education. They therefore lacked sufficient understanding of both the environment and the industry in which they wished to operate. Given the limited support provided to them, it was unsurprising that they were able to achieve sustainable livelihoods, especially when they were soon faced with adverse economic changes far beyond their control.

It seems likely that the current population of Margaret River will face adverse climatic changes that are also beyond their control. However, this population has a very different composition. Although it is diverse, containing as it does vignerons, retirees, alternative life-stylers and electronic cottagers, many, if not most, of them were familiar with the region before they settled there. The vignerons in particular had the benefit of accurate and scientific knowledge of the potential of the properties that they obtained and, in most cases, possessed the financial capital to withstand the delay between land purchase and the sale of their finished products. Many of the surfies and alternative life-stylers had a strong awareness of and commitment to environmental values. They were therefore able to see the potential of a range of 'green' business initiatives both in and beyond (eco)tourism.

Once this scenic area began to be populated by such people, this selective demographic process has become self-perpetuating in Margaret River and elsewhere. As Argent et al. (2013, 97) argue:

> Our analysis of the ecumene of southern Australia shows that creative workers are more likely than the general population to be attracted to rural areas offering diverse physical landscapes and gentrified socio-economic and cultural settings. Moreover, our analysis indicates that population density is also important, suggestive of the need for a particular 'critical mass' of economic and socio-cultural activity to attract this type of worker.

In these circumstances, the confidence of the subjects of our investigations in both their and their community's ability to surmount the challenges of climate change is less surprising. The population of Margaret River is both well placed and well suited to draw on the best evidence that is available to it; to utilise the networks its members possess with industry, government and academia; to engage and partner widely; to identify and work with other frontrunners and early adopters; and, more generally, to accept that continual adaptation to change is the only path to sustainability.

Certainly, there are examples of other rural communities in Australia (e.g. Armidale, New South Wales (Sorensen, 2016)) and elsewhere (e.g. Totnes, the first Transition Town) that are engaging with climatic and economic change in this way. But "Australian rural communities typically have little accumulated knowledge of how to accomplish psychological re-orientation effectively" (Sorensen, 2016). The wider challenge is therefore how to use the lessons from the successful initiatives in places like Margaret River and Armidale to assist other rural communities, and particularly those in less environmentally, economically and/or demographically favoured circumstances. A major purpose of this chapter has therefore been to highlight the methods and techniques used by a small and remote rural and tourism community that is, in general terms, well-educated and environmentally aware, to combat some of the challenges presented to it by climate change. In doing so, we have sought to identify some of the ways in which rural and tourism-dependent communities can utilise both their own resources and the support available to them from 'outside' government, industry and academic sources to raise awareness, coordinate local support and devise strategies to combat sustainability challenges such as climate change.

Reflections

1   Successful local tourism industries can build upon the failure of previous economic initiatives – such as the interwar Group Settlement Scheme in Margaret River's case.
2   Tourism industries frequently develop in parallel with other local activities. In this case, these include viticulture, organic agriculture and environmental protection.

3   All industries have to adapt to ongoing social, economic and technological change. Coastal, gastro- and eco-tourism activities can also be severely impacted by climate change. Margaret River is particularly vulnerable in this regard.
4   Local tourism communities that possess populations with high educational and environmental awareness levels are more likely to possess the skills, networks and attitudes required to remain resilient and sustainable in the face of severe and ongoing climate change.

Questions

1   How might former local economic failures contribute to the subsequent development of successful tourism initiatives?
2   How might tourism enterprises work with other components of their local economy to obtain mutual benefits?
3   Why are certain components of the tourism industry more vulnerable than others to the threat of climate change?
4   What demographic characteristics do communities require for the maintenance of resilient and sustainable local tourism activities?

Note

1   Article previously published in Roy Jones. (2018). Rural sustainability in the face of climate change; consultation in Australia's south west corner, *Science & Technology Development Journal*, 2(2), 50–56.

Further reading

Harvey, D.C. and Perry, J. (eds.) *The future of heritage as climates change: loss, adaptation and creativity.* Routledge, New York (2015).

Jones, R., Wardell-Johnson, A., Gibberd, M., Pilgrim, A., Wardell-Johnson, G., Bizjak, S., Ward, D., Benjamin, K., and Carlsen, J. *The impact of climate change on the Margaret River wine region; developing adaptation and response strategies for the tourism industry.* Cooperative Research Centre for Sustainable Tourism, Gold Coast (2010).

Jopp, R., DeLacy, T. and Mair, J. Developing a framework for regional destination adaptation to climate change. *Current Issues in Tourism* 13, 591–505 (2010).

Kajan, E. and Saarinen, J. Tourism, climate change and adaptation: a review. *Current Issues in Tourism* 16, 167–195 (2013).

McDonald-Lee, T. Three generations of surfing nomads. *Your RAC Magazine*, June/July, 28–32 (2016).

Scott, T., Hall, C. M. and Gossling, S. *Tourism and climate change: impacts, adaptation and mitigation.* Routledge, London and New York (2012).

References

Argent, N., Tonts, M., Jones, R. and Holmes, J. *A Creativity–led Rural Renaissance? Amenity-led Migration, the Creative Turn and the Uneven Development of Rural Australia.* Applied Geography 44, 88–98 (2013).

Argent, N., Tonts, M., Jones, R. and Holmes, J. *The amenity principle, internal migration and rural development in Australia Annals of the Association of American Geographers* 104, 305–318 (2014).

Bednarik, R. *Pleistocene stone pendant from Western Australia. Australian Archaeology* 45, 32–34 (1997).

Brunger, A. and Selwood, H. J. *Settlement and land alienation in Western Australia: the Shire of Denmark. Journal of Historical Geography* 23, 478–495 (1997).

Burnley, I. and Murphy, P. *Sea change: movement from metropolitan to Arcadian Australia.* University of New South Wales Press, Sydney (2004).

Butler, R. W. *The concept of a tourist area cycle of evolution: implications for management. Canadian Geographer* 24, 5–12 (1980).

Butler, R. W. (ed.) *The tourism area life cycle. Vols. 1 and 2.* Channel View, Clevedon (2006).

Considine, S. *Unemployment in Britain between the wars.* Longman, Harlow (1980).

Curry, G. N., Koczberski, G. and Selwood, J. *Cashing out, cashing in: rural change on the south coast of Western Australia. Australian Geographer* 32, 109–124 (2001).

Gabbedy, J. P. *Group settlement. Part 1: Its origins, politics and administration.* University of Western Australia Press, Nedlands (1988).

Gladstones, J. S. The climate and soils of Western Australia in relation to vine growing. *Journal of the Australian Institute of Agricultural Science* 31, 275–288 (1965).

Gold, J. R. *Fishing in muddy waters: communication media and the myth of the electronic cottage.* pp. 327–341, in Brunn, S. D. and Leinbach, T. A. (eds.) *Collapsing space and time: geographic aspects of communication and information.* Harper Collins, London (1991).

Hennessey, K., Webb, L. Korono, D. and Ricketts, J. *Climate change scenarios for tourism sites: supplement for Cape Leeuwin.* CSIRO, Canberra (2008).

Hopkins, R. *The transition handbook: from oil dependence to local resilience.* UIT Cambridge Ltd., Cambridge (2008).

Jones, R., Diniz, A., Selwood, H. J., Brayshay, M. and Lacerda, E. Rural settlement schemes in the South West of Western Australia and Roraima State, Brazil: unsustainable rural systems? *Carpathian Journal of Earth and Environmental Science* 10, 125–132 (2015).

Jones, R., Wardell-Johnson, A., Gibberd, M., Pilgrim, A., Wardell-Johnson, G., Bizjak, S., Ward, D., Benjamin, K. and Carlsen, J. *The impact of climate change on the Margaret River wine region; developing adaptation and response strategies for the tourism industry.* Cooperative Research Centre for Sustainable Tourism, Gold Coast (2010).

McDonald-Lee, T. Three generations of surfing nomads. *Your RAC Magazine*, June/July, 28–32 (2016).

Sanders, D. *From colonial outpost to popular tourism destination: an historical geography of the Leeuwin-Naturaliste region 1829–2005.* PhD thesis, Murdoch University (2006).

Sorensen, A. Community development in an age of mounting uncertainty: Armidale, Australia. pp. 249–267, in Halseth, G. (ed.) *Transformation of resource towns and peripheries: political economy perspectives.* Routledge, London (2016).

Turney, C. S. M., Bird, M. I., Fifield, L. K., Roberts, R. G., Smith, M., Dortch, C. E., Grun, R., Lawson, E., Ayliffe L. K., Miller, G. H., Dortch, J. and Cresswell, R. G. Early human occupation at Devils Lair Western Australia 50,000 years ago. *Quaternary Research* 55, 3–13 (2001).

Turton, S., Hadwen, W. and Wilson, R. (eds.) *The impacts of climate change on Australian tourism destinations – a scoping study.* Cooperative Research Centre for Sustainable Tourism, Gold Coast (2009).

Western Australian Planning Commission. *Perth and peel @ 3.5 million.* Western Australian Planning Commission, Perth (2018).

20 The Sustainable Garden of Pirámides de Güímar

A living exhibition blending tourism and sustainability

David Valcárcel Ortiz

Summary

This chapter analyses the Sustainable Garden of Pirámides de Güímar, an innovative experiment conducted in the Canary Island of Tenerife. Pirámides de Güímar is an outdoor museum and botanical garden. Among its various specialised gardens we find the Sustainable Garden, a recreation of a typical Canarian ravine, including the representative flora and fauna associated with such environments. The garden, developed in collaboration with the Botany Department of the University of La Laguna (Tenerife), is separated into a dry area and a watercourse that includes specimens of the critically endangered European eel and many endemic aquatic plants. The watercourse also allows us to stress the importance of water as a vital and scarce resource. The garden was developed following the main environmental, economic and social principles of sustainability, its purpose being to become a model of how to develop gardens in the Canary Islands in a sustainable manner.

Precedents – an introduction

A brief explanation of what Pirámides de Güímar is and how it came to be can help us understand the purpose and value of the Sustainable Garden. The Ethnographic Park Pirámides de Güímar was founded in 1998 with the aim of conserving and studying six step pyramids located within the 67,000 m^2 of park premises. For the first decade of its existence, the exhibitions and collections of the museum revolved around the pyramid site itself, the scientific studies conducted in situ and the theories concerning the age, origin and purpose of the stone pyramidal structures. However, it is within the natural life cycle of a museum to evolve over time, to encompass new fields of study and to create new exhibitions; more so, when the majority of the museum's visitors are tourists, with only a small proportion (between 5% and 10% of our total number of visitors) consisting of local residents and school visits.

Despite Tenerife being a very touristic island, it mostly attracts visitors who are searching for sun, sandy beaches and sea resorts, with only 2.7% of visitors to the island considering cultural tourism as their main interest (ISTAC, 2017). This makes renewing and reinventing oneself all the more important, if one is to gain and maintain the interest of the visitors. The recession of 2008 made the transformation ever more urgent, since tourist visitor numbers arriving at the island subsequently descended, as did the purchasing power of those who did continue to travel abroad, i.e. to the Canary Islands. At Pirámides de Güímar we therefore had to invent something new, develop a new strategy or exhibition or change our praxis or our focus; we were not sure what, but we had to adapt to hard times and something had to evolve.

It was around this time when we discovered the solution standing directly in front of us. Apart from the pyramids themselves, an auditorium and a small ethnographic museum, Pirámides de Güímar, did not count with any proper collections that could be exhibited. Only it did. During the creation of the Ethnographic Park, vast accessible garden areas were planted alongside a pathway that surrounds the main pyramid complex. A large proportion of the flora planted was native vegetation, mostly endemic to Tenerife or the Canary Islands. Until then, the flora had played a mere ornamental role. It certainly made the visit to the site more pleasant, but it provided little else. Then we realised that this extraordinary botanical collection was a real, valuable and scientifically and culturally valid collection. The plants would step up into the limelight and become the protagonists of our new exhibition; they were to become the motor of many new projects and transform and expand Pirámides de Güímar.

It is surprising the amount of information that plants can provide about the nature, culture and history of a place: of the folklore, mysticism, customs and academic and social interests of a population. So that is precisely what we did. We created two outdoor, self-guided routes that accompanied the visitor to discover specimens of various interesting and important plant species. One route, the Canarian Botanical Route, presented some of the most emblematic and unique plant species native to the archipelago. The Export Products Route introduced those plants and elements that have represented the sustenance of the Canarian people over the centuries since the conquest by the Spaniards, such as sugar cane, wine or cochineal-bearing cacti. The routes allowed the plants themselves to tell their story, via information panels, period photographs, QR code access to videos, audioguide scripts and other museological tools; they allowed the visitors to wander at their leisure and discover interesting anecdotes in a pleasant setting.

These two routes earned Pirámides de Güímar a nomination to the European Museum of the Year Award in 2011. This award, created under the auspices of the Council of Europe, is the most prestigious and longest lasting award of the continent, as it promotes the enhancement of quality in museums. The great acceptance by our visitors of these new exhibitions, coupled with the recognition from the museum sector via the nomination, was a sign that we were going in the right direction. The expansion of the museum into the outdoors, thereby not restraining our exhibits to the small museum building, gave us the opportunity to exploit the tens of thousands of square metres of accessible garden spaces. Two other outdoor routes (called the Cultural Route and the Volcanic Route) and the specialised 'Poison Garden' (consisting of over 70 species of poisonous and even lethal plants) are shortly followed.

In the pursuit of scientific rigour in all our exhibitions, we started developing a relationship with professors of the Botany Department (Departamento de Botánica, Ecología y Fisiología Vegetal) of the local University of La Laguna. This relationship became official when we signed an agreement with the University to develop projects of 'Environmental Education for Sustainability'. This agreement resulted in the development of a multitude of actions and activities. Our role as a museum meant that we were eager to participate in the creation of environmentally friendly actions and in the dissemination of the importance of sustainability to as wide an audience as possible. Our varied spectrum of visitors, who come from dozens of different nations and encompass all manner of demographic backgrounds, allowed us to share these projects far and wide. Then we started to get ambitious. We wanted to create something permanent, a new exhibition that embraced the philosophy behind the agreement that we had declared, something that served to promote environmental education and training for sustainability, as well as the conservation and dissemination to the society of our natural and cultural heritage.

The Sustainable Garden – the beginning

The idea of creating a garden was clear enough from the beginning. All previous projects with the University had been botanically related, plus it would represent a permanent display of sustainability, as opposed to the more ephemeral activities we had developed previously. The trick was determining the exact focus we wanted to give to the garden, how to make it environmental, economic and social, how to make it relate to our local natural heritage, and last but certainly not least, how to make it appealing to our visitors. We had determined the location where the garden would be created: an area of approximately 1,000 m^2 just outside our Auditorium, at the beginning of the pathway that tours around the pyramid site. This is a strategically sound position within our grounds, which also complied with the necessary climatic conditions required by the vegetation as regards to exposition to sunlight, wind and so on. We knew this already because we had previously made a small, simple experiment on that terrain. We had marked a rectangular area of about 5 m^2 with small stones. This area was barren and covered simply in soil and volcanic pumice stones, with no vegetation at the time of delimiting it. Then we just let it be for some time. After a few months, fuelled solely by the natural resources available during that time – the little rain there was and the nutrient-rich soils – the marked area was covered in native vegetation. This was nature taking its course. Plants had gradually taken over the terrain and established themselves by their own means.

Then a period of unexpectedly strong storms came. The water poured down relentlessly and roared and gushed down our gardens, leaving large meandering marks along the area reserved for the Sustainable Garden. It reminded the eldest of us of how the Canarian ravines used to sound during the rainy months. They do not have flowing water anymore. Water rarely runs down the ravines nowadays (except on very stormy days), namely due to human intervention resulting in blocked watercourses, or the exhaustion and exploitation of the little water sporadically present in some ravines (Francisco-Ortega et al., 2000). There was something inspiring and even romantic in hearing a sound that is seldom heard in nature in the Canarian archipelago, the sound of a flowing stream of water. The storm passed but the pathway that the water had created, channelling its way down our allotted space, remained. The bottom part of the area quickly germinated and plants sprang everywhere. It then became clear that the garden would be a recreation of a typical Canarian ravine.

Many factors came into place to help us conclude that it would be a ravine. First, the watercourse is a fundamental part of it. Then the vegetation, Canarian ravines usually include three basic plant types associated with those environments (Arco & Rodríguez, 1999). They are *Phoenix canariensis* (Canary palm tree), *Salix canariensis* (Canary willow) and *Tamarix canariensis* (Canary tamarix). What defines them is their proximity to the water, with the Canary palm trees living furthest from it, in the flood areas, the Canary willow growing in close proximity to the watercourse, and the Canary tamarix salt cedars being found at the mouths of the ravines, by the sea, due to their notable tolerance to the high salinity levels characteristic to those areas. The willow and the salt cedars are reasonably easy to cultivate, the latter growing at a considerable rate, but the Canary palm trees are much slower growing. This was another reason why we selected the area we had chosen, because it had hardly any vegetation, with the exception of a number of well grown, over 20-year-old, palm trees. This meant that we already had one of the key species (and the most complicated to obtain) out of the three characteristic species found in ravines. One could argue that their presence helped in the decision of determining that the garden would be a recreation of a ravine. The other two key species were subsequently obtained and planted. The next step was to focus on how to create a garden that complied with and explained the principles of sustainability.

The creation

Water had already created the natural path it follows in the terrain, so the course of the future ravine was easy to define. It was decided that although the project would certainly have a watercourse, it would be located in the bottom half of the garden, rather than all along the terrain. This was for several reasons; on one hand, it would permit us to create an initial dry area with a palm grove. As mentioned previously, Canary palm trees live far from the watercourse, so the initial area would house the type of vegetation found at the same distance from the water as the palm trees. In fact, much of this flora appeared all by itself: the true, native inhabitants of that environment taking over the terrain. On the other hand, it would help us to develop the storyline, by raising awareness of the fact that most ravines nowadays are indeed dry, with the subsequent loss of biodiversity and increase in scarcity of fresh water. Since then, this area has particularly thrived with native species. A path runs along this first half of the garden (the 'dry' area), where information panels and audioguide descriptions introduce the visitor to the habitat they are entering and the characteristics of a typical Canarian ravine. Then the path turns unexpectedly and one crosses between two *Rumex lunaria* (a native flowering plant that grows into bushes) reaching the second half of the garden (the 'wet' area). This area includes the watercourse: a tailor-made water circuit created for the garden (Figure 20.1).

The watercourse was designed with the idea of showing both the flora and the fauna of these ecosystems, so a closed circuit aquaponics system was created. Aquaponics is a food production system that combines cultivating plants in water and raising aquatic animals, in a symbiotic environment (Goddek et al., 2015). In this system, the excretions of the animals are broken down into nitrates and nitrites which are reintroduced into the water circuit and used by the aquatic plants as nutrients. A small shed was created to house the water pumps and some biological filters, placed over a bed of volcanic pumice stones, which would remove the organic residues. These are the only man-made elements created for the Sustainable Garden. The water pumps require a small electrical consumption to recirculate the water, but other than that the system is totally sustainable. There is no residual contamination because the organic matter produced by the animals is broken down and reutilised. The watercourse was designed including a series of descending pools that allows the water to oxygenate itself as it flows downstream, thus achieving a clean and self-sustainable environment,

Figure 20.1 Aerial photo of the Sustainable Gardens.

devoid of an excess of organic matter, and with the only cost of replacing the volume of water lost by evaporation, which is relatively small.

The watercourse itself emanates as a small waterfall at the highest point of the 'wet' area, right after the visitor passes between the *R. lunaria*, and then flows along several pools that meander their way down towards a large pond at the bottom of the garden, surrounded by endemic vegetation. The water is then pumped uphill towards the shed, which is next to the cascade where the water re-enters the circuit (Figure 20.2).

The flora

An important aspect of the garden is the variety of the vegetation, which links with the environmentally friendly approach of the project. The aquatic plants distributed all along and within the watercourse were obtained and planted by our colleagues from the University, as well as a few specimens of other significant flora usually present in Canarian ravines. It was essential to show the three key plant species of the ravines mentioned before, but we also considered it important to show a variety of other

Figure 20.2 The watercourse.

ravine-based vegetation. Thus, a small number of specimens of representative species were planted throughout the garden, but especially along the watercourse area (each species at its required distance from the watercourse), in order to be able to illustrate not only which plants grow in these environments, but also the interactions that take place and the role each one plays. That was it as far as planting went. The rest of the vegetation now present in the Sustainable Garden arrived by itself, grew by itself and survived by itself. Our philosophy was to let nature follow its course. The only direct gardening intervention we undertake is eliminating invasive and exotic plants whenever they arise, but if other endemic vegetation appears, we let it strive. If it survives, it is testimony to the adaptation over time of native species to the particular environmental conditions of our valley.

And so, over time, the Sustainable Garden has become a catalogue of the same vegetation one finds in nature, outside the perimeter of our premises, alongside the ravines of the island. Much of the vegetation is endemic to Tenerife or the Canary Islands. Other plants are native to Macaronesia, perhaps not exclusive to our archipelago, but nonetheless examples of plants that have adapted to our ecosystem without affecting it negatively (Figure 2.3).

Figure 20.3 The Sustainable Gardens of the Pirámides de Güímar.

The fauna

Water attracts life. Several species of native birds and small reptiles, a hoard of insects, including dragonflies, butterflies, bees, wasps, bumblebees and many more, and even frogs have all found their way to the large water pond and the many water pools spread along the water circuit. The real star, however, became the European eel. The European eel (*Anguilla anguilla*) is the only freshwater fish found in the Canaries, although seldom, since its presence has decreased immensely. It is catalogued as 'Critically Endangered' in the Red List of threatened species (Jacoby & Gollock, 2014). Nowadays in the Canaries, they can only be observed in a handful of ravines that have not undergone works in their mouth and that still allow the ascent of fish. Despite their previous historical abundance, the European eel has been disappearing in recent decades due to overfishing, the destruction of suitable habitats and marine pollution.

The eels have a surprising life, since they are fish that live most of their lives in fresh water, yet they reproduce in the sea, following a complex cycle. The adults travel over 4,000 km to the Sargasso Sea (West Atlantic) to reproduce at depths of over 600 m and then die after laying the eggs. Next, the larvae travel to Europe with the aid of the marine currents, reaching the mouth of the continental rivers or the Canarian ravines, after swimming two to three years. They then ascend the water courses till they reach backwaters or lagoons where they will live until they become adults, which can be up to 12 years for males and 20 years for females. Afterwards they will return downstream to the sea and swim all the way back to the Sargasso Sea to reproduce and die.

The specimens of the Sustainable Garden are adults, so they feed on invertebrates and fish. We obtained them with the help of Fundación Neotrópico, the only Species Survival Network member in the Canary Islands. (The Species Survival Network is an international coalition of non-governmental organisations committed to the promotion of the Convention on International Trade in Endangered Species of Wild Fauna and Flora – CITES.) As such, this foundation managed to obtain adult specimens of European eel and monitor their introduction and adaptation to the watercourse we had created for them. The eels adapted well to their new environment and serve as an example of the grave problem of decreasing biodiversity. The remarkable life story of the eels, as well as information about the aquatic vegetation, is also illustrated in information panels and included in the audioguide script.

Sustainability

The visit to the Sustainable Garden, and the script it follows, finishes with reflections about its sustainable value, the importance of water as a vital and scarce resource and the need to use it wisely, as well as the necessity to conserve our natural resources and protect global biodiversity: an important 'take home message' delivered in a pleasant, natural and peaceful environment. It is appropriate to expand upon these reflections about sustainability that we pose to our visitors when they have seen the Sustainable Garden. We try to explain exactly how and why garden is sustainable, and why it could and should be copied as an example of how to create sustainable environments in an archipelago where, due to its touristic importance and volume of yearly visitors, there is a constant creation or restoration of numerous hotel gardens and private, as well as public, garden spaces.

The fact that we allow much of the vegetation of the garden to appear by itself is directly related to the sustainable approach proposed by our project. We wanted the garden to conform to the three pillars of sustainability: it had to be economic, it had to be environmental and it had to be social (Vega et al., 2007). The plants that adorn the ravine are true survivors that exist independent of human action and intervention. They mostly appeared by themselves. This means that we do not add fertilisers to the plants, nor do we water them, thus sparing us an irrigation system. We just let the plants be. This saves costs in fertilisers, water, irrigation materials and maintenance, and thus makes the project economic. After the initial expense of creating the water circuit, the only costs of the garden are those related to the previously mentioned replacement of water lost by evaporation. This makes the garden an inexpensive project and exhibition.

The garden is indeed also an exhibition. It pays tribute to the unique and irreplaceable endemic flora of the archipelago. It represents a catalogue of the native vegetation that covers the ravines of the Canaries, and it introduces us to aquatic vegetation that we no longer see in our weekend excursions to, or incursions into, nature. This represents the environmental pillar of the garden. The information panels and other informative elements convey the knowledge of some of the greatest scientific experts on Canarian geology and biology, while the landscape leads the visitor into a realistic recreation of a Canarian ravine. On a small scale, certainly, but reminiscent of what you would have found decades ago in the Canarian scenery.

The social aspect is met in different ways. The role of the garden as an example of sustainable gardening in the archipelago is discussed, as are the reasons why and how the garden manages to be environmental, economic and social, and ergo sustainable. We have received countless school visits, which are complemented with sustainability-themed workshops created for such visits. The aim of the workshops is to encourage the contact with and respect for nature, to raise the children's awareness of the need to protect and preserve it and to explain what sustainability is. We have also invited and given guided visits to landscape professionals, key representatives of hotels, public garden-planning councils, directors of gardening companies, botanists and anybody else related to the creation of gardens in the Canary Islands, with the intention of presenting an example of how one can create attractive gardens using local vegetation and projected in a sustainable manner. There is no need to plant exotic flora every time a new hotel garden is made, or a new seaside pedestrian path is developed. The Sustainable Garden aims to show that one can create just as enticing environments in a cheaper and more self-sufficient way, with the additional benefit of throwing in a bit of culture and raising awareness of important issues. Furthermore, a number of specialised courses have been organised for the University and for the professional tourist guides association, in order to present the Sustainable Garden to these equally important sectors. Finally, it represents an accessible way for tourists to discover such a symbolic environment of the Canary Islands.

Promotion

The visits offered to the local gardening, botanical and tourism experts from the public and private, as well as the academic and professional sectors, served to inform and interest the local population on the cultural and environmental value of the Sustainable Garden. Its inauguration made the front page of the two main local newspapers and was widely broadcast on regional radio and television. It is important to share the project with the resident population and to make them part of the idea. It is crucial, on the other hand, to introduce it to the largest part of our audience: the tourists.

As we mentioned in the introduction, about nine tenths of the visitors of Pirámides de Güímar are tourists. Our marketing and promotion plan is carefully mapped out on an annual basis. In such a highly touristic destination, with so much to offer, it is imperative to stand out and to ensure the visitor knows who you are, where you are and what you are. Despite the fact that the largest proportion of visitors to the island are not interested in cultural activities, there is a growing interest in the development and consumption of active tourism, trekking and the discovery of our natural heritage (ISTAC, 2017). The Sustainable Garden offered a chance to discover a significant part of this natural heritage, and this made it an appealing novelty to offer to this stimulated, eco-friendly public. Thus, the promotional campaign on the inauguration year of the garden was entirely focussed around this new addition to the park's exhibitions. We likewise aimed to announce it in a more academic sector, with surprising and rewarding results.

Results and concluding remarks

The results have been numerous and beyond our expectations. Visitor numbers clearly increased after the opening of the Sustainable Garden. It also became a feature visit for the schools that have come to the park since its opening. The philosophy and scope of the garden complements the new knowledge, respect for nature and importance of conservation that is being taught at schools. The garden represents the largest and most ambitious project developed so far with the University of La Laguna, within our 'environmental education for sustainability' collaboration agreement; but it is merely another stepping stone towards the dissemination and exposition of this compromise. It has become a great teaching tool to use with the younger generations and a positive 'wakeup call' for the older ones. Moreover, it adds to the other environmental and sustainable projects we had developed in the past, and it inspires the development of future ones.

The Sustainable Garden was nominated to the European Museum of the Year Award in 2017, the second nomination received by Pirámides de Güímar to this prestigious award. This in itself suggests that we are still going in the right direction; quite possibly, and despite it being a garden, the fact that we are a museum, makes the Sustainable Garden an unusual botanical collection. This is because, as a museum, we naturally gave the project a museological perspective: the end result could not be a mere showcase of vegetation, the plants and the landscape had to tell a story, the whole experience had to transmit a didactic message. This is what distinguishes this garden from other ones, since we consider our garden areas to be a living museum.

Additionally, and parallel to this nomination, the Sustainable Garden formed part of the various botanical collections presented by Pirámides de Güímar to the Asociación Ibero-Macaronesica de Jardines Botánicos (the Spanish-Portuguese Association of Botanical Gardens) in our petition to be accepted as a new member. That same year of 2017, the said association accepted us by unanimity as a new member, transforming us into the fifth botanical garden of the Canary Islands and expanding our official name to the 'Ethnographic Park and Botanical Garden Pirámides de Güímar'. Becoming a botanical garden implies complying with a number of conditions and requirements of the Association, such as having a variety of properly presented botanical collections; habilitated for their study, visit and recognition; and developed following scientific, cultural and educational objectives. The Sustainable Garden, we hope, is a valid example of this, and a worthy contribution to the development and promotion of sustainable tourism.

Reflections

We have aimed to produce a unique garden with the objective of transmitting the principles and values of sustainability, engaging the population in the cognisance of environmental education and becoming a reference model of how gardens and botanical exhibitions can be developed in our archipelago in a respectful, socially involving and environmentally friendly manner.

The increase in demand of school visits to the Park since we offer the Sustainable Garden, coupled with a sustainability-themed workshop, suggests that we finally seem, as a society, to realise the importance of sustainability and the need to introduce its principles to the new generations and integrate it in the academic curriculum.

Tenerife is a tremendously touristic destination, with circa 6million visitors a year (ISTAC, 2018), so it is important to protect, foster and exhibit the local biodiversity, which has been displaced in the past by introduced species. The Sustainable Garden has allowed us to do so in a respectable and educational manner, as well as paying tribute to the autochthonous flora of the Canary Islands, which is unique, unrepeatable and incomparable.

Questions

What is the purpose of a Sustainable Garden in an otherwise ethnographic museum? The Sustainable Garden has resulted in the nomination of the museum to an important continental award, but it has also paved the way for it to become an internationally recognised botanical garden. Is this definitive of a good praxis? Will combining a museum and a botanical garden be an appealing touristic offer, or will it backfire by confusing and scaring off potential visitors?

What other repercussions could these recognitions have? Will they reflect an increase in income due to higher visitor numbers, or an enhancement of the prestige of the institution?

Did we want to make a ravine because we already had palm trees present? Or was it because the storm created the watercourse and hence begged for the garden to be a ravine? Would it have been something else had we not had the palm trees? Does it matter? Isn't the dissemination of the principles of sustainability what most matters in this project, irrespective of whether it is portrayed and presented as a ravine, a gorge or any other type of geographical scenario? Or is the theme per se of the garden essential for the success of the project?

Further reading

Simon, N. (2016). *The art of relevance.* Museum2.0: Santa Cruz, California.

References

Arco Aguilar, M.J. & Rodríguez Delgado, O. (1999). *Flora y vegetación. La enciclopedia temática e ilustrada de Canarias.* La Laguna: Centro de la Cultura Popular Canaria.

Francisco-Ortega, J. et al. (2000). Plant genetic diversity in the Canary Islands: a conservation perspective. *American Journal of Botany,* 87 (7): 909–919.

Goddek, S. et al. (2015). Challenges of sustainable and Commercial Aquaponics. *Sustainability,* 4 (7): 4199–4224.

ISTAC (2017). *Encuesta sobre el gasto turístico.* https://turismodeislascanarias.com/sites/default/files/promotur_tenerife_2017_en.pdf

ISTAC (2018). Estadística de Movimientos Turísticos en Fronteras de Canarias. Islas de Canarias. 2012–2018. www.gobiernodecanarias.org/istac/.content/noticias/estadistica-movimientos-turisticos-fronteras-canarias-frontur-noticia.html

Jacoby, D. & Gollock, M. (2014). *Anguilla anguilla. The IUCN Red List of Threatened Species* 2014: e.T60344A45833138. http://dx.doi.org/10.2305/IUCN.UK.2014-1.RLTS.T60344A45833138.en

Vega Marcote, P. et al. (2007). Marco teórico y metodológico de educación ambiental e intercultural para un desarrollo sostenible. *Revista Eureka sobre Enseñanza y Divulgación de las Ciencias,* 4 (3): 539–554.

21 Inclusivity in cultural heritage sites as a means of sustainable tourism
The Istanbul Topkapi Palace Museum

Emir Çekmecelioğlu and Aslı Sungur

Summary

Cultural heritage sites stand as the common property of humanity and unique areas that have universal value. These areas are also home to intensive tourism. Cultural heritage sites, which have a sensitive environment and structure, can be affected and damaged by this intensity. On the other hand, well-managed tourism activities have important benefits on these areas. The study discusses the principles of inclusivity in the cultural heritage sites within the context of sustainable tourism. Istanbul Topkapi Palace Museum is examined and evaluated as a case within the context of inclusive design principles. As a result, conservation of cultural heritage sites and enhancing their values by developing proposals are aimed.

Introduction

Cultural heritage sites are unique and indispensable areas that reflect past civilisations to present and have important value in local, regional, national and international levels. These areas are of concern to all humanity due to their rich qualities and, being common heritage sites; they are visited by people from all over the world. In addition to the positive aspects of the interaction between the cultural heritage sites and intensive tourism, there are also negative aspects. Although cultural heritage sites are sensitive and need to be protected due to their historical and cultural characteristics, they are under threat of losing their original values, in places where tourism develops unrestrained. This situation causes irreversible losses to the heritage sites. In addition, tourism, which is well-managed and sustainably developed in the heritage sites, can provide significant contributions to the conservation of these sites. Therefore, experiencing cultural heritage sites by everyone through well-managed tourism movements are important, as they are common heritage of all humanity.

People who constitute the society do not have equal mobility and perception level. Also, cultural heritage sites do not ensure suitable conditions for all users. To make cultural heritage sites accessible by all through appropriate solutions increases the level of benefiting from the positive aspects of tourism and increases the awareness about the cultural, social and economic values of the sites. In this context, inclusivity in cultural heritage sites emerges as an important consideration with regard to sustainable tourism.

It is a challenge to discover applicable inclusivity solutions and to realise consistent applications in the heritage sites, which have unique properties. This challenge arises from the difficulty of establishing the balance between inclusive design principles and the notion of conservation of the historic environment. Deriving from this challenge, the study aims to discuss the principles of inclusive design in cultural heritage sites in the context of sustainable tourism, to make assessments and suggestions through the evaluations which are developed via the chosen area as the case and, consequently to serve as a guide for future studies.

In this study, the concepts of sustainable tourism and inclusivity in cultural heritage sites are discussed. Then, Istanbul Topkapı Palace Museum, which is the case study area, is introduced and examined systematically in terms of inclusivity. The case area was chosen for its original structure and its place in the UNESCO World Heritage List. In the conclusion part, discussions and suggestions in terms of inclusive design principles of the study area are made according to the items in the main text.

Sustainable tourism and inclusivity in cultural heritage sites

Cultural heritage sites have universal value in terms of human history and must be preserved and transferred to the future. The UNESCO World Heritage Convention defines cultural heritage sites as a relic that we inherit from the past, we live in today and we will carry into the future (UNESCO, 1972).

Cultural heritage sites are high-value areas for both locals and tourists due to their rich historical and natural qualifications. Together with all the features, the cultural heritage sites are important centres of attraction and constitute the backbone of the tourism industry.

Cultural heritage sites that host intense visitor population may be damaged by exposing to the external influences and interventions over time, and they are under the threat of losing their original values. Therefore, the development of tourism in the cultural heritage sites has always been controversial to conservation. At this point, some of the local governments are in hesitation about the development of tourism in the heritage sites, while some administrations ignore the potential threats of the uncontrolled development of tourism (Ruoss & Alfarè, 2013). The UNESCO World Heritage Committee states the concerns listed below, about the potential risks of tourism on the heritage sites, which are in the world cultural heritage list, in its 2010 report of Mogao Workshop:

- Alteration of social structure
- Loss of physical fabric with uncontrolled development in and around the historical sites
- Quality of the visits and values at risk
- Impacts on local culture
- Low suitability of the heritage sites for large-scale tourism
- Fail to reach the benefits of mass tourism to the local communities (UNESCO, 2010).

Besides to all these negative impacts, tourism has the potential to make significant contributions to the cultural heritage sites. Providing the necessary financing for the conservation of cultural heritage sites, improving the sensitivity to conservation, ensuring the recognition of culture and keeping traditions alive are some of the positive effects of tourism on the heritage sites. However, the obvious situation is the fact that the tourism industry will grow and will have an increasing impact on the cultural heritage sites (Molstad et al., 1999). World Tourism Organisation foresees that cultural tourism will be one of the five most important tourism market segments in the future and draws attention to the fact that the growth in this field will create difficulties for the management of visitors in cultural areas (UNWTO, 2017). Therefore, the achievement of bilateral benefits between tourism and cultural heritage sites passes through successfully managed sustainable tourism. Sustainable tourism meets the needs of visitors, industry, the environment and host communities. Besides, the economic, social and environmental impacts of sustainable tourism are taken into consideration (UNEP & WTO, 2005). The challenge is to minimise the negative impact on the environment and host communities with increasing visitor volume because of tourism growth to maximise the positive effects of tourism in terms of business, wealth, local culture and environmental protection (Molstad et al., 1999). On the one hand, it is necessary to find suitable solutions that increase the number of tourists in order to increase the income obtained from the tourism sector and, on the other hand, adopt environmentally friendly strategies to preserve the beauties and values of the natural and cultural heritage (Ruoss & Alfarè, 2013).

The most effective way of protecting man-made cultural heritage sites is sustaining actively the usage of these buildings. At this point, tourism is an important driving force. While cultural heritage sites are kept in use, the primary objective should be providing accessibility and availability for all (McClean, 2011).

The International Council on Monuments and Sites (ICOMOS), in the Charter on the Interpretation and Presentation of Cultural Heritage Sites, defends the necessity that the cultural heritage sites should be physically open to the public and promotes inclusive access (ICOMOS, 2008). As of all these approaches, inclusivity in cultural heritage sites emerges as an important condition. The universal design ("inclusive design", "universal design", "design for everyone" etc. are the terms that are used for the similar meaning, varying according to geography. In this study, the inclusive design is chosen to be mentioned). However, in the information obtained from the original sources, the term "universal design" is used as it is referred to the strategies applied to cultural heritage sites which aim to achieve the following goals in the areas where possible:

- Publicly accessible **site design**
- Accessible **entrances**, alternate entries when they are not accessible by everyone
- Accessible and understandable **spatial organisation**
- **Signage systems** that can understandable by anyone
- Accessible and understandable **exhibits and collections** (Danford & Tauke, 2001)
- Accessible environment and providing information about accessing this environment
- Trained personnel about the awareness of disability and equality (Donnely, 2011).

The compatibility of cultural heritage sites with inclusive design principles is quite variable. Because of the different eras, they were built in some heritage sites can easily adopt to the inclusive design principles, while in some areas, it is much more difficult to achieve this balance. At this point, a bilateral conflict arises between the preservation of the heritage site and the provision of inclusivity. Provision of inclusivity aims to remove obstacles by enabling each user to experience cultural heritage sites and to increase tourism capacity. On the other hand, conservation principles try to prevent the loss of cultural heritage values, which cannot be replaced. Therefore, it is not possible to fully implement the principles of inclusive design in the cultural heritage sites in all cases. Nevertheless, there are many cases in which it is possible to increase the inclusivity of heritage areas with innovative management practices, quality and sensitive design interventions. At this point, the main goal should be to ensure a delicate balance between the increase of the touristic value of the area through inclusivity and the preservation of original values of the heritage site.

Istanbul Topkapi Palace Museum

Istanbul Topkapi Palace Museum is located in the area on the eastern Roman acropolis in Sarayburnu, at the tip of the Historical Peninsula of Istanbul, between the Bosphorus, the Marmara Sea and the Golden Horn (Figure 21.1). The construction of the palace was started in 1460 in the ruling of Mehmet the Conqueror and was completed in 1478. For almost 400 years, the palace was used as the administrative centre of the Ottoman Empire and became the home of the sultans. Until the middle of the 19th century, despite the various changes in the palace, it has maintained its importance and significance in every period (Ertuğ, 2012).

Figure 21.1 Topkapi Palace location.
Source: Google Earth Pro, 2018, Modified.

Topkapi Palace was converted into a museum in 1924, being the first museum of the Republic of Turkey. Topkapi Palace is one of the largest palace-museums in the world with its architectural structure, collections and archival documents, and in 1985, it was included in the UNESCO World Heritage List (topkapisarayi.gov.tr, 2018). Along with its historical and cultural value, the Topkapi Palace Museum hosts a large number of tourist populations every year. According to the Ministry of Culture and Tourism data, in 2018, Topkapi Palace Museum was the most visited museum in Turkey, being visited by nearly two and a half million tourists (kulturvarliklari.gov.tr, 2019).

The Topkapı Palace Museum is to be reached from Imperial Gate near the Hagia Sophia Museum, and the museum consists of structures located around four interconnected courtyards (Figure 21.2). At Alay Square, the first courtyard, Hagia Irene Church, ticket offices, museum shop, cafes and toilets are located. The second courtyard is Council Square, where the state administration takes place; the Harem entrance and the palace kitchens are also located here. In the third courtyard called Enderun, the sultan's places and the units belonging to the palace school are located. In the fourth courtyard, there are kiosks and gardens belonging to the use of sultan. The Harem, the residence of sultan and his family, is located in the western part of the palace (topkapisarayi.gov.tr, 2018) (Aydin, 2012). In Figure 21.3, the units and spatial organisation of the palace can be seen in detail.

Figure 21.2 Topkapi Palace and surroundings.
Source: Google Earth Pro, 2018, Modified.

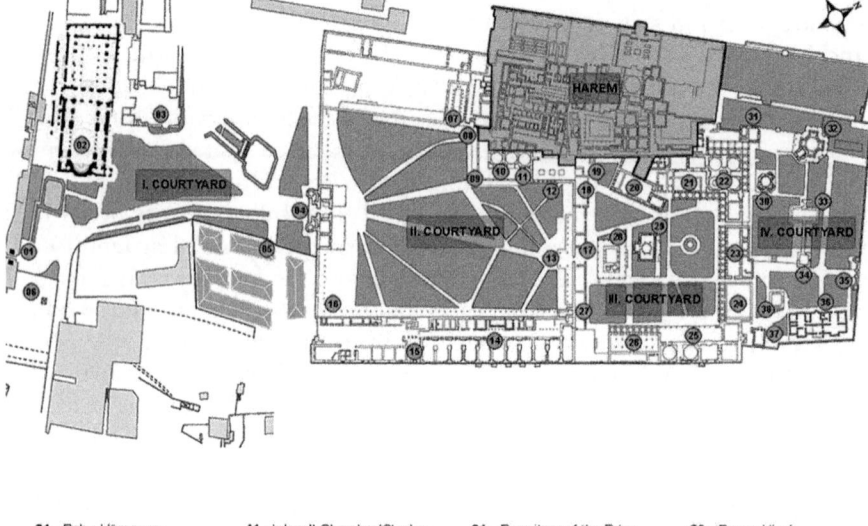

01 - Bab-ı Hümayun
    (Imperial Gate)
02 - Hagia Eirene Church
03 - The Imperial Mint
04 - Babüsselam Gate
05 - Ticket office - Cafe
06 - Gendarmerie
07 - Dormitory of the
    Haldberdiers with Tresses
08 - Entrance of Harem and
    Dormitory of the Haldberdiers
    with Tresses
09 - Imperial Council
10 - Tower of Justice

11 - Inkwell Chamber/Clocks
    Section
12 - Outer Treasury/Weapon and
    Armours Section
13 - Babüssaade Gate
14 - Palace Kitchens
15 - Cooks' Mosque
16 - Toilets
17 - Dormitory of the Akagalar
18 - Dormitory of the Small
    Chamber
19 - Harem Exit/Aviary Gate
20 - Agalar Mosque

21 - Dormitory of the Privy
    Chamber/Portraits of the Sultans
22 - Privy Chamber/Chamber of
    the Sacred Relics
23 - Dormitory of the Treasury
24 - Dormitory of the Kilerli
25- Fatih Kiosk/ Treasury
26 - Dormitory of the Seferli /
    Imperial Costumes
27- Dormitory of the Large
    Chamber
28- Chamber of Petitions
29- Library of the Ahmed III

30 - Revan Kiosk
31 - Circumcision Room
32 - Baghdad Kiosk
33 - Kara Mustafa Pasha
    Kiosk / Sofa Kiosk
34 - Tower of the Head
    Physician
35 - Tower/Gülhane Gate
36 - Mecidiye Kiosk
37 - Sofa Mosque
38 - Wardrobe Room

Figure 21.3 Topkapi Palace ground plans.
Source: commons.wikimedia.org, 2018, Modified.

Topkapi Palace Museum in the context of inclusivity: an analysis

In cultural heritage sites, both protection and accessibility requirements need to be tackled in an integrated way in order to provide inclusivity principles that will increase the tourism potential. This analysis provides guidance in order to determine the interventions that can be done without damaging the original values in line with inclusivity in the cultural heritage sites. In this context, the case area of Topkapı Palace Museum is examined in detail. While examining the case area, the method was used to determine the inclusivity conditions for cultural areas as it is presented in the Universal Design New York books. Five main topics were systematically examined in the case area: site design, entrances, spatial organisation, signage systems and exhibits and collections (Danford & Tauke, 2001; Levine, 2003). In this study, the implications from the Topkapı Palace Museum, as well as the implications from guidelines about connection of inclusivity and historical environment, have also been used (Danford & Tauke, 2001; Levine, 2003; Donnely, 2011; Sungur Ergenoğlu, 2013; Sawyer, 2015). Topkapı Palace Museum was also evaluated with Universal Design Audit Checklist, which was developed to analyse the inclusivity level quantitatively. (Levine, 2003). Through this systematic evaluation, a total score was obtained and the inclusivity level of the cultural environment was revealed to discuss.

Site design

An inclusive site design in a cultural heritage site, starting from the immediate vicinity of the facility, is the site where availability and accessibility requirements are provided in all areas such as public transportation, passenger loading zones, pathways, outdoor attractions and exhibits. Transportation to Topkapı Palace Museum is provided via Sultanahmet Square. Near the square, the tram station and *passenger loading zones* for tour buses are public transportation routes. The site, which is reached by pedestrian pathways over the east of Hagia Sophia Museum, is safe in terms of *pedestrian access* due to the fact that it is a closed area to the traffic (Figure 21.2). The Topkapı Palace Museum has a variety of flooring types at *pathways* such as cut stone, marble, paving stone and mosaic at the same time. It can be said that these flooring types are suitable for inclusive access in terms of features such as not being slippery and not having gradual changes of level. However, there are no tactile arrangements for access of visually impaired people in the floors throughout the museum (Figure 21.4). On the pathways or entries of Topkapı Palace Museum, *protection elements against weather conditions* are not designed. However, the museum hosts original landscaping arrangements in the courtyards and provides protection against weather conditions on pathways where there are many different plant species (Figure 21.4b). Topkapı Palace Museum is open to visitors at certain times of the day, so there is no *lighting* at exterior pathways due to not being visited after-hours. The Topkapı Palace Museum's website lists the recommended mode of transportation for the access to the museum, the opportunities that the disabled visitors can benefit from in the venue, and availability of accessibility of places (www.topkapisarayi.gov.tr, 2018).

Various *information services* are provided to the visitors within the site. The model of the palace and the information panels are located at the entrance to provide visitors with information about the site and the spatial features (Figure 21.4c). In the Topkapı Palace Museum, there are seating units at the outdoor spaces as *urban furniture*. It is seen that the seating units are gathered at some points instead of being placed at regular distances. The seating elements are not of an inclusive feature that can be used by all due to their dimensional features and material. However, these elements can be consider as suitable; hence, their dismountable joints do not damage the historical fabric (Figure 21.4d).

Based on these analyses and literature reviews, below are the inferences about inclusive site access in cultural heritage sites:

- It should be considered that a large number of visitors can arrive at the same time. Sufficient bus *passenger loading zones* and waiting areas should be designed. Easy access to public transport stops should be provided.
- Pedestrian priority transportation should be designed around the site, and necessary measures should be taken for *pedestrian access* such as crosswalks (Levine, 2003).
- Continuity should be provided on the *pathways* throughout the site, and the sudden changes in the level should be avoided. If there are changes in the level, ramp solutions with features suitable for everyone should be developed. Especially in cultural heritage sites, it is important that these structures are separated from the original fabric and that they will not harm. In the flooring of the pathways, the surfaces must be arranged so that they do not carry any danger of movement

Figure 21.4 Topkapi Palace Museum site.

for the visitors. In addition, the elements required for the access of the visually impaired people must be considered (Sawyer, 2015).

- Measures should be taken for *protection against weather effects* on pathways for visitors.
- Adequate *lighting* levels should be ensured on pathways (Levine, 2003).
- In areas where there is no accessible interior place for all visitors especially in cultural heritage sites, the necessary *information services* and activity areas should be constructed outdoors.
- *Urban furniture*, which is necessary for outdoor seating, resting, and can be used by everyone, should be placed in such a way that they cannot obstruct the access areas and must be suitable for the historical fabric (Sawyer, 2015).

Entrances

The entrance area in a cultural facility is the main access point where the publicity, ticketing and control are provided. An inclusive entrance needs to have appropriate features in terms of the main entry point, door systems, thresholds, waiting areas, amenities and disability supports. The entrance to the garden of the Topkapı Palace Museum is the Bab-ı Hümayun gate next to the Hagia Sophia Museum (Figure 21.5a).

A   B   C

D   E

Figure 21.5 Topkapi Palace Museum entrances.

Since the Topkapı Palace Museum has a system consisting of units settled around the courtyards, the palace has many entrances that connects interior and exterior spaces. In the *main entrance* of the museum, it is possible to access from the same place by everyone by means of dismantled and mounted ramp designs (Figure 21.5b–c). In some of the entrances to the interiors, access can be provided for everyone, while in some places, it is seen that the same access could not be achieved due to the original structural features. Topkapı Palace has many *doors* with special character. In general, the door openings appear to have a sufficient width. In all open to visit areas, it is seen that the doors are kept open during the visit hours and thus the barriers to accessibility have been largely abolished. There are *thresholds* on the door crossings at the Topkapı Palace Museum. It is seen that some doorways in the museum provide accessibility in these regions with temporary ramp analyses and in some regions, these solutions are not implemented (Figure 21.5c–d). The entrance and ticketing area of the Topkapı Palace Museum are located at the entrance of the second courtyard, Babüsselam Gate. This place provides *sufficient space* for reception. However, there is no lobby area designed in these areas. There are *public restrooms* near the entrance and a cafe place for drinks. Wheelchair support is provided in the entrance of the museum as a *disability support* (Figure 21.5e).

In this context, based on the research and literature reviews, below are the inferences about the inclusive entrances in cultural heritage sites;

- The first aim is to provide a *main entrance* space available for all, compatible with the principles of inclusivity. However, considering the original fabric and conservation principles, secondary access solutions can be implemented when an inclusive main entrance space is not possible.
- Automatic *door* systems with sufficient width should be preferred for all accessible entrances. However, in historic buildings, doors can be characteristic elements. Alternative solutions such as expanding the existing opening or creating a different opening in the door gaps that do not have sufficient width should be examined in detail considering the characteristics of the historical fabric. In the case where automatic door solutions cannot be applied, solutions can be provided such as keeping the doors open or having a bell to open the doors and finding auxiliary staff (Sawyer, 2015).
- In historical buildings, there are often *thresholds* in the entrance spaces. In these cases, the most accurate solution is the placement of disassembled ramp and platform solutions that will not damage the historical fabric (Donnely, 2011).
- In cultural facilities, lobby areas should be designed to provide *sufficient space* for high visitor density. In these areas, there must be seating elements where visitors can wait.
- *Amenities* such as public restrooms, vending machines and telephones should be found close to the entrance.
- *Disability support* services should be provided for visitors in need, such as wheelchair support and waiting area for service animals (Levine, 2003).

Spatial organisation

It is important that the spatial organisation in cultural facilities is designed in a way that is easily perceived and intuitively guided for the first time visitors to the site. However, it is not possible to intervene in the spatial organisation due to its unique fabrics in such. In this case, solutions such as route solutions, information and signal elements to facilitate the circulation within the field, and auxiliary staff can reduce the problems related to the organisation. In addition, lighting elements, seating and rest areas and emergency evacuation are the other critical points in terms of spatial organisation.

Topkapi Palace Museum has a unique spatial organisation consisting of units that settle around different courtyards and provide transitions within themselves. No specific *route solutions* has been developed within this organisation. The *entrance and exit areas* can be easily perceived thanks to their original textures and intuitive movement can be provided (Figure 21.6a). The main entrance of the museum has an *information* desk for advisory, and the catalog of the museum and the audio guide can be obtained (Figure 21.6b). Within the spaces, information and sign elements are located, for visitors to provide information about the units (Figure 21.6c). Due to the courtyards, the natural light effectively pass into many places. There is sufficient *lighting* for visitors in the exhibition areas. All of the exhibition spaces do not have a *seating and rest area* arrangement. This is due to the unique features of the exhibition spaces. For example, while the hall where the sacred relics are displayed cannot offer

A   B

C   D

Figure 21.6 Topkapi Palace Museum spatial organisation.

a suitable place to sit due to the rare works and the high number of visitors, there are seating units in the space of the kitchen exhibition (Figure 21.6d). Automatic fire and security systems are used, in addition to the intervention equipment located in certain areas, according to the ***emergency evacuation*** plan.

In this context;

- A ***route solution*** should be developed in order to allow visitors to experience all venues, and visitors should be informed about this.
- The ***entrance and exit areas*** should be clearly visible.
- Inclusive ***information*** should be provided at the main entrance, and various information systems and informational staff should be provided. Within the spaces, information elements that can be easily understood by everyone should be included.
- The interiors should be visually perceptible, and the ***lighting*** arrangement should be sufficient.

- **Seating and rest areas** that do not obstruct circulation areas should be included.
- **Emergency evacuation** should be planned, and at least two exits should be designed in each possible exhibition area (Levine, 2003).

Signage systems

Signage systems are critical elements of spatial orientation and information in cultural facilities. In these facilities, signage elements must be perceptible and understandable by all. Furthermore, due to historical fabric of the cultural heritage sites, signage elements should not damage the fabric and should have demountable joints.

The signage systems in Topkapı Palace Museum are organised in **two different languages**: Turkish and English. Perceptibility in terms of **colour and font** used in signage systems has a good level (Figure 21.7a). **Pictogram** expressions are used in the signs describing the rules and facilities of the site (Figure 21.7b–d). However, there is no **braille printing** for visually impaired visitors. **Colour-coding systems** were used in maps of spatial organisation, but this was not used in sign elements (Figure 21.7e). Moreover, the signage elements within the museum are moving, **dismountable elements**, so as not to damage the historical fabric.

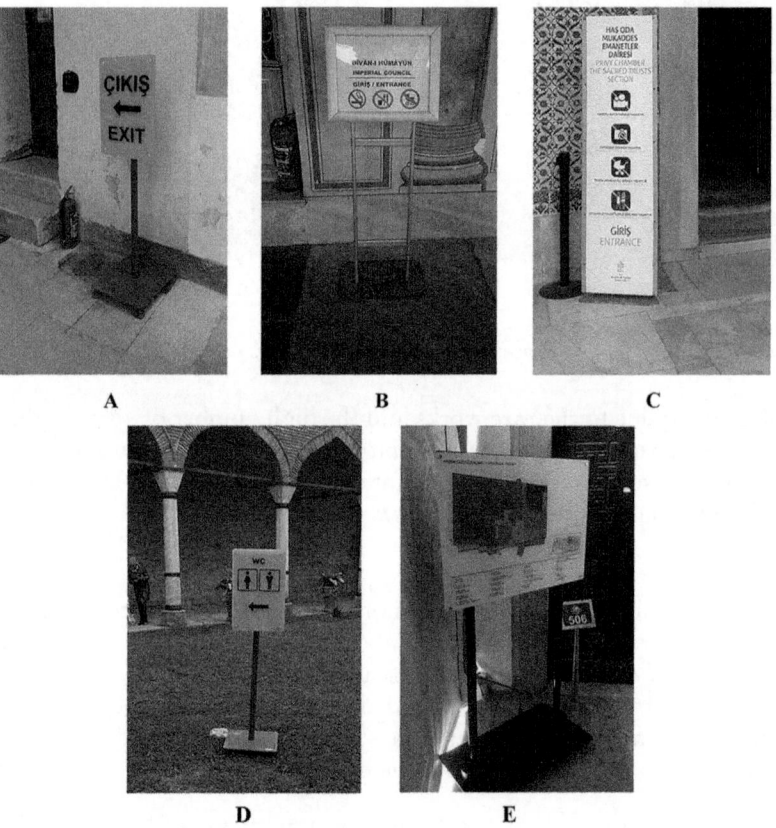

Figure 21.7 Topkapi Palace Museum signage system.

In this context,

- Signage systems should be organised in at least *two different languages*. The brochures and maps prepared about the place should be arranged in more languages.
- Sufficient contrast and embossed writing system in terms of *colour and font* in signage systems, supported with voice expression systems, should be provided.
- In signage elements, it is preferable to use universally understandable *pictogram* expressions together with the writing.
- Signage elements should be mounted in such a way that visitors with low vision may come close to read them, and *braille printing* should be used for the visually impaired.
- *Colour-coding system* must be used for different places in signage elements (Levine, 2003).
- The signage systems within the historical environment should not damage the original fabric and should be *dismountable elements*.

Exhibits and collections

The exhibits and collections, which are provided in a cultural facility, are the main attraction sources for visitors. In addition to the collections they host, cultural heritage sites are also an element of exhibition themselves.

Topkapı Palace Museum is home to many private collections and exhibitions as well as its own original values. Due to the unique architectural fabric of the building, there is not *sufficient space* allowance in some exhibition halls. For example, the harem section has restricted sufficient space allowance due to narrow and original texture, while there are sufficient space in the arms and armour exhibition areas (Figure 21.8a–d). In the exhibition halls, there is *information* about the space and collections offered with an alternative language option. In addition, audioguide also provides voice narration (Figure 21.8b). However, there are no braille printing options for visually impaired visitors. Within the halls, the exhibition elements' *counter heights* are at a height that every visitor can easily perceive (Figure 21.8c–d). *Lighting systems* focussed on collection items were used in the exhibition areas, and the items were successfully illuminated (Figure 21.8).

In this context,

- There must be sufficient *movement space* for all the visitors within the exhibition halls.
- Inclusive *information* about the exhibition items, alternative language options, alternative media, braille printing, voice aid and presentation should be provided. Information about presence of alternative expression types should also be included.
- Exhibitions and collections should have a suitable *counter height* that all visitors can easily perceive.
- Shaded surfaces should be reduced by creating appropriate *lighting systems* in exhibition areas (Levine, 2003).

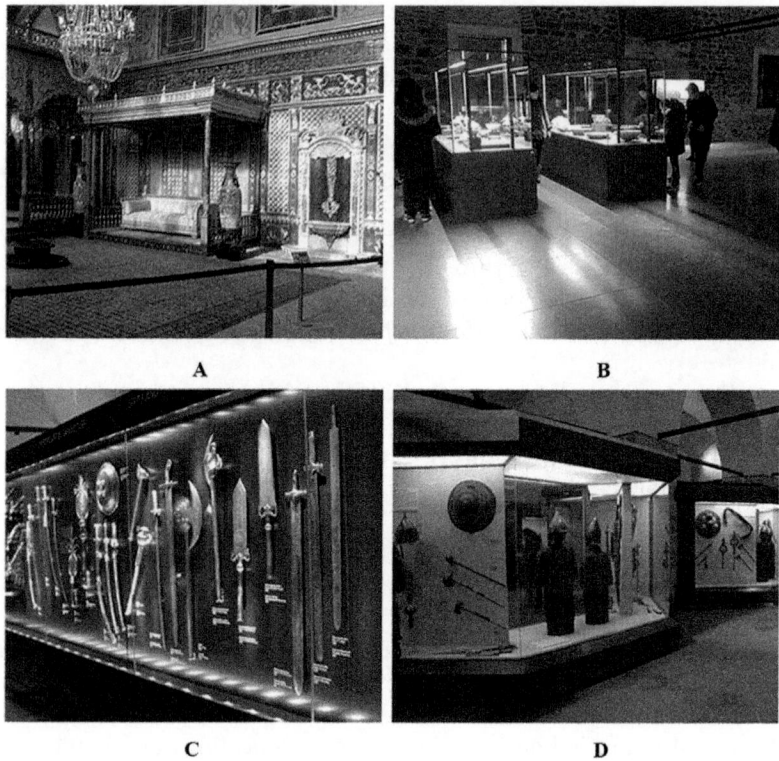

Figure 21.8 Topkapi Palace Museum exhibitions and collections.

UD *audit checklist*

In line with all these research, Topkapı Palace Museum was evaluated in terms of inclusivity with Levine's Universal Design Audit Checklist (Levine, 2003). The UD Audit Checklist is a universal assessment table that includes improved evaluation questions in terms of the inclusivity of the space and reinforcement features of a building, and serves to demonstrate the inclusive dimension of the structure. Appropriate matches are chosen for the places and facilities in the structure, and the total score is obtained by the scoring of the features of them (Table 21.1).

As a result, Topkapı Palace Museum's inclusivity score is calculated as 61%. The details of the calculation are not given here, but if this score is to be interpreted; it is a low score when compared to newly built environments, but it can be considered successful in terms of a historical environment built centuries ago. However, it is obvious that this level should come to a better point by supporting these studies more comprehensively and supporting them with innovative solutions. This evaluation table provides an incentive.

Table 21.1 Elements of Topkapı Palace Museum evaluated on the UD audit checklist

Site issues	Access points
	Parking
	Passenger loading zones
	Pathways
	Vertical circulation
	Amenities
	Walking surfaces
	Public restrooms
Building issues	Entry
	Reception area
	Doorways
	Vertical circulation
	Walking surfaces
	Restrooms
Environmental systems	Natural illumination
	Artificial illumination
Communication system	Information and direction signs
	Room identification information
	Emergency alarms
Program spaces	Exhibit spaces

Source: Levine (2003).

Conclusion

Cultural heritage sites, which are the common heritage of all humanity, are unique areas that host unique values that reflect the rich expressions of the past societies. Together with these characteristics, they are special areas that must be experienced by all, protected, kept alive and transferred to the future. These areas, which have significant attraction for all people, host a large number of visitors every year. At this point, the aim is to minimise the negative effects of tourism and to maximise the positive effects with the sustainable tourism approach. In this approach, the main goal is bringing these areas to the highest possible level of inclusivity. In this context, below are the main considerations, extracted from the case of Topkapı Palace Museum:

- *Site design:* Topkapı Palace Museum has a unique fabric in terms of its historical environment and structural features. Although the principles of inclusive design have not been fully achieved with the works carried out within this environment, it can be seen that the level of inclusivity can be increased with the support of administrative interventions, appropriate material selection and well-designed architectural solutions.
- *Entrances:* There are many and different entrances, but not all of them have equal inclusivity. It is understood that the constraints imposed by the original

fabric can be overcome in some proportion, but entrances that are more inclusive can be created with the help of the development of administrative solutions and innovative solutions.

- *Spatial organisation:* Since the revision of the spatial organisation in historical environments will harm the original values of the building, the interventions at this point are not possible. Topkapı Palace provides good conditions for inclusive access due to its comfortable perception and free circulation in terms of spatial organisation. However, it can be at a better level with the development of auxiliary elements such as managerial solutions and route solutions.
- *Signage systems* are the easiest to implement in terms of inclusive design principles because they are developed independently of the structural constraints in historical environments. In Topkapı Palace Museum, the signage elements are one of the most successful solutions in terms of inclusive design. These systems are compatible with the historical fabric and have perceptible characteristics. However, these elements may be more successful with the support of different sensory systems and especially with the addition of equipment for visually impaired visitors.
- *Exhibits and collections:* Topkapı Palace Museum is very rich in terms of exhibits and collections, besides, being an exhibition itself. Exhibition systems should include sensitive solutions compatible with the place and provide suitable conditions for visitors. The exhibition systems organised in Topkapı Palace Museum are compatible with the place and inclusivity norms. In these areas, level of inclusivity may increase with the development of solutions related to information elements.

It is possible to reach the target of full inclusivity in the historical environments, with the right material selection and good design, and provide suitable solutions for all humanity to benefit and learn from. Nowadays, it is possible to provide a higher level of inclusivity in historical environments with the increase of innovative solutions provided by the developing technology. In all historical environments, it is important to ensure that all facilities are handled in a balanced manner, that inclusivity is achieved at the its highest and that these areas are brought into society in the context of sustainable tourism. Topkapı Palace deserves to be dealt with in a more systematic way in terms of inclusivity with all its original qualities.

Assessment of cultural heritage sites in terms of inclusivity is a guide for the studies to be carried out in these environments. Thanks to these studies, it is possible to realise the necessary interventions in the field, take precautions and create awareness. This enables the area to maintain its values and to benefit more from tourism in the context of sustainable tourism. For this purpose, "an inclusive model" can be established to improve the inclusive design in the areas of cultural heritage. This model, which is both universal and has the flexibility to contain of geographic and local values, should include applicable solutions for heritage areas with common characteristics. In the field, solutions should be developed under the guidance of "the model", taking into account the specific characteristics, and the inclusivity conditions should be increased by increasing the benefits of tourism and reducing the losses. In management of cultural heritage sites, an international link can be established to create this model. A guideline to be established through international cooperation will be inclusive in terms of heritage sites and will increase the likelihood of success.

Reflections

1 Cultural heritage sites and tourism interaction involve a bilateral conflict. Sustainable approaches aiming to control the negative effects of tourism on heritage sites and increase their benefits make this conflict beneficial in both sides. It is expected that the volume of tourism will gradually increase in the cultural heritage sites. In this case, it is important to consider sustainable measures as soon as possible.

2 Inclusivity is critical for increasing tourism value. A balanced approach to both conservation and inclusivity needs is important for the sustainability of heritage sites.

3 Cultural heritage sites can only be seen as a common heritage for all humanity when all can experience them. Considering that, each member of the society has a different perception and movement capability, inclusivity is a key parameter in terms of heritage sites.

4 Since providing the principles of inclusivity in historical environments is a challenge in itself, analysing the situations of these areas is a guide for future studies. Interventions to be carried out in line with these evaluations can be handled with precision.

5 Universal guidelines for all the cultural heritage sites in the world can be critical for solutions to be developed with precise interventions to be carried out. An international linkage on the management of these areas will be useful for the creation of these guidelines.

Questions

1 What are sustainable solutions to reduce the harmful effects of tourism in cultural heritage sites and increase their benefits? What is the role of inclusivity here?

2 How can solutions be developed in order to develop inclusivity without damaging sensitive historical fabric in the cultural heritage sites?

3 What kind of guidelines can be developed to implement inclusivity in cultural heritage sites? Are these guidelines universally usable in all areas?

4 Can local, national and international management organisations be developed in order to make the principles of inclusivity prevail in historical environments?

Further reading

Donnely, J., ed. (2011). *Access Improving the Accessibility of Historic Buildings and Places*. Dublin: Stationery Office.

Levine, D. ed. (2003). *Universal Design New York 2*. New York: Idea Publications.

McClean, R. (2011). *Providing for Physical Access to Heritage Places*. Wellington: New Zealand Historic Places Trust Pouhere Taonga (NZHPT).

Ruoss, E. and Alfarè, L. eds. (2013). *Sustainable Tourism as Driving Force for Cultural Heritage Sites Development*. Roma: National Research Council of Italy.

Sawyer, A. (2015). *Easy Access to Historic Buildings*. 3rd ed. London: Historic England.

Sørmoen, O., ed. (2009). *Accessibility to Cultural Heritage Nordic Perspectives*. Copenhagen: TemaNord.

References

Aydin, H. (2012). Topkapi Sarayi Müzesi. In: *İslam Ansiklopedisi*. Ankara: Türkiye Diyanet Vakfı. Vol. 41, pp. 261–263.

Danford, G. S. and Tauke, B. eds. (2001). *Universal Design New York 1*. New York: City of New York Office of the Mayor Publication.

Donnely, J., ed. (2011). *Access Improving the Accessibility of Historic Buildings and Places*. Dublin: Stationery Office.

Ertuğ, Z. (2012). Topkapi Sarayi. In: *İslam Ansiklopedisi*. Ankara: Türkiye Diyanet Vakfı. Vol. 41, pp. 256–261.

Google Earth Pro 7.3.2 (2018a). *[Bosporus, Istanbul. Satellite view, 41°00'37.79"K 28°58'47.99"D, elevation 2KM]*. [Viewed 20 Jan. 2019]. Available from: www.google.com/earth/index.html

Google Earth Pro 7.3.2 (2018b). *[Topkapi Palace, Istanbul. Satellite view, 41°00'40.29"K 28°59'44.76"D, elevation 5.50KM]*. [Viewed 20 Jan. 2019]. Available from: www.google.com/earth/index.html

ICOMOS (2008). *Charter on the Interpretation and Presentation of Cultural Heritage Sites*. [online]. [Viewed 02 Feb. 2019]. Available from: www.icomos.org.tr/Dosyalar/ICOMOSTR_0397812001353671158.pdf

Levine, D. ed. (2003). *Universal Design New York 2*. New York: Idea Publications.

McClean, R. (2011). *Providing for Physical Access to Heritage Places*. Wellington: New Zealand Historic Places Trust Pouhere Taonga (NZHPT).

Molstad, A., Lindberg, K., Hawkins, D. and Jamieson, W. eds. (1999). *Sustainable Tourism and Cultural Heritage: A Review of Development Assistance and Its Potential to Promote Sustainability*. Oslo: NWHO.

Ruoss, E. and Alfarè, L. eds. (2013). *Sustainable Tourism as Driving Force for Cultural Heritage Sites Development*. Roma: National Research Council of Italy.

Sawyer, A. (2015). *Easy Access to Historic Buildings*. 3rd ed. London: Historic England.

Sungur Ergenoğlu, A. (2013). *Mimarlıkta Kapsayıcılık: "Herkes İçin Tasarım"*. İstanbul: Yildiz Teknik Üniversitesi Basım-Yayın Merkezi.

T.C. Kültür ve Turizm Bakanlığı – Kültür Varliklari ve Müzeler Genel Müdürlüğü. (2017). *Müze İstatistikleri* [online]. [Viewed: 08 Feb. 2019]. Available from: www.kulturvarliklari.gov.tr/TR-43336/muze-istatistikleri.html

T.C. Kültür ve Turizm Bakanlığı Topkapı Sarayı Müzesi Müdürlüğü. (2013). *Topkapı Sarayi* [online]. [Viewed: 02 Mar. 2018]. Available from: http://topkapisarayi.gov.tr/tr

Topkapi Plan.png (2008). *Wikimedia Commons*. [Viewed: 03 Mar. 2018]. Available from: https://commons.wikimedia.org/wiki/File:Topkapi_Plan.png

UNEP and WTO (2005). *Making Tourism More Sustainable: A Guide for Policy Makers*. Paris: UNEP.

UNESCO (1972). *World Heritage Convention* [online]. [Viewed 20 Feb. 2018]. Available from: www.unesco.org.tr/dokumanlar/somutkulturelmiras/somut_kulturel_miras.pdf

UNESCO (2010), *World Heritage Committee: Report on the International Workshop "Advancing Sustainable Tourism at Natural and Cultural Heritage Sites", Mogao Caves, World Heritage site, China, 26–29 September 2009* [online]. [Viewed 21 Jan. 2019]. Available from: https://whc.unesco.org/archive/2010/whc10-34com-INF.5F.1e.pdf

UNWTO and World Tourism Organization (2017). *2017 Annual Report* [online]. [Viewed: 23 Jan. 2019]. Available from: www.e-unwto.org/doi/pdf/10.18111/9789284419807

22 Social and environmental impacts of tourism mega projects in Mexico

Sandra Luz Zepeda Hernández and
Fabíola Cristina Costa de Carvalho

Introduction

Tourism is an important source of foreign currency in México. According to the World Tourism Organization – UNWTO Barometers, México is among the top tenth countries in tourism arrival since 2014 without interruption (*Secretaría de Turismo*, hereafter SECTUR, 2018), which is a distinctive position in Latin America. In 2017, it was the sixth country in the ranking of international arrivals and the fifteenth considering the foreign exchange income for tourism (UNWTO, 2018).

Tourism is a territorial-changing activity, especially on those hardly inhabited places to be transformed into dynamic centres of attractions. In México, the political attainment to develop tourism is mainly focussed on the coastal areas, associated with the discourse that tourism is a way to reach the growth of national economic indicators. Accordingly, it has a central position on the national agenda, being a state policy since the 1970s. The main strategy to develop the activity was to construct integrally planned tourism centres (*Centro Integralmente Planeado*, hereafter CIP). Though, tourism expansion represented a transformation on economic, social and environmental dimensions on Mexican territories. Meanwhile, that was incapable to extend social development to host communities.

On the present days, high attention is being given to tourism development in the region of *Bahía de Banderas*, located in the north-west coastal of the México. In this geographical area, seven out of every ten inhabitants are a migrant, a phenomenon that was also largely motivated by tourism megaprojects and the property model, expanded since the 1960s and strengthened in the 2000s. For the 2010 national census, 61.5% of the *Bahía de Banderas'* population were born in another entity, and this number increases to 70% estimated in the Inter-Census Survey Research by the National Institute of Statistics, Geography and Informatics (INEGI, 2015). Nevertheless, the region had its highest demographic growth from the year 2005 to 2010 with a corresponding increase of 48.3% (Zepeda, 2019), when it had the utmost investment collection at the national level. Then, it became the most important tourist corridor in the segment of beach and sun in the country, covering almost the 289 km of coast in Nayarit entity.

Merged in this coastline, *Bahía de Banderas* territory is composed by three municipalities: Puerto Vallarta and Cabo Corrientes, in the state of Jalisco, and *Bahía de Banderas*, in the state of Nayarit (see Figure 22.1).

That is worth noting that in Nayarit state, territory is marked by the coastline, where the tourism projects were primarily set up, and also by the valley and highlands,

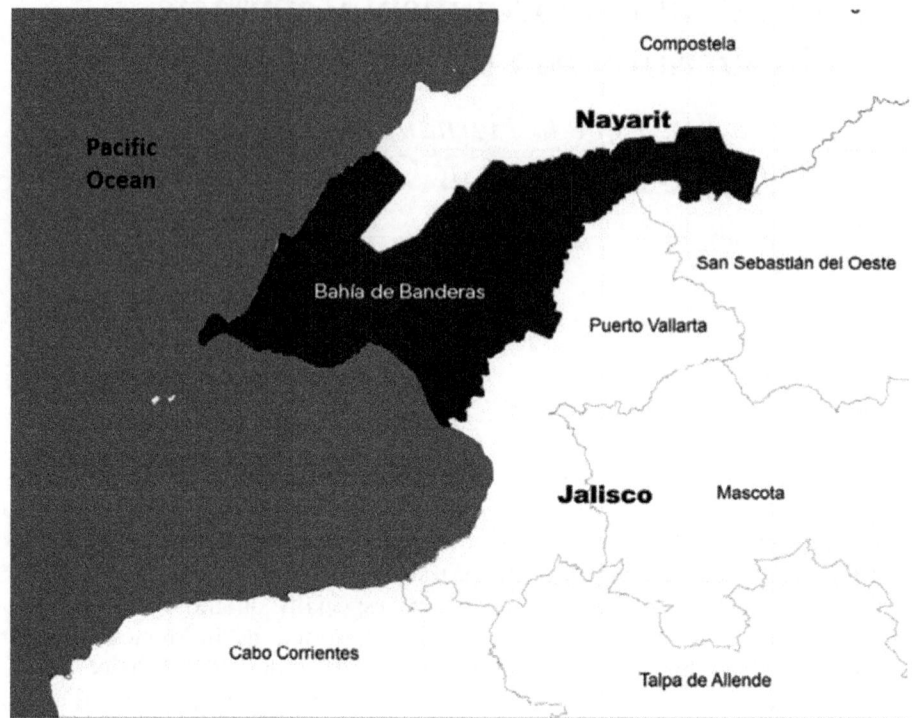

Figure 22.1 Map of Bahía de Banderas region.

that had some population stablished before the starting of tourism projects. Precisely, in *Bahía de Banderas* municipality the attraction of megaprojects, based on the neo-liberal economic model, has been the central strategy to develop the region since the 1980s, when it remarks the opening to large capitals to construct tourism infrastructure, as a policy plan to spread occupation and induce the economically growing on the territory.

From a historical perspective, primary sector was the main source of economics in the region since late 19th century, and this implied a population concentration in the highlands of the municipality, especially in *San Juan*, *El Colomo* and *Aguamilpa*, located on Vallejo's Mountain (Zepeda, 2019). However, as tourism industry increased, coastal communities began to grow in terms of population and infrastructure, in an expansion process until nowadays. It has drastically changed the demographic dynamics, as well as the coast and the valley territory. At present, the biggest part of the population has almost emptied the highlands, redirecting the economic activities in the third sector.

According to Zepeda (2019), an estimation from the 2010 census suggests that the coast area gathered 49.9% of the population, valley zone 45.0% and mountain communities barely 2.1% of population concentration. (Note: this does not match 100% since the results do not include human settlements scattered on the territory, so they were not considered in the estimation.) In this recent period, tourism became the first economic activity and 78.1% of the working population belonged to the third economic sector (National Institute of Statistics, Geography and Informatics (*Instituto Nacional de Estadística, Geografía e Informática*, hereafter INEGI, 2010).

As a result, in the region large capitals have generated an expectation in the generation of employment with the approval of the governments. Then, it shows a complex and contradictory reality in which tourism could not contribute to increase the well-being standards, even though it has effective tourism results in terms of the level of tourism infrastructure inside the centres of attractions and tourism arrivals.

In these initial considerations, this research identified the socioeconomic and environmental impact of the property model of tourism development in *Bahía de Banderas*, particularly regarding the initial expectations and its real effects caused by the model itself on the region. The study takes as a statement the conceptual discussion proposed by César & Arnaiz (2006, 2012) and César (2015), who claims that tourism is a "model of development" assumed by the State, being part of the framework of the hegemonic economical system. By doing so, it works in the maintenance of social structures, conducting the social behaviours and affecting the possibility of transformations in the government action towards social development.

The text is organised in six parts considering the introduction. In the second section, it presents the fundamental characteristics of Mexican policy to tourism and then how institutional discourse has changed through last four decades. Next, the methodology is described. In the fourth part, four case studies are analysed: *Corral del Risco*, developed in the 1990s, *Vidanta* and *Litibú* set up in the 2000s and *San Pancho* that is just being stablished. Finally, considerations are given about the main results of the study.

Tourism agenda and development in Mexico

The first policies to bias the tourism in México date from 1929 (Madrid, 2015). Later, in the 1940s, Ernesto Fernández-Hurtado, a junior researcher at the Central Bank of México (*Banco Central de México*, hereafter Banxico), suggested to calculate the foreign exchange generated by tourism, at that time an emerging activity, in the balance of payments, leading tourism to be addressed in the bank annual reports (Ambrosie, 2015).

However, the foundation of the first institutions responsible for designing and operating tourism in the 1970s remarked its achievement as a state policy (Madrid, 2015). Consideration should be given to the fact that Fernández-Hurtado ascended as Banxico General Director (Ambrosie, 2015). Then, Madrid (2015) claims that the weakness of the Balance of Payments makes Banxico to look for alternatives to obtain foreign currency. Additionally, the fact that the county hosted the 1968 Olympic Games and the 1970 World Cup demanded some attention on tourism organisation.

In the meantime, in 1974 the Tourism Promotion Law (Ley de Fomento Turístico) was promulgated, it created the National Fund for Tourism Promotion (*Fondo Nacional de Fomento al Turismo*, hereafter Fonatur) and it set the Ministry of Tourism (*Secretaría de Turismo*, hereafter Sectur) (Madrid, 2015). Thenceforth, it initiated the agenda of tourism in México that is operating ever since: the development of integrally planned tourism centres (CIP), constructed in strategic areas of the country that had low economic outputs or unproductive areas, without some real alternative of development (Inda and Gomez, 2015; Madrid, 2015; Ibañez Pérez, 2016).

Table 22.1 Construction of the integrally planned tourism centres according to its location and previous characteristics of the area

Year	Generation	Tourism integrated centre	State	Previous characteristics
1974	1st generation	Cancún	Quintana Roo	No tourism, almost nonpopulation
1974	1st generation	Ixtapa Zihuatanejo	Guerrero	Rustic tourism, short population
1976	1st generation	Los Cabos (Cabo San Lucas and San José del Cabo)	Baja California Sur	Rustic tourism, short population
1984	2nd generation	Huatulco	Oaxaca	Rustic tourism, short population
1976	2nd generation	Loreto	Baja California Sur	Occasional visitors, short population
2004	3rd generation	Bahía de Banderas	Nayarit	Tourist destination in growth
2009	3rd generation	Playa Espíritu (Escuinapa)	Sinaloa	No tourism – unfinished project.
2009	3rd generation	Costa Lora	Tamaulipas	Cancelled project

Source: Based on Inda and Gomez (2015).

Tourist growth was proposed to be developed in the medium and long term (Benseny, 2007; Ibañez Pérez, 2016). To manage the interventions, the State would provide the land and subsidies to hotels to be constructed, as well as to airline initial operations (Inda and Gomez, 2015). Besides, a commercial infrastructure and other tourist facilities should be constructed and a master plan elaborated for the operation of a support village, such as roads, parks, schools, health and centres. (Madrid, 2015). Regarding this policy in the last four decades, eight integrally planned tourism centres were set in México (see Figure 22.2).

All of these CIPs were constructed on the coast, being the first on the east side (Cancun project) and the others on the west side. Contradictions are observed in the operation of these projects. First, interventions were designed and implemented without attention to those involved in the areas where the projects would be carried out (Ibañez Pérez, 2016). According to Castro (2007) and Ibañez Pérez (2016), the land where the first CIPs were constructed was expropriated by changes of the Federal Constitution, exactly using an amendment to constitutional article 27, in the 1980s, that altered the prohibition to national territory to be disposed of by foreigners.

Considering the first and second generations of tourism centres formation (see Table 22.1), according to Inda and Gomez (2015), the main outcomes were

- Cancun grew continuously to become the most important CIP. The "all-inclusive" commercial strategy attracted mass tourism, producing an enormous expansion of the city, while the local purchasing power decreased and the social and environmental problems improved in the region due to tourism.

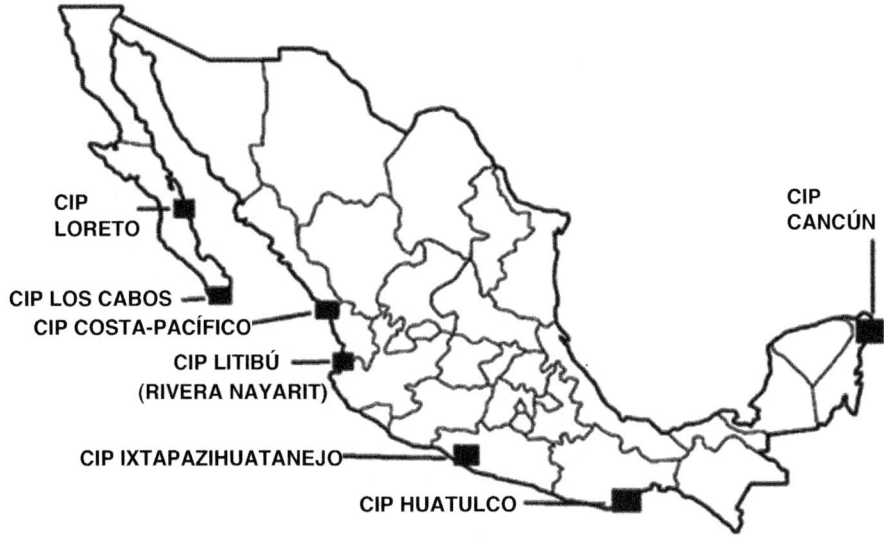

Figure 22.2 Integrally planned tourism centres setting in Mexican territory.

- Ixtapa, unlike Cancun, was an inhabited territory with some marginal tourist experience since 1946. On the other hand, after the centre was stablished, the transformations in the federal governments, in SECTUR and Fonatur, led to cease its consolidation as an international destination, limiting it to the middle-class national tourism.
- Los Cabos (Note: At the beginning, San José del Cabo received public investments, from Fonatur, while Cabo San Lucas had only private investment. Nevertheless, this second one developed more than the first. Both together became the second more successful CIP in México (Inda and Gomez, 2015) and Loreto, had been conceived as high-quality and low-density destinations and became the second most successful centre in the country. Recently, the all-inclusive marketing promotion and timeshare strategy started to attract mass tourism to that area. Moreover, in 2014 the Odile hurricane affected the region, generating economic and social crisis.

Among the first five projects, Cancun and Los Cabos (Cabo San Lucas and San José del Cabo) became the most important sun and beach destinations of the country; Ixtapa and Huatulco have some discreet operation; Loreto never reached its consolidation (Inda and Gomez, 2015).

Meanwhile, these projects represent the basis of tourism offer in México. Up until now, it is constituted by a vertical and centralist policy that is carried by Fonatur (Ibañez Pérez, 2016), in which public-private investment interests rule the decision-making on tourism interventions. In the centres, it operates a real state model of development, inputting economic and social dynamics around these territories. The results tend to be the concentration of economic interests instead of changing to more sustainable politics, getting as a result of social and environmental troubles associated with tourism growth.

Paradoxes of the actual political discourse: sustainability versus economy

In a review of the tourism policy of Mexico, in 2017 the Organization for Economic Cooperation and Development (*Organización para la Cooperación y el Desarrollo Económicos*, hereafter OCDE) recommended to improve tourism performance, based on competitiveness and innovation principles, to increase the governance on destinations, which not only denotes the adaptation to market trends and demand, but also applies better forms to issue the benefits of the activity, by promoting inclusive growth in smaller-scale systems and focussing on innovative projects with the inclusion of small and micro-enterprises, as well as using of public resources efficiently.

Indeed, the combination of the concepts of governance, partnership and sustainable destinations has been largely reproduced in institutional discourse. Zepeda and Costa de Carvalho (2017) argues that the stated recommendations are associated with the introduction of the theme of sustainability in the international agenda of tourism, which was disseminated since the 1980s in Europe and the United States, and in the 1990s in Latin America. From that time, mechanisms to encourage the participation of those involved in the productive chain of tourism and other social actors interested in its development became one of the foundations of tourism policies and its operating strategies.

Definitely, in the 1990s, the signing of the Free Trade Agreement with the United States and Canada impacted all Mexican government policy; meanwhile, the tourism sector went through a structural crisis. Benseny (2007) considers that there has been greater concern with the control of the exploitation of tourism, grounded on the promoting sustainable development. However, only in the 2000s the notion of sustainable destinations was incorporated in institutional documents.

Especially in the first two decades of the 21st century, the political discourse has associated the concept of sustainability with a possibility for social development, mainly stimulated by UNWTO. Hereby, the Tourism Sector Plan (Plan Sectorial de Turismo 2013–2018) included the participatory planning and integrative decision-making on tourism destinations, though it is mentioned in future form, which is indicative of its non-existence in their currently actions (Bifano-Oliveira and Costa de Carvalho, 2015).

Finally, the 2017 was declared by the United Nations as the International Year of Sustainable Tourism for Development (UNWTO and UNDP, 2017). Thus, UNWTO members, including México, signed the 17 sustainable objectives to transform the world, which must be considered in the political agendas until 2030.

Contradictorily, to reach the sustainable tourism agenda, proposed by the UNWTO, it is necessary to have a more complex perspective concerning the sustainability and what must be done that should integrate an organised interference, so that the problems generated in the destinations can be dealt with (Soares & Emmendoerfer, 2011).

Taking into account the third generation of the CIP policy agenda, *Bahía de Banderas* became the focus on the political attention. Associated with this main agenda, other actions to develop tourism in the region are also related to public-private relationship and based on the attraction of large capitals investments, while sustainable planning and operation is not undertaken. The research undergone identified some consequences of these political decisions and the strategies applied to stimulate tourism expansion. Considering this agenda of tourism, it examined the processes of implementation of these megaprojects, the rules that characterised the political decisions related to tourism developments, and how it impacted in the host community dynamics.

Methodology

The methodology used in this research was according to an interdisciplinary perspective (Wallerstein 1998, 2005), which allowed the apprehension of a reality of a complex nature derived from the multiplicity of components, so that they cannot be taken apart to be analysed separately; thus, referred to the rest, a new and contradictory reality is revealed.

In consequence, all qualitative techniques were used in order to collect information relating to the study cases, such as in-depth interview to specific community actors, on-site visits and participatory observation (Gil, 2008). Secondary data was collected at official sites to complement the description of the context around the study objects. Fieldwork started in August 2017 and finished in January 2019.

Megaprojects in *Bahía de Banderas*

A megaproject can be defined as something built with great dimensions (*Real Academia Española*, 2019). It may be for urban, residential and tourists' utility and using new financial techniques within public and private sectors (Lehrer & Laidley, 2006; quoted in Díaz, 2009: 194).

Under this definition, it presented four study cases that are considered as megaprojects with deep social and environmental impact on the territory. The projects are located among what is nowadays promoted as *Riviera Nayarit* brand in *Bahía de Banderas* (Figure 22.3).

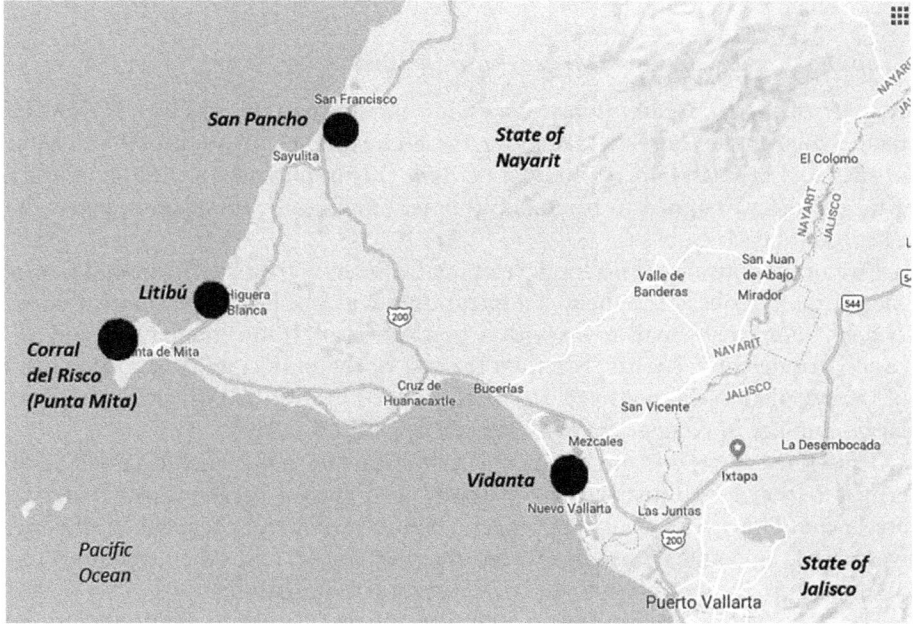

Figure 22.3 Map of the study cases localisation.

"Corral del Risco" in Punta Mita, the beginning

Corral del Risco was a little town placed until 1994 just over the first shoreline of the municipality. Since then, it has been removed from its original location to create a new town named *Nuevo Corral del Risco* obeying the government interest at federal and local levels, which moved towards economic investments from private sources. This way became possible touristic developments such as St. Regis and Four Seasons Punta Mita resorts, both targeted to upper level socioeconomic status, primarily foreigner.

According to Fonseca (2009), destitution was "necessary" since this little community of fishermen and was located in the middle of the territory sold to the developer. There was resistance to abandon the land, resulting in disturbances (1992–1994). This social issue was solved by security force. In consequence, the native people were destitute from their original living places in order to create a new one, far from the coastal line under the promise of DINE Group, the construction company, and the Government in turn, of endowing all public services increasing their well-being and, consequently, a better way of life. However, almost 25 years later social demands have not been resolved since DINE Group did not accomplished the resolution they had promised about, specifically related to the destruction of "El Anclote" beach and not giving land enough for urban growth.

Unfortunately, there is no better expectations for all these social issues since time has passed and local government did not focus on it. Thus, DINE Group continues participating in touristic developments and investing, and they also own a large part of front-bench land thanks to the benefits of the federal government, in turn, despite excluding local community development so that inhabitants suffer the impact: lack of water and dirty roads.

Litibú: a "great" employment generator in 2003

As part of the Mexican's public policy in tourism matters, in 2003 FONATUR intended to promote tourism, taken over 151.84 ha on the north side of Punta Mita, one of the most beautiful areas in *Bahía de Banderas* in pursuance of developing *Litibú*, a megaproject designed to reach 4,100 hotel units, golf course, mall, entertainment centre and beach clubs.

One of the considerations for developing *Litibú* as a Tourism Integrated Centre was the planning process and the social integration with the host community, in this case, *Higuera Blanca*, a small town with a population of 1,360 inhabitants and an education average of 7.2 years, less than the rest of the municipality. Additionally, 67% of the population did not have social security for health care which also represents a larger number in comparison with the whole (INEGI, 2010).

Therefore, social and environmental commitments were taken by the federal government in order to justify the construction of such a great infrastructure to create *Litibú*. However, during the process, deforestation and chemical land treatments were used, as could be usual, to keep the golf course and other amenities in good maintenance, in opposition to an environmental sustainability.

For José Valdivia (responsible for Higuera Blanca's municipal representation from 2002 to 2005, interviewed by the authors in 2017), a native citizen of *Higuera Blanca*, there has been irreversible damage in environmental and social matters, as he claims

...There were oil coconut palm trees and they were affected in consequence of deforestation ... yet government kept telling us we were lucky because of tourism development in our town.

(Fonatur official Press bulletin number 05/1)

Also, traditional activities such as fishing for local consumption were modified as the project has continued.

Since the first inhabitants here, people were dedicated to fishing to survive (...) we continue going to get some to eat but there is less product.

For federal government at that time, this megaproject represented a great employment generator since Felipe Calderón, Mexican president from 2006 to 2012, argues that "Litibú represents until today a total federal government investment of 750 million, added to a private investment estimated in five thousand million (...) allowing generate three thousand direct employments and almost ten thousand indirect ones".

Furthermore, it was said the finances recovering would begin in 2017, but according to official reports, this was not accomplished and, yet for that year, barely reached 508 room units corresponding to *La Tranquila* and *Iberostar* resorts. As a result, the employment generated was insufficient for enhancing life in *Higuera Blanca*.

On the other hand, the social commitments included facilities for local water supply for host community that never succeeded and restoring some of the main roads and free access to the beach called "sea windows", but it did not happen as promised. In México, difficulties in public accessing beaches are amply known once they are associated with the tourist developments. Even though it is not legal. Thus, for host communities to remain with access to their beach could be an achievement. Consequently, local people are used to have restrictions to access to their own beach and claim that "occasionally there is restrictions using private or military security" (local interview, 2017).

Vidanta Nuevo Vallarta, one of the most important tourist projects in México

Vidanta Group is a Mexican corporate emerged in 1974, and it has tourist developments in several national destinations. It owns one of the greatest resort investments in *Riviera Maya* (Cancun) and Los Cabos among others. Vidanta Group also operates golf courses around Mexican territory and has 15,000 employees.

The first Vidanta Group tourism project in *Bahía de Banderas* started in the 1990s. Ever since, it has expanded to reach a tourist complex of 1,000 ha including 5 resorts, 2 km beachfront, 3 golf courses, 2 tennis court, 1 gourmet market, 28 pools, and 40 bars and restaurants. But the greatest project is a conjoint investment with Cirque du Soleil to create a theme park, meaning the biggest bet in tourism in Mexico, at the same time that is the first in Latin America.

But the territory influenced has social and environmental effects: in this case *Las Jarretaderas* and *Boca de Tomates* localities. The first place, *Las Jarretaderas,* is a small site located on the line coast. Now it is stuck in the middle of the tourism development. For most of the people living there, that are low-middle class, have two realities: one surrounded by their own poverty and another one the opulence and luxury that tourism offers but inaccessible for them.

Also, the socioeconomic structure at *Las Jarretaderas* has been modified. Its location was one of the best to live when working on construction for Vidanta Group, as it can be assumed, it needs hundreds of workers in construction. As Vidanta generates jobs, the more immigrants settle down to *Las Jarretaderas*. Accordingly to Cárdenas (2014) most of them come from Chiapas, Oaxaca and Guerrero, located in the poorest region of the country. In 2010, this town already had a population of 6,262, and 7 out of 10 inhabitants were born in another state (INEGI, 2010).

This statement involves new social demands and changes in social structure, culture, habits and lifestyles. Fieldwork showed discrimination for indigenous kids, sons of immigrants who are separated from the natives for taking classes, even though in public education. People claim for better public services, in particular about transportation, security and residential trash duties, besides the continuous struggle for their right to access the beach.

Moreover, the Ameca River's bed has been modified in order to get the territory ready for the theme park constructed entitling several environmental and social problems, such as effects on the biodiversity and flooding in towns nearby. Some other environmental matters have been revealed, primarily in *Boca de Tomates*, a beach located at the south side from *Bahía de Banderas* and belonged to Jalisco State. This beach was the last one to survive to the real estate voracity until Vidanta got the federal permission for construction in 62,545.31 m². This area is also known for its natural reserve *Isla de Los Pájaros* (Bird Island) a refugee of migrant birds and crocodile, apart from birds and turtle natural habitat.

This place is also known because of the small rural restaurants called *palapas*, settled more than 40 years ago by local families, whose consumers are especially local market. Even though these families have not been moved out until now, dislodge is latent, getting over a traditional activity. Some of them claim "I have lived here all the time, I learned to walk here, my father is a native too" (local interview, 2018).

San Pancho, Punta Paraiso *development*

San Francisco is a little town located at the north of the municipality and is it better known just as *San Pancho*. It was originally planned in the 1970s by the federal government as a "model city", but unfortunately unsuccessfully the agenda policies changed. During the next decade, local and federal authorities focussed on developing different areas of the municipality and left *San Pancho* to grow by itself.

Though, in the last few years it has become a land of struggle between community members and foreign investors, since the growth of *Bahía de Banderas* as national and international destination. It is remarkable *San Pancho*'s capability of gathering an important number of foreigners, now settled down into this little town, and how they have become members of the active community whom concern for defending *San Pancho* territory. Therefore, a local group opposes the plan for developing the area primarily for environmental reasons.

One of the most important issues for *San Pancho*'s civil organisations is education and environment; for instance, there are more possibilities for a conscientiousness about the responsibility to protect and preserve natural areas for next generations. *Punta Paraíso* is a luxury oceanfront apartment development, including three buildings with 44 unities, and also offers amenities such as swimming pool, golf course and polo club. In order to get this development completed, some changes need to be done. Some of them include closing the beach for the community members and surfers, and also taking over a natural area, preserved for nesting marine turtle. Although community members claim that illegal procedures were applied in pursuance of getting the federal authorisation to construct this project, it has already sold many of its residential units according to developer's online information.

Although *San Pancho* was sold since the beginning as a low-impact destination and, for a long time, attracted by retired-old-visitors, now it is tempted by the mass tourism. Yet, now there is better expectation of the new federal government, which has already had official meetings with local activists concerned with the social and environmental impacts on the beach and general community, at least to earn precedents to prevent territory remains of these developments led by speculation and private investments.

Discussion

The tourist national agenda is framed into the development model, in which the institutional discourse is advocated as a way to bettering the quality of life of host communities, mainly by the creation of jobs, the expansion of infrastructure and services, as well as the preservation of the natural environment.

In this territory, the private investors and primarily the federal government by means of Fonatur have generated an expectation in the generation of employment with the consent of the local governments in turn. Nevertheless, not all of the megaprojects in Mexico are successful as a job generator. In an opposite way, real results show that tourism has generated contradictions and social problems associated with the projects conveyed to be centres of organised tourism.

The study cases presented show a disconnection between institutional discourse and the concrete actions of private and public sectors, to social and environmental intervention in pursuance of sustainability.

Besides the economic dimension, also fieldwork suggests that social and cultural components have been modified by host communities in order to adapt themselves to their new reality. In addition, host communities are starting to organise in order to participate in decision-making and defend their territory which can play an important role in the new politic actions from the federal government. However, a remarkable aspect about it is the active participation of foreign residents in the struggle to protect the territory, emphasising on environmental protection, as in *San Pancho*. This brings out some other considerations about the role of the local activists in decision-making process in the new federal government – that started in December 2018 – which has promised to attend the social and environmental problems in tourist destinations.

Conclusions

Results showed that the large capitals caused an expectation in the generation of employment with the approval of the governments. Nevertheless, it identified a complex and contradictory reality, considering the impacts on local population.

Tourism developments transformed the territories with the constructions that closed the public accesses to the beaches, generating social exclusion. Public demands increased as a reflection of tourism expansion, without the attention of public policies, as education, public transport and health services. Tourism expansion generated public instability, and failed expectation in social and economic dimensions by host communities. Finally, tourism affected the sense of belonging to people who live in altered sites.

According to the current national reality, it may be worth the effort to design and apply a new scheme for public policy in tourism, focus on local and regional development and promote a greater social participation, which would help to generate a sense of belonging and territorialisation. This action could give a better expectation for balance between speculation and social justice.

Finally, considerations should be given to reduce impacts and offer quality of life to population, contemplating the decision-making, tourism planning and organisation roles on these territories, to reach a sustainable model of tourism development.

Reflections

1   It may result very contradictorily how touristic development has social and environmental impacts when they are placed in a sustainable frame, according to the Sustainable Development Goals also subscribed by México.
2   Institutional discourse and practical action are about further extremes in Mexico political agenda of tourism?
3   How could a local community participate actively in public policy so that an equilibrium could be reached?

Questions

1   Is the tourism development in large scale a real option for human and social development so that local communities could embrace a better life?
2   Is it possible to reach an agreeable level between an effective, sustainable destination and large capital investments competitiveness?

Further reading

Lopez Torres, V., Moreno, L. & Antonio Meza Fregoso, J. (2016). Assessment of sustainable tourism in Mexico. *Global Journal of Business Research*, 10, 21–33.

References

Ambrosie, L. M. (2015). Myths of tourism institutionalization and Cancún. *Annals of Tourism Research*, 54, 65–83.

Benseny, G. (2007). El turismo en México. Apreciaciones sobre el turismo en espacio litoral. *Revista Aportes y transferencias*, 2(11), 13–34, enero-junio, Universidad Nacional de Mar del Plata, Argentina.

Bifano-Oliveira, M. C & Costa de Carvalho, F. C. (2015). Participación Social en el Proceso de Desarrollo Turístico. Topofilia Segunda Época. Revista de Arquitectura, Urbanismo y Territorios. Instituto de Ciencias Sociales y Humanidades "Alfonso Vélez Pliego" BUAP. V(1). 111–124.

Cárdenas, E. (2014). *Chiapanecos en la zona metropolitana de Puerto Vallarta*. México: Universidad de Guadalajara.

Castro, Á. (2007). El turismo como política central de desarrollo y sus repercusiones en el ámbito local: algunas consideraciones referentes al desarrollo de enclaves turísticos em México. *Revista TURyDES*, 1(1), 1–10.

César Dachary, A. (2015). El Turismo: un modelo de desarrollo. *Revista Latinoamericana de Turismologia – Rlat*, 1(1), 16–26.

César Dachary, A. & Arnaiz Burne, S. M. (2006). *Territorio y Turismo*. Puerto Vallarta: Universidad de Guadalajara.

César Dachary, A. & Arnaiz Burne, S. M. (2012). *Territorios Globalizados del Turismo Rural*. Puerto Vallarta: Universidad de Guadalajara.

Díaz, F. (2009). El impacto de los megaproyectos en las ciudades españolas. Hacia una agenda de investigación. *Estudios Demográficos y Urbanos*, 24(1), 193–218.

Fondo Nacional de Fomento al Turismo – FONATUR (s.f.). Official web page. Libros Blancos. Retrieved from FONATUR: www.fonatur.gob.mx/gobmx/transparencia/LibrosBlancos/4%20CIP%20Nayarit.pdf

Fonseca Morales, M. (2009). Punta Mita en la dinámica del desarrollo turístico regional. *El Periplo Sustentable*, (16), 85–108.

Gil, Antonio Carlos (2008). *Métodos e Técnicas de Pesquisa Social*. (6ª ed.) São Paulo: Atlas.

Ibáñez Pérez, R. M. (2016). Divergencias asociadas al desarrollo turístico en destinos costeros de la región noroeste de México. *Revista Iberoamericana de Turismo – RITUR, Penedo*, 2(6), 63–91.

Inda, M. T. & Gómez, A. S. (2015). Los Centros Integralmente Planeados (CIP´S) en México. *Rev. Latino-Am. Turismologia / RLAT, Juiz de Fora*, 1(1), 1–78.

Instituto Nacional de Estadística y Geografía. (2010). *Censo de Población y Vivienda 2010*. Gobierno Federal. Retrieved from www.inegi.org.mx

Instituto Nacional de Estadística y Geografía (2015). Encuesta Intercensal 2015. Gobierno Federal. Retrieved from https://www.inegi.org.mx/programas/intercensal/2015/

Lehrer, U. & Laidley, J. (2006). "Old Mega-Projects Newly Repackaged? Waterfront Redevelopment in Toronto", XVI World Congress of Sociology, Durban.

Madrid, F. (2015). La sostenibilidad en la política turística mexicana. PASOS. *Revista de Turismo y Patrimonio Cultural*, Special Issue, 6(13), 1301–1313.

Organización para la Cooperación y el Desarrollo Económicos – OCDE (2017). *OCDE Estudios en Turismo. Estudio de la Política Turística de México. Resumen Ejecutivo, Evaluación y Recomendaciones*. Paris: OCDE.

Real Academia Española (2019). Diccionario de la Lengua Española. Retrieved from https://dle.rae.es/?w=diccionario

Secretaría de Turismo de México – SECTUR (2018). Barómetro OMT, noviembre 2018.

Soares, E. B. S. & Emmendoerfer, M. L. (2011). Por um turismo sustentável? Uma análise à luz das abordagens de desenvolvimento no planejamento público do turismo em Minas Gerais (2007–2010). *Revista Anais Brasileiros de Estudos Turísticos /ABET, Juiz de Fora*, 2(1), 15–28, jul./dez.

Valdivia, J. (2017). "Percepción social en Higuera Blanca en torno a Litibú", September 28 (S. Zepeda, interviewer).

Wallerstein, I. (1998). *Impensar las Ciencias Sociales*. México: Siglo XXI Editores.

Wallerstein, I. (2005). *Análisis de Sistemas-mundo. Una introducción*. México: Siglo XXI Editores.

World Tourism Organization – UNWTO (2018). *UNWTO Tourism Highlights*. UNWTO: Madrid. doi:10.18111/9789284419876.

World Tourism Organization – UNWTO & United Nations Development Programme – UNDP (2017). *Tourism and the Sustainable Development Goals – Journey to 2030*. UNWTO: Madrid.

Zepeda, S. (2019). Desarrollo y Turismo en Bahía de Banderas, Nayarit. Doctoral Thesis. Universidad de Guadalajara.

Zepeda, S. & Costa, F. (2017). El Desarrollo turístico y la utopía de la sustentabilidad en Bahía de Banderas, Nayarit. *Revista Anais Brasileiros de Estudos Turísticos/ABET, Juiz de Fora* 7(3), 29–41.

23 Alto tâmega

Present heritage and future prospects

Sérgio Lira

Introduction

In this chapter the focus of the discussion is the touristic potential of a Portuguese region called *Alto Tâmega*. For the purpose an initial geographical, historical and sociocultural contextualisation is necessary, in order to explain the present situation of the region. Subsequently, tourism in Portugal and in Alto Tâmega at present is analysed. The text ends with the presentation of a case study – an innovative tourism project currently being developed in the region.

Alto Tâmega is a region in the north of Portugal, bordering with Spain. Because there are no formal administrative or political regions in the country, it is simply the gathering of six municipalities under the general designation of Inter-Municipal Community, or CIM, from the Portuguese acronym. It extends over 3,000 km^2 and counts circa 95,000 inhabitants. Population density is of circa 32 inhabitants per km^2, a figure well below the national average, which is around 110 inhabitants per km^2 (INE, https://www.ine.pt). River Tâmega cuts across from north-east to south-west and is deeply inscribed in the landscape. The climate is continental, given the distance to the sea, but humidity levels of the atmosphere and soils are still quite high, if compared with the centre of the Iberian Peninsula. The relief is at times sharp, combining mountains with fertile valleys, with great potential for agriculture and cattle breeding (Figure 23.1).

Thermal springs are a major marker of the territory and have been in use at least ever since the Roman occupation – the remarkable Roman spa in the city of Chaves (former *Acquae Flaviae*) being one of its major examples. The attractiveness of these resorts, both for their medicinal and their leisure characteristics, was particularly high by the end of the 19th century and early 20th century. A period of significant decay succeeded, during which the local business retracted, from hotels, to restaurants, to the transports network itself with the closing of the railway line. Only some of the sparkling water industries survived, but even those underwent difficulties.

At present, there is a new breath in the region's ambitions, notably on tourism and natural and cultural heritage. From infrastructures, to equipment, buildings, hotels and thermal resorts there is a whole new range of innovative projects that aim at revitalising the region. Furthermore, land connections were substantially improved (it takes approximately 90 minutes by car from Porto airport to get there). There is also a major effort to bridge this new endeavour with academic and entrepreneurial expertise on good practices. This is why this region is a relevant case study in natural tourism, heritage tourism and therefore responsible and sustainable tourism.

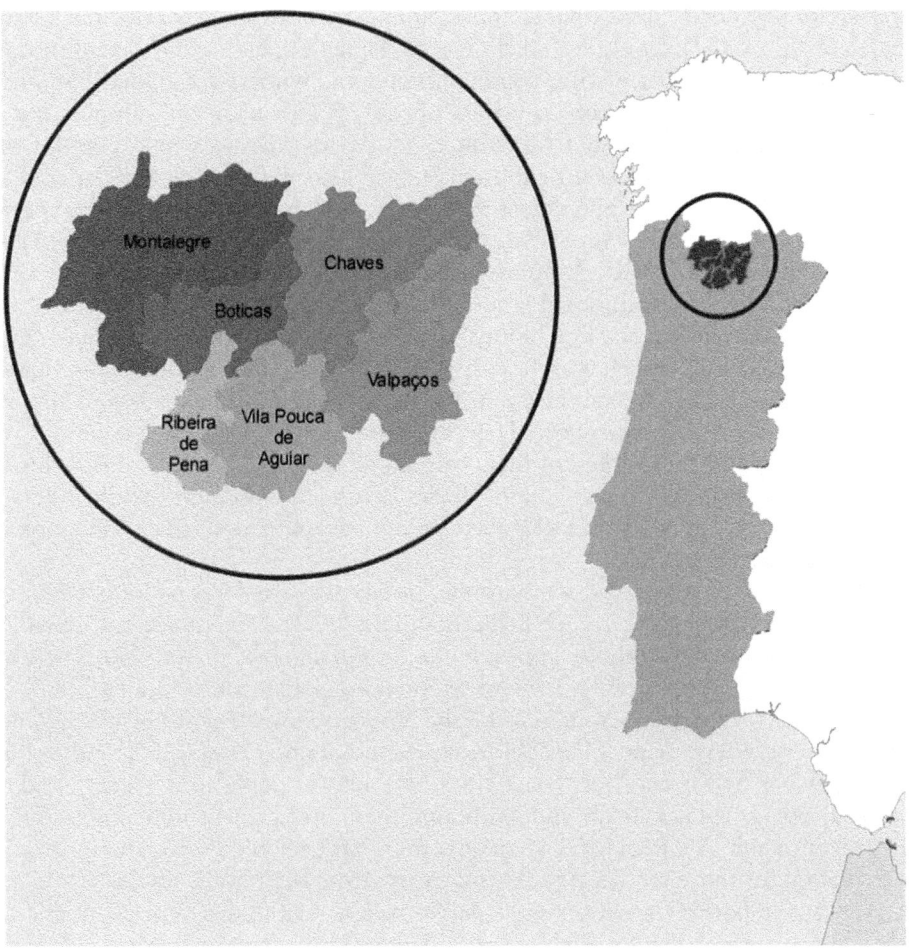

Figure 23.1 Portugal and Alto Tâmega in the context of the Iberia Peninsula.
Source: Author.

The context – Portugal and *Alto Tâmega*

Portugal is one of the medium-sized countries of Europe with a continental territory of approximately 90,000 km² and a total population of about 10.5 million inhabitants, of whom almost 3 million are concentrated in the region of Lisbon (the capital of the country) and more than 1 million in the area of Porto (the second biggest city). The continental territory is shaped as a rectangle (from North to South approximately 500/600 km and from East to West approximately 150/200 km): the North and East borders facing Spain, and the West and South borders facing the Atlantic Ocean. Most of the population is concentrated on the West coast, within a "corridor" of circa 50 km width. Latest statistics show a high HDI (0.847) and a Gini coefficient of 33.7 for an average GDP per capita in 2017–2018 of USD26,700 (INE, https://www.ine.pt; PORDATA, www.pordata.pt). However, no matter how interesting these figures may be they do not depict the reality of the Portuguese inner-land. In *Trás-os-Montes* (the expression means "behind the mountains" and is the name of all the Northeast part of the country) socio-demographic and economic realities are generally much harsher, partially due to the geography and climate of the region, but mainly due to the lack of population and investment. Summers are hotter and winters are colder than near the sea, and extreme temperatures can raise above 45° Celsius in the summer, but drop below 10° Celsius throughout the winter. This is the reason why a popular saying refers to *Trás-os-Montes* as a region of "9 months of winter and 3 months of hell". Despite the fact that the land is fertile, it is not appropriate for the same type of intensive agriculture within very small parcels as in the territory nearer to the Atlantic. Olives, almonds, vineyards, chestnuts, rye, forestry and cattle breeding were, and still are, some of the most traditional land-related activities of the region.

Throughout the 19th and first half of the 20th centuries one of the major emigration destinations from Portugal was Brazil; then, in the 1950s and the 1960s European countries as France, Luxembourg and Germany received thousands and thousands of (illegal) Portuguese emigrants. They were mainly trying to leave behind poverty, and a very significant number of them originated from the North and the Northeast parts of the country. That way, some villages became almost desert while others were populated mostly by women. Fields were abandoned and "desertification" took place in vast Northeastern areas.

More recently, because the demographic situation evolved it is no longer as extreme as before, but the ageing trend of the population is still there and an unavoidable social problem. In general, the ageing index for Portugal went from 101.6 in 2001 to 153.2 in 2017; but in the *Alto Tâmega* region it escalated from 158.6 to 303.0, in the same years. Also in this region, in 2017, the proportion was 1 new born for 2.6 deaths (INE, https://www.ine.pt; PORDATA, www.pordata.pt). Youngsters tend to flow to Porto, Lisboa and other West coast cities, notably for going to university and often they do not come back at the end. Although there is at present some university offer in Bragança and Vila Real (the two major cities in the region) Porto remains the major destination for those who decide to study away from their home towns.

Another important aspect is the relative weight of the different economic activities in the region. For example in *Alto Tâmega* and in recent years (2015–2017) agriculture was still the largest sector in number of enterprises (more than 42%) but representing only circa 6% of the wealth produced in the region, and commerce (15% of the enterprises) represented almost 45% of the product. The number of tourism-related enterprises is significant (circa 8%) but only generates approximately 3% of the region's product (CIMAT, www.cimat.pt).

In terms of potential, the region is in a favourable position, both geographically and strategically. The "far" Northeast of Portugal is no longer that far: back in the 1970s or 1980s, driving from Porto (the nearest international airport and major Northern city) to Chaves or Bragança used to be a 5–6 hours adventure (in good weather conditions); today both cities are reachable in less than 2 hours. On the contrary, the railway connections (e.g. *linha do Tua, linha do Corgo*) that were built during the late 19th/early 20th centuries (Chaves was reached in 1921; Vidago, where one of the most important water spring hotels of the region was built in 1910, received the railway on that same year) then decayed throughout the second half of the 20th century and are no longer in operation. This is commonly pointed out as an error, notably in terms of tourism development. However, new road accesses made this part of the territory reachable within reasonable travel times. From the strategic point of view,

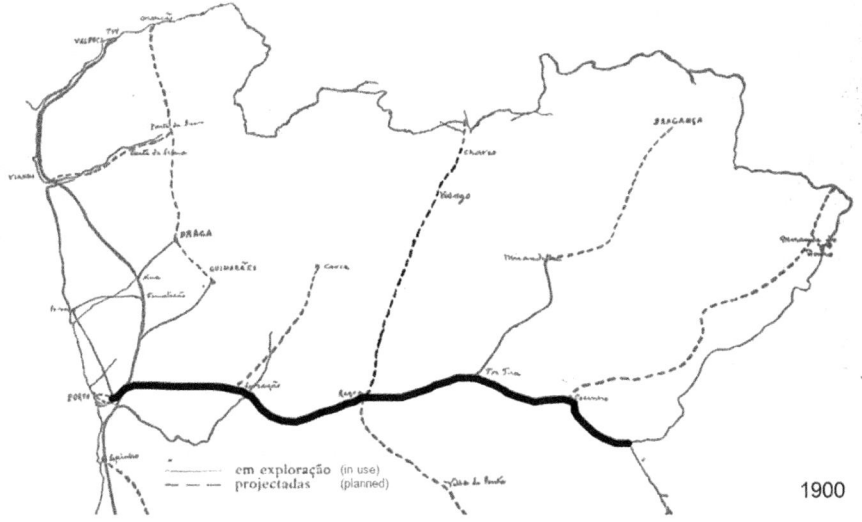

Figure 23.2 Railway lines in the North of Portugal (map dating 1900, adapted); in blue the Douro line, in red the Corgo line.
Source: Author.

the region of *Alto Tâmega* is a "cross-roads" for Spanish people living not far from the Portuguese border – it could be argued that within a range of about 100 km it is worth coming to Portugal (for the gastronomy or for the SPAs) instead of crossing the arid regions of Castile and Leon, in the centre of the Iberian Peninsula. At present, the region has three major assets to explore, in terms of visitors' attraction: natural heritage, cultural heritage and good travelling conditions. These are the aspects further discussed below (Figure 23.2).

Tourism in Portugal and in *Alto Tâmega*

Portugal has a long-lasting tradition in tourism, dating back to mid-20th century on what concerns massive attraction of foreigners mainly for the "sun & beach" of the Algarve. However, in recent years tourism trends in Portugal changed significantly with a substantial increase in the overall numbers of guests and nights and with some shift in the destinations: Algarve and Lisboa are still the most visited regions but the North is increasingly receiving more visitors, both national and foreigners.

Therefore, tourism offer, in terms of available beds, has increased steadily in the last decade: from circa 264,000 beds in 2005, Portugal reached 312,000 in 2015 (of which, almost 40% in 4 or 5 star hotels). The number of enterprises that promotes touristic activities considerably grew between 2010 and 2015 from less than 700 to 2,661 (INE, https://www.ine.pt; Turismo de Portugal, www.turismodeportugal.pt).

About 8 million foreign tourists visited Portugal in 2013, spending more than 29 million nights here; in 2017, these figures increased to almost 13 million people, staying a total of circa 42 million nights. Revenues from tourism activities reached more than 15,000 million Euros in 2017. Cities (Lisboa, Porto) are major attractions, but tourists are also searching for the countryside. The past concentration in the Algarve is no longer so extreme – for instance, one of the destinations that grew more visibly in 2017 were the Azores islands (both in terms of guests and number of nights). In any case, there is still a very strong asymmetry between the coast and the inner land: circa 90% of the nights spent by tourists in the country are indeed concentrated in the coastal areas (Algarve and West coast).

Despite this new tendency to visit the more distant country side, *Alto Tâmega* is not yet benefiting in a large scale from this new trend. In 2016, the North (and that includes Porto) represented 14% of the available beds in the country, and almost 13% of the nights spent by tourists. The occupation rate was one of the highest in Portugal (i.e. 50.2%; only Lisboa with 57.8% and Madeira with 71% were higher), but the total number of visitors the northern region is able to attract is still relatively low.

Even if almost all strategic assets as defined by the national authority in tourism (Turismo de Portugal) are present in *Alto Tâmega*, they are not yet explored to capacity (CIMAT, www.cimat.pt). Those assets are as follows: climate, history and cultural identity; the sea, nature, water, gastronomy and wines; and events (cultural, artistic, sports, etc.), well-being and quality of life in Portugal. Of these, *Alto Tâmega* only lacks the sea, as all the other are either present or possible. Therefore, the question that emerges is as follows: "why is *Alto Tâmega* performing so poorly in terms of tourism?". To answer this question it is worth going back a century in history, in order to fully understand the region, its potential, its present ways and future prospects.

By the end of the 19th century spa vacations and water treatments had become trendy. Portugal was no exception: the wealthy bourgeoisie of the time was very keen on spending generous amounts of money in luxury hotels associated with thermal springs. In the valley of the *Tâmega* the number and quality of thermal waters had been known (at least) since the Roman presence in that part of the Iberian Peninsula, and a number of spa hotels were built at the beginning of the 20th century. The outstanding case was the Vidago Palace, not least because it was King D. Carlos who had it built. For its remarkable characteristics and for a long time it was considered as the best hotel in the Iberian Peninsula. Its inauguration was set on the 5th October 1910, with the presence of King D. Manuel II (who had succeeded his father) but the Republican revolution occurred that exact day, thus postponing the inauguration on the 6th October, and obviously no longer with the presence of the king.

Another remarkable hotel was the Salus-Vidago, which was inaugurated a decade after the Palace. It was also a luxurious hotel, with 100 rooms, most of them *en suite* (what was then truly exceptional). This hotel had its own SPA facilities and water spring in the premises, so that guests could do all treatment (baths, showers, water-drinking, etc.) inside. A golf course was also part of the hotel amenities, which led to a change in the hotel's name, from the original to "The Golf Hotel". The quality of the water (and of the treatments) was often compared with the famous French Vichy springs, the hotel owners claiming that their water was even better than the French one

Therefore, in the first half of the 20th century the region benefited from this natural heritage – the water – and developed immensely, in terms of tourism. Not only the wealthy came to the *Tâmega* valley: there were accommodations for all prices and qualities, from the luxury hotels to the humble guest-houses where more modest people could still rent a room, and share the family toilet and the family dinners. During the "season" (mainly from the end of spring to the beginning of fall) the region would receive thousands of tourists who would spend significant amounts of money. Part of the local economy thus adjusted to this rhythm – making money in the high season and surviving the rest of the year.

However, by mid-20th century, water vacations were becoming less and less popular. The seaside had become the new attraction, and quite suddenly everybody wanted to go to the Algarve. The hotels decayed, many of them were closed down, the guesthouses no longer had guests, restaurants also closed and therefore the railway was no longer bringing tourists, to the point that it was finally decided to gradually shut down its services. By the end of the 1980s the railway line connecting Chaves to Régua and from there to Porto was finally closed. In terms of tourism, the second half of the century has been a long and painful decay for the region – the thermal springs were not updated to more modern requirements and no touristic strategy was designed in order to attract clients. Obviously, that was not a specificity of the *Alto Tâmega* region.

In recent years things have started to change, though. One of the main hotels, the Vidago Palace, was re-inaugurated exactly one century after the original opening, on the 6th October 2010. The restoration project was authored by Siza Vieira, one of the most famous Portuguese architects.

Other initiatives also concurred for the revival of tourism in *Alto Tâmega*. In Montalegre one of the most successful eco-museums of Portugal (the *Ecomuseu de Barroso*) was created. Besides, the municipality developed an original concept for a regular celebration of the "witches' day" in the medieval castle, which runs every Friday, 13th and which attracts a lot of visitors. A race track that receives world-class rallycross events was also built. The favourable natural conditions of the mountain of *Larouco* are being used to host the paraglider European championship. In *Pedras Salgadas*, another famous natural water spring, new accommodations were built inside the historical park. Equestrian events of national and international standard take regularly place there in high-quality facilities. Another example of tourism attraction is the *Tresminas* Roman site, a vast area that was once a gold mine, today transformed into an *in-situ* visitable heritage site, with an interpretative centre and guided visits to the caves. Biodiversity is also explored and explained there, as part of a holistic approach to heritage (both natural and historical-cultural).

At present, the CIM of the *Alto Tâmega* region is conducting several projects that directly or indirectly concern tourism development and related activities. Some good examples are projects focused on water and thermal water spots as a tourism destination, on biodiversity and preservation of natural heritage and on the signage of all the touristic resources of the region. Other projects will also have an impact on tourism activities, as is the case of projects in the areas of the academic qualification of local population, transports and public transports, urban mobility and support to entrepreneurship. As a general aim, these projects are all meant to attract permanent population to the region and thus interrupting the exodus to coastal cities.

An ambitious tourism project in *Alto Tâmega*

The *Vidago Valley – Eco-Holistic Project* is a recent and charismatic project being developed in the region. The project officially started in January 2017 and in May 2018 the formal licensing was concluded and received several official recognitions: Public Interest (Municipality of Chaves, 28-12-2016); approval of the architectural project (Tourism of Portugal, 06-04-2017); use of non-agricultural RAN soils (Portuguese

Environmental Agency, 08-05-2017); fire plan (National Civil Protection Authority, 06-06-2017); relevant public interest action in RAN soils (Tourism of Portugal, 29-06-2017; Secretary of State for Tourism and Secretary of State for Forests and Rural Development, joint decision, 09-02-2018).

It is presented here as a case study inside the study-case of *Alto Tâmega*, for its relevance in illustrating how the region is providing opportunities and finding new entrepreneurs. In this case, after 20 years of academic activity and research in the area of medieval history, and 20 years of work as tourism expert in a travel agency, Anísio Saraiva and Ana Valejo, respectively, decided to change their lives, looking for a new source of happiness and self-fulfilment. They changed everything in their lives: they quit their jobs, sold their property and left their town to create new roots in Vidago, a small town in the core of *Alto Tâmega*. They were attracted by this region that carries the scars of a long period of decay but holds to its natural richness (thermal waters, nature, forest, agriculture, landscape, gastronomy, culture) and decided to invest in a territory where they saw a high developing potential in the medium and the long term, coupled with good quality of life.

The enterprise – *Vidago Valley* – was created by this couple in December 2016 to be the institutional support of an "agriculture plus tourism" project, which encompasses two major activities:

tourism in a rural environment, aiming to provide the guests with an eco-holistic and inclusive experience, and real nature tourism in a health and well-being hotel;
biological agriculture, forestry and beekeeping, with an emphasis on local products (e.g. aromatic herbs).

One of Anísio's and Ana's first tasks was the acquisition and reorganisation of the property (they already owned some parts of it, and some of it having been abandoned for a long time). As proprietors, they carefully gathered parcels previously separated, having for the purpose studied the history of local property fragmentation in the Vidago parish and bringing back together the pieces of the puzzle (following a previous reorganisation that had happened from late-18th century to mid-19th century). Two years after, the *Vidago Valley* is established on a 15 ha property.

This is the area where a 4 star hotel with 48 rooms (96 beds) will be built, combining local-rural traditions of construction with modern materials and techniques, aiming at a sustainable, comfortable and aesthetic result. Local materials, such as stone and wood, will be used, combining traditional techniques with modern ones, in order to achieve maximum energetic sustainability. Linkage with the landscape and rural areas will be granted by using significant glass surfaces. Different elements of traditional and vernacular architecture will also be integrated in the buildings (balconies, yards, chimneys, etc.) evoking a long-lasting regional know-how. Both the architectonic project of the hotel and the planning of the surrounding agricultural areas were conceived under careful inclusiveness standards, allowing access to all handicapped persons. Furthermore, animals will also be part of the project – those connected with the agricultural activities, but also pets brought by the hotel guests.

The core objective of this project is to offer well-being – in the holistic sense of the word – allying a sensorially stimulating experience in cultural traditions and values, with modernity and comfort. Clients will be able to enjoy life in a rural and sustainable place that is intended to offer both tranquillity and inclusiveness. The project aims at being classified and certified as "Turismo de Natureza" by the ICNF and/or "Turismo Sustentável" by the Biosphere Responsible Tourism Portugal; "Construção Sustentável" / LEED; "Turismo Acessível e Inclusivo"; Bikotel and Pet Friendly. With reference to the latter, clients will have their own personalised program and experiences, in relation to their special needs and personal development. The hosts aim to bring together a very traditional, classy but warm, way of hosting, with guest-tailored programs to meet their guests' particular needs.

The project also highlights the role of water, in the rural context of the hotel. For the purpose, water will be present "everywhere" in the premises and surroundings: old agriculture-related structures (e.g. wells, aqueducts, norias) will be restored and exhibited alongside with interpretative information; water will be used for visual, tactile and sound experiences. Furthermore, all water resources will be used in sustainable ways, both for the hotel and for agricultural purposes.

The project targets a new breed of tourists, who crave for different and alternative travelling and accommodation solutions, exploring a market niche but also creating it: nature tourism, sensorial and inclusive, that is the product the *Vidago Valley* project aims to create. In the hotel the world traveller tourist and therefore a demanding costumer, seeking for culture, history, heritage, but also for vernacular food served with *gourmet* refinement will find it. Thermal treatments, meditation, yoga, Tai Chi and Chi Kung, among others, will complete a vast menu of possible activities. Local traditions, culture and different forms of intangible heritage will be brought into the hotel, for providing the guests with real experiences of local life and ways-of-doing (crafts, gastronomy, literature and performances, among others). Groups looking for a venue for personal coaching, training and workshops will also be welcome. In short, the main market for this project is an upscale segment of national and international tourism, with high added value, that seeks high-quality accommodation and complementary health- and well-being-related activities, and natural and cultural heritage experiencing.

The balance between hotel industry and actual agricultural activity is fundamental for the success of the project. The idea of a "rural hotel" requires not only an hotel within an agricultural area, but actually the integration of both activities – for instance, serving products from the local production in the hotel restaurant and making the same biological products available in the store.

The owners describe "harmony" as their key-concept and sought to achieve it by balancing different areas in the property: the hotel, but also agricultural fields, gardens for aromatic plants and for vegetables, beautiful fruit trees (chestnuts and hazelnuts), vineyards and groves. The project is also expected to have a very positive impact locally, by creating jobs both in the hotel and in agricultural activities, since considerable areas of fertile land that were abandoned for a long time are returning to production, under sustainable patterns. The (wrong) practices of unsustainable use of water and other natural resources will find an end here and "harmony" will, hopefully, be brought back to the *Valley*.

Reflections

Tourism is not a novelty of the 20th or 21st centuries, at least for some very particular regions. In Portugal, a SPA tourism phenomenon dating from the 19th century shaped the size and in many aspects the way-of-life of small countryside towns and villages, as is the case of some in the *Alto Tâmega*. Present-day tourism in those regions is inevitably linked to that period: transports, urban structures, roads, public buildings, hotels and people's memories, all account for a tendency to think about tourism promotion endeavours as mere reconstruction of patterns of the past, because the past was successful. And yet it cannot be brought back. These regions face new challenges and need new objectives. Fulfilling those demands with new approaches, new perspectives and new projects is imperative. On the contrary, trying to go back to the "golden years" will not be a solution, and it is the task both of governmental institutions and of private entrepreneurs to aim high and to create a new wave in natural and cultural heritage tourism. It seems that this process has already started in the *Alto Tâmega*.

Questions

- How can a "tourism tradition" and a collective memory of a successful period that occurred a century ago be used in a positive way, knowing that the "recipe" cannot be repeated and – if attempted – that it will not be successful?
- How can a region with a demographic deficit, strong tendency for depopulation and long-lasting lack of attractiveness for young people use its main assets (natural and cultural heritage, climate, fertile soil, good network of road connections and water springs, among others) to break the vicious cycle and head to sustainable development?
- In that process, what should the role of public institutions (like the CIM) and of private entrepreneurs be, in order to ensure the aim of sustainable tourism development? – Should tourism be considered an "anchor" for sustainable development (meaning one of the economic and social pillars of development) or merely a "means to an end" (meaning that tourism cannot be sustainable in the long-run, but must nevertheless be explored, in order to generate wealth and to allow reinvestment)?

Further reading

Chitty. G. & Baker, D. (eds.). (1999). *Managing Historic Sites and Buildings*. Routledge: London.

Convery, I., Corsane, G. & Davis, P. (eds.). (2012).*Making Sense of Place*. The Boydell Press: Woodbridge.

Crouch, D. & Lübbren, N. (eds.). (2003). *Visual Culture and Tourism*. Berg: Oxford.

Fayos-Sola, E. & Cooper, C. (eds.). (2018). *The Future of Tourism: Innovation and Sustainability*. Springer International: Cham.

Herbert, D. (ed.). (1997). *Heritage, Tourism and Society*. Pinter: London.

Honey, M. (1998). *Ecotourism and Sustainable Development: Who Owns Paradise?* Island Press: Washington, DC.

Timothy, D. (2011). *Cultural Heritage and Tourism: An Introduction*. Channel View Publications Ltd.: Bristol.

Vignati, F., Hawkins, D. & Priedeaux, B. (2016). *Sustainable Tourism: Driving Green Investment and Shared Prosperity in Developing Countries*. Createspace Independent Publishing Platform.

Wood, M. E. (2017). *Sustainable Tourism on a Finite Planet: Environmental, Business and Policy Solutions*. Routledge: London.

References

INE, National Institute of Statistics, https://www.ine.pt

PORDATA, Contemporaneous Portugal Data Base, https://www.pordata.pt

CIMAT, (https://cimat.pt/wp-content/uploads/2018/06/CIM-28062018.pdf

CIMAT, https://cimat.pt/caracterizacao

Turismo de Portugal, https://www.turismodeportugal.pt/SiteCollectionDocuments/dados-estatisticas/Dados-evolutivos-turismo-portugal-2017.pdf

CIMAT, https://cimat.pt/wp-content/uploads/2018/05/Estrategia-de-Desenvolvimento-Integrado-do-Alto-Tamega.pdf

24 Sustainable tourism development and its implementation

A case study of glamping accommodation providers in local tourism destinations

Maja Klančnik, Barbara Pavlakovič and Marko Koščak

Introduction

Tourism has become one of the fastest growing global economics sectors. It creates significant impacts on the earth, impacts which are both positive and also negative. The most negative impacts are caused by mass tourism, which brings about a degradation of the natural environment and the disturbance of many natural species. Tourism also has the ability to cause negative pressures on host communities, and in some situations, this may lead to a discord and ruin of traditional societies. At the same time, tourism has the capacity to bring positive impacts – preservation of the natural environment, creation of new workplaces and an improvement of cultural awareness (Adamič, 2012, p. 39).

As response to mass tourism, new concepts and types of tourism have arisen. They are known by different names – sustainable tourism, green tourism, responsible tourism and ecological tourism. Despite these different names, the concept of all of these sub-divisions of tourism activity is closely related – they have a common purpose and goals and also similar methods for creating more sustainability in a tourism activity (Suša, Vodopivec, and Brecelj, 2011, p. 6).

The concept of ecotourism was developed in both the practical and theoretical concept over the last 20 years, and it continues to be developed (Drumm and Moore, 2005, p. 15). Ecotourism is becoming more and more popular and demands higher levels of access and service (Fennel, in Kraševec, 2009, p. 7). This is not always compatible with theoretical definitions of ecotourism given the concept of ecotourism is a vehicle for better promotion and the providers frequently fail to fulfil the underlying concepts and objectives of ecotourism. Many providers see opportunities in ecotourism, due to the rising interest for glamping. They often fail to realise and accept their responsibility to the environment which is one of the necessary demands of ecotourism (Parks T. H., Parks, T. A. and Allen, in Kraševec, 2009, p. 7). The concept of ecotourism is based on the inclusion of only small groups of visitors who have a low ecological footprint and is diametrically opposed to mass tourism. Reality indicates that this approach may not be acceptable for many tourism providers – usually due to economic reasons which may dictate their intervention into the natural environment. The use of energy in the construction of tourism facilities may be counter-productive towards the ecological and sustainable approach. Similarly, with some ecotourism projects, there are problems in dealing with waste (Bodi eko, 2011).

A potential danger of not following the concept of sustainability is also present during the development of glamping accommodation. Glamping that is luxurious represents one of the sustainable strategies, which follows the demands of ecotourism (Bodi eko, 2011). Camping is exactly that kind of offer, where tourist can spend time in the authentic natural environment. Glamping offers more comfort and exclusivity to the tourists, than the classical way of camping. This could mean also a higher consumption of the energy and more extensive damage of the local environment. For the reasons above, we have performed the research, where we tried to discover how strictly the providers are following the concept of sustainable development. Are they following sustainability, even though demand for glamping is reaching higher levels?

Our research was performed through a case study of glamping providers in Slovenia, which are offering their services on a year-round basis.

A number of manuals and guidelines dealing with three pillars (ecological, socio-cultural and economic) and three requirements (ecological responsibility, visitor satisfaction and participation of all stakeholders in the destination) were issued in order to prevent the negative consequences that may be caused by tourism industry activities. In the study, we focussed on key areas where providers can integrate sustainable practices. These are

- *corporate strategy;*
- *internal management* – in particular in the management of human resources and material;
- *management of the supply chain,* where they can pay more attention to the choice of suppliers, which include sustainability principles;
- *product management* with product planning or glamping accommodation that reduces negative social, economic and environmental impacts;
- *raising awareness* by providing authentic information and raising awareness of responsible behaviour at the destination;
- *cooperation with the destination* and supporting all stakeholders in sustainable development.

Ecological tourism

The concept of ecotourism is relatively new and often misinterpreted or poorly defined. Commentators frequently use the term "ecological tourism" to create a greater sense of attractiveness towards the ecologically sensitive tourism sector. Yet, in reality such a supply or service belongs to the concept of natural tourism, which can have a negative impact on both the natural and the social environment (Drumm and Moore, 2005, p. 15). The authors have different opinions about the origin of the word ecotourism but agree the origin of the description "ecotourism" which was first coined by Ceballos-Lascuráin in the early 1980s of the 20th century. Ecotourism has been defined as "travelling to relatively unspoiled and unpolluted natural areas with specific intentions – studying, admiring and enjoying nature and wild plants and animals, and in any cultural manifestations (from the past or present) of the region" (Fennell, in Kraševec, 2009, p. 5).

In 1990, the International Ecotourism Society adopted and issued the first definition of ecotourism, which was named as a responsible travel to nature that preserves the natural environment and contributes to the well-being of the local community. Ecological tourism awareness increased over time and led to the need to improve the basic definition and define more precise definition of the concept. Thus, in 1999,

Marta Honey issued a more in-depth definition of ecological tourism. It defined it as a journey into a delicate, unspoiled and often protected area that aims to minimise the impact on the natural environment. It helps to raise awareness of tourists, provides the means for preserving and improving the natural, social and economic environment, encourages respect for different cultures and traditions, and tends to respect human rights (Drumm and Moore, 2005, p. 15).

The International Ecological Society states that tourism can be ecotourism only if it is focussed on six key principles (Drumm and Moore, 2005, p. 15):

- ecotourism should have as little impact on protected natural areas;
- involve all stakeholders (individuals, communities, ecotourists, tour operators, political institutions) in the process of planning, development, implementation and monitoring of tourism;
- respects local culture and traditions;
- provides a sustainable and equitable profit to the local community and other stakeholders, including tour operators;
- provides income for the conservation of nature;
- raise awareness among stakeholders of their role in nature conservation.

Glamping

Glamping is a composite word that connects "glamorous" and "camping". It is a campsite that is in touch with nature, while it offers the comfort of a hotel, similar to a kind of mobile hotel room (Borštnik, 2013). Glamping was first introduced in 2005 in the United Kingdom (Wikipedia, 2017), and according to some sources, it had appeared even before that date. Despite the fact that the term has been present for more than a decade, the very concept of glamping has become more recognisable at a popular level in the last five years. The *Journal of Outdoor Recreation and Tourism* exposed the term "glamping" in 2013. According to them, glamping occurred at a time when the economy recovered from recession (Spitler, 2017).

The reason for growing trends of this type of accommodation is the need for comfortable and luxurious accommodation. Luxurious camping originates from African safaris, where demanding European and American tourists were staying in luxury tents to avoid some negative factors that are sometimes present in classic camping. These are, for example, lack of heavy rain protection, inappropriate temperature, improvised meals, unhygienic sleeping bags and lack of hygiene. (Ternovšek Kolar, 2017, pp. 6–7).

Glamping is nowadays a trend in the offer of tourist accommodation and frequent upgrade of the existing campsite offer. The total number of glamping accommodation around the globe is 33,051, according to the Glamping Hub website. In North America, there are 25,957 glamping facilities (Figure 24.1). They are followed by Australia and New Zealand, where it is possible to spend the night in 3,398 different glamping facilities and Europe with the total number of 2,551. The lowest amount of glamping locations are currently located in Asia (Glamping Hub, b.d.a).

With the data from Glamping Hub web portal, we also conducted an analysis of the number of glamping accommodation facilities per country (Figure 24.2). The results showed that most glamping sites are to be found in the United States. The highest concentration is in the state of California with 2,754 glamping locations, followed

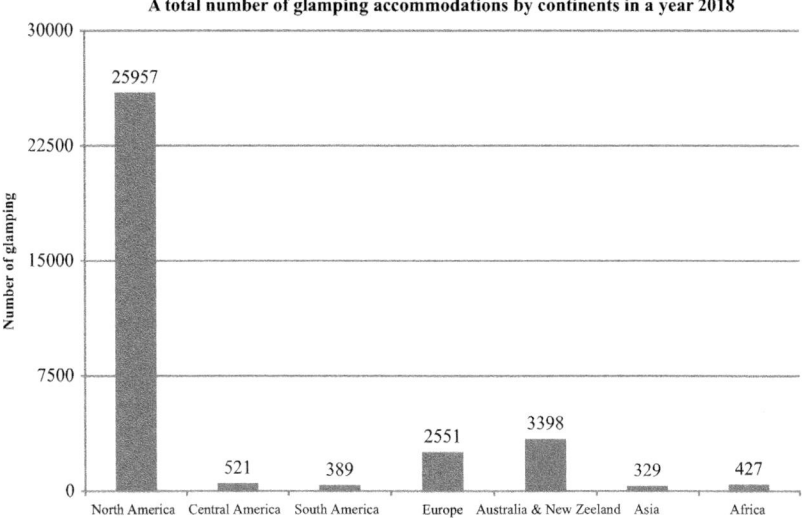

Figure 24.1 Glamping by continent.
Source: Glamping Hub (b.d.a), Made by: M. Klančnik.

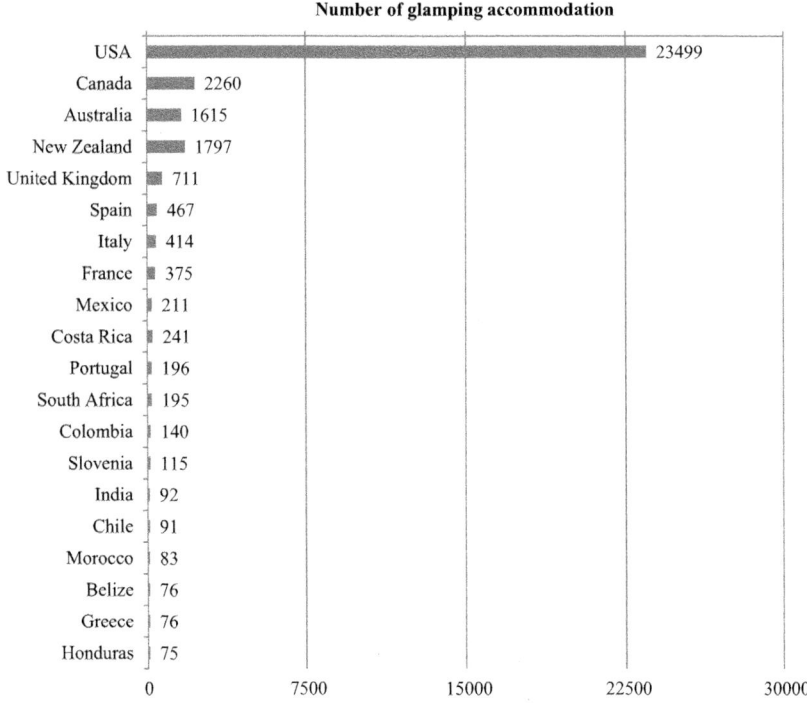

Figure 24.2 Top 20 glamping countries.
Source: Glamping Hub (b.d.a), Made by: M. Klančnik.

by the state of Colorado and Texas. Canada ranks second with 2,260 glamping locations. Most of them are in the province of Ontario, where there are 887 facilities, followed by the provinces of British Columbia and Quebec. Third and fourth place are Australia and New Zealand. In Australia, most of the glampings (412) are in Queensland, followed by New South Wales and Victoria. The North American states and Australia and New Zealand are followed by European countries – United Kingdom, Spain, Italy and France. Slovenia (in which we carried out the survey) is ranked 14th in terms of the number of glamping accommodation in a global scale, and 6th among the European countries. In the Central American countries, glamping accommodation prevails in Costa Rica (ibid.).

It is necessary to highlight that the results of glamping analysis in the global scale can be misleading and the reality may be different from the analysis shows. The data is based solely on the information from the Glamping Hub web portal, which is considered to be the largest global portal intended to market only glamping accommodation. We assume that in the world, there are many glamping objects that are not included in the portal, so the real numbers are probably slightly different.

Forms/types of glamping

Today, it is possible to find on the tourist market different types of glamping, which differ in shape, material from which they are built, location of objects, etc. The number of individual forms of glamping today is 27, and these are the following (Glamping Hub, b.d.b):

tree houses: built directly on or next to the trees, mostly wooden, accessible by ladder or hanging bridges;

yurts: originate from Mongolia; they are of low and circular shape; the frame is mostly wooden and covered with tent cloths, resistant to strong winds;

safari tents: represent the main type of glamping accommodation in the area of Africa, especially when organising safaris, they are in the form of large tents, the framework is mostly wooden or aluminium covered with tent cloths;

camper-vans and caravans: they represent miniature cottages on wheels. They can be quite simple or slightly more luxurious, depending on the equipment they offer;

tipis tents: originated from Indian villages, in the form of a pyramid and covered with a resilient tent cloth;

domes: they are built from a combination of wood, iron, steel and polyester; the bottom is slightly raised from the floor, and therefore, domes have a minimal impact on the environment;

Eco-pods: they are the basic and most classic form of glamping. They are considered to be more secure accommodation, as they can be locked;

nature lodges, cabins, cottages: represent the most numerous type of glamping accommodation and are present practically all over the world;

caves: they represent an alternative form of accommodation, as they are built directly in caves formed by nature;

barns: farm buildings, which are converted into comfortable and luxurious tourist accommodations, are mostly located on farms or in their vicinity.

huts: they originate from the tradition of nomads; they are made of various materials such as straw, wood, snow, grass, palm leaves, ice, branches, animal skin or commodities;

igloos: they are dome shapes, mostly built of snow. Once in the tradition of the Inuit people, the inhabitants of the Arctic, Greenland, Canada and the United States (ibid.);

cabooses: accommodation, rearranged in a cargo train.

villas: they were very popular in Roman times; they are usually placed on a location that provides with a superb view;

luxurious tents: represent a more comfortable version of classic camping with a tent; there are several types of luxurious tents (e.g. safari tents);

towers: a unique accommodation, towers are part of a wind mill, lighthouse or castle building;

tiny houses: mostly located near forests, ponds or lakes.

tented cabins: tents that make the appearance of the cottage, since the fabric surrounding it is so dense that it gives the feeling that the cottage is built of solid material;

islands: accommodation on islands constitutes one of the most expensive forms of glamping, mostly located on private islands;

log cabins: mostly wooden, with some so-called hot tubs or jacuzzis and rooms for socialising and relaxation, they are very suitable for larger groups or for families;

A-frame cabins: houses are in the form of a pyramid or letter A; **A-frame cabins** represent a cheaper form of glamping;

bell tents: their structure and design are simple and apply to the most popular form of tents in the world. A large number of people can sleep in them;

floating hubs: the houses are placed above the water, so they give a feeling as if they were floating above the water. They are built on a structure that is attached to the bottom of standing water;

elevated cabins: represent a mixture of a classical house and house on a tree. They stand on wooden beams, and they can be located both above water and above solid floors;

caravans: they are mostly placed on a permanent location. Some are built into a wooden frame, which does not create the look of a caravan (Glamping Hub, b.d.a).

Global trends and trends

The demand for glamping has increased dramatically in the last decade, which has led to the establishment of a special category of trips on the tourism market (Glamping. com Forecast, 2017). It is also evident from the number of searches on this topic in Google's web browser, as it points to a sharp increase in demand from 2012 to 2017 (see Figure 24.3). Trend also indicates the seasonality of glamping, where it is possible to detect the greatest demand in the summer months (Spitler, 2017).

In October 2017, the experts from the Glamping.com glamping website published five trends on the basis of the current behaviour of glamping tourists, which they expect to continue in the future. The first trend, which they expect to continue, are types of accommodation that are unique and unusual, such as accommodation in railway wagons, caves, igloos, ice hotels, glass towers and planes. The second trend predicts the greatest demand for glamping accommodation located in Slovenia. Glamping. com has published 11 glamping accommodation in Slovenia, which ranks 6th in the number of such accommodation. The third trend is glamping, which is organised in the time of special space or star events, such as the sun eclipse. The fourth trend in the field of glamping is expected to be an increasing interest in accommodation, which

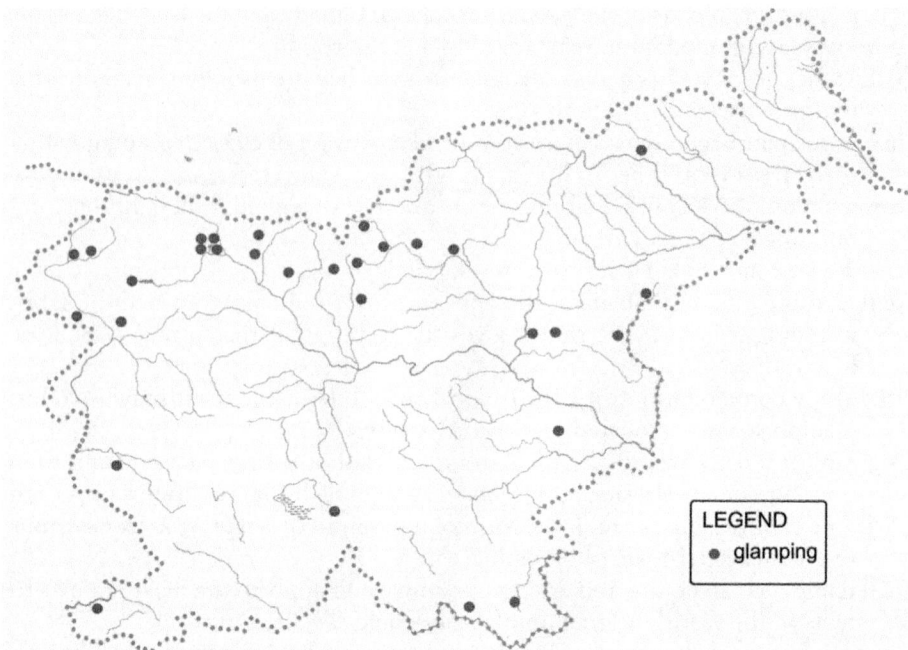

Figure 24.3 Map of Slovenian glamping.

allows guests to contact all four elements: air (e.g. tree houses), soil (e.g. caves), fire (near volcanoes) and water or over water. As a fifth trend, experts report staying on tourist farms, for example in livestock farms and in vineyard areas ("Glamping.com Forecast", 2017).

Research on the business of glamping accommodation in the field of sustainability among providers in Slovenia

In the survey, we investigated the number of Slovenian providers of glamping accommodation which included sustainable development in their business activity. In order to obtain primary data, we selected a survey methodology. The questionnaire was composed of six sections covering all seven topics discussed in the previous chapter. These are

- knowledge of the concept of sustainable tourism development;
- corporate strategy;
- energy;
- water and waste;
- supply chain management and employee involvement;
- cooperation with the destination and customer awareness.

The survey included 30 providers of glamping accommodation, which are shown in Figure 24.4. The number covers the entire population of providers that offer a year-round tourist offer in the Slovenian area. The final number of all units that have at

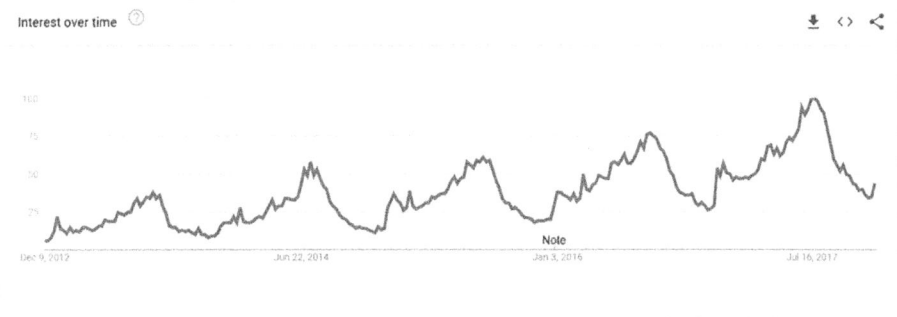

Figure 24.4 Glamping and the Green Scheme of Slovenian Tourism.
Made by: Maja Klančnik.

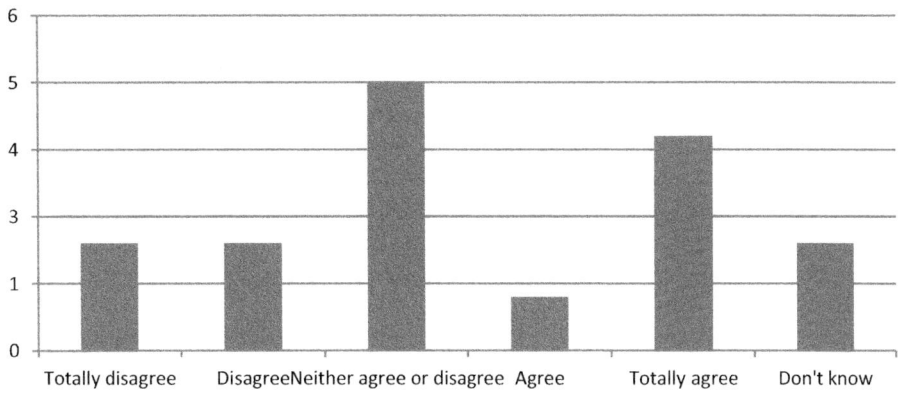

Figure 24.5 Optimal use of the natural environment.
Source: Glamping Hub (b.d.a), Made by: M. Klančnik.

least partially completed the questionnaire is 22 and completely completed was from 19 providers.

The first part of the questionnaires is related to knowledge of the concept of sustainable tourism development. The providers were very unified, which is also shown by a small statistical deviation of around 0.5. The respondents agreed or completely agreed with the claims. The providers were the most uneven in the claims about the company strategy. The highest standard deviation is to be seen in the claim about the involvement of companies in the Green Scheme of Slovenian Tourism, which suggests that there is still considerable confusion among the providers in the area of environmental schemes. It should also be noted that all the involved companies are relatively young and that is probably also one of the reasons why providers are so undefined about this topic (Figure 24.5).

The providers completely agree with 11 out of 27 claims. To a large extent, the providers agree that it is important to ensure optimal use of the natural environment and to help with protection of natural resources, and with the development of tourism, it is necessary to bear in mind the contentment of visitors. They also fully agree with the need to respect the culture of the local population and that the development of tourism depends also on the environmental awareness of the company

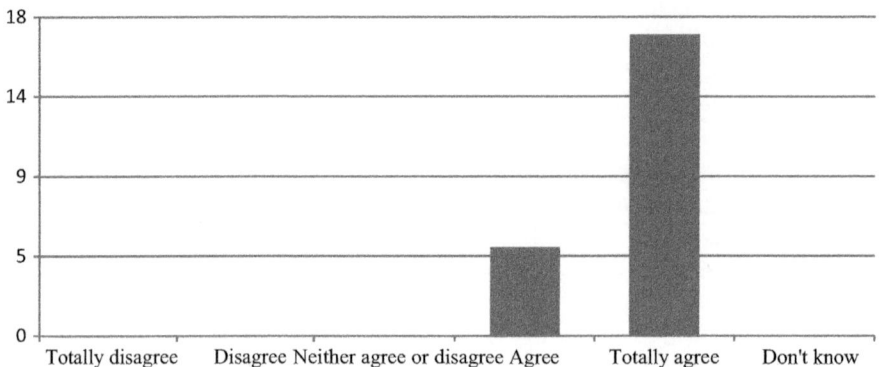

Figure 24.6 Electricity from renewable sources.
Source: Glamping Hub (b.d.a), Made by: M. Klančnik.

and the visitors. The companies have stated their orientation towards sustainable business, and the respondents fully agree with the fact that they allow the guests to adjust the provision and exchange of towels and sheets, to carry out separate collection of waste and to take care of the environmentally friendly disposal of hazardous waste. Respondents also agree with the claim to choose between the companies that are in the local environment, in respecting human rights, ensuring that employees have good working conditions and encouraging guests to buy local products (Figure 24.6).

In general, the respondents at least agreed or would be classified with the answer on four critical issues that they

- applied and observed environmental schemes;
- were included in the Green Scheme of Slovenian Tourism;
- had obtained electricity from renewable energy sources;
- used rainwater and/or recycled wastewater, which most bidders have not yet fully regulated.

With all other issues, the respondents agreed. Descriptive statistics thus indicate the extremely good awareness of Slovenian glamping providers on the sustainable development of tourism and the successful integration of the principles of the latter in everyday business.

Key findings

Companies that provide glamping accommodation in Slovenia are very small and mostly belong to the category of "micro"-companies employing up to 10 people. The result is as expected, since glamping is considered a boutique offer, intended for only a small number of guests, providing guests with a slightly higher level of privacy and luxury. The majority of respondents, that is 50%, offer over 20 beds in their glamping facilities, 28% of glamping complexes offer from 10 to 20 beds, and the smallest number of companies (22%) offer only up to ten guests at the same time.

They are also relatively young enterprises, since most of them (39%) have operated from one to three years, followed by others (34%) for more than ten years, and the remainder (27%) from four to six years or from seven to nine years.

These results show that the largest number of overnight stays (more than 20%) are offered by companies operating from one to three years. These are about 45%, followed by the companies that have been operating for more than ten years, with a share of over 30%. Similarly, the average category of providers in regard to the number of overnight stays is 10–20, where the smallest companies account for 40% of the shares, and that is the proportion of companies that operate from four to six years. The least capacity (up to 10) is offered by the oldest companies that have been operating for more than ten years. The share of the latter is about 50%. The other share is equally distributed among younger companies that operate from one to three years, or from four to six years.

In order to facilitate the analysis and presentation of results, we have merged companies that operate from one to three years and from four to six years into the category of younger companies, while older companies represent those that operate from seven to nine years and more than ten years.

Statistical tests have shown that the younger the company, the more selective is their choice of business partners from the local environment. This may be attributable to the fact that providers are increasingly aware of the importance of local food supply and the benefits that it brings. The analysis also shows that older companies agree somewhat more with the claim that the company respects human rights and that employees have good working conditions and equal rights. This is also reflected by the link that includes the number of overnight stays, as the most strongly supported are companies that offer up to 10 beds or from 10 to 20 beds. In the latter categories, the total share of older enterprises is around 70%.

Staff applying efficient waste management, water and energy, and utilising the correct dosage of detergents and cleaning products tend to be more intensively trained by younger companies and smaller companies. The result is explained by the fact that fewer employees are more easily trained in the efficient handling of raw materials, and less time-saving providers are likely to function more sustainably, as environmental awareness of people is increasing.

In organising events that support local culture, the most active are older companies or companies that offer a smaller number of overnight stays. The latter can be attributed to the fact that older companies have already introduced a tradition that enables them to work more easily and more actively with the local environment. In addition, business that have already reached the level at which they can focus on such local projects, while younger companies remain engaged in projects in the start-up phase.

Guests in the purchase of local products are most encouraged by the youngest companies, which operate from one to three years or from four to six years. This is also confirmed by the connection, where we included the number of overnight stays, as the larger companies are the most active in promoting guests. Also, younger companies are somewhat more active in raising guests' awareness of water and electricity saving methods. The result can be explained by the fact that companies with a higher number of overnight stays also consume more raw materials, which makes them seek to be more economical in this area. Raising guests' awareness and actually carrying out such activities by guests can lead to more efficient savings, which has a positive impact on both the nature and the company's business.

The analysis showed that younger companies are those who are leading in the offer of using environmentally friendly means of transport. Given the number of overnight stays, the use of such means of transportation mainly offered by the companies which are offering between 10 and 20 or more than 20 overnights. The result is expected, since younger companies are the ones that pay more attention to the sustainable aspects than the older ones. Also from a profitability perspective, the offer of such means of transport is the most rational in the larger companies, where economies of scale in the means of transport will be applied.

Interpretation of individual statistical links indicates that providers operating from one to three years or from four to six years are more perceptive in including the concept of sustainability in the operation of glamping accommodation compared to older companies. Depending on the number of overnight stays, more intensively sustainable business can be detected in glamping accommodation which offers between 10 and 20 beds.

Lessons learned for more successful integration of the concept of sustainable development into glamping accommodation

The survey showed that, in general, clamping providers are including very well the concept of sustainability in their business models. However, in the future, they will require to focus even better in this area and ensure greater direction of sustainable development into their business.

In the following text, we have presented several ways in which glamping accommodation providers can provide a more sustainable business. For example:

- saving energy and water;
- the relationships between employees and guests;
- contributing to the well-being of local communities;

This guidance is mainly summarised in the Travelife environmental travel guide (Travelife, b.d.).

Method 1: Energy saving

Energy saving can first be started with the regular shut-off of lights and other electrical devices when not in operation. This can significantly extend the life of devices and lights, less maintenance is required, and costs are also significantly reduced. However, regular shutdown can also become a constant by using automatic switch off lights and devices. It is also important to educate employees on how to save energy and, consequently, to implement the latter on their side. It is also recommended to use energy-saving machines and appliances to save energy (ibid., Page 3).

Method 2: Use Energy-saving lights

Many accommodation facilities are predominantly supplied with classical lights, which can be quite energy-consuming, as they can contribute up to 25% of the total cost of electricity consumption. It is therefore a good idea for suppliers to replace classical lights with economical ones. The best alternative is LEDs that are environmentally friendly, have a longer lifetime and use even less electricity (Tihec, 2017).

Method 3: Reduce water flow in bathrooms

In the bathroom, it drains into an empty lot of clean drinking water. The most is consumed when showering and flushing toilets. However, small changes can bring great water saving effects, which can save a lot of energy. The water flow in conventional shower systems is quite high and therefore consumes excessive water and energy. It is recommended to use systems that allow the flow of water to be only up to 10 litres per minute, which can be achieved quite easily and also cheap (Travelife, b.d., Page 2). One of the options for saving water is the installation of flow restrictors or air vents that are installed on pipes or showers. It is also recommended to use thermostatic fittings to adjust the water temperature and cause the hot water to flow out immediately (Ozmec, 2017) at the moment the user opens the tap.

Method 4: Re-use of towels and bedding

Daily change of bedding and towels is still a practice in more than 70% of all accommodation facilities around the world. With re-use providers, they can save a lot of money both in electricity and in water, which is consequently also more environmentally friendly. Flexible change also brings other benefits such as longer bedding and towels, less need for repair of washing machines and irons, less wastewater and less chemicals (Travelife, b.d., Page 3).

Method 5: Careful handling of waste

In addition to regular and careful separation of waste, it is recommended that providers try to minimise the amount of waste as much as possible. This can be achieved by reducing consumption, reusing and recycling. Providers should avoid buying products in small individual packs and disposable cups and dishes as much as possible. They can reuse bottles or encourage guests to fill their bottles with water from larger water fountains. It is recommended that they print on both sides of the paper and use refillable cartridges. It is necessary to recycle paper, glass, plastic, metal products, steel, copper and brass, used cooking oil and motor oil (ibid., Page 2).

Method 6: Integration and fair treatment of employees

Accommodation providers can contribute a lot to the more successful business by creating an efficient and friendly environment for employees. Well-motivated and rewarded employees perform their work more efficiently and better, which consequently leads to improved guest experience. In order to improve employee relations even better, it is recommended that providers check employees' salaries (are they are high enough), enable employees to complete and educate themselves in additional skills, providing some additional benefits to employees, such as free meals, organising team building, etc. (ibid.).

Method 7: Work locally

It is good that providers buy as much as possible from the services and products of local producers as they contribute to a more successful development of the local community.

In addition, with the help of local products, providers can create a unique offer, so they can improve their reputation and record more successful business. Suppliers can buy food, souvenirs and other hand-made products, furniture, cosmetics and clothing from the local community. Providers can also encourage guests to buy local products through organising social evenings that allow guests to contact the local community, or invite local souvenir makers to demonstrate their products (ibid.) to their guests.

Conclusion

In this case study, we have presented the concept of glamping, current trends and a specific example from Slovenia. We found that such clamping accommodation prevails on the American continent, followed by Australia and New Zealand and then Europe (Glamping Hub, b.d.a). Glamping is based on nature and sustainability, but it offers tourists a bit more comfort and luxury. Demand is rising, and as a result, pressure on the environment is increasing. Therefore, we carried out a survey in which we tried to recognise whether providers know the concept of sustainable development and whether they take into account the concept of sustainable development in their business. The survey was carried out in Slovenia, which ranked 14th in terms of the number of glamping accommodations in the world. According to the demand on the Google web browser, it reached the second place on the world in 2017 (Spitler, 2017). We conducted a survey among glamping providers that allow tourists to stay throughout the year-round. Through the results of the research, we wanted to prove the importance and role of such types of accommodation, which they represent the implementation of sustainable aspects in their operation of accommodation facilities.

The research we undertook covered 30 providers with year-round tourist offer of glamping accommodation. Twenty-two providers answered the survey, which is the base pattern of the survey. The research is based on a statistical analysis, which gives us a good insight into the knowledge of the concept of sustainable development of tourism and its implementation in the performance of glamping providers.

In the survey, we assumed that Slovenian providers of glamping accommodation, which provide a year-round tourist offer, are well aware of the sustainable development of tourism. According to the results, we can confirm the correctness of the thesis, as the providers are aware that for successful sustainable development, environmental awareness of both themselves and visitors and society is necessary. In addition to environmental awareness, successful sustainable development also requires the preservation of cultural heritage and the natural environment, which is also agreed by all providers. According to the analysis carried out in the SPSS program, providers who operate from one to three years or from four to six years are more aware of sustainable development than the ones who are in this business even longer.

We also assumed that the majority of Slovenian glamping providers, which offer a year-round tourist offer, already implemented these measures in order to achieve higher level of sustainable development in tourism. We can only partially confirm this, as most providers successfully implement measures to achieve sustainable development, but they are not fully implemented. The results of the sustainable policy record in the company strategy are encouraging, since all providers are registered, but rarely anyone is using the environmental schemes. The least of the measures for achieving sustainability are implemented in environmental management, since they mostly do not acquire electricity from renewable energy sources, while non-organic products are still used more frequently in washing and cleaning, and they use rainwater and wastewater only in small quantities.

With the help of the analysis carried out in the SPSS program, we found out that the integration of the concept of sustainable development is more successful within providers that are doing business for a short time, which is from one to three years and four to six years. This can be linked to the fact that people are generally more and more ecologically and sustainably aware. In addition, tourists are increasingly demanding, which is reflected in the growing inquiries for sustainable housing, which is why the number of such accommodations is increasing. The analysis also showed that the concept of sustainability in glamping accommodation operations is most successfully implemented by providers offering between 10 and 20 beds.

With the help of the research, we have confirmed that glamping plays a significant role in the implementation of sustainable development in the operation of accommodation facilities. We found out that greater luxury and comfort does not always mean more pollution and pressure on the environment, but we realised that in the concept of glamping, it can be a manner that represents a unique offer, which is located in pristine nature with wonderful views and, at the same time, offers comfort based on durability, which is actually a luxury. Considering that glamping on the tourist market has been officially inaugurated for just over 10 years, we can conclude that the concept of sustainable development in the operation of such facilities will only be present more and more intensively. The latter applies to destinations around the globe, where glamping is already occurring and also where it is currently not yet available. The fact is that people are becoming more and more aware of the importance of sustainable development and consequently, they are more attracted to the sustainability-based offer, which works well for glamping.

Reflections

1   Sustainable practices can be integrated in five business areas, which are company strategy, internal business, management of the supply chain, product management, raising awareness and cooperation with the destination.
2   Glamping is a composite word of "glamorous" and "camping". It is a campsite that is in touch with nature, while it offers the comfort of a hotel, similar to a kind of mobile hotel room.
3   The total number of glamping accommodation around the globe is approximately 33.000. Most glamping sites can be found in North America, followed by Australia and New Zealand and then Europe.
4   There are many different types of glamping, which differ in shape, material from which they are built, location of object, etc. The number of individual forms of glamping today is 27.
5   The demand for glamping has increased dramatically in the last decade, which has led to the establishment of a special category of trips on the tourism market. Trend also indicates the seasonality of glamping, where it is possible to detect the greatest demand in the summer months.
6   Providers can provide more sustainable business in a several ways, for example with energy saving through the regular shut-off lights, reducing water flow in bathrooms, re-using of towels and bedding, careful handling of waste, integration and fair treatment of employees and with working locally.

Questions

1   What are six key principles of a concept of ecotourism?
2   What is the definition of glamping?
3   Why is glamping growing trend in the tourism market?
4   Where does glamping originate?
5   How many different types of glamping exist? Define five of them.
6   Which methods can be used in order to reduce negative impacts on the environment?

Further reading

Drumm, A. and Moore, A. (2005). *An Introduction to Ecotourism Planning* (Vol. 1.). Arlington, VA, The Nature Conservancy.
Font, X. and Cochrane, J. (2005). *Integrating Sustainability into Business, an Implementation Guide for Responsible Tour Coordinators.* Paris, United Nations Environment Programme.
Giraldo, A. and Koschwitz, G. (2008). *Corporate Social Responsibility (CSR): Guidelines CSR – Reporting in Tourism.* Stuttgart, KATE.
Greening the WSSD Initiative. (2003). *Responsible Tourism Handbook: A Guide to Good Practice for Tourism Operators.* Johannesburg, Greening the WSSD Initiative.
UNEP and WTO. (2005). *Making Tourism More Sustainable; A Guide for Policy Makers.* France, Spain, United Nations Environment Programme and World Tourism Organization.

References

Adamič, L. (2012). *Uresničevanje trajnostnega razvoja turizma: primer slovenskih organizatorjev potovanj.* (Magistrsko delo). Univerza v Ljubljani, Ekonomska fakulteta, Ljubljana.
Bodi eko. (2011, September 19). Kaj je ekoturizem. Pridobljeno iz. www.bodieko.si/kaj-je-ekoturizem. *Bodi eko.* 25.5.2018.
Borštnik, B. (2013). *MP intervju: Peter Ličen – Lushna.* Mladi podjetnik. Pridobljeno iz. http://mladipodjetnik.si/podjetniski-koticek/mp-intervju/mp-intervju-peter-licen-lushna, 4.1.2018.
Drumm, A. and Moore, A. (2005). *An Introduction to Ecotourism Planning* (Vol. 1.). Arlington: The Nature Conservancy.
Glamping Hub. (b.d.a). Pridobljeno iz. https://glampinghub.com/, 04.01.2019.
Glamping Hub. (b.d.b). *Types of Glamping.* Pridobljeno iz. https://glampinghub.com/types-of-glamping/, 7.1.2018.
Glamping.com. (2017). Forecast Top Five 2018 Experiential Travel Trends, 24.10.2017. *Cision, PRWeb.* Pridobljeno iz. www.prweb.com/releases/2017/10/prweb14834438.htm, 13.1.2018.
Kraševec, V. (2009). *Primera ekološkega turizma v Sloveniji.* (Diplomsko delo). Univerza v Ljubljani, Ekonomska fakulteta, Ljubljana.
Ozmec, S. (2017, September 18). Varčevanje z vodo se začne v kopalnici. *Delo in dom.* Pridobljeno iz. www.deloindom.si/kopalnica/varcevanje-z-vodo-se-zacne-v-kopalnici, 8.3.2018.
Spitler, L. (2017, December 14). Going glamping? [Web log post]. Pridobljeno iz. www.sabre.com/insights/going-glamping/, 22.12.2017.
Suša, R., Vodopivec, B. and Brecelj, G. (2011). *Nova destinacija: odgovornost. Kako delovati skladno z načeli pravične trgovine in odgovornega turizma? Nabor idej za lokalne skupnosti, podjetja in posameznike.* Ljubljana, Društvo za človekove pravice in človeku prijazne dejavnosti Humanitas.

Ternovšek Kolar, E. (2017). *Arhitekturna interakcija narave- glamping ob jezeru.* (Diplomsko delo). Univerza v Mariboru, Fakulteta za gradbeništvo, prometno inženirstvo in arhitekturo, Maribor.

Tihec, S. (2017, June 16). Od varčnih čim prej do led sijalk. *Varčujem z energijo.* Pridobljeno iz. www.varcevanje-energije.si/novice-rss-zanimivosti/od-varcnih-cim-prej-do-led-sijalk.html, 8.3.2018.

Travelife. (b.d.). *Sustainable Tourism Is Good for Business.* London: Travelife. 15.08.19

Wikipedia. (2017). *Glamping.* Pridobljeno iz. https://en.wikipedia.org/wiki/Glamping, 6.1.2018.

Part C

The business impacts of ethical sustainable development

25 Queensland-Gold Coast tourism, the Japanese era 1980–1997 and single market strategies

A case study

Lesley Crowe-Delaney

Overview

This case study will briefly touch on this tourism phenomenon and includes an interview with one of the major players in Queensland at the time. However, first, this period needs to discuss the type of tourism in Queensland at the time, a synopsis that provides at once a voyeuristic account and one that overnight caused a sensation that was to mimic other coastal destinations worldwide-holiday hospitality.

Introduction – trade and tourism

In February 2016, several universities met at a two-day symposium with tourism and wine industry stakeholders and role-players to discuss the tourism industry, wine and gourmet foods. Under the banner of Are You China-Ready, an industry education accreditation supported by the Tourism Council Western Australia in conjunction with the international body for China Accreditation® (2018) (Xia et al., 2018) the symposium was held at Margaret River, Western Australia. This region is already a well-established tourism destination holding various events and is a prime holiday coastal destination, with holiday and second homes and a local population with schools, Technical & Further Education and a small university campus. Local and international industry, academic, government and financial folk discussed the 'latest ideas' in attracting and keeping China tourists and investors in the region. Topics included managing the Chinese tourists, their accommodation, food, how to sell wine and other products to China.

The interest in this latest 'flavour of the month' single-focus tourism market (SFTM) had surpassed that of the Japanese tourist the popular single market of the late 1980s and early 1990s. As early as 2006, at The Council for Australasian Tourism and Hospitality Education (CAUTHE) conference at Victoria University, tourism academics and industry pundits were well aware that the Golden Week of August moved over 200 million Chinese annually since its inception just under a decade earlier. To attract even 5% to Australia would be a bonus to the economy there. These similar strategy topics to attract the Chinese tourist were used in the Queensland tourist strategies for retail, tourism and hospitality but with much less organised features. There are consequences in SFTM strategies where both industry and government tourism stakeholders and role-players still do not acknowledge the impacts of the Japanese tourism of that period. Loyalty to foreign single-focussed tourism can be troublesome for tourism-focussed towns and localities.

History has a habit of repeating itself. Until 2007, Japan had held status with Australia as its largest trading partner for over 35 years. From 2008, China and Australian trade relations have become more contiguous, and in 2008, China became Australia's largest trading partner. Japan had overtaken Britain as Australia's largest export market where a significant margin still exists between these two markets. Chinese outbound tourism began to increase as China's visa policies relaxed, and its nationals had a spending ability. In 2017 the multi-entry visa has meant an ease of entrance into Australia (Xia et al., 2018, 15).

A note: research and industry

Looking at the early 21st-century webpages of tourism clusters throughout academic institutions in Australia, there is a danger of a precedent being set that research focusses entirely on one market at a time in a kind of one-way relationship tunnel. In this current tourism climate, for Australia and the rest of the world, it is China. However, in the 1980s through to the early 1990s, it was Japan. The Australian tourism landscape focus was Queensland and Sydney. For the Japanese, any natural curiosity of an outside world was further prompted by the government-owned tourism agencies with aggressive advertising campaigns. They also owned the majority of Japanese-focused tourism souvenir and goods shops in the early stages in Queensland. Very little information remains regarding these outlets, the agencies and tourism operators. This was always controversial as connections within the Queensland Joh Bjelke-Petersen government were rumoured with Japanese and other foreign and local developers (Mitchell, 2015).

Japanese tourists and property acquisition

Whilst Japanese international tourism expansion from the 1980's had a global impact, Japanese tourists also began to dominate the more popular Australian tourist destinations, including Queensland. It is uncertain whether Queensland tourist providers and property developers were surprised by the groups of Japanese, particularly since there were few Asian tourists in Queensland at this time. However, the influx of Japanese tourists also resurrect latent fears amongst some members of the population who related to the threat of Japanese invasion of Queensland in the 1941–1945 period, when there were extensive military camps throughout the state. Such attitudes created a complex dichotomy between the views of local residents and those of inward investors. Thus on 29th November 1980, the central coastal town of Yepoon was bombed by protesters causing AUD200,000 of damage. The purchasing of the militarily iconic Lone Pine Koala Sanctuary and a subsequent 177 ha of bushland in Redbank Plains to supplement the sanctuary by Japanese investment company Kimihito-Kanko led to a public furore of a former enemy purchasing a commemorative-named site. Along with other large property acquisitions by wealthy and prominent Japanese, some who had survived imprisonment in WWII, this was seen as a betrayal to locals who still held WWI ANZAC and Gallipoli in their hearts due to family loss and more recent losses in WWII. This became a national debate and the anti-Japanese sentiment to property ownership ensued. Public demonstrations and the upcoming Queensland and federal elections threatened change and right-wing policies, and the White Australia Policy empathy was again reignited in the minds of fearful Australians (Hajdu, 2005, 104–126).

That the now popular coastal areas of Queensland were developed by British, Sydney and Melbourne developers, decades earlier, was forgotten in this heated period due to local media reporting, television and radio reports. One of the well-known local entrepreneurs who attended every opening of a development was Max Christmas of Max Christmas Pty Ltd. Actually, the Gold Coast was a frenzy of excitement and wealth, and at the same time, a 365-day lifestyle that attracted many international investors as well as Australians. Queensland mineral resources, particularly coal, were entangled in all this debate, but the trade continued (ibid.).

For Japanese and the global community, an insularity from international understanding had developed due to two hundred years of exclusion, followed by two world wars and re-integration into the global relationships of its once declared 'enemies' (McCormack, 1994; Tada, 2000). Yet trade and tourism thrived and emigration grew. By the 1980s approximately 1,000 Japanese found Southeast Queensland an escape from their homeland. These residents and tourists were separate social groups. Retirees and some younger families established a lifestyle on the Gold Coast region, filling jobs that required their Japanese language skills, understanding of Japanese business and the like (Denman, 2014, 17–26). These permanent residents left their home country where, as noted in the Japanese chapter (*please see Section 1, Chapter 12, Part C*), historically the Japanese as tourists have enjoyed and expected, a cultural experience of good hospitality, one that services the guest from welcome to goodbyes and generations of tourism language (Moeran, 1983).

The mass tourism phenomenon of the Japanese outbound market of the 1980s was an international experience and one which mirrors the Chinese mass market in the second decade of the 21st century. The Japanese government had deregulated the Japanese airline industry and was strongly advised by the US government to repair the US-Japan trade imbalance. To remedy this imbalance, one strategy was for luxury goods and leisure industry brands such as golf to enter the Japanese home market (Donzé and Fujioka, 2015). The other strategy was for the Japanese government to aim for 10 million outbound travellers and encouraged their outbound tourists to spend. The Japanese had already experienced the luxury market, but luxury items and leisure activities in Japan were expensive for desiring middle-income earners who found these unaffordable as the cost of living was rising as was the disposable income, the highest it had been since the Supreme Commanders of the Allied Powers had left Japan under a new constitution following its defeat in WWII.

By the 1980s, the Japanese had a high disposable income and greater purchasing power than Australia which offered a bargain to purchase less expensive luxury goods, to play on the branded golf courses and to stay in international status 4 and 5 star hotels as well as those provided by Japanese property and construction companies such as Daikyo Kanko and Kumagai-gumi. This was part of the 'two-way' tourist flow expected by the Japanese government as it realised the income potential of tourism (Cha et al., 1995). Japanese tourists knew the value of the US dollar as well and utilised it in the Australian tourist destinations. This initially caused issues such as cash flow and travellers' cheques. Credit cards were mostly used by American tourists.

Single-focus tourism markets

Immature SFTM is a term coined for the purpose of this case study. It is where a national market is new to tourism (or a new generation stemming from previous generations who have reduced their travel) and has, at the same time, a per capita disposable with this freedom and ability to travel internationally. For the host country, it is a major target for marketing and advertising, encouraged to make certain and major adjustments to its tourism and hospitality systems in order to attract the SFTM to encourage spending. Japan was one of the first post-WWII nations to allow its citizens to travel internationally for tourism *en masse*. Pre-WWII, it was predominantly either the wealthy who undertook foreign tourism or Japanese academics – for example geographers and anthropologists.

Some background: Gold Coast tourism in the 1950s–1960s

By the period of 1980–1997, Queensland, and in particular Surfers Paradise and the Gold Coast, was already a tourism mecca. From the 1920s it was promoted as a place of health, fun and later fabulous locations for Rest and Recreation (R & R) for the visiting American troops of WWII. While tourism-based infrastructure boomed from the 1950s, it was not until the 1960s that growth occurred in a different fashion and architecture from the laid-back appeal of camping, caravanning and simple beach houses. Development along the coastal highway and near the beaches included hotels and (drive-in) motels, high-rise accommodation, large second or holiday homes. Eventually early canal development of the marshes and mangroves led to the latest architectural homes for the wealthy Australians and self-repatriated Americans who returned after WWII.

Coastal urbanism has been a strong factor in tourism development of the Gold Coast and Surfers Paradise. More rural developments on the nearby islands of Tangalooma, Bribie and Stradbroke were also holiday havens for the local Brisbane and suburbs populations. While Tangalooma was a popular 'watering hole', the other islands were destinations for family stays; eventually as they gentrified, they were holiday destinations for 'southerners' holiday makers from Victoria and NSW. Tourism, of course, in Queensland was not just based on a single market, although Americans and English were the international tourists of this period. The Gold Coast was developed early between the two world wars; it certainly did not grow as a tourist destination overnight. Holiday making in Australia after WWII depended on several factors: to own a car, to be able to afford fuel and to have the time to travel. From the 1950s, the Gold Coast and Brisbane became a tourist destination for Australian travellers, who mostly travelled by car and bus.

Prior to the 1950s–1960s tourism developments began to change the Australian Gold Coast landscape from a natural, unbuilt environment focused on the beach camping scenario to the development of hotel accommodation. By the late 1960s and early 1970s, further accommodation development meant that numerous multi-storied accommodation for some early campers who would travel to the Gold Coast could now enjoy a new Miami style coastal holiday experience.

There was a homogeneity of Australian and adopted American culture. Long gone were the Las Vegas named hotels such as the Beachcomber and the Silver Sands hotels, replaced by newer hotels and skyscraper apartments. The Pink Poodle hotel sign, remnants of the Surfers Paradise iconicism, is an indicator of the American culture that was introduced following the R & R for the Allied troops in the state in the 1940s; the American boom of the 1960s architecture led to the American tourism hotel styles (Laughlin, 2015).

There was a strong comparison to the United States holiday resorts for the middle-income groups, with street names being Americanised as a result of US military settling in the area. Developers were either US based or had been impressed by US coastal tourism culture. Though the landscape had changed local communities, entrepreneurs had adapted to this area of the coast with schools, hospitals and public facilities and administrative buildings planned separately from the tourism zones. Account must also be taken of the engagement of US forces in Queensland during WWII as they sought to manage the potential Japanese threat against Australia. Yet it was not a just European threat, but a Japanese one. As controversial research now indicates, the threats of invasion being confused with incapacitation (Wilson, 2002): due to the Sydney harbour discovery of two man submarines and the fatal bombings on Darwin 19th February 1942. Despite these immediate past issues, Trade was re-established with Australia from the late 1950s. By the time of the 1960 World Expo, which was held in Tokyo with and industry staff introduction programmes such as with Nissan car manufacturers (Private communication with a former Nissan engineer) and with later educational scholarships to Japan for language and cultural studies, Japan seemed to be re-entering the global economy and establishing trade relationships.

The scenario 1980–1997

The fear of Japan was reignited when tourists from Japan discovered Queensland in the 1980s. It was also the heyday of Japanese tourism to the state, the development of tourism infrastructure and the lifestyle of the time that this author spent in the industry. Queensland tourism was swept up and invigorated by the promise of increased profits, safari-suited, white leather shod entrepreneurs, that as rapidly plummeted to economic despair.

Local and Australian tourists were shunned by retailers quick to take up the Japanese customer who had a desire to spend on the various array of foreign and local goods on sale. Japanese language 'barkers' in the street touted to any free independent travellers (FITs) who spilled out of the regimented bus tour groups. Increasingly this cacophony was bilingual as those retailers who could not supply the Japanese realised that non-Japanese tourists had money to spend as well. However, the luxury goods retailers quickly took up leaseholds of shiny new developments and the lower market retailers found this a difficult competition. Street signs in Japanese, large Japanese signs with small English subtitles or none at all, restaurants catering only in Japanese language for Japanese tourists also increased at the lower end markets. This scenario drove away the 'bread and butter' tourists (Executive of Daikyo Kanko, 2019).

Development

Development was rapid. Swathes of condominium apartments along the coastline and into the hinterland often meant that any bush environment could be chain dragged (often at night) and completely cleared for the breaking of ground the next day. This caused local anguish as locals felt that their homes would be also taken up for redevelopment, and they were as large amounts of money were paid for small pieces of sand blocks. High-rise apartments filled with Japanese tourists, owners or renters led to an uncomfortable co-habitation. As the hinterland developed into Nerang, local Queensland people sold to the developers and moved to comfortable homes, but which had limited retail and supermarket access.

Tourism development on the Gold Coast and Surfers Paradise had followed a growth pattern of development and upgrades. From repaint of the Cavill Avenue hotel corner that remained an open window bar for beer-swilling locals and holiday makers in the summer to the gradual changes the Hard Rock Café, the redevelopment of the Lennon and Chevron Hotels, the Oasis gardens shopping centre and the Raptis Plaza with the copy of statue of David, gardens and fountains amidst coffee shops, restaurants and fashion boutiques which gracefully led to the extensive food courts to the Sheraton Hotel.

Along the main highway were cheaper goods stores fitting in amongst the Japanese-only stores. The Queensland government allowed the Japanese to develop tourism retail outlets, hotels and golf resorts in the main established tourist hubs, as was tourism and hospitality, and food industries. This was a controversial relationship which incorporated graft and corruption rumours. In a period of political upheaval, controversy and eventual downfall of the longest sitting premier in Australia, Joh Bjelke-Petersen, Queensland tourism flourished in particular areas (Mitchell, 2015).

On the Gold Coast first and then later at Cairns and Townsville, Japanese tourism agencies expanded their souvenir shops, real estate companies and offices filled Cavil Avenue, as shorts-only men, tourists and locals strolled around the Cavill Avenue ('Cav-Av') district of Surfers Paradise. No longer do these tourists and locals just look at the bikini-clad meter maids, but also at busloads of queuing Japanese tourists. At first, private local bus companies were hired to move the tourists with Japanese travel guides who had limited English, to several hotels in and around the shopping precinct.

The 1980s, however, was also the boom time of the Japanese economy. The Gold Coast skies in the Cavill Avenue quarter quickly filled with towering cranes to build even higher multi-storied hotels. The Gold Coast was a rush of competitive unfettered development. American, Canadian and Australian property developers quickly took the opportunity to fill the accommodation needs of the area. Intent on keeping low-priced accommodation, local motel owners of un-renovated 1960's accommodation competed with up-market and luxury-end high-rise hotels. The 1982 Commonwealth Games attracted a broad international attention to Queensland and Surfers Paradise became a busier holiday playground.

Tourism in the 1981 period was being recognised as a growth industry, nationally employing over 5% of the workforce and contributing the 5% to Australia's GDP. Domestic tourism was 85% of the tourist expenditure, and international growth was gaining industry interest. By 1985, tourists from Japan, Singapore, Malaysia and Hong Kong had overtaken America as the main source of visitors (Tisdell, 1987). By the end of the 1980s, from the Surfers Paradise boardwalk to Southport and to Broad beach, the overuse of the area, constant redevelopments, new construction and crowded streets and pavements led to a contrasting tourism environment from the earlier pristine beaches. Locals and Australian tourists accepted the Japanese tourists and vice versa. Not only had the Japanese tourists brought extra investment interest to this already established but by now this rather tawdry entertainment sector, with drab peripheral tourist accommodation extending to Southport, but a new tourist attraction in itself grew for the low-budget accommodation tourist, Japanese and Korean university student and working tourist market. This was in older holiday homes and rundown motels.

The pilot strike of 1989; the new direction for Gold Coast tourism

Already there were signs that Japanese tourism was a maturing market with more than just a focus on the coast. Brisbane was a popular city to add to the Surfers Paradise Gold Coast tours. Resort developments grew and attracted Japanese and other remaining wealthy tourists to Palm Meadows Golf Resort. The luxury market in Melbourne attracted tourists as did Sydney and even Western Australia. The very young tourism market of Western Australia (mostly based on accommodation) attracted international tourists to its wildflower attractions and other scenic phenomena. The Gold Coast entrepreneurs were showing signs of stress. High-end real estate sales were plateauing and retracting back to local markets with some pursuing the now incoming Korean investors. However, redevelopment of Southport and the hinterland meant that more affordable housing and holiday accommodation were available.

Then as quickly as the rise of the Gold Coast over this almost ten-year period, it came to a halt with the Australian pilot's strike of 1989 causing immediate havoc and a political fight that led to the military taking over many of the flights. This also led to the demise of two Australian airlines: Ansett Australia 1935–2002 and the short-lived Compass Airlines 1990–1993 closure while others amalgamated. A local restaurant magazine DiningOut recorded 30 restaurant closures a month in the strike period (Executive of Daikyo Kanko, 2019). This led to a political upheaval in Australia as the Prime Minister Bob Hawke had accused the pilots of a glorification of their roles, media translated it to 'glorified bus drivers' (Hawke, 1989).

Impact of the Japanese economy

The Japanese economy had been affected by several impacts to its economy. The 1973 oil shock led to high oil prices and inflation compared to wage growth. It was cheaper to live as a tourist than to live in Japan. The pressure from the Japanese government for its nationals to travel in order to ease the US-Japanese trade imbalance took its toll on middle-income savings. The higher cost of other macroeconomic factors including the cost of building materials for the construction industry, the only sector that had any growth in this period, together with other pressures for the Japanese economy was taking its toll and a recession was rolling in, despite manipulation, subsidisation and other more dubious measures (McCormack, 1996; Jiménez-Rodríguez and Sánchez, 2012).

Once the mass tourism trips slowed, the Japanese owned travel agencies and retail outlets closed their premises. This further impacted other businesses in the Surfers Paradise area and led to a change in the overall tourist strip of the Gold Coast. Its tourism industry, devoid of its big spending Japanese visitors as well as Cairns taking up a relaxed lifestyle for these outdoors and laid-back tourists, began to crumble like the roman ornamentation it had depicted. 'Last days of sale' signs were rapidly followed by 'For Lease' signs. The commercial real estate industry had suffered and commercial property sales declined, instead leasing became an option. By then, however, the Japanese national economy had moved into stagnation and the Japanese government had appealed to its people to become conservative in their leisure spending and to travel judiciously. Additionally, the Joh Bjelke-Petersen government had used the last of its highly controversial methods to obtain power, construction and expansive developments.

What remained of the development period of the 1980s for Queensland with a focus on the southern region between Beenleigh and Caloundra meant that tourism and construction minister Russ Hinze was able to finalise the last of the massive transportation system that was arguable ten year too late for domestic tourists to travel from Brisbane to the Gold Coast to fill the tourist void left by the Japanese. Domestic real estate also fell as wealthy Japanese visitors and temporary visa holders moved elsewhere in Australia to more stable economic regions and real estate investments were sold at a loss to South Koreans, who were willing to take up bargains (Mullins, 1991, 332).

The end of the golden era

By the 1990s, Japanese tourists did what other tourists did, lived the life of locals or chose their own accommodation and travel experiences. The Japanese economy was already in a free fall as the Japanese economy began to retract into what was to become the ten-year recession. Otherwise spending money on accommodation, food and organised outdoor activities such as windsurfing or jet skiing, Japanese tourists straight from college or university studies and before serious employment were a younger cohort who also enjoyed cycling and surfing locally, gaining deep suntans, blonding their hair, wearing the beach clothes of the locals and generally 'laying back'. Others took long cycling journeys and it was not unusual for them to be seen along the highways of Queensland to Melbourne, or on longer trips across the Nullarbor in the heat of summer.

By 2002, Australia had lost one of its oldest national airline carriers, and Japan's airlines, tourism industry and domestic economy became heavily dependent on government subsidisation and the construction industry. Peppered throughout were SARs and terrorism.

The Gold Coast had become a seedy and dangerous tourist hub and Surfers Paradise has retained this image, even though infrastructure has been updated and an international events calendar that includes the Gold Coast Indy 300 (1991–2008) and the 600 motor racing events.

Another peak time is now schoolies week, the last weeks in November after Year 12 examinations are completed (Surething, 2019). The area is filled with under-age tourists, extra police who try to fend off drug dealers and bad social behaviours. For two weeks schoolies 'week' makes the destination undesirable and unsafe for other tourists. Now inevitable are the deaths and permanent injuries of young people as a result of the promotion of concerts, a sense of freedom to drink alcohol and take illegal drugs.

Insider's stories

As a role-player and stakeholder in the tourism industry in Brisbane and the Gold Coast in the 1980s–1990s, in that first five years, I witnessed the daily bombardment of Japanese tourists into downtown Gold Coast alighting from buses hired by Japanese tourist agencies, and shepherded to Japanese-owned restaurants, souvenir shops the size of small department stores and other Japanese-titled retail outlets and businesses. Group tourism was fashionable in that period as many Japanese found that their English lessons from secondary school and college days (mostly US based) were not sufficient for managing the Australian drawl. The Queenslanders too were not prepared for the intimate transaction language required, and idiomatic language, loudly expressed, did not stand the test of tourist time.

Non-Japanese-owned businesses gradually gave way to this, hiring Japanese staff, non-native speakers or just placing window signage and Japanese descriptions of products. The local government council helped a great deal. Producing bi-lingual signage, it directed non-group Japanese tourists (mostly honeymooners and business men) to the Japanese-centric tourism districts. Such Japan-town tourism streets, repelled the Australian tourist, determined to experience his tourism ethnocentrism as far away as possible from the former potential invaders of coastal Queensland. Pockets of Japanese-focussed districts became no-go districts for 'Aussie' tourists, while staff and business owners in the non-Japanese areas of small retail and cafes could make it difficult for the Japanese tourist who often walked out of shops and cafes unserved or poorly treated.

Compounding this was the large-scale Japanese developments. Palms Meadow Golf Course, the ANA Hotel, the Gold Coast International and high-end restaurants such as Yamagen, owned by Daikyo Kanko, hosted and entertained Japanese multi-millionaires. They were served exclusive foods and drank thousand-dollar bottles of wine and alcohol made in Australia or exclusive imports. Japanese-only female staff, specially migrated for short-term services in the hospitality industry and administration, would attend within the decadence of comfort, dining and leisure. The atmosphere was always as the *nomikai* or drinking group, as much as staff within the company as between company directors as well.

At each opening of a large-scale development, equally large and decadent celebrations were held, including the flying out of visiting guests, such as government VIPs and their entire families from Japan. These would include major shareholders and Japanese government officials, mostly from the developer's prefectures, their wives and children, sometimes parents if the business were several generations owned. Australian officials were mid-level government office bearers or public-sector staff, mostly on their own. The Queensland premier and vice premier of the day rarely attended any of these ceremonies.

In that period of time and in a social climate that precluded political correctness, social inclusion and where sexism, age-ism and celebrity was manifested in the tourism and hospitality industry, the end of the economic boom in Japan (mid 1990s) was not considered and the heyday of the Gold Coast was at its zenith as every new high-rise hotel was marked by openings of decadence, grandeur and celebrity.

Medium to small businesses rode on the economic wave of the big corporations from Australia, Canada, the USA opening Sanctuary Cove and real estate development for canal housing, Pacific Fair shopping centre and a monorail. It was the Japanese who made the greatest cultural impact in terms of tourism and property development, even attracting the location of Australian rules football field in Carrara, near Daikyo's exclusive golf course, Palm Meadows.

Conclusion: a tourism divided

From the late 1880s until the 1950s, property investors and an early tourism industry had focussed on tourism, attracting lifestyles changers, later retirees, housing development for those American and Australian soldiers who decided to live in Queensland. An ageing population and a tourism industry, while internationally focussed, also attracted its fair share of domestic tourists. For locals, they saw the Japanese tourism agency behaviours of herding their customers into the Japanese-owned souvenir shops to purchase goods to take home to Japan, or to have them sent by Japanese couriers. These people were quickly herded out again onto air-conditioned buses and whisked away to capture glimpses and take passing photographs of the beaches, people and animal parks. These tourists were then directed into Japanese-owned hotels, such as the Gold Coast International.

In terms of Australian media, however (Tada notes, 2000), there was a negative media war, almost a striking up of a perceived takeover of Australia by 'Asian hordes' a term used by White Australia policy pundits about the Chinese who came to the gold mines in the 1880s!

Together with the local talk of the Japanese coming to claim what they could not take in WWII (a common phrase in real estate conversations) the reality for non-Japanese tourists was not being attended to if Japanese tourists were in a shop or kiosk, completely ignoring non-Japanese customers or bad sales service. Fun parks supplemented this tourist spillover demand and was well rewarded. However, this also created a divide where the Japanese mostly attended Movie World and SeaWorld only if their time afforded it or to get married in unusual and often ludicrous scenarios with Bugs Bunny or underwater with a dolphin. Marriage tourism became popular with Japanese Christians seeking our small chapels. Other marriages were also held in pseudo chapels as one-stop marriage experiences, where within hours a couple could choose the dress, chapel ceremony and celebrations to be held on the same day.

While this was an exciting and prosperous period for luxury brand retailers, others captured the spillover economic effects either from increasingly singles or couples Japanese tourists and other tourists who did not find the large bustle of hotels, discount stores and services to their liking. Product labelling in Japanese on store front signs and employment of Japanese language students in the largest retail department stores across Australia, were all strategies used to entice Japanese tourists and business people and encourage the parting of the hard earned, but value-for-dollar yen. Double degree translators, particularly in economics, business and accounting, were hired by the Japanese property developers to expedite government negotiations for planning permissions and property sales.

At the same time, the uptake of Japanese language in Australian schools and universities curricula included teachers of European languages expanding their skills to include Japanese basic language for introducing Japanese language into schools and the immigration of native language teachers from Japan. Universities courses that included Japanese language and studies experienced larger numbers of interested students. Those students initially saw their future employment in tourism and hospitality, both here and in Japan, or in industrial and the corporate sectors as interpreters and translators. For a few academically minded, a career in tertiary education and research beckoned.

The encouragement also came from Japan in the form of various scholarships, the establishment of sister-city trade and educational exchanges and collaboration. School resources developed and were introduced to assist non-native teachers to better engage their students, while grants for graduated scholars and the Japanese Exchange Teachers and Public sector exchanges drew Australia's brightest to Japan for temporary, but beneficial terms of stay and education.

Then came the crash of the Japanese economy. Cairns was the second exciting tourism destination and property development focus for local entrepreneurs to capitalise on the new wave of Japanese tourists suffered. The Japanese economic bubble had burst, and local Cairns opportunistic hoteliers, accommodation and tourism operators were left with expensive and over-inflated investments rapidly under booked. Mostly local investors did not prepare for a broad-based tourism industry and the collapse of the local economy was worse as the pilots' strike made for overnight empty rooms.

This double effect of the pilot strike caused the demise of many Australian and Australian-internationally supported companies who retreated to their home countries, such as a Canadian consortium at Sanctuary Cove. Discord was heard from disgruntled entrepreneurs. Japanese entrepreneurs of the retail, real-estate and restaurant sectors either sold their valueless investments or left them empty. The pilots suffered too as did suburbs as far south as Sunbury in Victoria, where many pilots lost their homes to bank for outstanding mortgages. Sunbury was never to recover to the luxury regional haven of airline pilots and engineers.

As Japan-bashing in the USA had yielded much literature in the academic and public fora, so too did the public dissent arise in Australia. Little attention had been paid to the local, Canadian and US withdrawal from the tourism and hospitality sector at the time, with the journalists leading the foray, encouraged by remnant of a white Australia attitudes in their readership. Meanwhile, Japan too had a perceived viewpoint of Australia (Tada, 2000), and the Australia debate was the fall of both Queensland Premier Joh Bjelke-Petersen and Australian Prime Minister Robert Lee Hawke.

In hindsight, research (Tada, 2000) has answered many questions of the tensions that lay between Japan and Australia 1970–1996. Prompted by media and later anti-Asian activists (and anti-Australian Japanese), it was evident that on the streets of the Gold Coast there was little tourist interaction with retail outlets divided into two sectors. Additionally, the comparatively cheap luxury goods market that included golf wear (and always had at least one Japanese speaker-salesperson on hand) and lower end retailers who welcomed Japanese with signage, also with a Japanese-speaking salesperson and gradually introducing Japanese desired products became the next wave of Japanese tourism. These tourists were tired of the regimental style of tourism in a country where other international tourists were happy to travel through freely at will.

The Japanese travel agencies did not want their tourists to wander. By the time Japanese mass tourism was entrenched in Australia, elsewhere in the world, Japanese tourists were making their own way. This meant that Japanese-owned retail souvenir shops were at risk of local and cheaper accommodation, recreation and other tourist activities.

Reflections

Single-focus tourist marketing for a specific market or country focus creates a shadow over overall visitor statistics (Anon, 2007). While visitor statistics are important obviously to watch trends and understand patterns, what visitors spend is also important and under what category they consider themselves as indicated in the chapter on Japan.

Data gathering includes sophisticated data collection, but there needs to be and awareness of the equally sophisticated way that Japanese tourists know how to add to survey material. Japanese citizens are used to census taking, surveys and questionnaires. Japanese employees in the past have had travel restrictions and, as Japanese employees working internationally, cannot always state that they will have been touring.

Underlying and outside factors contribute to uncertainty in tourism. What is certain is that particular incidents in modern tourism industry history should be acknowledged so that host industry role-players and stakeholders can learn to make home tourism industries more economically resilient. To a certain extent this has happened. Off-season deals, packages and other marketing tools can offset upcoming low incomes.

With better WEB 2.0 data crawling and the understanding of social media, hosts may now be able to protect themselves in times of tourist fluctuations and long-term changes in tourist behaviour. Selling gourmet meals and bottles of wine will not protect a tourist industry. Understanding the market and making decisions for business resilience and sustainable development for the tourism industry should be the focus and not just on a single-focus market tourism opportunity.

Questions

1 Consider why tourists are now referred to as visitors under the Tourism Research Australia's categorisation.
2 Why do you think that academic literature is scarce in this period of tourism activity?
3 What role do you think the media played, in this vacuum of informed research from academic and educational institutions, in portraying Japanese tourism in Australia?
4 Can sport be a tourism/entertainment/ event? Discuss.
5 What roles does academic literature now play in tourism knowledge acquisition?
6 What would you like to know in terms of the above case study? How will you best protect yourself from biased opinion?
7 What role do diaspora play in tourism growth in Australia? Consider and list the positives and negatives.
8 How will you manage stereotyping yourself and in others in the workplace?
9 What are the implications of single-market tourism strategies:

a   For rural and regional tourism industries
b   For city tourism?

10 Should single-market tourism be first on a lagging tourism economy?
11 Do state tourism strategies match national overarching statements?
12 Consider the papers by Tada and Hadju. Through comparison and contrast, discuss the role the media and academia play in Australian tourism studies.
13 What is a mature tourism market? What is an immature tourism market? Are these terms too simplistic?
14 Read McCormack's argument with Japan's then discuss this is a very torrid communique. How would you manage both protagonists should they come to a conference or event?

Further reading

Australian Government Department of Foreign Affairs and Trade. 2008. *Australia and Japan: How Distance and Complementarity Shape a Remarkable Commercial Relationship*.

Dredge, D. & Jamal, T. 2013. Mobilities on the Gold Coast, Australia: Implications for Destination Governance and Sustainable Tourism. *Journal of Sustainable Tourism*, 21:4, 557–579. doi:10.1080/09669582.2013.776064.

Executive of Daikyo Kanko. 2019. *RE: The Gold Coast 1980–1990*. Internal memo. Type to Crowe-Delaney, L.

Faulkner, B. 2002. Rejuvenating a Maturing Tourist Destination: The Case of the Gold Coast. *Current Issues in Tourism*, 5:6, 472–520.

National Archives Queensland beach culture.

Tourism Australia. 2019. *Direct Aviation Capacity from Japan to Australia* [Online]. Available: Tourism Asutralia.com.

References

Note: This author was an undergraduate and tourism industry consultant in Brisbane and the Gold Coast; the second informant was a senior executive of a tourism and leisure development company.

2018. *China Ready Accreditation Training Program* [Online]. Available: https://chinareadyandaccredited.com/about-us.

Anon. 2007. Drop in Japanese Tourists Worries Qld. *The Sydney Morning Herald*, July 18, 2017.

Cha, S., Mccleary, K. W. & Uysal, M. 1995. Travel Motivations of Japanese Overseas Travelers: A Factor-Cluster Segmentation Approach. *Journal of Travel Research*, 34, 33–39.

Denman, J. 2014. *Japanese lifestyle migrants in Southeast Queensland: Narratives of Long-Term Residency, Mobility and Personal Communities*. Honours: The University of Queensland.

Donzé, P.-Y. & Fujioka, R. 2015. European Luxury Big Business and Emerging Asian Markets, 1960–2010. *Business History*, 57, 822–840.

Executive of Daikyo Kanko. 2019. *RE: The Gold Coast 1980–1990*. Type to Crowe-Delaney, L.

Hajdu, J. 2005. *Samurai in the Surf: The Arrival of the Japanese on the Gold Coast in the 1980s*. Canberra, Australia: Pandanus Books.Hawke, R. 1989. Transcript of Doorstop, ABC Studio, Melbourne – 21 August 1989, 7719. *Doorstop*. Melbourne: Department of the Prime Minister and Cabinet.

Jiménez-Rodríguez, R. & Sánchez, M. 2012. Oil Price Shocks and Japanese Macroeconomic Developments. *Asian-Pacific Economic Literature*, 26, 69–83.

Laughlin, S. 2015. The Iconic Pink Poodle neon sign in Surfers Paradise to Feature on New Stamps. *Gold Coast Bulletin*, 31 August 2015. https://www.goldcoastbulletin.com.au/news/gold-coast/the-iconic-pink-poodle-neon-sign-in-surfers-paradise-to-feature-on-new-stamps/news-story/e8fd3f35947ecd5868226d021bcf4023.

Mccormack, G. 1994. Kokusaika, Nichibunken, and the question of Japan-Bashing. *Asian Studies Review*, 17, 166–172.

Mccormack, G. 1996. *The Emptiness of Japanese Affluence*. St. Leonards, Australia: Allen & Unwin.

Mitchell, A. 2015. Queensland: Knocking off the Hillbilly Dictator: Joh's Corruption Finally Comes Out. *Crikey*.

Moeran, B. 1983. The language of tourism. *Annals of Tourism Research*, 10, 93–108.

Mullins, P. 1991. Tourism Urbanization. *International Journal of Urban and Regional Research*, 15, 326–342.

Surething. 2019. *Schoolies Week* [Online]. Available: https://surething.com.au/schoolies/.

Tada, M. 2000. Japanese Newspaper Representations of Australia 1970–1996. *Journal of Australian Studies*, 24, 169–179.

Tisdell, C. 1987. Tourism, the Environment and Profit. *Economic Analysis and Policy*, 17, 13–30.

Wilson, S. 2002. Rethinking Nation and Nationalism in Japan. In: Wilson, S. (ed.) *Nation and Nationalism in Japan*. London: Routledge Curzon.

Xia, J. C., Crowe-Delaney, L., Holmes, K., Adriano, R., Zea, M. P. C., Li, Y. & Chen, Z. 2018. Are We China Ready? *Chinese Tourism in Western Australia*. Bankwest Curtin Economic Centre (ed.).

26 Managing a sustainable tourism destination

Aleksa Panić, Barbara Pavlakovič and Marko Koščak

Overview

As with any industry, tourism faces modifications that are stimulated with technological, social and environmental changes. New concepts of tourism have now emerged that understand tourism on a different, more socially responsible and educative way. Therefore, tourism has developed new branches which emphasise socio-ecological awareness, clear goals and a more comprehensive approach to tourism management. Tourists who are interested in this kind of tourism experience request a higher level of sustainable and responsible attention, which is more positive for local residents and assists in the promotion of local unique values – such as local culture, history, cuisine and events. Therefore, there is a need for well-organised tourism management which will gather all of these requirements and convert them to a unique tourism offer. There are many successful practices, not only in Europe but overseas, which could use as an example of good and sustainable tourism management. On the other hand, Belgrade, the capital of Serbia, struggles to achieve this kind of tourism attractiveness. Many complaints about the city's tourism offer are persistent, as well as criticisms regarding the sustainable and responsible standards and the cleanliness of the city. Because of that, this chapter will provide an overview of the current circumstances in Belgrade and also provide examples and suggestions on steps which require to be undertaken in order to create a better environment for both tourists and local society.

Introductory concept

With the massive development and popularisation of tourism, many countries quickly realised the numerous benefits of this industry. These benefits were primarily reflected in the fact that the development of tourism brings with it greater economic prosperity. In the middle of the 20th century, a tourist concept was being implemented which stimulated exclusively economic goals – i.e. to achieve as much profit as possible from tourism. Strengthening and spreading of traditional mass tourism in that period resulted in a real danger of devastation and the disappearance of resources and authenticity of tourist destinations. Motivated by this problem, at the end of the 20th century, individual countries began to advocate a greater role in the conservation of natural resources and the preservation of the ecosystem. This subsequently expanded to a range of connected social and cultural aspects and thereby created a completely new concept of sustainable tourism. The idea of sustainable tourism involves the use of local resources, but in a responsible and sustainable way; in addition, it engages in the promotion of local specialities and lifestyles, whilst seeking to avoid the impact of mass tourism. This without doubt engages the involvement of the local tourist community – directly or indirectly – in order to contribute to the development of its tourism area, whilst achieving economic well-being. Furthermore, one of the fundamental objectives of this concept is ecological awareness, which requires the preservation of natural resources as one of the key priorities.

This concept began to expand rapidly across the European continent, but it is not widely developed in a number of countries, especially in Eastern Europe, which include Serbia. Considering its position, its numerous natural and social resources, Serbia certainly has the potential to develop this concept of tourism. Belgrade, for example, may have significant economic and cultural benefits from tourism. With a good strategy and a sustainable way of organising and developing this destination, Belgrade should have the ability to create positive effects for the improvement of all segments of its tourist offer and achieve better positioning in the European and regional tourist markets, thus creating the possibility for opening new jobs (primarily in the catering industry) and making profits for a longer period. In addition, such a concept would have positive effects on the local population, as well as new jobs, and more healthy living conditions would be created which is particularly important in large cities where there is a large fluctuation of traffic and where exhaust gases damage the environment. Finally, a successfully implemented and applied concept could serve as an example to other cities in the country. In this way, the social and natural resources of the country would be used in a sustainable way on a larger scale.

Sustainable and Responsible Tourism

With its development in recent years in addition to economic and social importance, tourism has played a significant role in the context of promotion and implementation of plans and systems for sustainable development. According to the UNWTO (2017), the number of trips in 2015 will exceed 1 billion; according to UNWTO forecasts for 2020, this figure will exceed 1.5 billion tourists annually on a global basis. Despite the many security challenges that it has faced, Europe has attracted more than half of world's tourists in 2015 (608 million). This indicates that interest in the European continent is not extinguished and that in the future, the number of tourists will continue to be very high. This however leads to a legitimate conclusion that despite the economic benefits, serious risks will arise in terms of endangering the environment, the well-being of the population, the preservation of the tourist potential and the attractiveness of the destination for a longer period, which endangers the entire tourism sector. The greatest dangers come from the continuing neglect of the environment and its significance, which is a consequence of poor organisation and poorly planned tourism management.

Up until the mid-1980s, the primary focus of the tourism industry was on economic profit – e.g. on direct, indirect and multi-faceted economic effects connected to the economic consumption of domestic and foreign tourists and their positive impact on a country's economy. Such an approach has brought many condemnations and criticisms, primarily because of its negligence towards society, as well as to tourists themselves: first of all, an unacceptable treatment of the natural environment and disreputable constructions for tourist purposes. In addition to the destruction of space, there has also been a commercialisation of cultural and historical heritage, as well as the loss of authenticity of the destination. Because of the loss of this authenticity, numerous destinations have also lost the interest of tourists to visit these towns (Bakić, 2010, pp. 24–25). Due to such practice and such development of tourism, there has been the development of "alternative forms of tourism", of "more humane", "healthier" and "responsible" tourism.

The concept of sustainable tourism development is a relatively new trend in the tourism industry and as such has not yet been applied on a larger scale. The United Nations Environment and Development Conference adopted the Agenda defining the Action Plan for a Sustainable Development Conference in Rio de Janeiro in 1992 (Krivošejev, 2014, p. 50). However, due to its characteristics and the goal that this concept aims at and the idea connected with it, it has become very popular and, on a scientific basis, highly desirable for studying and further upgrading. As such, it has been and remains the subject of numerous analyses and discussions from which various definitions and explanations of this concept emerged. Butler (1999, p. 10) in his work cites several definitions, first of all Eber (1992, p. 3) which emphasises that sustainable tourism is

> tourism and appropriate infrastructure that: both now and in the future act within the natural capacities for regeneration and future productivity of natural resources; Recognises the contribution that people and communities, customs and lifestyles give for a tourist experience; It acknowledges that people must have an equal share in the economic benefits of the local community and people in tourism areas.

Butler quotes the Countryside Commission (1995, p. 2) that focuses on the local economy: "A tourism that can sustain a local economy without damaging the environment on which it depends". Swarbrooke (1999, p. 13), to its definition of sustainable tourism, comes through the emphasis on the importance of the economic, natural and social elements of the tourist system – "tourism that is economically viable, but which does not destroy the resources on which the future of tourism will depend, in particular the physical environment and social material of the local community".

Similarly, Hetzer (1965, pp. 1–3), quoted in his work by Cheia (2013, p. 56), claims that there are four most important factors, namely: "the smallest possible impact on nature and environment, respect for domestic (local) culture, greater benefits for the local population and greater satisfaction for tourists". Taking into account all of this, we come to several major following factors of sustainable development in tourism (Vujić, 2011, p. 476):

- Tourists, who influence sustainability with their acts;
- Tourism employees, who directly or indirectly influence sustainability;
- Business entities in tourism, within basic and related activities;
- Public services;
- Local people.

Despite different definitions, science has recognised and agreed on the core, or the main, pillars of sustainable development. These are social, ecological (and cultural) and economical moments. It is therefore clear to define the goals of the concept of sustainable tourism development. First, through the protection of cultural and historical heritage and natural resources, the preservation of a destinations uniqueness prolongs the length of local resources. Second, by including other industries and service activities, the tourist offer of the destination is enhanced. This primarily means that the local community, in a direct or indirect manner, is included in the tourist offer and with its goods or services additionally promotes the local culture and the specificities of this destination. For example, by engaging local farmers, tourists would have the opportunity to enjoy local products, which means that these producers are also indirectly (and sometimes directly) included in the tourist offer. This can also define the third importance of this concept, which is the economic development of the local community. Namely, when other local producers and suppliers of goods and services are included, employment of new people in local tourist centres, generating money from the sale of tourist services and goods (such as souvenirs), leads to an increase in the economic well-being of the local community.

SWOT Analysis

To provide a better insight into Belgrade sustainable tourism situation, we have made a SWOT analysis of the city. In Table 26.1 there are presented the strengths and weaknesses of Belgrade, which will be explained subsequently.

    When we discuss the advantages that Belgrade has as a tourist destination, its position is in the first place. Belgrade is at the crossroads of two international waterways – the Danube and Sava rivers – which allow it to generate an influx of tourists directly to their shores. Further, Belgrade is characterised by a positive climate, which contributes to tourism activities throughout the year. In almost all countries, the capital is also the most developed place in the country, so Serbia is no exception. This is supported by the fact that with the establishment of a new national airline and consequent networking with numerous destinations, as well as raising the quality of service at the airport, Belgrade has seen a significant increase in the number of tourists. In addition, Belgrade is rich in cultural and historical content, which may be interesting to tourists, given its history and the different cultures and people that have changed in this city. There is also the traditional cordiality and hospitality of the Serbian people, which leaves perhaps the strongest impression on the guests.

Table 26.1 Strengths and weaknesses of Belgrade

Strengths	Weaknesses
Geographical location – the hub of road and river corridors	Lack of strategy for sustainable destination development
Climate characteristics	Traffic infrastructure
Accommodation capacities – price and quality ratio versus competition in the region	Pollution of rivers, coastal areas and green areas (ecology)
The most developed city in the country	Insufficient utilisation of MICE capacity
New national airline/connections with numerous European and international destinations	Taxi transportation
Rich cultural and historical heritage	
Hospitality of the local population	

Source: Author.

Unfortunately, large crowds, an uncompleted city bypass, an international transit corridor that passes through the urban part of the city, a lack of parking spaces and undeveloped metro links, all create a major problem for travelling in respect of tourists and for the local population. The great problem of the capital, and which is especially important for the topic of this work, is ecology. In addition to official data and the European Commission's assessment, this is visible on rivers, coasts and green areas. Furthermore, Belgrade has only four 5-star hotels, for Meetings, Incentives, Conferences and Exhibitions (MICE) tourism, which Belgrade aims to develop, this is an extremely small number. On the other hand, although a "Strategy for Tourism" has been adopted, there is still no clear definition of how Belgrade seeks to develop tourism. MICE capacities are significant, as we have already analysed, however, it seems that the economic entities that have these capacities are left to promote their own capacities and attract interested clients. The next step in SWOT analysis is to define opportunities and threats of Belgrade, which are presented in Table 26.2.

In discussing the opportunities of Belgrade to improve its position on the tourism market, we should mention the current biggest project in the country, which is "Belgrade Waterfront". Unfortunately, the finalisation of this project will be seriously delayed due to the fact that the total deadline for project completion covers 30 years. Until then, Belgrade should make more use of international trade fairs, tourist rallies and all legitimate marketing assets in order to more effectively promote its tourist offer in the foreign market. In that, we should expect the help of the state that is investing more and more in the promotion of domestic tourism in recent years. As we have already pointed out, the arrival of new large hotel chains will be announced and the capacity for accommodation and the service of guests will be even more significant. In addition to investing efforts to bring foreign hotel chains, the state is also working to improve the transport infrastructure, and in this regard it is working on the completion of the bypass around Belgrade, which should significantly reduce crowds in the city. There should be a space for attracting ecologically conscious tourists, which without the development of the concept of sustainable tourism and a clear strategy in this direction is not possible. Finally, another big chance is the influx of more passengers after reconstruction of the airport and the establishment of new air connections. This will undoubtedly strengthen the existing connections and open new markets in Europe as well as in the East and the West.

Table 26.2 Opportunities and threats of Belgrade

Opportunities	Threats
Finalisation of the project "Belgrade Waterfront"	Unstable political and economic situation in the country and the region
Promotion of Belgrade on the international market	A large number of terrorist attacks across Europe
Country's interest in the tourism sector	City break destinations in the region
Increase in the number of large hotel chains	Slow reconstruction of tourist infrastructure
Investing in traffic and tourist infrastructure	Global economic recession
Attracting foreign and domestic investments into tourist facilities and infrastructure	

Source: Author.

When we consider the factors that pose a threat to the further development of tourism in Belgrade, we must mention the problematic and unstable economic and political situation in the country and the region mentioned in the first place. First of all, the low standard of living of citizens from most of the countries of the former Yugoslavia prevents a higher flow of regional tourists. There is also a factor that burdens the political stability of the country, which is the issue of the southern Serbian province of Kosovo and Metohija. In addition, there are frequent verbal conflicts between the countries of the Balkan Peninsula, which have intensified with the onset of a migrant influx. All of these factors affect the willingness of tourists to choose Belgrade as their visit destination. The aforementioned economic instability was caused by a major global recession from 2008. However, the last parameters give reasons for optimism, since there is a steady increase in tourists. Of course, if a similar situation would recur, it would drastically affect tourism in Belgrade. There is also a threat from the competition, primarily from the region. Far ahead of everyone in the region is Budapest, however, the increase in the number of tourists recorded by Belgrade is an indicator that tourists are increasingly choosing the Serbian capital for their vacation. When it comes to raising the quality of the tourist offer, it should be said that the reconstruction of the existing and the construction of a new tourist infrastructure must be quick and efficient. At a time when technology is constantly advancing, it is unacceptable that a tourist destination that seeks to record a serious result of the tourism market has an old and inadequate infrastructure.

Finally, there was lately a growth of terrorist attacks. The attacks in Paris, Brussels, Nice, London, Manchester, Saint Petersburg and cities across Turkey has significantly influenced the reduction of travel and created fear among tourists from travelling. Belgrade and Serbia do not fall into high-risk areas, but given the large number of people from the Middle East passing through Belgrade, such a risk cannot be excluded or taken as frivolous.

Research and analysis of the current situation, plans and future activities for sustainable development of the tourist offer of Belgrade

Empirical research of the current state of tourism in the city of Belgrade was performed by using semi-structured interviews as a research method. Interviews were conducted with responsible persons from different tourism sectors. The research was carried out in two relevant touristic subjects. First of all, the basic and most important part of the research process was carried out at the Tourist Organization of Belgrade (TOB) as the main organisation for the promotion and planning of city tourism development. The purpose of the interview was to gather the necessary primary information on how this organisation plans to further improve the city's tourist offer. Besides that, interview was also made at the tourist agency "Sabra" which helped to gain important information in the sphere of receptive tourism, as well as observations and impressions that foreign tourists carry from Belgrade.

Finally, this helped to define the basic shortcomings in the current organisation of the destination and based on that, through the benchmarking analysis with foreign example of good practice (the capital of Slovenia, Ljubljana and its concept "Green Ljubljana"), the best possible solutions are proposed for such defects.

Analysis of the interviews

Initially, the questions were related to the results of the tourism in 2017, from the aspect of the attendance, the recorded trends and individual visits of foreign and domestic tourists. The largest number of registered foreign tourists, according to the data of the agency "Sabra", is from Asian countries, primarily from China and Taiwan. This fact confirms the thesis that Belgrade and Serbia are becoming more and more attractive to tourists from the Far East. The enormous potential that the Asian market brings with it moves the focus of receptive travel agencies into that part of the world. It is also expected to continue recording a positive trend in terms of tourists from the East in the coming years, especially according to the tourism campaign that targets this tourism market. In addition to Asian tourists, there is noticeable presence of tourist groups from Europe, primarily from Austria and Italy. However, according to the data of this travel agency, the smallest number of tourists comes from Germany. So far, in 2017, over a million overnight stays have been recorded and an increase of 12% over the previous year. According to a comprehensive survey conducted by TOB in 2016, as many as 85% of the tourists surveyed feel safe in Belgrade. When it comes to the city's most visited attractions, those are as follows: Beli dvor; Kalemegdan; Skadarlija, the coastal area along the river tours (additional popularisation and the visit of this part of the city is expected with the construction of the project "Belgrade Waterfront"); Savamala (where tourists, among other things, go because of the restoration of karaoke as a form of popular entertainment); Cetinjska Street, the city centre; and Novi Beograd as a business and walking area.

According to TOB, most foreign tourists come to Belgrade from Turkey. Only in 2017 was growth of as many as 52% of Turkish tourists in Belgrade. The reason lies in the introduction of new direct flights from Istanbul, including low-cost companies. In addition, more and more Turkish companies in Serbia are also bringing an additional influx of Turkish citizens. What is a novelty is that Belgrade is recording a high growth trend when it comes to visiting tourists from Israel. As in the case of Turkey, a large number of direct flights, but also a growing number of business opportunities in the capital of Serbia, attract people from Israel. What is even more interesting is, according to TOB, unlike most tourists who stay in Belgrade for up to three days, guests from Israel stay for up to seven days. Bearing in mind their payment power, it is clear that Belgrade has a huge economic benefit from it. Motives for visiting are mostly the same; according to the aforementioned research, the strongest impression that tourists bring from Belgrade are the kindness, hospitality of the citizens of Belgrade, as well as a very good atmosphere in the city.

Speaking about the presence of domestic tourists visiting Belgrade, the situation began to improve since last year, when the Government of the Republic of Serbia, led by the Ministry of Trade, Tourism and Telecommunications, launched the action of sharing vouchers for holidays in Serbia. This action had a big echo, especially in the oldest population, and the participation of domestic guests was very high. When it comes to utilising the fact that Belgrade lies on two rivers, and that tourists have the opportunity to get to know Belgrade from another perspective, TOB makes a distinction between seeing a city from a river and a cruiser that sails to Belgrade via the international river route, most often across the Danube. Namely, TOB uses and promotes private companies that provide such services and perform tours when they collect enough number of interested ones. When it comes to the second category of tourist exploitation of the river, the number of consignments in the Belgrade port is increasing from year to year.

Age profile

Research showed that the majority of people who visit Belgrade belong to the oldest group of people over 65 years of age. They also point out the hospitality, good and cheap food and atmosphere in the city as the biggest advantage of Belgrade. Even 83% of respondents said they were the first time in Belgrade and a large percentage expressed their desire to come again, but also to recommend Belgrade as a tourist destination to their friends, which is a confirmation that they take positive impressions from Serbia's capital. When it comes to positive criticism of tourists, the most important ones are hospitality, delicious food, people who know the English language well, as well as good training and professional behaviour of tour guides. On the other hand, negative reviews are most often related to poor traffic infrastructure, ecology, insufficient information boards, souvenir shops, internet and Wi-Fi zones, undeveloped dock and lack of waste bins, shopping distance, as well as the need to provide better access to people with disabilities. In any case, there is room for improvement of services for tourists who are among the best paying and with the most free time.

The highest inflow of foreign tourists was recorded in the period from April to October. This is for all "city break" destinations, and so for Belgrade, the main period of the tourist season. It is interesting that the period during New Year's and Christmas holidays was not highlighted, although a lot of funds were invested in order to be recognised as a New Year's tourist destination.

Green tourism

On the other hand, Belgrade started with "green" or "eco-friendly" tours. Although it is still not massive, Belgrade is part of the international bicycle network, and there are even special cruisers that bring tourists for cycling along the Belgrade biking trails. In addition, there are also "sag way" tours, which are shorter (they include the lower and upper Kalemegdan with sights) and longer (they include the centre of the city with Knez Mihailova street, the Patriarchy building and the Belgrade port). In the case of river tours and in the case of "green" sightseeing tours of the city, it is necessary to organise a group, therefore, there are no regularly scheduled tours for individual tourists. On the other hand, when talking about the needs for additional MICE capacities, the TOB points to the fact that an increasing number of hotel chains are opening facilities in Belgrade. The best example is that in 2018, the first hotel of the Hilton Corporation is opened in the very centre of the city, prior to this was the arrival of "Intercontinental", "Starwood", "Marriott", "Falkensteiner", "Accor" and others in Belgrade. The current problems that the city has, when it comes to this topic, are, according to TOB, the lack of congress and accommodation capacities in organising large events.

Benchmark Analysis – Project "Green Ljubljana" and its application to Belgrade

In order to reward efforts for facing environmental challenges in European cities, the European Commission set up the European Green Capital award in 2010. In particular, the prize is awarded to a city that has a consistent outcome on achieving high ecological criteria, and is committed to ambitious goals for further improvement of the environment and sustainable development, and that it can act as a model that inspires other cities and promotes good practices in all other European cities.

(European Commission, 2018)

The city authorities of Ljubljana devoted themselves to the goal of creating a place where the local population will live healthier and ecologically organised, and to which the tourists will come in greater numbers contributing to the development of Ljubljana as a tourist destination. The development of Ljubljana as a "green" or ecologically and sustainably oriented destination began with the "Vision of Ljubljana 2025" in which 93 projects worth at least 3 billion euros were defined (Mestna obc̆ina Ljubljana, 2018). As the two most important projects Mr. Kož̌elj, an architect and the vice mayor of Ljubljana, pointed out the construction of three hydropower plants on the Sava River, which would shift the city to renewable energy sources, but also to the arrangement of a large Sava Park and the development of sports and recreational facilities. The second most important project, according to Mr. Kož̌elj, was the reinforcement of the railway, bearing in mind that Ljubljana crosses two large railway corridors. This project is also related to the development of sustainable transport, which would, as such, solve the traffic problems of the city (Kos, 2008).

In order to get the status of the "green capital", Ljubljana had to make many changes in the city's existing functioning. In order to get closer to the ecological picture of Ljubljana, the official website of Green Ljubljana (Mestna občina Ljubljana, 2015a) published data shows the extent to which the capital of Slovenia has advanced in terms of sustainable development, with particular emphasis on ecology and the use of renewable energy sources (Mestna občina Ljubljana, 2015b):

- 74% of households are heated remotely and have natural gas distribution;
- Drinking water can be used completely without prior processing;
- The city centre is now mostly for pedestrians and cyclists;
- 63% of the collected waste makes Ljubljana the leader in Europe;
- 542 m^2 of public green areas per capita;
- 80 ha of newly maintained green areas;
- New green areas are made from degraded urban land;
- Ljubljana is on the list of the best cities for sustainable development.

It would be said that Belgrade, as well as Ljubljana at the time, needs a certain vision, supported
by numerous projects that would make their move and contribute to sustainability. Nevertheless, when comparing Belgrade and Ljubljana, one should first point out some differences that should be taken into account when discussing the possibility that the Serbian capital moves in the same way as Ljubljana. First of all, Belgrade is a much larger city than Ljubljana, both in terms of population and area. Consequently, the frequency of traffic is much larger and more complex. In addition, when it started on such projects, Slovenia was largely a full member of the European Union, while Serbia is still on its way to becoming it. This is important because EU funds for the development and financing of projects are important, and Serbia, although the official candidate, cannot use these funds at full capacity. Belgrade could capitalise on

the experience of Ljubljana in a way to make numerous projects with which it would apply to funds that would provide funding for financing. However, before that, much would have to be done on educating the population and explaining the need for a sustainable and ecological organisation of the city. It is very important that such a concept be accepted by the local population so that it can be developed and implemented at full capacity.

As a multiple winner of the awards for sustainable tourism development and for the ecological organisation of the city, Ljubljana can indeed represent a model that Belgrade could and should follow. First of all, Belgrade's city authorities should use good relations with Ljubljana officials to discuss projects that the largest Slovenian city realised and what are the effects of such changes. The transfer of experience is very important because it represents new knowledge and the opening of new horizons that can be used in the further development of the city as a tourist destination.

Proposals and discussion for the future development of Belgrade as tourist destination

In order to best define the most important tasks that Belgrade must do in order to develop in the future as a responsible and sustainable tourist destination, three main priorities are defined. These are concrete steps that must be implemented in order to make Belgrade a planned city and become a destination with better conditions for the development of the tourism industry. These priorities are as follows:

- Priority I: Solving traffic problems in the city and improving the traffic infrastructure;
- Priority II: Reconstruction and construction of tourist infrastructure;
- Priority III: Improvement of ecological image and focus on environmental protection and town planning.

Priority I: Solving traffic problems in the city and improving the traffic infrastructure

The main focus should be on relocating or limiting traffic to the city centre. In this way, conditions for several pedestrian zones would be created, and noise, pollution and traffic jams would be much smaller. As one of the most important steps towards a permanent solution to the problem of traffic in the city, it is necessary to totally complete the bypass around Belgrade, but also to disperse the traffic that is currently passing through the very centre of the city by building new roads that would serve as an additional bypass around the city centre. Expanding pedestrian zones and using environmentally friendly means of transport would be a positive step towards improving the ecological image of the city. In addition, several pedestrian zones in the city centre would be more attractive to tourists, and the level of noise and pollution in the city centre would be much smaller than now. By blocking or limiting traffic in the city centre, the need for so many parking spaces would be reduced, and in the meantime, this would be economically good for the city, as more people would be using public transport. In order to do this, adequate conditions must be created.

This implies the construction of the necessary infrastructure that would accept all traffic and enable a better flow around the city centre. Furthermore, it is necessary to continue with the reconstruction of the city roads, especially those that connect the most important tourist attractions. First of all, it refers to "refreshment" and adaptation of roads leading to or located in tourist zones. By investing in quality rehabilitation of road infrastructure, Belgrade would get better quality roads, and pedestrians would be safer.

In addition, Belgrade's metro has been mentioned as the biggest project for decades. Construction of the metro network would enable better frequency and connection of all parts of the city, while at the same time reducing the concentration of motor vehicles in the city, which would reduce crowds and the number of motor vehicles on city roads. Finally, it is urgent that the authorities start solving the problem of unregistered taxi drivers. The largest concentration of such taxis is, logically, in the places where there are most tourists, such as airports, bus and train stations and major tourist zones.

Priority II: Reconstruction and construction of tourist infrastructure

Quality tourism content is one of the basics of successful development and management of the tourist destination. In order to attract tourists, local authorities must create the conditions for utilising the tourist potentials of the destinations and display them in the best way. This means good infrastructure, offering tourist objects with quality and unique contents, as well as new innovative contents that will enrich and strengthen the tourist offer. Such content must be based on the expectations and real needs of tourists, and at the same time try to preserve the basic characteristics and culture of the tourist destination. The focus of the authorities should be on making the current tourism infrastructure fully accessible, especially those that have great cultural and historical significance and great importance in the promotion of Belgrade and Serbia. In addition to the reconstruction itself, it is necessary to carry out modernisation that would follow the modern tourist flows and needs of today's tourists. In this way, the promotion of Belgrade on the international tourist market would be meaningful and of higher quality, which would undoubtedly attract even more tourists.

In addition to completing the commenced reconstruction work, it is necessary to make an analysis and plans to bring other tourism attractions to a representative and usable level. Cultural and historical heritage, which is also one of the bearers of Belgrade's tourist offer, must be fully equipped to be used for tourist purposes of the city. In the first place, the expert commission should deal with this work, which would make an analysis of devastated objects that are of great cultural and historical significance for this city and country. Then it is necessary to find funds and invest them in a complete reconstruction, in order to present such objects in from of museum or tourist sites. Besides this, it is necessary to build a new tourist infrastructure that would not disturb the harmony, authenticity and tourist concept of the city. Such projects do not necessarily have to be great. The construction of a new viewpoint, free use of bicycles in tourist zones, theme hiking tours and similar projects can greatly enhance the quality of the tourist offer.

Priority III: Improvement of ecological image and focus on environmental protection and town planning

In order for the city to attract more tourists, besides tourist facilities and necessary infrastructure, it must also have adequate ecological conditions. For example, without the introduction of recycling and adequate containers for sorting waste, it is not possible to imagine successful waste management. And it is just something that currently ruins the city's image and affects the overall impression of tourists. This gives the city a label that it is "dirty" or "messy", and this kind of campaign undoes the great efforts the tourist organisation invests in the promotion of the capital and state. Green oases, such as city parks or botanical gardens, need to be managed better with significant promotion and better content. In this way, the city would demonstrate its ecological commitment; tourists would be much more attracted to the city, and the local population would live in a healthier environment. In addition, regular cleaning of streets, watering green areas, and more stringent control and prevention of the destruction of public areas and properties would change the image of the city for the better. Greater commitment to the use of renewable energy sources would improve the ecological image of the city and the country. The other parts of Serbia should also apply the same principle, hence the long-term economic benefit would be very significant. Given that Serbia does not have much practical experience with the use of renewable sources, it should apply examples of good practice from other countries, such as Slovenia, Austria or Germany.

In the process of deciding on the choice of tourist destination tourists will visit, they pay more attention to the ecological segment, that is, to general treatment of environmental protection. Insufficient good rating in this segment can result in a large number of tourists who repel from visiting a tourist destination, which means a smaller financial inflow for the local economy. In addition, the local population would have to benefit first and foremost from the correct and quality relationship to environmental principles, as this would bring healthier living conditions and a better environment in which they live, and the local government would also have financial benefits from recycling.

Conclusion

Tourist demand is influenced by many factors that contribute to the radical changes in the perception of tourism as an industry that records high rates of growth and progress. First of all, tourists are significantly more interested in using their free time to understand the culture and history of a destination. Preserving the tourist destination is the main precondition for tourists to return to this same destination in future years. This is one of the main initiators of the sustainable tourism development in the conceptual emergence of sustainable tourist destinations: first of all, nurturing and promoting local tourism products and services as a basis for the survival of the authenticity of the destination; second, encouraging the application of ecological norms in order to protect the natural resources; and finally, the development of jobs and the employment of the local population. This concept contributes to the stability of the tourist destination and opens the perspective for long-term development. It contributes to the economic benefits of the local population, which is one of the biggest features of the tourism industry. Also, this concept encourages reduction of adverse impacts on nature, preservation of the environment, as well as the use of renewable energy sources.

One of the conditions for a tourist destination to successfully and responsibly use its resources is to care for and preserve the environment and ecosystems. Raising the level of cleanliness and the care of green areas must be one of the priorities when it comes to further development of Belgrade as a tourist destination. It is precisely this segment where foreign tourists have the most objections. The regulation of municipal waste, the reduction of the level of exhaust gases and noise in the main tourist zones, the regulation of pedestrian zones, the reduction of traffic jams, cleaner streets and prevention of plotting graffiti on buildings facades are aspects that must be given special attention. The example of Ljubljana as a tourist destination that has made enormous progress in the area of sustainable and ecological management of a tourist destination is a model that Belgrade could follow. Taking into account all the differences that exist between these two main cities, the principle applied by Ljubljana, concerning the preparation of a large number of projects, including the relocation of traffic from the very centre of the city, is also applicable in Belgrade. Of course, all projects should be synchronised, with the ultimate goal of how Belgrade should function as a tourist destination. Undoubtedly, it takes a lot of effort to move this segment to a better one, and this is not possible without the clear and determined steps of the city authorities to bring the state of the environment and better regulation of the city to a representative European level. This includes, among other things, the use of renewable energy sources, which would contribute to more efficient and longer-term use of existing resources in order to improve the ecological picture and reduce the emission of harmful gases and fuels.

In addition to improving the ecological image and appearance of the city, it is necessary to invest effort and resources in improving the tourist infrastructure. Every additional tourist component, regardless of its scope, which does not undermine the sustainability and city's authenticity, contributes to the enrichment and empowerment of the city's tourist offer. Also, accessible tourism is not something with which the capital of Serbia can be proud of. Access to a number of tourist attractions is not enabled for people with disabilities. Since TOB regularly monitors tourist facilities and tourist infrastructure, this is one of the areas that should be dealt with much more in the future, together with the relevant city authorities.

Finally, one of the main problems of the city concerns traffic regulation and traffic infrastructure. In the first place, a large amount of traffic consists of transit vehicles that are forced to enter the city because the bypass around the Serbian capital is not fully completed. Completion of this bypass must be a priority, and this will be the first step in solving the problems of transport. The second traffic problem is reflected in poor traffic infrastructure, primarily roads and railways. The rehabilitation of existing roads and the construction of new access roads and bridges that connect parts of the city are crucial for relieving the main city roads. In addition, the construction of new roads and bridges connecting other parts of the city would result in fewer motor vehicles at the access to the main city core, which is also the main tourist zone. This would open the possibility for opening several pedestrian zones that would additionally bring the city to tourists, but also contribute to a better ecological image of the tourist destination. One of the solutions for reducing the use of motor vehicles in the tourist zones of the city is to encourage the use of public transport, especially ecological buses that already exist in Belgrade. In addition, taxi transportation must be more regulated, especially in places where tourists get first contact with the city, such as airports and bus and train stations. A final solution to the traffic collapses, and a long-term contribution to better traffic fluctuations is to build a metro system. The plan for the construction of the metro which has been delayed and changed for decades has to be realised in order for a large number of people to move more easily from one part of the city to another, including tourists, which would thus quickly and easily reach different tourist attractions, and at the same time use their time in a more efficient way.

The concept of sustainable development of a tourist destination is necessary in the capital of Serbia, because only in this way could local residents and tourists feel benefit. First of all, there will be improvement in city transport infrastructure and therefore better mobility. Then, the ecological orientation of the city would greatly contribute to a better image of the city. In addition, the use of renewable energy sources would bring the economic, which would increase the financing of new development projects. Involvement of local providers in the tourist offer would lead to the economic benefits of the local economy, as well as the population through new jobs and better working conditions. Tourists, on the other hand, would enjoy a more organised and cleaner city, with additional contents that best represent the history and culture of Belgrade. Such management of the tourist destination will provide better and more sophisticated touristic content, improved road infrastructure, cleaner and greener city zones and, most importantly, higher revenues and more tourists.

Reflections

1 There should be a clear plan what should be considered as the main tourism offer and what is the additional advantage.
2 Tourists recognise Belgrade as the nightlife destination and that is the brand which Belgrade currently has.
3 Tourists who are looking for short-term fun will not spend their time and money to visit some museums or other cultural sites.
4 From economical point of view, they cannot participate on the tourism market because their "target customers" are discouraged to come because of the overall market picture of the city. In order to change this perception Belgrade needs to make strategic changes and to come out with new tourism offer.
5 The capital city must attract visitors because of its beauty and cultural uniqueness. That means that public areas need to be clean and tidy. That includes well-organised waste management, traffic relocation (from the main tourism areas) which should further bring more pedestrian zones and less pollution. Furthermore, Belgrade needs to open more green areas, such as public parks, gardens, eco-friendly zones and pedestrian boulevards.
6 Moreover, local citizens would enjoy more beautiful and less polluted environment.
7 The capital of Slovenia, Ljubljana, could be a bright example of how it can be done. Series of capital projects which would, one by one, change the urban picture of the city and therefore create a new brand which would be represented to tourist.
8 What is also important when it comes to systematic changes such as re-branding of tourist destination is acceptance level of the local community. That means that local citizens need to support these kinds of changes.
9 What they need to change is their behaviour which is consequentially responsible for how Belgrade looks at the moment.
10 Education needs to be equally important (if not even more important) as any capital urban project. Nobody can expect that, for example, people would use recycling containers if they are not informed and educated why that is so important.
11 Once the locals accept and understand the idea of "green or eco Belgrade" local Government would be able to process the projects more efficiently and with better outcome.

Questions

1 Would making Belgrade a sustainable tourism destination be an issue which would open important discussions?
2 Are such processes in Belgrade justified since this kind of progression would require significant funds and inputs which in a country where there are many poor people and where the average salary is not on the acceptable level, it is difficult to explain such spending?
3 How may local and state governments justify this type of public spending to the local population given that is may be to explain how Belgrade would generate more income from these changes?
4 Therefore, we may suggest that perhaps education is a crucial element in this process. That leads to the view that how may the government operate to educate people so they may understand the importance of this process?
5 Having in mind financial and economic power of Serbia, it is clear that there should be additional ways of financing. That brings us to the next, very important question: where and how local and state governments will find additional funds to finance the process of sustainable development?
6 Essentially, Belgrade requires to change the marketing approach in terms of the foreign tourism market and to invest more in marketing activities. But is Belgrade capable to find sufficient resources to promote such a new image and to approach to its target market in such an efficient way?

Further reading

Arbuthnott, K. D.: Education for sustainable development beyond attitude change. *International Journal of Sustainability in Higher Education*, 10(2), 152–163, 2009.

Buhalis, D.: Marketing the competitive destination of the future. *Tourism Management*, 21(1), 97–116, 2000.

Kharas, H., Prizzon, A., & Rogerson, A.: *Financing the Post-2015 Sustainable Development Goals*. London: Overseas Development Institute, 2014.

Konecnik Ruzzier, M., Petek, N., & Ruzzier, M.: Incorporating sustainability in branding: I feel Slovenia. *The IUP Journal of Brand Management*, 12(1), 7–21, 2015.

Sachs, J. D.: *The Age of Sustainable Development*. New York: Columbia University Press, 2015.

Sharpley, R.: Tourism and sustainable development: Exploring the theoretical divide. *Journal of Sustainable Tourism*, 8(1), 1–19, 2000.

Shen, B., Wang, J., Li, M., Li, J., Price, L., & Zeng, L.: China's approaches to financing sustainable development: Policies, practices, and issues. *Wiley Interdisciplinary Reviews: Energy and Environment*, 2(2), 178–198, 2013.

References

Bakić, O.: *Mareting u turizmu*. Beograd: Univerzitet Singidunum, 2010.

Butler, R. W.: Sustainable tourism: A state-of-the-art review. *Tourism Geographies*, 1(1), 7–25, 1999.

Cheia, G.: Ecotourism: Definition and concepts. *Revista de turism-studii si cercetari in turism*, 15, 56–60, 2013.

Countryside Commission: Sustaining Rural Tourism. Cheltenham: Countryside Commission (CCP 483), 1995.

Eber, S.: Beyond the Green Horizon: A Discussion Paper on Principles for Sustainable Tourism. *WWF UK (World Wide Fund for Nature)*, 1992.

European Commission: About EGCA. Retrieved from: http://ec.europa.eu/environment/europeangreencapital/about-the-award/, 2018.

European Comission: Winning Cities. Retrieved from: European Green Capitals: http://ec.europa.eu/environment/europeangreencapital/winning-cities/, 2018.

Hetzer, W.: *Environment, tourism, culture.* UNNS, Reported Ecosphere, 1–3, 1965.

Kos, D.: *Vizija Ljubljane 2025.* Retrieved from: SiolNET: https://siol.net/novice/slovenija/vizija-ljubljane-2025–76462, 2008.

Krivošejev, V.: *Upravljanje baštinom i održivi turizam.* Narodni muzej Valjevo, 2014.

Mestna Občina Ljubljana: Dobrošli v Ljubljani. Retrieved from: Zelena prestolnica Evrope 2017: www.zelenaljubljana.si/, 2015a.

Mestna občina Ljubljana: European Green Capital 2016. Retrieved from: Welcome to Ljubljana: www.greenljubljana.com/, 2015b.

Mestna občina Ljubljana: Vizija Ljubljane 2025. Retrieved from: www.ljubljana.si/sl/o-ljubljani/vizija-ljubljane-2025/, 2018.

Swarbrooke, J.: *Sustainable Tourism Management.* New York: Cabi, 1999.

UNWTO: Definition. Retrieved from: World Tourism Organization Sustainable Development of Tourism: http://sdt.unwto.org/content/about-us-5, 2017.

Vujić, T.: *Upravljanje održivim razvojem turizma sa osvrtom na Republiku Srpsku.* Bijeljina: Univerzitet Sinergija, 2012.

27 Promoting the "Legacy Businesses" of San Francisco

An incentive-based approach to the protection of intangible heritage

Brian Roberts Turner

Summary

Policy tools to protect cultural heritage in the United States have traditionally focused on safeguarding physical assets. While this approach has often yielded the successful protection of historic sites, architecture and artefacts, it overlooks the intangible contributions that define American life. This case study will examine a policy in the City and County of San Francisco, California (USA) which focuses on the protection of one particular class of intangible assets: businesses with demonstrated contributions to their neighbourhood's history and identity. The policy introduces a roadmap for other municipalities that takes into account a broader definition of cultural heritage.

Introduction

The historic preservation movement in the United States has traditionally focused on the protection of material objects. The National Historic Preservation Act, the 1966 federal law which established the framework for state and local policy, set out to foster conditions under which our modern society and our historic property can exist in productive harmony and fulfil the social, economic, and other requirements of present and future generations (National Historic Preservation Act, 1966).

The law authorised the National Park Service to develop criteria for a National Register of Historic Places. The Park Service thereby limited the scope of what is eligible for recognition to "districts, sites, buildings, structures, and objects." Many states, counties and localities across the United States have mimicked these criteria in creating their own historic registries. The Park Service rules have helped aid cultural literacy and enabled future generations to experience places that spark their imagines (National Register of Historic Places, 2019).

However, one serious criticism of the preservation movement is that the conservation of historic material may come at the expense of a buildings' function. A long-standing business that has become a cultural fixture in a neighbourhood may have no legal authority to appeal to when faced with steep rises in rent. The controversy swirling around landmark status for the New York City building housing The Strand Bookstore is one of the latest incarnations of this debate (Advisory Council on Historic Preservation, 2016).

The City and County of San Francisco, California has challenged this norm. Its Legacy Business Registry celebrates the immaterial and intangible values of businesses. Unlike traditional historic preservation laws, the programme is incentive-based and, for the most part, non-regulatory. There is one exception to this rule in the City's Calle 24 Latino Cultural District, which requires a conditional use permit for any new non-residential use where the immediately prior use was a Legacy Business and where the property has been vacant for less than three years (S.F. Planning Code § 249.59(d)(2)(B)). Other cultural districts in the City do not have this regulatory provision including Japan town, SoMa Pilipinas – Filipino Cultural Heritage District; Compton's Transgender Cultural District; LGBTQ Cultural District; and the African American Arts and Cultural District (S.F. Admin Code §107.3).

The Registry is an evolving list of long-standing local businesses including, but not limited to retailers, service providers, manufacturers and non-profit organisations that operate in San Francisco. This case study will demonstrate how the programme holds promise as a replicable model for other cities seeking to complement their land use policies with a tool that recognises immaterial cultural assets.

Traditional regulation of historic properties in San Francisco

San Francisco is known for its restrictive land use regulations to protect its world-renowned stock of older and historic buildings. In addition to maintaining a City Landmarks programme, San Francisco has a deserved reputation of ensuring that new development respects its historic assets. Even if a building has not been formally declared a landmark, the City requires a determination of its eligibility for historic status prior to permitting structural alterations or demolition. The courts have ruled that the City's authority can extend to interior spaces that are open to the public. In Martin III v. City and County of San Francisco (37 Cal.Rptr.3d 470, 2005), the court grappled with the question of whether the City had discretion to review changes to a historically significant interior of a private residence not open to the public. It referred to California Environmental Quality Act's (CEQA's) definition of "environment" – i.e. within its scope of protection – as a "very broad concept encompassing both tangible and intangible factors. But the intangible has CEQA consequence only if there is a nexus to a *physically perceivable reality*" (37 Cal.Rptr.3d 477, 2005).

San Francisco has discretionary review of such permits under the "CEQA". CEQA is modelled on federal law and provides legal protections for the "environment" throughout California, a definition which includes historic resources. It provides substantive protection to these places, meaning the City has the legal obligation to deny permit applications that might result in demolition or substantial alteration of eligible historic sites if "there are feasible alternatives or feasible mitigation measures available that would substantially lessen the environmental effects of such projects"(Deering, Lexis Advance 2018).

While CEQA has become critically important to preserving San Francisco's historic resources, there are aspects of the City's social and cultural history that it is simply not designed to protect. To be eligible for protection CEQA relies on the criterion of the California Register of Historic Resources (Deering, Lexis Advance 2018). The California Register is largely modelled on its federal predecessor, the National Register of Historic Places, which, in accordance with national preservation policy, maintains a focus on material objects.

While effective in conserving architectural resources, traditional historic preservation protections are ill-suited to address the challenges facing cultural heritage assets. Historic designation is not always feasible or appropriate, nor does it protect against rent increases, evictions and other factors that threaten long-time institutions.

Origins of the Legacy Business Registry

In recent years economic inequality in San Francisco has been reported to be growing faster than any U.S. city and has driven commercial rents to unprecedented levels. In a landmark report in September 2014 the non-profit organisation San Francisco Heritage (SF Heritage) advocated for a "conservation-driven, incentive-based response to the loss of cultural heritage assets." In *Sustaining San Francisco's Living History: Strategies for Conserving Cultural Heritage Assets* the group provided policy makers 16 specific case studies, including examples from Barcelona, Buenos Aires, London and Paris, where city policies have been established to recognise and sustain elements of intangible cultural heritage.

Since it was first established in 1971, SF Heritage – formerly named the Foundation for San Francisco's Architectural Heritage – had primarily focused on the preservation of the City's built environment. However, its charge has expanded in recent years. As the *Sustaining SF's Living History* report (SF Heritage, 2014) acknowledged, long-standing businesses, non-profits and other arts and cultural institutions were being lost at an "alarming rate." The report called on the City to take action.

One of the policies that emerged from the SF Heritage report is the focus of this case study: the Legacy Business Registry. In 2014, an analysis from the City's Budget and Legislative Analyst's Office substantiated the concerns of the report, recognising that over a thousand small businesses in San Francisco were closing as a result of rapidly rising commercial rents (City & County of San Francisco, 2014). And while the City's rent control laws aim to protect a majority of leased residential units from rapid rent hikes, California state law forbids rent stabilisation measures for commercial leases.

The City's report was particularly startling in its review of relatively established businesses that had been at the same location for at least five years. For instance, between 1992 and 2011 business closures and location changes increased 606%. Moreover, in a span of 15 years from 1999 to 2014 commercial property rates increased by 256.3% (City & County of San Francisco, 2014).

The City takes action

In March 2015 the San Francisco Board of Supervisors adopted the Legacy Business Registry. The legislation, carried forward by former Supervisor David Campos, recognised that "longstanding, community serving businesses can be valuable cultural assets of the City" and created "a tool for providing educational and promotional assistance to Legacy Businesses to encourage their continued viability and success"(https://sfgov.legistar.com, 2015).

A business must first be nominated by a member of the Board of Supervisors or the Mayor. The City's Small Business Commission is the final arbiter of what is listed on the Registry. The Commission reviews applications, prepared by the businesses, which must make meet three specific criteria:

- The applicant has operated in San Francisco for 30 or more years, with no break in San Francisco operations exceeding 3 years (note that businesses that face a "significant risk of displacement" can apply if they are 20 years or older);

- The applicant has contributed to the neighbourhood's history and/or the identity of a particular neighbourhood or community;
- The applicant has committed to maintaining the physical features or traditions that define the business, including craft, culinary or art forms.

The criteria do not ignore the material spaces that businesses occupy, but treat them as one of several factors in determining whether a business has sufficient cultural value to be recognised. Regarding the tangible elements of a business, the City's Historic Preservation Commission has the opportunity to weigh in and recommend specific material features. That body uses its expertise to evaluate a detailed Historical Narrative prepared by the applicant.

The supporting documentation for the roughly 170 businesses that have been placed on the Registry is available to the public on the Commission's website. The applications contain critically important historical information that would not otherwise be gathered. Collectively these nominations help illuminate San Francisco's authentic communities, culture and social history.

The voters take action

The Legacy Business Registry offered significant new promotional value as well as general public awareness of cultural assets in San Francisco. But initially it was a list only; the City had not committed actual funding to help the businesses survive as real estate values continued to soar, tempting landlords where businesses may be located to seek higher paying tenants. This changed in November 2015 when voters passed a ballot initiative that allowed the Small Business Commission to manage two-grant programme for the businesses listed on the Registry.

The Business Assistance Grant recognises all Legacy Businesses including those that own property as well as those that lease space. Building owners are eligible to receive up to $500 per full-time equivalent employee per year, capped at USD 50,000 annually. The Rent Stabilisation Grant for tenants provides funding to building owners who provide commercial leases for businesses on the Registry for at least ten years or extend existing commercial leases to at least ten years. The landlords are eligible to receive grants of up to USD 4.50 per square foot of space leased per year, capped at USD 22,500 a year.

The Legacy Business Registry application process

The Legacy Business Registry allows for a competitive nomination process that helps document unique aspects of San Francisco's cultural history. It offers both financial and promotional incentives to prospective applicants. By emphasising the value of the intangible aspects of the business first, it fills a gap that more traditional historic registers miss. And for some businesses in noteworthy buildings, the opportunity in the process to describe notable physical features might assist in subsequent designation efforts for more architecturally focused registries.

A Historical Narrative is the heart of the business's application. It contains a standard questionnaire asking for evidence of how the businesses meet the three main criteria (duration, contribution and commitment). It is typically supplemented with additional documentation from the applicant, such as media and historical photographs. The exercise of writing the narrative can be didactic, encouraging businesses to research their history and engage their patrons and supporters. Many businesses may not otherwise have an opportunity to evaluate their status as institutions in possession of cultural heritage as well as work to articulate the economic, social and political value of their tangible and intangible assets for posterity.

A brief survey of a select eight narratives is useful for understanding the application process and profiling the types of businesses the City seeks to support through the programme.

Establishing a role for personal histories and oral interviews

The Legacy Business Registry application allows businesses to document both their significance as cultural institutions and the personal stories of business owners and workers. The Castro Country Club is a worthy example of how personal narrative conveys the nature of the institutions' value to the community it serves. It is a non-profit organisation formed in 1983 as a social alternative to gay bars, providing clean and sober gathering place in the Castro neighbourhood. Recognising the disproportionate effect that alcoholism and drug addiction had had on the LGBTQ community, the club's founders built a comforting space for recovery. Soon after its founding the club became a second home for people living with and impacted by AIDS.

The Club's Legacy Business Registry application contains moving letters of support which testify to its crucial role in providing services for AIDS patients. One particularly moving testimonial is a letter from James Moore, one of the Castro Country Club's long-standing members:

> *Many of the men I met in my first months and years at the Country Club did not survive the scourge of AIDS as it ravaged the gay community. The Club was ground zero for me, a place I sought recovery from drugs and alcohol, a place I sought solace from the incredible sense of loss, a place I sought soothing for the anger and hopelessness that seemed to crash upon me and my community over and over. Hope. Recovery. Love. Community. I found these things at the Castro Country Club.*

The use of personal histories provides citizens new access to the role these institutions have played in the life of the City as well as make the Legacy Business Registry process an important self-education tool for the businesses themselves.

Recognition of long-standing community service

The Richmond District in the northwest corner of San Francisco is not a typical stop on tourist itineraries. But the neighbourhood shows a slice of the City's roots as a multicultural, middle-class hub. Joe's Ice Cream on Geary Street is the oldest independent ice cream parlour in the neighbourhood and has been a gathering place for youth since 1959. One of the features highlighted in Joe's Ice Cream's Legacy Business application is the role it has played in providing community service. The application emphasises its commitment to hiring local kids to work in the shop and awards programme that rewards high academic performance with coupons for free ice cream.

Historical narrative as an historical record

Specs' Twelve Adler Museum Café's has been based in San Francisco's North Beach neighbourhood since 1968. Its Legacy Business application is particularly creative and a good model to demonstrate how the application process itself can be used as a tool to engage its community of supporters. The historical narrative includes photographs from birthday parties, a variety of letters of support and art and poetry from long-time patrons of the quirky establishment – part bar, part museum. It is a fitting representation of the business's role sustaining the bohemian culture in North Beach.

Role in averting development threats

The taps at the legendary bar Zeitgeist (once known as the "Rainbow Cattle Company") have been flowing since 1972, and its beer garden is electric even on the foggiest of summer days. It is also in an area where real estate values have skyrocketed in recent years. The bar has benefited from small grants from the Legacy Business programme. But the designation also proved its value for an unexpected purpose when a proposed new building across the street threatened to shade over its outdoor beer garden. The fact of its Legacy Business status was a factor the City Planning Commission considered in limiting the height of the new building (Brinklow, 2017).

The role of the business in maintaining artistic traditions

Muralism

Precita Eyes Muralist Association is a non-profit community arts organisation that promotes mural arts, a well-recognised tradition in the Mission district. The association's application to become a Legacy Business documents its work with youth to bring vibrant art to the neighbourhood. The group offers weekly tours on Saturdays.

Culinary arts

The fortune cookie was invented in San Francisco, and the city is still home to the last remaining factory that, tucked into one of Chinatown's back alleys, is making the cookies in the traditional, hand-folded fashion. The Golden Gate Fortune Cookie factory's application for the Legacy Business Registry highlights that the building holds what are likely the last vintage machines that prepare the batter for folding.

Literary arts

The October 3, 2016, Small Business Commission hearing featured a number of independent San Francisco bookstores vying for Legacy Business designation. Dog Eared Books had a particularly compelling argument for being listed: it was facing a steep rent increase at its prominent Mission district location. The bookstore met the criteria, and its designation on the Registry proved effective in negotiations with the landlord, who has since extended its lease.

Musical traditions

San Francisco is known around the world for its contribution to the musical arts, particularly in shaping the sound of Rock and Roll. The Blue Bear School of Music was established in 1971 and is currently located at Fort Mason Center in the Marina neighbourhood. Its Legacy Business application documents its role in providing affordable musical programming to underprivileged students and schools.

Accounting for businesses that have moved locations and changed ownership

The Legacy Business Registry application accounts for the fact that many businesses have multiple locations and/or have moved operations. Tracing the trajectory of the business, from the date of establishment to present day-creates, is critical for proving its 30-plus year contribution.

The application supporting the nomination of Brownies Hardware, a local hardware shop and repair service business in the "Polk Gulch" area, is one example of how a business's provenance – and even name – can be mutable. The first incarnation of the business, called "Brownie's Bazaar," on Golden Gate Avenue, was destroyed in San Francisco's devastating 1906 earthquake. Since its destruction it went on to occupy three different locations on Polk Street, and has been a fixture of that neighbourhood ever since. Brownies Hardware's application also recognises that the original owner of a Legacy Business need not still own the shop as long as there is no cease in operations for more than two years. The original owner Edgar Brownstone (for whom it is named) operated the business for its first 40 years until 1945. Since that year it has been owned by four successive owners.

Conclusion

In a city that is changing at breakneck speed, the Legacy Businesses Registry is one small step to help establish cultural continuity. By codifying a new class of heritage assets, San Francisco has created a unique policy for the preservation of its intangible values.

Nonetheless, challenges lay ahead. While the City has allocated USD 4 m over four years through its general fund for the Small Business Assistance grants, the programme still has no permanently dedicated funding source. And as more businesses are listed on the Registry funding has become more competitive. Without further action the grants could expire by 2020.

Though the prospective loss of funding would be a blow, the Legacy Businesses programme can remain an important model for other cities to celebrate their community culture and value systems. The Historical Narratives required by applicants are an educational tool, illuminating histories that might otherwise be lost. The flexibility in rules surrounding the physical manifestations of a property is also critically important to keep the programme from overlapping with more traditional historic registers focused on architecture and materials conservation.

Most importantly, a programme that honouring the contributions of long-standing businesses has helped create a shift how our cultural heritage is perceived. They allow us access to the places and people which have shaped our culinary, literary, social and artistic roots. Though fleeting and always subject to the vagaries of the market-place, they serve in the present as touchstones to the traditions which shape our modern identity.

Reflections

1   The traditional historic preservation movement in America has failed to recognise intangible values of cultural heritage in the United States. San Francisco's Legacy Business Registry is an important step in recognising intangible contributions by offering promotion of and small incentives for long-standing businesses.

2   Applicants to the Registry not only must prove continued operations for over 30 years, but document how they have contributed to a neighbourhood's history and/or the identity of a particular neighbourhood or community. This documentation is not necessary for more traditional historic registers (such as the National Register of Historic Places), yet is invaluable for filling important gaps in the historical record to help future generations better understand the social dimensions of our history.

3   The Legacy Business Registry does not entirely discard tangible features; applications must document physical features or traditions that define the business, including craft, culinary or art forms. In doing so the Registry recognises the visual landscape which long-standing businesses have helped create and strive to create cultural continuity by keeping these features in place.

4   San Francisco's Legacy Businesses programme in its infancy will continue to evolve can be an effective model for other municipalities looking to enhance recognition of the value of long-standing businesses.

Questions

1   Critics of the Legacy Business initiative in San Francisco have argued that businesses should survive in their own right by adapting their business model to shifting market conditions. A business that fails is antiquated and should make way for a new institution. Is San Francisco's desire to assist long-standing businesses justifiable in your view? Why?

2   The City and County of San Francisco uses incentives to promote legacy businesses – recognition and small grants. It did not pursue a regulatory approach. What are the advantages to structuring the programme this way? The disadvantages?

3   Do you think the 30-year threshold is appropriate? How might another city determine what age is appropriate for inclusion on a legacy business registry. What would be the consequences of extending the age criterion affect the programme?

4   Legacy businesses in San Francisco need not have the same ownership through time nor be located in the same structure. What are the reasons the City might have for allowing for this flexibility?

Further reading

Mike Buhler & Desiree Smith, *Mobilizing to Sustain San Francisco's Living History*, December 9, 2014, https://forum.savingplaces.org/blogs/special-contributor/2014/12/09/mobilizing-to-sustain-san-franciscos-living-history.

San Francisco's Legacy Business Registry: https://sfosb.org/legacy-business/registry.

San Francisco's Legacy Bars and Restaurants: https://www.sfheritage.org/legacy/.

San Francisco Small Business Commission, meeting minutes and supporting documentation for Legacy Businesses cited in this chapter: https://sfosb.org/meetings/10.

References

36 C.F.R. § 60.4- National Register of Historic Places criteria (Lexis Advance through February 1, 2019).

Adam Brinklow, *City shaves five feet off top of condos to accommodate popular Mission bar*, SF Curbed, https://sf.curbed.com/2017/2/17/14651122/san-francisco-bar-zeitgeist-shadow-shade-valencia, 2017.

Advisory Council on Historic Preservation, "The National Historic Preservation Program at 50: Priorities and recommendations for the future," June 2016.

Cal. Pub. Res. Code § 21002 (Deering, Lexis Advance 2018).

Cal. Pub. Resources Code, § 5024.1; *note that "eligibility" alone is sufficient, the resource need not be formally listed to be protected under the law.*

City and County of San Francisco Board of Supervisors Budget and Legislative Analyst, Memo to Supervisor Campos re: Analysis of Small Business Displacement dated Oct. 14, 2014 http://sfbos.org/sites/default/files/FileCenter/Documents/50557-BLA%20Small%20 Business%20Displace.101014.pdf.

Martin IIIv. City and County of San Francisco, 37 Cal.Rptr.3d 470 (2005).

Martin IIIv. City and County of San Francisco, 37 Cal.Rptr.3d 477 (2005).

National Historic Preservation Act of 1966 § 1, Pub. L. No. 89–665 (2018).

San Francisco, Cal., Admin. Code § 2A.242 (2015), https://sfgov.legistar.com/View. ashx?M=F&ID=3675421&GUID=76048692-98DF-4225-BE79-0A75393B3E64.

SF Heritage, *Sustaining San Francisco's Living History: Strategies for Conserving Cultural Heritage Assets*, September 2014, https://www.sfheritage.org/Cultural-Heritage-Assets-Final.pdf.

28 Building success on the edge of Europe – the Inishbofin case study

Tony O'Rourke

Introduction

This case study relates to a very small community in population terms and to a geographic locality which is very small in global terms. Nonetheless, the case study should have significant resonance in making clear the significant problem faced by small, peripheral communities. Yet the size of the community should not, it would be suggested, reflect disproportionally on the importance of the case study.

Europe has some 1,639 small islands, with a total population of around 355,000; major concerns for these islands – which tend to be peripheral and often marginalised from the mainlands – are maintaining and developing their cultural identity whilst at the same time ensuring economic development through such areas as tourism, marine harvesting and low-impact energy development. Finding the correct balance between environmental sustainability, protection of the cultural and natural heritage, and ensuring economic development for the benefit of island inhabitants is a highly delicate task.

This case study is based on a small island which is in effect mega-peripheral. The entire western coast of Ireland, from Cork in the southwest, through Clare, Galway and Mayo in the west, to Donegal in the north-west are not only peripheral to the more populated east of the country, but peripheral to Europe as a whole. Thus, the western offshore islands have an added sense of remoteness, magnified by often tenuous transport connections which are at the mercy of an uncertain Atlantic climate. They also tend to have reliance on a few industries – primarily tourism, but augmented by fishing and agriculture. Whilst the advent of high-speed broadband technology has brought some benefits, such areas as second-level (age 11 onwards) educational provision require children to stay on the mainland during the school week. Medical provision can often be limited, with emergencies dealt with through air cover.

The Irish offshore islands

In 2016, the Irish Census revealed that there were 23 inhabited offshore islands, a decline from the 2011 census total of 27. The total population of the Irish offshore islands in 2016 was 2,734, which compared to 2,879 in 2011, represented a decline over the five-year period of 5%. In 2016, 73% of the population of the offshore islands were classified as having Irish as their first language, with the remaining 27% having English as their first language. Interestingly, those islands that have displayed the best rate of population growth between 2011 and 2016 are the Irish-speaking (Gaeltacht) islands – Inis Cléire (19% increase), Inis Meáin (17% increase) and Inis Oírr (13% increase). Inishbofin has only reported a 9% increase in that same period.

It is however a rather complex concept to seek to relate the linguistic issue to the general socio-economic development of island communities.

For the Galway offshore islands, of which Inishbofin is one, there were 6 inhabited in 2016 (8 in 2011) with a total population of 1,405 (1,416 in 2011), a highly marginal decline over the five-year period of 0.8% (An Phríomh-Oifig Staidrimh, 2016). The economic development of these islands is under the responsibility of Comhar na nOileán Teo (Federation of Irish Islands, 2017, http://oileain.ie), the LEADER/EU partnership company which operates under the Irish government department An Roinn Cultúir, Oidhreachta agus Gaeltachta (Culture, Heritage & the Gaeltacht, https://www.chg.gov.ie/ga). Comhar na nOileán Teo is also the Irish representative on the European Association of Small Islands (ESIN, https: europeansmallislands.com).

The island of Inishbofin

Inishbofin (Inis Bó Finne – "the Island of the White Cow") is one of the 24 inhabited Irish offshore islands and is located 10 km from the west coast of Galway; it is 5.7 km by 4 km. The main activities are tourism and farming; fishing has declined over recent years with only two full-time fishing vessels. There are five main settlements on the island – West Quarter, Fawnmore, Middle Quarter, Cloonamore and Knock.

Archaeological evidence points to the island have been inhabited from around 8000 BC, although the first documentary evidence of the island dates from the early Christian period (430 AD onwards). St Colman's monastery indicates the importance of the island as a centre for religion and culture during the period from 700 to 1000 AD. A striking historical feature of the island is Cromwell's Barracks, dating from the invasion of Ireland in 1,651 by the English Republican army.

Inishbofin has three official looped walks of varying difficulties, each offering spectacular views of the island's wild Atlantic scenery. It has EU Blue Flag status, with sandy beaches which due to the clear nature of the sea water are good for swimming, snorkelling and diving. Two of the beaches on Inishbofin have been awarded a "Green Coast Award" to denote their exceptional water quality and natural, unspoilt environment. Inishbofin is also special area of conservation as it is a breeding area for many species of birds. The rarest and most threatened species on the island at present are the Corncrake.

The population stood at 1,404 in 1841 (prior to the great famine of 1845–1847), falling to 909 in 1851. A century later, the 1951 census revealed a population of 291. By 2011 it had fallen to 160 but grew to 175 (2016 census). The current number of permanent residents is estimated at 210. During the height of the summer tourism the population expands significantly. There is a passenger ferry connection (35 minutes) from the mainland port of Cleggan (which has an express bus link with Galway and rail/bus connections to other Irish cities and airports); the ferry operates two return sailings daily with an additional sailing in the summer. In addition, there is a cargo ferry service twice a week. There is no passenger car ferry access, which limits the capacity of traffic to the island.

Tourism background

Structured tourism began on the island in 1969, when two hotels were established; by 1995 there were 3 hotels, a youth hostel, 4 Bed & Breakfasts and 38 holiday homes. In 2018, there were 3 hotels, 6 Bed & Breakfasts, a hostel, a campsite and

23 self-catering holiday homes. It is estimated that there are a further 40 privately owned holiday cottages. The holiday season on Inishbofin tends to operate from Easter through until the end of October. The tourism market is focused on a high level of repeat business, which is predominantly from the Irish domestic market. In terms of the holiday home accommodation this will often relate to third and fourth generations of visitors – a distinctive level of repeat business covering the great-grand children of original summer visitors. For the hotel market, although the domestic market is the largest at around 80% (and again highly dependent on repeat visitors) the next largest market is from the UK, followed by France. For day visitors, again the Irish domestic market is predominant, followed by France, Germany, Italy, Spain and USA.

It appears that word-of-mouth and personal referrals have a significant part in the tourism inflows. The island has not had to resort to expensive marketing campaigns, although it participates in the national tourism marketing activities through Fáilte Ireland (http://www.failteireland. ie), the national tourism authority. Clearly tourism inflow is limited to the actual capacity on the ferry service (90) and the total capacity of the island's accommodation facilities (around 400). This tends to ensure that carrying capacity will not reach levels at which damage could be made to what is a relatively fragile ecological environment.

Tourism organisational structure

In 1989, the existing island Community Council and the crowd-funding group that had been formed to build a Community Centre merged to create the Inishbofin Development Association, a voluntary organisation tasked to assist in a wide range of tourist, ecological and community development plans. In 1993, this was replaced by a legally constituted company limited by guarantee (i.e. a not-for-profit entity) – the Inishbofin Development Company (IDC – http://www.inishbofin. com). This has the mission of improving:

1   the quality of life for the island through the establishment, development and provision of support and services;
2   the socio-economic, economic, infrastructure, environmental, cultural, heritage and administrative requirements of the island.

It is clear that on Inishbofin, the community seeks to take a different approach to tourism, aiming to achieve sustainable tourism that does not negatively impact upon the island's natural environment, whilst at the same time benefitting and supporting the local community. This precarious balance between ethical and environmental engagement over the longer-term and the shorter-term socio-economic needs of inhabitants reflects the major dilemma that faces all rural and peripheral communities.

The island has, in the words of Simon Murray, Chairman of the IDC, been driven by external events and its peripherality to maintain its existence. The abandonment of a nearby island (Inishark) in the 1960s created a strong sense of shock for the inhabitants of Inishbofin, and created an urgent need to ensure that the island remained populated and viable. Importantly, the island did not await the provision of government or EU grants before seeking to improve and structure its tourism and related offers.

Rather it relied on a process of self-resourcing, and then when it had achieved viable products, it began to seek grants and financial support.

This is an interesting learning point, as it indicates that tourism-driven communities can be self-sufficient, independent of grant/loan support and only applying for such support once they have developed a tangible project. The focus on tourism activity from Easter-October has traditionally been part of the socio-economic model for the island population; it has then enabled a focus on other economic activities from November through to March (e.g. farming, fishing, tourism marketing and development). However, it has become clear that there is surplus capacity in the "shoulder" periods (mid-April to end-May and end-August to end-October). Whilst the Irish school holidays occupy an eight-week period from the beginning of July to the end of August, there are periods outwith that peak season which could be further exploited. The shoulder seasons have now become a primary area for the development of outdoor cultural and natural heritage activities which are by their nature not weather-dependent.

Ecotourism developments

Inishbofin was the first Irish offshore island to have international EcoTourism status; it is tourism car-free. Only residents may have motor vehicles on the island, and these generally tend to be relatively old; an important ecological issue has been the removal of old and discarded vehicle from the island using the occasional cargo ferry service.

Inishbofin achieved Gold Certification from EcoTourism Ireland (http://www.ecotourismireland.ie) for its Cultúr na nOileáin tours run in conjunction with the Community Centre. These tours offer ecotourism experiences in the most environmentally friendly way (i.e. walking). This has led to EcoTourism being viewed as a major force in the "greening" of the island – with EcoTourism Ireland certifications covering more than 23 tourism activities. This includes such diverse activities as historical tours and studies, equestrian activities, stand-up paddle-boarding, self-guided walking, horse riding, nature photography, birdwatching and sailing. In addition, the community is also engaged in a number of festivals – food, Fair Trade, walking, arts, yoga, sailing, dancing and a half-marathon. Importantly, the IDC has been able to operate to a fairly tight schedule in developing these actions. Utilising grant aid from the state's Environmental Protection Agency, it was able to gain certification for the main ecotourism activities.

Leave No Trace

Importantly, both Cultúr na nOileáin and the Inishbofin Community Centre are members of the Leave No Trace network (LNT – www.leavenotraceireland.org, 2019), with the guided walks keeping to the LNT code of conduct and adhering to the minimal impact hillwalking, birdwatching and marine megafauna viewing codes where relevant. The tour maximum group size is fixed at 25 people per guide. For larger groups they employ a secondary guide to lead a walk on a different route. Particular care is taken to highlight features of the Special Areas of Conservation, and how to avoid negatively impacting upon these. Currently, there are two EcoTourism experiences – an exploration of Inishbofin and a guided tour to the unpopulated island of Inishark. Inishbofin is the first Irish island to have been given

LNT status. The Inishbofin LNT Network currently includes seven businesses on the island, and many inhabitants have taken the certified Awareness Sessions that LNT operate. LNT is an outdoor ethics programme which has devised a series of guidelines for outdoor recreation, intended to ensure that visitors have a minimal impact on environments by promoting and inspiring responsible outdoor recreation through education, research and partnerships (http://www.leavenotraceireland.org, 2019). Its seven principles, which are applied educationally as well as in communities, are as follows:

1   Plan Ahead and Prepare
2   Be Considerate of Others
3   Respect Farm Animals and Wildlife
4   Travel and Camp on Durable Ground
5   Leave What You Find
6   Dispose of Waste Properly
7   Minimise the Effects of Fire

Training

It should be noted that LNT Ireland is a not-for-profit company made up of partner organisations with a shared interest in encouraging responsible enjoyment of Ireland's natural environment. Their mission is to promote and inspire responsible outdoor recreation through education, research and partnership throughout the island of Ireland. The programme strives to inspire those who enjoy outdoor recreation to take personal responsibility and to reduce their impact on the environment teaching simple skills and techniques to minimise the impact of visitors on the environment.

In Inishbofin the LNT training (Leave No Trace, 2018) was delivered at various levels, including Awareness Training, Trainer Courses and Advanced Trainer Courses. The LNT message was adopted enthusiastically by the local community due to previous issues of the dumping of various forms of waste on the coast, on farming areas and in settlements. A key factor is that tourism recreation across the island of Ireland takes place in harmony and in balance with nature and that all recreational users value and support efforts to protect Ireland's natural environment.

The problem of island communities

Island communities face a number of intensive problems, and these relate strongly to ethical and sustainable development and the protection of the frequently fragile environment on such islands. A Swedish case study (Hellén, 2016) indicated that the potential for young families to live on an island which had an irregular ferry service to the mainland was poor, and that such islands would only be populated in the summer by tourists.

Often we may see situations where islands may provide good conditions for the development of ethically sustainable and environmentally friendly activities – e.g. growing fruits and vegetables, which may then develop into other food production activities. Fishing may often be a traditional activity, but the cost of operating and maintaining fishing vessels is high and also generally seasonal. This means that fishing businesses will need to rely on off-season activities such as marine tourism.

A major issue is often the availability of high-speed internet connectivity; islands that have such connectivity will become attractive to entrepreneurs who are excited by the potential of living on an island, but have the same connectivity they would have in a big city. Whilst such entrepreneurs may not initially understand or share the existing island culture, they may in due time become embedded in that culture. The disadvantage of remote communities is often their physical disconnection from mainstream society and socio-economic development. At the same time, this very disconnection is appealing to tourists and to new settlers on these islands.

However, globally, tourism may be an answer for small island communities in that it may provide economic benefits, but the social benefits to the wider community may be elusive and more difficult to calculate. Income from holiday rentals and tourism stays may inevitably focus on those who hold relevant property assets – hotels, guest houses, holiday cottages and holiday homes. Whilst some of this income may also spill over into local communities – restaurants, cafes, bars and shops – it may not necessarily improve and augment the conditions of island residents who live there for the whole year and who are engaged– for example – in farming or fishing. At the same time, tourism may have a depressing effect on local culture and local languages, and also provide an indirect magnet to pull young people away to urban and more sophisticated centres.

Access to finance has and will remain a major issue for any peripheral community. The retrenchment of the financial sector after the 2017–2018 financial crisis was followed by a full-scale reduction of banking facilities in rural environments. We have yet to see the full social impact of such a reduction, but it is clear that large numbers of communities no longer have ease of access to financial capabilities that were available in the past. Added to this problem, it has been a general reduction in community and co-operative credit facilities (e.g. credit unions and rural credit co-operatives), often prompted by the higher demands for capital adequacy as a result of the financial crisis. Micro and small businesses have therefore less access to finance both for start-up and development situations than were previously possible. At the same time, new SMART technology applications such as crowd-funding, peer-to-peer funding and crowd-equity platforms tend to be located in urban areas and are not accessible to more remote rural and peripheral communities. Innovative solutions to these problems certainly exist, but how they may be effectively rolled out and be accessible is a difficult issue. Importantly, it is an issue that we require to seriously address, as many islands provide a repository for culture, tradition and understanding of the past. If that is swept away as a result of depopulation or abandonment of these unique island communities, then we have lost a hugely significant part of our cultural heritage.

Ultimately the fundamental problem is how we protect fragile island communities, whilst balancing ethical, sustainable and environmental protection against the needs of island communities to seek to match the living standards and socio-economic status of their mainland neighbours is a serious issue.

Conclusion

Despite the issues of location (e.g. peripherality, lack of developed infrastructure and dependence on a single transport link), this appears to be a community which has built cohesion in its efforts to attract sustainable and environmentally friendly tourism activity. This task has been carried out through self-reliance and self-support, using the cohesion of the island community and the skills of the islanders themselves. The Community Centre is clearly the island's activity hub, including tourism information, cultural/heritage activities as well as community support (e.g. nursery/childcare).

1   The first critical success factor is the engagement of the permanent community who see building a sustainable tourism product and extending the tourism season as helping to ensure the long-term survival of the island. Connected to that has been embracing environmental and ecosystem controls to ensure that the flow of visitors does not damage a fragile environment. Carrying capacity is effectively restricted to the size of the passenger vessel, which effectively even in high season can only transport around 200 passengers per day in each direction – some of whom will stay and others will be only day visitors.
2   The second critical success factor is the level of community cohesion which has been bottom-up driven, to reflect the boundaries existing in a peripheral island environment. This has been underpinned by the driving force of self-reliance and self-support.

Undoubtedly, Inishbofin is a very small tourism destination. However, it presents a microcosm of the situation affecting Europe's offshore island tourism facilities. In a sense, size is an attraction, as it presents a compact and easily visited environment.

Reflections

This case study seeks to enable an understanding of how community development structures evolve and how they meet the challenges of the environment in which they operate. It focuses on the potentials for community cohesion and self-generated funding, rather than over-reliance on public funding – whether local, national or international). It is suggested that in this specific case study, the important elements are as follows:

- An extensive level of community cohesion due to the potentially precarious nature of the socio-economic and geographic environment;
- A strong willingness of the community to engage in self-financing at the outset, rather than being reliant on regional, national or European funding in the first stage thereafter using the self-funding track record as a methodology to plug into regional, national and European funding;
- The role of the IDC, a community-generated social enterprise, in seeking to improve the quality of life of the inhabitants of the island and to a degree of the visitors to the island, by the establishment, development and provision of support and services through the Development Company to improve the socio-economic, economic, infrastructure, environmental, cultural, heritage and administrative requirements of the island;
- The facilitation of environmentally appropriate policies for the island to ensure sustainable tourism development. They seek to take a different approach to tourism by achieving sustainable tourism that does not negatively impact upon the island's natural environment, whilst at the same time benefiting and supporting their local community. This has resulted in the wide range of tourism providers on Inishbofin seeking methods of achieving this goal and equally importantly, conveying that message of sustainable tourism to all visitors to Inishbofin.

This is evidenced by the EcoTourism Ireland and LNT Ireland awards for sustainable tourism development;

- The critical success factor is the engagement of the permanent community who see building a sustainable tourism product and extending the tourism season as helping to ensure the long-term survival of the island. Importantly, the community cohesion has been bottom-up driven, to reflect the boundaries existing in a peripheral island environment. Undoubtedly, Inishbofin is a very small tourism destination. However, it presents a microcosm of the situation affecting Europe's many offshore island tourism facilities;
- Clearly with Inishbofin, the restriction of the capacity of tourism access (a boat with limited daily capacity) minimises the potential of excessive and potentially damaging tourism flows.

Questions

1   Should we give thought to the fact that fragile communities that achieve benefit from their engagement ecotourism will inevitably move towards an all-year-round tourism product (i.e. not solely during the June-September holiday season)?

2   Are methodologies that manage, and where necessary, restrict tourism capacity access to ensure that fragile environments are not damaged by excessive tourism flows important in small remote communities?

3   On Inishbofin, a primary driving factor has been a community that has built cohesion in its efforts to attract sustainable and environmentally friendly tourism activity. This task has been carried out through self-reliance and self-support, using the integrated aspect of the island community and the skills of the islanders themselves. Is this an appropriate model?

4   May tourism be easily distinguished or separated from socio-economic activity in remote communities, or is it an organic part of the community?

Further reading

Comhar na nOileán Teo (Federation of Irish Islands) (2017). [online]. Accessed 21.09.19: http://oileain.ie *(website also available in English)*.

European Small Islands Network (2017). List of small islands activities [online]. Accessed 21.05.19:https: europeansmallislands.com.

References

An Phríomh-Oifig Staidrimh Roinn Cultúir, Oidhreachta agus Gaeltachta (2016). [online]. Accessed 21.09.19: www.chg.gov.ie/ga.

EcoTourism Ireland (2018). [online]. Accessed: 20.06.18:www.ecotourismireland.ie.

Inishbofin Development Company (2016). [online]. Accessed: 30.04.16: www.inishbofin.com).

Leave No Trace network (2019). [online]. Accessed: 21.05.19:www.leavenotraceireland.org.

Leave No Trace training guidelines (2018). [online]. Accessed 21.05.19:www.dropbox.com/s/azfumxyleej6vdx/Leave%20No%20Trace%20Ireland%20Training%20Guidelines%20Dec%202018%20Updated.pdf.

RoseMarie Hellén (2016). *Threats and possibilities of a small island society in the middle of Sweden.* [online]. Accessed 21.05.19: https://europeansmallislands.files.wordpress.com/2016/10/threats-and-possibilities-of-a-small-island-society-in-the-middle-of-sweden.pdf.

29 An assessment of the case studies

Marko Koščak and Tony O'Rourke

Discussion

The purpose of the Discussion section is to seek to review the main contents of each of the Case Studies (Chapters 14–28) by theme.

Destination management aspects of ethical sustainable development

In Chapter 14, entitled "The ethics of sufficiency: the Edelsbach Tulip Festival as a best practice example of sustainable event culture," authors Daniel Binder, Harald A. Friedl and James W. Miller examine how events, when managed in a truly sustainable way, may contribute to the identity of a rural community, whilst at the same way helping to preserve its economic and social foundations. In this case study, the authors began with a discussion of the ethical aspects of sustainable development and how they are connected to questions of community identity. A specific case, the Edelsbach Tulip Festival, illustrates how concentrating on core values such as sustainability and sufficiency when designing and managing an event can help fend off rural decline. The way the event was originally conceived and then organically developed has resulted in the strengthening of local identity. In the process, the residents have also committed themselves to sustainable event management practices.

Chapter 15, with the title "The cycle network is a soil project between sustainability and resilience: Montesilvano as a case study," is written by Antonio Alberto Clemente. This review of experiences has clearly shown that the cycle path can be an environmental infrastructure capable of responding to both the needs of slow mobility and to contribute to a better collection and management of water in urban areas. Applying it to Montesilvano, in Abruzzo, means integrating a multiplicity of lines of action. The first concerns the need to change the point of view – the cycle path is not a ring road which, by always staying on the side of something, fails to activate any link with it. On the contrary, it is a work that relates to the places it passes through; this establishes privileged relationships with the public space and thereby opens to the interdependence between infrastructure and environment. Working on this hypothesis, the author offers and proposes different concepts about traffic engineering which in Italy, since the second post-war period, have imposed the idea that to solve mobility and accessibility problems, one had to invest only in big infrastructure networks. Montesilvano was no exception: the construction of the city was strongly influenced by the Adriatic Railway, of the Strada Statale 16, the Autostrada A 14 and the interchanges connecting to the urban viability. It is essential to re-start again from the smaller networks and, in particular, from the cycling ones. And this is precisely the premise from which the second line of action must start. The municipality of Montesilvano, which has built all its part of the Ciclovia Adriatica and a significant number of kilometres of other cycle paths, is now called upon to take the next step: building the network.

In Chapter 16, entitled "The importance of stakeholder involvement in the strategic development of destination management: the Mirna Valley case study," authors Maja Žibert, Boris Prevolšek and Marko Koščak develop the suggestion of the importance of stakeholder involvement in the strategic process of destination management, which has the purpose of achieving a deeper understanding of how different stakeholders perceive the critical features of destination management. The key concepts of strategy and of destination management are explained in the theoretical part of the chapter. Based on this, authors have developed the following critical research question: What are the desires of different stakeholders in the development of the destination in the light of strategic management? Results confirmed the findings that the life of the local population should be included and engaged actively when developing the destination and identifying the potential of that destination. Each group of stakeholders plays a specific role in the development of the destination, and thereby, this case study offers an overview of the analytical challenges and trends in the development of a small tourist destination. The most effective and appropriate structure for small destinations is to operate on a "bottom-up" basis and to consider a common brand, which will provide recognition of the place and its key tourism products.

In Chapter 17, entitled "Evolution of a gentle mobility in an Alpine rural municipality: the case of Werfenweng, Province of Salzburg, Austria," author Milan Ilić offers an example of a village with 1,000 inhabitants and a summer & winter tourist resort with 2,000 beds and 290,000 overnight stays per year. Village Werfenweng developed a concept of "gentle mobility" (*Sanfte Mobilität* – SAMO) in the late 1990s. Supported by the federal and provincial government and launched in the winter season 1999/2000, the SAMO gradually became more successful as a role model for a holiday without the privately owned car. The example of Werfenweng shows that success for the concept is based on the deliberate, gradual introduction of new, attractive, high-quality, reasonably priced mobility services, as well as the voluntary participation of both tourist enterprises and guests. The smart concept of alternative mobility during holidays addressed social trends relevant to marketing in target markets, such as the increased environmental awareness of tourists. The municipality continues to register a constant tourism growth, particularly of guests who arrive by train. However, daily visitors and their avalanche of private cars on many weekends in the area continues to be a significant challenge.

In Chapter 18, entitled "Experience design in interpreting cultural heritage: a case study on the Land of Hayracks, Slovenia," authors Bogdan Turnšek and Maja Turnšek introduce the concepts of experience design within the so-called "experience economy" and apply the model of the 4Es in experience design to heritage interpretation: the 4Es being education, entertainment, aesthetics and escape. They apply the model to a case study from the village Šentrupert in SE Slovenia, namely The Land of Hayracks and discuss on the implications the model has for the management of the product and its value in interpreting local cultural heritage to tourists.

In essence, "Dežela kozolcev" (The Land of Hayracks) doubles up as an outdoor ethnological museum and a tourist product that displays and interprets a diverse typography of Slovenian cultural heritage – all in one location. Its success with incorporating modern tourist trends was appraised by a qualitative content analysis and a quantitative survey research conducted on a random sample of Slovenian museum visitors. The study revealed that the managers of the "Dežela kozolcev" tourist product are not very familiar with the most recently developed cutting-edge concepts that ensure high-quality experiences.

Environmental & social aspects of ethical sustainable development

In Chapter 19, entitled "Climate change, tourism and rural sustainability in the Margaret River wine region of Western Australia," authors Roy Jones, Garry Burke and Laura Stocker offer the experience from the Margaret River. The region is within a biodiversity "hot spot" and is an agricultural region famous for its premium wine production and wine, gastronomic and ecotourism. These activities are vulnerable to climate change, especially to reductions in rainfall and runoff. The region has experienced demographic growth as the wine and tourism industries have expanded and as an educated and affluent population of retirees, second home owners, "electronic cottagers" and alternative lifestylers have moved into the area. Two projects, a local study as part of a national evaluation of the adaptation of tourist areas to climate change and a more focused identification of vulnerable locations and activities, were supported by local government, business and community organisations, and several adaptive strategies were identified. The success of these projects can in part be attributed to the relatively high levels of both education and environmental awareness possessed by the local population as a matter of happenstance. Nevertheless, the original contention of this chapter is that these initiatives also allow communities like Margaret River to take on the role of front-runners, providing demonstrations and learning opportunities on how to manage the transition to sustainability and guidance on how such methods might be adapted in other tourism areas facing the challenges of climate change.

In Chapter 20, entitled "The Sustainable Garden of Pirámides de Güímar: a living exhibition blending tourism and sustainability," author David Valcárcel Ortiz analyses the Sustainable Garden of Pirámides de Güímar, an innovative experiment conducted in the Canary island of Tenerife. Pirámides de Güímar is an outdoor museum and botanical garden. Among its various specialised gardens, the author finds the Sustainable Garden, a re-creation of a typical Canarian ravine, including the representative flora and fauna associated with such environments. The garden, developed in collaboration with the Botany Department of the University of La Laguna (Tenerife), is separated into a dry area and a watercourse that includes specimens of the critically endangered European eel and many endemic aquatic plants. The watercourse also allows us to stress the importance of water as a vital and scarce resource. The garden was developed following the main environmental, economic and social principles of sustainability, its purpose being to become a model of how to develop gardens in the Canary Islands in a sustainable manner.

In Chapter 21, entitled "Inclusivity in cultural heritage sites as a means of sustainable tourism: the Istanbul Topkapi Palace Museum," authors Emir Cekmecelioğlu and Asli Sungur suggest that cultural heritage sites stand as the common property of humanity and as unique areas that have universal value. These areas are also home to intensive tourism. Cultural heritage sites, which have a sensitive environment and structure, can be affected and damaged by this intensity. On the other hand, well-managed tourism activities have important benefits on these areas. The case study discusses the principles of inclusivity in the cultural heritage sites within the context of sustainable tourism. Istanbul Topkapi Palace Museum is examined and evaluated as a case within the context of inclusive design principles. As a result, conservation of cultural heritage sites and enhancing their values by developing proposals are aimed.

In Chapter 22, entitled "Social and environmental impacts of tourism mega projects in Mexico," authors Sandra Luz Zepeda Hernández and Fabíola Cristina Costa de Carvalho suggest that tourism is a territorial-changing activity, especially on those hardly inhabited places to be transformed into dynamic centres of attractions. In México, the political attainment to develop tourism is mainly focused on the coastal areas, associated to the discourse that tourism is as a way to reach the growth of national economic indicators. Accordingly, it has a central position on the national agenda, being a state policy since the 1970s decade. The main strategy to develop the activity was to construct integrally planned tourism centres (*Centro Integralmente Planeado*). Tourism expansion represented a transformation on economic, social and environmental dimensions on Mexican territories. Meanwhile, that was incapable to extend social development to host communities. This case study discusses tourism development in the region of *Bahía de Banderas*, located in the north-west coast of 1960s México. In this geographical area, seven out of every ten inhabitants are migrants, a phenomenon that was also largely motivated by tourism megaprojects and the property model, expanded since the 1960s and strengthened in the 2000s. Nevertheless, the region had its highest demographic growth from the year 2005 to 2010 when it had the utmost investment collection at the national level. Then it became the most important tourist corridor in the segment of beach and sun in the country, covering almost the 289 km of coast in Nayarit entity.

In Chapter 23, entitled "Alto Tâmega: present heritage and future prospects," author Sérgio Lira discusses the touristic potential of a Portuguese region called *Alto Tâmega*. *Alto Tâmega* is a region in the North of Portugal, bordering with Spain. Because there are no formal administrative or political regions in the country, it is simply the gathering of six municipalities under the general designation of an Inter-Municipal Community. It extends over 3,000 km² and counts for around 95,000 inhabitants. The author offers an initial geographical, historical and sociocultural contextualisation, which is necessary to explain the present situation of the region. In addition, the case study offers beside this an analysis of the tourism situation in Portugal and as well in *Alto Tâmega* an innovative tourism project, which is currently being developed in the region. Thermal springs are a major marker of the territory and have been in use at least since the Roman occupation – the remarkable Roman spa in the city of Chaves (former *Acquae Flaviae*) being one of its major examples. At present, there is a new breath in the region's ambitions, notably on tourism and natural and cultural heritage. From infrastructure to equipment, buildings, hotels and thermal resorts, there is a whole new range of innovative projects that aim to revitalise the region.

In Chapter 24, entitled "Sustainable tourism development and its implementation: a case study of glamping accommodation providers in local tourism destinations," authors Maja Klančnik, Barbara Pavlakovič and Marko Koščak discuss the response to mass tourism, with new concepts and types of tourism, which are known by different names – sustainable tourism, green tourism, responsible tourism and ecological tourism. Despite these differing names, the concepts of all of these sub-divisions of tourism activity are closely related – they have a common purpose and common goals and also similar methods for creating better sustainability in a tourism activity. A potential danger of not following the concept of sustainability is also present during the development of glamping accommodation. Glamping represents one of the sustainable strategies, which follows the demands of ecotourism, and it represents a luxurious glamping. Glamping is exactly that kind of offer, where tourists can spend time in the authentic natural environment. Glamping offers more comfort and exclusivity to the tourists than the classical way of camping. This could mean also a higher consumption of the energy and more extensive damage of the local environment. For the reasons above, authors have performed the research, where they tried to discover how strictly the providers are following the concept of sustainable development.

The business impacts of ethical sustainable development

In Chapter 25, entitled "Queensland-Gold Coast tourism, the Japanese era 1980–1997 and single market strategies: a case study," author Lesley Crowe-Delaney touches on a tourism phenomenon based on inflows from a specific tourism source – in this case Japan. However, the case study is placed within an overall concept of why this type of tourism in Queensland was so favoured at the time. The author places this narrative within the concept of the fact that Queensland tourism had, in the period from 1880 to 1950, focused on attracting domestic tourists, then lifestyle changers and latterly those Australians retiring to a warm and attractive climate. Japanese tourism appeared very much akin to cruise tourism; the visitors arrived on short visits, bought souvenirs and then left for hotels which were frequently Japanese owned. Whilst an economically successful period for luxury brand retailers, and a resulting cascade effect on the orientation of the local tourism industry towards Japan, the author makes clear that there were some serious reactions from local communities. The situation was then seriously affected by the Japanese economic crash from 1991 to 2000 – hotels became empty, and Japanese-owned property became valueless. Added to this, the author makes clear that, in such a period of economic instability, latent anti-Japanese sentiments came to the fore.

In Chapter 26, entitled "Managing a sustainable tourism destination," authors Aleksa Panić, Marko Koščak and Barbara Pavlaković stress that as with any industry, tourism faces modifications that are stimulated with technological, social and environmental changes. They propose that tourists engaged in sustainable tourism require a higher level of sustainable and responsible attention – manifesting their concerns to understand local culture, history, cuisine and events. The authors focus on an urban destination – Belgrade – which has, it would appear, a poor record in seeking to attract sustainable tourism. The case study is therefore extremely useful in elaborating what the city tourism authorities require to carry out to create a "green city" environment. Undoubtedly, Belgrade has a rich cultural and historic environment, but the case study indicates how this is in many ways obscured by issues of pollution from traffic and poor management of cultural spaces. An interesting part of the case study is the analysis of the success of the Slovenian capital, Ljubljana, in creating a dynamic green environment and suggesting that Belgrade could follow this example.

In Chapter 27, entitled "Promoting the 'Legacy Businesses' of San Francisco: an incentive-based approach to the protection of intangible heritage," author

Brian Roberts Turner takes a unique perspective on intangible cultural and historic assets. We are often used to regard culture and heritage as consisting of sustainable and ethical physical assets which are clearly tangible. The author, however, gives us a highly refreshing approach to the intangible contributions that in this case define American life in San Francisco and demonstrate the rich cultural heritage of that city. Furthermore, he focuses on businesses with demonstrated contributions to their neighbourhood's history and identity. The author explains the role of the Legacy Businesses Registry as a methodology to establish cultural continuity and the preservation of those intangible values. This has a powerful effect in allowing access to the places and people which have shaped culinary, literary, social and artistic roots and are thus touchstones to the traditions which shape modern identity.

In Chapter 28, with the title "Building success on the edge of Europe: the Inishbofin case study," author Tony O'Rourke relates a case study connected to a very small community in population terms. Nonetheless, the case study has resonance in making clear the significant problem faced by small, peripheral communities. The author suggests that the size of the community should not reflect disproportionally on the importance of the case study, which focuses on the remote nature of offshore island communities – of which there are 1,639 in Europe – and the challenges they face. The case study emphasises two key factors – (a) the engagement of a community seeking to build an ethical and sustainable tourism product and (b) a level of community cohesion which is bottom-up driven and has been self-reliant in financial terms.

Learning points

The Learning Points are an addition to the Reflections in the Case Studies. In a sense, they seek to summarise some of the key factors and may be used to demonstrate a number of critical issues which affect Ethical and Sustainable Tourism at a local level.

Destination management aspects of ethical sustainable development

- Self-understanding and reflection are prerequisites for ethical and sustainable behaviour. This applies to both individuals and groups. In times in which change is the only constant, it is especially important for a community to know its residents and what they want to achieve. Only then can common goals be identified and reached. If community residents begin to define themselves through common goals that lead to a steady state in which all of them can survive economically, then unlimited growth may lose its meaning as the be all and end all of economic development. The local population then can decide which activities are conducive to the steady state and which are not. Taking control is an important prerequisite for sustainable development of societies.
- Sustainable economic activity at the local level means minimising waste and conserving resources, while ensuring that the income generated by such economic activity remains to as large a degree as possible within the community. For this to work, the local population has to be led in their actions by these guiding principles of sustainability, which will lead them to make use of local products and labor. The better the inclusion of local residents works, the lower the potential for conflict that might interfere with the success of such economic activity in the long term.

- The starting point of any strategic tourism policy is a tourist destination (city, region, country, site) as a group of interconnected stakeholders. The activity of each individual affects the activity of the others. Certain common objectives must be defined and achieved in a coordinated way. The public sector should be responsible for the future development of the destination (the development plans). The tasks of the public sector are interest rate subsidies, employment assistance, infrastructure in the Municipality, taking care of monuments, organization of events and market research, etc.

Environment & social aspects of ethical sustainable development

- Glamping is a composite word of "glamorous" and "camping." It is a campsite that is in touch with nature, while it offers the comfort of a hotel, similar to a kind of mobile hotel room. Sustainable practices of this kind can be integrated in six business areas, which are company strategy, internal business, management of the supply chain, product management, raising awareness and cooperation with the destination. The demand for glamping has increased dramatically in the last decade, which has led to the establishment of a special category of trips on the tourism market. Trend also indicates the seasonality of glamping, where it is possible to detect the greatest demand in the summer months. Providers can provide more sustainable businesses in several ways, for example, with energy saving through the regular shut-off lights, reducing water flow in bathrooms, reusing of towels and bedding, careful handling of waste, integration and fair treatment of employees and with working locally.
- Tourism developments transformed the territories with the constructions that closed the public accesses to the beaches, generating social exclusion. Public demands increased as a reflection of tourism expansion, without the attention of public policies, as education, public transport and health services. Tourism expansion generated public instability and failed expectation in social and economic dimensions by host communities. Finally, tourism affected the sense of belonging to people who lived in altered sites. According to the current reality in many destinations, it may be worth an effort to design and apply a new scheme for public policy in tourism, focused on local and regional development and promote a greater social participation, which would help to generate a sense of belonging and territorialisation. This action could give a better expectation for balance between speculation and social justice. Considerations should be given to reduce impacts and offer quality of life to population, contemplating the decision making, tourism planning and organisation roles on these territories, to reach a sustainable model of tourism development.
- Cultural heritage sites and tourism interaction involve a bilateral conflict. Sustainable approaches aiming to control the negative effects of tourism on heritage sites and increase their benefits make this conflict beneficial in both sides. It is expected that the volume of tourism will gradually increase in the cultural heritage sites. In this case, it is important to consider sustainable measures as soon as possible. Inclusivity is critical for increasing tourism value. A balanced approach to both conservation and inclusivity needs is important for the sustainability of heritage sites. Cultural heritage sites can only be seen as a common heritage for all humanity when all can experience them. Considering that each member of

the society has a different perception and movement capability, inclusivity is a key parameter in terms of heritage sites. Local tourism communities that possess populations with high educational and environmental awareness levels are more likely to possess the skills, networks and attitudes required to remain resilient and sustainable in the face of future challenges in tourism destinations.

The business impacts of ethical sustainable development

- Single-focus tourist marketing is clearly tenuous in that it is based on the economic ability of the home base of the tourists. Reliance on a specific market (e.g. as shown in the Queensland tourism case study) indicates the potential problems that arise from reliance on a single tourism market. It will tend to lack resilience and will become hugely dependent on the economic success for the origin of the home group. If that home market enters economic decline, then the highly focused reliance on such a market will result in severe failures for the destination market.
- A green tourism location cannot rely only on the unique values of its culture; it must also ensure waste management, traffic relocation, pedestrian zones and low pollution. This must engage the local community and their support for the radical changes required. The example of Belgrade is that there appears to be no clear civic consensus to enable the necessary steps to create a green/ecocity. Thus, progress will continue to be hampered by a lack of such consensus as well as failures at a political level.
- We have often failed to recognise intangible values of cultural heritage and how they contribute to the place in which they are located – thereby contributing to a neighbourhood's history and identity. This does not minimise the connectivity to the more tangible cultural and heritage issues – e.g. craft, culinary or art forms. By helping businesses and organisations which have a target in protecting the intangible heritage, we are effectively protecting a sustainable future.
- A critical concept is how community development structures evolve and meet the challenges of the environment in which they operate. Communities which display robust cohesion and an ability to self-generate funding appear to have an edge over communities reliant on public funding. Primarily, the case study exhibits the fact that a community who regard building an ethical and sustainable tourism product may ensure the long-term survival of their environment. Importantly, that community cohesion is bottom-up driven and based on a multi-agency approach of public, private and social agencies.

Further questions

The further questions are connected to the issues raised from the Case Studies; they may be used for teaching or training purposes or as a method for stimulating concepts and ideas about the fundamental topics in this book.

Destination management aspects of ethical sustainable development

- How may regional sustainable development contribute in the long run to protecting local jobs that might otherwise be threatened by global and digital competition or alternatively how can a well-developed local cultural identity influence tendencies towards outmigration in rural regions? What role does heritage interpretation play in local destination management?

- How is it possible to enable and motivate cross-sectoral development of local destination management strategy when there is a mix of sectoral partners from public, private, social and voluntary sectors?
- What may be done at the EU, national and regional levels to promote environmentally friendlier transportation in tourism? What is the role of regional, national and international transport companies in gentle mobility development at the local level, and what should be the main motivational factors for tourists to change their transportation habits?

Environmental & social aspects of ethical sustainable development

- How might former local economic failures contribute to the subsequent development of successful tourism initiatives? How might tourism enterprises work with other components of their local economy to obtain mutual benefits?
- Why are certain components of the tourism industry more vulnerable than others to the threat of climate change?
- The Sustainable Garden has resulted in the nomination of the museum to an important continental award, but it has also paved the way for it to become an internationally recognised botanical garden. Is this definitive of a good praxis? Will combining a museum and a botanical garden be an appealing touristic offer or will it backfire by confusing and scaring off potential visitors?
- What are sustainable solutions to reduce the harmful effects of tourism in cultural heritage sites and increase their benefits and what is the role of inclusivity here? How can solutions be developed in order to develop inclusivity without damaging sensitive historical fabric in the cultural heritage sites?
- Is the tourism development in large scale a real option for human, social and environmental development so that local communities could embrace a better life? Is it possible to reach an agreeable level between an effective, sustainable destination and large capital investments competitiveness?
- How can a region with a demographic deficit, strong tendency for depopulation and long-lasting lack of attractiveness for young people use its main assets (natural and cultural heritage, climate, fertile soil, good network of road connections, water springs, among others) to break the vicious cycle and head to sustainable development?

The business impacts of ethical sustainable development

- What are the implications of single-market tourism strategies; these are strategies which focus and rely heavily on one specific group of tourists and develop the entire tourism product around that group? Is it possible to develop ethical and sustainable tourism policies in such a situation?
- Would it be appropriate to suggest that creating an ethical and sustainable form of tourism activity in a city which has significant ecological management problems requires not only a strong political commitment by the city authorities, but also an equal level of commitment by the local population? Importantly, how can such an initiative be financed when resources are already stretched and limited?

- The concept of protecting the intangible heritage through the support of legacy businesses challenges the concept that business should succeed or fail on purely economic grounds. Yet the importance of our ethical and sustainable heritage cannot be measured wholly in economic terms. Is it therefore appropriate to help to protect business and economic activities which have a profound and valuable legacy for now and the future?
- Are we able to view ethical and sustainable tourism in remote communities as an organic component of those communities in terms of the basis of unique cultural and heritage systems? At the same time, may the existence of such unique culture and heritage encourage a form of voyeuristic tourism which is not fully appreciative of the values and systems of such communities?

Section 3

Final thoughts

30 The theoretical reflections

*Marcela Costa Bifano de Oliveira and
Thiago Duarte Pimentel*

Introduction & explanation of the theoretical reflections
(Editors: Marko Koščak and Tony O'Rourke)

In this chapter, we have two interesting and supportive inputs of theoretical reflections as a part of our final conclusions which develop critical thinking in regard to the overall subject of this book.

The first input on the topic, the section "Volume of capital and collective action in tourism fields: a comparative perspective in Latin America," has been prepared by our colleagues Marcela Costa Bifano de Oliveira and Thiago Duarte Pimentel. This chapter takes a critical view of the different actors embedded in the tourism field, in three countries – Brazil, Mexico and Ecuador. The authors conduct their study through the theoretical lens of Pierre Bourdieu's social theory to consider

- framing the problem of action in the tourism field
- how actors compete in a social space in order to influence the final decisions of this space
- how the interaction of collective actors with tourism policies has evolved.

The authors focus their analysis in three specific locations across the three countries – Juiz de Fora (Brazil), Mazatlán (México) and Quito (Ecuador), by reconstructing a social field in each location and using historiographic, qualitative and quantitative techniques. The results from the three cities indicate the roles of differing actors – the centralised state (Quito), the private sector (Mazatlán) and organised civil society (Juiz de Fora).

The second input on the topic, the section "The ODIT method revisited: some lessons from Brazilian experience and directions to the future," has been prepared by Thiago Duarte Pimentel. It investigates the approaches that the Brazilian federal, regional and local governments have attempted over some 25 years to develop the tourism system. The author explains that although a multiplicity of approaches have been attempted, they have not been conducted in a systematic and logical manner. This has led to the fragmentation of effect and the resulting poor performance. The study therefore looks at the value of ODIT (Observation, Development and Tourism Engineering) as a methodology for tourism management and planning, supported by one decade of empirical studies and applications in the Federal State of Minas Gerais. The author examines the four dimensions of ODIT – economic, social, ethical and environmental – and how these operate. He suggests that the ODIT method differs from other tourism planning models by being flexible and interactive. At the same time, the author explains that the method presents some limitations – e.g. the creation of new dimensions and indicators for analysis – but if constantly reviewed, it may be seen as a methodology leading to a better margin for strategic initiatives and the achievement of beneficial results in the development of the planned visit.

Volume of capital and collective action in tourism fields: a comparative perspective in Latin America (*Marcela Costa Bifano de Oliveira and Thiago Duarte Pimentel*)

Summary

This section analyses, in a comparative way, the interactive dynamics of the different agents (actors) embedded in the tourism field, in three different countries of Latin America: in Brazil, Mexico and Ecuador. Particularly, we wanted to see through the theoretical lens of Pierre Bourdieu's social theory to frame the problem of action in the tourism field, how the agents compete in a social space in order to influence the final decisions of this space and their outcomes. Since the elaboration of tourism public policies is supposed to involve a large part of the agents in the field, we have focused on this process to analyse empirically the interactive dynamics of the agents involved in Juiz de Fora (Brazil), Mazatlán (México) and Quito (Ecuador). Following Bourdieu, we have reconstructed a social field in each case, and in order to do so, different sorts of techniques – historiographic, qualitative and quantitative techniques – were used to reconstruct these tourist fields, as well as to analyse the mechanisms that structure the action of the agents. The results show that, in the three cities, the process of elaboration of tourism policies is predominantly influenced by the powerful agents. In conclusion, in Quito, it is the public power that makes the decisions related to the tourist policy; in Mazatlán, the private sector and in Juiz de Fora, the organised civil society.

Introduction

This work aimed to analyse the social field of tourism from its agents and its interactive dynamics (collective action) based on the common object of tourism policy in Juiz de Fora (Brazil), Quito (Ecuador) and Mazatlán (Mexico). To fulfil this objective, Pierre Bourdieu's theory of social fields was used to frame the problem of collective action in the tourist field, which is empirically considered a social field. The central argument is that agents with more capital have a greater capacity to influence the field. Specifically, we argue that the collective interaction between the agents of a particular field, in particular, collective (or institutional) agents, demonstrates its evolutionary degree and its capacity of action of aggregate form in the social field of tourism.

The sociological theory of social fields (Bourdieu, 2001a) is considered in this work as a heuristic referential model (Harré, 1988), potentially useful for the framing of social agents who are somehow involved in a social space their own rules, resources and objects of dispute, to which they devote their attention, energy, time and effort. According to Pimentel, the notion of field is prior to Bourdieu, originating in French philosophy of the first half of the twentieth century (Bachelard, 2010); it is important because it allows incorporating the political dimension (which goes beyond the functions and values, as seen in the systems analysis) according to the logic of competition among agents for scarce resources. In this sense, the general logic of social field theory has been used in the analysis of what Pimentel proposed to call the tourist field (Pimenetel et al., 2013, 2014, 2015a, 2015b, 2016b).

The emphasis of *Bourdieusian* analysis is predominantly on the agents constrained by the structure of the field, which depends on the volume of capital they possess, which, by its turn, distinguishes them from each other, as well as their capacity for influence in reality. Besides the identification of the central agents according to their volumes of capital and, therefore, their capacities (or probabilities) of influence and intervention in the reality, more attention here will be given to the process and the results of formation of the agents' interaction in the field, seen as a mechanism to interfere in the decisions regarding tourist policies and rule the field.

We point out that the theoretical proposal presented in this research is original, since it makes one of the first systematic and structured approximations of the sociological theory of Bourdieu as a whole and its application to tourism, contrary to some previous works that resort to Bourdieu (Anaya, 2005; Kay and Laberge, 2002; Kane, 2010; Ahmad, 2013), selectively considering aspects of his theory, often limiting the discussion of "social distinction" (Bruner, 1991; Aledo, Martinez & Terán, 2007; Belhassen and Caton, 2009). In any case, the use of Bourdieusian theory in tourism studies is patently an unexplored area (Pimentel et al., 2014). This work, in addition to this introduction, is divided into four parts. In the first section (theoretical reference), a discussion is made on Pierre Bourdieu's theory of social fields, followed by the theory of "Organized Collective Action." The second section presents the method used in this work. Then comes the analysis with the categories of Bourdieu's theory and "Organized Collective Action," identifying the position, disposition and collective action of the agents present in the tourist field of Juiz de Fora (Brazil), Quito (Ecuador) and Mazatlán (Mexico). Finally, we present the final considerations.

The theory of social fields by Pierre Bourdieu

Pierre Bourdieu is a cornerstone in social theory. More than this, given the breadth and transversality with which he built his theoretical *corpus* in various fields of social interaction, economy, education, religion, art, politics, etc., he is a central reference in the human sciences that if there is a paradigm (in the Kuhnian sense of the term) in the social sciences – or, at least, in contemporary sociology – it is definitely Bourdieusian. Bourdieu sought to understand social phenomena from a proper view based in his structural generative perspective, interposing dominant and dominated agents in a particular social field. He believed that the intellectual should serve the interests of a true praxis of social transformation, demonstrating the reproduction of all symbolic domination.

According to Wacquant (2002), Bourdieu in his research practice combined the theory of several renowned authors such as Marx, Durkheim, Bachelard, Weber, Husserl and Merleau-Ponty, among others, resulting in an original theoretical field, unveiling the dialectic of structures' social and mental processes in the process of domination, in a general world theory of social fields.

Bourdieu (1990, p. 2004) characterises his work as structural constructivism. It considers structuralism in the sense of Levi-Strauss, where there are in the social world objective structures (language, myth, etc.) that guide or constrain the practices and representations of agents, regardless of their consciousness or will. By constructivism, it is understood that there is a social genesis of the schemes of perception (thoughts and actions), which on the one hand are built by the *habitus* and on the other hand by social structures, which are the field, groups and social classes.

According to Pimentel et al. (2014), it is important to recognise that the analysis of objective structures is the central axis in Bourdieu's genetic structuralism. He does not attach in a fixed way to Strauss's classical structuralism but in the analysis of the structures of the relations system that are located in space-time. The field structure designates an externality (which is not the field) and an interiority (which are the institutions and the agents); in this way, the field is analysed as the incorporation of the preexisting structures. Social fields are products of the history of positions and dispositions that reproduce them (Thiry-Cherques, 2006). In this sense, Bourdieu develops the theory that incorporates the concepts of field, capital and *habitus* to identify the relations between individual or collective agents that through strategies struggle to achieve their interests and have the domination of the field.

According to Bourdieu (1993), the field is a space of individual, collective or institutional relations that compete for the domination of the specific goods. Each field has an interest that is common to all agents, which is linked to the existence of the proper field through to the various forms of capital, determining and reproducing social positions (Thiry-Cherques, 2006). The objective relationships are the relations between the positions occupied in the distribution of resources, economic capital, cultural capital, social capital (recognised as legitimate). Thus, agents are distributed in the social space, first according to their volume of capital and then according to the relative weight of the different kinds of capital (Bourdieu, 1990 [2004]).

The positions are imposed on the agents or institutions in relation to their current and potential situation in the structure of the distribution of power (or capital), whose disposition commands the access to the benefits that are at stake in the field. The dynamics of a field lies in the particular configuration of its structure, in the distances between the differences of specific forces that compete in it. Capital types confer power in the field, and their distribution constitutes the very structure of the field, which is given by position (Bourdieu, 1993).

By capital, Bourdieu considers economic capital (money, goods, material wealth), cultural capital (knowledge, skills, information), social capital (social accesses, networks of contacts) and symbolic capital (prestige, honour, synthesis of the other capitals). These forms of capital mean forms of power. For the author, capital is labour accumulated in the form of matter, internalised or incorporated, and time is required for its acquisition (Bourdieu, 2001a).

The social space or social field is constructed by the distribution of the agents in function of their position. Each class of positions corresponds to a class of *habitus*; that is, agents with similar or close positions tend to have the same *habitus*. *Habitus* is the style of an agent, which is tied to his practices and his assets. Position in the field is related to positioning, which depends on the intermediation of dispositions (Bourdieu, 1996).

The concept of *habitus* has a wide history, going through Aristotle, Aquinas, Mauss, Hegel, Husserl. In the definition adopted by Bourdieu, *habitus* is a system of dispositions (way of thinking, doing, feeling) that lead us to act in a certain way and circumstance. The provisions are flexible; they are acquired by the internalisation of social structures. They are carriers of individual and collective history; they are internalised in ways that ignore their existence. "It is the unconscious bodily and mental routines that allow us to act without thinking" (Thiry-Cherques, 2006, p. 33). The opportunity for a mobilised group in defence of their interests to be more successful is related to the proximity of agents in space, so that agents are more inclined to recognise each other on the same project (Bourdieu, 1996). The agents' strategies for positioning, however, depend on the position they occupy in the field, which through dispositions inclines them to conserve or transform the distribution structure (perpetuating the rules of the game or changing them). The strategies, through the objectives of struggle, also depend on the availability of space inherited from previous struggles, which will define the space of position taking (Bourdieu, 1996).

In a synthetic way, Bourdieu's theory describes that the relations existing in the social field are determined by the *habitus* and quantity of capital that each agent possesses. The types of capital will determine positions in the field of agents; the *habitus* or dispositions will determine what the agent is predisposed to do or not to do and the way he does (strategies). These individual or collective agents, from their position and their *habitus* can take a position, that is, have a decision regarding their action, that will maintain or change the social space. From this review of Pierre Bourdieu's theory of social fields, we can say that despite the existence of a structure, transformations can occur from the action of the individual or collective agent. This concept of structure implies that powerful institutions struggle to maintain the power and *habitus* of the countryside, which often does not correspond with societal needs.

Methodology

This study starts from a theoretical-critical perspective, anchored epistemologically in the historical rationalism of Bachelard (2010) and developed by Pierre Bourdieu (1983, 2001, 2001b, among others), which manifests itself methodologically in a proper form of structural-constructivism. This means that the research undertaken according to the Bourdieusian *métier* follows its own form of production, not accepting the Manichean dichotomies (quantitative vs. qualitative, survey vs. case study, questionnaire vs. interview, just to name a few). Instead, it assumes the active role of the researcher in artificial construction (*since it is not automatically given "by nature," e.g. taken for granted*) from the research object. In this sense, the researcher resorts to several research methods and techniques, selected and delineated according to rational criteria of their pertinence and necessity, which are being elaborated, as is a *bricoleur* in the sense of constructing a specific theoretical-empirical landscape of reality (Jenkins, 2006).

In the Bourdieusian theory, what is sought to study are the "social theories, methodologically, the field concept is used as a heuristic tool to conduct the study. The interactive dynamics of the agents involved in the elaboration of tourism public policies in the municipalities of Juiz de Fora (Brazil), Quito (Ecuador) and Mazatlan (Mexico) provide empirical evidence. It is assumed that this process would involve a large part of the agents of the field in either its formulation or implementation, since these are mechanisms that, once created, exert normativity and coercibility on all those who are in the field (Bourdieu, 2001b, 2004).

Thus, the design of this research is guided by the mixed method, done in two Phases (described in Table 30.1). For that, the first point was to make a historical review of the tourism context of each country to trace the genesis of the formation of the countryside, its historicity, the key agents, its interests and objects of dispute. As part of this historicity, we sought, as Bourdieu recommends, screening for proximity to the bureaucratic field, where a historical reconstruction of the main tourism policies in Brazil, Ecuador and Mexico was made at different levels: federal, state and municipal. Next, a current public tourism policy was chosen that was relevant in the

Table 30.1 Criteria to frame the data collection

Dimensions	Environmental	Economic	Social	Governance
Subspecific criteria to frame thematic analysis of each dimension	Renovation	Profitability	Recognition	Governability
	Prevention	Territorial integration	Employment absorption	Disclosure and accountability
	Environmental appreciation	Flexibility	Collectivity practices	Solidarity
	Quality of life	Durability	Access to tourism by locals	Tolerance

Source: Adapted by author from AFIT (2001).

sense that it could affect multiple agents. With the definition of specific, this served as reference for the analysis of all agents in relation to the same object (the policy).

In the following stage, agents were analysed in the tourist field – the individual ones, of organisations, entities and formal institutions that compose the tourist field of each studied municipality (Juiz de Fora, Quito and Mazatlán). The individual agents were divided collectively in public, private and civil society. Finally, semistructured interviews, observation, notes in the field diary and questionnaires were made for the quantitative data related to the calculation of the capital volume.

Based on this empirical object of dispute (a particular tourism public policy), all these steps were carried out, and it was moved to phase 2 (data analysis), which took place in two more stages according to the set of categories analysed. In this way, the position, disposition and position of agents in relation to tourism policies were first verified. These categories allow us to visualise that the agents' actions are determined by their position, that is, by their power in the field and their capacity to influence decisions according to their interest, their willingness to do something, and they are the effective actions in this field. These three categories are oriented by agents' habitus.

The tourism field in analysis: three examples from Latin America – analysis of the tourism field

Position in the field

Methodologically, the agents' position was identified from primary data (interviews) and secondary data (electronic sites); we created a scale of 1–8 for each capital, checking the volume of capital of each actor and each sector (public, private and organised civil society). For economic capital, a scale of 1–8 was made from the annual income of each organisation interviewed. For cultural capital, we analysed the school level of each representative of the organisations on a scale of 1–8. There are eight levels of school in the order Elementary School, High School, Higher Technician, Specialisation/MBA, Masters, Doctorate and last, Postdoctoral Degree. For social capital, we analysed the number of links or relationships maintained by the actor with other organisations, which may be related to (1) government, (2) academics, (3) businessmen and (4) civil society organized at the levels of (i) friendship, (ii) work and (iii) known. In this way, 12 is the maximum number of relationships an organisation can maintain; we specify who the actors are (4) and their respective (iii) levels. That is, 8 (maximum scale number) divided by 12 (number of relations), we have a scale of 0.67 for each relation that the agent maintains.

In Juiz de Fora (Brazil), from the capital distribution of the actors in the field, we can say that the private sector (capital volume: 106.5) occupies a central position in the field, followed by the public sector (capital volume: 60, 76). Organised civil society has a lower volume of capital (36.73) but is represented by few organisations.

It is important to point out that, because there is a Municipal Tourism Council in the city of Juiz de Fora, and because tourism involves different actors and sectors for its organisation, there are many actors present in the discussions about tourism in the city, mainly from the private sector, which is represented by a large number of actors. In this way, we analyse the actors directly related to the tourist activity, in order to verify the position of the agents in this segment, so we have a total of ten actors distributed as follows.

In this way, organised civil society has a greater volume of capital in the field, followed by the private sector and the public sector, respectively. On the other hand, the strongest actors in the field, or with a better position, are those who have greater capacity and are those who tend to influence the actions that must be developed in Juiz de Fora. The other actors have a secondary role in this scenario.

In Quito (Ecuador), we can say that the public sector (capital volume: 52.73) has the best position in the field, followed by the private sector (capital volume: 28.04) and finally the organised civil society (volume of capital: 27.05). In this sense, it is the public companies that have a greater power and strength oriented to the tourism and possess greater economic capital in the field; thus, they have a legitimacy and autonomy to handle the tourism in the way that suits them.

In Mazatlán (Mexico), we can say that the public sector (capital volume: 60.11) is the one with the best position in the field, followed by the private sector (capital volume: 53.77). Organised civil society also has a good volume of capital (46.76) if we consider that it is represented by fewer organisations. Regarding the policy analysed, the actors CODESIN, CONSELVA and SECTUR are the dominant players in their sectors; they are the proponents of actions to make south of Sinaloa competitive and sustainable. The other actors are co-operative in the tourist scene.

Disposition in the field

In Juiz de Fora (Brazil), the *dispositions* of the agents in the field are different. There is a very large fragmentation; the actors have very different visions, which makes it difficult to generate homogeneity in the habitus of the field. On the other hand, it is possible to verify that one idea stands out in relation to another; in practice, there is a tendency, although it is common sense, to reproduce the logic of the market. There is a central axis in considering that the focus of the activity in the city is business tourism and events, which is precisely the business discourse, which reproduces the logic of the market and has an advantage since it is common sense, and the different actors repeat this same discourse of economic improvements. In addition, it verifies that, in the city, there is an inertia of the actors in relation to concrete actions; they expect the public sector to solve the problems and challenges related to the activity; there is also little tourist awareness of the general population in seeing/recognising the city as a potential tourist destination.

In Quito (Ecuador), the dispositions of the actors are identified in some points, such as to bring better economic development to the city and to the communities, besides the subject of sustainability. The interests of agents also intertwine in the aspect of making tourism bring greater economic development and a better quality of life for all involved. It is noticed that the public sector has a great interest in developing the municipality economically, providing quality services for the visitors, as well as that proposed in the policy analysed by Quito Tourism. The private sector is the one that most aims at the economic benefit in relation to the other benefits of tourism. Organised civil society is the agent that focuses more on the quality of life of communities, conservation of nature and their customs. In this way, the policy analysed legitimises the public sector's disposition, while leaving isolated the questions demanded by the organised civil society.

In Mazatlán (Mexico), the dispositions of the actors in the field are different in some points, and each sector has its priorities. On the other hand, it is possible to verify that all the sectors are in search of an improvement in the quality of the tourist product to attract more tourists; that is, they want to promote the tourist destination to have greater economic growth. Thus, all seek economic growth to have social and environmental achievements.

Taking of position in the field

Taking into account the data analysed, we can infer that, in Juiz de Fora (Brazil), the different actors are present in the discussions on tourism policies, due to the existence of COMTUR, trying to influence the path of these policies. On the other hand, the council is only consultative and not deliberative, which limits the decision-making by the different actors. This shows a great influence of the three sectors in the determinations of the public policies, influencing in a certain way which policies and actions will be executed.

By its turn, in Quito (Ecuador), the data shows that the different agents present in the field make decisions regarding their organisations and responsibilities, but there is no room to interfere in tourism policies, even if there is a given emphasis by the state to promote democratisation and citizen participation in public decision-making. In this way, the public sector is responsible for deciding which policies are going to enter the agenda; there is no participation that leads to a consensus to generate the best for all those involved.

Finally, in Mazatlán (Mexico), we could verify that the different actors are present in the discussions on tourism policies, trying to influence their way. The public and private sectors are the ones who interfere and decide the policies that will enter the agenda; their positions and provisions maintain the rules of the game of making tourism an economic detonator. Organised civil society tries to participate more actively but is often not heard.

Comparative analysis among the tourism fields and concluding remarks

From the analysis in Juiz de Fora (Brazil), Quito (Ecuador) and Mazatlan (Mexico), we verified that there are substantial differences in the interactive dynamics between the actors in the three cases analysed. Even with the different interactive dynamics in the analysed cities, we find that the actors who participate in the empirical process of shaping public policies are the ones that have the largest volume of capital (i.e. accumulation of cultural, social and economic capital), which allows them to interfere in policies according to their interests. Thus, it can be said that the resultant in terms of action in each field depends on the distribution of power in the field (volume of capital and position of agents) as well as the forms of interaction, contextually manifested in a given conjuncture.

In addition, we find that the social domains seem to be affected socioculturally and institutionally by the national systems, and in Quito, the public power makes the decisions related to tourism policies; this occurs in function of the planned economy model established from the national level, where decisions are taken centrally by the state (Senplades, 2013) since the state is the actor that has a greater concentration of all types of capital. Thus, it is not possible to verify the formation of a collective action; the actors in the field are not recognised.

In Mazatlán (Mexico), it is the private sector that decides the orientations related to tourism, since the implementation of the neo-liberal model favours the interest of the predominant sectors for the economy, as is the case of tourism (Rojas, 2014). This actor has a greater capacity to intervene in public tourist policies and consequently in the field in general, leading the direction that the tourist activity should follow. In this way, the policies implemented favour the interest of the market, and the other actors have a secondary role.

In Juiz de Fora (Brazil), it is the organised civil society that makes the decisions; this is due to the reactivation of the tourist councils in 2003, which allowed a space for democratic discussion regarding the guidelines and actions for the tourist activity (Emmendoerfer, Silva, Lima, 2014). Even in the interviews with COMTUR/JF members, when asked if they participated in the proposals, debates and decision-making in public policies, most answered that they did participate through COMTUR: "Yes, COMTUR is for this, to unite society with the public sector." (SCS); "Through COMTUR, through votes and proposals." (Municipal Guard); "Yes, with proposals and responsibilities." (ABAV); "Yes, within COMTUR, helping to build this new moment of doing tourism in the city." (ACRBA). Thus, here there is a greater participation of organised civil society in the elaboration of public tourist policies. This is due to the existence of the Municipal Councils, which allow a greater participation of the different actors. However, the actors do not achieve a common identity, a coalition, which does not allow an effective collective action, which promotes concrete results.

As a final word, and recalling the objective of this study, which was to study the social field of tourism based on its agents and its interactive dynamics based on the common objective of tourism policies in Juiz de Fora (Brazil), Quito (Ecuador) and Mazatlan (Mexico) and the possibility of intervening in them, we can say and verify the following supported by the data collected and analysed: in Quito, Ecuador, *the tourism field is state oriented (e.g. directed and centralised by the state)*; in Mazatlan, Mexico, it is *market oriented*; meanwhile in Brazil, it is *civil-society oriented*. These patterns, by their turn, seem to be related to the political regimes and the path dependence trajectory of each country, which may be a new development of the agenda for future studies.

The ODIT method revisited: some lessons from Brazilian experience and directions to the future (*Thiago Duarte Pimentel*)

Summary

Despite more than a century of tourism planning in the world, Brazil has faced an acute question in the last 25 years. The government, at federal, regional and local levels, has tried differing approaches to guide the tourism planning process in order to develop the tourism system. Many references and models have been used but not in a systematic and logical manner, thus leading to a fragmentary and non-cumulative theoretical perspective. Further, these fragmented attempts have practical implications (e.g. the low-level performance or even the lack of effective results to the local communities and municipalities). In this context, this theoretical chapter aims to present and discuss ODIT (Observation, Development and Tourism Engineering) as a methodology of tourism management and planning, supported by one decade of empirical studies and applications in the *Minas Gerais* state, also generating a reflexive balance about its contributions and possibilities to improvement.

Introduction

Despite discussions regarding the historical data of the beginning of tourism in the world, a dilemma intertwined with competition over the very definition of what tourism is, there is a form of consensus that planning and organisation of tourism are recent, assuming as a point of reference the institution of this new phase in the last quarter of the 19th century (Costa, 2001), whose intensification and massive use only occurred in the second half of the 20th century.

The growth of tourism and the conditions of its development began to be increasingly important for its accomplishment. However, as it intensified its complexity, the dependence on new factors also increased. Since tourism has changed the social dynamic and productive spaces where it exists, it is essential to intervene in the activity of controlling its harmful effects and maximising its benefits. In this context, several models have emerged to understand tourism and also been developed to serve as a reference for rational intervention, under planning, in this activity (Lohmann and Panosso Netto, 2008).

The planning process has historically been treated as an administrative task (Fayol, 1931). The administrative task, in turn, was seen as a process including the following actions: (1) planning, (2) organising, (3) control, (4) command and (5) coordination. However, quite often in tourism, this process is metonymically confused with the management as a whole. This synthetic understanding of tourism management in terms of a single activity-planning has been done consistently and can be verified through the emphasis, sometimes excessive, on the proposals and planning models (1985).

These models collaborated in the management of destinations, since they allowed the planning of activity by visualising the tourist system as a whole. In turn, they created the means to intervene and control the flow of tourists, adapt the infrastructure and qualify the tourist destination, among other factors. On the other hand, in most cases, they were limited to applying the knowledge of other areas in tourism – particularly administration and economy – without developing from their own tourism systems the techniques, procedures and information systems specific to the management of destinations.

- From 1990 to 2000, an innovative action undertaken by the French government convened a group of experts in tourism planning and elaborated, based on a series of preliminary studies, a synthesis document entitled *Driving Sustainable Tourism in Territories and Companies: a "know-how" guide*. This document, prepared by the French Agency for Tourism Engineering (now the French Tourism Development Agency/*Atout France*), was used as official methodological reference for territorial tourism planning by several French public bodies, such as the Department of State for Tourism and the Ministry of Territorial Planning and Environment. *Atout France* was created, in 2009, as a new governmental agency, by the integration of two existing agencies:

- *ODIT France*, initially a public interest association specialising in tourism planning that dealt with the structure of tourism specifically with local communities and private operators
- *Maison de la France*, an economic interest group in charge of the promotion of tourism in France.

To carry out the necessary operations of planning, management and development of tourism in France, the agency *Atout France* has established a triple objective:

- the promotion of tourism in France
- tourism planning operations
- application of a policy of quality and competitiveness in tourism, in both the public and private sectors.

In Brazil, the Ministry of Tourism published at the end of the 2010s, a set of *know-how guides* in order to promote the self-organisation of tourism at the local level. Thus, the same process of institutionalisation of tourism planning and management methods, already used in other countries, was put into practice as a toolbox for tourism operation.

Basically, these instruments were intended to "normalise" the development of inbound tourism, guiding the actions and the ways in which they would be carried out in a common direction. However, the absence of a deep background and professionalisation of the sector, at the lower level (e.g. for local and regional staff), makes the operation difficult. In this context, the "generic tools" can oversimplify the process by transforming it into an application of common sense. A planning model without a method, and a method without a parametric system, cannot be helpful or constructive.

In this section, we aim to present and discuss the ODIT (Observation, Development and Tourism Engineering) method of tourism management and planning, supported by one decade of empirical studies and applications in the *Minas Gerais* state, and at the same time generate balanced reflections about the contributions and possibilities of ODIT as a system of improvement. Particularly, we aim to

- present the ODIT premises and background
- explain its operation through its phases and main characteristics, dimensions and scales
- illustrate the development process of tourism indicators, which is based on the ODIT methodology.

These indicators are useful for the management of tourist destinations.

The French ODIT method: observation, development and tourism engineering

Tourism in France went through a period of fast quantitative growth in the last century, particularly after the end of World War II, between the 1950 and 1989

(Boyer, 2003). After that, the increasing demands of immaterial goods and services in the context of a post-industrial society were a way to express a symbolic new alternative and emerging identities as well to expand the interests of the ordinary life to a broader cycle of events. This reflected also in the increasing demand for inbound and outbound tourism and thereby required the French tourism industry to adapt itself. It sought qualitative development to adapt to the growth of the global tourism supply. As tourism evolved in France, despite being a young activity, it had already acquired a degree of maturity and progressively began to focus on the empirical application of sustainable tourism in the national territories. This demonstrated a willingness to apply this type of tourism and also provide the necessary organisation to achieve it.

The age of Sustainable Tourism (Jafari, 2005) gave the necessary umbrella to provide quality stays to tourists while seeking to improve the lives of people, without dismissing competitiveness. It was also directly interested in the impacts of tourism activities on the development of the territory and in ensuring equitable benefits for local populations. In terms of production, sustainable tourism advocates mainly the development of practices that allow tourism companies to maximise the creation of wealth, preserving and optimising the environmental and human capital of the territory, the necessary durability and the attractions of the destination. Durability is a key concept in understanding sustainability, as it is very representative of the fusion between the economic discourse and the environmental discourse. Whilst the second furnishes a legitimacy with appeal to the new form of behaviour (individual and collective), the first guarantees that the economic operation would maintain the logic of the capitalist system, without radical changes that might break the expectations of investors.

However, for tourism to develop in the territories in a sustainable manner, as proposed by the ODIT method, a number of factors must be taken into consideration. The broader conception of sustainability is framed to encompass the economic, social and environmental ones. Thus, first, one needs to be aware of the relationship between the territory and the companies located there. Therefore, it is necessary to observe the practices and strategies that the actors exercise in the tourism activity, both at the organisational and at the territorial scales.

Secondly, an action plan must be built as a result of the planning process of sustainable tourism in the territory, in a specific and proper way, and carried out systematically and professionally. The planning process consists of organising the necessary actions to achieve the previously established objectives. In addition, it is the most important management device, since it acts as an element of orientation of the action (plan) and also as a correction tool (evaluation). Therefore, to guide the development of a sustainable tourism plan in accordance with local needs and wishes, it is necessary to use the information collected in advance from the territory and the organisations present in it.

Finally, the diversity of actors involved in tourism must be taken into account, so that their effect on the environment is the most beneficial for the development of sustainable tourism. This is necessary because tourism is not an isolated activity in the territory; but on the contrary, it exercises and is influenced by the environment in which it operates, which could significantly affect the possibilities of sustainable tourism development (Pimentel & Pimentel, 2015).

In spite of the difficulty to take into consideration the diversity of actors, in order to respond to multiple local demands, a way to deal with the diversity of actors is articulated somehow in a democratic and equitable manner to guarantee the recipro-cal right to express their ideas and claim their interests. In this sense, it is necessary that some entity (for example, a consulting firm, a state agency, a research center or a university), whenever possible outside the territory, occupy the role of mediator in this process. This process of mediation (known in French terminology as "animation" of the actors) leads them to reflect collectively on their tourism practices and to value di-versity through the organisation of favourable devices for their expression, creativity and validation of the guidelines necessary to achieve sustainable tourism.

In summary, the ODIT method takes into account different premises – local sus-tainability, collective participation, transparency – which are gathered in a very par-ticular way and are also set in motion through a systematic and professional dynamic (AFIT – Agence Française de l'Ingénierie Touristique, 2001). To devote more detail to issues related to the French experience of tourism planning and management, this section will deal with the logic of the operation of the ODIT method, from a theoret-ical point of view but empirically validated by a series of empirical applications in the last decade (see Pimentel, 2010, 2018; Pimentel et al., 2014).

The modus operandi *of ODIT*

Each tourism planning model presents a sequence of phases that must be followed to achieve the expected effects. Collecting data, interpreting them, diagnosing problems and pointing out interventions are steps that lead to the formulation of a formal plan, which can then be applied or not, depending on the context. In the case of the ODIT methodology, the sequence of the phases occurs in the following way: (1) the portrait of the place, (2) the diagnosis, (3) the definition of the strategic axes and (4) the plan of action (AFIT, 2001) (Figure 30.1).

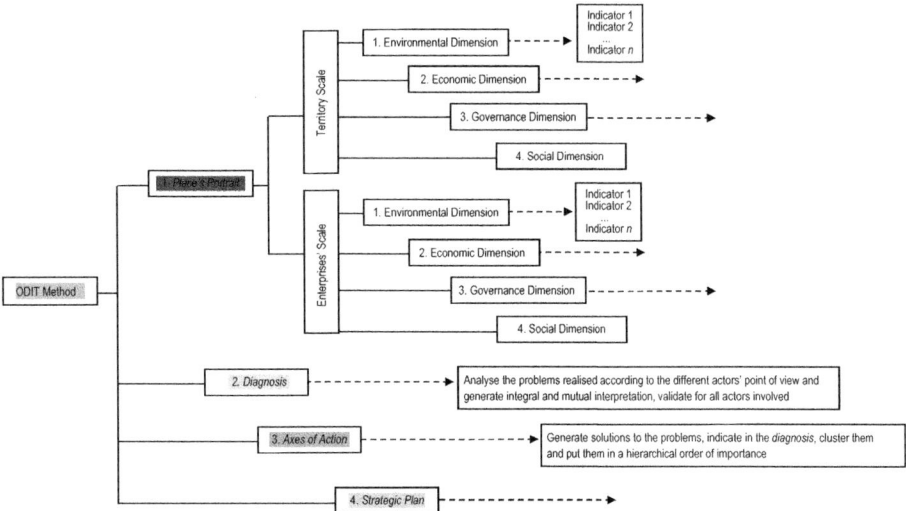

Figure 30.1 The modus operandi of ODIT.

Phase 1: the portrait of the place

The first stage of the application of the ODIT method is to conduct the "portrait" of the place, that is, the extensive data collection identifying the relationship between tourism activity and the environment; in a broader sense, this implies the economic, social, environmental and governance conditions in which it operates. The objective is to identify with as much precision and detail as possible the diversity of actors (public, private and organised civil society) and their practices (actions, habits, beliefs and traditions) and interests. In addition, it requires investigation into the dynamics existing in the territory (how tourism events and conditions occur in that place, who conducts these events and conditions, how they are created, how often they are held) (AFIT, 2001). The answers to such questions will resemble a puzzle, which requires to be configured in order to make sense of the whole picture. Once it is possible to make sense of that information, then we will have a "portrait"; this is the sense-making generated and valid for a specific context (place and time) but requires to be updated from time to time.

Therefore, the important question in this stage is to analyse the diversity of individual actors (residents, tourists, workers, among others), groups and collectivities (associations, organisations, companies, etc.) and the practices associated with them. More than that, it is necessary to involve them in the commitment to collectively build a set of indicators for the direction of sustainable tourism in the territory (AFIT, 2001).

However, due to the diversity of the actors, we must keep in mind that different data cannot always be comparable (AFIT, 2001). For example, the opinion of an inhabitant of the city differs in reality from the institutional opinion of a municipality or of a collective actor (e.g. a firm). The latter refers to an opinion from a collective group, and due to that it, has a form of institutional value. Traditionally, in sociology, it is acknowledged that reality may be studied through various social levels: micro, meso and macro (Brante, 2001). Therefore, the comparison of the opinion of an individual or an organisation may lead to misunderstandings in the interpretation of the data, and, of course, it is necessary to consider methodological parameters that protect the analysis.

To avoid this type of situation, which may significantly influence the diagnosis and, therefore, the overall result of the tourism plan, the ODIT method suggests dividing the data collection and its analysis into two levels: that of the territory and that of the company, in order to delimit the focus of analysis and of different and non-overlapping cycles of action.

In the first level, the *territorial analysis*, the objective is to identify the issues related to the territory and tourism by the actors. Therefore, the diversity of logic and rationalities of the actors is the guide of that phase. The second level, the *organisational analysis*, has an emphasis on tourism with the objective of identifying the types of practices and their methods for evaluating sustainability and possible improvements. This analysis allows prefiguring the organisational mode to facilitate participation (AFIT, 2001).

With regard to the territory, it is necessary to deepen its dynamics with tourism, economy, quality of life, etc. We must have a greater focus on tourism, seeking, for example, to observe the interrelation between visitors and local inhabitants, who take advantage of the opportunity to develop the tourist city economically, and the impacts of the actions between them. Knowing how to enjoy this activity and its benefits requires planning, if possible, within the logic of sustainable tourism, so that everyone benefits.

Within firms, it is necessary to analyse and identify the key points related to their operating processes and tourism, for example, how tourism is developed in the locality, what is its progress, is it being carried out in a sustainable way, what needs to be improved and how to manage it. This will develop tourism more easily, with better quality and with the participation of all stakeholders.

These two stages culminate in a series of key questions for the understanding of local tourism dynamics, where (AFIT, 2001)

- the diversity of the representations in the territory will be identified and brought together and will characterise the tourism practices that depend on it
- the ways of carrying out the touristic practices of the organisations will be taken into account
- the expectations and priorities of the organisations will be known regarding territorial policies and supervisory structures
- what will govern the behaviour of the actors in the territory and tourism will be clearly identified.

At the second level, the micro/organisational concepts which may be envisaged as the production units connect to the collection of data and related analysis. For example, a number of questions (AFIT, 2001) may arise such as

- what are the management practices of the environment (environmental dimension) that are carried out?
- do companies generate profits that allow them to reinvest in the territory, increasing, for example, their business and the creation of jobs (economic dimension)?
- if the labour relations are formalised in the companies, consequently will the rights and working conditions be appropriate (social dimension)?
- is there transparency in the information and/or participation of workers in decisions (ethical dimension)?

In addition to these vertical levels of analysis, the ODIT method proposes, in the *portrait of the place* phase, the thematic or dimensional concept, which involves framing the information and data collected into clusters in order to organise and ensure an easier task of sense-making. In this, it is possible to observe the reality composed of the environmental, economic, social and ethical dimensions, through analysis – horizontal and dimensional – which in summary will generate the tourist panorama of the investigated destination. For each of them, there is also a set of indicators or measurement elements for control, such as tourists or general socio-economic practices that are being developed in the territory (AFIT, 2001) (Table 30.2).

Indicators are in all aspects "information tools" to support management. Indicators are essentially numerical data relating to at least two variables and have a unit of measurement and reference/comparison (OECD, 1994). As decision support tools, indicators have simplified reality models with the ability to facilitate the understanding of phenomena, the ability to communicate raw data and the adaptation of information to the language of decision makers. The different categories of indicators have been used throughout the world for different purposes: environmental, social, cultural, historical, tourist, among others.

Table 30.2 Examples of indicators

Driving question: does the tourism enable the environmental resources' renovation, over that it is supported? Are these resources treated by others' activities or even by the tourism in the territory?	
Possible indicators	Assessment criteria (absolute numbers or percentile)
Landscape attractiveness and biodiversity	Tax of changing landscape and biodiversity
Water consumption	Amount of days without (or with limited disposal) of water
Air quality	Amount of days with air pollution
Sound and olfactive quality	Number of polluting firms in a geographical area
Architectural quality	Conservation conditions of the heritage
Tourism intensity	Density of visitors in a geographical area (m^2 or Km^2)

Source: Author adapted from AFIT (2001).

An indication of the importance and priority of a tourist area, in terms of actions, investments and dissemination, is the availability of tourist information. Despite the increasing appreciation and impact of tourism on society, the measures for the creation and use of tourism indicators are still incipient, often remaining (when they are) restricted to large cities and established tourist centres, depending on their physical, scenic or scenic attraction, for their economic and/or political centres and for their historical-cultural relevance.

The use of indicators enhances the ability to transmit information, add value to it and allow deeper analysis through the correlation between information. The differential treatment of the data may generate more objective information and be accessible to users, facilitating communication between the technical and scientific community and society. As an example, one may cite the capacity of environmental indicators to portray the potential of space tourism and the response capacity of the indicators to monitor the actions and initiatives of tourism management.

It is precisely in this sense that the table of indicators is inserted in the ODIT method, which has a double function: to be a rigorous tool for data collection and scientific research and also to provide reliable bases for the control and management of tourism. Each indicator provides specific information; a set of indicators for each dimension offers a portrait of this dimension. In turn, the sum of the portraits of the four dimensions of the place (economic, social, environmental and ethical), regarding their application at organisational and/or territorial level, should offer a global view of tourism at any destination.

As an example of tourism indicators, one may create an indicator regarding the "impact of tourism in the locality with the objective to determine how much financial investment is injected into the locality in terms of tourism and thus to estimate the proportion in which this affects other activities. This would require obtaining data concerning the volume of income from tourism and cross-referencing this data with the volume of companies in the key sectors – e.g. primary (agriculture), secondary (industry) and tertiary (services) that provide products for tourism in a specific period (e.g. a year).

Phase 2: the diagnosis

The objective is to interpret, in terms of development, the signs and directions observed in the *portrait of the place*. The signals may be translated as SWOT (strengths, weaknesses, opportunities and threats), according to the different types of actors. Sustainability must be defined to interpret the implications of tourism practices (AFIT, 2001). The diagnosis focuses on tourism and its integration with other types of activities and sectors, which is closely involved with

- the problems originally identified, that is, the common thread of the entire analysis
- the quality of the methods used for the *portrait of the place* and their capacity to consider the diversity of actors and their representations
- the ability to list the preliminary "conclusions" for the diagnosis of the elements observed in the *portrait of the place*
- control of the volume of information collected to generate indicators of sustainable tourism
- the way to organise collectively in building and validating the interpretations (quality of animation and diversity of representation).

Experience shows that the practices are not dichotomous, that is, exclusively sustainable or unsustainable. They never manifest in the whole in the same way but in degrees of preponderance. Making a diagnosis, therefore, does not have the ambition to consider everything and to make a state of the art of the place but to observe the actors involved and their actions that interfere in sustainable development.

Thus, the diagnostic stage concerns three main questions:

- the first is to collectively identify and validate priority topics for interpretation, seeking to test whether the sustainability of tourism practices responds to priority issues of the territory
- the second deals with encouraging the development of contradictory interpretations (in the territory, statements and opinions may be contradictory). This discussion implies argument and induces a debate which is based on the indicator framework, with the objective of rectification and collective validation. The objective is thus to take a dynamic generating a minimally shared and consensual tourist diagnosis
- the last question refers precisely to a collective discussion and debate focussed on the completion of the diagnosis of the tourist territory. Creating a base of clear and common indicators with problems, practices and representations of work and including a diversity of points of view (contradictory interpretations) makes it possible to collectively validate the diagnosis of the territory. As a result of this stage, a list of suggestions is drawn up on the aspects that should be improved in the territory and on the organisational levels (AFIT, 2001).

Phase 3: Elaboration of the strategic axis

Based on the diagnosis validated by all the actors involved, in this phase, the main lines of work are defined to compare the strengths and improve the weaknesses of tourism. The idea is to design actions that have some degree of stability over time. In general, a time frame of three to five years is used as a reference to devise an action plan (AFIT, 2001).

This implies that the areas of strategic intervention in the territory must be defined and prioritised collectively. The axes are the development objectives of the intermediaries of the place (e.g. improving water quality, improving the profitability of business activities, etc.) and are extracted from the points identified in the diagnosis to be improved.

To validate the strategic axis to be jointly debated by the local group, it is required (AFIT, 2001) to

- analyse the links between sustainability and the types of tourism practices carried out in the territory and their impact in the region
- propose strategic axis taking into account the set of elements validated in the diagnosis
- organise the debate to establish priorities and collectively validate the strategic axes that must be conserved for the territory (the temporal dimension is one of the elements that requires reflection).

The proposed organisation – linked to the research method – facilitates the synthesis, as at this stage, the actors have two common types of references. The first is to identify the types of tourism and its practice with sustainability, and the second is to evaluate the impact of these practices on the development of the territory. The concept is developed from a common tool – the local tourism indicators table.

To establish the hierarchy of intermediate objectives (also called lines of action), this question must be taken into account: do the proposed guidelines allow the observations initially made to be addressed (corrected/mitigated)?

Therefore this stage allows the relation of the coherence of the trilogy of the procedure: search/interpretation/priority development goals.

Phase 4: the action plan

This phase consists in the creation of a formal document organising and prioritising in time and space the actions corresponding to the main development objectives identified above (at the stage of the strategic axis). The action plan acts as a guide to implementation as well as monitoring the execution of the activities and corrections prior to analysis. The central task rests on the question: "do the proposed actions meet the purpose of correctly oriented development and strategic priorities?" (AFIT, 2001).

To clarify this issue (elaboration of the action plan and collective validation), it is useful to return to what has already been completed. Thus, it is necessary to return to the findings made in the *portrait of the place*, which is full of lessons to guide the debate of the proposed adapted actions.

It is recommended to have a discussion about the facts (e.g. the improvement of water quality – Strategic Axis 1 – which may not be perceived as a priority of all stakeholders). Each stakeholder may have their focus on a subject which might require different actions to deal with the problem. For example, certain actors may have a problem of conscience; others may discern an economic problem.

The question that arises here is whether one may act simultaneously on a series of existing instruments or only a few instruments (i.e. one at a time). To clarify such a doubt, a committed systemic analysis is necessary, so the actors must systematically develop the plan to achieve the medium, the human element and the necessary logistics to implement each designated investment action.

Monitoring and assessment: a transversal process

Monitoring and evaluation are carried out twice: at the end of each stage and with a guide for decision-making. In case you have the indicator framework, you should look for the registration information along each step to reveal the reasons and choose a path and at the same time build a temporary database. It can be done directly with the actors in the indicator framework. The second is at the end of the cycle of the four stages where the elaboration of the plan ends. The same may occur when it is put into practice, with evaluations at each stage and also at the end of each cycle (AFIT, 2001).

Concluding thoughts

Studies on tourism planning will go through a long period of stagnation, especially when reaching the stage of theorising and expanding knowledge concerning the planning process per se. The ODIT method differs from other tourism planning models by being guided by the search for the interrelation between all the actors involved in the tourism industry and the flexibility to create indicators aligned to the reality of each destination. Other planning models restrict the participation of stakeholders in the process (centralised planning). On the other hand, interactive planning methodologies are often more successful in individual contexts; therefore, they are not absolutely reproducible in other contexts.

In the case of the ODIT, it is based on criteria of flexibility for the creation of markers and promotes the adaptation of the model for different contexts. In addition, ODIT exceeds the actions of mapping and the preparation of rigid plans, which provide analytical tools for the control and evaluation of the need for adaptation measures, in the form of tourism indicators, resulting in decision-making and the implementation of qualified plans.

Therefore, the merit of the ODIT methodology represents an indisputable advance, but it also presents some limitations, in which progress is needed, such as the creation of new dimensions and indicators for analysis. It is also recommended to review the operational logic to specify the actions and deepen the precision of the process. The deepening of empirical research in the context of Brazil may test and extend the methodology leading to a better margin for strategic initiatives and achievement of beneficial results in the development of the planned visit.

However, empirical data suggests that the use of this method imposes a double challenge: on one hand, it requires some basic and precedent conditions of data and information (which not always is available in the Brazilian context), and, on the other hand, the method itself could be improved by incorporating some new dimensions and indicators.

References

AFIT – Agence Française de l'Ingénierie Touristique (2001). *Piloter le Tourisme Durable dans les Territoires et les Enterprises: guide de savoir-faire.* Paris: AFIT.

Aledo, A., Martinez, T. M. Y., and Terán, A. M. (2007). La insostenibilidad del turismo residencial. In: D. Lagunas (coord.). *Antropología y turismo: claves culturales y disciplinares* (pp. 185–208). Ciudad de México, México: Plaza y Valdés.

Anaya, J. (2005). El estudio del turismo a partir de la teoría de los campos de Pierre Bourdieu. In: A. Palafox (Ed.). *Turismo Teoría y Praxis.* Ciudad de México, México: Plaza y Valdés.

Bachelard, G. (2010). *A experiência do espaço na física contemporânea.* Rio de Janeiro, Brasil: Contraponto.

Belhassen, Y. and Caton, K. (2009). Advancing Understandings: a Linguistic Approach to Tourism Epistemology. *Annals of Tourism Research*, 36 (2), pp. 335–352.

Bourdieu, P. (1983). Algumas Propriedades sobre os Campos. In R. Ortiz (Ed.) *Questões de sociologia* (pp. 89–94). Rio de Janeiro, Brasil: Marco Zero.

Bourdieu, P. (1990). *Coisas Ditas* (pp. 149–159). São Paulo, Brasil: Brasiliense.

Bourdieu, P. (1993). Entrevista a Pierre Bourdieu, La lógica de los campos. *Zona Erógena (16),* pp. 1–14. Recuperado de: www.educa.ar.

Bourdieu, P. (1996). *Razões Práticas: Sobre a teoria da ação.* Campinas, Brasil: Papirus.

Bourdieu, P. (2001a). *Las Estructuras Sociales de la Economía.* Buenos Aires, Argentina: Ediciones Manantial SRL.

Bourdieu, P. (2001b). *Poder, Derecho y Clases Sociales.* España: Desclée de Brouwer.

Bourdieu, P. (2004). From the King's House to the Reason of State: A Model of the Genesis of the Bureaucratic Field. *Constellations,* 11, pp. 16–36. doi: 10.1111/j.1351–0487.2004.00359.

Boyer, M. (2003). *História do turismo de massa.* São Paulo: Editora EDUSC.

Brante, T. (2001). Consequências do realismo na construção de teoria sociológica. *Sociologia, Problemas e Práticas [online],* 36, pp. 9–38. ISSN 0873–6529.

Bruner, E. M. (1991). Transformation of Self in Tourism. *Annals of Tourism Research,* 18, pp. 238–250.

Costa, C. (2001). An Emerging Tourism Planning Paradigm? A Comparative Analysis between Town and Tourism Planning. *International Journal of Tourism Research,* 3, pp. 425–441.

Emmendoerfer, M. L., Silva, F. C., and Lima, A. A. T. F.C. (2014). Inovação social na gestão pública do turismo: uma análise dos circuitos turísticos em Minas Gerais. In: Pimentel, T. D., Emmendoerfer, M. L., and Tomazzonni, E. L. (Ed.). *Gestão Pública do Turismo no Brasil: teorias, metodologias e aplicações* (pp. 528). Caxias do Sul (RS): Editora da Universidade Caxias do Sul / EDUCS.

Fayol, H. (1931). *Administration industrielle et generale: prevoyance, organisation, commandement, coordination; controle* (p. 174). Paris: Dunod.

Harré, R. (1988). *As Filosofias da Ciência.* Lisboa, Espanha: Edições 70.

Jafari, J. (2005). El turismo como disciplina científica. *Política y Sociedad,* 42 (1), pp. 39–56.

Jenkins, R. (2006). Pierre Bourdieu: Key Sociologists. New York (USA), Routledge: Taylor & Francis e-Library, (Series: The Open University), 1992.

Kane, M. J. (2010). Adventure as a Cultural Foundation: Sport and Tourism in New Zealand. *Journal of Sport & Tourism,* 15 (1), pp. 27–44.

Kay, J. and Laberge, S. (2002). Mapping the Field of "AR": Adventure Racing and the Bourdieu's Concept of Field. *Sociology of Sport Journal,* 19 (2), pp. 25–46.

Lohman, G. and Panosso Netto, A. (2008). *Teoria do turismo. Conceitos, modelos e sistemas* (p. 468). São Paulo: Editora Aleph, (Série Turismo).

OECD – Organization for Economic Cooperation and Development (1994). *Environmental Indicators* (pp. 124–176). Paris: OECD. pp. 124–176.

Pimentel, T. D. (Org.). (2010, julho) *Plano Estratégico para o Desenvolvimento Sustentável do Turismo no município de Lima Duarte/MG.* Relatório Final da Disciplina de Planejamento e Organização do Turismo II. Versão não publicada. Universidade Federal de Juiz de Fora.

Pimentel, T. D. (Org.). (2018, julho) *Plano Estratégico para o Desenvolvimento Sustentável do Turismo no município de Juiz de Fora/MG.* Relatório Final da Disciplina Gestão de Destinos Turísticos. Versão não publicada. Universidade Federal de Juiz de Fora.

Pimentel, T. D.; Emmendoerfer, Magnus L. & Tomazzonni, Edegar L. (Org.). (2014) *Gestão Pública do Turismo no Brasil: teorias, metodologias e aplicações.* (1. Ed., vol. 1, p. 528). Caxias do Sul (RS): Editora da Universidade de Caxias do Sul / EDUCS.

Pimentel, Thiago D. and Pimentel, Mariana P. C. (2015) Destino Turístico como Construção Coletiva: os atores envolvidos e sua necessidade de articulação. *TURyDES (Málaga),* 8, p. 1–13.

Rojas, M. A. M. (2014). Es México un Estado reproductor de las desigualdades regionales. *Finanzas, Política y Economía,* 6 (2), pp. 403–426.

Senplades, Secretaria Nacional de Planificación y Desarrollo (2013). *Plan Nacional de Desarrollo/Plan Nacional para el Buen Vivir 2013–2017.* Quito, Equator.

Thiry-Cherques, H. R. (2006). Pierre Bourdieu: A teoria na prática. *Revista de Administração Pública,* 40 (1), pp. 27–55.

31 Conclusions

Marko Koščak and Tony O'Rourke

The aim of this concluding part of the book is to answer the open questions regarding environmental sustainability, the protection of our common heritage and culture and the role of tourism as a driver or as a participant in the process of developing ethical & responsible tourism and thereby managing sustainability in local tourism destinations.

In the following pages we consider

- *the Thematic Approach*
- *the use of "Links"*
- *key issues arising from the Topics and the Case Studies*
- *critical issues in the development of ethical & sustainable tourism in local destinations*
- *understanding the longer-term view.*

The thematic approach

We do not see this conclusion as being based wholly on a repetition of our analyses of the Topics (Chapters 2–12) or the Case Studies (Chapters 14–28). We suggest that these are covered adequately in our overview assessments of the Topics (Chapter 13) and the Case Studies (Chapter 29).

What we seek to find in this part of the book is a realisation and understanding of what may be seen as critical issues – indeed we hope to be able to initiate on ongoing discussion regarding the fashioning and crafting of these issues into critical success factors as well as critical failure factors.

It is therefore appropriate to use the three thematic areas as a guide in this process.

Theme A: Destination management aspects of ethical sustainable development

This theme covers the following issues:

- adventure & active tourism
- cultural & heritage tourism at a local level
- developing green transport systems
- destination & event planning
- interpreting cultural history

- responsible gastronomy & viniculture
- spatial planning connected to active tourism and sustainable transportation
- stakeholder engagement, sustainable ethical event planning.

Theme B: Environmental & social aspects of ethical sustainable development

This theme covers the following issues:

- developing ethical and environmentally supportive projects in a peripheral region
- effects of climate change on rural tourism
- inclusivity in protecting an historic urban heritage attraction
- inter-generational concepts of sustainability
- low-environmental-impact tourism in the landscape
- maintaining biodiversity and responsible tourism in a natural attraction
- mega-tourism – creating environmental and social disaster
- preservation of fragile historic natural environments
- sustainable urban tourism
- slow adventures in a responsible way.

Theme C: The business impacts of ethical sustainable development

This theme covers the following issues:

- economic recovery through tourism development
- economic sustainability of island communities
- effect of single-market-focused tourism strategies
- ethical financing of rural projects
- managing sustainable capital city tourism
- promoting intangible heritage businesses
- SMART sustainable finance.

As previously explained, an essential component of this book has been to serve a multiplicity of purposes in terms of

1 connecting theory and practice
2 bridging the existing gaps between academics and practitioners operating in ethical and responsible tourism
3 bringing in those concerned with planning ethical, regenerative and sustainable tourism
4 engaging those seeking to invest in or seek investment in ethical and responsible tourism actions at a local level.

The use of "Links"

Whilst using a thematic approach to categorise the Topics and Case Studies, we have also sought to make connections that cross the thematic boundaries. Essentially, the themes were intended as signposts; they placed the Topics and Case Studies in hopefully specific and relevant areas. But those boundaries were not fixed or immobile; signposts may be structured to point in different directions and thus follow parallel or alternative routes. The possibility to cross over the thematic boundaries and more importantly to link and connect the Topics (as indicative of broad ideas) with the Case Studies (as indicative of practice) was found by devising the "Links."

In most of the Topics, there are links (indicated at the beginning of the chapter) to a wide range of Case Studies. These will not only be for the same theme, but will frequently link to other themes. This then explains why in **Appendix 1 – the Guide to the book,** we indicate suggested readings from the book depending upon the background and interests of the reader. The "Links" then provide some compelling evidence of the need to look at the material contributed in terms of the three overall themes and, at the same time, to clearly understand that there is a high degree of interaction across the thematic boundaries.

Key issues arising from the topic chapters & the case studies

We are proposing that the key issues can be exemplified by the use of the following key words, which are applicable to each of the Themes and which resonate throughout the Topics (Chapters 2–12) and the Case Studies (Chapters 14–28). These key words are as follows.

Theme A

1   *Destination management* – successful performance requires a new and practical tourism paradigm combining excellence, co-creation and co-operation, and high quality services. Development of innovative tourism products is aimed at increasing competitiveness, facilitating sustainable tourism development, and consequently increasing tourism turnover. A systematic approach is important if you are to achieve organisational synergy, with creation of new jobs, development of new skills, and ecological innovations in tourism. This takes into account the competitive adjustments required for sustainable development

2   *Responsible Tourism & sustainability* – we offer a description of this made by Dr. Harold Goodwin who said: "Responsible Tourism is about using tourism to make better places for people to live in and better places for people to visit, which means also in that order. It is different from sustainable tourism in that it focuses on what people, businesses and governments do to maximise the positive economic, social and environmental impacts of tourism. It is about identifying the important issues locally and addressing those, transparently reporting progress towards using tourism for sustainable development. Responsible Tourism is not the same thing as sustainable tourism. Sustainability is the goal, a goal which can only be achieved by people taking responsibility, together with others, to achieve it. Responsible Tourism is about taking responsibility for making tourism sustainable, it is about what people do to address the many specific challenges we face" (Goodwin, 2007)

3   *Participatory planning* – effective collaborative planning depends on a number of internal factors including adequate representation of interests, a shared vision, goal accomplishment, good working relationships, and open communication between members. This requires strong leaders and administrative support.

In this way, firstly, participatory planning forms an integral part of future place-making processes and planning by which our aim is to capture the importance of incorporating public perspective into the place-making process when considering future tourism planning. Secondly, our aim is to stress the importance of the creative participatory processes to attract stakeholders and enhance their willingness to partake in the participatory planning processes. And thirdly, our aim is to identify creative participatory planning tools that can be used to enhance participatory planning within the place-making process

4   *Carrying capacity* – the carrying capacity study is necessary in order to identify environmentally and culturally sensitive areas and ensure that the tourism destination is sustainable. The purpose of the carrying capacity assessment is to ensure that the tourists and day visitors attracted to the particular destination will not have a deleterious impact on the cultural or natural sites, that overcrowding will not result in visitor dissatisfaction and that local people will not feel antagonistic towards their "guests." This is essential if tourism is to contribute to the conservation of cultural and natural heritage though the realisation of economic value and raising awareness of, and commitment to, the local patrimony. Local people must be consulted in the assessment of landscapes and cultural and natural heritage assets. It is essential to ensure that the local impact of increased heritage tourism is brought within the process of developing and marketing tourism products

5   *Community-led development* – this is an approach that turns traditional "top down" development policy on its head. Under community-led development, local people take the reins and form a local partnership that designs and implements an integrated development strategy. We are talking about the bottom-up approach. The development strategy is designed to build on the community's social, environmental and economic strengths or "assets" rather than simply compensate for its problems. In the phase of implementation of strategy, the partners receives long-term funding, and they decide how it is spent. Many cases described in the book are examples of such approach

6   *Experiential & multi-sensorial* – experiential travel is a form of tourism in which people focus on experiencing a country, city or particular place by connecting to its history, people and culture. Travellers can experience intimate encounters with real people and places without distraction – focus is on travelling to less-travelled destinations while still providing a high-standard customer service. The key to making that happen is in respecting and keeping in mind the traveller, the place they travel to and the people who live there. In addition, it is shared opinion that sight, sound, smell, taste and touch are in a direct connection to the customers' emotions; therefore, it is crucial to understand and react to the emotional needs of customers (joy, awe, excitement, delight). Tourism experiences are increasingly determined by experience of co-creation and technology use.

Theme B

1   *Environment* – tourism may be a lucrative source of revenue for a destination, but equally it may also have major negative impacts on that destination. Whenever the negative impacts on the natural environment are dealt with, it should be considered that these impacts rarely affect only one entity but the ecological impacts of tourism usually impact on ecosystems as a whole. The impacts on the natural

environment do affect not only pristine nature areas but also cultivated land, which is an important part of the natural and cultural heritage of a region and ecologically valuable because it is the habitat of many species. Environmental impacts that primarily have effects on the local and regional level may also affect the environment globally in the long run (UNESCO, 2009)

2 *Social responsibility* – tourism aids change and development and thus has major effects on the cultural development of a society. The reactions of societies towards tourism are diverse: some reject changes; others inculcate them into their traditions; and some will abandon their cultural roots altogether. Whilst cultural change is an unavoidable, natural part of human culture, the sudden and forced changes that tourism often brings may cause the complete breakdown of a society and may consequentially cause the loss of entire cultural tradition. Socio-cultural impacts of tourism are often hard to identify or to measure and a subject of personal value judgments. Generally spoken, tourism brings about changes in value systems and behaviour of the people and causes changes in the structure of communities, family relationships, collective traditional life styles, ceremonies and morality. The ambiguity of socio-cultural impacts is due to the fact that tourism may have impacts that are beneficial for one group of a society but negative for others (UNESCO, 2009)

3 *Local community* – one motive for responsible travelling is the desire to interact with people in local tourist destination and to get to know their cultures. Cultural exchange supports understanding between peoples and cultures, can lead to the reduction of prejudices and thus contribute to the decrease of tension between societies. Our contributions show and discuss that the initiatives and experiences of local inhabitants with tourists who appreciate local cultures, show interest and value their traditions and enjoy participating with local inhabitants have the potential to increase the sense of regional identity and pride. Tourists' demand for the original and authentic elements of a destination's culture may cause a revaluation of that local heritage and tradition, leading to a renaissance of indigenous cultures, cultural arts and crafts and the rejuvenation of events and festivals that are becoming forgotten due to modern developments and adaptation to developed economy lifestyles (UNESCO, 2009)

4 *Networking* – in the majority of case studies, there is a clear message from the contributor's texts for a need to ensure that tourism is developed in a way that is ecological, economic and socially sustainable. To achieve this, adequate management and monitoring requires to be established. To provide optimal solution to these aims, good networking between many institutions and individuals is needed. It is important to note that different stakeholders involved in the tourism business are responsible for the implementation of multiple parts of the guiding principles. Governments, tourism businesses, local communities, NGOs and the tourists should all contribute in ensuring that tourism becomes more sustainable. In order to achieve the goals of sustainable tourism, the various actors should co-operate and stimulate each other to place the principles into practice. This must be achieved on all levels, namely international, national, regional and in particular local (UNESCO, 2009)

5 *Climate change* – it is clear that many fragile and biodiverse tourism destinations are particularly sensitive to the effects of climate change. This is not only apparent in, for example, the Arctic, Antarctic, and tropical regions where large-scale

tourism appears to be on the increase but is also obvious in more temperate regions where changes in rainfall (increase or decrease) as well as flooding and more dynamic storm patterns have become evident. Whilst tourism may have an impact on such fragile environments – e.g. degradation of coastal paths – climate change may also lead to a rapid withdrawal of tourism – e.g. Japan. There we should therefore begin to view climate change as an issue in which tourism may have an effect on or be affected by

6   *Renewable energy* – a number of our contributors have included the value of renewable energy in the tourism destination offer. It is clear that mass tourism – whether large-scale hotel resort developments or the cruise ship industry – have tended to be focused in the past on the use of non-renewable energy sources. Whilst this is changing – e.g. the use of renewable power for hotel developments and the switch to hybrid energy cruise ships – local tourism has the greatest ability to benefit from localised renewable power schemes. This includes the use of wind, solar and hydro power at a local community level; there are now many examples of peripheral rural and coastal communities using community power generation schemes. At the same time, we should be aware of the use of off-grid energy, water and waste consumption. Holiday homes in rural communities have the capacity to use alternative power sources for heating, grey water from rainfall for showers and bio-degradable technologies for the management of waste.

Theme C

1   *Business adaptation* – the material we have collected indicates a wide potential for assessing how businesses may embrace ethical and responsible development at a local level whilst maintaining financial stability. This should of course require looking at new models of business activity that have a strong base in local communities and to an extent focus on self-generation of community funding within an overall regenerative community concept

2   *Financing ethical and responsible tourism at a local level* – local tourism activities will always be constrained by the availability of capital through traditional sources. There are however useful models for developing community, co-operative and mutual systems to finance local actions. Blending differing methodologies and looking at new ways to create financing structures is becoming an important feature, particularly if is it necessary to escape from total reliance on grant-aided models

3   *Investment through SMART technology* – powerful growth in technology-enabled systems of financing has suggested the potential for accessing wider pools of investment opportunity for ethical and responsible tourism enterprises in peripheral regions. Traditionally peripheral and remote regions have suffered from a lack of direct access to financial markets – new technology, such as crowdfunding, enables a more direct and potentially sustainable approach

4   *Assessing market changes* – tourism markets are in a continual process of change, and over the last three decades, we have seen a number of shifts; whilst this has included a greater interest in responsible tourism and the reduction of the size of tourism groups to match footfall, at the same time, we have seen a dynamic growth in cruise tourism as the size of cruise vessels expands to meet market expectations

5 *Community-driven management* – stakeholder engagement tends to bring in a mixture of public, private and social sector actors. Building on community engagement links the management and operation of local tourism destination organisations with the actual community. This then requires a review of ownership models and a potential for greater interest in mutual and co-operative structures which localise ownership but do provide access to improved management capacities and solutions

6 *Partnership* – we should seek to distance ourselves from a simple dichotomy between tourism providers (individuals and organisations) and tourism recipients (consumers). We should also look at other agents in the community process; decision-making is often in the hands of the older members of society, whilst the future of ethical and responsible development will without doubt be in the hands of today's younger generation.

Critical issues in the development of ethical & sustainable tourism in local destinations

In many of the Topic Chapters and Case Studies, authors have identified situations, issues and trends which either created success or contributed to failure. Our concept of the management of tourism at the local level, which is explored in the book, distinctly implies that such *critical success factors* and such *critical failure factors* have a significant and profound influence on how locally driven ethical and sustainable tourism may (or may not) operate in a specific area or region. Indeed, much of the material provided by our contributors illustrates rather graphically how projects have succeeded as a result of critical inputs and how others have failed through the absence of such critical inputs. The factors proposed below are drawn from the material in the book but are not intended to be exhaustive or exclusive:

Critical success factors

• The building of local coalitions of actors and agents is a primary success factor; however, it is also clear that there is a need to bring into the coalition elements of regional, national and international organisations to achieve the maximum effect
• Ethical and responsible event management, as a part of local tourism activity, appears to be successful not only in attracting tourism input, but also in engaging the support of local residents. Minimising waste from tourism is a potent example
• Promoting tourism all year round, particularly in peripheral regions which are not weather dependent, has a major economic benefit and, by spreading the tourism season over a wider base, has a less detrimental environmental effect
• Flexible and imaginative financial solutions, blending different funding methodologies (credit, equity and crowd funding finance), appear to be effective in financing local, ethical and responsible tourism development
• Tourism projects which have an environmentally friendly approach have the potential to push wider society into infrastructure developments which themselves articulate environmental responsibility and also will bring longer term socio-economic benefits
• Regeneration of local environments with appropriate educational developments and community engagement, potentially helps to secure and enhance the local

culture and heritage. Local inhabitants who are aware and understanding of their own culture and heritage (and its future) will be more willing and receptive to the idea of sharing this unique inheritance with tourists

- Major urban heritage sites which are able to protect their unique physical and heritage environments, whilst at the same time offering inclusive experiences for all types of tourists (e.g. the mobile as well as the less mobile) may have a positive economic impact on local communities.

Critical failure factors

- We would suggest that there are a number of capacity challenges at a local level which minimise the opportunity to develop sustainable activity. These include poor financial capacity, poor marketing and promotional capacity and poor management capacity. These capacity problems are often due to a lack of co-operation between actors and agents as well as an unwillingness to create financial/management/marketing coalitions
- A serious failure is where local tourism actors and agents fail to create destination management structures; this failure then means that the opportunity to co-operatively and collectively promote and market a destination in a meaningful and targeted way is totally lost
- Overtourism remains a massive critical failure; it not only degrades the environment and escalates the living costs of local inhabitants, but it also creates antagonism between tourists and local residents. Furthermore the effects of overtourism do apply not just to major urban tourism destinations, but more increasingly to rural tourism centres as well
- Failing to understand the necessary balance between people and the environment – at whatever level – has the potential not only to diminish local culture and heritage but also to undermine economic stability and development. This is frequent and the result of failing to engage all sectors of society in the planning of tourism activity
- Tourism cannot be seen as a means of injecting a new format for economic growth into economies which have significant structural imbalances. In the short term, tourism may well provide economic growth and foreign exchange inputs; but tourism trends are tenuous and extremely affected by global economic and security trends. Today's favoured tourism destination may swiftly become abandoned and underutilised tomorrow

Understanding the longer-term view

We tend towards a view that the development of ethical and responsible tourism at the local level has been blighted and constrained by short-term thinking. Often this is driven by the blind acceptance of previously fashionable neo-liberal economic principles which predicated success based on contribution to GDP or significant gross income inflows. The evidence of the past two decades, particularly through the global economic crisis of 2007–2009 and the subsequent economic depression, indicates how short-term thinking by major financial and investment institutions brought about the near collapse of the advanced economies.

Equally mass tourism – whether large-scale hotel developments or cruise ships of an increasingly massive size – are developments which are ethically challenging and potentially non-sustainable. Such developments, by the very capital required, may only be possible through the engagement of large-scale corporate investment which is dependent on hedge funds and private venture capital investors who will clearly not necessarily have an ethical and responsible outlook on their investment scenarios. At the same time, mass tourism is hugely sensitive to events and trends; the unwillingness of US tourists to travel after 9/11 was responsible for the collapse of a number of major airlines; we also saw a major shift of tourism flows from North Africa and Turkey after terrorist attacks in those regions.

But it is clear from the contributions in this book that short-term economic inflows tend to benefit organisations, corporations and individuals outside local areas. The economic benefits of cruise tourism, for example, are primarily directed to international cruise companies and port facilities; they fail to provide immediate benefit to communities where tourism footfall damages and destroys both the tangible and intangible cultural and heritage environment. Clearly seeking to find a balance between the importance of economic growth (particularly in peripheral coastal or rural regions) and protection of fragile environments and cultures is a complex and frequently dangerous balancing act.

It is possible to suggest that local tourism appears to be less sensitive, and certainly the emergence of responsible tourism and travel has engaged the interests of three important groups (Koščak & O'Rourke, 2018):

- the "silver tourism market" – those above 60 years who are retired/semi-retired, remain physically active and have the financial assets to engage in independent organised vacations in places with significant cultural and heritage content
- the "family market" – families with children who are dissatisfied with mass tourism offers and seek a more authentic family experience which will gravitate towards active and adventure tourism
- the "back-packer market" – those who are between 20 and 30 years of age, seeking authentic local experiences, demonstrate a strong degree of flexibility in the travel plans and wish to engage with local communities.

So how do we seek to determine the potential for meaningful longer-term planning? Perhaps this does involve looking at alternative planning perspectives which encourage ethical and responsible tourism at a local destination level.

Involvement of stakeholders in strategic management of a destination is important in each stage of development. We would suggest that this emphasises the importance of a "bottom-up" approach in local tourism management. This involves growing tourism actions and activity from a local level, as well as building strong coalitions of local actors and dynamic connectivity into the regional/national level, and will not only meet the focus on the bottom-up methodology but will satisfactorily address the problematic failures.

We suggest that many of the problematic failures are due to the fact that, in general, top-down models tend to suffer from weakened impact, unfocused resourcing and a diffusion of structural energy at the point of local delivery due to the bureaucratic elements present in such models (Koščak & O'Rourke, 2018). The top-down method drips down resources from the top, but at the point of local delivery, the impact is potentially diminished. This perhaps explains why, for example, European Union programmes committed to improving sustainable economic activity in both rural and coastal regions (through LAGs and FLAGs respectively) are implemented by direct relationships between the Commission and the local programme agencies.

Seeking a conclusion

At the outset, we made the statement that we perceived distinctive gaps between theory and practice and between methodology and actuality. We suggested that a publication in this format may make an effort to bridge those gaps.

Our interaction with the contributors and the opportunities we have had to engage with them have made clear to us that local problems require local solutions. They have also underlined our support for the concept that local destination issues require an interdisciplinary approach and the contribution of different disciplines and expertise in resolving development challenges. The ability to cross disciplinary boundaries and to include such a wide range of contributors has been immensely pleasing and productive.

Yet trying to find an accurate conclusion is difficult; as editors, we have been fortunate in sharing a common view of the issues addressed in this book. We have also been equally fortunate in gathering a wide group of contributors who have all given unique and fascinating perspectives. At the same time, we also realise that there is an immense multiplicity of approaches about how we manage ethical and responsible tourism in a local environment. Perhaps what we see as potentially different is the approach in seeking to blend practice and theory and to draw ideas and concepts from both.

References

Goodwin, H. (2019). *Personalised academic internships.* [online] Accessed 27.05.19, www.lets gointernship.com/en/blog/there-difference-between-sustainable-and-responsible-tourism.

Koščak, M. & O'Rourke, T. (2018). *Practical and conceptual strategies for the re-evaluation of local tourism destinations.* Harlow: Pearson UK.

UNESCO (2009). *Sustainable Tourism Development in UNESCO Designated Sites in South-Eastern Europe,* Ecological tourism in Europe – ETE.

Appendix

Table A.1 A matrix-based guide for the use of this book

Reader classification	Complete book	Topic chapter numbers	Case study chapter numbers	Theoretical reflections (Chapter 30)	Editorial (Chapters 1, 13, 29, 31)
Undergraduate tourism		2, 5, 12	16, 18, 19, 22, 25, 28	YES	YES
Undergraduate ethical-sustainable areas		4, 7, 8, 10, 11	14–24 + 26	YES	YES
Masters tourism	YES				
Masters ethical-sustainable areas	YES				
Doctoral students in all areas covered	YES				
Academic staff	YES				
Professional trainers in tourism/ethical, etc.		2–12	14–28		YES
Destination management professionals		2–12	14–28		YES
Tourism managers and other practitioners		2–12	14–28		YES
National tourism agencies		2–12	14–28		YES
Cultural and natural heritage managers		2–12	14–24 + 26, 27, 28		YES
Event managers in tourism destinations		5, 7, 12	14, 17, 18, 20, 25, 26		YES
Rural and town planners		2, 5, 18	16, 18, 23, 24		YES
Tourism entrepreneurs		3, 4, 6, 10, 11	16, 18, 23, 24		YES
Ethical and sustainable tourism consultants		2–9 and 10, 11	14, 15, 17, 19–24, 27, 28		YES
Ethical and sustainable tourism researchers		2, 3, 4, 6, 7, 8, 9	14–24, 26, 28	YES	YES
Tourism project managers		2–12	14–28		YES
Tour operators – responsible tourism		2–12	14–28		YES
Community development co-operatives and NGOs		10, 11	16, 20, 21, 22, 23, 25–28		YES
Investors in ethical and sustainable tourism		2, 3, 4, 6, 10	15, 16, 18, 22, 24, 27		YES
Ethical crowd funding platforms		2, 3, 4, 6, 10	15, 16, 18, 22, 24, 27		YES

Index